To the Land of Gold and Wickedness

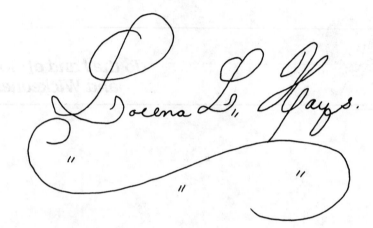

Lovena L. Hays.

To the Land of Gold and Wickedness

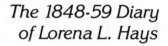

The 1848-59 Diary
of Lorena L. Hays

Edited by

Jeanne Hamilton Watson

The Patrice Press
St. Louis, Missouri

Library of Congress
Cataloging-In-Publication Data

Hays, Lorena L. (Lorena Lenity), b. 1827.
  To the land of gold and wickedness.
  Bibliography: p.
  Includes index.
  1. West (U.S.)—Description and travel—1848-1859. 2. Overland journeys to the Pacific. 3. California—Description and travel—1848-1859. 4. Hays, Lorena L. (Lorena Lenity), b. 1827—Diaries. 5. Pioneers—West (U.S.)—Diaries.
I. Watson, Jeanne Hamilton.   II. Title.
F593.H36 1988 978′.02′0924 [B]   88-19590
ISBN 0-935284-87-7

      The preparation of this volume was made possible, in part, by grants from:
        The Program for Editions of the National Endowment for the Humanities, an independent federal agency,
           and
        The Educational Foundation of the American Association of University Women.

The Patrice Press
1701 S. Eighth Street
St. Louis, Missouri 63104
1-800-367-9242

Printed in the United States of America

Dedicated to the pioneers who followed the trails west and to their twentieth century counterparts who work to preserve our frontier heritage.

Contents

Part 3—The California Years

Foreword

THE DIARY OF LORENA HAYS is in many ways a unique document. Diaries of American women written in the mid-nineteenth century have been published previously, as have innumerable accounts of Oregon-California Trail travel, but Lorena's writing has some special qualities.

She was a bit of a hypochondriac, but she generally looked forward to feeling better. She agonized over her sins (and sometimes the sins of others), but was genuine in her religious feelings and seldom was "holier than thou." Falling in love was difficult for her, but she married and worked at being a wife and mother.

She longed for more formal education, yet she was talented enough to be a correspondent for *The Golden Era* and other newspapers. She also was a schoolteacher. She was alert to the world around her and commented on national politics, politicians, and social issues. She was a foe of intemperance, but generally was a tolerant person.

Lorena had misgivings about making the journey to California, but she enjoyed the trip. She noted the hardships and fears of the trail, mourned the death of fellow travelers, and paid attention to the standard landmarks and crossings. She viewed the completion of the trip with some regret: "I am no longer to live a camp life, no longer walk, ride and to be almost constantly in the fresh, free air of Heaven. A roof must now intervene between me and the blue dome above. . . ."

The diary does much for the understanding of state and local history. Lorena's comments on education, religion, parties, and town meetings in Illinois; her view of the new California and its infant communities, businesses, and social institutions; and her observations across the plains and mountains shed new light on some aspects of American culture between the Mexican and Civil wars.

Despite her physical and philosophical concerns about herself and members of her family and her doubts about the future, Lorena was not inclined to look back or to dwell on regrets. She persevered in her quest for more knowledge, was not afraid of new surroundings, and was inquisitive about the activities around her.

Anyone who is interested in the viewpoint of an enlightened pioneering woman in the West should be glad that Lorena Hays kept her diary and that Jeanne Watson pursued its editing and publication.

Robert W. Richmond
Kansas State Historical Society
Past-president, American Association
for State and Local History

Preface

S ILVER LAKE LIES shimmering in a high Sierra Nevada basin surrounded by peaks that form a region south of Lake Tahoe known as the Carson Pass of California. Here Highway 88, designated as one of America's scenic routes, criss-crosses a trail traveled by pioneers of the gold rush era. Known in the mid-nineteenth century as the "Carson Route," it was named for Kit Carson, mountain man and scout. He was with the Fremont Expedition that crossed these mountains in the winter of 1843-44. This route, opened for covered wagons in 1848, became part of the California Overland Trail. It was one of three major roads leading from the Nevada desert across the Sierra into California and was used throughout the 1850s. Today it is called the "Carson Emigrant Road." My family and I have kept it marked for nearly twenty years. It is also the road traveled in 1853 by Lorena L. Hays and her family, who came from Illinois to settle in California.

I became acquainted with Lorena during a 1969 vacation at Silver Lake when Ellis E. Eckland, Lorena's grandnephew, let me read a typescript of her diary. At first Lorena's account was only one of many pioneer journals read to enhance my family's summer hikes along the Carson Emigrant Road. Often we stopped to read typed excerpts from such diaries while taking photographs to illustrate these descriptions of the road where covered wagons once rolled.

My interest in the Carson Emigrant Road dates back to my childhood and many summers spent at Silver Lake with my family. I first heard stories about the Carson Emigrant Road when we stayed at the Stockton Municipal Camp and later learned more about it at the Silver Lake cabin of Lyle and Alice Mewhirter, who collected artifacts from wagons abandoned by the pioneers. Most of these artifacts had been gathered in the 1940s when Lyle walked with Irene Paden and her husband along the old emigrant road across part of the Utah-Nevada desert. Paden's books, *The Wake of the Prairie Schooner* and *Prairie Schooner Detours*, are now considered classics. These were the first books I read upon returning to the Mewhirter cabin at Silver Lake. While my husband taught our son and daughter how to fish, I read about the gold rush pioneers and wondered how they managed to cross the adjacent mountains. The Carson Emigrant Road over the Sierra Nevada climbs to 9,600 feet, the highest point that covered wagons traveled in the United States.

When our children were old enough, we began hiking sections of the Carson Emigrant Road. In 1970 at Silver Lake we met Jess Machado, a friend of my family from the Stockton Municipal Camp days. Jess had kept the Carson Emigrant Road marked since the late 1930s. During the next two summers we walked with him, identifying and marking approximately forty miles of the Carson Emigrant Road through Alpine and Amador counties in California. Beginning at the Carson Canyon on the Nevada side of the mountains, we have retraced this gold rush trail over the top of the Sierra and west as far as the Leek Springs turn-off from Highway 88. In 1979-80 the Forest Service joined in preserving the Eldorado National Forest section of the Carson Emigrant Road.

Our high Sierra summers appeared to end in 1973 because my husband was transferred east. We spent two years in Illinois before moving to New Jersey. In both states, while working at three historic house museums, I discovered additional information about gold rush pioneers. Several times during the late 1970s we returned to California for Silver Lake vacations and continued our work on remarking the Carson Emigrant Road. In 1977 I asked Lorena's descendants, the Eckland family, if I could write the introduction and footnotes for her diary. This included the 1848-53 section that had not been previously transcribed.

Research trips were made possible by grants from the National Endowment for the Humanities and the Educational Foundation of the American Association of University Women. At the Newberry Library in Chicago I found the names of Lorena's uncles in another 1853 overland travel journal, the fifty-third of more than 130 pioneer diaries, letters and reminiscences I have read for that year. In the Illinois community where Lorena lived for fourteen years I was able to review Baptist church records from 1829. Dance invitations Lorena and one of her sisters received in 1853-54 were in the California Historical Society library in San Francisco. Stereoptican views, taken by the photographer who rented Lorena's California house, turned up in the collections of the Huntington Library in San Mario, California.

While doing this research I also became acquainted with other descendants of the Hay(e)s clan. After moving to Summit, New Jersey, I met Rutherford P. Hayes, a grandson of Lorena's distant cousin, President Rutherford B. Hayes. Bernice Hoover, a granddaughter of Lorena's aunt and uncle, wrote from Fort Collins, Colorado, upon learning of my research from a friend living in the California gold rush town where Lorena settled. Hoover shared family pictures, geneology, and old letters, including one that tells about Lorena and her mother. Often it has seemed as if Lorena were looking over my shoulder, ready to call my attention to an important piece of information in census records, other 1853 trail diaries and reminiscences, newspapers and county histories, as well as court and church records. Otherwise, it would be difficult to explain why Lorena's married name caught my attention as I read the May 28, 1979, issue of *The New York Times*. This newspaper article led me to her great-grandson, whose whereabouts was unknown to other relatives. He was the late Angus L. Bowmer, founder of the renowned Shakespearean Festival in Ashland, Oregon, and a member of the National Council of the Arts. His wife, Gertrude Bowmer, sent me a copy of his book about the festival as well as information about the family and a picture of Lorena's son and grandchildren, thus helping to complete her story.

The search for Lorena has been long but fascinating, often exciting, and always rewarding. Her story has dominated our family dinner table conversations to such an extent that Lorena, according to my husband, has become "our illegitimate relative." Surely it could only have been Lorena who dropped an 1840 dime for me to find in August 1978 near the upper Sierra Nevada summit of the Carson Emigrant Road — believed to be the first nineteenth century coin discovered along this gold rush trail in the mountains above Silver Lake.

—Jeanne Hamilton Watson
June 1988
Summit, New Jersey

Acknowledgments

THE SEARCH FOR LORENA has involved the help of many people at libraries, archives, universities, museums, courthouses, churches, and historical societies across the country. I am indeed indebted to them for taking the time to answer questions and letters, to arrange interlibrary loans, and to provide other research assistance. I would especially like to thank Dr. George P. Hammond, director emeritus of the Bancroft Library, University of California-Berkeley, for guidance and assistance, and Evelyn Angier, a local historian in Ione, California, whose interest led me to finding one of Lorena's cousins in Colorado. My thanks, also, to Merrill J. Mattes, historian and author, for providing a copy of the Isaiah Bryant diary from among his papers at the Nebraska State Historical Society. I am also appreciative of his suggestions as well as the time and interest he has taken in this project. Researching western history while living in the East turned out to be easier than anticipated, thanks to the material and the helpful staff at the New York Public Library, particularly in the special collections and the rare books rooms; the Beinecke Rare Book and Manuscript Library at Yale University; the western Americana collection at the Princeton University Library; the Library of Congress, especially its newspaper division; the National Archives in Washington, D.C.; and the Federal Archives and Record Center in Bayonne, New Jersey.

At the National Archives, Ken Hall located information about the *Die Vernon,* a Mississippi River steamer, in the form of its 1840s and 1850s boiler inspection records, with edges burnt by the fire that destroyed the 1890 census. James Walker found 1853 army records from Fort Laramie and John Porter Bloom shared knowledge as editor of the territorial papers project to locate other 1853 journals. Walter A. Deiss of the Smithsonian Institution archives dug out the letterpress correspondence concerning J. Soule Bowman's overland journey.

In New Jersey Ezra C. Fitch, Ulla Volk, and Pepper Pathe of the Friendship Library, Fairleigh Dickinson University-Madison, arranged innumerable loans and Dr. L. M. Renzulli and Professor John Fritz of the FDU history department served as unofficial consultants. My thanks also to the staff of the Drew University Library, Madison, and to Dr. Kenneth Rowe of the United Methodist Church Archives there. His files helped identify ministers in Illinois and California. Background information about nineteenth century women was obtained from the Victorian Research Library at Acorn Hall, headquarters of the Morris County Historical Society, Morristown; the Newark Public Library; and the library at the Newark Museum. Help was also given by the staff of the Summit Public Library. Information about Lorena's family in western Pennsylvania came from the Erie County courthouse. John Sigler and R. Norton Walther of Barry, Illinois, answered questions about that community. Additional information about Pike County was given by Josephine McLaughlin of Griggsville; Fay Gray and Warren Winston of the Pike County Historical Society and Austin Altizer's staff at the Pike County courthouse, both in Pittsfield; as well as by Dr. and Mrs. Benjamin Carey, former Pike County residents now living in New Jersey. I am also most appreciative of the courtesy extended by Mr. and Mrs. Russell Yelton in allowing me to read the records of the First Baptist Church at their home in Barry.

In addition I would like to acknowledge the encouragement and advice offered by the late Warren Howell of San Francisco, whose ancestors (the Belshaws) made the overland trip to Oregon in 1853. Lowell Volkel and Wayne Temple of the Illinois State Archives also provided research help, as did staff members at the Illinois State Historical Society and Library, Springfield. My thanks also to the staff of the Chicago Historical Society and the Newberry Library of Chicago.

Dr. Robert Becker and others at the Bancroft Library helped solve research problems and also called attention to additional unpublished 1853 diaries. In San Francisco research was made easier by J. Roger Jobson and Deborah Ginberg of the Society of California Pioneers and by Maude Swingle and Karl Feicktmeir of the California Historical Society Library. Also providing information were staff members of the history room at Wells Fargo Bank, San Francisco; the Henry E. Huntington Library, San Marino; and the Holt-Atherton-Pacific Center for Western History, University of the Pacific, Stockton.

My appreciation and thanks also to Dave and Heidi Casebolt of the Pardee Home Museum in Oakland, California, for calling my attention to letters that contain information about Lorena's husband.

Information about the Methodist church in California was provided by Oscar Burdict and Will P. Ralph at the library of the Pacific School of Religion, Berkeley. And material about the early days of the Baptist church in the Ione Valley was located at the library of the Berkeley Baptist Theological Seminary. Others helping to answer questions about various aspects of California history included Rudy Miskulin, California State Fair, Sacramento; Ray Hillman, Pioneer Museum and Haggin Gallery, Stockton; and staff members at the Amador County courthouse, Jackson, as well as the Jackson Public Library.

Copies of Mormon diaries were made available by Donald T. Schmidt, Church of Jesus Christ of Latter-day Saints, and Steven R. Wood, Utah State Historical Society, Salt Lake City. My thanks for information about other 1853 overland travelers to: Discovery Hall Museum, South Bend, Indiana; the Idaho State Historical Society; the Iowa State Historical Society; the Kansas State Historical Society; the Kansas City (Missouri) Historical Society and Museum; the Lane County Historical Society and Pioneer Museum, Eugene, Oregon; the Missouri Historical Society, St. Louis; the Nebraska State Historical Society; the Oregon Historical Society; the Wyandotte County Historical Society, Kansas; the State Historical Society of Wisconsin; and the Wyoming State Historical Society.

In addition I am indebted to Gregory Franzwa and Betty Burnett, Ph.D., for editorial direction on behalf of The Patrice Press.

For the use of photographs, my thanks to Mrs. Angus L. Bowmer; Dennis Chapman, Curator, Fort Caspar Museum; Ellis E. Eckland; Bernice Hoover; The Bancroft Library, University of California-Berkeley; California Historical Society; California State Library; The Huntington Library; Missouri Historical Society; National Park Service; Dean Decker and the Bureau of Land Management; The Margaret Woodbury Strong Museum; Gregory Franzwa; Mort Sumberg; and Tom Hunt. All pictures are by Bill and Jeanne Watson unless otherwise stated.

My thanks also to Art Randall of the Natrona County Historical Society for sharing his research about the Reshaw Bridge and walking the north bank with me in hopes of locating the grave of Lorena's cousin. I am especially grateful to Andrew F. Johnson, librarian at the University of Washington, Seattle, for finding at 1893 biography of Lorena's son and to the Ashland Shakespearean Festival for putting me in touch with the wife of her great-grandson. And last, but certainly not least, a special "thank you" to my husband and family for encouragement as well as great patience with piles of papers and books throughout the house.

To the Land of Gold
and Wickedness

Introduction

A HINT OF SPRING touched the air that January evening of 1848 as a young woman made her way through the gaslit streets of St. Louis. It had been a remarkably pleasant day and now, on this unseasonably mild night, the city offered among its many diversions both a performance of the circus and a lecture on history, one in a series that "promises to be the best ever in St. Louis . . . a rare intellectual feast." But neither of these entertainments, nor any of the other amusements announced in the newspapers, attracted the attention of twenty-year-old Lorena L. Hays. Her destination was the white building, resembling a Greek temple topped by a New England spire, that stood at the corner of Fifth and Walnut streets not far from the city's bustling Mississippi River levee.[1]

By seven o'clock Lorena had taken her seat in one of the free pews in the eight-year-old Second Presbyterian Church where "quite a revival" was in progress "under the ministrations of Dr. Hall."[2] Lorena found these meetings both stimulating and emotionally confusing. On January 10, after nearly a week of revivalist sermons and exhortations, she became so agitated about the state of her soul that she began the diary she would keep for the next eleven years. In it Lorena recorded the anxieties and hopes of her life during the next five years in a small Illinois village, her overland journey west in 1853, and six years in a California gold rush community.

Lorena made her diary from folded paper, unevenly cut and hand-stitched together with two strands of white thread to form six small booklets. She used white paper and lined blue ledger sheets with a cover of plain, light blue paper. The first booklet, a little larger than the rest, was separate from the other five, which she sewed together to form a 202-page volume 6¼ " x 8 ". Lorena designed these booklets with a

Lorena Hays made her diary by stitching together blue and white paper to form six slim volumes. The first, a separate booklet (right), records her life in Illinois, 1848-52. The other five (left) tell about her 1853 trip to California and life in a small gold rush community.

formal heading at the top of each page separated from the text by double lines. Except for three-quarters of a page at the end of the first book, she filled every inch of space. Usually she wrote in ink but occasionally resorted to pencil.

Lorena was concerned primarily with things of the spirit and of the mind. Her first entries dealt solely with the religious crisis of her life. She could not decide which church to join but felt impelled to profess a faith. She sampled all the churches available in her small community and then agonized over the choice, filling page after page in an agitated hand, in contrast to her usually legible script. When she finally made her decision, two-and-a-half years later, it brought little happiness, contentment, or peace of mind. She felt she had received inadequate counseling and guidance from her minister. Such intense concern about religion was not unusual for a young woman of the 1840s and 1850s. "Daily self-examination" was considered proper for "the harmonious development of Christian character," according to a *Young Lady's Guide.* The questions Lorena posed for herself about her activities and feelings were those outlined in just such books.[3]

Church membership played an important role in almost everyone's life and, to some degree, social acceptance in a small town depended upon it. In those days attending more than one church service on a Sunday was not considered an indication of religious zeal. It was merely another symptom of the enthusiastic and feverish revivalism that swept through frontier and rural areas with great regularity during the early nineteenth century. Church attendance also offered women one

This entry for June 2, 1850, was written while Lorena agonized over the decision about which church to join.

of the few legitimate reasons to escape from the chores and isolation at home in exchange for a few hours of socially approved activity.[4]

Gradually, Lorena gained more perspective on her life and began to write about her other interests and activities. Education was always very important to her and she longed to continue her schooling, taking advantage of any opportunity to learn. This desire was not without family precedent. Her paternal grandfather and one uncle had attended college. While higher education for women was one of the most controversial issues of the Victorian era, western Illinois offered women college-level classes in nearby Jacksonville as early as 1833, when the Female Academy was organized as an adjunct to Illinois College. However, Lorena could not afford the tuition of four to eight dollars a quarter to attend one of the local female seminaries that would have provided the necessary high school preparation for college.[5]

Although she always regretted the lack of formal instruction, Lorena's diary indicates that she was fairly well educated, with a good background in history. Her writing style might seem eccentric by twentieth century standards, but the capitalization, punctuation, odd divisions of words, and inconsistencies of spelling were not unusual for many educated people in the mid-nineteenth century. A similar style appears in the 1853 overland travel letters of a Wisconsin doctor, Joseph R. Bradway, who graduated from Rush Medical College in 1847.[6]

Except for a very brief period while attending school, Lorena did not use the "long s" that resembled an "f." As late as the 1850s this eighteenth century form of script was still being widely used by many of her contemporaries for words such as "Mifsifsippi."

To help earn a living Lorena taught school while continually worrying about whether she was really qualified for the job. Her desire for improvement led her to attend the first two teachers' institutes held in Pike County, Illinois, in 1850. As the eldest daughter in a family that had not found wealth and prosperity by moving west, Lorena also helped her widowed mother. But she longed to be someone important, rather than "an unknown," to achieve "a name and influence."

Throughout the years, Lorena's drive for self-improvement turned her into an avid reader of every magazine, newspaper, and book that she picked up. Spurred by ambition, she worked to become an "authoress." Writing was one of the few socially acceptable careers open to women during the early Victorian years. Such aspirations were not particularly welcomed, however, as indicated by the somewhat testy response from one western Illinois newspaper editor in the summer of 1851 to an unknown correspondent:

> An article handed us by a lady on religious subjects, we must decline publishing. We like to please the ladies when we can; but we think they fill the place the Almighty intended for them in nursing babies rather than writing poetry or discussing theological points. But if they must write let them write well.[7]

Lorena's efforts were rewarded the following year when the rival county newspaper printed her first two articles in the fall and winter of 1852. What subjects she chose to write about may never be known, however, because existing files of the *Pike County Union* are incomplete: apparently no copies of the two issues containing Lorena's first published articles have survived.[8] In California Lorena also enjoyed a brief career, cut short by the duties of marriage and motherhood. She wrote for *The Golden Era,* one of the foremost literary periodicals of the 1850s and 60s. Her stories sometimes appeared on the front page of this San Francisco weekly newspaper, whose columns also encouraged such writers as Charles Warren Stoddard, Alonzo ("Old Block") Delano, Joaquin Miller, Mark Twain, and Bret Harte.[9]

Several times Lorena used the pages of her diary to draft her newspaper articles, but she also recorded in it many items never submitted for publication. She took an interest in local and national politics, commenting upon election campaigns and issues, including slavery and women's rights. Lorena became aware of women's status when she realized that they had never been trained to speak out in church. After her marriage in 1855, her comments upon this topic became much more outspoken but apparently were never expressed outside of her diary.

Reticence has always been associated with the image of the Victorian woman, and in this respect Lorena was typical of her times. As she moved west she conformed to Victorian traditions, which continued to cling to the edges of her pioneer skirts. While she enthusiastically endorsed many of the reform movements of the nineteenth century, the radical change in dress advocated by Amelia Bloomer did not interest her, even though a small number of women did favor this costume for overland travel in 1852 and 1853. Straight-laced Victorian attitudes of primness and propriety also dictated that Lorena avoid mentioning the unpleasant task of cooking over a fire built from buffalo chips when wood became scarce on the California Trail. This was one aspect of overland travel almost always recorded in other diaries and reminiscences.[10]

While pioneer women ususally are not considered to be "Victorian" in the late nineteenth-century meaning, the "Cult of Domesticity" had its origins before 1840.[11] The elaborate code of conduct and etiquette which came to be synonymous with Victorian did influence the lives of women who made the overland trip west, as Lorena's diary and those of other 1853 travelers indicate.

Many of Lorena's sentiments and opinions fit the staid Victorian mold of respectability. As a married woman in California, she followed the rigid social etiquette of "calling" in a small gold rush community.

After the first romance of her marriage faded, Lorena ceased to use her husband's name and referred to him as "Mr. B." and "husband" in her diary. And even though no one else was ever expected to read these pages, she never openly wrote about her two pregnancies but only hinted at them.

In several aspects, however, Lorena did not fit the traditional pattern of sheltered and pampered Victorian womanhood. Her great interest in politics, religion, and education reached far beyond the confines of her own parlor. In one other significant respect the stereotyped picture did not apply to her. While other young women might devote considerable time and attention to elaborate dress and personal appearance, these were of little consequence to her. *Godey's Lady's Book* brought the fashionable world into many remote western households in the 1850s, but Lorena's diary never tells about a new dress or bonnet for herself or her sisters. Nor is there any mention of hand-me-downs. Yet store bills in Illinois show that the six Hays women bought yardage and sewing notions frequently.[12] Even when Lorena was married she did not record anything about her wedding attire.

A shy, self-conscious, and serious young woman, Lorena longed for romance, but never found it in Illinois. There was little fun in her life. When she did enjoy herself, she was inclined to feel guilty afterwards. At twenty-three, Lorena was somewhat older than many unmarried women in 1850, when the median age for women was 18.8 years. There were probably few eligible single men of her own age group in the community. While there were a number of older widowers with ready-made families in Pike County, this undoubtedly held little appeal for a young woman who had helped raise nine younger brothers and sisters.[13] Society, in those days, considered it to be:

> Folly — for girls to expect to be happy without marriage. Every woman was made for motherhood; consequently babies are as necessary to their "peace of mind" as health. If you wish to look at melancholy and indigestion, look at an old maid. If you would take a peep at sunshine look in the face of a young mother.[14]

Lorena endured the agonies of spinsterhood. While the early years of her diary contain a few hints of possible romantic attachments, none developed into the special relationship Lorena sought. Marriage proved not to be the answer to her soul's longings. When she married, her husband soon became too busy to take an interest in her intellectual pursuits and apparently could not give her the intimate companionship she wanted. Without a special friend in whom to confide her innermost thoughts and hopes, Lorena continued to pour out her heart in the pages of her diary. She must have found great comfort in this, although she frequently let many days go by without writing, even during the five-month trip to California.

Lorena's diary provides few clues about her family or her early years, but because she was very distantly related to the nineteenth president of the United States, Rutherford B. Hayes (1877-81), some of this information can be found in a formal genealogy of the Hay(e)s family printed in 1884. It was a large family, and, although President Hayes and Lorena were both of the sixth generation, they did not know each other. The president, five years older than she, grew up in Ohio while Lorena spent the first twelve years of her life in western Pennsylvania. His side of the family was descended from the eldest son of the first Hayes in America; hers came from the fourth son in this family of seven children.[15]

Although descended from the same ancestor, Lorena's branch of the family spelled their last name differently than did the president. Sometime during their westward migration the Hays dropped the "e", although records in Pennsylvania, Illinois, and California show their name spelled both ways. Boldly and with a considerable flourish, Lorena signed her name — without the "e" — on the blue cover of her diary in June 1852.

The westward migration of Lorena's family from Great Britain to California during the course of two centuries was not an unusual story for early Americans. It was the pattern repeated by countless others seeking the elusive golden promise at the end of the western rainbow. Like so many others, George Hayes, Lorena's ancestor, believed that opportunity would be found in the West. He began his search for wealth and prosperity when he was about twenty-five years old, arriving in Connecticut in the early 1670s.

Family speculation, again based upon the spelling of the last name, claims he could have been either a Scot or an Englishman. Little is known about George's origins or his previous life, but it is known that he settled in Windsor, just north of Hartford. His name first appears in Connecticut records in 1683, when he married a second wife five months after the death of his first. Fifteen years later the couple and their seven children lived in Granby, northwest of Hartford. George later moved his family six miles south to Simsbury, where he died in 1725.[16] Lorena's grandfather was one of George's thirty-nine great-grandsons. Born March 31, 1776, Martin Hays was the seventh son and last child in a family of ten children. His mother was the former Rosanne Holcomb; Samuel Hays II, his father, served in the Simsbury militia company during the Revolutionary War. Apparently Martin's parents believed in the English tradition which decreed that in a large, multi-son family, one of the sons should enter the church. Martin (Lorena's grandfather), destined for the ministry, became the only son to attend college. When ill health forced him to give up his studies, he turned to farming and also became one of a growing number of mechanics during the eighteenth century to be praised for their industry and ingenuity. In this he followed a family tradition.

Through the generations, most of the Hay(e)s men had been described as "ingenious mechanics and inventors," as well as wagon and carriage makers, coopers, carpenters, shoemakers, and farmers. Lorena's paternal grandfather was also a man of "considerable literary taste and talent, undeveloped for want of opportunities of culture." This description was provided by his youngest son, a Presbyterian minister, for the 1884 family genealogy. "A restless visionary, like several of his brothers," Martin was only moderately successful in business. He was also portrayed as having "perfect integrity and deep religious principles."[17]

While members of the second and third generations of the Hay(e)s clan remained in New England, the footsteps of the fourth led many of them west to the lands of New York and Pennsylvania. In 1800 Lorena's grandfather followed the lead of an older brother, Pliny, who has been credited with beginning their family's exodus from Connecticut. (The oldest brother had inherited the family home.) With Martin was his wife of two years, the former Mary Camp, daughter of Rev. Samuel and Hannah Guernsey Camp of Ridgeway, Connecticut. Mary, Lorena's grandmother, was considered a "woman of fine mental and moral qualities and much natural refinement."[18]

Martin and Mary Hays were married December 25, 1797. Their first move was to the small New York community of Marcellus, about ten miles southwest of Syracuse. There Lorena's father, Alson, was born on August 18, 1801, the second in a family of three sons and two daughters. A second move, again to the west, brought the Hays family to Plattsburg in Steuben County, where two of Martin's older brothers had settled by 1806. Family recollections do not agree about the date of the third move, but the Hays family ended up in western Pennsylvania in present-day Erie County. One account says the journey was made in 1814-15 while another claims it was six years later.[19]

One of the attractions of northwestern Pennsylvania for Martin Hays might well have been the low price of land. After the War of 1812 property there could be purchased for as little as twenty cents an acre. The area around the community of Erie became one of the most heavily settled in the region.[20]

In later years Lorena's grandfather was considered an early settler of Greene, as the area was known when its name was changed from Beaver Dam. One nineteenth century history of Erie County states that between 1816 and 1818 a colony of New England people settled in that township, "including Martin Hayes and sons." How much land Lorena's grandfather may have owned at any one time cannot be ascertained but according to his will, dated September 2, 1846, he had "about fifty acres" at that time.[21]

While the youngest son, Joseph Martin, studied at Jefferson College (now Washington and Jefferson College in Washington, Pennsylvania) and continued his ministerial training at Ohio's Western Reserve College, the two older Hays sons, Lester and Alson, married and settled near their parents. On April 12, 1826, Alson married Susannah Woodward, the eighteen-year-old daughter of Oliver and Lenity Segar Woodward. Susannah was seven years younger than Alson Hays, the first of the three husbands she would outlive.[22]

Susannah was born January 14, 1808, in Bradford County, Pennsylvania, according to the Hays genealogy, although her birthplace was given as Ohio in the 1850 Illinois census. Her mother, Lenity, was the second wife of Oliver Woodward; Susannah was their oldest daughter and fourth child in a family of seven. Susannah presumably never learned to read or write, since she signed legal documents with an "X."[23]

The Woodwards must have moved frequently because Susannah's immediate younger sister, Caroline, was born two years later on February 6, in Elmira, New York. Caroline and three brothers would later join Susannah as she moved west to Illinois and on to California. Little more is known about the Woodwards, but they apparently returned to Pennsylvania by 1830, if not earlier, because an "Oliver Woodward" and family were listed in that census for Greenfield township, Erie County.[24]

The marriage of Lorena's parents marked the beginning of a relationship between the Woodward and Hays families that lasted throughout the nineteenth century. A year after their marriage, Lorena arrived on May 29, the first of ten children during the next twenty years. She was given the middle name of Lenity after her maternal grandmother and later modified it to "Lenita" for one of her pen names. Two brothers were soon followed by four sisters, all born in Greene, Pennsylvania, in the 1830s. The youngest of the Hays children were born during the 1840s.[25]

It cannot be determined with any sort of certainty that Lorena's father owned land. The fifth federal census lists only "heads of households" and the number of people in each home by age and sex, but not by name. There is no "Alson Hays" listed. However, an "Alonzo Hays" was recorded in Mill Creek township, population 1,783, where Lorena's grandparents resided. If "Alonzo" and "Alson" could have been the same person, then the extra female, between the ages of fifteen and twenty years old, listed in that household must have been either a younger relative or a live-in servant girl. According to the Hays genealogy, in 1830 Alson and Susannah were the parents of a daughter,

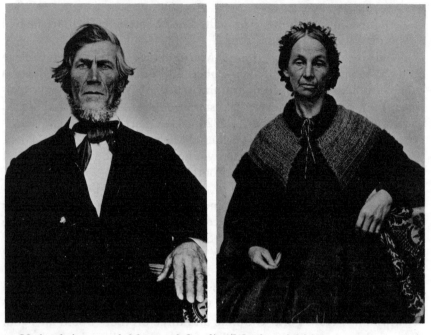

Undated tintypes of Adam and Caroline Woodward Lithgow, Lorena's uncle and aunt, probably from the 1860s.

Lorena, and a son, Flavel Horatio, born August 24, 1828. Their second son, William Philander, was born July 24, 1830, and might not have been recorded in the census for that year.[26]

Exactly when Lorena's father decided to move west is not known. By 1833 a distant relative by marriage had settled in western Illinois, in a section formerly part of the Military Tract established to provide bounty lands for 18,000 veterans of the War of 1812.[27] This family relationship, centering upon the Woodwards, was a complicated one, but it provides an example of the strength of kinship bonds in an extensive, yet close, nineteenth century extended family. In 1833 Caroline Woodward, Lorena's maternal aunt, married Adam Lithgow, whose family apparently also lived in Erie County in the 1830s. One of Adam's sisters, Elizabeth Lithgow, later married Lauristan H. Brown, a cooper and carpenter from New York state. Lauristan's brother, B(en-jamin) D. Brown, became the first one of the expanded family circle to move west, arriving in Illinois in 1833-34, where he began work as a millwright in Rockport. In later years B. D. Brown played a prominent role in the development of western Pike County.[28]

The next member of the Hays-Woodward-Lithgow-Brown clan to feel the lure of the West was Lorena's uncle, Adam Lithgow. Church records show that he must have been in Illinois sometime before the late summer of 1838. After the annual meeting in August of that year he became a member, by baptism, of the First Baptist Church, which had been established in Pike County in 1829. Whether his wife and two small daughters accompanied him to Illinois at that time or waited to come with the Hayses in 1839 is unknown. Between the third Saturday of August 1839 and the same time in 1840, the Lithgow name appears in church records with the notation "1 baptized, 1 excluded, 2 dead." One death might have been that of their son, James, who died at birth on August 1, 1840. However, the other death cannot be explained in light of the known Lithgow genealogy.[29]

Susannah Woodward Hays Hull Gould, Lorena's mother, who outlived three husbands.

The Lithgows probably made the trip west to Illinois in 1837 at the same time that the Lauristan Browns and the John Dehavens did. Mrs. Dehaven (Leah) and Mrs. Brown (Elizabeth) were sisters of Adam Lithgow, Lorena's uncle. Their mother, Elizabeth Lithgow, may have accompanied them, because she was listed as a member of the Dehaven household in Illinois in 1850. The Dehaven family came from the same area of Pennsylvania (Mill Creek Township in Erie County) as did Lorena's family. A similarity of names in the 1830, 1840, and 1850 census records also suggests that other Pennsylvania neighbors moved to Illinois about the same time, including the McDaniel and Morey families, acquaintances of the Hays.[30]

With a number of relatives and friends already in Illinois, word must have reached Lorena's father about the advantages of moving. Whether letters were exchanged between the Hayses and Lithgows can not be determined, but favorable reports from a new area were usually responsible for relatives moving west. Many small communities were held together by kinship bonds.

The thought of moving west must have been in the back of Alson Hays's mind for some time before he decided to take the step in 1839. That was a good year to seek prosperity elsewhere because the United States was struggling to recover from the grip of the second of the five great panics that periodically depressed the economy during the nineteenth century. As the Panic of 1837 moved from New Orleans to New York, editor Horace Greeley of the *New York Tribune* made an indelible impression on the public with his advice to "go West." At first it seemed a logical enough move because the West had managed to survive the early stages of the depression. Crops were plentiful and prices high. But during the next four years farm prices declined and Illinois was deeply affected by the aftermath of the panic. Tempting men like Lorena's father to move west was the bargain price of $1.25 an acre for land in the public domain. When the Preemption Act became law in June 1838, it opened up a new range of possibilities and alternatives.[31]

Uncle Henry Woodward in 1875.

Alson Hays packed up his family and left Pennsylvania behind. The restlessness attributed to his father seemed to have settled upon his shoulders alone — his two brothers and the youngest Hays sister, Roxy Ann Hays Hilborn, remained in Pennsylvania near their parents. Probably accompanying Alson and his family were another sister, Mary Marinda, and her husband, Thomas Jefferson West, with their three sons and three daughters. The Wests were listed as residents of Pike County in the 1840 census. Henry Woodward, Lorena's youngest maternal uncle, was also in Illinois by this time and an older Woodward uncle, Arnold, had moved to Pike County and purchased land in November 1833.[32]

Lorena was nearly twelve years old when she joined her younger brothers and sisters in bidding good-bye to their grandparents, aunts and uncles, cousins and schoolmates, friends and neighbors. She would never see any of them again. Twelve years later she still longed to return to the "scenes of my childhood" and envied Aunt Caroline Lithgow and Leah Dehaven their visits to Pennsylvania.

Lorena never wrote about her family's 1839 move to Illinois, so how the Hays family reached their destination remains another unanswered question. Steamboats and schooners plied the Great Lakes between

Buffalo, New York, and Detroit, Michigan, stopping along the shores of Lake Erie at the towns of Erie in Pennsylvania and Ashtabula, Cleveland, and Sandusky in Ohio. From Detroit another boat took emigrants to the new city of Chicago. The "most expedient and pleasant way" to travel at that time was by steamboat down the Illinois River. Stagecoaches also ran between Chicago and Peru, Illinois, for a fare of six cents a mile and 37 ½ cents a meal at the taverns along the route. From Peru, river steamers to St. Louis, Missouri, stopped at Montezuma, on the eastern edge of Pike County. Expenses for such a trip could be cut by making the Illinois lap on horseback for an estimated seventy cents to $1.50 a day. Emigrants going by water were advised to take their wagons with them because they would need them at the end of the trip.[33]

An overland route could have taken the Hays family south to the National Road, which they could have followed into Illinois. This road, which reached Columbus, Ohio, by 1833, entered Illinois at the northeast corner of Clark County and crossed the state diagonally, ninety miles southwest to Vandalia, the old state capital. The Illinois section of the National Road was described in 1834 as being eighty feet wide with a thirty-foot center section raised above standing water. An 1841 traveler reported it was still "nothing more than a track." From Vandalia a network of roads built between 1817 and 1822 led emigrants to the Mississippi River and St. Louis.[34]

A third alternative also existed. It would have been possible then for emigrants to make the entire trip by water, as did other Hays relatives in the spring of 1840. T. J. West, whose wife, Mary Hays West, was Lorena's paternal aunt, leased a sawmill in order to prepare lumber for a raft that would take his family on the first part of the journey. As Wells Wallis West, the sixth West child, later recalled, "The raft was put together on a large creek below the sawmill and one day we moved with a team to the raft where some men were building a cabin on it." The Wests "went down different streams" — one of these might have been French Creek — to the Allegheny and Ohio rivers. At Louisville they sold the raft and transferred to a steamboat for the trip up the Mississippi River to Cincinnati Landing, which was thirty miles below Quincy in Illinois.[35]

Whichever route they took, the journey ended for the Hays family at the home of relatives in the low, rolling river bluffs of Pike County, where 800 square miles had been divided into twenty-two townships by 1837.[36]

The advantages of this part of Illinois were widely touted in the mid-1830s by booster publications announcing that "no state in the Great West has attracted so much attention or elicited so many enquiries from those who desire to avail themselves to the advantages of settlement in a new and rising country.'' Illinois was reputed to ''offer every possible inducement to emigrants'' because it had the ''richest soil in the Union.'' Prospective settlers were told there existed ''vast quantities of first rate land lying in every direction uncultivated, which may be had very cheap.'' One acre was guaranteed to produce ''at least three times as much as the same amount of land in most of the eastern states,'' while produce would ''spring up almost spontaneously, less than one-third of the labor being necessary on farms here than is required of farms in the east.''[37]

Pike County, the oldest county in the Military Tract, was bordered along the Mississippi River with a sandy soil that was ''mostly inundated land at spring floods'' but provided ''a great summer and winter range for stock.'' At flood season the Snycartee Slough on the western edge of the county supposedly would make steamboat navigation possible as far as the small community of Atlas on the edge of the bluffs. Two to three miles inland from the river, the prairie was cut by ravines with streams, ''chiefly timbered.'' The interior of Pike County was ''quite rolling with excellent prairie and timbered upland.'' The earnest emigrant was also told ''this must eventually become a rich and populous country.'' In spite of the nation's economic problems, western Illinois beckoned enticingly in the late 1830s.[38]

Part 1—The Illinois Years

The Illinois Years 1848-53

LORENA AND HER FAMILY reached their destination in western Pike County sometime in 1839. In November her father bought land in Pleasant Vale Township, between the small communities of Barry and New Canton. On November 7 he paid Isaac and Eleanor Crouch $140 for 50.75 acres in section 4. The following day, November 8, he purchased an adjoining 85.19 acres in section 3 from the United States government. For this property Alson Hays paid $106.49 based upon the standard Preemption Act price of $1.25 an acre. Federal land policy required that he pay the entire amount in cash, either gold or silver coin, at the time of purchase, but he was not required to make any improvements.[1]

The Hays were relative latecomers to this area since most of their immediate neighbors purchased land in 1836-37. Lorena's father owned one of the larger parcels, however, as most of the other holdings in that part of Pike County averaged between forty and forty-five acres in the late 1830s. The land the Hays family bought was located on the low bluffs, immediately east of the Mississippi River flood plain.[2]

Many acres in this region of Pike County were prairie, designated in 1819 as "very rich first rate soil" and "excellent second rate soil." However, much of the land that Lorena's father purchased consisted of hillsides and ravines, covered with heavy underbrush and a dense forest of oak, elm, walnut, hickory, hackberry, hazel, and maple. Alson Hays faced the problem of clearing land with help from two sons, nine and eleven years old. A small stream ran between the two sections while a spring issued from a hillside near a level area where the Hays may have built their home in section 3. Lorena's father received the patent to this land on March 10, 1843. The three-and-one-half-year delay was typical of the time required in those days for the federal

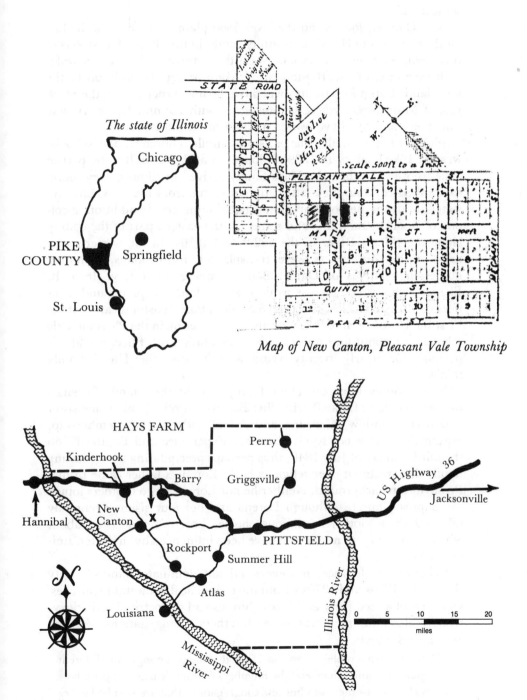

The state of Illinois

Map of New Canton, Pleasant Vale Township

Location of the Hays farm in Pike County, Illinois

government to verify that the land had not been previously sold to someone else.[3]

New Canton, located on the level flood plain at the base of the low bluffs, became the Hays' community center in the 1840s. The streets of this town, with seventy-six lots, were thirty-three and sixty feet wide, with exception of the 100-foot wide Main Street. In addition to the farm land, Lorena's parents owned two facing corner lots on the north side of Main Street where it intersected with Palmira Street. At one time they may also have owned another lot in block four.[4]

With its many small villages, stores, mills, churches, and schools, western Pike County in 1839 no longer considered itself to be part of "the frontier." When the Hays family arrived in Illinois, they found established communities settled by emigrants from the New England states and from the South in almost equal numbers. In addition, a colony of English emigrants had settled in the eastern part of the county along the Illinois River in the 1820s and 1830s. In the western area most of the southerners were transplanted Kentuckians, including numerous relatives of Daniel Boone, among them Rev. Jesse B. Elledge, whose mother was a niece of the famed explorer and frontiersman. In 1833 Elledge received a call to take "pastoral care" of the First Baptist Church of Pike County, then meeting in the Pleasant Vale schoolhouse about four miles south of the Hays farm. Elledge held this position for nearly twenty years and became the Hays' family minister.[5]

Nine months after the Hays family bought their land, Lorena's mother became affiliated with this Baptist church, joining her sister and brother-in-law, Caroline and Adam Lithgow, in membership. Susannah Hays was "received on her Experience and Baptized" on the third Sunday of July 1840, thus perhaps precipitating a long-lasting family disagreement over religious faith. Lorena's father came from a Presbyterian background. Neither he nor Lorena's two brothers joined the Baptist Church, although Lorena and her four sisters eventually followed their mother's religious choice. Lorena's indecision about which church to join might well have been influenced by this interfamily conflict.[6]

Religious intolerance, however, did not dominate Illinois society during the 1830s and 1840s within the evangelical Protestant churches, which emphasized piety and fellowship instead of doctrinal orthodoxy, while welcoming members of each others' congregations. As one traveler observed:

> There is considerable expression of good feelings amongst the different religious denominations and the members frequently hear the preachers of each other as there are but few congregations that are supplied every Sabbath.[7]

One of Lorena's younger cousins, Louisa E. Lithgow, later went against her parents' Baptist convictions to join the Congregational Church in Barry.[8] So it was not unseemly for Lorena to attend services of other denominations while trying to decide whether to join the Baptist Church.

For two-and-a-half years Lorena considered alternatives, enduring family and social pressures to make up her mind. She felt out of place at a Baptist Fourth of July picnic because she did not belong to the church in her own right. Yet she continued to lack the confidence to go forward in search of salvation. Only once during these years did Lorena gather up the necessary courage to walk, tremblingly, up the church aisle. This occurred at the 1848 revival meeting in St. Louis. Back home in Pike County she found it difficult to repeat such a profession of faith.

Lorena finally made her decision nearly two years after her father's death. In August 1850 she managed to overcome her fear of total immersion to become a member of the United Baptist faith "through experience and baptism."[9]

Church membership was not an unmixed blessing nor was it to be undertaken lightly. Once the choice became final, the congregation expected strict adherence to its rules. Lorena found it difficult to do her "duty" because this meant she must speak out at covenant meetings, held the fourth Saturday of each month. Members of the First Baptist Church were required to "express his or her feelings, at least in a few words, so that the church may know what progress they are making in the divine Life." This would enable others "to participate with them in their joys and sorrows, to pray with and for each other and help in our Christian endeavors." Hesitant to volunteer, Lorena wished the meetings could be conducted in the manner of a school class, where members were encouraged to speak, rather than ridiculed for refraining. She felt men did not understand that women were unaccustomed to speaking in public. It also was the duty of each member of the congregation to attend covenant meetings "unless providentially hindered."[10] No wonder Lorena felt guilty when she could not muster the courage to attend these meetings. She often stayed away from church services as well because she felt unworthy.

Baptist "Rules of Decorum" also required a standing committee on vigilance to report on the "state of mind in regard to Religion of the members in the different neighborhoods." Lorena's third youngest sister, Amanda Malvina Hays, came under this scrutiny in December 1852, when she admitted she had "sinned in her irrevident conduct for which she was sorrow and wishes the church to forgive." Three women were appointed to visit the Hays household and ascertain the facts. At the January 1853 covenant meeting this committee reported they were "satisfied that the sister had sincerely repented" so the congregation forgave Lorena's fifteen-year-old sister.[11]

Once her religious problems were resolved, Lorena's attention focused upon her consuming desire for more education. She probably attended her first classes while in Greene, Pennsylvania, where church and private pay schools had been established by 1830. The first public school in that area was built in 1837, four years after the passage of the Pennsylvania Public School Law and two years before the Hays family moved west. In Illinois Lorena, her brothers, and sisters could attend school whenever time and money permitted, because in 1836 a log schoolhouse was built in New Canton, less than two miles from the Hays' home. The fee for this common school probably matched that charged by the school in nearby Pleasant Hill Township: $2 per scholar per term.[12]

In the Midwest during the 1830s and 1840s, a more liberal attitude prevailed towards female education than in the East, where it was often considered an unnecessary accomplishment for young ladies. In 1834 the *Chicago Democrat* declared that female education was of "immense importance as connected with domestic life." It imparted an "elevated and improved character . . . [and] eminently exalts the dignity and multiplies the charms of every female that can excel it." In Pike County additional education for girls became available in 1836 when a private seminary opened in Griggsville for young ladies, eight to eighteen years of age, including some pupils from Alton, Illinois, and St. Louis, Missouri.[13]

By 1852 Pike County seminaries and academies offered girls a preparatory level curriculum of geography, grammar, arithmetic, and composition at $8 for a twenty-week session. Lorena could not afford this tuition, let alone the $12 fee to enroll in the "senior department" for advanced courses in English, mathematics "pure and mixed," the natural sciences, classical and modern languages and phonetic writing. After completing such studies a few fortunate girls then attended the Female College, organized by the Methodist-Episcopal Church in Jacksonville, Illinois, where "the attention paid to female education indicates a new era in society." One of Lorena's acquaintances, Sophrenia F. Naylor of Barry, was graduated from there in 1852 with a "Mistress of English Literature" degree.[14] Lorena must have longed for a similar education.

The Illinois years had not been kind to Alson Hays and his family. He had to settle on timbered land in an area where most of the tall-grass prairie was already claimed by the time the Hays arrived in 1839. How much land he cleared to farm is not known but thirty years later much of the property was still heavily wooded. To judge from the records, Alson Hays cleared and farmed only enough land to provide

Land in Section 4, between the communities of Barry and New Canton, belonged to Lorena's father in the 1840s.

his family with food. Otherwise, he earned their living by working as a carpenter.[15]

Six months of store bills in the spring and summer of 1848 provide a brief profile of the Hays family lifestyle and of their community. These bills imply that Alson Hays did not grow crops to be sold commercially, although he did raise most of the family's food supply. Beets grew quite well in Pike County (in the fall of 1847 one was harvested with a "good weight" of 19 pounds, 2 ounces), so the following spring Lorena's father purchased "1 paper beet seed" for ten cents at one of the New Canton stores.[16]

Almost every day some member of the family made the four-mile round trip to New Canton to pick up supplies at the two "groceries." Staple items on the Hays shopping list included molasses and sugar, dried apples, "tatters," matches, coffee, "Imported Tea," flour, saleratus, salt, and vinegar. Once they bought a pound of ginger. A most unusual purchase was butter, which the Hays bought frequently, four to six pounds at a time. Either their two cows had gone dry that summer or there was not enough milk left to make butter for a family of ten persons, including baby Augustus Harvey. He died at age seven-and-one-half months on August 15, 1848. (The Hays family earlier lost another baby, Susanna, on April 18, 1844, six days after birth.)[17]

At the New Canton stores the Hays also bought small tools and

A spring from the wooded hillside becomes a small stream which could have provided water for the Hays household.

nails. A currycomb cost them fifteen cents as did one and a quarter pounds of powder plus a bar of lead, while a pocket knife was charged for twenty-five cents. In May 1848 they bought a set of china teacups and plates, three bowls, and a platter for a total of $1.76. They purchased wicking to make candles, augmented in the spring by one pound of candles at fifteen cents. The New Canton stores also carried yardage of calico, muslin, cottonade, "Jeans," gingham, linen, and cambric, as well as the requisite sewing notions. On March 14, 1848, five yards of silk fringe at eighteen-and-three-quarter cents a yard were charged for a total of ninety-four cents. Slippers, gaiter boots, and pumps were also sold by the New Canton stores, as were ivory hair combs. In mid-February 1848 the Hays family charged half a quire of paper for ten cents.[18]

For a family in debt there were few luxuries in life, but the store bills show that Lorena's father was a man who enjoyed an occasional cigar. Alson Hays indulged himself every three or four weeks by purchasing cigars in dozen or half-dozen lots, priced at ten cents a dozen. In between, he bought tobacco in half-pound packages for twelve or thirteen cents, depending upon which store he patronized. In mid-April 1848 three strings of beads, total price twenty-five cents, were charged, perhaps intended as May birthday gifts for Lorena and her fourth sister, Sarah Louise.[19]

The promises of prosperity held out so alluringly by western Illinois

In November 1839 Lorena's father bought 85.19 acres on the west side of Section 3 in Pleasant Vale Township.

failed to materialize for the Hays family. A long period of depression, punctuated by brief intervals of economic revival, during most of the early 1840s extended well into 1848. Although agricultural production was abundant, prices remained low and money was in short supply throughout the United States during these years. Since 1845 Lorena's father had been borrowing small sums which he could seldom afford to repay at the six to twelve percent interest rates.[20]

The area in which the Hays family lived was close to the edge of the Mississippi River sloughs and swamps, where a variety of "malarious diseases" lurked. Regardless of all the publicity attesting to the healthfulness of the region, Illinois in the 1840s was noted for "diseases of a bilious nature, which sometime assume an aggravated character, when it speedily carries off a number of victims." Chills, fever, and ague added up to an affliction, widespread among the population each fall, that was known as the "Illinois shakes." It was not considered fatal if quickly and properly treated. "A kind of miasma floating around in the atmosphere was absorbed into the system," an 1880 county history stated. In the spring of 1846 Lorena's youngest sister, Mary Melissa, died at the age of five years; her maternal aunt, Mary Marinda Hays West, also died that year, in August.[21]

The cause of Alson Hays' death on October 4, 1848, at the age of forty-seven years, is unknown. Pike County death records do not date back that far and not all deaths were reported in the weekly county

Juniper tree in old section of graveyard near New Canton.

newspapers. Although Lorena's father was attended during his last ill-ness by Drs. A. C. Baker and P. Parker, their bill did not include any medical information. Their $10 fee covered a visit and two consulta-tions for Alson Hays in 1848 as well as three visits made in March 1846, when the youngest Hays daughter died. Apparently the bill for these three earlier house calls had never been paid. Also charged against the estate of Alson Hays was the bill of $7 for his coffin and fourteen signed promissory notes plus two others that were unsigned. Most of these unpaid notes had been for cash lent to redeem, in part, a mortgage on the Hays house. In addition, the family also owed $70 for groceries and sundry items charged at the New Canton stores owned by James Shipman and Hugh Barker.[22]

Seven days after the death of Lorena's father, her mother (Susannah Hays) declined to serve as administrator of the estate, declaring to the probate court judge that "it is my wish that H. Barker be appointed in my stead." Her statement, signed with an "X" which was identified as "her mark," was witnessed on October 11, 1848, by Lorena, whose shaky signature testifies to her emotional state that day. The Hays family was indebted to the administrator, who also served as a justice of the peace, for $20.52 in groceries, $1.25 in fees and a note of $13.32. Hugh Barker posted a $600 bond for the position of administrator, as required by the county court. [23]

Lorena and her family were left destitute. "There is no money on hands no loom, provisions, fuel, feed for the cows, no sheep, a deficien-

cy of $8 on the horse, no saddle or bridle,'' reported administrator
Barker on December 7, 1848. After appraising the Hays personal property, he set aside a portion to serve as the "widow's dower," which
should have amounted to one-third of her husband's estate, according
to both custom and the common law of England and Colonial
America.[24]

The remaining household goods were put up for sale at an auction
on December 25, 1848. Conducting such an event on Christmas Day
would not have been considered inappropriate because the holiday was
rarely celebrated with the type of festivities observed later in the nineteenth century. The auctioneer, Thomas R. Russell, sold carpenter's
tools, supplies, and lumber appraised at a total value of $112.59. Nine-
teen neighbors, friends, and relatives in Pleasant Vale Township attended the auction; their purchases amounted to $62.73.

This sale of personal property did little to help clear the Hays family
debts of more than $400. Between December 4, 1848, and November
29, 1849, the administrator disbursed $99.03 to the Hays family. This
included $30.97 as the "widow's specific property" as well as another
$30 and then, as an "absolute allowance," $16.67 more. Lorena's
family was also alloted $3.87 on the "year's provisions." Taxes for
1847-49 amounted to $9.50 and it cost another $3 for a trip to the
federal land office in Quincy, Hancock County, to "perfect the title to
the land." To balance the books, the administrator, whose fee was
three dollars, charged himself the sum of $30.97 to cover the difference,
resulting in a total of $102.03 in credits and $102.41 in debits.[25]

On March 1, 1848, Hugh Barker announced in the *Pike County Free
Press* that as administrator he would appear before the probate court in
Pittsfield on March 5, "for the adjustment of claims" against the estate
of Lorena's father. "All persons interested may appear. Those knowing themselves indebted to said estate are requested to make immediate
payment." The outcome of this hearing is unknown because it was not
filed with the Hays' estate papers at the county courthouse in
Pittsfield.[26]

By 1849 the Hays' property had been reduced to "more or less"
45.1 acres in section 3 and 26.57 acres in section 4, Pleasant Vale
Township, plus the two village lots in New Canton. A year after Alson
Hays' death, his wife, Susannah, voluntarily relinquished all claims
and dower rights to this property "for and in consideration of the sum
of one dollar to me in hand, paid by Hugh Barker, administrator."
Perhaps this was done to clear the remaining debts. The transfer of title
was witnessed on November 3, 1849, by Lorena and Stephen R. Gray,
an acting justice of the peace and formerly postmaster in the community of Barry. Two months earlier, before Susannah Hays signed over title to the land, administrator Barker applied to the circuit court for per-

mission to sell it.[27]

These legal proceedings reveal an almost unnoticed paradox concerning women's status at mid-century. When Susannah Hays signed over the real estate, she acted on her own behalf. She did so without any attempt by the justice of the peace to make sure she fully understood the implications of what she was doing. As a widow in 1849 her situation was much different than it had been a year earlier when she and her husband sold twenty-five acres of their land. As a married woman in February 1848, Susannah had been taken aside by the justice of the peace, who later wrote:

> Susannah, wife of Alson Hays, having been by now made acquainted with the contents of said deed and being by me examined separate and apart from her Husband acknowledged that she had executed the same and relinquished her right to dower in and to the premises without compulsion of said husband.[28]

This was apparently standard legal practice in the 1840s and 1850s to provide protection when married women were involved. In California twelve years later Lorena received the same type of explanation, in almost identical words, when she and her husband sold their house and lot in June 1860.[29]

Representing Lorena's mother throughout these estate hearings were William A. and J. Grimshaw, well-to-do Pittsfield attorneys who were remembered in later years for helping widows and orphans. Their fee amounted to $66.42, while other legal costs came to an additional $33.43.[30]

On January 5, 1850, administrator Barker sold the Hays land at an auction, conducted on the steps of the courthouse, as was the custom of the day. It brought $105.60. Five months later Barker received another $100.20 as payment on a note from the purchaser. In his report to the court, Barker did not specify the exact number of acres sold nor did he mention the two lots in New Canton, so presumably he had disposed of all the Hays property.[31]

Considering that this was a forced estate sale to settle debts, the total price for the Hays property was probably fair enough. However, only two years earlier Lorena's parents sold half of their land in section 4 for approximately six dollars an acre. In the 1850 sale the remainder brought much less. Even if the land in section 3 was not worth as much as it had been, 1849 and 1850 were years of increasing prosperity throughout the United States, so Pike County prices would be expected to reflect something of the improved economic climate. Perhaps the seemingly low price for the Hays land can be explained by the fact that production of wheat, corn, and potato crops was below average in western Pike County during these years.[32]

From existing estate and land records it is now nearly impossible to

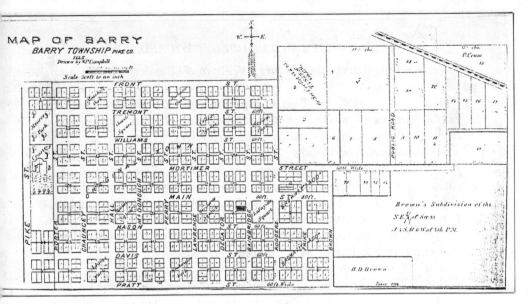

Map of Barry, Illinois

tell which of the debts were discounted, how many paid in full or what remained to the Hays family after the administrator's costs and the lawyers' fees were paid. It seems certain, however, that Lorena and her family were left with very little to begin anew.

Adding to their problems was the death of Lorena's eldest brother, twenty-one-year-old Flavel Horatio, on November 6, 1849. A year younger than Lorena, he died in Galena, Illinois. Whether his death occurred from an accident while mining for lead or from the cholera epidemic rampaging throughout the United States that year is unknown. In 1849 the dreaded disease killed an estimated 4,285 persons in St. Louis alone: half the total known deaths for that city in that year.[33]

In December 1849, a month after her brother's death, Lorena again began to write in her diary, this time on a more regular basis. A notation at the top of page six shows that the Hays family had now moved four miles up the bluffs to the thriving community of Barry. Established in 1836, Barry had a population of 400 in 1850. It was described as a "pleasant and business village eligibly situated on the north-west of a beautiful and well-cultivated prairie extending some 10-12 miles from east to west and 4-5 miles north to south."[34]

Three of the four mercantile houses were doing "a fair business" in Barry when Lorena and her family moved there. "Mechanics appear to have plenty of trade of late, especially carpenters who have several store-houses and dwellings in process of erection," observed one county newspaper. A pork processing house, a steam flour mill, sawmills, and a woolen factory were also located in or near Barry. It was the hometown of six wheelwrights, sixteen blacksmiths, twenty carpenters and forty-three men who gave their occupation as "cooper," including

Lorena's only surviving brother, William Philander, twenty years old.[35]

The community of Barry supported a grog shop and the establishments of ten merchants, two tailors, a "hat maker," two cabinetmakers, three shoemakers, three saddlers, a harness maker and a tanner. Employed in other trades were three painters, a plasterer, three masons and a "stone mason," a stage driver, a potter, a broom maker, and a woodchopper. Another thirty-one men were listed in the 1850 census as "laborers." Professional men included four school-teachers, seven doctors, an engineer, a surveyor, a river pilot, and a lawyer. Although women's work was not recorded, one female clerk was employed in Barry, as were eight male clerks.[36]

The village was depicted as a "reading community" and the editor added, "That *we* can testify." Although there were no public libraries in the western division of Pike County, four Sunday school libraries provided readers like Lorena with a selection of 450 volumes. The Methodist Church was the first religious denomination to build a house of worship in Barry. It was soon followed by the Baptists, the Christians, and the Congregationalists.[37]

Lorena and her family moved their few belongings from the farm in Pleasant Vale Township into a house near what was then the west side of Bainbridge Street, which was 60 feet wide, and one lot down from the corner of 80-foot wide Main Street. The Hays house faced Lafayette Square, one of ten public parks and squares in the village. Barry was laid out in such a way that crossing alleys, fifteen feet wide, separated every two lots from the other six in each square block.[38]

In the 1850s it was customary for families to take in at least one unrelated lodger. Many were artisans living with their employers' families. Others were unrelated to their landlords but took lodgings because there was a housing shortage in western Illinois. However, the 1850 census does not show anyone other than the seven immediate family members living in the Hays household, at least not on the day when the census taker came to their door. Lorena never openly wrote about how they supported themselves, but several times alluded to some employment, either taking in sewing or boarders. Perhaps the Hays women did both, but the latter is more likely because renting space to lodgers at approximately two dollars a week for room and board provided an assured income for a widow who had no other way to earn a living.[39]

"Duty" kept Lorena at home when she desperately wanted to earn enough money to go away to school, to replace physical labor around the house with intellectual accomplishments. Had she followed these inclinations, her mother would have been "thrown out of work, too, without my assistance" because May 1850 was a "hurrying time" in

Barry. The village was crowded again in September of that year when teachers attended a county-wide meeting. Lorena wrote: "Last week has been one of bustle and commotion on account of the Institute are having boarders and many coming in and out."

Lorena and her sister Caroline, eighteen, began teaching school in the spring of 1850 without any specific training or instruction for these assignments. Until mid-century the teaching profession had been almost completely dominated by young men, but the California gold rush attracted so many of them that rural village schools throughout the country were in danger of closing for lack of teachers. This provided women, especially those in the Midwest, with a greater opportunity than ever before to enter the teaching profession. This phenomenon was noted in 1853 by Sarah Josepha Hale, the renowned editor of *Godey's Lady's Book:*

> While the Great West, California and the wide Ocean invite young men to wealth and adventure, and while the labors of the school room offer so little recompense or honor, the twenty thousand teachers needed cannot be obtained from their ranks, and therefore the young women of our country must become teachers of the common schools or these must be given up.[40]

Room and board often supplemented teachers' salaries but women were paid less, usually only half the salary for male teachers. It was assumed that women teachers did not need higher wages because they were only working temporarily until they married and were not supporting families, as were their male counterparts. Although no records exist for Pike County schools at this time, the superintendent once announced in the newspapers that "the lowest amount of monthly compensation is five dollars."[41]

Lorena's first teaching experience was a disappointment because she had few students and her school was in an isolated area. Due to "unfavorable weather and other circumstances," which she never explained, Lorena closed school after three weeks and returned to Barry. She then decided, after some hesitation, that she could improve her education by attending the Teachers' Institute scheduled for mid-May at the Congregational Church in Griggsville.

Controversy surrounded this meeting of teachers in 1850 who wished to improve their profession. Many Pike County residents thought the institute to be unnecessary, although the superintendent of schools believed:

> The best method of securing good teachers and raising the standards of their qualifications is to convince people of the great difference there is between good and poor teachers — convince them that a good teacher will do more in one quarter than a poor one will do at 10 dollars per month.[42]

Disapproving letters appeared in the two newspapers but the editors "earnestly" recommended to all teachers "the propriety of dismissing their schools" to attend the two-week meeting, which was open to "all persons now teaching or intending to teach." The Teachers' Institute of May 1850 was the first held in Pike County in nearly fourteen years; earlier attempts to form a county educational society "to which the ladies are invited" had failed. Each community in the county named a committee to observe and report on the proceedings of the institute. Those attending were requested to bring slates, pencils, Bibles, the *Eclectic Fourth Reader,* and any other text books they owned. [43]

Lorena and her sister were among the twenty-seven teachers from western Pike County who attended the institute. Only four of the ninety-seven teachers in the county were absent. Lorena thoroughly enjoyed the sessions, which began at "8½ o'clock a.m." with roll call, scripture readings, and prayers. The institute ended each day at 4:30 P.M., after lessons in map drawing and elocution. In between were scheduled eleven short classes on various aspects of mathematics, grammar, punctuation, composition, and spelling, with an hour-and-a-half lunch break and three recesses, plus singing. More lectures and discussions took place each evening and one topic concerned the issue of early childhood education. Pike County teachers, including Lorena, debated and then voted that children "should not be sent to school under six years of age." Qualifications of teachers and textbooks were also discussed and plans made to hold another Institute in the fall.[44]

In late September 1850 the institute convened again, with fifty-five teachers in attendance at the Baptist Church in Barry. Lorena was appointed to serve as "map drawer" on the second day and was also named to the "court of errors" for the first week. In the evenings she participated as one of the "select readers." Her sister Caroline did not attend this institute, but their brother, William Philander, was elected "sheriff" and also served as one of the "declaimers" during the two weeks. Cousin Louisa Lithgow took her turn as "map drawer" on the third day.[45]

Principal instructor for the Barry institute was Professor Jonathan Baldwin Turner, a former faculty member at Illinois College in Jacksonville and a leader in the Illinois public school movement. A graduate of Yale University, he advocated state-supported universities for the industrial classes when he spoke in Barry and has been credited with instigating the campaign for land grant colleges.[46]

Although Lorena enjoyed the two Teachers' Institutes, she did not resume her teaching career until the following year. In December 1851 she left home to take a position at a small country school eighteen miles from Barry, perhaps in the community of Summer Hill. Lorena kept school until early March 1852 and then went home for a brief vacation, fully expecting to return and teach the spring term. Friends intervened and instead, on March 30, she was hired to teach in one of the three Barry schools.

Two weeks later she was joined by Jon Shastid, who had played major roles in the two Teachers' Institutes of 1850. The same age as Lorena, he was a graduate of Illinois College and already held a prominent position in Pike County educational circles. Lorena continued to teach in the school room next door to Shastid during the summer and fall terms of 1852. However, she did not attend the Teachers' Institute held that April in the nearby community of Perry. Interest in these meetings had apparently waned. No report of the proceedings was printed in the county newspapers, unlike the 1850 institutes which had received wide publicity.[47]

Between teaching positions, Lorena fretted about her health and occupied her free hours by reading and by attending church functions, temperance meetings, and singing schools. Once, she had a chance to continue her studies by attending a six-week writing school in August 1851, taught by a Mrs. Barker. This was probably Ellen Barker, the English-born wife of James Barker, who then lived in Perry. Two years later Jon Shastid visited one of Mrs. Barker's classes and praised her instruction:

> Mrs. Barker deserves great credit for her energy and I hope the pedagogues of the county will have the benefit of her presence and example sometime during the coming summer at a Teachers' Institute.[48]

Shastid also discovered that Mrs. Barker's students "enunciated clearly and could be heard without any painful effort by the audience."[49]

While attending Mrs. Barker's school in 1851, Lorena discovered that she loved to write but disliked reading her own compositions aloud, especially when visitors were present. It was not unusual for school classes to have an audience on oral examination days or at the Friday rhetorical exercises because these occasions provided a form of community entertainment. Young men made it a practice to visit on Friday afternoons when compositions were read so they could preview the latest crop of prospective brides. That alone obviously contributed greatly to Lorena's nervousness and self-consciousness.[50]

More pleasurable times were provided by the singing schools, which also afforded legitimate opportunities for young women and men to meet. "A very good one," taught in February 1853, was described in a letter to Lorena's cousin by another Pike County young lady, who did not appear to be overly interested in the music:

> And I tell you what we had the *best kind* of times. it was three nights this week — Monday, Tuesday and Wednesday. the gents were *very* kind. they came after us each night, if it was to bad to walk. they had

some conveyances for us. they came for us once in a Sleigh and we were so glad for we wanted a Sleigh ride very much, although we had not far to go.[51]

Lorena enjoyed the singing. Music was important to members of the First Baptist Church of Barry. At church a "singing clerk" led "such tunes as will be likely to unite the greatest number of the congregation in singing the songs of Zion." It was hoped that this would result in "further improvements and harmony among the different modes of singing." Music was an approved activity for women during the Victorian years because it was thought to provide a refining influence in the home.[52] In California Lorena attempted to master the violin and later considered taking piano lessons, if she could ever find the time and the money.

During the winter months church activities claimed Lorena's attention. In addition to two services each Sunday (at 11 A.M. and 7 P.M.) there were mid-week prayer meetings on Wednesday evenings. Protracted and quarterly meetings augmented this schedule and Lorena's diary provides a detailed calendar of such religious events during her years in Barry, although she did not attend them all. In some communities protracted meetings could last all winter as various churches took turns, in succession, holding sessions that lasted between three and five weeks each. These protracted meetings were held in the hope that "all the church members would get new zeal and all the non-church members would 'get religion'." As the name implies, quarterly meetings were held four times a year with the presiding elder of the church always in attendance.[53]

Local meetings of the Sons of Temperance also interested Lorena. Divisions of this national organization, founded in 1842 in New York City, existed in Pike County to "shield us from the evils of Intemperance, afford mutual assistance in case of sickness and elevate our character as men." Dues were "not more than 6¼ cents a week with benefits not less than $3 weekly." The Sons of Temperance also functioned as a fraternal lodge and the Pike County division paid $30 towards funeral expenses for a member, but only $15 for a wife. During the 1850s membership in temperance societies was considered a sign of respectability. It also promoted self-perfection in an egalitarian setting. While women supposedly had "every right and privilege" in the Sons of Temperance, the Pike County division made no mention of them in the 1848 constitution and bylaws. Perhaps an unofficial women's auxiliary existed. At least once Lorena participated in a Sons of Temperance outdoor parade, which was the standard form of non-partisan persuasion for total abstinence. Throughout her lifetime she remained devoted to the temperance cause.[54]

Books and newspapers enlarged Lorena's view of the world, exposing her to political issues of national importance. But she also enjoyed reading the romantic novels of the day, despite widespread Victorian disapproval of such books because they did not offer a true view of life and duty. In 1852, six months after publication, Lorena read *Uncle Tom's Cabin* and became concerned about slavery.[55]

Slavery was not a new issue in Illinois, although many of the early settlers had come from the South. Illinois entered the Union as a "free state" in 1818. Nineteen years later in 1837 the issue became inflamed in western Illinois when Elijah Lovejoy, editor of an anti-slavery newspaper, was murdered by a mob because he called for an abolition convention. This occurred in the community of Alton, slightly south of Pike County. By 1850 blacks in Illinois were either indentured servants or free. The most noted of the forty-three blacks in Pike County was seventy-three-year-old "Free Frank" McWhorter, a farmer in the Hadley area. While a slave he had worked to buy his own freedom and later that of his wife, children, and at least two grand-children.[56] These incidents in the history of Illinois and Pike County might well have made *Uncle Tom's Cabin* a meaningful book for Lorena, who recorded anti-slavery sentiments in her diary.

Lorena's increasing interest in politics led her to attend an election campaign meeting in the fall of 1852. Orville Hickman Browning, a friend of Abraham Lincoln, spoke in Barry on Saturday, September 11, when he ran unsuccessfully for the United States Senate. At the meeting, held in the Methodist Church after dinner, he spoke for two-and-a-half hours. He related in his diary: "Quite a number of ladies were out to hear me." Browning stopped at the Dehaven tavern, owned by Mrs. Leah Lithgow Dehaven, a sister of Lorena's uncle, Adam Lithgow. The Republican politician dined with Dr. Alfred Baker, the Hays family doctor, and stayed the night with the Elisha Hurts. Lorena was favorably impressed by the tall candidate, who was also noted for the beruffled shirts he wore.[57] She became fascinated by politics and in later years preferred the new Republican party of 1856 and its first presidential candidate John C. Fremont.

When not intellectually or emotionally involved in other matters, Lorena continued to worry about her health. Between 1849 and the spring of 1853 when she left for California, her symptoms (as she recorded them) almost fit this classic description of the "Illinois Shakes":

> After the fever went down, you still didn't feel much better. You felt as if you had gone through some sort of collision and came out not killed but badly demoralized — weak, languid, stupid or sore, "down at the mouth" and heel and partially ravelled out, so to speak. Your back was out of fix and your appetite in worse condition. Your head ached and your eyes had more white than usual. You felt "poor, disconsolate and

sad." You didn't think much of yourself and didn't believe others did either and you didn't care. . . .[58]

While Lorena's almost constant worry about illness and death appears morbid by twentieth century standards, this was a typical concern during the Victorian era. In the middle of the nineteenth century whole families were sick at one time; death was a well-known visitor in many households, especially those with small children. Death was a topic that dominated many conversations and funerals were frequent occurrences in Barry, as Lorena's diary indicates. Her anxieties became intensified when her two uncles and then her brother joined other gold rush pioneers heading west. In Pike County the fate of the Donner-Reed Party was well known because local newspapers carried stories about this overland journey to California in 1846-47. Amid the snows of the Sierra Nevada of California, forty of the eighty-seven members in this emigrant party perished. Many of them had lived in west-central Illinois.[59] Prayer meetings, held in the Baptist Church for the lives and safety of those residents from Barry making overland trips west, show that Lorena's fears were widely shared by others left at home.

Exactly when her uncles, Henry Woodward and Adam Lithgow, first went to California is not certain because Lorena did not write regularly in her diary until the end of 1849. In those years the community of Barry did not have its own newspaper. The names of all the gold rush pioneers from Pike County in 1849 and 1850 were not reported by the two local newspapers because there simply was not enough space in the four-page weekly editions to give complete county-wide coverage.

It is impossible to ascertain from diaries and scattered newspaper accounts how many from Pike County went to California in both years. In 1849 a number of wagon trains did leave from Pike County for the gold regions. On April 5 William T. Stackpole, who had left his home in Pekin, Illinois, to join the gold rush, wrote: "The little village of Barry (which we passed through today) and vicinity sends eighty persons to California." Stackpole recorded in his diary the times and places where he saw wagon trains from Barry and other Pike County communities along the California Trail in 1849, but gave no names. His diary ended in mid-sentence on July 5, near the Green River in Wyoming.[60]

It seems likely that Lorena's uncles might have made their first trips west in 1849, but whether or not they traveled together is also unknown. Neither of their names appear in the 1850 census for Pike County, Illinois, nor for California that same year. Yet in December 1850 Uncle Adam Lithgow had returned to Barry, where his wife, Aunt Caroline, and their daughters lived while he was in California.

Family recollections claim that he made at least one other trip to California, perhaps as early as 1848. According to these accounts by his descendants, on one trip west Adam Lithgow led a wagon train of some 300 persons; when he suffered an attack of measles the train halted for two days while he recovered.[61]

Upon his return to Illinois in December 1850, it became apparent that Adam Lithgow had prospered in the California gold mines — to what extent is unknown. He gave Lorena and two of her four sisters enough gold to be made into rings by Pike County jewelers. This must have made quite an impression upon eleven-year-old Sarah Louise, the youngest Hays sister, who undoubtedly was envious of her sisters' good fortune. In later years she would recall that their uncle had brought back "plenty of gold." In February 1851 Uncle Adam bought 101.95 acres of farm land west of Barry: on September 17, the Lithgows' fourth daughter, Helen Annette, was born. [62]

Confusion surrounds Lorena's other uncle, Henry Woodward, and his wife, Sarah. They had no children, according to Lithgow-Woodward descendants, but the 1840 census does show a "Henry Woodward" and wife (unnamed) with a family of three sons and two daughters living in Pike County. Ten years later a "Sarah Woodward," without a husband listed, lived near the community of Perry with six sons and three daughters. Perhaps between 1840 and 1850 there were two men named "Henry Woodward" in Pike County, but only one at home the day the census was taken in 1840. However, a number of other persons with the surname of "Woodward" also were recorded as living in Pike County in 1850; none was related to Lorena's family, so far as can be determined. When and how many times Uncle Henry Woodward made the trip to California cannot be determined either, but once he was accompanied by his wife, Sarah. When he returned to Barry in April 1851 and again in December 1852, she remained in California. However, neither of their names appeared in the California special census of 1852.[63]

Lorena's only surviving brother left home in April 1851, the same week their Uncle Henry arrived in Barry. William Philander Hays, twenty-one, headed for Oregon because that spring gold had been "discovered in abundance in the valley of the Klamath." According to the newspapers, "Lumps valued at $450-500 have been taken out and exhibited." William ended up in northern California, in the gold rush community of Shasta, hoping to find a more profitable way of making a living than working as a cooper in Illinois. When an ounce of gold a day — $16 in the 1850s — was considered a "fair wage" in California, a cooper's wage of $18 a month in Illinois looked rather meager. Other wages in western Pike County at this time could not begin to compare with the riches promised by the gold mines of California.[64]

Lorena began to worry about her brother's moral character when he left Barry. She became especially distressed when reports of California society depicted it as corrupt and dissolute:

> Suffice to say that we know of no country in which there is so much corruption, villainy, outlawry, intemperance, licentiousness and every variety of crime, folly and meanness. Words fail us to express the shameful depravity and unexampled turpitude of California society.[65]

Descriptions of a similar nature appeared in midwestern and eastern newspapers announcing that the mining areas were filled with gambling and drinking saloons, "dens of thieving iniquity." The *Pike County Free Press* on March 1, 1849, reprinted the following statement from a Chicago newspaper:

> The accounts previously received respecting the terrible state of society which was existing are confirmed. The state of affairs grows worse and worse, murders and robberies are of daily occurrence.[66]

The inhabitants "gamble, drink and cheat," according to one Pike County emigrant, who found the only "good" that could be said in California's favor was that "it is healthy."[67]

In early December 1852, when Uncle Henry Woodward made another visit to Barry, Lorena, her four sisters, and their mother talked about going to California with him in the spring. The idea had wide appeal within the Hays-Woodward-Lithgow clan. On December 29, 1852, Uncle Adam Lithgow sold his farm land for $1,500 and began making plans to move his family to California. He hoped that the overland trip and the western climate would improve the health of their eldest daughter, Louisa, eighteen, who suffered from consumption (tuberculosis), a disease prevalent in the nineteenth century.[68]

With close relatives planning to move west permanently and her brother already there, Lorena found little reason to remain in Illinois. Offering added inducement were newspapers stories about how women could better their positions in California. Because there were more men than women in California during the gold rush years, women were told they "could command enormous wages and are sure of constant employment and good pay," especially if they worked as cooks and laundresses. "Women of some refinement" were warned, however, that they might soon become "uncivilized" by life in mining communities, where they would be in the minority.[69]

Few women, it has been claimed, participated in decisions to move west but instead faithfully followed fathers and husbands along overland trails to the unknown wilderness of Oregon, Washington, Utah, and California.[70] However true this might have been for other women pioneers of the 1840s and 50s, it was not the situation faced by Lorena and her family. In January 1853 the six women decided of their own accord to undertake the five-month trip to California.

The Hays women spent January and February "preparing for California." Although Lorena did not specify what these chores included, they were undoubtedly similar to those reported on April 18, 1853, by a teenager in Dartford, Wisconsin, whose parents, William T. and Harriet Sherrill Ward, were getting ready to move their family to California. In a brief diary Frances ("Frankie") Elizabeth Ward, seventeen, described these activities:

> All engaged . . . Hannah Randall at work on wagon cover. Aunt Harriet and Elizabeth making ginger cookies. Dear Anna washed and at eve Father gave the girls a ride in the covered wagon.[71]

Mary Hite Sanford's account of her family's preparations for the trip tells of preparing food supplies to last six months. She also wrote about how wagon covers were made from "heavy domestic," explaining that it took three widths to cover the bows while two additional widths formed a double cover to shed rain. Mary added:

> Then Mother with the help of other ladies, made a tent. It was about 9 ft. x 11 ft., all sewed by hand. There were many button-holes to be worked, both in the tent and wagon covers, so they could be buttoned to the wagon body.[72]

For Lorena, "preparing for California" also meant going through letters and papers, regretfully throwing out those she could not take with her because of space limitations. Perhaps she packed her personal belongings in a small leather trunk and a carpet bag, as did each woman in the Reynolds-Salmon train of forty wagons that left Grant County, Wisconsin, on April 25, for California. The Hays family wagon might also have been equipped inside with the "long boxes like window gardens" that Virginia Wilcox Ivins found useful for storing "sewing materials & other odds & ends dear to the housewife's heart."[73]

Lorena may well have packed several pairs of shoes as did two other women pioneers of 1853: Mary Ellen Murdock Compton and Rachel Bond. Mary Ellen in later years recalled she left Independence, Missouri, on March 23 with ten pairs of shoes. On the California Trail she wore out all except the last pair, which she saved by going barefoot. Rachel, who married Allen Bond the day before they started west in the McClure train, received as wedding gifts a purse and clothing for the journey as well as seven pairs of shoes, the number considered sufficient for such a trip. Rachel's first pair gave out after 300 miles and she found the rest hurt her feet so she discarded them to walk barefoot, too.[74] While Lorena did not report similar problems, she once considered buying a pair of Indian moccasins, but these were probably intended to be a souvenir of the trail rather than for actual wear while

Sister Caroline Hays M'Neely

Sister Sarepta Hays Shoemaker

walking along it.

It is not known if Lorena had her photograph taken before she left Illinois as did her cousin, Louisa Lithgow. This photograph of Louisa was described as "a shadow of yourself" by a friend living in the nearby community of Perry. Her February 7 letter to Louisa continued: "You will not want that back will you? Well, if you do, we can take a copy before we send it back. There is a Mr. Clark here now. I do not know how good he is at taking pictures."[75] However, neither this photograph of Louisa nor any of Lorena are known to exist, although those taken in later years of other members of the Hays-Woodward-Lithgow clan remain among family mementos.

Church records show that at the February 23 covenant meeting of the First Baptist congregation in Barry, the Lithgow family (Uncle Adam Lithgow, who served as deacon and was also a member of the building committee; his wife, Caroline; and their second daughter, Mary Jane) "called for letters of dismission." So did "Sister Hays & daughters Lorena, Caroline, Amanda, & Sarah." Why the name of Sarepta, Lorena's second sister, was omitted is unknown. At the same time "letters of dismission" were granted to Willard Hart and William T. Young, who apparently also planned to travel with the Hays-Woodward-Lithgow families. Young's letter of February 26, signed by Stephen R. Whitaker "Ch. Clk.," still exists, folded but badly torn, never presented to a church in California. Nor was the letter written the following day for Lorena's cousin, Louisa, who had not joined the rest of the Lithgow family in the Baptist faith.[76]

These "letters of dismission" served as certificates of transfer and allowed church members to take their religious affiliations with them or to join a new faith in full membership upon arrival at their destinations, thus assuring immediate social acceptance in their new communities.[77] Louisa's letter remains among family papers. Signed by the church clerk, G. G. Shipman, it states:

> This certifies that Miss Louisa Lithcoe is a member of the Congregational church in Barry in good and regular standing and at her request is dismissed by a unanimous vote of the church to the christian care and fellowship of any orthodox church she may present this letter.[78]

With these essentials taken care of there remained only one more thing to be done before departure. On March 10, two days before leaving for California, Lorena's mother sold the house and lot on Bainbridge Street. Their next-door neighbor, B. D. Brown, and his partner, Lewis Angle, paid $300 for the Hays' property.[79] And in the midst of her farewells, Lorena, who had discovered since her father's death that there were few opportunities for a "poor orphan," wondered what fate awaited them on the California Trail and what the future held for them in California, that "land of gold and wickedness."

Note to the Reader

Lorena's diary has been presented with her spelling, punctuation, and capitalization. The use of *sic* has been omitted except where needed for clarification. The same has been done with quotations from other 1840s and 1850s sources. Lorena's use of the long "s" which resembles an "f" in mid-nineteenth century manuscripts has also been omitted due to the confusion it can create for a twentieth century reader.

Because it covers eleven years, the diary offers a multi-faceted view of mid-nineteenth century life. It reflects the prevailing concerns about religion, which influenced all aspects of Lorena's life, as well as her ardent desire for an education both in Illinois and California. Lorena's diary also provides a unique view of a woman's status in the 1850s, thus recording additional information for interpreting early and mid-Victorian social history.

Readers primarily interested in Lorena's account of her 1853 overland trip to California will find her first comment about the gold rush dated April 14, 1850. Although she wrote about her brother and their uncles going to California at different times, it was not until the fall of 1852 that the idea of making the trip west was considered seriously by Lorena's family. They started "preparing for California" on March 2, 1853.

The design for the sunbonneted "California Belle" has been taken from an article in the January 1, 1853, issue of *The Pictorial Union*, published in Sacramento, California.

"Seek On, Hope On & Pray On"

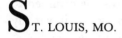

St. LOUIS, MO.

Monday, January 10th, 1848 — I have been to hear preaching almost every evening for one week and also on the two last sabbath days. Almost the first sermon I felt some interest on the subject of religion, felt that it was necessary that I "should be born again". . . I have often felt as though I would like to ask someone to pray for me, that I might feel a deeper concern for my souls salvation — but as often as I felt as though it would relieve me to express my sorrows and conflicts & dreams to someone, I found, that when an opportunity did occur, I became so agitated, my ideas so scattered, that it became impossible to express my feelings with any degree of inteligence — this inability I fear arrose from pride & a want of deep concern which I ought to have felt — from the commencement of the meeting I have felt a great desire to attend & indeed found that I felt very much disappointed if any thing occurred that I could not attend & have always when enquirers were invited to remain in their seats to be conversed with by the ministers of the gospel, found that I could not — feel willing to come away without manifesting a desire to be for christ.[1]

Last eve heard Dr. H. preach from the tent "Come, for all things are now ready," a sermon which I thought quite applicable to my case, which enabled me to take some courage. I felt that I had a small hope, & more fully determined than ever that I would seek on, hope on & pray on, until I should obtain a full hope in god through christ, but let the consequences be as they might I felt that I must try & that I must let my determination be known — as soon as I can that Mr. H was about to invite mourners to the anxious bench I felt very much aggitated & began to tremble violently[2] — I solemnly asked myself the questions, shall I let my determination be known by going, or shall I risk the salavation of my soul, I felt that by going forward that I should strengthen that determination & that if I had any hope it would be increased I did go. — I did have courage, to go al the way down the aisle, in presence of hundreds who were almost every one of them strangers, a thing that a few days before (with my timidity) I would not have believed I could have done — god has enabled me to do this much for him . . . this evening heard a good sermon & yet feel disharding. . . Oh I want faith, I want sincerity & energy — felt no relief from going forward last night except from a sense of having performed my duty in letting my determination to forsake the world be known — to day have felt very disconsolate and as if it were of no use for me to do anything more. have felt that my prayers were useless & when praying that god did not hear me.

13th did not go forward to the enquirers seat though I greatly feit the need of the prayers of the church & that I still was determined to seek god — but my heart was so hard so void of feeling . . . it was my desire to have a new heart — yesterday went to enquiring meeting & experienced some pleasure from hearing the prayers & conversation of god's people. was enabled to express my feelings more freely & was glad to receive the instruction given me — last eve heard a good sermon[3]

15th today have had many doubts & fears . . . a thought struck me that I been so great a sinner, so often refused to hear his voice, that god just intended to make me feel enough so as to make me uneasy, not enough to make me realize that i was a lost-sinner & that I must throw my self in to his arms & make me feel it enough so that I should be willing so to do; but just anxiety sufficient to make me unhappy — why this sinful though[t] should enter my heart (for enter in cannot be reality) I know not expect it is Satin tempting me. Oh! what impression do I not give God! . . .

27th It is impossible to describe the various feelings I have experienced during the last ten days — sometimes almost hoping other times despairing & sometimes without any feeling, scarsely at all; but at all times with to little time I fear has been my greatest hindrance . . . I am therefore determined by the grace of God that I will renew my energies, strive to enter in at the straight gate, that I may not be one of those that seek & shall not be able to enter in, I am to inactive, O that God would give strength & fortitutde to my cry for mercy —

Pleasant Vale [Illinois]

Feb. 28th, 1848 Another month has flown & with it has fled (I have often feared & almost believed) true happiness forever. Oh! the Agony I have experienced the past month; How shall I describe it? I could not, had I the eloquence of Cicero or Demosthenese . . . to say the least, my feeling have been of such a nature as to have kept me from writing any, or doing much of anything; my mind & body both having been reduced to such a state of weakness and inabillity as at times, to have rendered me entirely incapable of doing anything; whether it was physical debility that rendered my mental distress so much more accute I can scarce tell; this has been the opinion of friends, but I was not aware of any bodily weakness until mental anguish became so great, as to deprive me of any desposition to eat & little to sleep, which consequently, would cause debility of body as well as of mind.—

If what I have suffered has in a great degree been caused by over study & anxiety, & has been the exaggeration of a weak but imaginative mind, then I may hope "there's a better time coming" . . . fear seems to have been the most prominent trait in my character of late. . .

Oct 1st . . . O that I could do or feel right — that I might find that peace that surpasseth understanding —

Barry [Illinois]

Dec. 2nd 1849 Almost *two years* have elapsed since I have attempted to write any in this little book. And now what shall I write? Surely I do not lack matter though it be sad & mournfull — in that short time I have lost A father, grandfather, two brothers & three cousins. A year ago my youngest brother, father & grandfather & cousin and this fall two cousins, one a young lady, the other just my own age or only 10 days older a little over 22. She has left a beloved husband & child to mourn her irraparable loss for she was an estimable person and will be long remembered by all who knew her and appreciated her — how little did we think when she was passing away that her cousin, too, lay on his death-bed. Oh brother how little do I realize your death — how little do I feel like one that has lost so many very near relatives.[4] Can it be possible that I am the same creature that I once was? no, I *surely* I am changed, or I never could have survived such afflictions; but I have not only survived them, but, have passed through them, with out scarscely feeling the losses I have sustained. hardly feeling or knowing that I have been seperated by death from the dearest friends I possessed on earth. Surely mine is a heart incapable of feeling the ties of common friendship, least of all those that should bind cousins or brother and Sister. oh what spell has come over me that should have caused such apathy of feeling, such stoicism, such stupor of soul for the last year and a half . . . In former years, I have experienced the deepest distress and irrepressable anxiety, when one of the family have been ill. Indeed it seemed (if possible) that I was the greatest sufferer sometimes so great was my anxiety; but, now it is hard work to get myself to feel as much as I ought . . . I can only hope that it may not always be so but,

that I may someday feel as others do, enjoy life as others do and indulge in hopes of future happiness looking at the bright side of things
rather than *always* on the *dark* — Oh! that I *might have* happy thoughts
again . . .

Feb. 9th 1850 — I must not neglect to say though that I have thought
that the unhappy state of mind I have so much labored under has in a
great degree been caused by my neglecting to perform supposed
religious duties. I know that this was the first cause and beginning of
my troubles, and though I have refused to perform my *necessary* duties,
yet I believe that I have supposed many things to have been duties
which were not: and the fear of being thought foolish, and absurd, has
kept me from asking advise . . . I am tossed to and fro with contending
thoughts and emotions, and scarsce ever wishing to pursue the right
course though I know it to be the best . . . it would be impossible for me
to describe the contending emotions and thoughts, that I have experienced in the last two years of my life, though I had thought to have
attempted it. indeed when I commenced this practice of putting my
thoughts on paper, I meant to have done it every day or as often as time
would admit, but did not follow up my resolutions long, ere my mind
became so distracted that I could not bear to feeling again to mind and
so have neglected it until quite lately not keeping regular date always
when I have written; but I mean hereafter to write every or almost
every day or evening, giving an account of how I have occupied the
day, what I have done and said that I ought not to have said, or done,
and also to note any other matters of interest or incident worthy of
notice, hoping that I may be benefitted by such a course. to day is
monday, the 11 day of Feb I have read more than usual and have enjoyed myself better having read good works mostly a number of the
'ladies repository' and some in the beauties of Washington Irving[5] —
to night in conversation made one or two thoughtless remarks, for
which I am shamed and sorry too I hope. I ever do suffer after have
said thoughtless or unwise things; which happens quite too often, so
that I should think I would have learned ere this to speake with more
wisdom and discretion.

12th — Shall again retire with a heavy & I fear conscience striken
heart for I have been wild and thoughtless to day and am just now
returned from spelling school where I may have given others pain by
"thought word or deed" there all was mirth and joyessness and most
seemed to be happy, and, I too might have been but for the thought
that I was inflicting pain upon another, by having deceived him by
having said or as much as said, that I was not going so that I fear that I
have been guilty of falsehood in a greater or lesser degree for I was not
really determined not to go, when I said so: when, shall I learn to do
right? . . .

18th it is late. I have just finished a lettere to grandmother. I have neglected for several days to record any thing here and have only time to say that I have had many bad thoughts and feeingss and but few good in comparison to the evil — if I could only think every time before I speak or act. how much more wisely I might act, but, also, I do not always think wisely either

19th almost all of the young ladies in town have commenced going to school to day, how I long to go too. It has been a long time since I have attended, and, I do not much expect to ever go again however much I feel the necessisty of a better education. if there were none except myself that my time should be spent for, nothing would hinder me from going except sickness. but alas: for the poor, they must work, work, in this country, have as good a chance to gain knowledge and arrive at distinction as the richest. but I see it not so in my case —

March 7th thursday — a week ago last tuesday I went to the country and did not come home until yesterday excepting a week ago to night I was at home a short time. I shall not forget it, for I had some to regret being at home that night 'A casued no little commotion for I presume that the joke carried to such an extent, would not have been thought off, had we not have taken such a wild goose chase as coming to town that night. the joke was this, there was a wedding close by at which there was a ''picked'' party and several of us getting together who were not invited, took it into our heads to have a little 'fun' by playing a joke on the wedding party or some one there — So after thinking of, proposing and rejecting several things we at last concluded that some one would go to bed and fain sickness while some one else, should be sent for the doctor, who was groomsman — the thing was no sooner said then done. brother faining sickness and the boy who was sent for the doctor arriving there just as the party were about to sit down to supper which had to be postponed, until the doctor could view his patient, which detained him nearly an hour. he found out the joke however and in order to be revenged administered a dose of epicack which however failed to have any effect. the joke did not end here however as the doctor took it as an insult offered to him, and next morning put into the constable's hands a bill of two dollars against brother. he did not think proper to pay it, as some were inclined to lay the blame all on him, and by not paying he thought to have an opportunity of proving who was most forward in the scrape but the doctor has done nothing more about it, so it will be likely to end here[6] it was no credit to any of us, to play such a joke on any one and we were all sorry enough for it afterwards & although, it was scarsely intended to insult or to hurt the feelings of any one, but we were thoughtless and foolish, and I think that it will prove a lesson to us in future. for we should do by others as we would be done by. . . .

Sunday 10th I have attended church both to day and to night and have enjoyed preaching better than sometimes is the case . . . I have read a very interesting piece to day which reminded me of what I have often thought and regretted, that is, the loss of the freshness of the susceptibilities and impressions of childhood. why is it, that we cannot always have the same purity of thought and feelings as when we were children. . . .

March 15th I have been attending school this week and have consequently found not time to write as I have had so many other duties to attend to — I find much pleasure in studying but also find that I do not learn so easily as when formerly going to school but hope that I shall learn more easily after getting accustomed to study — we have a very good teacher he is particular in having the rules of school obeyed, but I must confess that I have not obeyed in every respect. I have in one or two instances showed disatisfaction in recitations, at least, some deggree perhaps more than was becoming, for I imagined that he was rather too particular in regard to our being just so correct in our answers. He is very srict in regard to having rules obeyed for I shall like him the better — a short time since, I little expected to attend school so soon as I almost feel sometimes, that I am neglecting other duties but, then I ask what is more beneficial or lasting than knowledge? and then, I do not think, in after years, that I shall regret having sacrificed a little time for the purpose of getting an education —

29 have not went to school any this week, expecting to commence teaching and have been very busy getting my work done up —

31st there has been considerable sickness with in a fortnight past and several deaths, one very Sudden one the funeral was preached on Sunday a week ago to day, and to day another funeral sermon was preached an is now being preached at the same Church. how very little do I reflect upon such events; how little realize that I shall one day be clasped in the cold embraces of death — I am expecting to commence teaching school tomorrow I hope that I shall realize the responsibility resting upon me, and endeavor to discharge my duty faithfully which cannot be done without labor and preserverance.

April 7th What a lonesome week the last has been it has been such rainy, gloomy weather that to be shut up in a school house with but few scholars, makes it not very pleasant, especially to one subject to low spirits. the school house too is situated in a very lonely place. I have already most wished that school was ended. for I fear that I shall have hard work to keep up courage, but I must try for it is of no use to get discouraged. I hope that I shall endeavor to do the best that I can, to learn the scholars —

April 14th the Snow has fallen quite fast to day, an occurence quite unusual in this climate, but this Spring has been very late and backward. the flowers are but just begging to peep forth, some times they are blown by the 18the and 20th of March. they will make but a poor show to day for the ground is entirely covered with Snow — I fear that the Californians will have rather unpleasant times to day. what a vast emigration there is this spring to the Eldorado of North America, more famed that of Sir Walter Raleigh: and visited by greater numbers. may it not prove to them, but a land of visions & dreams as did his, though doubtless we may have heard some almost as flattering accounts of it as those Sir Walter presented to queen Elizabeth, though perhaps not quite So absurd — it is quite probable that there is a great quantity of gold in California, but it cannot be probable or possible that all of the hundreds of thousands who have gone there, will return, laden with the gold. they do fully expect and for which they undergo so great privations & hardships; they will sacrifice almost every thing. thinking to be many times rewarded, almost as soon as they shall reached the land of gold. but there will be many sadly disappointed. many have bid their friends and relatives farewell, forever. Children, parents, & husbands their wives brothers their sisters; all fondly anticipating a happy return with money enough to make them comfortable and happy hereafter. Oh! we little realize how little power riches has to make us happy, though they might add to our happiness were they put to wise purpose — last week was not quite so lonesome as the former though I still have but few scholars which makes teaching seem rather dull; I have to board around and I also have some distance to walk which renders my situation a little more unpleasant at least to me, as I have but little opportunity then to read or write. Should I otherwise get time and feel disposed to spend in that way. to day is sunday and I am at home which is about all the time I have to spend in reading and writing.

April 21st Sunday again and it still continues to be quite unpleasant weather most of the time. So much so that with other causes combined I have closed School for a fortnight, at least, & I should scarsely be surprised, if altogether, as most circumstances seem to be rather unfavorable at present. Sister C. has been teaching 2 weeks and has quite a full School — received a letter from Cousin M. in which he scolds me pretty severely for not having answered his last.[7]

May 2nd Shall not commence my school again — last evening met (with one or two others) with the little girls to help them make arrangements for a "may party." they expect to have a very happy time and we hope they will but we do not know what may take place &c ten days may pass by, to mar our pleasure, but happy children; they will enjoy a great deal, even in anticipation, which at most is the greatest of our enjoyments. if we could ever be fancying bright and beautiful pictures, it were better than to be ever looking upon the *dark side* of suffer-

ing ourselves to have disappointments, or even [ever?] rest in reality[8]
—

Sunday, May 12*th* All has been hury and hustle this week getting
ready for the institute at griggsville which is to be of two weeks conti-
nuence. it is called the *normal* institute and is for the benefit of teachers,
though none are excluded in the county commences tomorrow. I was
very anxious and determined upon going when first informed of it as
the expense is very triffling indeed only one dollar for ladies board and
all — but it seems almost wrong for me to spend the time under my
present circumstances, as the present is a hurrying time, and mother
will be thrown our of work too, without my assistance; were it not that I
am so anxious to improve my education (which I have almost dispaired
of doing) and that I thought the present a good and cheap opportunity,
both in respect to time and money. were it not for these things, I should
not go, but when will another such an opportunity be afforded me, or if
it should would my time be less precious than now? a great many are
going all of the teachers, though there has been something said by one
or two about its being all a humbug. though I do not see why we cannot
have such an institute in Illinois as well as in other states or why it
should not prove beneficial[9]

Griggsville [Illinois]

My 13th attended school to day have not time to State all of the exercises all which were interesting. after school our boarding places were
appointed us at which we have all become pleasantly established and
situated. I think that I shall enjoy myself very much, this is a very
pleasant place and the people are kind and intelligent. in the evening
attended a lecture by a profssor and others, the subject was "what is
the most proper age for a child to commence going to school before or
at six"

14th it is almost school time and I have not studied my lesson any
yet. School opens with singing and prayer — exercises have been very
interesting to day especially elocution. quite a debate was carried on
this evening on question mentioned. the resolution was passed that a
child should not go to school under the age of six[10]

16th tired, tired and dont see that I make much progress. Some are
rather displeased with the Proffessor at times he is so severe, I myself
was once to day, but perhaps he is not too much so for the benefit of the
scholars — did not to prayer meeting last evening. this evening in company of a school mate went home called on some others, I find that I
am not always happy, as the rest seem to be I can hardly ever enjoy
company or entertain others as well as I would like or as others do, why
is it? is it for the want of ability or of a disposition . . . to night must attend the institute lectures —

Sunday attended methodist this forenoon and Baptist afternoon. liked afternoon service best but, enjoy none very much. Oh! as the minister said, one is miserable, this is deprived of hope, ever in the things of this world, I almost think sometimes that I have very little, indeed I have but little joy. I think some times that it arises from some physical derangement. I form new acquaintances almost every day, but these do not seem to add to my happiness as is naturally the case. I do indeed take some pleasure in attending the institute, going to church is my chief delight. Could I but go all the time

Sunday at home, again. arived yesterday, institute closed in forenoon I have not had time to write much though I have been much interested yesterday especially several very able addresses were delivered by institute scholars, and valedictory adress by an Honorary member, and a short one by the Proffsor in which he bid us farewell. We have spent a delightful fortnight and I hope a profitable one. We have formed many acquaintances which I hope may prove lasting and pleasant. yesterday received a letter from Cousin M., which gave us intlenigence of his brothers death, how many of us are taken away! we are as the flowers of the field that bloom and fade in a day — every body is going to church, and I dont know but I ought too but as I was some tired & not very well, I thought I would not[11]

Barry

June 2nd Sunday *eve* more than usual cast down, I know not but for staying from Church, that I am doing wrong. but I was almost afraid that I should do wrong if I went: The *Christians* are holding a meeting & it is their custom after sermon always to open the doors of the Church to any that may come forward for baptism. When such calls are made, it seems almost as if I were neglecting by duty in not accepting such an opportunity. . . . It has long seemed to me that that to join some church, is a duty that I am neglecting yet I know not what church, scarsely I prefer, I think that I dread somewhat, baptism by imersion & I should feel almost afraid to adopt any other mode least that dread, had influenced me. I know not what to do & ever feel as if I were delaying and neglecting what I should not especially if I attend Church where any such invitations are given and this has kept me from church, for I was afraid I should come home disatisfied and unhappy as I have many times . . . I wish that I had courage to do my duty promtly and decidely; I should save my self so much trouble and wretchedness, but I am ever so undecided and affraid, lest that I should do something that would not be thought proper by some. but we cannot do or act so that *all* will approve our conduct. we should to do we think God will approve . . . I am tired and will put by my pen though it be such a consolation & give me some pleasure when alone as I am to night. I attended S.S. [Sunday School] this morning & church twice to day

June 15th I deeply deplore (and not so much as I ought) this evening the want of a Charitable & generous disposition, for I have indulged in ungrateful and unkind thoughts towards those I last of all should, for who is kinder than my Aunt C. & I so Careless and thoughtless of my actions and perhaps words, thought I have felt as though I could not repay her for her past kindeness and she has been more kind than ever to day. . . .[12]

June 13 today's the Sabbath. it is quite rainy so that we have staid at home which I do not much regret, I think; I sometimes feel as if I would not be sorry to have a good excuse for staying at home on Sunday, which I suppose is wrong, for I ought to feel it is a priviledge to attend Church or Sabbath School, and regret that I do not appreciate such a priviledge more . . . I have often felt as if it was my duty to attend the means of grace, Such as prayer meeting, or church meeting but when the time comes to go, am willing to make the most trivial thing an excuse — i did think it my duty and thought I must go the last time to Church meeting but did as I have often before, excused my self or rather stayed at home with out an excuse this I find makes me very unhappy . . . I have just finished reading a Sunday School book, which I might learn much good from as regards duty &c — I have had but little time to read or write for two weeks past —

July 8th the fourth is past which I spent at home, there 'pic nic' I could not convenitantly attend.[13] the party in the evening I did not for several reasons, one of which was, I feared it was hardly right — all of the Church members there are young people do attend them. perhaps there can be no harm in doing so. yesterday was sunday, I went to S.S. and Church, Still troubled about somethings I imagine to be duty; O! that I had the courage I should have. . . .

July *18th* How swiftly time flies! days and weeks glide by & what do I accomplish? what do I learn, or do, that is good & true. I work, and I think sometimes that, that, is all I can do, that I have time for nothing more for the improvement of my mind, which I think is so necessary — I feel very unhappy & discontended Sometimes, when I think of my lot in life, when I see so many who have every advantage in an intelectual point of view, who think so little of improving them, I think that I would be very thankful could I enjoy their unappreciated advantages . . . at least I should endeavor to preserve a contented mind and to strive after a better heart —

20th yesterday a Colporteur[14] called with Books to sell and I think by some remarks he made, I been led to think a little more than usual, or perhaps not to think, but to feel rather more — I was struck with the simplicity of his manner and the conscientiousness with which he seemed to perform his duty —

yesterday (monday) — attended Church, in the afternoon heard Mr. Malong he said much about the condemned state that a sinner feels himself in. I thought my own feelings were exactly portrayed & felt so condemned and guilty that it seemed to me I could hardly hide my feeling much longer & thought I must surely say something to my mother, before I could rest in peace, relative to the duties which have given me so much trouble, and which it seemed I ought no long delay to perform, but I soon found myself, as often before, desiring some excuse and again retired with out saying anything. . . . I ought to do my duty at least and if it bea duty for us to attend the family prayer, I hope that we shall conquer all difficulties and do as we should —

Aug. *4th* Another has instituted family prayer at evening. I have not experienced so much pleasure by it as I expected. perhaps it is because I did not speak of it to her when it gave so much anxiety, or when it seemed to me a duty that ought not be neglected . . . I did not attend prayer meeting, and though I did not feel like it perhaps I ought to have done so. . . . The weather is exceedingly warm & I have but little to do. Last week made a visit to the country. I have heard indirectly from my friends in St. Louis, would they believe that the two years and a half, since I left them, have been such years of wretchedness and perhaps unprofitableness to me. . . .

August *22nd* various have been my feelings and thoughts since last writing . . . I have been to prayer meeting and we have been thrown into confusion by a circumstance of nature to be regretted. Brother considering himself very highly insulted by a person who ought to be noticed so little as to be paid no attention at all, (although he is very insulting person) sufered himself to get so angry as to appear almost like a deranged person I hope that he will be sorry when he gets it and try to control his temper better in future, for he says things that he will wish he had not. . . .

26th Monday — have united with the Church by Baptism unworthy as I felt myself to be yet it has been urged upon me as a duty which ought to be done[15] — but I had hoped it to be an ordinance which I should engage in with feelings of solemn pleasure which I should remember with delight — I hope that I did not wish to shrink from it, or put it off, because I did not wish to bear the Cross, but it ever seemed to me that I was no yet a fit subject for that ordinance, though our Minister and others have urged it as my duty, the neglect of which they seemed to think caused so much darkness and sorrow or unhappiness, which he said would be removed upon the performance of duty, and I often myself would feel condemned to think how long I have delayed it and ever when an opportunity of uniting with any church has been offered, have had to persuade myself that it was not my duty, even as unfit as I thought I was — I had wished to and thought I ought to give a more particular account of my feeling to a minister, than I felt as if I could publickly, but as I went to covenant meeting without doing so, although I had an opportunity (but my courage failed) there which I sincerely regretted, or rather regretted that I had not the opportunity to conversing entirely alone with him, as I think that I should have received both comfort and instruction which he could not well give me with out better knowing my mind and which I sincerely wished him to know. He expressed it as his sincere belief, that until I united with the Church, I would never enjoy my mind as I wished to, as I went to covenant meeting, and there being an opportunity given to any who wished to unite with the Church, I felt as if I should, as I had done before, come home unhappy and distressed, giving my consent to be baptized the next day, it occurred to me that perhaps I ought to have delayed it until I could have the opportunity of expressing the state of my mind more freely than I found I could before the Church but I did not have an opportunity as I hoped to have of doing so, which gave me so much anxiety that I had no enjoyment, for I could but think and feel myself guilty and sinful, with nothing but sinful and wicked thoughts, entirely unworthy and unprepared, to name the name of Christ before the world, although I did not think that I was ashamed to. . . .

August 9th — A quarterly meeting of the freewill baptists has been in progress two days & there is to be meeting this evening if the shower does no prevent, it seems as if it ought to be a joyful time for me — but alas! unlike others who are called Christians, I can ever say that I "experience joys unspeakable" . . . Oh! when Shall I become willing to do every thing, trusting in god for grace. surely he will bless me then and enable me to rejoice, but not while I doubt his goodness and promises or disobey his commands. Oh that my pride were all gone and that I could be as a little child, obeying and confiding, in every thing . . . I often thought it would be an honor, rather than otherwise, to be a member of any Christian Church, one which I was unworthy to enjoy & one which I feared would tend to fill my heart with pride, rather than shame, except on account of my exceeding unworthiness, & I think that should have been my only excuse for delaying to fulfill that command . . . .

Sept. 21st Neglecting to do my duty at convenant meeting today, although young members were particularly advised to speak of the state of their feelings, both by our dear pastor and deacon; how much he feels for us, yet how little do I feel for myself, yet I do want to feel more

Sundy' if it be a cold & Phlegmatic temperament that renders me so incapable of sympathising & feeling for others or of feeling sorry on account of my own sins, surely are they fortunate who possess such a temperament . . . it sometimes seems that one so sinful has no right to have faith, and if I did all things as I should, faith would come as a natural consequence to day for the first time patook of of sacrament, although I felt unworthy and condemned — I almost thought that I ought not to do so, and came almost to the conclusion not to, on account of my feelings. I know not whether I did right or wrong. . . .

I do not see why duties should appear to me such mountains, especially public ones, and when I engage in them it is with so much fear and undecision, that I experience little benefit — so it was to day although I felt no fear of the world or any unwillingness to show to the world my profession, but I feared that I was partaking unworthily. . . .

Sunday Eve 30th — I have nothing but sin to mourn over. It seems as if I had given every to every evil passion this last week. have had no Control over my feelings at all letting every anger or any other wicked feeling alike carry me away from the path of reason. Last week has been one of bustle and commotion on account of the Institute are having boarders and many coming in and out — Proffessor Turner preached today and this evening[16]

Oct. 6th Our Institute has closed — the last week has been very Interesting and I think highly beneficial to many — The Closing scene yesterday was very affecting the valedictorian in his last remarks himself much affected — Also Proffessor Turner could scarscely refrain from weeping in addressing his last remarks to us — there was scare a dry eye in the house — I very much enjoyed the last week, and most of the exercises have been interesting to all — The compositions yesterday were Interesting . . . received a letter cousin Myron — How I should like to visit Old Pa. the scenes of my childhood and friends there too! Oh how hard the lot of the poor, no enjoyments for them sometimes I think — but if they could only receive an education equal to the rich, it would be almost all I could ask, or at least I think so now but I ought rather to ask a contented mind, and a thoughtful heart for the blessings I do enjoy — I certainly enjoy a great deal while attending Teachers Institute, and never shall forget all, I hope that I heard and saw, all the good lessons taught us, by an amiable Proffessor either mental or moral — yes his mild and amiable deportment on all occasions, will make impressions long to be remembered. O if I could always have enjoyed such a blessed privellige, as to have been under the guidance and government of such an instructor how different might have been my disposition, how much more useful and happy myself but I ought not to complain. I am alive and well, while many of my relatives are gone from this world, only one year since my poor brother died, young and beautiful, just in the quick of life — poor boy, no friends were near to console you — who could have known the depths of your sorrows? who know the dreadfulness of your anguish — or how much you might have wished to pour out your trouble to some sympathising heart, in that dreadful dying hour. none can tell or know thy sufferings, though we know they were great —

Sabbath — I feel unhappy to day. It seems to me the more I try to read good books the less I find in myself that is Christian like therefore I can take but little comfort in reading the biographies of eminent Christians . . . Oh that I could, as I have long desired, have an opportunity of giving my Pastor *some* account of my feelings — it has been said by our deacon, that we ought to tell out trials of mind &c at covenant meeting. It seems as if it were impossible for me to give a satisfactory account of my own, so publick — perhaps it is pride that hinders me, yet I do not feel as if I were ashamed to be a Christian I only wish that I may truly be one —

The weather is getting quite cool — I love fall the best of all the seasons. I know not why unless, that the melancholy pensiveness which nature seems to assume, coincides with my own disposition, its fading foliage, mild sunbeams and smoky horizon, all inspire feelings that no other season can[17]

16th The "Sons" haveing been invited to go to Canton to help organize a division, with some of the Ladies went down to day, but took the Canton people by surprise it seems as there had been no preperation for lectures our people, not willing to come home without doing something the whole Company took circle around the Groceries, the majority them going by Kenderhook where after singing one or two temperance songs we came home. I do not think much good was accomplished and I guess some of the natives were astonished never having seen any sons of temperance before especially with their regalia on[18] — we had rather a lively time & I fear some of us were rather to frivolus to set a very good example for others — I for one

Nov. 10th To day has been rainy so that I could not very well go to Church. The Sabbath is not so pleasant a day to me as it should be & for the last time, I have found it very hard to keep my mind on the things I should . . . Some of the Californians have returned. We are expecting Uncle Adam,[19] but do not know but he is detained with a sick person, his nephew who was just starting for home. How many have died in that far of land, and can never see their loved homes and friends. How much Sorrow has the land of gold caused. How many hearts has it not made Sad.

Nov. 18th. More from California have arrived to day. Poor Jhn Dehaven I suppose is no more, taken away just as he was anticipating a return home, to see friends & relatives. friend N. gone to day for his licence. I may go to his wedding ere long. Have thought to much of wordly things to day & do not feel that sorrow for sin that I ought. Heard Mr. Shunk preach. did not stay at class meeting although rather thought I ought to. . . . [20]

Nov. 29th Sunday Again. Last week attended a wedding of very intimate friends, so at some surprized at the choice made of bridesmaid & I said more than I ought to about it[21] Sister C. sick and could not go, was better yesterday but seems not well to day — feel very much disappointed at not receiving letters from friends that I have written too . . . It seem to me that I can scarsely be contented to remain at home this long winter to come. I know not why it is, but it seems as if I am happier away from home than at home & love friends & mother & sisters &c when away from them — the best — I do not have so much love & sympathy for them as I ought to have. O there is such a change come o'er my heart! Such a calm indifference towards every thing . . . It seems to me *sometimes,* as if I had lost all hope of true happiness.

Dec. 1st To day has been rainy and gloomy. At home all day, and spent it too much, in my usually despairing mood.

Dec. 8th Went to church this evening and seemed to feel more than usually interested, but do not feel so great an interest as I should, upon so great a subject as religion. Uncle Adam returned from California last week All were glad to see him. He does not seem to have changed very much in any way. The hardships of such a journey do not seem to have affected him, and his health seems better than before going, gave myself, Sister C. and Sister S. enough gold for a ring[22] — Wrote a letter to grandmother last Sabbath & hope to get an answer as soon as convenient as I long to hear from her. I have read but little to day. hope that I shall not give way to despondency in future *so much* as I have done. . . .

Dec. Heard three sermons to day & hope they may do me some good, but still feel that my heart is very hard and proud and an unwillingness to do many things that may be my duty . . . expect to be very busy this week.

January 8th 1851 Christmas & New Years past, though they were holy days to most, yet they have not been much so to me, as I have been confined by work even Closer than usual — Oh how tired I am some times — This evening received a letter from Grandmother. I can perceive that she is failing. She is very old and may not live long — we have a singing school, which I attended & I hope to learn a little but can never make a good singer. O! if I were but as fortunate as 'Jenny Lind ',[23] but I ask not for *supernatural* powers! If those I possess could have a proper education, if I could hope to posess a well cultivated mind it would be a compensation for all the trials and trouble I have to undergo, but I almost dispair whenever I think of it, for there seems nothing but continual toil and labor, in store for me, with hope of little opportunity to improve my education, but I am afraid that I indulge too much in discontent

Feb. 2nd. Sabbath. Heard Mr. Cady[24] preach to day . . . I like him much better than the first time I heard him it was a good sermon — I have been spending some few days at Uncle Adams, am returning to day, found a letter from an acquaintance formed last summer at Griggsville. it was a good letter — I have a great desire to attend school and though I have little to encourage me to hope to do so [illegible] yet, I can scarscely repress the ardent desire I have — There is no wordly object that would give me more pleasure to possess than the means of acquiring a good education. It seems to me there is more pleasure in acquiring knowledge, than in any other pursuit —

9th Last evening Singing School

Feb. 10 Our Temperance meeting was rather an odd affair last monday evening — Singing School passed off very well tuesday evening I hope we shall improve — attempted to write letter this morning but am not in mood and so have postponed it to some future time my visit to Pittsfield[25] was not as pleasant as I anticipated it would be some time previous to going an unexpected opportunity presented or I should not have went at present or at the time I did, it being sabbath. I do not know but it was wrong to go but as I seldom have an opportunity of going, I accepted the invitation without hesitation at first, though I was almost sorry after — I cannot write letters to day, dont know what is the matter, as I generally delight in writing

March 15th How time flies! I have not written for sometime. How delightful the weather is at present and such beautiful moonlight nights! just right for the protracted meeting being commenced this evening by Mr. Cody & Ellege. may it prove a blessing to all though I feel little of that hungering & thirsting after righteausness which Mr. Cody preached of this evening. . . .

Tuesday 17th The meeting still progresses and bids fair to prove a blessing to many. Christians seem to be awaking up to a sense of their duty & to mourn their past neglect of priveliges, their coolness barrenness. The conference meeting to day and yesterday has been quite interesting to most, surely so those who have had the courage to do their duty. most have done so. most can mourn and weep bitter tears of penitence on account of the hardness of their hearts & those tears and signs and confessions bring relief and even joy and peace to the heart. . . . So impossible does it seem for me to speak on Conference meeting, that when I think I will try, and almost am on the point of doing so, my agitation is such that I again give it up even though I feel as if I were commiting one of the greatest sins & know that I shall go away burdened with guilt and sorrow. I believe that by discharging my duty, I should save my self much very much of that unhappiness which it seems constantly my lot to share — I think too, many times, that I might feel a tenderness and sympathy for others, which I have not felt of late if could feel more free to confide my own troubles to others but then I think again, that no one cares to be troubled with my complaints and sorrows, no one can feel interested with my troubles, and ere disclosing, I again lock my sorrows within my own already unchanged and aching heart. O — for some sympathizing friend, some one to care for me, that I could feel free to confide in. . .

18th Last evening the house was crowded. Mr. Cody delivered a sermon in refrance to those who have died in California. I felt quite discouraged last evening after my return from church, when contemplating my own condition. I have no confidence in myself . . . .

The weather is delightfuly pleasant so that few have an excuse for not attending meeting.

22nd feel some degree of enjoyment since this afternoons service was in some degree enabled to do my duty but have not done it all yet or all perhaps that I ought to have done — the meeting was a very interesting one although it was rainy and muddy a considerable number seem to have a trembling hope —

23 yesterday was sabbath — Mr. Ellege preached twice Mr.Cody once . . . — a sermon to backsliders; it seemed to me, my faith and confidence seem to be entirely gone sometimes, but perhaps my prayers will be heard, sometime. May I be kept from giving up in despair — It is very pleasant this morning, but I arose with a heavy heart. It is not unusual for me to have, when first awaking, a very painful heaviness of heart, a feeling as if there was no joy or happiness for me in anything — I know not what causes it. There may be some Physical cause for it, for years I have suffered more or less, but there is scarscely a time that I do not feel in some degree desponding and low spirited — there is a something weighing down my spirits, so that my heart can not give or go out in enjoyment. If I for a moment think that I *will be* happy, some thought of some act will crowd itself upon my mind and drive it all away again

25th Two days have passed — I thought surely I could have spoken yesterday and then again to day — but I am most discouraged It seems impossible for me to do it. I know I that I want to do it — I believe that if our conference meeting were conducted more as class meeting it would be far better, for young persons or those who are timid, to get in a habit of expressing their minds — I think it would be encouraging to any one who feels so backward and timid, for those who conduct the meeting to say to such a one, will you express your feelings? I know that for one, nothing would have given me more pleasure, than such an invitation, although it would have drawn forth every effort, to have done it. But I have felt it duty to do, and have wished and tried to do so and none can know how I have suffered — I do not believe as some, that it is pride, that prevents all from doing this duty And men, who scarsce know what timidity is, comparatively speaking, I think can hardly know how to judge of, or sympathize in the feelings of a female, who never was acustomed to address a congregation, upon any subject whatever. I think it would make but little difference, as to that. They would feel the same diffidence — I think, then we should have charity, and not accuse one another of being ashamed of Christ. I do not wish to be ashamed of being a Christian. . . .

29th Meeting not closed yet — I have not attended all of this week, being absent two days. Attending young ladies prayer meeting this evening — hardly knew as it was my duty to pray — It seems to me that I can not feel enough or as much as I ought — perhaps it is a sin, for me to engage in such duties —

April 1st — tuesday — It was Mr. Cody's request, Sunday After-noon, that we should every twilight pray with him, for our selves, and those, who have during the past meeting experienced a hope in Christ — I think last evening, after engaging in that prayer, (as well as I could) that I felt more peace and tranquility of mind, than I have before for a very long time. I begin to *hope* that I may see better times.

Apr. 9th I think I enjoyed the sermon last Sabbath Mrs. Barker commenced her school yesterday.[26] I have an irrepresable desire to go to school, and often get very discontented and unhappy to think there is no way for me but to work, work, from morning till night with no op-portunity of improving my mind. Surely what enjoyment is there to be had if the mind can not have that knowledge, or rather food, for which it thirsts. But poverty, what a hard master: If it could only but give an education, what richer legacy could I desire of earthes riches. Sometimes I almost resolve that I will set myself to work to get an education. If I go without every thing beside and if there were none to think of a care for but myself, I Should do it. I believe that I could, but there are others to care for and it would be wrong — as it is I need a more contented mind, that I need not look upon my lot as one so hard.

April 19th Saturday convenent meeting 9 joined the church, most to be baptized tomorrow. I did not do my duty by speaking today

21st yesterday Church meeting of Mr. Cody's Church one joined the Church, to day baptized by sprinkling — have been quite unwell for two days and feel very low spirited sometimes. do no feel the enjoy-ment a Christian might. Surely, I do very wrong some way. Uncle Henry came today & Brother started for Oregon thursday, left home last monday for a long time perhaps forever. May God keep him in the path of truth and virtue wherever he may be — may we all be kept from sin. . . .[27]

27th To day Mrs. Barker took a class of young ladies in the Sabbath School, of which I am a member. Our Sabbath School assumed a more interesting appearance to day then it has for a long time previous. Two persons were baptized to day. I have had to many trifling thoughts to day and have paid to little attention to the things I ought most to prize, and fear I have not set a very good example before others. Visited Mrs. Barker's school friday. Oh! how much I wish to attend. It seems to me that I can never be satisfied until I can go to school, for I feel the necessity more and more of a proper education. I enjoy myself so much better, when engaged in study than at any other time.

[May] 20th Christian meeting in progress. Mr. Brown minister.[28]

29th more Baptized today by the Christian and baptist ministers. Mr. Brown the Christian minister seems to be a sincere and candid man. . . . Many of other denominations attend his discourses and some are very much pleased with them. I like to hear him myself though I cannot believe just as he does upon some points — We have an interesting Sabbath School at present. Mr. Presy is now Superintendent.[29] The lessons in the bible class are very interesting and instructive. I did not attend church meeting yesterday and fear I did wrong in not doing so — I have a great deal to do and find that I have not time to devote to the things I am most anxious to and therefore feel that I enjoy life much less than I could if I only had the chance I long to have —

May 30th yesterday was my birthday again 24 years of my life are gone, and how very little good have I ever accomplished. I hope that I may improve my time better in future than I have in time past. I do feel more and more anxious every day of my life, to improve my mind, I can hardly persuade myself sometimes that it is not wright for me to spend more of my time in studying. It is the most earnest wish of my heart, that the time may soon come when I can devote as much of my time as I could wish to acquirement of knowledge. Oh! how I thirst and long for it. How my mind reaches after that, which it scarce dare hope to obtain. How little the prospect of realizing my most ardent desires

June 12th I have been in rather an unhappy state of mind for several days past. I scarse Can tell what has caused it unless it was because I have been quite unwell — every thing has went wrong, as I felt quite out of humor with myself and every one else and I feel quite ashamed and sorry that I been so foolish as to let my feelings influence my conduct so much as I have — I fear I have in some degree lost the confidence of friends. I hope that I shall have more patience in future

19th To day Mrs. Whyke was buried. We hurried home directly after preaching but were caught by the rain so that those who went to the burial must have been very wet[30] — I have not felt very Serious minded today, and fear that my thoughts and actions have been rather too trifling — and undignified. indeed I ever lack dignity

I find it very hard to confine my thoughts to the subject of religion. There are so many other subjects that seem to interest my mind, so much, and which seem to demand all of the few leisure moments I have, that it seems as if there was no time for that — Oh! I think Sometimes, If I were only *free* to act, to do, as I would how dilligently would I improve the time in gaining knowledge. But Oh! I see no prospect, not a single ray of hope seems to beam upon the dark horizon that stretches itself out before my imagination. My life seems almost a blank and I am a tool, an instrument just made to work, work with my hands — nothing more. The mind with all it's capacities for enjoyment, it's susceptibilities and longings — that that may be dormant, uncultivated, unsatiated, uncared for and all of our time, spent in caring and working for the body, that soon perisheth. . . .

July 6th Sunday The 4th I spent at home, nothing was going on more than usual — Today Mr. Cody preached last night sat up with Mrs. Bushnel, other thoughts have occupied my mind, so that I cannot get settled upon things befitting the day as I should.

13 Three ladies have died the last week in town other persons are sick and one or two are not expected to live. The flux seems to be the prevelent disease. It seems to be very fatal, yet people are not frightened, as they are sometimes. I think perhaps its assumed the nature of cholera more than formerly, which is quite prevalent in other parts of the country.[31] Mr. Cody appointed a meeting this afternoon for prayers on account of sickness. poor Mr. Blair. I believe he is thought to have been a universalist,[32] He does not expect to recover, but I do not know how he feels in regard to dying — I have thought it was the duty of some one to see him — perhaps they have — I wonder that my heart is not more drawn out in sympathy, when there seems so much need for sympathy on the part of the afflicted. — Sister Sarepta came home to day, having taught a week. She seemed pleased.

21 There are some sick yet but all are getting better. Next week School commences I would that I knew whether I ought to go or forever give up the idea. I think sometimes, that I will go regardless of consequences, but then I think again if it is my duty to stay at home, it would be but little benefit that I should receive from going

Aug. 10th It is sabbath again and a very rainy and desagreeable day it is, especially for the association which is in progress at parson. I have not spent this day in the manner I should. It seems almost impossible for me to fix my mind upon the subjects most suitable for a day which we are commanded to keep holy. I have at length commenced attending school and enjoy it as much as I expected, but not so much as if I had more leisure for study out of school. I have had a composition to write last week, an exercise which I ever enjoy, though one that requires a little hard study.

Aug. 31st. Last evening the young ladies of the school met as usual, at the school room for the purpose of holding prayer meeting. Mrs.

Barker meets with us — last friday we had to read composition. I did not succeed in reading mine though I made two attempts. It is a very hard task for those who are not accustomed to it —

Sep, the 22nd. Only 4 weeks more of school How I dread to have it close. It seems as if I should be perfectly miserable if I were to attend no more. I cannot be content, to think that I must no more have the privelege of attending school. can I give up the idea of treasuring up knowledge, when I feel the need of it so much, when I feel it is so essential to true enjoyment — I have enjoyed my self very well since going to school, and at times extremely so. Oh may my present priveliges long continue, and may use them to the best advantage — we had visitors one day when compositions were being read. How I love to write

To day Mr. Ellege preached the funeral sermon of Miss Triplet.[33] There has been several deaths by flux within a short time. Oh that I might look upon death as I should — I little realize it solemnity. May I live in such a way as to meet death with joy. I fear that I do not try to do others as much good as I might. I am too selfish — too unwilling to deny myself. At present my time is taken up with my studies. I feel so anxious to improve my mind, that I may be better qualified for the various duties which may devolve upon me — Oh! I cannot give up the idea of getting an education.

Sabbath Oc 19th Heard a new minister to day, & thought he preached quite an able sermon. I know not why it is that I do not enjoy Sabbath days more. I get discouraged trying to fix my attention upon those things I should. I scarsely no interest in those thing I should most delight in. It is strange that I can be so cold and indifferent. Oh! that I could once more feel as Christian does, if I ever had any such feelings — Next friday is the last day of School, will it be the last quarter I can attend? I shall be more unhappy than ever if it is. How little I know yet and if I were to live a long time and go to school all of my time how little still would I know. I am anxious to have a *good* composition for the last day but *fear* I shall not succeed.

[Nov.] 10th School closed two weeks since. the evening of the examination the church was filled with spectators. that morning, for the first time, I succeeded in reading my own composition after many efforts. In the evening I read again, with many other young ladies. It is a very hard task to read one's own composition, but one we should do, that we may have confidence in ourselves. School commences again in two weeks I do not expect much to attend, though I am very anxious to & can hardly give up hoping that I may be able to do so, though I see no prospect yet. We have a new singing school taught by a very celebrated singing master, through the kindness of a generous friend, I have the pleasure of attending. Last night for the first this fall, we had snow attended a social party last evening, and the evening previous.

Perhaps said, and done many wrongs things. at least have not enjoyed myself to day as a Christian should the Sabbath. I fear that in one instance, I wounded the feelings of a kind friend, by thoughtless conduct.

26th Have engaged to teach school this winter, and shall soon have to bid adieu to singing school, and give up all idea of attending school, which I so much desired to do.

Dec. 7th One week more and I shall leave home and all the pleasures attached to it. I expect to be very lonesome, it can hardly be otherwise in a country School but if I do all the good I can, and exercise a right spirit at all times, I shall have nothing to regret, though I be deprived of some priveliges. I should very much like to enjoy the singing school and Seminary I can hardly consent to leave when I allow myself to think of them.

Dec. 14th Sunday. Here I am 18 miles away from home among strangers. I know not how I shall like it here, though I have a pleasant boarding place and have enjoyed myself very well to day having had a plentiful supply of interesting books to read. Oh! such a ride as I had yesterday. I never was so thoroughly jolted in all my life. I thought it would almost kill me at first. Tomorrow I commence school, may I succeed in teaching well so that it my be interesting to myself and scholars

28 Christmas is past and New years is close at hand another year of my life gone and how has it been spent? I feel lonesome tonight. O for some kind, attentive friend, into whose *willing* ear, I might pour the *burthen* of my heart's pent up feelings, with the consciousness that, that heart did readily sympathise with my own either in joy, or sorrow. How few — how *very few* are there who feel interested for others than themselves, and the sensitive, where can they find that sympathy which their quick feelings, and susceptible natures ever need? Oh! is there so holy, so heavenly a sentiment, as pure, disinterested friendship or love? Such as eyes may read from eyes. Sentiments so deep, so earnest, that words were powerless to express? Oh! when heart, with heart, thus comingles, it were worth while to *name* it *friendship!* or — *love!*

Feb. 1st [1852] the sixth week of my school has closed, week before last last spent at home, on account sister S., being sick. and very sick she was, with the erysipelas.[34] Some had died with it — I hope to commence school tomorrow with renewed energy, and hope that I may succeed in being useful to my pupils. I must be diligent, and do them all the good I can that I may not have cause to mourn over neglect of duty. May I try to be a kind, and faithful teacher. I was very unhappy last week, so much so, that I had little appetite to eat, or disposition to work. it was a bitter wound my heart received from the conduct of one, whom I estemed a friend, one to whom I thought I had reason to be grateful, who are true friends? Is friendship but a name, and are none to be trusted? Oh! may I ever be careful not to wound the feeling of others.

5th this morning awaked at 4 oclock. the moon was shinning most brilliantly, as it had all night. I could not sleep any more but spent the time in meditation and prayer & felt more earnesteness than usual. . . .

Sunday 8 Feb — I think that I have not spent this day altogether unprofitably, though it has not been without troubles. I spent most of the day in reading and I think I some wiser & hope better than before. Oh! wish that I might daily grow better & wiser. I hope that I may be better than ever prepared to enter upon my duties in teaching tomorrow. I intend to read at least one chapter daily in the bible in future.

Monday 16 Yesterday went to Perry, to Church in Company with friends from Barry, whom I found on my return from A[tlas] Saturday who I was much rejoiced to see.[35]

22 of February Sunday Today is Washingtons birth day, a glorious day to all Americans. as it is Sabbath, I suppose that tomorrow will be celebrated. I went home Friday, went to the examination of Mrs. B's school in the afternoon and evening, found it very interesting, as I always do such occasions. There was a very interesting meeting in progress in the baptist Church which however I did not attend any. I know not but I ought to have went friday evening. I did not enjoy the examination so well for thinking, perhaps that I did wrong in not attending church. I was told that many were serious I would liked to have stayed to attend last evening & today as I feel that I have need of spiritual consolation and instruction. . . . I ask not for riches, or the goods of this world to make a display, but I do long for those treasures which adorn the heart, and mind, those *jewels,* and *gems,* which I may never grow weary of, and which would procure for me a happier residence in the highest realms of the future insomuch as they would render me more cappable of that exquisite enjoyment which is in store for those who are diligent, and faithful. But oh! the poor — those who have not money, how shall they succeed in cultivating, and rendering qualified, that intellect which God has given them as their only inheritance in this world, and which both poor, and rich, will alike retain in their possession in that world, where mind will not be fettered by a prison house of clay;

March 1st Such a delightful time as I have had reading this evening! — or rather such delightful pieces? Sweet "Lilly"! may I be as fortunate as thou wert — but I am not skilled in preparing favorite dishes to regale the appetites of poet-or of musician. . . . Oh! can poets love a second time? Can a tender, sensitive heart, once stripped of the idolized object of its affections find another to fill its vacancy, another to call forth those tender emotions into life and vigor, which they once thought no other one could cherish?[36]

8th My School has closed one week sooner than I anticipated and I came home yesterday, and found a very interesting meeting in progress. quite a number have joined the church among the rest, Sister C., so that we all have now made a profession of religion. May we adorn that cause which we have espoused, but, also I am so cold, and hard hearted. Mr. Esty is the most faithful minister and very many seem to to deeply interested.[37]

Sund. 14th meeting still in progress. I am very much depressed in mind. There is comfort and consolation for every one but me. For me there seems no encouragement . . . I am too fearful of doing my duty, too afraid of what might be said or thought of me, and allow too many doubts to enter my mind.

21st Mr. Estey is still laboring with us. The meetings are very interesting, especially the afternoon meetings, the conversations of the anxious &c One circumstance of a young man, a stranger accidentally thrown among us he acknowledged that he had never prayed. Many hearts were enlisted and many prayers offerd in behalf of the stranger penitent, and in strangers he has found the best of friends, those to whom he will feel attached. One week from tomorrow I expect to commence school again; among strangers, I shall be placed, with not a friend, or an acquaintance to be near me.

March 31 Commenced School yesterday at home instead of among strangers, as I expected. There being a chance for me to do much better here, my friends thought it would be my duty to do so, though I may have disappointed others. Our meeting closed Sunday evening & Mr. Esty left us yesterday. The meeting Sunday evening was very affecting. . . . Many were the tears that were shed, and the sighs, heard as the parting hand was given Sunday evening. If I could feel but half what he feels, how exceedingly would I rejoice.

Apr 4th A week of my school has passed. I think I feel satisfied that I have done what I could for the advancement of those under my charge. May I be as faithful as I can. Mr. Shastid commences tomorrow in the room adjoining.[38]

6th to day, had to dismiss School, on account of town meeting, which was to be held in the School room.

12th friday evening heard Rev. Kettin preach . . . . Yesterday heard Rev. Carter preach . . . . In the afternoon Mr. C. & Nolly lectured on Baptism & administered Bap. & sacrament. Evening lectures by Ketlin & Nolly on home missions & Fletcher on foreign missions, and some very apt remarks by Rev. Rutlege & a sermon this evening by him . . . . [39]

20th To day heard Mr. Ellege twice, in the he preached the funeral sermon of Sister Harriet Bulkley. She was a very amiable young lady, and a christian.[40] Many are sick a present time Tomorrow is the third monday of my School I like it better that I expected that I should like teaching so many young children.

28th The other teachers have closed their schools for the purpose of attending the teacher's institute this week.[41]

2nd of May. I did not attend Church today, but have enjoyed myself in reading the Bible, especially in reading some incidents about the prophet Elisah, which I did not recollect of reading before. Very few attended the institute. I am glad that I did not go.

9th Have not been to Church to day, it has been so rainy. My School is half out.

19th Have just finished reading an account of Grandmother's sickness and death.[42] She was deranged most of the time for a year, and was very old (78) and very helpless. . . .

29th to day is the anniversary of my birthday. I am 25 years old — and I more than ever anxious to improve my mind that I may be more useful than I have ever yet been. I sometimes feel as if I had no time for the necessary duties of every day. I am so anxious to have more time to study. I am particularly desireous to have a better opportunity to learn music. Had a ride to the country one evening last week in company with several young people did not find it very pleasant as there was but little conversation in which I was interested. There was a party which I did not attend: prepared but gave it up as there was prayer meeting.

Sund. attended Sabbath S., and prayer meeting — was constantly thinking of curious things — Have been reading of a new plan to keep a private journal in some respects, intend to adopt it — I have been much interested (and profited I hope) this few weeks past in reading Goodriche's School History — I think it a valuable work[43]

Private Journal

Barry

June 18th — To day my school closed. The day passed off quite pleasantly. Mr. S. and some of his scholars called. One day last week Mr. B. favored me with a call. I am ever pleased to receive the attention of those who are interested in the subject of education. Sunday, heard an interesting sermon from Mr. Ballard.[44]

June 29th Second day of my second term of school. Not so many scholars as before. These are beautiful moonlight evenings, so delightful for walking Tomorrow evening our singing school — it will soon close and our faithful and kind teacher will have bid us adieu. May I remember and practice his instructions. I consider them invaluable, yet I am afraid they will not profit me so much as he desires to see his pupils benefited.

July Our singing school has closed and as have no teacher any longer, we shall have to depend entirely upon our own exertions for improvement in music. I am through the history. I intend to finish Laribee's Evidences.[45]

Sund — Very well pleased with Mr. Lyman's sermon — Subject on bridling the tongue.

Aug 1st Have been very much interested reading "Uncle Tom's Cabin." It certainly is a very affecting book, and I think a useful one, too. I hope that I may be benefitted by it. The evils of slavery very very clearly portrayed, and the influence of Christianity upon the negro heart is well sustained. What an angel was Eva. What a practical Christian her and Mrs. Shelby. Poor St. Clair — he knew but never did, like so many others. Tom was the very personality of affection and confidence.[46]

Aug 23 My school has been vacated three weeks, 2 of these I have spent at an Uncle's helping Aunt get ready to start on her journey to Erie. How very much I should like to go with them that I might once more behold the scene of my childhood. Those were happy days, and those are hallowed associations which would recall tender emotions in a heart, now alas, grown so cold — I have some horseback rides in the last fortnight, but cannot say they were very delightful, though I did enjoy them. One time visited the place father bought and improved when we first came to Illinois, 13 years since. The buildings are torn down and the place in ruins — Both sad and pleasant recollections were recalled. Tomorrow commence school again.

Sep Went to hear Mr. Browning's speech. He is a candidate for Senator, is thought to be a very smart man. I was interested and pleased with his remarks.[47]

Personal Journal   Barry 1852
On cultivating the intellect

Sund Sep 25 — Have been very much interested for some time in reading "Laribee's Evidences of Nat. and Revealed Religion". It certainly contains a vast deal of scientific knowledge which everyone should be acquainted with. I wish that I might be able to remember it all — This evening have been reading in the "Young Christian" some hints in reference to intellectual improvement[48] — it is a duty incumbent upon all Christians to improve & cultivate their intellects. I feel a great desire to do so, and experience more pleasure in reading and trying to treasure up knowledge than in doing anything else. I feel sometimes as if I have no time, and as if it were a task almost to do anything else, so eager do I get sometimes, and so late have I learned the importance and the pleasure there is connected with knowledge. "The objects of study should be 'First' — To increase our intellectual powers. Sec — the acquisition of knowledge. Thirdly — the acquisition of skill." May I endeavor to hold these objects in view herafter as much as possible.

Thoughts suggested by a dream

Sep What beautiful impressions do dreams sometimes leave upon our hearts — yes, as we lay in the gentle embrace of Somnus the sweetest sentiments and happiest emotions will visit us, prevade our whole hearts — we feel the purest love and utmost confidence as we receive the affectionate embrace or approving kiss of a dear and sometimes new found friend. We believe we are loved and we love in return unconscious of evil. Oh! that such soul harassing doubts and fears and realities of evil should so fill our waking hours; we are so often deceived, so often find coldness and indifference where we looked for love and kindness that we soon dare not love or trust where we would . . . . O! that we might often dream of love and kindness — if 'tis but a dream 'twill do us good. We may recall those light and joyous feelings again, and live them over in our day dreams. Those gladsome sunny pictures of dreamland — let them often be wafted to us on memory's light wing. . . .

O 10 School is at last ended. I am glad to be released. What am I to do, and where go next? I should like to have some pleasant visits in "country and village" but may be disappointed. I must be prepared for disappointments for very bitter ones come sometimes. Mrs. D. returned from E.[49] a few days ago and brought from our old home a thousand miles away some little presents in the way of grapes, a few quinces, apples & etc. from the old homestead — I am through "Evidences" and hope I am wiser for it. Have read the memoirs of Francke, a German, and founder of the Orphan house in Hulle, and have also been reading "Greenwood leaves from over the Sea". They are charming.[50] I envy Grace her good fortune and happiness, almost . . . . Yet I have many blessings for which I am not sufficiently thankful.

17th Accidently I came across the "Christian era". Read first the story of "Nobility and High Life". I liked it well enough. I then read Grace Greenwood's letters which are most interesting and instructive. The political matter was also interesting, especially Sumner's and Mann's speeches on the fugitive slave law. "Democracy of Science" is a useful article in favor of the acquisition and diffusion of knowledge among men.

Nov. 23 Started to school yesterday. Find it quite pleasant after being confined at home several weeks. Study Astronomy for the first.

Dec. 6th Have not been to school for a week. Cannot study, read or sew on account of sore eyes. A brother of the Columbians will teach in singing class I suppose. I wish to attend — don't know how I can, O! I want money so much. Uncle Henry came from California a few days since. We want to go back with him very much. There seems to be a good prospect for females to make good wages there. I trust our Heavenly Father will direct our steps aright, and if it be his will that we shall go I pray that we may be prepared both spiritually and temporally. Brother is in Shasta, Cal. I earnestly hope that he will do well & especially *keep* himself free from the temptations which surround him

Christmas Have been staying a fortnight at aunt's. was sick a day or two — I have felt quite interested about going to California for a few days. I should not wonder if we go in the spring. If we do I hope we may be prospered and that we may spend our lives usefully and profitably in that land of gold and wickedness — Had the pleasure of reading some of my own compositions in print in To day's paper. It is the second piece that has been printed in the "Union".[51] I have a desire to become an authoress but cannot expect that my hopes will be realized further opportunity to improve my mind. My eyes are still very weak so that I dare not study much.

1853

Jan 6th The sixth day of the new year! How many of our great men have fallen prey to the conqueror, Death. Webster, that giant of intellect, has passed away within a few months. Clay, another of our mighty statesman, too, has fallen, respected and lamented by many, within the past year. I have been reading some numbers of the "National Era" lent me by a friend. I find them most interesting papers, strongly anti slavery as they should be. They contain the great speeches of Sumner, Mann, Giddings, &c, and many other original pieces from the pens of popular and gifted authors.[52]

Jan. 30th I have been anticipating much pleasure to come, as we have made up our minds to go to California next spring. It is only two months until starting time & we shall have to be quite busy making preparations. I hope we shall have a pleasant time, and I know there will be many trials and petty vexations attending such a very long fatiguing journey. I do hope I shall have strength to endure everything with patience, and I hope we shall be prospered and blessed with good health. Uncle Henry is very kind in assisting mother and each one of us to go. I hope God will guide safely through the journey and preserve us from temptation in that land of dangers. I trust I may be useful in some way to others, and I also hope that my own opportunities for getting knowledge will be increased. How can I impart it to others if I have so little myself? Oh! that I could have the opportunities that others have wasted, and thrown away. . . . But I know not as my desires can ever be realized, yet I hope to have grace to enable me to be as useful as I may be in my humble way. If I do the best I can, perhaps I shall not have lived in vain. I have been writing to brother & cousins in Cal. Cousin seems to be doing very well — Sometimes since experienced great pleasure in hearing "Sunny Side" read aloud. I think it a most beautiful book.[53] It called up emotions in my heart which it had long been almost a stranger to, and I had to press back the teardrops to keep them from wilfully gushing forth when I did'ent want them to.

Mar 2nd — Barry

Preparing for California

Cousin Orlando has arrived from California.[54] I was anticipating a meeting with him on the plains. I have seen him but a few moments. He does not seem changed much, I hope to see him again, but we start in one week and I may not. Have been reading over old letters and papers and burning up those with which I could part best. I did not like to spare any but had to some. I cannot carry them all. I like to read old letters & papers as they recall past and interesting incidents. It will be a busy time until we start. Many things to arrange and friends to bid good bye. Last Saturday we attended the last covenant meeting. Some of our friends seemed very sorry to think it was the last time they should meet us thus. I may never see them again, but if I live I may be privileged to correspond with some. . . .

Saturday, 5th Many persons have been in to day. Mrs. and Mr. Hart, Clara & Orlando among the rest. I feel almost discouraged tonight. Orlando says the society is so bad I am affraid we will want to come back very much, but I hope we may like it and that we shall be useful to others. I promised to write to Mrs. Hart.[55] I feel so lonely tonight. I want someone in whom I can confide all my thoughts. But there is no one I can open my heart to, none who would care to listen to my tale of woe. I often think of some who have professed friendship for me, and O! if those professions were real, how much should I prize them. But alas! how soon are they forgotten. Perhaps there was no meaning in those words or looks of tenderness. I bid them all adieu forever. They are for me no more.

10th Attended the donation party last night. Enjoyed it as much as any party I have ever attended. It is the last one I shall ever attend in Barry, perhaps anywhere. Sometimes I almost wish I was not going. . . . Last evening formed some new acquaintances, but what good will it do. I shall never see them again. As it was a donation party Elder Wallace had singing & prayer which I enjoyed. I came from the party without that feeling of regret which I often feel after attending one. We start tomorrow, I suppose. I dread it somewhat[56]

11th at Uncle Adams got into the ox wagons & came through the mud. Rec'd from C. Foot "Deeds of Noble Women", from Mrs. Shields, "Bible Women", from Mrs. Angle, a neck ribbon and some other little keepsakes from others. Promised to write to Mary Hull, Mrs. Harny. Stayed at Mrs. Dehavens last night. took dinner at Mr. Harvey's to day. Heard Mr. Wallace preach last night. How long will it be before I go to church again? Heard Mr. Lillis had died on his road home.[57] Who of us will die on our way to California?

Part 2—The Trip to California

The Trip to California 1853

I N 1853 A TRIP OVERLAND to California could be considered "easy and interesting." Lorena, despite forebodings, found it so and other emigrants that year agreed. After nearly two months of travel, Mrs. Harriet Sherrill Ward declared:

> Indeed, I think what is often termed suffering is merely a little inconvenience, for I had so often read and heard of the difficulties and dangers of the overland route to California, and I find from experience that the pleasure thus far quite over-balances it all.[1]

William Taylor, who made two cross-country trips in two years, also recalled his 1853 journey as "one of the most pleasant I ever enjoyed. The trip the year before was hard but I really enjoyed this."[2]

Lorena's overland adventure began on a cold, disagreeable day in March when she left Illinois behind, never to return. March 11, her last day in Barry, was spent visiting friends and attending church. On Saturday morning, March 12, the six Hays women and Uncle Henry Woodward began their western journey without the Adam Lithgow family, who planned to catch up with them later. The first day of wagon travel brought Lorena and her family to the banks of the Mississippi River, thirteen miles west of Barry, over roads transformed into a sea of mud after a week of "freezing hard at night and thawing some during the day."[3]

The Woodward-Hays party probably crossed the Mississippi River by steam ferry to Hannibal, Missouri, although an alternative would have been another ferry, farther south in Pike County, across the river to the community of Louisiana, Missouri. The steamer *Die Vernon* stopped at Hannibal, but not at Louisiana, four times a week on round-trip voyages between St. Louis and Keokuk, Iowa. On the even-

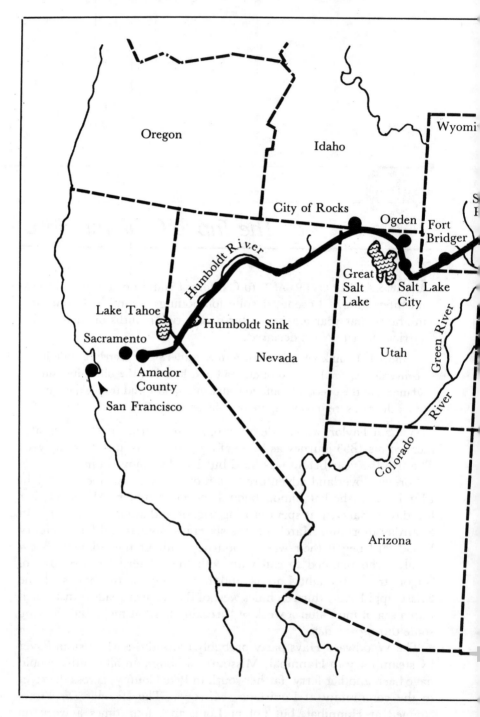

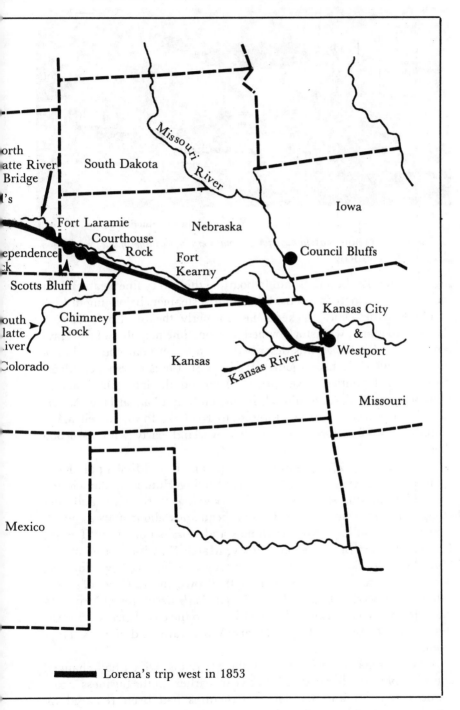

orth
atte River
Bridge

's

Fort Laramie

Courthouse
Rock

ependence
k

Scotts Bluff ▲

outh
latte
iver

Colorado

South Dakota

Nebraska

Fort
Kearny

Chimney
Rock

Kansas

Missouri River

Iowa

● Council Bluffs

Kansas City
&
Westport

Kansas River

Missouri

Mexico

━━━ Lorena's trip west in 1853

Missouri Historical Society, St. Louis

The Die Vernon *was named for Diana Vernon, heroine of the Sir Walter Scott novel,* Rob Roy.

ing of March 12, Lorena's family boarded this "very fine steamer" for the overnight trip to St. Louis. One of three steamers belonging in 1853 to the Keokuk Daily Packet Line (formerly the St. Louis-Keokuk Packet Company, with stock owned by a onetime neighbor of the Hays family), the *Die Vernon* was described as "a better boat you could not find upon which to take a journey," by a St. Louis newspaper advertisement that omitted ticket prices. Two months later Dr. Thomas Flint observed his twenty-ninth birthday on May 13 aboard the *Die Vernon* en route from Warsaw, Illinois, to Keokuk, Iowa, to sell 6,410 pounds of wool before rejoining his overland party with its 1,880 sheep.[4]

Like that of Flint, Lorena's trip on this Mississippi River steamer was uneventful. Shortly after leaving Hannibal, the 446-ton *Die Vernon* met the steamer *Kate Kearney* going up the river and later stopped briefly near Cap au Gris, a headlands about halfway to St. Louis at the confluence of the Illinois and Mississippi rivers. The *Die Vernon* arrived in St. Louis on Sunday, March 13, with a cargo of "77 bbl. pork, 203 sks. bran, 46 bbl. whiskey, bacon, ale, eggs, turkeys, Mr. Woodward, and three wagons, Mr. Brown and 130 head of sheep, fish and flax seed." Thus did the *Missouri Daily Republican* of March 14 inadvertently record Lorena's second visit to the city, because this was indeed a reference to Uncle Henry Woodward and the six Hays women.[5]

Again Lorena neglected to describe St. Louis, which had changed considerably since her first visit five years earlier. In the business areas, frame tenements and temporary structures had been replaced by "substantial buildings of brick and stone." By 1853 St. Louis had a population of nearly 100,000, "exclusive of the suburbs," and forty-

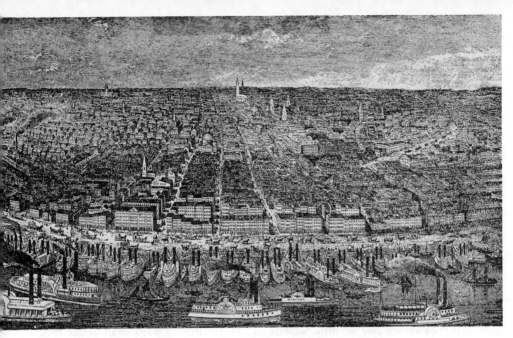

Lorena stayed overnight in St. Louis before leaving for the West in March 1853. This engraving was done about that time by Charles Magnus.

four places of Protestant worship, according to a brief sketch written by an anonymous citizen. It was also described as a "hard looking place" by Calvin H. Graham, who stopped there April 15-16.[6]

However, a month earlier Celinda Hines had been "very much pleased with the city." St. Louis charmed Celinda with its "superb appearance of everything together with the rich and tasty apparel of the ladies we saw in the street." Basil Longworth, who arrived there on March 24, was surprised by the "wealth and magnificence" of St. Louis, with its "splendid mansions, cathedrals, churchs and court house."[7] Another visitor to the busy port city that spring described it as "much larger and more densely built than any yet seen on the route." On May 14 Dr. James G. Cooper, a surgeon and naturalist who filled the pages of his small diary with notes about birds, added:

> The streets near the river are mostly devoted to business and have some very extensive whole sale establishments on them. Further back, wider and pleasanter streets are lined by many fine dwellings, churches and other unpublic buildings. The want of large shade trees must make it very hot here in summer.[8]

Lorena's omission of such information about St. Louis can be excused. She spent only a couple of days there, primarily in the port area, which Longworth described as

> one of the most business-like places I ever saw. The shore for a mile and a half is lined with boats while the wharf is piled high with merchandise

of every kind and description and drays and wagons make a continual hum.[9]

Upon arrival Lorena was unable to visit former acquaintances and friends because her Uncle Henry immediately booked passage on the side-wheeler *Clara* for the trip up the Missouri River. The 248-ton *Clara,* then in its third season, was one of the regular packet boats that made the trip between St. Louis and towns along the Missouri, as far as Council Bluffs, Iowa, during the spring flood season when the river was high.[10]

Eight days behind schedule, the *Clara* arrived in St. Louis on March 13 from New Orleans, where she had wintered. Her cargo consisted of leather and mackerel, as well as most of the ingredients a St. Louis resident might need to mix a bowl of punch: sugar, liquor, lemons, oranges, and molasses. Recently renovated, this steamboat was "unsurpassed for her accomodations . . . no trouble or pain shall be spared to make them who travel on the 'Clara' comfortable and the trip agreeable," while the twenty-five foot cabin was "furnished in a style of comfort and elegance that will far excel that of any boat now plying the river."[11]

According to a pre-announced schedule, the *Clara* should have made her first trip of 1853 up the Missouri River on March 5, returning to St. Louis in time for a second voyage on March 19. Instead, the *Clara* did not leave port until either March 15 or 16. This departure was not accurately reported by St. Louis newspapers, whose columns gave conflicting dates.[12] Lorena's diary indicates that the *Clara* did sail on March 15. She and her family, therefore, were passengers on the *Clara* for the first voyage of the season up the Missouri River.

The trip took six days because the *Clara* stopped at several of the small communities along the river. According to Calvin H. Graham, who sailed on the *Clara* a month later (April 16) to Independence, Missouri, the fare was $2.50. Graham also paid a provision bill of eighty-four cents. These prices may have been only for deck passage, however, because cabin accommodations on a rival Missouri River boat, the *Banner State,* cost Basil Longworth $12 on March 24.[13]

Lorena's immediate destination was the community of Kansas City, located on the Missouri side of the river before it turns north to Iowa. Known for many years as merely the landing place for the older frontier community of Westport, Kansas City outgrew this youthful reputation to develop its own identity in 1853. On April 4 the first municipal elections were held to name a mayor, a council president, and four council members. Lorena did not report this event, but Celinda Hines, who was with her family, did: "On Tuesday Kansas was made a city."[14]

Celinda stayed in Kansas City sixteen days and devoted most of her time to helping with chores and sewing covers for the wagons. Phoebe Goodell Judson, who spent five weeks in nearby Westport before she and her husband joined the Hines company, also made covers of white cotton drilling, lined with "colored muslin to subdue the light and heat of the sun."[15]

Lorena spent nearly six weeks in Kansas City and had time for sight-seeing. She visited the Catholic Church founded in 1835 by Father Benedict Roux and toured bustling Water Street along the river with Uncle Henry. Lorena found Kansas City now rivaled St. Joseph, Independence, and Council Bluffs as a "jumping-off place" for western travelers. One such traveler was John C. Fremont, who passed through Kansas City in September 1853 at the start of his fifth-and-last-exploring expedition.[16] While only a few miles farther west than Independence, Kansas City had one distinct advantage over its rivals: emigrants beginning overland trips from there did not have to cross the Missouri River because they were already on its western bank.

Lorena enjoyed her stay in Kansas City and wrote a description supplying more details than did Celinda Hines. Both young women met Margaret Clark (Mrs. Hiram M.) Northrup, the Wyandot Indian wife of a prominent merchant and trader.[17] During these weeks Lorena and her family lived in rented quarters, holding frequent "open house" for other emigrants from their home town. Who these other pioneers might have been is unknown because the Pike County (Illinois) newspapers of 1853 did not report their names and no newspaper was printed in Kansas City that spring. Lorena's diary provides but few clues and only one name can be identified with any certainty. Ahead of her on the trail was Dr. A. C. Baker, who had attended her father in 1848 during his last illness[18]

In Kansas City Uncle Adam Lithgow and his family caught up with the Hays-Woodward party and then decided to go ahead along a different route with other friends and former neighbors. This time it was the Hays-Woodward party that remained behind. Lorena and her family waited in Kansas City until Uncle Henry returned from a trip to purchase cattle to drive to California.

Finally, on April 23, the Hays-Woodward wagons got under way and that evening Lorena camped out for the first time, only seven miles from Kansas City. From Kansas City and Westport, the road she and her family traveled soon became part of the California-Oregon Trail, well-traveled and well-marked during the preceding decade of western emigration. Lorena's route to California held few surprises because the trail and its major cutoffs had been charted and mapped by 1853. In many places well-worn wheel ruts marked much of the way.

A number of guidebooks for overland travelers had also been printed by 1853, but Lorena preferred to compare her trip with Fremont's exploring expeditions insofar as the two routes coincided. First printed in 1845, his *Report to Congress* was still considered one of the best of the many overland guides.[19] Lorena had a copy of it with her in the wagon and jotted down her own observations as they agreed with those in the *Report.* Such information was primarily for her own personal enjoyment, however, because her two uncles had made the trip to California before and would have been quite familiar with the trail.

Lorena never reported who traveled in their party, but thirty years later her youngest sister, Sarah Louis Hays (Mrs. Daniel) Whitlatch, provided some of these details:

> Thers was a mixed company; a gentleman who had been in California & returned with plenty of gold to his family, who had found his eldest child, a daughter of seventeen, wasting with consumption and was returning to California now with the hope that the journey across the plains and the healthful climate of California would effect a cure. there was his wife and three daughters younger another gentleman whose wife was in Cal and he had gone east & was bringing out stock on a speculation - a widowed sister of the same with five daughters, of whom I was the youngest, fourteen — a lady and daughter coming out to a husband and father who had made some money and sent for them, a widow with three sons, a Mosourian proprietor of an immense "prairie Schooner" and four hands and two hundred head of cattle, two Kentuckians, one Tennessean, A Missippininan, a jolly Irishman — a sedate dutchman and a dozen others, mostly young men & boys seeking their fortunes in the West.[20]

The first gentlemen mentioned in this account was Uncle Adam Lithgow and the second, Uncle Henry Woodward, while the "widowed sister of the same with five daughters" described Lorena and her family. According to Wells West, Lorena's cousin, the combined Lithgow and Woodward-Hays parties consisted of "18 men, 3 women and enough young ladies and girls to make the whole number about 30," with six wagons drawn by ox teams, one spring wagon, two mules, and several riding horses.[21]

The others cannot be identified, but among the company may well have been the widower Thomas Jefferson West, Lorena's paternal uncle by marriage, who died in Drytown, California, on December 25, 1853. Whether or not the other West sons also went to California at this time is unknown, but in later years they lived in the same area as their Hays relatives. How many of Lorena's Woodward relatives might have also joined the company cannot be ascertained either, but several of them were later reported living in California.[22]

From Westport Lorena and her company headed west to ford the

Wakarusa River on May 3. Then they followed a trail north to the Kansas River, camping near the Baptist Mission while waiting to be ferried across on May 9. Much to Lorena's regret this crossing was made on a Sunday; she did not feel that it was quite right to travel on the Sabbath, regardless of what other emigrants might do. On the north side of the Kansas River, the Woodward-Hays company met Uncle Adam Lithgow and his family, and on May 10 the enlarged wagon train passed the Catholic mission of St. Mary's. The progress of the Woodward-Hays-Lithgow wagon train at this point was recorded by another emigrant of 1853, Elizabeth Julia Ellison Goltra from Jacksonville, Illinois. The twenty-two-year-old woman and her husband, Nelson, had left Kansas City a day behind Lorena's party, crossed the Wakarusa River on May 3, and ferried the Kansas River on May 9. The Goltras, who were going to Oregon, became separated from their own wagon train, and on Tuesday, May 10, Mrs. Goltra wrote: "Started in Company with Lithcoe and Woodard travelled till noon and one of the wagons broke at the Catholic Mission."[23]

Apparently, the Goltras joined Lorena's company for only part of the day because Mrs. Goltra added: "We camped alone for the first time as our company did not come up." On May 10, both Lorena and Mrs. Goltra wrote about the "very bad creeks" along this section of the trail. The Goltras must then have dropped behind Lorena's company because the following day, May 11, they again waited for their own train. When their wagons did not catch up, the Goltras moved on alone.[24] During the next few weeks both companies stopped near the same location each day. Mrs. Goltra did not again mention the "Lithcoe-Woodard" party, although Lorena wrote about seeing a number of acquaintances from western Illinois.

In addition to the diaries kept by Lorena and Mrs. Goltra, sixteen others are known to have been written by women during overland trips west in 1853. Four of these journals, including Lorena's, describe travel to California. Another ten, besides Goltra's account, record women's experiences along the Oregon Trail. Of the thirty-seven men's diaries consulted, eighteen were written en route to California and another thirteen on the way to Oregon. There were also five other accounts by men, and one by a woman, with Salt Lake City as their destination; seven additional diaries tell about the adventures of various transcontinental railroad survey parties that year.

Men also wrote the majority of letters about overland travel, including those printed in Midwestern and Eastern newspapers. However, the letters from 1852 of Cornelia Woodcock (Mrs. B. G.) Ferris, wife of the U.S. secretary for Utah, were later compiled and eventually printed as a book.[25] Although the first part of Mrs. Ferris's overland journey was made in that same year (she spent the winter in Salt Lake City),

CROSSING THE PLAINS.

Views Drawn from Nature, in 1853, by George H. Baker.

EMIGRANT TRAIN PASSING WIND RIVER MOUNTAINS.

SIOUX INDIANS.

CALIFORNIA INDIANS.

INDIANS CHASING BUFFALOES, SCOTT'S BLUFFS.

COURT HOUSE ROCK.

MOUTH OF ASH HOLLOW.

FIRST NIGHT ON THE PLAINS.

CHIMNEY ROCK.

DEVIL'S GATE.

LARAMIE PEAK.

SCENE ON THE DESERT.

CASTLE ROCK.

DRIVING STOCK ACROSS THE PLAINS.

Published by Barber & Baker, Sacramento. Copyright secured.

Pictorial lettersheets, such as this, were designed for sale to California miners, who sent them to the home folks. This one was prepared in 1853 by George H. Baker, a forty-niner.

she and her husband left Utah the following spring to join emigrants on the California Trail. Her letters about this part of the trip cover 1853. The same holds true for several letters by Lucy Rutledge Cook, who spent the same winter in Salt Lake City before continuing her trip to California in late March 1853.[26] By far the busiest writer on the overland trail must have been Dr. Joseph R. Bradway. He kept a detailed travel diary and also wrote numerous long letters to relatives and friends in Delavan, Wisconsin.[27]

For eleven wagon companies, more than one diary or reminiscence exists. While some of these companion pieces were written by relatives, several were kept by travelers who did not stay together for the entire trip. Similar cross-references include James Farmer's diary mentioning the progress of another Mormon train and three reminiscences by families traveling together to Oregon. In later years at least thirty-one men and fourteen women recalled their emigrant experiences in 1853 and of these, Capt. John Lewis and Sarah Jane Watson Hamilton chose to write in verse. There was also one reminiscence, written almost as fiction, about Allen and Rachel Bond's honeymoon trip to Oregon while members of the McClure train.

The 1853 emigration was recorded pictorially by two artists whose work has been published. Frederick H. Piercy's drawings for his Mormon guidebook are well known and have been reprinted many times.[28] Cyrenius Hall, whose artistic career (1852-94) included exhibiting at the 1887 International Exposition in Chicago, made pencil sketches of the trail in 1853. Five have been printed twice but further use has been "restricted." How many other emigrants might have illustrated overland journals, as did Robert Eccleston, remains unknown, but Lorena was not one of them, since her talents and aspirations were literary rather than artistic.[29]

The fact that men wrote the majority of diaries and reminiscences about 1853 overland travel is not surprising: women were always outnumbered in emigrant companies. Exactly how many emigrants made the overland journey that year cannot be precisely counted, of course. At one time registers kept by soldiers stationed at Forts Kearny and Laramie did exist, but these have long since disappeared. For 1853 the only figures available are those reported in letters to newspapers and copied into their journals by a few of the pioneers. Lorena did not record such information because her company did not stop at Fort Kearny but bypassed it on May 25. Nor was a soldier sent out to register members of the Woodward-Hays-Lithgow train as was sometimes done. So it is unlikely that Lorena and her traveling companions were included in the count of 18,726 emigrants registered at Fort Kearny as of August 15.[30]

This was by no means the total number of emigrants for 1853

Camping Scene.

These scenes of camp life along the trail and crossing the Platte River were published in Sacramento on January 1, 1853. California State Library, Sacramento

Fording the Platte.

Emigrant Party on the Road.

California State Library, Sacramento

This illustration was published by the Sacramento Pictorial Union *in January 1853.*

because it did not take into account the numerous companies traveling along the north bank of the Platte River. Because they did not cross the river, these emigrants were not registered at Fort Kearny. While a number of pioneers commented upon the many wagons that could be seen across the shallow Platte, Maria Parsons Belshaw once provided an estimate of how many followed the north side trail. On May 19 she was told by a ferryman at the Elkhorn River that 1,500 wagons had already crossed. This was early in the season but on June 1, at the crossing of the Loup Fork, another ferryman told William W. Gilbert he had already counted 2,400 wagons.[31]

Some idea of the traffic along the north side of the Platte in 1853 can be obtained through the number of diaries and reminiscences written by those who took this road. There were twenty-eight diaries (twenty by men and eight by women) as well as forty-eight reminiscences of travel along this Mormon Trail, so named because it was the route followed in 1847 by Mormons leaving "Winter Quarters" near Council Bluffs, Iowa, to travel to the Great Salt Lake Valley under the leadership of Brigham Young. In contrast, twenty-six diaries (eighteen by men and eight by women) and nine recollections describe the journey along the south side of the river. Despite these figures there is no way to ascertain which bank of the Platte River saw heavier travel in 1853. Henry Allyn, who camped on the north side May 19, observed that emigrants were "pouring in like locusts." Two days later he discovered "trains of wagons in sight behind us as far as the eye can reach." And Hannah Cornaby, a Mormon emigrant from England, later recalled the "long train of wagons stretching itself out like a huge snake and winding its slow length along the boundless prairies."[32]

It was predicted in early May that "from all accounts, the number of emigrants will fall far below that of former years." According to this Illinois newspaper, although the California emigration of 1852 totaled "upwards of 50,000," the number in 1853 was "not expected to exceed 20,000." A "great number" would be from Iowa, Michigan, Wisconsin, Illinois, and Indiana. While a large part of the emigration would consist of Mormons headed for Utah, Oregon was said to be the final destination for many pioneers. This contemporary estimate of some 20,000 emigrants has sometimes been accepted as the total number of overland travelers for 1853, regardless of the fact that it referred only to those bound for California.[33]

One study of the trans-Mississippi West, published in 1979, indicates the total emigration to the West Coast in 1853 was considerably larger: 27,500 persons. Approximately 7,500 emigrants were headed for Oregon, while California remained the destination for the other 20,000. In addition, another 8,000 emigrants were Mormons en route to Utah. These statistics agree more closely with an 1853 newspaper story from Fort Laramie that reported 23,000 persons and 6,000 wagons had passed as of late June.[34]

While Lorena and her relatives would have been included in this number, not every emigrant registered at Fort Laramie. Although the majority of travelers made an effort to visit the fort, in 1853 a few companies did not. Such was the case with the Henry Allyn wagon train as well as that of Isaiah Bryant, since neither crossed the North Platte River to visit the fort.

Also, there has never been a way to count the "number of large parties of emigrants to California from the southern and southwestern states, who are driving out immense herds of cattle" and came into the main trail well beyond Fort Laramie, as did Dillis Ward and Joseph Williams.[35] Nor will it ever be known how many emigrants from Texas traveled directly west to southern California. Trips along that route in 1853 were recorded in later years by Basil G. Parker and Maggie Hall, who was nine years old when she made the journey with her family and their slave, Delia. Arthur Pendry Welchman chronicled a similar trip to Utah when he learned to be a "cow-boy" while driving cattle for a group of Texas Saints.

Therefore, if the 27,500-plus figure is fairly accurate, 1853 constituted the third largest overland emigration in the history of the westward movement during the 1840s and 1850s. The largest migration occurred in 1852, when an estimated 10,000 pioneers headed for

Oregon while another 50,000 followed trails into California. In the major gold rush year of 1849, the emigration totaled 25,450 with only 450 going to Oregon, according to the same 1979 study. As for the Mormons, 1853 would be the second largest emigration in their history as compared with 10,000 the previous year.[36] This 1853 Mormon migration included the first large company of Saints from Scandinavia, led by Elder John E. Forsgren. Their journey from Copenhagen was recorded by an unknown member of the Forsgren company who wrote from St. Louis on April 23, that "135 of the brethern and sisters left for Keokuk [Iowa]" to begin their overland trek.[37]

Lorena and her company were in the first half of the 1853 emigration since they reached the vicinity of Fort Kearny by May 23. Three days earlier 3,348 men, 905 women, and 1,207 children were registered at the fort. Eight days later, on May 31, the count had risen to 4,937 men, 1,900 women, and 2,630 children.

How many women made overland trips west during the 1850s can only be estimated, but in 1853 they made up approximately fifteen percent of the 15,219 emigrants recorded at Fort Kearney by mid-August. Lorena, her four sisters and their mother, as well as her aunt and the two eldest of her Lithgow cousins, were among the 2,252-plus women traveling to California along the south side of the Platte River, while another 761 women were listed as going to Oregon. The same newspaper reported 9,909 men and 3,058 children in California companies while Oregon remained the destination of another 1,661 men and 1,085 children. Later in the year the number of emigrants to reach Oregon was cited as at least 6,499 persons: 2,630 men, 898 women, 1,408 sons, and 1,513 daughters.[38]

In only one instance was a report given about the number of blacks participating in the 1853 emigration. At Fort Kearny as of the Fourth of July, 400 were registered. How many were "free" was not indicated, but it was recorded that a male slave accompanied the William R. Taylor family from Kentucky. This unexpected statistic appeared in the August 23 edition of the *New York Times* as a reprint from the St. Joseph (Missouri) *Gazette* twenty days earlier. While the accuracy of this report cannot be ascertained, the chances of a typographical error occuring in the small, hand-set type of one or both newspapers should not be overlooked. Several episodes involving blacks on the trail were reported in the press but the name of only one free black, who passed Fort Kearny on May 5, has been found. Vardaman Bullard traveled with Harriet Tarleton Gill and her husband, William, from St. Louis. Nothing more is known of him because Harriet, anxious about her husband's health, did not keep her diary after reaching the Humboldt River on July 1.[39]

All these statistics do not, however, provide any indication of the number of explorers traveling across the plains in 1853 to survey possible routes for the future transcontinental railroad to the Pacific Coast. Each proposal had its outspoken partisans, so the question of where the railroad should go became an important issue of the day. Strong support for the railroad to run through the Southwest, via New Mexico, came from Kit Carson in a March 27 letter to the press, while Senator Thomas Hart Benton campaigned for a central route. Lorena missed hearing the senator explain his views in Kansas City and Westport on May 6 and 7 because her wagon train had started for California a week earlier.[40]

To help solve the railroad route dilemma, in March 1853 Congress passed a $150,000 appropriation to defray expenses of six survey parties. The three expeditions best remembered today were those commanded by Isaac I. Stevens, who later served as governor of the Washington Territory; Capt. John W. Gunnison, killed on October 26, along with eight others in his "scientific party," by "Pah Utah" Indians south of the Great Salt Lake; and Lt. A. W. Whipple, leader of one of the four official companies assigned to explore southern routes. Each party had its own artist(s) to illustrate the official reports.[41] In addition to these government-sponsored explorations, "many more private expeditions were set on foot," according to Samuel F. Baird, assistant secretary of the Smithsonian Institution. Among these was one company led by Lt. Edward F. Beale, returning to the West Coast to assume his new position as superintendent of Indian Affairs for California and Nevada. Another privately financed party was commanded by John C. Fremont, whose men barely managed to survive the snows of the Sangre de Cristo Mountains during this mid-winter survey.[42]

In 1853 the American West claimed the attention of two representatives of European royalty. William Nicholas, known as "the Prince of Nassau," and four traveling companions, including a mysterious "Prince de Viede," arrived in Kansas City on May 29. Upon returning to Fort Kearny in mid-October from a "pleasure trip," Nicholas was identified as "a grandson (I think) of old Prince Paul of Wurtenberg, who has passed many years in Indian country. . . ." Meanwhile, Count Leonetto Cipriani, a patriot active in the Risorgimento movement to unify Italy, prepared for what he claimed would be a "scientific exploration" for a transcontinental railroad route.[43]

Also on the plains in 1853 was Col. Joseph B. Chiles, a member of the 1841 Bidwell-Bartleson party, the first company to make an overland trip to California. Colonel Chiles, credited with taking the first wagons over the Carson Pass of the Sierra Nevada in the fall of 1848, left his home in Napa, California, in the spring of 1853 to visit relatives in Missouri, thus making his sixth cross-country trip in a dozen years. At about the same time, "Chiles & Co.," led by one of his elder brothers, undertook the first drive of the season from Jackson County, Missouri, with 400 head of cattle.[44] Another cattle drive from the same county was directed by Joel W. Hudspeth, whose surname is associated with a cutoff that bypassed Fort Hall, thanks to the 1849 exploring efforts of his relative, Benoni Hudspeth, mountain man and trail guide.[45]

Two of the most famous mountain men in the history of the West were on the trail that year as well. Thomas "Broken Hand" Fitzpatrick followed the emigrants' route as far as Fort Laramie late in the summer to meet with the Sioux Indians and negotiate yet another treaty. Kit Carson, his companion in leading the second Fremont expedition (1843-44), came into the main overland trail at Fort Laramie, driving sheep from New Mexico. His progress was reported by the newspapers, and William Rowe had "the pleasure" of shaking hands with Carson when they met near the Humboldt River. As Rowe later recalled, Carson "sat there in his fancy looking covered carriage."[46]

A possible explanation for this choice of vehicle, a most unlikely form of transportation for such a famous frontiersman, appeared forty-six years afterwards in D. A. Shaw's memoirs. Shaw, a member of the Southern California Academy of Sciences, traveled with Carson along the upper Humboldt River in 1853 and camped with him in the Sierra Nevada, not far from the emigrant trail named the Carson Route in honor of his 1844 exploration through the same territory. Shaw wrote: "I came again in contact with the celebrated Kit Carson, who with his wife and several Spaniards in his employ were on their way to California . . . with 400 sheep. . . ."[47]

Only one woman on the overland trail that year might have attracted attention from contemporaries. Cornelia Woodcock Ferris lived in Salt Lake City "among the Mormons" for six months while her husband, Benjamin, served as the U.S. secretary for Utah. In the spring of 1853 Cornelia and her husband continued on to California.[48]

As in other years, these pioneer women remained anonymous except for a few diaries, letters, and reminiscences. Like Lorena, they were primarily seeking "a happy home," rather than pursuing fortune, as did so many of the men, including one twenty-year-old from South Bend, Indiana. In mid-August 1853 John M. Studebaker arrived in Hangtown, now Placerville, and immediatley began making wheelbarrows for miners rather than digging for gold himself. Five years later Studebaker, who had acquired a nest egg of $8,000 along with the nickname "Wheelbarrow John," returned home to help his brother develop what later became the Studebaker automobile company.[49]

Lorena did not meet anyone famous during her trip. But the number

National Park Service

Tremendous thunderstorms crashed around emigrants on the prairies of Kansas. This one was painted from life in 1866 by the noted William Henry Jackson.

of overland travelers that year, including those of some prominence, provides reason enough why 1853 deserves more attention in the history of the westward movement than it has received. Traveling conditions were different than those in 1849, 1850, and 1852, years that have been more intensively studied. The spring of 1853 was described by contemporary newspapers as "cold and backward." And in retrospect it proved to be a remarkably wet year for overland travel. Pioneers discovered water available and grass growing in places seldom found in other years.[50]

Frequent storms with rain, thunder, lightning, hail, and driving winds plagued emigrants, including Lorena and her family, during their first weeks of travel, stampeding livestock, overturning tents, and soaking clothing and provisions. Esther Brakeman Lymon readily believed it when told ". . . 24 hours seldom pass together while on the Platte without some kind of storm either rain or hail." The only emigrant with any sense of humor about these storms appears to have been Dr. Joseph R. Bradway, who commented: "We are compelled to submit to hydropathy treatment daily with occasionally a wet pack at night as our bed clothes are occasionally quite wet."[51]

He also noted on June 1 that his boots were not high enough to keep out water, so each day he took "a walking footbath." More to the point were the sentiments Dr. John Smith confided in his journal while crossing Iowa. Twice in late April, while describing the thunder, rain, and winds which blew down his tent, he wrote: "We saw a little of the Elephant to day" and "We See a little more of the Elephant this morning." Smith's use of this gold rush phrase indicates that he felt he had already encountered and overcome considerable hardships on his Oregon trip, which had only just begun.[52]

Horace Seaver, reporting on his cross-country adventures, wrote to his father that it had "rained for 32 days every day . . . the roads were almost impassable." Every "little ways" his company became stuck and had "to pack our loads through on our backs, go 40 rods & the same thing over again." Although wet for two or three days at a time, Seaver found he "never enjoyed as good health in my life" and did not even "seem to have a cold."[53]

While stormy weather was not at all unusual along the valley of the Platte River, in 1853 it was reported that "an almost incessant rain [fell] for the past 40 days" in the region of Fort Kearny. This June 21 newspaper account, written by "A Friend," added "all stock lost has been in consequence of the frequent stampedes caused by the alarming character of electrical phenomena." Roads near the fort were depicted as "miserable" and in "a most abominable condition." It was reported that "all streams except for the South Platte are unusually full," making crossings difficult as well as dangerous. And in mid-May a mail carrier traveling east between Salt Lake City and Fort Laramie encountered "great difficulty and suffered severe hardships" due to deep snow. Readers were assured that normally "the snows are never over 14 inches east of South Pass and rarely over five inches west of that point."[54]

Newspapers reported "grass has not furnished as good a support for the stock of the emigrants as they needed" but there was enough to enable them to move "slowly forward." Harriet and William Gill, who began their trip "early [April 6] to keep ahead of the greatest of the spring migration," found there was not "sufficient grass for the cattle to travel fast."[55]

Others discovered that "it only requires a little trouble to find grass by looking for it." Many emigrants were "in a hurry to push forward," and one train of seventeen wagons and 100 men from St. Louis were reported beyond the Little Blue River as early as April 25, the day Lorena and her company left Kansas City. "This year more energy has been shown in pushing onward than ever before . . . we hope they meet with no trouble," commented one western Illinois newspaper. By early May a number of companies were already hundreds of miles upon the road before the grass "was fairly out of the grave. Those in the greatest haste to leave are now lying by at Fort Kearny, the Little Blue and other places, waiting for the grass to grow."[56]

Despite the backwardness of the season and the wet weather, many sections of the overland trail must still have been incredibly dusty in 1853, one of the three peak years for livestock drives. Amelia Stewart Knight traveled behind fifty wagons and two large droves of cattle along the north side of the Platte River at the end of May. She soon discovered

> we either had to stay poking behind them in the dust or hurry up and drive past them. It was no fool job to be mixed up with several hundred head cattle and only one road to travel in and the drovers threatening to drive their cattle over you if you attempted to pass them. They even took out their pistols.[57]

It was predicted "if the emigration of people is smaller, the amount of stock will be larger than ever before." By August 15 the count at Fort Kearny reached 105,792 head of cattle, 5,477 horses, 2,190 mules, and 48,495 sheep. In addition, seventy-two goats, one hog, and five asses had been recorded earlier. The amount of livestock driven along the north side of the Platte is unknown, but in late August it was estimated that 150,000 head of cattle had passed Fort Laramie. Of this livestock, only 6,518 cows, 9,077 oxen, 2,009 horses, 327 mules, and 1,500 sheep reached Oregon in 1853.[58]

The rest was intended to be sold on the California market because "a great scarcity of beef cattle" had driven prices up to an unprecedented $50 a head in San Francisco during the winter of 1852-53. Lamented one California newspaper:

> The large ranches . . . that have long boasted of their large herds of stock, are daily being reduced and instead of the large droves that formerly blackened the plains, there are to be seen a few small herds here and there . . . We find it the same with every description of stock: the falling off is almost incredible . . . unless our farmers turn their attention more to stock raising, which will require some time, our market must be supplied by stock driven across the plains, or meats of every description advance to a much higher price.[59]

The press also reported, "We hear of several parties who are on their way to the Altantic States, for the purpose of purchasing stock in large quantites for the California market." These private entrepreneurs were assured they could "realize a handsome profit on their investment." Count Leonetto Cipriani, who left Westport on June 3, confidently expected to make a profit of $200,000 on an investment of

$35,000 — even if half his livestock were lost during the trip.[60]

Others with the same hope of easy profit-on-the-hoof decided to drive sheep when they returned to California. Dr. Thomas Flint and company herded 1,880 sheep, "young and old," while Robert Eccleston and his companions had to contend with 1,040 sheep "not including the lambs." Col. W. W. Hollister started with 6,000 sheep, but lost two-thirds of his flock en route. Eccleston met Hollister on June 25 at the lower ford of the South Platte River and helped him "to cross his sheep to an island," rather than go on to the upper ford where 12,000 sheep waited ahead of them. Kit Carson also could not resist the temptation and purchased 6,500 sheep for a few cents a head from Navaho Indians in New Mexico, and his partner Lucien Maxwell bought 2,000. In California Carson's sheep sold for $5.50 each and later he recalled, "We did very well."[61]

The financial aspirations of Lorena's uncles apparently were more modest. Uncle Henry purchased only 200 head of cattle as "a speculative venture" before leaving Kansas City, but there is no record of how much livestock Uncle Adam decided to drive west. The two brothers-in-law may well have been able to make a nice profit, too, because a large portion of the Ione Valley in Amador County, California (where they planned to settle), "had been overflowed and the whole country . . . was under water" during early January 1853. As the result, "a large amount of stock has been destroyed on the tule lands between Dry Creek and the Cosumnes [River]. . . ."[62]

Aside from large livestock drives and wet weather, 1853 is noteworthy in yet another respect: a much-feared Asiatic cholera epidemic did not haunt overland trails as it did in 1849, 1850, and 1852. George Himes, who made the trip in 1853 as a boy and grew up to become curator/secretary of the Oregon Historical Society, in later years estimated 5,000 emigrants died in 1852 from "plains cholera." Himes and his family left Illinois March 21, 1853, and along the Platte River he recalled seeing the remains of a train of fifteen or twenty wagons whose members were said to have died of this enteric disease. However, this incident was not remembered by Mrs. M. A. Looney, who was eleven years old when the Himes family and other Illinois friends joined her parents for the trip to Oregon.[63]

At mid-century the germ theory of disease was as yet unknown. When cholera did break out along the overland trail, some emigrants thought the disease was caused by drinking alkali water. Col. W. W. Hollister in 1878 believed that "cholera morbus and dysentery" were induced by "change of water and perhaps by bad water." He recalled, "The river water of the Platte was always good or generally so, the best water on the route" and was puzzled when fellow emigrants "would go out to the lowlands and dig holes in the ground and I think the water percolated through the alkaline soils and a great many got sick and a good many died.''[64]

No one realized at this time that cholera spread through contaminated water due to the lack of sanitary facilities. A subject seldom mentioned in overland trail diaries, this was certainly something many proper Victorian ladies might not write about. But Charlotte Stearns Pengra was not quite so reticent. Her 1853 account of a trailside rest area is one of the few that exists. Also rather candid for a woman of that day were Rebecca Ketcham's comments upon the changing state of her digestive tract.[65]

With fewer emigrants than in 1850 and 1852, the rainstorms of 1853 proved to be a blessing in disguise, because water supplies tended to be less polluted. Most emigrants found that overall it was a healthy year for overland travel. Fewer newly dug graves existed because ''there is no sickness on the plains this season [and] there never were as many persons traveled the same distance who were so healthy.'' A letter mailed from Fort Kearny also reported: ''I have seen or heard of little or no sickness on the Plains this far. About the only complaint in our train is a most prodigious appetite which seems to prevail generally among all hands.''[66]

Letters from one of the doctors who kept travel journals that year support these statements. On May 15 and again on May 31 Dr. J. R. Bradway, who had treated a few travelers for ''intermitent fevers,'' noted, ''The emigration continues remarkably healthy.'' He saw the first new grave on May 31, several days' travel beyond Fort Kearny.[67]

Although Lorena did not adopt the habit of counting graves, as did many others diarists, including Maria Belshaw, she did write about those of particular interest. On May 26, three days west of Fort Kearny, Lorena recorded the burial of a woman.

On June 2 Michael Luark, who had crossed to the north side of the Platte, told about stopping ''a spell where a family from Indiana was burrying a young lady who died of consumption.''[68] It was consumption, the nineteenth century term for tuberculosis, that depleted the health of Lorena's cousin in Illinois. Now, as the Woodward-Hays-Lithgow party traveled along the Platte, Louisa's health took a turn for the worse. Lorena, whose own health and spirits improved greatly during the trip, feared her cousin ''will not live to get across the plains.''

Although this threat continued to hang over the company, Lorena's attention soon turned to other matters. With the first sighting of buffalo, one of her uncles led a successful hunting expedition and Lorena enjoyed ''the most excellent flavor'' of the meat. She also observed, ''They think buffalo hunting quite rare sport,'' a view widely shared by many other emigrants. By 1853 the slaughter of buffalo had reached such proportions that bones littered some areas along the trail.

Lorena's train found an ingenious use for them upon reaching the Upper California Crossing. Large bones, placed under the four corners of the wagon beds, raised loads above the water when it came time to cross to the north side of the river. One other emigrant told about doing the same thing that year. "Luckily," recalled John B. Haas, "there was any amount of bleached buffalo skulls scattered over the plains which served admirably to prop up the wagon beds."[69]

In the "Valley of the Platte," wood was extremely scarce, so another by-product of the buffalo proved even more useful, as emigrants soon discovered. Dried buffalo chips burned well and most cooking fires depended upon their use, distasteful as this might seem. While this was a common experience, Lorena never wrote about anyone in her company using such a fire. Neither did Celinda Hines or Elizabeth Goltra. Perhaps such omissions could be attributed to Victorian sensibilities, or else it was such an accepted practice that some did not bother to record it. For others, the experience of cooking over buffalo chip fires made quite an impression. Henry J. Hazard was eight years old, but he long remembered, "The ladies in the train started on a fast immediatley after we got onto the Platte — the fuel was not the proper kind. After we had been there about a week, however, they got *grandly* over that."[70]

Lorena made a point of recording diligently whenever wood could be found, and so did Bradway, but he also noted the frequent necessity of gathering chips. By 1853 these offensive chips were "mostly used up near the road" by travelers of previous years, according to John Haas.[71] Collecting them could be a chore and, with four younger sisters, Lorena may not have had to do such things.

She also, apparently, did not have to cope with the details and problems of covered wagon housekeeping as did her mother and her aunt. The only time Lorena mentioned food during the trip was the dinner menu for the Fourth of July. And while others were doing the laundry in convenient nearby streams, she usually wrote in her diary. Exactly what her assigned camp duties were cannot be determined. For Lorena, never one to enjoy housework, there would be little reason to write about such mundane things. Rebecca Ketcham, however, recorded more details of domestic life on the trail than did many other single women. Ketcham found that while "some of the folks are busying themselves about dinner [there] seemed to be nothing for me to do." Like Lorena, she tried "to improve the few leisure moments by putting down a few incidents that have occurred. . . ."[72]

The 1853 diaries of married women did not devote much space to descriptions of daily living, nor did they provide many practical household hints.[73] "How we manage to build a fire since we left the stove," was explained by Esther Lymon. "We dig a trench about six inches in depth, one foot in width and between three and four feet in length. We lay small bars of iron across the trench, after the fire is kindled, then it is ready for use."[74]

Her "worst trouble" arose from not having a baking pan. Her husband finally found a "bake kettle" that lacked a cover so that she had to borrow one whenever she wished to use it. Lymon had a recipe to make the "waters of the Platte, saturated with moist earthy lime stone and sand . . . quite clear and palatable and wholesome." She recommended, "Before using it for drinking or cooking, it should be settled by sprinkling a handful of corn meal slowly into a pail and stirring it at the same time."[75]

Many a pioneer woman could not help but brag in the privacy of her diary about culinary triumphs achieved over a campfire. Men could also be talented campfire cooks, proud of the meals they produced. But surely first prize in a bake-off contest should be awarded to the mother of Henrietta Catherine (Kate) McDaniel Furniss. While camped near Castle Rock on July 4, her husband's thirty-first birthday, Kate's mother turned out "a big plate of cookies made in the shape of animals — the surprise & delight of the dinner." Kate, who had been a pleased eight-year-old at the time, recalled seventy-eight years later:

> Mother had been artist enough in cutting them out, that we could pick out the different shapes. We cherished our little cookies & were loth to eat them. But finally we could not resist the temptation to take just a wee taste; so few sweets did we get those days. We would just take a bit of a nibble like mice. We would try to make them last as long as possible.[76]

This special meal also included "ham, bacon, & dried-apple sauce and a big pan of rolls in a tin can with the side cut-out & used as a reflector of heat from the campfire."[77]

These household chores occupied only part of a woman's time while traveling west. For many, this journey became an adventure because it meant freedom from the constraints of small-town society. This was especially true for women, like Lorena, who had not yet undertaken the responsibilities of marriage and motherhood. In 1853 "the ladies seem to enjoy themselves very well indeed," wrote Bradway. He explained, "They amuse themselves walking, riding horse back, & occassionaly assist to drive cattle."[78]

Such tomboyishness was not frowned upon during the overland journey. When a horse slipped his halter to escape, "Frankie" (Frances) Ward "exercised her Yankee ingenuity and caught him, much to the amusement of some of our company, who remarked that she should have been a boy," her mother, Harriet Ward, wrote. Later in the trip Ward cast aside all sense of propriety to ride horseback in "a position not altogether compatible with the delicy of an American lady," much to her husband's great merriment. This forty-nine-year-

Margaret Woodbury Strong Museum, Rochester, N.Y.

This is the board from "The Mansions of Happiness," a game that taught moral precepts. It was played by Frankie Ward in her family's wagon during her 1853 transit to the West.

old mother of teenagers wrote about her "pleasant walks" with other women "in advance of the train and a laughing merry set we were, I assure you." She also noted the young people in her company spent many a pleasant evening playing "The Mansions of Happiness," considered the first American board game. Introduced in 1843, it had a moralistic focus upon virtuous and evil traits; the object was to reach an ethereal mansion by overcoming vice and temptation.[79]

Lorena, whose company camped opposite Courthouse Rock on June 7, delighted in climbing nearby Chimney Rock to the base of the shaft. Her skirts presumably flapped around her ankles because she had not adopted the new bloomer costume. When a Wisconsin traveling companion wore this outfit, Ward confessed she found this friend "not withstanding her bloomer dress . . . to be a sensible and pleasant woman."[80]

Upon reaching Chimney Rock, Bradway was amazed to discover the names of several ladies inscribed "as high as any on record." He could only assume "some friends in pants" had done this for them "or they must have worn bloomers as no long skirts could have clamered a way so difficult to a height so giddy." Bradway was puzzled since "none of the ladies which I have seen yet have had, as manifested the good sense to don the bloomer costume."[81]

Early in the trip, John Haas met some "real bloomers," whom he described as "a couple of young women dressed in wide blue trousers, tied to the ankles, and short skirts reaching to the knees. Broad brimed hats shaded their faces; to protect them, each had a Colt revolver slung to her hips."[82]

An idea of travel attire favored by other pioneer women can be ascertained from the journal of fashion-conscious Rebecca Ketcham. She began the trip wearing her "palm leaf muslin delaine," which soon became "very dirty and has been torn nearly if not quite twenty times." She decided to stick with it "as long as I can. . . . As long as I look as well as the rest, I don't care."[83]

At some time during the trip almost everyone commented on the scenery, especially upon the picturesqueness of the country around Scotts Bluff. Ketcham wished that "our people would be more desirous of seeing their own country before going to Europe. I am sure they can find no greater variety of scenery and surely none more beautiful than in different parts of our country."[84]

Lorena also admired the scenery and enjoyed the wildflowers along the trail, as did Clarissa E. Taylor, who must have written more than just the one letter that survives among her husband's correspondence to the Watertown, Wisconsin, newspaper. On July 6 Taylor wrote about "the most beautiful and splendid, the grandest specimens of the floral kingdom" and added, "I would attempt sending more of the dried flowers but fear they will break to pieces so you cannot distinguish them." She reported, "Hellen has dried a great many flowers, expecting to send them to her mates in W. and is very much disappointed that a letter will not hold them."[85] Lorena, taking her cue from the Fremont *Report,* also described the varieties of prairie flowers, as well as the rock formations she saw. The number of emigrants knowledgeable about botany and geology has never been counted, but many jotted down observations on these subjects in diaries and letters. Emigrants were also fascinated by the prairie dogs, snakes, and small owls inhabiting the same burrows in numerous "dog cities," as described in the Dinwiddie journal, written either by John or his brother David. But in 1853 no one could have been as interested in the fauna of the trail as J. Soule Bowman, a would-be natural scientist who voluntarily collected specimens for the Smithsonian Institution.[86]

While definitely not interested in the zoology of the overland trail, Lorena continued to be intrigued by the Indians. Again influenced by Fremont's reporting of a decade earlier, she described several unevent-

Many covered wagon pioneers skirted Scotts Bluff, which crowded up against the North Platte River, by going over the Robidoux Pass six miles to the south, as did Lorena's party. However, others passed through the bluff by means of Mitchell Pass, opened two years earlier.

ful meetings with members of various tribes. Emigrants of 1853 had relatively little serious trouble with the Plains Indians, although cases of harassment were recorded, especially along the north side of the Platte River. On May 22, a day after crossing the Elkhorn River, James S. Cowden reported a missing cow had been found "with five arrows in it." The MacMurphy party, traveling through the future state of Nebraska, discovered "Indians are constantly committing depredations on the emigrants," according to this anonymous woman's diary. [87]

A similar comment was made on June 4 by Rachel Taylor, a teenager from Rockford, Illinois, when her company reached the Loup Fork: "Reports are continually reaching us of Indian depredations." James H. B. Royal, whose family traveled part of the way with the Taylor clan, did not begin his diary until the following day and did not mention such reports. However, Rachel's uncle, S. H. Taylor, in a letter also dated June 4, assured friends in Wisconsin that although 200

Lorena's company would have seen this view of Scotts Bluff. They decided to skirt the formation to the left.

Pawnees were encamped nearby

> we are not afraid of our lives — but we find them very annoying. It is impossible to keep their hands off property when they attempt to get it. They will almost steal a horse from under his rider.[88]

Eleven days later the Dinwiddie brothers reported "quite a number" of Indians, crossing the Loup Fork to hunt buffalo, "stopped at our camp. They appeared very friendly but all were begging something." After Benjamin Franklin Owen crossed the Platte River at a ford four miles west of Fort Kearny, he wrote: "We were then on the Paunee side of the River & they Hostile, & of the Indians of the Plains, they were thought to be the worst to be feared at that time."[89]

Two accounts, both printed later, tell of Indians attacking wagon trains on the plains in 1853. N. C. Fanaker, hired at $35 a month in gold to drive a four-ox team with a load of 6,000 pounds between Fort Leavenworth and Fort Laramie, recalled, "Indians had surrounded a camp and killed all but three, who returned to the Fort with the news." In these "early day reminiscences," Fanaker added that the soldiers were sent in pursuit on June 10, "without success."[90]

John Beeson's *A Plea for the Indians,* printed five years after he made the overland trip, included an account of Indian retaliation. After Indians were accused of shooting a mail carrier from Fort Laramie, soldiers pursued and killed eleven of them, burned their camp, and captured twenty horses. That same night the Indians "surprised a company of travelers, killed the men, took a white woman prisoner and captured a number of animals with a considerable property."[91] However, according to a study printed in 1979, only seven emigrants and nine Indians were killed during a few, brief confrontations in 1853 as compared with forty-five emigrants and seventy Indians the preceeding year.[92]

In mid-June of 1853 many emigrants wrote, as did Lorena, about meeting large bands of the Sioux on both sides of the North Platte River, east of Fort Laramie. Twice, on June 9 and 24, Lorena, whose company followed the trail along the south side of the river, described these Indians. Henry Allyn, traveling on the north side along the Mormon Trail, encountered a band of 250-300 Sioux on June 14, three days before he saw the fort across the river. Allyn found these Indians to be "very friendly and sociable" as did Dr. John Smith, also on the north side. After trading hard bread for six pairs of "mockisans" at a Sioux village on June 18 he wrote, "They are the most pleasant friendly set of Indians that I ever saw."[93]

Most emigrants were impressed by the Sioux, "the finest looking Indians male & Female that I ever saw," stated Benjamin Owen. John Beeson met "several hundreds of the Sioux tribe at Fort Laramy" and his brief description augments the longer one written by Lorena. Beeson said the Sioux

> appeared to be fine people — clad in dressed skins, profusely decorated with feathers, beads and paint and most of them mounted on fair and well feed ponies . . . [they] appeared clean in their person and dress.[94]

There are also accounts by emigrants who stopped at Sioux villages as did Benjamin Owen's company on June 14. This village consisted of forty-four lodges and Owen found "more than a hundred imigrants besides our train stoped there at the same time."[95]

A company of English Saints from Norwich, led by Hannah Cornaby's husband, also camped near a Sioux village "where we held a big pow-wow, smoked the pipe of peace and paid them a tribute of sugar and flour for the privilege of travelling through their domain." Hannah also recalled that they purchased buffalo robes and dried meat from these "quite friendly indians." Upon reaching Fort Laramie, "many Indians visited our camp. The squaws were particularly anxious to exchange their commodities for grociers etc."[96]

To reach Fort Laramie travelers on the south side of the North Platte River had to cross the Laramie Fork, as did the Woodward-Hays-Lithgow train. In April 1853, anticipating "a profitable and infallible speculation," a toll bridge, constructed the previous year, was purchased by Alexander Barclay, mountain man and trader, whose colorful career included a stint as a London corsetier before he became a Canadian farmer and then a St. Louis bookkeeper. The toll bridge and Barclay's $2,200 disappeared twenty days after he made his investment due to an "unprecedented flood" or "late freshet," according to both Robert Eccleston and J. Soule Bowman.[97]

As in other years, emigrants had to ferry across the swift Laramie

Fork, one of the largest affluents of the North Platte River. On June 14 Elizabeth and Nelson Goltra found 300 wagons waiting ahead of them and the next day it was still "uncertain when we can cross on the ferry." In exasperation Elizabeth Goltra added, "They do not as they would wish to be done by with their ferry." The Goltra company caulked their wagon beds and crossed safely "while word comes that the ferry boat had sunk with a heavy wagon."[98]

William Zilhart, who found 500 wagons waiting at the ferry June 11, reported a similar occurrence earlier in the week. Jotham Newton, arriving on June 13 "and hearing that the bridge had been carried away by high water and that the water was now too [deep to] ford," waited a day to cross. "A complete hoggish grab game is carried on at the ferry," he grumbled. Bradway commented the next day about the "very large crowd of teams about the ferry . . . many waiting their turn for several days." He also noted the presence of "a large number of Sioux."[99]

After crossing, Bradway visited Fort Laramie, which, "like Fort Kearney cannot be considered a fortified post but merely a trading station." He then fumed about being taxed five cents "in advance" on each letter mailed at the post office, calling the "two cents extra a contemptible swindle." Fort Laramie in 1853 presented the "first place for a long way back that looked like civilization" to William Taylor, but Rev. S. H. Taylor (no relation to William), declared "it does not answer my expectations at all." Seeing it from a distance of two miles, Taylor stated the fort was "nothing more than a few log houses enclosed by a wooden picket fence . . . the buildings are on the flats, which gives them a mean appearance after viewing the grandest specimens of bluffs." In compiling a Mormon guidebook based upon his overland journey, Frederick H. Piercy described the fort as having fifteen-foot adobe walls and a court 130 feet square.[100]

Fort Laramie was built "partly of plank, partly brick, and partly of sod," according to Andrew McClure. Celinda Hines visited the fort on June 23 and expressed "surprise at seeing no fortification." But Count Leonetto Cipriani reported, "it had four exceedingly well-kept field guns, four mounted cannons and a garrison of sixty men under a captain." James Farmer discovered "there are stores here where we can purchase anything we need but very high, flour is $15 a sack." Thomas Flint found "the old adobe fort going to ruin" with two old wooden buildings, two stables, the officers' quarters and a store "all in dilapidated condition." When Helen Stewart took time to visit the adjoining graveyard, she became dismayed because "it [is] in a runis condition for so many idle fellows lounging about . . . it is all broken down cattle and everything else can go in and tramp all over it."[101]

Although Fort Laramie was a peaceful place when Lorena arrived on

June 11, three days later a "serious incident" occurred, one that has since been credited with setting off twenty-five years of intermittent warfare on the plains. This "little difficulty" with the Indians was described for readers of the July 26 issue of the *Missouri Daily Republican* in a letter signed "Yours, Yankton" that provided a few particulars:

> On the other side of the Platte, near the ferry, a party of Sioux had pitched their lodges and become troublesome to the emigrants by begging &c. They also troubled the ferryman by taking the boat away. A party of United States soldiers who were returning to the Fort from the farm, which is on the opposite side of the Platte, had found Indians in possession of the boat and had taken it away. The Indians fired at them and came near hitting a sergeant.[102]

In this letter, written June 28, "Yankton" explained that twenty-four soldiers were then sent to "apprehend the one who fired and bring him to the Fort." Frightened Indians were discovered hiding in their lodges, and when soldiers attempted to enter, an exchange of shots killed four Indians. Two others were taken prisoner but were turned loose the next day after "the head chief expressed himself satisfied that all was all right and his young men deserved what they got." Concluded "Yankton,"

> No Doubt reports will reach the states that the whole Sioux nation is armed against the whites, and cause some unnecessary uneasiness to those who have friends upon the road to California and Oregon.[103]

Emigrants were more than uneasy, of course, about this event, since no one could predict its eventual outcome. The ferry incident smoldered until August the following year when it erupted as the Grattan massacre in which thirty soldiers were killed.[104]

Apparently none of the emigrants who kept diaries or later wrote their reminiscences saw either the seizure of the ferry or its recapture, because no eyewitness account of these events has been found. Lorena's company, having visited the fort the preceding day, "started early" on June 14, so she missed the excitement. So did Samuel Handsacker, who considered Fort Laramie really "a credit" to the government. Although Bradway spent most of the day in the vicinity of the fort, he did not learn about the confrontation until nearly a week later and then called it "a rumor."[105]

Reports of what actually happened at Fort Laramie on June 14 easily became confused and distorted. Henry Allyn thought a quarrel between Indians and a Frenchman trying to deliver letters to the fort had "ended, if it be ended, in the death of six Indians." Both Benjamin Owen and James Woodworth heard three Indians were killed, but John Smith claimed the total was five.[106]

Maria Belshaw agreed with this number and added that the soldiers

Gregory M. Franzwa

Although there is no record of members of Lorena's company carving their names on Register Cliff, thousands of other pioneers did so. Hundreds of names are still legible.

L. N. Breed was one of at least thirteen 1853 emigrants who left their names on Register Cliff.

also "wounded two and took two prisoners." On June 22, five days after leaving the fort, Belshaw wrote,

> The news came this evening that a husband, wife and two children were murdered Monday the 20th near the Fort on the south side of the Platte river. The alarm was given at the Fort, soldiers came and killed one Indian and wounded one.[107]

Several days before he reached the fort, Basil Longworth heard Indians "killed a large number of cattle, some emigrants and nine of the soldiers at the fort and that four hundred warriors were camped near the river and were determined to murder every emigrant." According to Charlotte Pengra, "one hundred and fifty Indians attempted to cross over the ferry which is a violation of their treaty." When Indians refused to surrender, three of them were killed and two wounded. Pengra believed "they have dug up the tomahawk not to bury it again until they are liberated and declare their intention of falling on the Emigrants." Farther back along the trail, Helen Stewart became anxious because "they say that there is five hundred of them going to fight we hear that they laid down blankets that is a sine for the emigrants not dare govern them." Despite Helen's fears, her sister Agnes did not

Countless covered wagons grooved the clay and sandstone surface west of Guernsey to create what is known today as ''Deep Rut Hill.''

The trail led west over the Wyoming horizon near Guernsey, with no end in sight.

report this rumor in her diary.[108]

As rumors flew back and forth along the trail, many emigrant trains took precautions against Indian attacks, which did not occur. On June 16, the day before reaching the fort, George Belshaw corralled the wagons, called out sixteen men for guard duty and ordered all guns loaded, "ready at a moment's notice." After the "red chaps did not come," he boasted, "we could have given them over 100 shots without reloading."[109] Upon hearing about the ferry incident two days after it occurred, Basil Longworth's company stopped for several hours

> until a number of small trains joined in. We then numbered forty or fifty wagons and perhaps one hundred men, when we mustered all our arms and resolved to clear the road of every obstruction, and marched forward over a deep sand road to the ferry. On arriving there we found everything quiet.[110]

Dr. Thomas Flint also arrived at Fort Laramie on June 16 but did not write about the current Indian threat although, when Charlotte Pengra's group reached the fort the next day, "the captain advised us to form a company — and be prepared for battle."[111]

Lorena, whose description of camping facilities near Fort Laramie is unique for 1853, reported none of these things. Nor did she mention

Gregory M. Franzwa

Today the North Platte River looks anything but threatening. Its once swift and treacherous current has been subdued by many irrigation dams.

the ferry incident until ten days later and only briefly at the end of a long passage about the "very large train of Sioux" she had seen east of the fort. There was a good reason for her delay in writing about these events. While other wagon trains traveled peacefully through the Black Hills, once fears of Indian attacks subsided, tragedy struck the Woodward-Hays-Lithgow families. On June 20, a day before reaching the bridge across the North Platte River, Louisa Lithgow died.

Cousin Louisa was buried the next day on the north side of the river, on high ground a few rods from a blacksmith shop and "a small cluster of huts and tents." Thirty years later Lorena's account of the funeral and burial was elaborated upon by her youngest sister, fourteen years old at that time. Sarah, who also wrote an emotional poem of seventeen four-line stanzas about Louisa's death, recalled "services were held as 'at home' — the long funeral procession filed across the long bridge." Her essay, included with her poem in the appendix, concludes:

> there were strangers present who did not even know her name no doubt many still remember the funeral of a young girl of eighteen they attended on the North Platte in '53 — while on their way to California.[112]

No contemporary reports have been found about Louisa's funeral or her grave, marked with a carved wooden headboard, a transplanted spruce bush, and a cairn. These "lonely little mounds of stones," were used, as William Taylor explained years later, to keep the "ciotes and wolves from devouring the flesh of the dead." To William Hoffman, "A burial on the plains has something peculiarly affecting about it." Maria Belshaw, who meticulously recorded such details earlier in her trip, failed to note Louisa's grave on June 27 when her company, traveling along the north side, "camped on the river at the old ferry place and passed the bridge this afternoon."[113]

This plank bridge, located six or seven miles below the upper crossing of the North Platte River, competed with a Mormon ferry in operation since 1847. "The property of four Canadian brothers," the toll bridge was built with Indian help, according to Count Leonetto Cipriani. He described the bridge in detail, consisting of "twelve arches, entirely of cedar, with piers formed of huge tree trunks and filled with gravel." The 300-foot span was the second bridge built at this location by John Richard, mountain man, Indian trader, and ferry owner. Years later the autobiography of William K. Sloan, another 1853 traveler, identified Richard as a "Canadian Frenchman," whose name was often pronounced "Reshaw." The first Richard-Reshaw bridge, built sometime in 1851, lasted until June 11 the following year, when it was "chopped down," supposedly by rival ferrymen bent upon eliminating the competition. The enterprising Richard joined forces in early 1853 with two other trading firms to build another substantial bridge that would be "ready for the earliest trains."[114]

On June 24 Bradway reported the bridge "is built too low and to insure its safety, they will be under the necessity of raising it, which they informed me they intend to do." Others were not so critical. Calvin Graham declared it to be "a very good bridge," while Michael Luark thought it was "good looking" as well. Thomas Flint found it to be a "very strong bridge of hewn timbers." In 1966 three large handhewn timbers, remnants of the north ends of the bridge, were found at Evansville, Wyoming, east of Casper. Also discovered at the same time were "several piles of man-placed rocks" marking locations for some of the piers.[115]

Construction cost estimates of the Reshaw bridge varied between $14,000 and $16,000. Sloan claimed it was built for only $5,000. He saw this as a "good investment," expecting that the 1853 profits would total $40,000. Fees charged for crossing varied; most emigrants paid five or six dollars per wagon, but Newton was charged seven dollars in mid-June and Eccleston paid three dollars a wagon on July 22.[116]

Lorena, who neglected to report the number of miles traveled each day, did not keep a record of expenses during the trip either. But Agnes Stewart wrote that when her company crossed the bridge on July 3,

> We paid five dollars for each wagon and four yoke of oxen and 12½ cents per head for the rest of the cattle and the same for each man except one driver for each team. The ladies went across free for their dear little feet would not wear out the bridge.[117]

According to a February 1853 newspaper advertisement, Richard and his partners promised,

> There will also be at the Bridge two Blacksmith and wagon maker's shops, for the accomodation of emigrants. The company will have a good Grocery store and eating house, and all kinds of Indian handled peltries, also oxen, cows, horses and mules at low prices.[118]

James Cowden's report of July 11 matches, in most respects, these claims because he found near the bridge "several log houses or huts, one Blacksmith, a grocery and one dry goods store." Robert Eccleston noted a place serving refreshments and commented upon the number of cattle dealers present. These details were not recorded by Lorena, who was understandably preoccupied with her cousin's death. However, her diary contains little or no information about the many trading posts that flourished along the trail in 1853, especially when compared to other women's diaries. Lorena's company may not have patronized these establishments, but why she did not write about them is unknown. These frequent trading stations provided an opportunity to replenish provisions, albeit at high prices, and helped, as did numerous blacksmith shops mentioned by other emigrants, to make overland travel easier. That year many new bridges also made travel more convenient.[119]

Shortly after Lorena's party crossed the Reshaw bridge, they left the Platte River country entirely. To Rachel Taylor, "it seems like leaving an old friend," as her company encamped for the last time near the "river of Silver" on July 16. Beyond the bridge, emigrant trails from both sides of the North Platte River converged to form essentially one road, despite a number of short optional detours, for approximately the next 176 miles through South Pass to a junction with the trail to Salt Lake City. This route brought pioneers to the Sweetwater River, where there were nine fords in 1853, according to tallies kept by James Woodworth and Flint.[120]

It also lead past two of the most famous landmarks along the overland trail: Independence Rock and Devil's Gate, six miles apart. Rachel Taylor described this scene as "a frightful as well as romantic situation. Just back of us Independence Rock stands out in bold relief and in front of us yawns the Devil's Gate." Lorena, tired from exploring Independence Rock, did not visit Devil's Gate, which was "a little

Dennis Chapman, Fort Caspar Museum

The historic 1853 Richard's (Reshaw's) Bridge east of Casper has been partially reconstructed. Here, in this "dreary place," Lorena's cousin was buried on June 21.

distance from the road." But at sunset on July 6 Harriet Ward found it to be "the most gloriously magnificent spectacle upon which my eyes have ever delighted to dwell." Ward decided the best view was from the east end of Devil's Gate and added, "No one will regret spending half an hour admiring its granduer, even en route to California."[121]

In late June and early July, while approaching South Pass, emigrants encountered "weather as cold as winter," according to Ward. Along the north fork of the Sweetwater River James Compton found snow and ice "twelve to fifteen feet deep" on July 7. Charlotte Pengra wore her thickest clothing and still "was obliged to wrap up in a

Independence Rock, the great "Register of the Desert," looms up from the stark plain, a natural magnet for inscription-minded emigrants. Thousands of their souvenirs remain on the granite mound.

comforter to keep any ways comfortable," while Henry Allyn donned his "winter clothes." When it snowed all day on June 27 Catherine Amanda Stansbury Washburn wrote, "The men wore two coats and then were cold." William Zilhart's company found a better way to keep warm — they drank whiskey and brandy slings chilled with snow. "It was fine," reported Zilhart, who also gave a detailed weather report for June 27 when it "blowed and snowed so awful hard . . . hail and snow fell in abundance." He added, "The dust [was] so thick you could not see at all . . . the wind blew hard in the states but not like this."[122]

Enos Ellmaker recalled in his 1898 memoirs that one day, nearing the summit of the Rocky Mountains, "we were unable to go any further . . . owing to the sand and gravel storm which was very severe. it blew so hard that it was a rain of sand and hail of gravel, it was so severe that our teams would not move."[123]

The wind and dust, combined with the raw weather, resulted in "parched lips and sore eyes," which Lorena found "are not very agreeable." This was quite an understatement on Lorena's part because thirty-four years later George B. Currey still remembered,

> To wipe the fine dust from watery eyes with a rough coat sleeve or dirty apron was neither pleasant nor ornamental. But the very acme of petty torture and facial deformity was to lick a circle around a pair of raw lips.[124]

It took Lorena's company five days to travel from Devil's Gate to South Pass, which they reached on June 30. She remarked, as did many others, upon the gradual ascent of the road through the Rocky Mountains. Rebecca Ketcham announced, "We would none of us known when we passed if we had not been told," while Samuel Handsacker decided "the Rocky Mountains are not half so difficult to cross as a great many imagine." Andrew McClure agreed,

> This is not as many suppose it to be, steep, craggy and mountainous but the ascent is so graduated that it can hardly be discovered with the naked eye and it requires close observation to discover you are on the ridge.[125]

Benjamin Owen reported there were "only two business places at Southpass" in 1853, a small trading post and an "ox shoeing device," where the "ox was swung up bodily without consulting his wishes, giving the Stalwart Blacksmith all the advantage."[126] A poetic description of "the summit of the great South Pass of the Rocky Mountains, where northward hang eternal snow on mountains high with grass below," was written by Isaiah William Bryant, who did not notice the blacksmith shop. Bryant continued,

> Gently rolling prairie surround it on every side. Nature seems to have intended that here alone should be the gateway of the great highway of nations . . . away to the north are to be seen the great Wind River Mountains. Fremont snowy peak reaching to the highth of fourteen thousand five hundred above the level of the ocean. To the south rocks upon rocks stretch away commencing the descent which is gently indeed.[127]

Beyond South Pass emigrants came to Pacific Springs, "the first waters of the Pacific Ocean." Here Basil Longworth found "good water . . . but the greatest quagmire I ever saw." To John Haas the springs appeared to be "a mass of black mud covered with stocky looking wire grass." Although alkali swamps and streams, as well as ponds and lakes covered with a soapsuds-like scum, existed on the eastern side of the Rocky Mountains, poisonous water did not begin to take a large toll of livestock until wagon trains crossed the Continental Divide. With "good water" scarce, the road soon became "strewn with dead cattle and the stench is awful," wrote Amelia Knight.

Knight might have been bothered unduly by the smell because she was six months pregnant at the time, a fact she did not reveal in her diary until early September when her eighth child was born in Oregon. However, Dillis B. Ward later recalled that while the sight of dead cattle by now had become "a familiar one," the stench arising here from the great number of carcasses was indeed "something awful." And Charlotte Pengra, usually rather outspoken, voiced her displeasure as an understatement: "The stench," she said, "is very unpleasant."[128]

The trail then led to the "Sandys," three streams described in reverse by John Haas as "big, little and dry." Knight discovered "as far as the eye can reach it is nothing but sandy desert," while Henry Allyn began to worry because "the emigration is far too large for what little grass there is in this desert." Upon reaching the Dry Sandy July 31, the Taylor-Royal company stopped to hold communion service because it was "the first Sabbath Day in Oregon," according to William Hoffman, who traveled in the same train. This event was also recorded by James Royal and Rachel Taylor, whose father and uncle officiated. To Rachel's satisfaction ". . . the Lord's supper was administered properly for the first time between the Missouri River and the settlements of Oregon."[129]

Between the Dry and the Little Sandys the trail divided with the right fork leading north to Fort Hall and on to the Oregon and Washington territories. The trail to the left of this junction, approximately twenty miles west of South Pass, was considered the main road to Salt Lake City. Both Jotham Newton and Robert Eccleston noted another route, presumably opened the preceding year, that "follows down the Pacific Creek to its entrance to Green River." In Eccleston's opinion emigrants would avoid problems by keeping on the well-known trail to the Mormon settlements.[130]

The Woodward-Hays-Lithgow company made the same decision and did not take either of the two major cutoffs that soon came into view. As Jotham Newton observed, "By coming the Salt Lake road we save crossing a desert of 40 miles without water or grass." Both Sublette's and the newer Kinney's cutoffs, which bypassed Fort Bridger and Salt Lake City, were used in 1853 by pioneers not interested in visiting the city of the Saints and by those headed for the Pacific Northwest.[131]

So the decision made by Samuel Handsacker, who wrote under the newspaper nom de plume of "Quail," to detour via Salt Lake City can be considered unusual for an Oregon-bound pioneer. Handsacker must have startled other emigrants considerably eighteen days later when he reached the western end of what he called the junction of the Salt Lake road and Sublette's Cutoff. He turned east "to back track on the cut-off road" until he reached the Fort Hall road and then the

William Henry Jackson's view of the great South Pass shows several lines of wagons making the transit.

Oregon Trail. Handsacker reported the Fort Hall road "but little traveled by the California emigrants as the other is said to be a better and nearer route."[132]

Emigrants following the Salt Lake road crossed the Big Sandy twice, passing out of Oregon Territory and into Utah Territory as they made their way towards the Green River. In 1853 the "traveling public" was encouraged to take this road by Brigham Young, who pointed out, "If you take Salt Lake in your route you can procure many articles there much cheaper than to haul them." He offered a few suggestions that he considered "might be timely and profitable" in an early March letter that probably influenced no one since it was not printed in St. Louis newspapers until May 22. Young also counseled emigrants to take care of their livestock but added, "Exchanges of property are frequently made much to the benefit of the traveler and, when stock has recruited, also the benefit of the citizens. . . ." Years later Elias Jackson Baldwin, nicknamed "Lucky," stated, "In 1853 Brigham Young was prospering too greatly from the emigrant trade to imperil it."[133]

In spite of Young's advice, when Harriet Ward reached the Salt Lake road on July 15, it looked to her as if "much of the emigration has gone other routes and consequently we hope to escape their dust." William Gilbert also wrote, "dont see as many teams on the road as we have seen great many have taken the cut off and Oregon roads. . . ." Both may have been correct. Aside from Mormon accounts, there are at least fourteen diaries, including Lorena's, and seven reminiscences noting travel along the Salt Lake road.[134]

Regardless of which route emigrants followed, they had to cross the Green River, described by George Miller West as "not very wide but deep and swift. . . ." Emigrants found Mormon-owned ferries in operation with either ten or eleven boats plying the river at three different locations in 1853. Charges ranged from five to twelve dollars a wagon. One dollar per head for loose stock seems to have been the standard rate at all three crossings. West, who had taken the Sublette Cutoff, observed many travelers "do not want to pay such prices." So, when cattle "were loath to swim," wrote Celinda Hines, whose company followed the Kinney route, "it was necessary to drive them in with a drove to get them across." Phoebe Goodell Judson at the age of ninety-five wrote about her "pioneer's search for an ideal home" and recalled, "The lives of our men were in constant danger as they ferried these perilous streams on horseback swimming the cattle." Since the Judsons and the Hines traveled together, no doubt Mrs. Judson remembered Celinda's father drowning under just such circumstances, only a few days before the end of their trip to Oregon.[135]

Lorena's company crossed the Green River on July 4 and stopped for the afternoon to prepare and enjoy a special dinner consisting of thirteen different kinds of food. Most emigrants, men as well as women, took time to record the variety and abundance that could be produced from precious stores, often hoarded for this festive occasion. Elias Johnson Draper enjoyed a Fourth of July "feast" of a potpie made from a hare "much larger than our jack rabbits." While almost everyone tried to observe this holiday with a spirit reminiscent of celebrations back home, members of Draper's party made an extra effort. "Our women put on their white dresses and we marched in military style, beating on an old tin bucket for a drum," he wrote in his autobiography.[136]

Another few days of travel brought the Woodward-Hays-Lithgow wagon train to the valley of Black's Fork and Fort Bridger, located in "a fertile plain in the neighborhood of some five or six mountain streams," according to Robert Eccleston. In 1853 not many emigrants visited the ten-year-old trading post of mountain man Jim Bridger and his partner Louis Vasquez, perhaps discouraged by Bridger's sign erected a mile and a half from the fort. "On a board was written a re-

William H. Jackson sketched this view of Echo Canyon during his trip as a bullwhacker in 1866.

quest for emigrants to keep a mile away from his place," said Frederick Piercy. John Haas proved to be an exception, however, and purchased tobacco at "a terrible price." He described the fort as "continuous rows of one-story log huts surrounding an open square with its doors and windows opening into the inside. A stout gate offered the only entrance."[137]

William Gilbert discovered Fort Bridger to be "nothing but a trading post a Store and Black Smith Shop," while Samuel Handsacker agreed "this is not what is generally considered a fort but the residence of a Mr. Bridger, formerly from the American bottom." The summer of 1853 was the last season Bridger and Vasquez profited from either emigrant or Indian trade. On August 27 Dr. Thomas Flint's company found the fort "in possession of the territorial officer. Mormons who had twenty-four hours before driven old man Bridger out and taken possession." Accused of supplying Ute Indians in attacks against Mormon settlements, Bridger barely escaped arrest by a Mormon posse.[138]

Upon leaving Fort Bridger, Frederick Piercy observed "a new road, now altogether traveled, leads to the right." The trail through the rugged "Salt Lake mountains," as Lorena called the Wasatch, crossed numerous small streams, as well as the Bear and Weber rivers. It led through Echo and Emigrant canyons and across a summit considered "the highest land passed over between the States and Salt Lake." As the diaries of Lorena and Dr. J. R. Bradway indicate, it took at least twelve days of steady travel to cross this country. Virginia Wilcox Ivins, hoping to rest and recuperate in Salt Lake City, remembered "one steep surface, perfectly bald and so steep that in order to climb the road the cattle had to be driven zigzag." John Haas, who decided to spend the winter in the Mormon capital, described Echo Canyon as having "almost perpendicular walls," while Ivins wrote the cliffs were "several hundred feet high." She added,

> The sun shines in its dim recesses a short time during each day. The road croses the creek a dozen times and the banks [are] worn away by wagons and cattle to a steep pitch.[139]

Haas claimed Echo Canyon was twenty-six miles long and the stream through it had to be crossed "at least as many times." Other emigrants agreed with Bradway that there were only seventeen crossings, "some of which were very bad."[140]

In mid-July at the mouth of Echo Canyon, both Lorena and James Compton met "a family living in the Weber River valley with all sorts of plants such as corn, tomatoes, pumpkins, watermellons, musk mellons, pease and beans." In the same area four weeks later Eccleston reported "a deserted log house which looks to have been [left] in a hurry — everything scattered about . . . everything denoted a disturbance with Indians and a hasty leave of the premises." On August 10 Count Leonetto Cipriani found "a house nearby had been burned down and there were four charred corpses whose bones were being gnawed by a pack of wolves."[141]

After crossing the Weber River emigrants were warned by guidebooks, "You will find a much worse road from here to Salt Lake City than you have found since leaving the Missouri river." According to Haas, "The road is hardly wide enough for wagons to pass between the holes and large boulders." At the foot of one summit he discovered "a brush hut as a trading post" with a sign reading "beer." This he disgustedly labeled "a fraud liquid."[142]

In Emigrant Canyon the stream had to be crossed thirteen times and here the narrow road was "hemmed in on both sides by dense brush." Before reaching the Salt Lake Valley emigrants still had to cross several more creeks and two mountain summits. As Jotham Newton observed, "Since leaving Fort Bridger the route has been very wearisome to teams as well as to the emigration." On July 19 James Woodworth described this section of the trail "jammed with trains pushing into Salt Lake." At the entrance to the valley William Gilbert noted a "quarantine Station where all of the Sick are taken care of and those affected with any disease are not allowed to go on to the city. . . ."[143]

Lorena and her family reached Salt Lake City on July 19. Unlike many others, they did not spend any time there but passed through the community in one day. Salt Lake City in 1853 had a population of approximately 9,000 and "the whole valley between 30 & 40 Thousand," according to William Gilbert, who heard Brigham Young preach. The city was pictured in Frederick Piercy's guidebook with a view *"taken from a camera lucida."* This showed "a pretty town, laid off in a beautiful manner," in Samuel Handsacker's estimation. He added,

> The whole town is kept neat and clean. Several springs of water, that come from the mountains, run through the streets and water the gardens. There is not a street but what has a good stream of water running through it.[144]

According to Gilbert,

> The city is situated in a nice level valley Streets wide and Straight with nice square blocks most of the houses are built of unburnt brick called Dobies very neat and comfortable houses   there are several elegant buildings Governor Young residence Council house Post office Tithings office and church. . . . Several Saw mills and Grist mills near the city and woolen factorys. . . .[145]

But Jacob H. Schiel, official geologist and surgeon for the Gunnison railroad survey, thought Salt Lake City "does not make a very friendly impression" because "almost every house has a little piece of enclosed land." Schiel, who spent the winter of 1853-54 there, added, "everything bears the mark of poverty and makeshift."[146]

A "temporary Temple" was in use that summer because "the great one is now being built," Eccleston wrote. According to William Rowe, only the basement of the new temple had been completed. Harriet Ward was told it would "far surpass that of Nauvoo [Illinois]." The Ward family stayed a day and a half at the "U.S. Hotel," which Irvin Ayres considered "the best house there." Ward was not enthusiastic about the accommodations because they were "annoyed by the most miserable of insects, which actually drove us from our beds to our wagons to sleep. . . ." Woodworth and Bradway both dined at the same hotel and afterward Bradway attended the theater for an evening of "very good music and performance pretty good."[147]

For Stephen Forsdick, an eighteen-year-old Mormon from England, Salt Lake City was the end of the line. He traveled in a "10 pound Company," explaining this meant not only the amount of money put up but also ten people assigned to a wagon. Upon reaching the city the "wagons, tents and cattle [were] given up to the Tithing office and sold" to repay the initial ten pounds advanced by the Mormon Perpetual Emigrating Fund.[148]

Eccleston noted Salt Lake City had "three or four large trading establishments and any amount of smaller ones as well as blacksmiths,

Bakeries and Markets &c abound . . . tanneries, founderies &c have been erected.'' Ward went shopping and discovered, ''They have some fine stores and sell their goods very high, in consequence of their being obliged to transport them from St. Louis by land.'' And Wood-worth described ''the place swarming with emigrants making pur-chases & the merchants, who were driving a fine business. . . .''[149]

By selling a cow for twenty dollars and ''some peaches at 30 cents per pound,'' William Browder made a profit of ''$39.25 cents worth.'' He recorded this information in his *Pocket Diary for the Year 1853 for the purpose of registering events of past, present or future occurrence.* A more unusual account of trading in Salt Lake City was provided years later by ''Lucky'' Baldwin, a shrewd hotel owner from Wisconsin. Before leaving home he loaded one wagon ''entirely with brandy and another with tobacco and tea for trading purposes.'' Baldwin, who later became a prominent San Francisco hotel operator, traded some of his supplies at Fort Laramie. Upon reaching Salt Lake City he ''made a deal with the firm of Walker Brothers.'' They purchased ''tobacco at one dollar a plug, tea and coffee at similar prices.''[150]

Baldwin, who always maintained his luck was due to ''careful plan-ning,'' then called upon Brigham Young and was invited by him to stay for dinner. Baldwin later claimed he was ''referred'' to Young's brother for the ''sale of his brandy and the liquor was cashed in at six-teen dollars a gallon'' for a $3-4,000 profit. Baldwin recalled that Young's brother ''urged us to take a different road from other travellers insisting it was easier and had more feed for the horses . . . he assured us we would avoid all danger by following his advice.'' Two days later Baldwin's wagons were attacked by Indians and he ''always believed'' Young's brother ''caused the attack and was with them, disguised as an Indian.'' In his memoirs D. A. Shaw wrote that the In-dians ''were thought to have been instigated by some of the Mormon officials.'' A reproduction of a painting depicting this battle, commis-sioned twenty-two years later by Baldwin, appeared in Shaw's *Eldorado.*[151]

''Indian rumors afloat'' in the city that summer were noted by Ec-cleston, who reported two teamsters killed and another wounded near a sawmill in the valley. A day before reaching the city Harriet Ward heard ''a report that the Mormons are having trouble with the Utah Indians.''[152]

''Owing to Indians difficulties,'' a wall twelve feet high and six feet thick at the base, tapering towards the top, was under construction. However, Horace Seaver wrote, ''They are enclosing 10 acres with a wall 22 feet in heighth it is splendid work I think they intend to fortify their city well then to declare their independence.'' John Haas called this ''Young's attempt to make it a walled city'' and explained an earth rampart was being built with "tithing work and paid by a tithing tax of 1/10 of all produce." When Arthur Pendry Welchman arrived from Texas, he helped to build "the mud (adobie) wall that was started, but never finished, around the north side of the city."[153]

On July 30 Gilbert also noted "some excitement here on account of some Trouble with the Indians at the South." Eight days later his company began "getting ready as fast as we can to get off . . . the Indians at the South have killed 4 Mormons. . . ."[154]

With reports such as these, it is no wonder that both Lorena and Harriet Ward were alarmed when they encountered a lone Indian, perhaps the same one, on the road west of Salt Lake City. Lorena, although afraid, boldly shook hands with him; six days later Ward, whose company was behind the Woodward-Hays-Lithgow wagons, told of meeting a similar Indian and finding him "very friendly indeed."[155]

In early August Ward reported constantly hearing accounts of hostile Indians and added Mormon settlers were "converting their dwellings into fortifications" for defense purposes. Several days later she wrote that the Utah Chief Walker threatened to destroy the Saints, so they were building a fort and "removing their families for safety."[156]

In August Brigham Young "issued an order to abandon the smaller settlements," according to one report "From the West." Chief Walker had "already attacked settlements and murdered some inhabitants," this newspaper account explained, because the Utah Indians

> who have naturally been disatisfied since their departure from their old residence and forced to settle in the Colorado Valley have become thoroughly exasperated and determined to carry on a predatory and murdurous conflict with the Mormons.[157]

When Lt. Edward F. Beale and his cousin, Gwinn Harris Heap, arrived August 2 in southern Utah, they found Mormon settlers "in a state of great alarm and excitement." Mormons were also surprised that these travelers "had passed in safety through Walkah's territory."[158]

Members of the Gunnison Railroad survey team, off on a separate exploration of Sevier Lake, were not so fortunate in late October. Capt. John W. Gunnison and eight companions, including the artist Richard H. Kern, were attacked and killed "at day break as they sat at breakfast by a strong company of Utah Indians." Jacob Schiel, the German scientist who remained with the main party, added there had been "no inkling of impending danger." In the same region Fremont and his men, attempting to prove a central railroad route would be feasible in winter, encountered hostile Indians, too, later in the year but were not attacked.[159]

City of Rocks, near the Idaho-Utah border, still is one of the most spectacular sights along the California Trail.

The Walker War did not seriously affect California emigrants because, upon leaving Salt Lake City, the majority followed the trail north along the east side of the lake. This route took Lorena's company through Ogden City, described by Cornelia Ferris as "a merely thickly settled neighborhood." According to Handsacker, Ogden City had sixty houses, although there was "no store in the 'town' but several groceries, a post office, a grist and a saw mill."[160]

Passing through the northern Mormon settlements, emigrants began to observe numerous "collections" of warm and mineral springs along the trail. As Elias Draper recalled, "Some were warm, some were salty and some were pure." While Lorena wrote in detail about these curiosities, she did not devote much space to crossing the Bear River again, this time at its western end with a "deep, swift, turbid and gloomy current," according to Ferris. In this region, when the weather turned "very warm" in late July, the trail turned to dust "a foot or more deep," wrote Virginia Ivins. She wore a veil attached to a silk cap but still found the dust "perfectly unbearable" when her company "overtook an immense drove of cattle" after crossing the Bear River.[161]

Seven days later the Woodward-Hays-Lithgow wagons reached the City of Rocks, also called Pyramid Circle and Steeple Rock Valley.

Nathaniel Myer, who arrived at this landmark two weeks earlier, said, "It is really delightful to see the many Pyramids of rock standing in a plain as they are."The circle, or "city,"measured "3 m. wide by 5 m. long surrounded by mountains composed principally of gray granite with many high pyramidal shaped rocks," wrote Bradway.[162]

Here James Compton saw on the right side of the road "a rock like some big Church burnt down" and also noted "a pillar runs up about 150 feet high." To Rachel Taylor the "pyramids resemble more than anything else, petrified hay stacks." Studying these rock formations, Joseph Williams reported the circle contained

> tall white and green stones from 60 to 150 feet high, from 10-40 feet in diameter at the foot . . . some of them running almost to a point at the top . . . Upon these stones are written, painted and engraved the names of many visitors with the dates.

He added that Pyramid Circle had an "inlet at the east end of about 50 yards, and an outlet at the west end, of 20 yards."[163]

West of these rocks the trails to California again became one for a short distance since Pyramid Circle, according to James Woodworth, was the place "through which Sublettes Cutof[f] runs and where it joins the G.S.L. road." And, in more precise detail, Joseph Williams explained the junction of the California and Fort Hall roads took place on the west branch of the Raft River, east of the circle, while that of the Great Salt Lake and California roads occurred "one mile next to the west end of the circle."[164]

When William Hoffman reached this point, approximately 167 miles from Salt Lake City, he expressed regret that he had not visited the Mormon capital: "It would have given satisfaction to see it and the difference in the distance would have been trifling."[165]

From City of Rocks or Pyramid Circle in southern Idaho, the "main California road" became a "rough, hilly" one crossing several small streams as well as Goose Creek and Valley. This was the "worst road I ever saw," declared Rachel Taylor:

> Up and down hill all day long — sometimes on top of a high mountain and then again in the valley. Sometimes crossing creeks and then wandering through mazes of luxuriant sage brush.[166]

It was along this section of the trail that Cornelia Ferris, who had left Salt Lake City on May 1 after spending the winter there, decided, "This journey is only for those who have health and spirits to enjoy and to endure; to those who are unfortunate, it is a chapter of woe."[167]

Many emigrants, upon reaching Goose Creek, echoed Jotham Newton's observation that "the grass is mostly eaten off by the earlier emigration." Upon reaching Thousand Springs Valley farther south, Newton, who was in the early part of the emigration and four days ahead of Lorena's party at this point, added, "Grass may be found by the early but those that come late cannot find much." The accuracy of Newton's statement can be judged by James Royal's reaction when his company reached Thousand Springs Valley at the end of August. Royal wrote: "No grass — NO GRASS!"[168]

Neither Lorena nor Harriet Ward described Thousand Springs Valley, which was really "two valleys separated by a ridge of about 2 miles in extent with good water besides mineral springs," according to Bradway. Of one he reported, "The water is quite hot 140 [degrees] said some of them are 180 [degrees] impregenated with sulphur and some other minerals." James Cowden found "the water looks clear and cold, yet it has an offensive smell," and John Pratt Welsh reported some "boiling springs" with a temperature of 142 degrees while "cold springs" 100 yards away were forty-seven degrees. William Hoffman camped twice in this valley and wrote, "The water is contained in natural wells, some of them 12 feet deep and the water in some of them is very good. The deep ones contain small fishes." Isaiah Bryant believed Thousand Springs Valley must "have once been a sort of lake and from time to time has grown over with a sod."[169]

In this valley Joel Miller became "much annoyed with dust" and felt "crowded with the trains and droves of cattle." Newton thought everyone "seems to be hurrying on to reach the Humboldt river."[170] Although others described two roads leading from the valley, Lorena did not keep a record of this section of the trail, either. After a day and a half of travel she wrote only about "coming through a narrow rock Kanyon" to reach the Humboldt River on August 7.

The Humboldt, also known as Mary's River, served as a lifeline through the desert country of eastern and central Nevada. Surrounded by mountains with tops "clad in everlasting snow," the river held forth promise of an easy trip because at its headwaters on the east and north forks emigrants found "plenty of grass" as well as large trout. Harriet Ward and Lorena both commented upon the river's beauty at this point. But the Humboldt proved to be deceptive, becoming smaller and more alkaline as it made its way through approximately 320 miles of increasingly barren countryside before disappearing completely in the desert sands.[171]

It took the Woodward-Hays-Lithgow company three weeks to complete this part of the overland journey, while the Ward train required two days more. Soon Ward and Lorena were writing about the "humboldt dust," a "mixture of alkali and clay, which imparts a roughness to the skin very uncomfortable indeed." Ward added, "I will credit every story I may hear after this with regard to the depths of the dust." Calvin Graham agreed: "The dust could not well be worse."[172]

Cowden reported, "There is so much alkali in the soil here the dust is poison and keeps my legs and mouth sore.'' He claimed it tasted and smelled ''like lime dust or ashes'' and Velina Williams thought so, too. Rachel Taylor commented, ''The dust is very oppressive, in some places being half-way up to the wagon hubs.'' And William Rowe remembered, ''We were a black looking crowd hurrying along in a cloud of dust.'' In addition to the ''terrible'' dust, John Welsh reported ''towards night the mosquitoes [become] intolerable.'' Cornelia Ferris found a ''veil invaluable'' against both mosquitoes and buffalo gnats, which ''come out of the foliage in perfect clouds.'' Newton discovered ''Traveling on this river is anything but pleasant — thick dust by day and mosquotes by night.''[173]

Changeable weather also contributed to the unpleasantness of travel along the Humboldt, with daytime temperatures reaching ''95 degrees in the shade'' on July 17 as recorded by Welsh. Bradway kept a record of morning temperatures during the second week of August and found they ranged from twenty-eight to thirty-eight degrees. Other emigrants' diaries for 1853 tell of cool weather as well as cold winds and rains along the Humboldt in late August, including at least one ''severe storm of hail.''[174]

Despite the ''dreary and monotonous'' days, Ward, unlike Lorena, wrote daily in her journal. Lorena's diary contains only eight entries for these three weeks, so it is not known whether her company stayed on the north side of the river the entire distance. It was customary for wagon trains to cross the Humboldt several times and to drive cattle back and forth in search of better grass. The Ward train crossed the river four times, traveling much of the way on the south side. ''I think the emigrants, most of them, are upon the north,'' wrote Ward on September 4. A month earlier William Zilhart, also on the south side, discovered it ''but little travelled'' because ''all the emigration has went down the north side except one or two trains.''[175] A disgruntled James Woodworth explained the situation on August 28:

> A great many heavy trains and droves passed along the road to day having recently crossed the river. The emigration which has before been mostly traveling on the south side are now crossing at every ford to the north side and though we have been almost by ourselves so far there is a prospect of our having more company than is agreeable for the rest of the way down the river. The cause of leaving the south side is the scarcity of grass on that side.[176]

In other years this part of the overland journey could be harrowing, but in 1853 emigrants had an easier time along the Humboldt. ''I presume,'' wrote Ward, that

> the present season is much more favorable for travellers than previous ones have been, or else the evils of this section of the country have been

much exaggerated, for we find it thus far quite comfortable as any other part of our route.[177]

Robert Eccleston, who called the Humboldt "the terror of the plains," pointed out that in 1853 its reputation was worse than its reality. Upon reaching the Humboldt, a traveler finds "it less terrible then he is led to suppose," said Eccleston.[178]

An explanation of these statements, which differ considerably from those of other years, was given by Benjamin G. Ferris and his wife, who arrived in "the valley of the Humboldt" on June 3. Both commented upon the "swollen state of the river" and the floods that made "the ordinary emigrant road, which runs mostly on the north side, nearly impassable" early in the season. In late July Joel Miller noted, "There are sloughs running through the bottom which, when the river is high, cattle cannot cross." Several days later he reported, "The river is falling and the ground drying," but miry bottoms "in consequence of the late overflow" still proved troublesome. He also reported, "Feed [is] in abundance all along the river." In late September Eccleston wrote, "In fact, the entire route along it, with the exception of the last 60 or 70 miles, abounds in grass and contains no greater quality of alkaly than is met previously in the journey."[179]

While trying to avoid "alkaly" water that killed livestock, emigrants also kept a close lookout for Digger Indians, who were "awfully given to stealing." Emigrants experienced considerable harassment from these Indians, but in early September Royal reported, "We have heard of some depredations having been committed by these Diggers this year though they have not disturbed us." He also noted "four Indians shot near us (horrible sight)."[180]

On August 31, according to William Gilbert, a company "campt within 80 rods of us last night lost 50 head of cattle" when Indians attacked at 2 A.M., stampeding livestock. "These Digger Indians are very Sly," Gilbert asserted. "We cannot see them in the Day time at all they keep along the willows on the river road following down the valley."[181]

When "a lot of Digger Indians" visited camp, Rachel Taylor decided, "They would not scruple to take a person's life if it could be done without risking their own." Hoffman, traveling in the same company, said of these Indians: "They do not hesitate to kill a man if they can't plunder otherwise." S. H. Taylor, Rachel's uncle, added, ". . . we heard of the Humboldt Indians — the Diggers — of their extinction by the small pox. We found it partially so — and no one comes over the plains without wishing it were so of all these tribes."[182]

However, Lucy Rutledge Cook managed to trade advantageously with the Diggers, acquiring a "Pretty robe of 10 prairie dog skins" for an old blanket while an "old red flannel shirt" was exchanged for "some beautiful mink skins." These she made into a flat boa "so two tails are sufficient." Cook was very pleased with herself: "Dont you think I got a bargain!" She also received as gifts a wildcat skin to use as "a pretty muff" and a wolf skin.[183]

In addition to writing about Digger Indians, alkali water, and Humboldt dust, emigrants described meeting pack trains from California going east. A number of diaries also mention trading posts scattered along the Humboldt, including one consisting of twelve or fifteen large wagons. On August 25 Bradway passed a trading post run by "Capt Jane Shed a woman who dresses in mens apparel." He further described her as "probably about 40 yrs." Nothing else is known about her since no one else seems to have met her in 1853.[184]

These trading establishments were welcomed by emigrants beginning to run short of provisions, like the Royal-Taylor train still "400 miles from settlement." Rather than travel on the Sabbath to reach Oregon sooner, the company split up. "We think the Lord can provide for us in the wilderness," declared James Royal. "After travelling so far without travelling on Sunday we thought it not right to start out from grass, water and wood on Sunday morning," he explained. The Royal family bought "some 33 pounds of beef from a trader for $1.25 per pound," and William Hoffman reported flour sold at "150 cents per pound." Then, having reached Lassen's Meadow, this company turned northwest from the California-Humboldt road, en route to the Rogue River Valley of southern Oregon, later to be met by government rescue parties with additional supplies.[185]

Also called Lawson Meadows, the area "contain[s] many hundreds of acres of rich land and produces a growth of excellent grass," according to Isaiah Bryant. Harriet Ward described these meadows as "a perfect little paradise." Here emigrants who planned to go to northern California or southern Oregon, cut and dried grass in preparation for crossing the desert of the Lassen Cutoff. This road, known variously as the Applegate-Lassen-Nobles route, was traveled by a "great many going a new route to Shasta City [California]," explained Eccleston.[186]

James Cowden, whose destination was the Yuba River in northern California, stated "the other road is the old trail and follows down the river to the Sink, as it is called. . . ." Starting out on the Lassen road, William Hoffman encountered "the first abondonment of property of any considerable amount" along the trail in 1853. But he declared his gladness at leaving the "swampy Humboldt." William Carey Bailey, who also took the Lassen Cutoff, later recalled his trip "down the sickening, dead Humboldt" as "days of desert and walk and hunger, days when we felt like kicking the dogs that ate the bacon skins and crusts around camp."[187]

A few miles beyond this meadow and the cutoff, emigrants began to remark upon the increasing bareness of the country away from the river itself. "Not a green thing can be seen," wrote Jotham Newton on August 16; he also described the nearby mountains as "gloomey and forbidding in the extreme." The California Trail in this region led over bluffs and ridges as well as through deep ravines and "kanyons," detouring from the river bottom and back again. In mid-June Cornelia Ferris, who now found "a new and abominable plague" in the "vile wood tick," told of crossing a "saleratus plain as smooth and hard as a house floor." She added that these "extensive saleratus flats" were formed by water overflowing to form temporary lakes that "left salts as they dried up."[188]

According to Eccleston, "the early emigration was obliged to climb the mountains, travel on their rocky slopes and take routes before unused to make their journey down the river at all" because high water covered the trail through the bottoms. In late September, after leaving "Lawsons meadows," he wrote, "The grass becomes scarce, the river bottom is small and Dry and barren is the general appearance of the country."[189]

Then came days of "very tedious" travel through sand four to eighteen inches deep. Lucy Cook lamented, "Oh what a loss I'm at to know how to amuse myself for tho I have a little sewing yet its nothing that must be done. . . ." Her principal job was to sew the "bosom and wrist" on two of her husband's shirts; although she had some red yarn, it was too near summer "to commence woolen socks." Instead, Cook wished for muslin so "I could be preparing our under clothes for we are all quite destitute."[190]

Joel Miller announced, "The river seems to have fallen but little down here, so we are compelled to travel on the high bottoms where the sand is deep." Isaiah Bryant's company encountered "the wind blowing a perfect hurricane and dust to almost suffocation." Remarked Zilhart, "The soil looks solid but it will mire down even a toad." To him the Humboldt seemed "an awful stream to travel on." At this point in the overland journey, other emigrants undoubtedly agreed with Zilhart and especially with Horace Seaver when he wrote how glad he was "to get of[f] that curssed stream."[191]

Finally, after continuing down the Humboldt several more days, emigrants reached the sink where the river ended in a large slough and a lake. Looking back on August 18 Zilhart noted "wagons as far as your eye could see up and down the river." In describing this area, Woodworth wrote that the Humboldt

> does not go any farther, but here spreads out into a vast, shallow lake, of several hundred acres extent, called the "Sink" which, as it has no outlet, is supposed to discharge the water received into it, by allowing it to sink into the earth.[192]

Twelve miles after Lorena left the Humboldt Sink she crossed the little Salt Creek, the last water before embarking on the bitter Forty-mile Desert.

The sink, to Ward, had "the appearance of a silver lake," while Eccleston called it "one of the greatest natural curiosities of the continent." He also reported "the waters of the Humboldt spread in different streams and form a marsh," ten miles long and two to four miles wide. Ferris wrote that the sink was "a large basin, somewhat circular, from 10 to 14 miles wide and 25 to 30 miles long, bordered by hills." The lake itself she described as two to five miles long with a "gravelly beach."[193]

Here the Big Meadows consisted of a "belt of deep green grass and bulrushes." Virginia Ivins used the word "pretty" to describe both the lake and the meadows, which she found "covered with coarse grass, long and luxuriant." Newton described the area as "a broad tract of land extending from one mountain to the other and nearly all overflowed." He added, "The river here spreads itself out and near the edge where it is shallow, becomes salty and the ground mirey." William Browder advised against stopping "at the commencement of the meder [meadow]" where the grass was "Brachis and Salty," while Eccleston noted the water was only "tolerable."[194]

Lorena's company arrived at these great meadows the evening of August 28 and spent the next couple of days recuperating while preparing to cross the Forty-mile Desert. This entailed cutting and drying grass to feed livestock during the long march, an ordeal that could take as long as forty-eight hours. Zilhart cut grass "in the darndest, wettest, mirist place I ever saw," while Calvin Graham and his companions "had to waid in the water up to our waists ¼ mile Sow as to get to grass water being high grass verry hard to get at." One of Graham's friends drowned while

> waiding the Slew when he steped in a hole where he could not touch bottom He was berried at dusk with his best Soot on in a sand mound at the head of the Big Meadows near the River.[195]

For others, the stay at the Big Meadows served as a very pleasant interlude. The evening before he crossed the desert, James Compton took part in a ball, attended by 150 persons.[196]

In 1853 emigrants discovered the desert crossing to be somewhat less dreadful than anticipated because "the longest reach on this desert is thirty-five miles, until the present year, and here-to-fore it has been forty." Isaiah Bryant also observed the lake had a sixteen-mile shoreline in mid-September, thus considerably shortening the distance to be traveled. This occurred, Bryant wrote,

> in consequence of the lake basin filling up with sand and sediment and this forming a sort of bed and the quick sand has made its way ten or twelve miles in to the desert towards Carson River and before many years will perhaps form a junction with that stream.[197]

This unusual condition was also reported three weeks earlier by Newton:

> Formerly no water ran out of the sink but on account of the very high water last spring, it broke its way through and ran down on to the desert about 12 mi, making a stream as large as the Humboldt river. By this means a large quantity of grass and plenty of water for the emigration is obtained.[198]

In later years Remembrance Hughes Campbell recalled that the Carson River also overflowed into the desert, forming its own sink at that end "owing to extreme high water." As he pointed out, "this, of course, made the drive without water shorter" in 1853. When Gilbert camped "near the outlet of the Lake" on September 5, he reported two trading posts and a ferry doing business. Although emigrants "can save about 12 miles by ferrying," Gilbert's company decided "to follow the road around the Slew" instead.[199]

Beyond the lake and sink, the California Trail again divided. Emigrants who took the right-hand road crossed the Nevada desert on the Truckee Route, so called because it then led along a river with the same Indian name. This trail, followed by the ill-fated Donner Party in 1846, took emigrants across the Sierra Nevada north of Lake Tahoe

Lorena's company attacked the Forty-mile Desert at night and would have seen this desolation the next day. Wagon parts are still visible here.

and on to the northern gold mines. Those who chose the road to the left of the sink crossed the same mountain range, but south of Lake Tahoe. Known as the Carson Route, this road ran through country explored during the winter of 1843-44 by Fremont's second expedition, led by scouts Kit Carson and Thomas "Broken Hand" Fitzpatrick.

Because it had been traveled for five years, the Carson Route could be considered "the old emigrant road." At least one emigrant of 1852 recommended it "especially for families" due to the "abundance of excellent grass and pure water" found after reaching the Carson River, according to an 1853 newspaper article. Harriet Ward's party would have taken this trail except they received word that her son awaited them at an encampment on the Truckee River. Lorena's uncles decided upon the Carson Route since it would bring them into California closer to their final destination.[200]

The Woodward-Hays-Lithgow wagons left Big Meadows on the afternoon of August 30. Lorena's next journal entry, on September 3, told briefly about crossing the desert at night, a procedure followed by the majority of emigrants. Since the trip usually took another full day and part of the next night, it was no wonder that cattle gave out, especially during the last twelve miles of deep sand. Years later Washington Bailey recalled:

> the sand was so light and fine that one foot would go down until I would set the other foot on top of the sand and pull that foot out, before I could step one foot ahead of the other.[201]

This style of walking, he said, was "as slow as treading water." When Count Cipriani reached the desert, he insisted the soil "was not sand but much worse since it is clayey soil reduced to powder finer than flour in which the animals sink up to their shoulders and vanished without a trace."[202]

The desert did not present Lorena's company with any exceptional difficulties, because halfway across they found "a little dry bunch grass off the road" for the livestock and later the weather turned cold and windy. Arriving at the Carson River at about 2 A.M. the second night, they found the bank bare of grass. The wagons moved on because "the cattle are very hungery and weak, quite a number having given out on the desert."

Gilbert counted "1019 head of Dead cattle & horses and mules during the 48 miles," but added "the greatest part of the Stock died last year. . . ." He also noted "an immense amount of property of waggon irons and other kinds of tools in some places the road on each side was perfectly lined with iron and Dead Stock." To Cornelia Ferris, who was in the early part of the emigration, "death alone appeared to be the presiding deity" in this "vast waste of sand, drifted into little hillocks around stunted grese wood and the carcasses of dead animals." In mid-July the number of emigrants between the Humboldt and the Carson rivers was reported as "immense — 1,000 wagons and 300,000 cattle."[203]

Along this section of the trail in other years emigrants had been met by relief parties sent out from California to provide aid for those who had exhausted food supplies and also needed help with transportation. This type of rescue effort, begun in 1849 and paid for with public and private contributions, was also designed to help latecomers threatened with being trapped in the Sierra by snow. In 1853 no such operations appear to have been organized along the Carson Route, and Ward did not report anything similar on the Truckee trail. But Mary Hite Sanford who was thirteen years old when her family followed the Truckee road, remembered her brother being charged ten cents for a half-pint of water at one trading post. She added:

> We found out afterwards that the government had paid those men well and fitted them up with small supply & barrels & team to haul water out and meet suffering emigrants, and there was suffering, *especially* for water, but they charged for everything.[204]

However, California-bound travelers in general fared better in 1853 than did those emigrants who left the Lassen Cutoff for southern Oregon. Relief was essential for these companies, said one Portland newspaper, because "whole families [are] left destitute on the plains with no hope of reaching Oregon" since their cattle perished. Some 1,500 emigrants with 250 wagons apparently "took a wrong turn and got lost to the south" while following "a new route over the Cascades." Citizens of Lane and Linn counties in southern Oregon

The sand of the Forty-mile Desert was blown into hummocks. Jaded animals were often unhitched here to find their way to the Carson River, ten miles beyond this point.

sent teams and provisions to help relieve this suffering.[205]

By now tempers had grown short and flared much more easily than earlier in the journey. Lorena wrote about one such episode on the Carson Route: a murder that occurred during a disagreement about ownership of a steer. Her account, written several days later, sounds remarkably like the one included by Elias Draper in his 1904 memoirs, since both took place on approximately the same section of the desert trail. Draper was present for the jury trial that sentenced the guilty party, "a man named Blankenship," to be "hanged at the end of a wagon tongue" for first degree murder, according to "Emigrant Law." In return for a bill of sale for all stock, wrote Draper, the lawyer declared the trial illegal and announced he would take Blankenship to California for a new trial. A preliminary hearing was later held in Placerville, according to Draper, but "no one appeared to prove his guilt so he was set at liberty and reclaimed his stock."[206]

The night of September 3 found Lorena's wagon train encamped near a small settlement called Ragtown at the end of the desert in present-day Nevada. Supposedly, Ragtown acquired its distinctive name because emigrants hung tattered but freshly laundered garments, washed in the nearby Carson River, on the surrounding sagebrush to dry. In 1850 this had been the location of Johnson's Station, which provided relief for emigrants on the Carson Route. Three years later Gilbert found "this place is a few tents [and] Trading Posts. . . ." But Newton considered it "quite a little town." According to "Lucky" Baldwin, this "town of the desert" consisted of "one clapboard house, five cloth houses, a log cabin and two willow shelters." The appearance of some of these wind-whipped flimsy shelters might also have accounted for Ragtown's name.[207]

In an interview given to the *Placerville Herald* on August 6, 1853, Baldwin added, "The six houses gave meals at $1 each and the meals consists of bread, fresh beef, thin coffee and sugar." At Ragtown R. H. Campbell remembered seeing "a grave yard fenced with wagon tires and log chains." Washington Bailey also saw "a trader's pound, the size of an ordinary city lot" constructed in the same manner, with "tires lengthwise and cross-wise, hind wheel tires and front wheel tires and log chains bound together in all kinds of shapes." He added that another trader's pound was made from two rows of 100-foot logs.[208]

When Zilhart arrived at Ragtown on August 24 he found 200 people there. Zilhart, who had an easy and quick trip across the desert, arrived at 5 A.M. for breakfast after traveling only one night. He stayed at Ragtown for two days to "recruit stock" and the evening of August 25 "danced to mid-night." Since Zilhart obviously did not dance alone, other emigrants must have had an easy crossing, too, and still had enough energy for merry-making.[209]

Upon leaving Ragtown, emigrants faced another twelve-mile stretch of desert plus a second detour before returning to the river where it entered the fertile Carson Valley. Cornelia Ferris wrote of this valley: "Surely, a more lovely place the sun never shown upon." She described the "thickly settled neighborhood, the fine large farms, luxuriant crops, rail fences and numerous herds of cattle." Jotham Newton also saw a "number of ranchos here," as well as trading posts, and declared, "I believe [the traders] are a gang of thieves" because his company was "constantly loosing cattle."[210]

However, neither Lorena nor Newton mentioned Mormon Station, near present-day Genoa, Nevada, although Isaiah Bryant called it "a considerable trading establishment." Mormon Station was developed in 1851 when Col. John Reese, a Mormon trader, purchased the site and erected a two-story building with kitchen, dining room, storeroom, and two upstairs rooms. Surrounded by log houses as well as fenced and planted fields, Mormon Station had become "an establishment on a large scale," wrote Ferris. She and her husband enjoyed "the freely-tendered hospitalities" of Reese. This station reminded Benjamin Ferris, who had just completed a year as U.S. secretary for Utah, of "the comforts and conveniences of Eastern life."[211]

Traveling slowly by now, Newton felt, "The star of Hope still lends its cheering ways." And Lorena wrote that she hoped the journey would end in another two weeks. While emigrants might breathe a sigh of relief upon reaching the Carson Valley, one last major obstacle awaited them. Ahead loomed the high Sierra. On September 7 Newton "went to the top of the mountains that border this valley on the west" and found "the scenery wild and beautiful" with "some snow" on the mountain tops and in deep canyons.[212]

When emigrants reached the Carson Valley they faced another decision: to continue following the Carson Route, opened in 1848 by members of the former Mormon Battalion en route to Salt Lake City from Sutter's Mill in Coloma, California, or to try one of two "new" roads. The first, called "the Walker river road a new route" by Gilbert, forked to the left and crossed the Carson River twice, as well as "a very bad ridge," before reaching the Walker River farther south. Also known as the Sonora Road, it was promoted as a much shorter route. By early summer of 1853 "citizens" of this mining community had already confidently suscribed $1,408 to ensure the road being built, thus hoping "to direct a large portion of the incoming emigration to their vicinity." The diaries of Joseph Williams and William Browder tell about following this "very small road" with "very little grass" through the Sierra in 1853 to the southern gold mining region.[213]

The second "new" road, known as the Johnson Cutoff, had been opened the preceding year. It led across the first dividing range of the Sierra Nevada and south along the valley of Lake Tahoe, then called Truckee Lake or Lake Bigler, in honor of California's governor. This trail climbed another mountainside to cross the Sierra summit at a lower altitude than the Carson Road, on the way to Placerville. Although the Carson or "main road" was considered preferable by some emigrants, Gilbert's company chose this new road, the Johnson Cutoff, to save "some 40 miles."[214]

This close to the end of their journey, Calvin Graham and his companions decided to backpack. They were among the few 1853 emigrants who "sold our team & waggon . . . for $575.00 Sold some of our provisions throwed away a great many little articles Packed up our things took them on our backs."[215]

While others tried their luck on these cutoffs, the Woodward-Hays-Lithgow company continued along the "old" Carson Route. Lorena, refreshed in spirit, resumed writing each day and described in detail the time spent in crossing the Sierra. How deceptive this route must have looked at first, because "the road ascends a gentle slope of the foot of the mountains," according to Isaiah Bryant, before it turned right between two low peaks to the "mouth of a Big Canyon." Here Bryant found "a saw mill . . . built this spring and the only one in the valley." Cornelia Ferris wrote that at a similar location, "the mouth of the canon," she saw "a tent with a table kept by a tiddy-appearing female."[216]

Turning into Carson Canyon, emigrants encountered the west branch of the Carson River rushing between huge boulders with the trail in many places directly in the stream bed. In earlier years, following this part of the trail was described as "a harder day's travel we had not made on the entire trip." By 1853 the road through this "notable Kanyon" was greatly improved. Jotham Newton wrote about several bridges across the river and also noted "some large rocks removed from the road." Isaiah Bryant commented upon how steep and rocky the road became as it climbed but he enjoyed the scenery: "In many places solid granite cliffs rise to several thousand feet in height" with fir, pine and cedar giving it "a romantic and beautiful appearance." Although this section of the California Trail was only about six miles long, it could take the better part of a day to travel it with wagons.[217]

At the top of the Carson Canyon lay Hope Valley, where many emigrants camped overnight to take advantage of "pretty good grass" and water. At the southwestern end of this valley the "road being quite sideling" skirted Red Lake, described as "a small lake with mirey shores." This brought travelers to the foot of the first summit, considered "the steepest and rather the most difficult mountain which you have to ascend on the whole route." On September 9 Jotham Newton found that "on account of the great crowd of wagons on the mountain, we are obliged to postpone our assent till morning."[218]

It took Isaiah Bryant four hours to reach the top, although the trail here was only about three-quarters of a mile long. He described it as "steep, crooked and rocky." Climbing nearly 700 feet in that short distance, the trail twisted and turned with a sharp "S" curve halfway up the steep slope. Both Bryant and Jotham Newton decided the greatest obstacle here consisted of "a smooth rock between three and four roods in width laying at an angle of thirty-five degrees." Newton's party was "obliged to double team on account of a large smooth rock over which it is difficult for cattle to pass without being hitched to something." Cornelia Ferris wrote about a similar large, smooth, flat rock "upon which the animals could not stand to draw the carriage." When Bryant reached this summit area, he declared, "We are now in the midst of the Nevadas and tall peaks of granite rock surround us on every side."[219]

Five miles more of crooked roads led over an irregular descent into a "beautiful valley," known variously — and misleadingly — as Lake,

Hope Valley, at the head of Carson Canyon, presented a sylvan setting to the exhausted emigrants. It is near the first dividing ridge of the Sierra Nevada.

Deer, or Mountain Valley [today Caples Lake]. Newton wrote about its "small lake which spreads out its silvery bosom with high snow-capped mountains on every side." Usually "flats covered with the best of grass" could be found here, but in September 1853 Newton said very little grass was still available because earlier emigrants "have taken all."[220]

Above this valley and lake towered Snow-Top Mountain, the second summit of the Sierra and the last high ridge to be crossed. At approximately 9,600 feet above sea level, West Pass on the Carson Route was the highest in the United States ever crossed by covered wagons. Bryant said of the summit, it "arises at a considerable height in the world." To cover some four miles of trail could take as long as half a day or more, with the road leading at first through dense forests and then above the timber line, a climb of 1,600 feet from the valley floor. Guidebooks warned:

> Here you commence ascending a very difficult mountain, in consequence of the deep snow over which you pass; and stony, rocky and sideling places to the summit . . . It always has more or less snow upon it.[221]

California Historical Society, San Francisco

This view of the "miry shores" of Red Lake was drawn by J. Wesley Jones in 1851. He depicted a wagon tumbling off the cliff in the center of the view. Two years later, when Lorena arrived here, traffic jams were reported.

Newton was again "detained by the crowds of wagons on the mountain." He reported the weather "very cool" on September 11 as "our wheels rolled over snow." After some "hard pulling," he reached the summit but found his "team very much fatigued." Again, improvements had been made along the trail where it crossed the face of the mountain near the snowbank, which could be fifteen to twenty feet deep. Large rocks banked the downhill side of the roadbed, as had been done in many other steep mountainous sections of the Sierra crossing. According to one authority, "You have now passed over 24¼ the longest miles ever measured by wheels."[222] Lorena, who had walked most of the way for several days, agreed: "We have truly had a hard day of it."

Cornelia Ferris admired the "grand view" from the Sierra summit. This "boundless panorama," she said, consisted of "a wilderness of snowy ridges, rocky peaks and deep cavities." And Horace Seaver, who also did not precisely identify which trail he followed, wrote home, "the road over the Nevadas beats all I ever saw." It took D. A. Shaw, who followed a "fool's cut-off" from the summit, two days of wandering through granite canyons and dense forests before he rejoined the main road. Those emigrants who had followed the regular trail found

Red Lake today is dammed and hence larger and deeper than in emigrant days.
The trail winds up through the center trees to the low point at right.

Wells West, Lorena's cousin, called this "a slippery rock." He wrote, "we had to unhich the oxen from the wagons and drive them up over the Rock and then hich them to the end of the tongue with long chains and pull them up" Red Lake grade.

Above Red Lake the emigrants reinforced the trail with rocks placed on the downhill side. Ropes probably were looped around the large red fir tree on the right, causing the massive bulge around its base.

that it led from the high Sierra summit through desert-like sands and then descended into green meadows. Now emigrants faced only a few more days of travel "over numerous hills, with more descent than ascent," for the last 75-100 miles down into the Sacramento Valley.[223]

On September 18 Lorena's wagon train left the main road for the small mining community of Volcano, just four days after Jotham Newton took the same route leading towards the Ione Valley. According to John Doble, who had prospected for gold in the surrounding hills, on July 10 "several teams and about 40 men" arrived in Volcano from Salt Lake, "being the first of the Season crossing the plains." Doble reported similar arrivals throughout the next three months as well as "traders going out regularly" to meet wagon trains. In mid-October he wrote, "The Emigration is supposed to be all in or nearly so as there has none passed through here for the last three days."[224]

So neither Newton's company nor Lorena's was among the first —

John C. Fremont's cartographer, Charles Preuss, drew this view of the men of the second Fremont expedition, possibly above Red Lake, during 1844.

California Historical Society, San Francisco

J. Wesley Jones made this view of a lone covered wagon, lower right, on the way to the summit of Carson Pass.

"Flats of the very best grass" were found in this valley until 1919, when the single Caples Lake was formed by damming two small lakes. This was a popular emigrant campground. The "eternal snowbank" is the large mass to the right of center. The small gap to the left is West Pass, at 9,600 feet the highest point in the United States ever crossed by covered wagons.

or the last — to reach California in 1853. The honor of being first belonged to another Illinois company, one from Galena, whose journey ended in Sacramento on July 4 "but one day later than the van of the immigration of '52," according to the newspapers. Led by Capt. Isaac Evans, "a famous overland traveler," this company was considered "the first of the great overland army." It consisted of twelve men with four wagons and twenty-five "handsome horses."[225]

Two and a half months after his arrival in California, James Cowden, who had taken the Lassen Cutoff, summed up the 1853 experience thus:

An overland trip to California or Oregon is not difficult or dangerous. I really enjoyed it and could spend several years very pleasantly traveling through the hills & mountains of the western country, it[s] wild scenery is very interesting to me & I do not see how any person can help enjoying it.[226]

Well-worn rocks, streaked with rust from the iron wagon tires, mark the route across the face of Snowy Mountain, above Caples Lake.

To the left of the "eternal snowbank" the wagons cut the trail through rocky soil, leading Lorena to her "Land of Gold and Wickedness."

*A towering turret of rock hovers above the crest of West Pass. This was con-
sidered the boundary of California by the emigrants.*

A narrow lane led between the rocks to the southwest of West Pass, wide enough only for the passage of one wagon at a time.

Emigrants moved larger boulders aside, but this one was too small to be a problem. It still retains the scars left by all the wagons which followed the Carson route.

"Oh! What Times We Shall Have"

13TH YESTERDAY CAME through the mud to the river. At night took the boat and now on the Di'vernon, a very pleasant boat. Now stopping a Capul Gray.[1]

14th On the "Clara" bound for Kanzas. Stay at St. Louis till tomorrow evening. I want to visit some acquaintances here, but do not expect I can.[2]

16th Horrible! Horrible! I never was in such a dreadful crowd in my life. Dutch, dutch, nothing but dutch except a very few gentlemen who seem to have been better raised, but we can't enjoy anything at all. Here we must be a week. Yesterday some of the hands came near fighting. I was very much frightened. Nearly all the passengers are going to California. If it is not better on the plains, I cant stand it.[3]

18th Have formed some quite agreeable acquaintances if they only hold out so, but I have found there is no trusting anyone hardly. Several gentlemen who are married have been passing themselves off as unmarried. The Engineer is very kind. We get along slowly, river is so low.

21st Last evening left the "Clara". Now at the hotel in Kansas.[4] It was with some feelings of regret I left the boat as I had formed some attachments that were not altogether disagreeable. [three lines crossed out here so that they can not be read] — How lonesome I felt when the boat moved off. I should dearly love to travel all the time, yet it is with some misgivings that I think of starting across the plains. I expect to see some very trying times. I hope I may have patience to endure all things, and that I may be able to contribute to the happiness and comfort of others. I think I am willing to be placed in such circumstances as God in his wisdom has designed. I know I shall be happiest in doing his will whatever it may be. I feel weak and unable to do anything but if he

The view from the Clara *in 1853 would have been about the same as the one above—the Missouri River a few miles downstream from Westport Landing.*

has a work for me to do I trust he will strengthen me. i hope I may be useful. I long for the friendship of the good and wise. True friendship is such a support, such a bright star to shine upon our pathway through life, but it seems as if we were going where we can scarcely expect to find much true friendship, yet I will hope for the best and try to believe we shall find many of them. I wish I were able, I should go to St. Louis while our folks were staying here. It would be so pleasant a way to pass the time that may otherwise hang heavily, for I dont know how we will be situated yet, whether pleasantly, or not. Kansas seems to be quite a pleasant little place so far as I can judge yet. I have had no opportunity to see it yet. I must write some letters while staying here.

Kansas

23rd Monday Uncle found a house and we are now at home for a little while at least. I was disappointed in its being so far from the river. I just now hear a steamboat, but we cannot see them which would be some variety in our strange home. heard the church bells to night which seemed pleasant once more. When we leave here we shall be out of the sound of Church bells. I have had no opportunity to see the place yet. There are Indians in town every day. We are only two miles from

National Park Service

William Henry Jackson painted this view of the Westport Landing, now part of downtown Kansas City, Missouri.

the territory[5] —

24th The Clara went down the river to day, one day sooner than I expected. We were kindly enquired after by some of the officers of the boat, Uncle said. It will be up again in ten days. I shall look for the boat.

March 31st — Last Sunday went to church. The time passes off quite pleasantly. Yesterday Uncle accompanied us down upon Water Street. I saw some Indians, some of the Wyandotte tribe. They are quite civilized, only live 2 or 3 miles from Kanzas. The women are in town every day. They get drunk. We also saw two of the "Caws." They were on their way to St. Louis and were dressed in true Indian style — looked grotesque enough. I did not have an opportunity of observing as attentively as I wished. To day we received some letters from Barry. One was from Aunt Sarah. times have been truly hard in California. I must write some letters soon to Barry and also to California.[6]

Kanzas

April 1st Walked half a mile yesterday to a Catholic Church. It was built of logs. Seemed quite antique. It was very tastefully adorned with pictures and vases of beautiful artificial flowers. in the graveyard almost every grave had a cross on it. Strange feelings came over my heart as I thought of the fate of those buried there when all must have been a wilderness here, when the red man was roaming in his primitive wildness. His home is here yet but he seems quite civilized.[7]

April 6th I find but little interesting enough to write, yet it seems that I ought to find a great deal in a place so closely connected by the ties of friendship and situation with the aborigines of our country, but I have had little opportunity to form any acqaintance with them or to learn much respecting their history. Many of the Wyandottes have intermarried with the french and americans. I feel a peculiar interest in the indians, especially if they have become connected in any way with the whites. They seem to possess a great deal of pride, and dignity. A half-breed lady starts tomorrow to her husband in Ohio. There is little variety in our situation here. The "Clara" was up yesterday which was quite an interesting incident to us, for it seemed as if we should meet old friends, almost, when she came, but we were disappointed. No one off her came to see us. Perhaps she will be down tomorrow. I have but little to do so I can read considerable which suits me very well. Why dont I like work better? I am affraid I am very selfish and like enjoyment too well, and am not desirous as I should be of being useful, yet I do sometimes think I want to be but perhaps I do not improve every opportunity that I have. I am ever longing for more means and self improvement. I know my own incapabilities and feel the need for greater proficiency in many things. I long for the privilege of moving in interesting and refined circles, but oh! how long it will be, if ever, before we shall have such privileges — five months before we get to our journey's end, and then we know not what kind of people we shall have to mingle with. I hope we shall find good friends and that we may be in some degree useful to others, that we may discourage vice, and in some degree aid in bringing about a reform, and improvement in the morals of so poluted a community as that of the gold land is said to be. I hope that not half we hear of it may be true in so sad a respect. Oh! may I be firm and try ever to set a good example.

Kanzas

Apr 8th Walked yesterday by the river. Could see Wyandotte away up the river, just where the Kanzas comes in. Its few log houses nestles quietly on a hillside as do all of the towns on the Missouri, or the most of them at least are built on points of bluffs and extending back on the hills. but little of Jefferson City is seen, though the penitentiary is in sight, and the court house is situated on a very pretty elevation, a high hill & seemingly no other houses with it. Boonville was a pretty place & they all have a considerable air of romance and neatness. Some Wyandotte Indians came up on the boat yesterday who had been down the

Missippi. Some were playing the flute, Mr. L. said. I did not see them. I should like to have an opportunity of forming some personal acquaintances among them, but I shall not, I suppose.[8]

Mr. V was telling last night of one young woman who had been drunk three days. She is called Mary and is said to be highly educated, understanding ours, and the french and some of the dead languages. I do not see why she is so intemperate. I should like to know her history — The "Clara" went down to day.

13th Yesterday Mrs. Northup, an Indian lady, wife of a merchant, and Mrs. Cants called on us. Mrs. N. is quite interesting, modest and simple in her manners and very good looking. She is from Ohio, has been here ten years. I do not know of what tribe.[9] Last evening mother and I called at Mr. Pealfry's. They expect to go in company with us; appear like pleasant people. One of our "Clara" acquaintances went through town yesterday. He did not call. I felt sorry for him on the boat, he seemed so lonely and discouraged, is young and inexperienced. He has a chance to go and was after cattle for his employer. I hope that he will do well.

17th Mr. Conroy called on us. He has not got a place to go yet. Seems quite discouraged, I think — this morning five Caw Indians came to our house begging. We gave them their breakfast. One or two were chiefs, were very good looking men if they had been dressed well. The youngest female seemed to be wife to one and had a very amiable, quiet appearance. The oldest one begged some needles & thread. The child had a medal on his neck, presented by a gentleman of Hartford, Conn. I suppose they formerly lived there and it had been given to his ancestors. Uncle has not returned yet, but will be here to start next week, then good bye to Kanzas. I shall look for the rest of our Company this week. I hope we shall have good times and enjoy ourselves.[10]

Kanzas

Apr 20th The wish to be floating on the moonlit surface of the missouri river such a brilliant night, is irresistible. The broad bosom lies so temptingly near, and then when is a more fit time to be on the water than a bright moonlight night? "Such nights and such a place were meet for love". The bluffs and hills, & vales are beginning to be covered with green, and the houses of our almost "seven hilled city" seem scattered here and there upon the sloping hills or green velvet covered mounds. Upon the whole, I think this place might be rendered a most romantic and delightful place of residence. Some of the buildings command a fine view of the river. There is talk that the great Pacific railroad will pass through here.[11]

23 Our house is quite a depot for Californians at present. All of the trains from Barry have arrived, but Uncle has not yet returned from buying cattle. Oh dear! how I wish we were all ready to start out with the other trains. I am afraid we shall get behind. Uncle Adam came yesterday but left his company ten miles above & will not be with us until we cross Caw River which will be 80 miles from here. We shall not see any of them. Some of our folks have gone down to the camp to see how they get along. They have just returned. Mrs. Isreal came to day and is staying with us. We had a storm last night, the rain came in so badly that our beds got wet and we had to get up and sit by the fire. Oh! what times we shall have camping out when it rains and blows.[12]

25th Went to church for the last time last evening, I suppose, until we arrive in California. We had rather a funny time, the minister was a perfect oddity, so much so that it was impossible for the most sedate to keep on a sober face some times. I liked to hear him pray and sing, he was so earnest, although I could not repress laughter when he sang, he had such strange nasal tones and made such gestures. Mr. Alkire's and Israel's trains intend starting tomorrow. They are busy as bees preparing; all are jolly and good natured. They call to see us quite often & have a good deal of sport about cooking, &c I see no need of quarreling as some have done before. I think we shall all get very much attached to each other.

Kanzas

27th Went down to the camp night before last. the next day they all started, and we are still waiting for Uncle Henry. Uncle Lithgow is going up the otherside of Caw River. Mr. Alkire said they would go slow and thought we would overtake them. I am afraid we shall not. Mrs. Israel was very anxious to have us all start together. She will be lonely as there are no more women along. It would have been very pleasant for us all to go in the same train, and all seemed sorry that it happened so we could not.[13]

29 Well, camped out last night for the first time. Started at three oclock. Came seven miles. Westport, four miles, is a very thriving place.[14] The road was very pleasant, but now we are on the vast plains. When we first came into them a feeling of lonliness came over me. They look dreary after leaving pleasant woods, and I thought I could account for the change. I often heard asserted that comes over all persons when on the plains, that want of friendship and disposition to quarrel, that, they say, so universally pervades all hearts, whether friends or foes. I dont believe our hearts can love so well where there are no trees or none of the attractions of hill and vale. But we have a good company and we shall have to exercise patience and bring into ac-

National Park Service

The Pawnees roamed along the north side of the Platte River, harrassing emigrants in 1853. Photographer/artist William H. Jackson painted them in 1866.

tion all the better faculties of our natures as much as possible. The oxen were all rather wild yesterday but no accidents happened, only one ox fell down and they had some trouble to get him up — they ran out of the road and he got thrown down by a bush. We are not out of sight of the woods yet. There are a great many strawberry blossoms here. We sleep in our wagon. I slept most sweetly, and did not fear any thing, save once in the night I heard a mule which awakened me and made me think of Indians.

30th Passed over most beautiful prairie yesterday. Came about ten miles. Walked some — it was a beautiful day & we all enjoyed ourselves fine. Four had to be on watch last night. The cattle (a hundred) were herded Close by our wagons so the men were close by us. A german overtook us, packing everything he had on his back, going to California to day is Sunday & it has been raining. We do not get very wet yet, but may when the wind blows very hard. We are just preparing to start. I dont believe it is quite right, but Uncle is anxious to get up with the other trains for fear we will be left behind — I cannot read much, especially any thing that requires much thinking. Ideas are soon jolted out of my head.

Indian Territory[15]

May 2nd Just stopped to camp. We pass over very beautiful prairie. See but little to relieve the monotony save emigrants and herds of cattle and occasionally a few indians who want to beg something. I walk some every day — think it will be beneficial to me — we have left pleasant villages, farmhouses and cultivated farms far behind. What a long, long waste wilderness we shall have to pass through yet before we shall be at home again —

3rd To day have not had quite so good road. Crossed the Waukalousa. Came out of our way some to ford it. Found very good ford.[16] Are not on the other road yet. I should think we would be at the Caw River tomorrow. Find very fragrant flowers resembling garden sweet williams. Walked considerable to day on account of the bad roads; was afraid to ride.

6th Two miles from Kansas River. Camped in sight of the Baptist Mission house, built of stone. it is quite a pleasant, romantic situation from here.[17] A small stream passes by along which is scattered a few trees. We have a very pretty view of the scenery around us. A great many cattle are in sight scattered here and there over the green sloping hillsides, as if they were all in one large pasture. Tents and wagons are all around us. We are never lonely for we see people continually. we saw a number of log houses and a few fields fenced in which made us think of home. We expect to cross the river to night and hope to meet our friends soon — Israel and Alkire crossed night before last.

7th Came to the river this morning. It rained last night as was cold and unpleasant until now it has the appearance of clearing off. I dont know when we will get across. There are forty wagons here — Uncle has just got back from the ferry and we are going to the upper middle ferry. Cant cross here.[18]

8th Sunday Came up here yesterday. Came over very pretty country. Camped in a pretty place two miles from the river. Came to the river this morning. Some bad places in the road, but romantic scenery. Saw indian graves and the interpreter's house, himself & family. He is the largest indian I have seen. They all looked very well. This is the Potawatamie tribe. Expect to cross to day. I am sorry we have to cross Sunday. Perhaps we will not get over — there so many cattle to cross yet before we do — It is pleasant to day. The Caw or Kanzas is quite a pretty stream. A very narrow strip of timber along its banks, and beautiful rolling prairie in sight each side. Two ferrys run here. There is another about five miles above called Union Town ferry, two below —[19]

Plains

9th Monday Crossed the river this morning. Came six or seven miles & found Uncle Adam's camp. We came around a beautiful bend in the river. No trees this side around the bend, but beautiful prairie. Just now as some of the girls and some of the men were taking some things out of the wagons one of them picked up a pistol and while he had it, it went off, the ball passing through another's hat and the powder burning his face. It was a very narrow escape and I hope it will learn them to be more careful about loaded guns and pistols.[20] I have been some alarmed about the smallpox as it is said to be along in some of the trains which have passed us and which we have passed several times.

10th Came by the Catholic mission to day. There is a log church in the shape of a cross. most of the best houses were white washed and the place had a very neat appearance.[21] The indians dress very fine in broadcloth but wear their clothes in rather an odd and slovenly manner. Had a bad road, or rather, a good many small creeks to cross all of which are deep sloughy places. There is timber on most of these creeks. We are not yet off the Caw river bottom. The country is beautiful to behold, and also good farming country. Grass does not seem so plenty. There is such an immense sight of stock passed over it. I wish we were five or six days earlier. Only came twelve miles to day. It has been a warm and pleasant day. I am anxious to have a better chance to read but shall not have so good an opportunity as I anticipated. There is always confusion when we stop and it is a trouble to keep books where one can get them without their getting soiled badly.

13th We have traveled farther the last two days than usual. We get up early, stop but a little while at noon and have traveled quite late. Yesterday I counted forty wagons in sight and five droves of cattle. We crossed a large stream of water. Some called it the little and some the big vermillion. To day we crossed another. I could not learn whether it was the big vermillion or the big Blue. Had to raise the wagon beds. Saw a grave by the roadside. Some one had died on the way to the land of his hopes. It must be very sad to think we must die and be left all alone in the great prairie, only a small crude stone to mark our last resting place out to the patient emigrants as they wend their way over the beautiful plains as they stretch far, far away to the setting sun. One day by the road side we saw a rude log pen covered over, and underneath the skull and other remains of an Indian we supposed, also

Lorena's company crossed the Big Vermillion River, north of Louisville, Kansas. A Pottawatomie, Louis Vieux, operated a toll bridge there as early as 1850.

a small kettle and other accouteraments. I suppose he was left in a sitting posture and such things as they thought he would need in his hunting grounds, left with him. What a long lonely time he has been sitting there. But though so close to the road side, he was not even conscious of passerby or of the oft-repeated peep of curiosity that is almost sure to peer through the crevices of his rude tomb many moons have passed away since he was placed in his solitary resting place. One of our men, Mr. Kisinggeer, has been sick the last few days. he is better to night, he thinks. Tis bad to be sick on such a journey.[22]

14th It was the Blue we crossed yesterday. To day the wind blows so very hard that I can scarcely write in the wagon with the cover fastened down. It seems as if they will turn over, almost, and the wind seem to increase. Came into the St. Jo road this forenoon. Saw several graves by the roadside.[23]

15th We had quite a hard windstorm last night. I expect we shall have a good many storms for a few weeks to come. I dread them some. We are resting to day, or at least we are not travelling. Some are washing, some at one thing, some at another, all as busy as if it were not Sunday, and one can hardly make it seem like Sunday if they try ever so hard.

Afternoon. I have been reading some and enjoyed it much. I was reading of some instances of conjugal affection. Those of Lady Fanshawe and Mrs. Hutchison and husbands are particularly interesting. If such love were more common, happiness would not be so rare a thing in our world. Oh! That true love could more often be experienced by those who take upon themselves vows of constancy to each other. Oh! If I ever love, may it be as ardently reciprocated, but I doubt whether that happiness is reserved for me. It were too exquisite a happiness for one so undeserving of any, least of all, so great a one of God's best gifts to sinful and ungrateful creatures. The love of an earnest, noble heart is no trifling valueless thing. This is the seventeenth day since we left Kansas. To day has been warm and pleasant.

Gregory M. Franzwa

T. S. Prather's trail came to an end on the near bank of the Big Vermillion. He died of cholera on May 27, 1849.

17th It rained yesterday morning so we did not get an early start. rained again last night. It is very disagreeable when it rains much. If it were always pleasant weather we should have nothing but a pleasure trip, that is, if none of us were ever sick. Sarah was quite unwell yesterday, but is better this morning. We camped in a pretty place last night but the water is bad. It is a little muddy stream which runs around our camp, leaving it a semicircle with a few scattered trees on its banks and a rise of green prairie outside, the road passing along the straight side of semicircle along which our wagons and tents are stretched. The majority of both camps (Uncle Adam's and ours) arranged themselves around our stove and prevailed upon Mr. Smith to sing some dutch songs. We sang a little "by the light of the moon" and then bid each other good evening.

18th Crossed the big Sandy yesterday. One place we came down into a valley intersected by ravines, along which grew a few scattered oaks. It was quite a romantic landscape. Crossed little Sandy, Turkey Creek and several other pretty streams to day.[24] They are very meandering with green sloping banks, and here and there upon them is scattered a few pretty green trees. All the country is one continuous,

The Louis Vieux Elm, located just west of the crossing, is ninety-nine feet high and the second largest elm in the United States.

The Kansas prairie assumes a limitless aspect west of the Big Vermillion River.

lovely green pasture. We have seen several graves both days, one fresh one in a pretty place on the bank of a creek yesterday. To night we camp on the banks of the little Blue on a pretty little bottom, or flat, but the grass is poor for the cattle. We pass and repass trains every day or two. I think we will get quite well acquainted after awhile.

19th Traveled most of the day on the banks of the Blue. The scenery was very pretty. Saw a good many graves to day.

21st Traveled yesterday on the Blue most of the time. left it last evening to camp. It is now 26 miles to the Platte. We are just now cross a small stream six miles from the Blue. Last night was a most beautiful night — moonlight, still and pleasant. To day is warm and pleasanter than usual.

22nd Sabath Last night had a severe wind storm. All of the tents blew down, left the boys under asleep, most of them, it came so suddenly. I was very much alarmed — but the storm did no material injury. I suppose we shall experience even harder ones. The cattle always run with the storm. Mr. Smith kept ahead of them so none were lost this morning.[25] He is a very faithful hand. Uncle was out all day yesterday hunting a cow and did not get to camp till this morning. We have just started for the Platte as there is no wood or water here, and we may not find any there. Yesterday found a train from near Barry in which was one or two acquaintances bound for Oregon.

23rd Traveled over most beautiful, level plains all day. have constantly been in sight of timbers which lies on the river. On the other, or left side lies a low range of hillocks where the high plains just off the bottom. We can see a very great distance so that tops of trees and hills appear like little dark clouds resting a short distance above the horizon, or some times we might deceive ourselves with the idea that water intervenes between us and distant objects. it is the phenomenon of the air which looks like small waves of shining water. Wagons at a great distance appear elongated perpendicularly so that they might easily be taken for large white graves stones. We passed Fort Kearny but did no go within a quarter of a mile, which was quite a disappointment. There were half a dozen good sized buildings.[26]

Platte river

26th day before yesterday traveled over the same level bottom of the Platte. Yesterday it rained and we stopped all day at camp, which was near the river, where we had plenty of wood and water. To day we have traveled along the river bank. The Platte is very wide and shallow. It is also a very straight stream, is interspersed with most beautiful grass covered islands, of all sizes, with pretty, graceful cotton wood trees on them, so that they look like grass plots with shade trees planted on them. Some islands are very long and narrow, covered with dry grass of last year's growth, which the fire has not reached, and at a distance looks like a field of grain. There are no trees scarsely except

Fort Kearny, in present-day Nebraska, is just a few miles west of the point where the wagon trains first encountered the Platte River. It was established in 1848. This painting is by William H. Jackson.

those on the islands, which are only scattering, and not large so that, where there are not too many islands we can look across the river which is so wide, that the distant shore looks almost like the opposite shore of a lake. The banks are one long continued green, grassy meadow. The water is muddy but does not taste badly. We saw where one train was burrying a woman.[27] Cousin Louisa has been much worse for several days. I fear she will not live to get across the plains, sometimes. The weather is cold, and damp, which is bad for a consumptive, to be so exposed. Her parents were in hopes the trip would restore her to health.

28th   Last night camped in the prairie — poor grass, no wood except a little we brought with us and one mile and a half to water in the river. After dark we heard three reports of a pistol in quick succession. our men answered by the same signal. Pretty soon we heard men hallooing. our men also answered the same way. It was not long before five or six men came to camp. They had been out hunting and had got lost from their own train. Our boys gave them some supper and a place to sleep. They had not more than got settled before one of our men (who had been our since morning with Uncle, hunting) came saying they had killed a buffalo, So three of our men prepared and started on their horses to return two or three miles where Uncle was guarding the hams from the wolves. They had got that far when the horse got his blindfold off and they could get no further with the buffalo meat. Horses cannot be made to carry it at all unless they are blindfolded so they cannot see it, then they are affraid when they smell it. All of the horses took a "stampede" as soon as the man came in with the one which had brought it only part way to camp. We had some of the meat for breakfast which was of most excellent flavor, equal to the very best quality of beef. It is the first time any of our men have been on a hunting expedition. They saw seventeen buffalo and quite a number of antelope. They think buffalo hunting quite rare sport.[28]

Today is Saturday again. I do not think we have traveled far this week. There has been a good deal of rain which causes hard traveling. I suppose we will travel tomorrow as there is neither wood or good water near us & grass poor. We heard this afternoon that Alkire's train camped near here night before last. I am not tired of the journey yet. hope that we shall see no harder times; if not we shall find it a pleasant trip. The boys have just gone to get wood which is more than a mile off, I suppose. we will have to wait some time for our supper, I am thinking — but no matter, it will taste good when it is ready. I never slept so well in my life as since I have been "camping out."

30th Stopped yesterday noon in a very pretty place near the bluffs which were quite rugged and much nearer the river than usual. Cedar grew in the gulches. This morning it rained again. A good many pretty flowers where we are stopping for dinner on the bluff or high plains. Thought we saw some buffalo running toward the river. We cross their paths very frequently which run from the bluff to the river.

31st Have passed the forks of the river about two miles. Now on the South Platte. No timber on the river. it is a broad stream rolling its muddy waters through the smooth level plains, nothing to mark its way but a low range of bluffs or sand hills some distance from its edge. Rained again last night.[29]

(June) 2nd Rained all day and turned off very cold in the evening. To day we have lain by because Louisa was very much worse and could not travel. We have washed and got all ready, we hope, to start early in the morning. I feel very sorry for Cousin. She cannot enjoy the journey at all. hope on her account that we may have pleasanter weather — have had a very pleasant day to day. We see some very pretty flowers most every day, prickly pears and an other specimen of cactus with a pretty flower on it. Mr. King brought Louisa one today, in bloom, the first I have seen.[30]

4th Saturday Arrived at the Platte half past one. Blocked up the wagon beds with bones, and what few pieces of timber could be found. got safely across by five O'clock. Some of the blocks came out and so many things got wet, which we had just sunned the day before. We

Gregory M. Franzwa

The braided North Platte River, where Lorena's company camped the night of June 4, 1853.

were half an hour crossing the river, which I suppose was nearly one mile wide.³¹ It commenced raining while we were crossing, and about dark poured down so that all the wagons and tents leaked sadly. many things got wet. we could hardly manage to sleep dry. In the midst of our troubles five strangers were to be lodged. Four had left a train on account of hard treatment, and were packing through without a tent, for what reason I did not learn. The other man had been out Buffalo hunting and could not reach his train. This morning it is more pleasant, and we are all safe, and sound I believe, through the night's troubles. I dont see how the men keep so well as they do, all having got very wet yesterday.³² We camped two miles from the river (South Platte). The country is quite hilly as far as we have come. We go to the North Platte to day.

Evening.   Travelled over high rolling plains until ascending a rise when a sight quite gratifying to us met our view. An expanse of rugged sterile hills was immediately before us, on, some distance, was Ash Hollow in which we could see green trees once more. On beyond the Hollow lay the broad bosom of the North Platte. While the wagons were passing round the ridge to descend the steep point we took a path

The first gut-wrenching obstacle on the trail was a downhill plunge into Ash Hollow. It is near the point where the wagons reached the North Platte River.

The trail is shown here along the top of the ridge. It is about to go over the edge of Windlass Hill and down into Ash Hollow.

The first of the great, uniquely shaped rocks encountered by the emigrants is Courthouse Rock, south of Bridgeport, Nebraska.

down a hollow which cut off much of the distance to Ash Hollow. It was a great treat to run over the rocks and down the crevices and to pluck a few new species of flowers. There is a creek meandering down Ash Hollow, and a few low stunted ash trees are scattered along, from which it derives its name — ledges of rocks and hills enclose it. We have camped at its mouth on the North Platte.[33]

Sunday 5th Traveled by bold rugged bluffs & over very sandy roads most of the day. A tree, or even a rock, is quite a relief to the traveler after traveling over many miles of country where the eye can rest upon no object but grass. Although the road has not been near so good, yet I have, and could have enjoyed the scenery much more if it had not been so very windy. The wind has turned to the west and we have a prospect of having a fair night, which we have not had for a long time. The river is a broad, beautiful stream, not a tree along it banks to day. There is emigration both sides. We can count ten trains this evening on the other side of the river.[34]

7th About one Oclock came in sight of Courthouse rock & Chimney rock. Camped opposite the first. It is a very pretty rock. The top when first seen resembles the cupola of a courthouse. It is on an elevation and looks some like an old antique castle. There is another singular rock

Another "singular rock," next to Courthouse, was named, predictably, "Jail Rock."

very near it as if it were a gate or a part of a wall which had been left standing after the rest had been torn down. Chimney rock from here puts one in mind of Pompey's piller somewhat.[35]

June 8th & 9th North Platte

Noon. Took dinner nearly oppsite Chimney rock. After dinner, rode out to it. It is said to be five miles from the road. The base is shaped like a cone from which issues the chimney, or straight shaft which is ninety feet high. The base and shaft together are three hundred feet high, it is said. I ascended to the shaft and had a hard climb of it. The summit seems cracked and looks as if in danger of falling at any moment. It is nothing but hard clay — scarcely any rock to support it, and liable to be washed by all rain storms. We all thought we would hardly run the risk of ascending it again. There were many names written on it but they become obliterated by the rain.[36] Camped this evening between two indian camps, tents made of Buffalo skin, nearly a

Chimney Rock is now only a fraction of its old self. The spire towered to about five times this height in Lorena's day. Lorena was one of many emigrants who climbed the cone to the base of the spire.

National Park Service

Sand hills rim the valley of the North Platte, as shown in this William H. Jackson painting.

dozen children close by the wagon where I am writing wanting to trade beads for bread. Some very fancifully trimmed off in beads. They are very friendly and want sugar and bread — shake hands, look at our dresses, and examine our finger rings.[37]

Thursday, 9th Walked this morning until we came to a collection of wigwams. They are buffalo skins sewed together, the smooth side out, supported by poles crossing at the top, a place being left in the center for the smoke to ascend. The squaws were dressing buffalo skins, drying meat. One Indian wanted to sell me some moccsins last night, said they were at his wigwam and that he would bring them in the morning, pointing to the west, and then to east to make me understand that he would bring them when the sun had risen as he could not talk any English. He kept his word, came and took his seat, looked at all of us, then pointing to one of us showed his moccasins wishing to know which one had enquired for them the night before. He thought I was the one, but I had changed my dress some, and he was not quite sure at first. They did not fit & I thought he felt disappointed. We gave him some biscuits which pleased him very much. This is the Sioux tribe. We came through a most beautiful valley today, leaving Scotts bluffs to the right. The valley was surrounded by bold bluffs and hills dotted over with cedars and pines. The high rocks are of various shapes giving plenty of scope for fancy to build old castles, walls, domes, &c. The valley was fifteen miles in length but looked as if one might soon walk from one end to the other in a short time. We often get very much deceived in reckoning distances. Objects appear much nearer than they really are. There was a cool spring at the end of the valley where we all got a good drink, after which we drove over the hill into another valley where we camped, two miles from the spring. Just before we stopped, came to a pretty mound-like hill over which ran a pretty path worn by travellers. On the top is a soft rock on which are cut many names. We left our initials, several of us who ascended.[38]

Fort Laramee

J[une] 11th Sunday — arrived in the forenoon at Larimee Fork. Started at sunrise. Had pretty roads and country. There are a great number of wagons here, all placed in close together, in rows, one behind another, an alley and then another row of wagons.[39]

12th Stayed here last night. I was quite amused last night after getting to bed, listening to people talking. It put me in mind of a city, only our wagons answering for houses, and being so much nearer together, no one could talk without being heard by a good many of his neighbors — have been writing letters to put in the office at the Fort. It has a pret-

Many emigrant diarists mentioned Scotts Bluff, and most likened the sandstone and clay formation to European castles.

Many emigrants threaded their way through Mitchell Pass, but Lorena's company took an alternate route leading over Robidoux Pass.

More than 500 wagons were here, at Laramie Fork, awaiting ferry service when Lorena's train rolled up. A bridge had washed out a week or two earlier.

National Park Service

William Henry Jackson depicted the adobe Fort Laramie. From here, on June 14, 1853, Lorena could see snow on the summit of Laramie Peak, in the background.

Gregory M. Franzwa

This sight would have greeted Lorena upon her visit to Fort Laramie. "Old Bedlam," the officers' quarters built in 1851, is in the foreground.

ty appearance from here, is just opposite us. We expect to cross today. I wish to visit the fort— do not know how it will be.[40]

13th Crossed the river, visited the Fort. It is most beautifully situated. There is one quite pretty house, the officers' quarters. The mud wall, or battery, I should think but a poor defense — We went to the post office. No letters. Mail came in just as we started. We could not wait. I was sorry. Mail passed us to day for Salt Lake.[41]

Black Hills

Tuesday, June 14th Started early, pleasant morning. Stopped at the warm springs. The water is so clear and sparkling, not so warm as to be unpleasant to drink. Brought some along to drink.[42] Came up a pretty hill from it; on a pretty eminence was a grave. Crossed Muddy, or bitter cotton wood creek, quite a number of times — It is a pretty stream — the largest cotton wood trees we have passed in a long while. Camped near the creek and in full view of Larimee peak. I just asked Uncle how far off it is. He says he has not a doubt but it is 30 miles. I was very much astonished, it does not look more than five or six miles from us. This morning I thought it only a few miles. it did not seem as though any thing intervened between us and the mountain, yet we have traveled toward it, and come over the hills and through deep valleys. Snow is visible on its summit.

15th The summit was enveloped in clouds. Had a much better view of it after traveling a few hours. The snow appeared in large quantities.

National Park Service

The wagon trains pulled away from the North Platte River forever when they came abreast of Red Buttes, southwest of present-day Casper, Wyoming. William H. Jackson saw the formation in 1866.

Came by a small rivulet, then over steep hills. pretty valley off to the right with pines scattered over it. roads very hilly. crossed cotton wood creek, a beautiful, cold mountain stream, running swiftly, one or two other pretty little streams, and a very long hill to ascend. I do not know why these are denominated Black hills, except it be on account of the pitch, and yellow pine on some of them which at a distance gives them a very dark somber appearance .[43] One of the men killed a buffalo this afternoon. Have gone with horses to bring a piece

June 16th Thursday ["Wednesday" was crossed out and "Thursday" inserted here] We have camped in a pretty place this evening, mountains off to the left, a fine view off to the right toward Platte River, and in front as far as the eye can see.

16th Very hilly road, river and hill road came together in the fore-noon. Crossed many pretty streams. Big timber creek for one. This afternoon came over red hills.[44] The road is a very red found various pretty flowers, some flax, and large white ones resembling tulips. on the campground is beautiful bunches of mountain moss, its snow-white flowers contrasting prettily with the red ground. The first I discovered was on Chimney rock.

Saturday 18th   Passed yesterday, Boisse creek and some pretty springs. one was delightful, the water dripped out of ledges of rocks. Took dinner two days under shade trees, which was very delightful as it was the first since we have traveled. To day have not been travelling. Stopped to rest the cattle. Some trees and a spring near us. We travel this afternoon.

Deer Creek North Platte Bridge[45]

19th Came to Deer creek, crossed came up it half a mile and camped last night. It is quite a pretty stream. A great many camped on it last evening. To day is Sunday. We do not travel this forenoon. We came to the N. Platte a little while before coming to Deer creek. it is much narrower and far more meandering than before the Larimee Fork emptied into it. A few clumps of pretty trees are scattered along its banks which gives it quite a romantic appearance. We have travelled about five days since leaving Fort Larimee, and before coming on to the river have had, most of the way, rough hilly road, but good water and plenty of wood. I have been delighted with the flowers. We find new varieties almost every day, none very large or gaudy, but pretty, delicate mountain flowers, ever cheering and welcome to the heart of the weary traveler. There are quite enough to afford interest, and pleasure for many a leisure hour. We are just going to see a tree, in the top of which is an indian buried. Our tree proved not to have an indian in it. There were only buffalo skins and sticks fastened up in the tree. Some thought one had been buried and others not.[46]

North Platte bridge

21st We had not travelled far yesterday before word came to us, from the back, that Louisa was worse. We supposed was fainting, but they soon said she was dying, and before we could get back from our wagons to the buggy she was gone. Poor girl! She hoped to get to California before she should die, but it was her lot to have to lie alone on these sandy plains, a sad lot indeed, and a hard thing for her parents to bear. We prepared her for the cold grave. Came on to the bridge where Mr. King had come to prepare a coffin. We could only get a rough one made as there were no tools to work with. This morning a grave was dug on the opposite side of the river where we followed her to her lonely resting place. A dreary place, to one of her sensitive feelings. She has often remarked that she wondered why people did not bury their friends under a tree when they could, or in some prettier place than by the roadside or where it was sandy & barren, but, poor girl! we were obliged to lay her where there is no tree or flower to shade her grave from the scorching rays of the sun. The ground was too low this side the river where there were a few trees, and her father thought it best to bury her near the bridge where there is a small cluster of huts, and tents. We wished to procure some rose bushes or ceder to plant on her grave, but cannot get any cedar and roses would hardly grow in so sandy a spot. She was very fond of roses. I carried her a bunch the night before she died, when she said, "O! I do like them so well." This was the last time I saw or spoke with her. We little thought she would die so soon. She had time to speak only with her father who was with her. Her last words were, "O! Pa, what does hurt me so"? Her pain only lasted a moment for she ceased to breathe. We cross the river in the morning.[47]

North Platte

Thursday 23   Crossed the North Platte yesterday morning. Some got out to look at Louisa's grave. The men had brought from the mountains a spruce bush which the girls placed at the head of the grave. We had to leave her in her lonely resting place, where no friend will ever be near to look upon her grave, perhaps, again. Her father had promised her that if she died on the plains he would send a tomb-stone to mark the place of her repose.[48] We came a few miles up the river when the road separated, one keeping up the river, the other which we took, passing over the hills by the willow springs which we hoped to reach last night, but could not. This morning started at sunrise, without breakfast, on account of poor water, which we did not like to use or have the cattle drink. Breakfasted at the spring. The trees have all been cut down for wood — We used sage brush last night and this morning, which makes very good stove wood. This morning camped near Fish creek where we use the same fuel, have not struck the river again, but think we are not far from it, the bluffs or mountains on its right bank appearing quite near and in plain view.

June 24th Since crossing Deer creek they have become very high and snow appears in some places which with their ruggedness gives them a very picturesque appearance. They are nearly covered in some places with large pine and spruce, luxuriant grass growing upon the slopes. I have just been reading Colonel Fremonts account of his travels, on his exploring expedition in 1842.[49] He has been very accurate in recounting almost every daily incident, and in noting all astronomical, botanical and geological variations, which renders his work truly interesting. This puts me in mind that I have, in my hurry, forgotten to put down some little incidents which I thought to have done. One day, the other side of Fort Larimee, we saw a very large train of Sioux moving. They fasten their long wigwam poles to their ponies something as

Dennis Chapman

The opposite (north) bank of the North Platte River is the location of the grave of Louisa E. Lithgrow. Richard (Reshaw) Bridge crossed at this point. It is in Evansville, just east of present-day Casper, Wyoming.

the shafts of a carriage are fastened to horses. Across these, and on the horses' backs are placed all of their baggage and babies, the squaws going before and leading the ponies, while the men ride on hourseback without saddles or bridles except a sort which they make of buffalo skins without bits. They are, some of them, dressed very fancifully in gay colored blankets and deer skin leggings and moccasins tastefully embroidered with beads and fringe. Some of the men, and most of the children, are often quite naked. In the train were dogs trotting along carrying loads in the same manner as the horses. They look more like wolves than dogs, but seem to have lost their wolfish propensities and follow along in the family circle very domestic like. One poor dog seemed to have too heavy a load and laid down howling most piteously — no one seemed to notice him while passing, and at last he got up and followed on again. Two or three squaws were walking together, one of whom has a red and white parasol holding over her head. We supposed her to be the chief's wife as she had on a deerskin dress fringed around the skirt, which was cut in large points or scallops, and very heavily embroidered with differently colored beads. A cape trimmed similarly hung over the shoulders. A pretty pony, which one of them was leading, was also very finely trimmed with beads, on which was placed a prettily painted skin basket and other etcetra which, I suppose, belonged to her indian majesty. The deer skin dress mentioned above, of which I have seen several, with pretty moccasins, make a very pretty, romantic robe-like dress, and exhibits much native taste and female ingenuity, which, with all the drudgery and rough work they have to perform, they still find time to cultivate, always paying much more attention to the dress of their husbands and sons than their own. We have heard it said that the Sioux boast of never having shed a white mans blood. This I doubt the truth of very much. I think if a fit opportunity offered, their savage propensity would exhibit itself. Mother and I were walking before the teams some distance, when two or three rode towards us. I supposed they would pass by us without notice, but as they came very close and reined their horses immediately toward us, I stepped out of the road, at the same time watching one who had a tomahawk in his hand, which he seemed to shelter under his blanket. He salauted us with "How do do", and as I stepped out of the road followed after me giving me a very savage look. I continued stepping away and told him to leave. He soon ceased to follow me, smiled and rode on. I suppose he wished to frighten me seeing that I looked rather timid, but I did not like the strange, wild expression of his countenance, and since then I have felt more aversion to their presence than before. I have, since leaving the fort, heard that these Sioux have had a skirmish with the whites in reference to the ferry boat, the indians claiming one which the emigrants had built.[50]

Sweet water June 24th

Friday This evening have camped on a beautiful, swift running creek, an affluent of the Sweet water river. The crystal waters and the bright green pasturage through which it meanders most circuitously, afford a pleasing contrast to the continuous bed of sand through which we traveled all the forenoon, where no vegetation grew save a shrub called Greece-wood, somewhat resembling in its appearance, low Cedar trees. Where there were no roots to support it the sand had blown away leaving small mounds and ridges covered over with this abundant sand-loving shurb. About noon we struck the Sweet water near Independance rock, below which there was a broken-looking bridge, and some Crow Indian lodges. above was a ford, about a half mile, to which our train drove, where they stopped for dinner. Some of us left the wagons and walked to Independance rock while they were passing round. We passed over it, and came to the wagons above it. In

Mort Sumberg

The Sweetwater River rushes through the 400-foot-deep cleft in the Devil's Gate, six miles west of Independence Rock.

approaching it, its appearance does not strike the eye as anything wonderful, the granite hills surrounding it being much higher than it is, but as one ascends and surveys its huge mass, its immensity fills one with wonder. It stands all alone surrounded by a pretty green level bottom of the river, it passing near the south end of the rock.[51]

Sweet water

June 25th I did not pass around it as I should like to have done in order to have read more names, owing to the Shortness of time, the fatigue in passing over it. Sister and [I] were separated from the others and were hunting a place to get down, when a gentleman with whom we had formed an acquaintance, observed us and came and assisted us down steep places. He owns a train of cattle and a wagon which has received the title of ''Prairie Schooner'' from the oddity of its shape. There is no other one like it and every one distinguishes it by some odd title. In five miles after crossing the river, we came to Devil's Gate. I had not time, or strength to visit it, it being a little distance from the road, but being out of the wagon, we thought to pass over the lower point of the ledge of granite adjoining it. We had a hard climb over the steep rocks, and crevices, but at last got over, and hurried on to the wagons which had quite a distance a head of us. The gate through which the river passes presents a pretty appearance when getting a front view of it. It is an opening in perpendicular rocks, four hundred feet high. Some of our men went to visit it, and in hunting the camp, went the wrong road, so did not get in until this morning. In order to pass off the joke, one of them said that "the keeper of his majesty's gate would not let them pass through, and so they had to go round" which took them much longer. The Artemesia around the point of the rocks near the gate is quite large, being three or four feet high, with tough twisted trunks. It gives to the air a very aromatic scent.[52]

Evening Camp This morning was a bright, pleasant one, but as we proceeded, the wind rose to a steady gale, and as yesterday, blew the sand into our faces so that we could see but little. The dryness of the air, and sand, caused parched lips and sore eyes which are not very agreeable. One of the men is nearly blind to day. Our course lay up the river over a sterile, sandy plain where the artemesia has usurped the place of the grass. To the right, and on the left bank of the Sweet water extends a high ridge of granite, sterile and bare, save where a few hardy pines have succeeded in procuring a scanty growth up along in the crevices of rock. The summits of this high wall are broken and rugged. One, more elevated, is dominated Devil's Peak. Indeed he seems to have quite an extended line of fortifications along here. To the left of our road extends a range of dark mountains on which spots of snow are often visible. The valley between appears green, and at the foot of the mountains and bordering on the river, perhaps might be found luxuriant grass, but between lays a wide, sandy and sterile waste, only producing sufficient nourishment for the artemisia and sage, excluding every thing else. The scenery is, as Fremont says, highly picturesque, the bold, high hills of granite on the one side, on the other the mountains in the smoky distance, and in front an open valley of green, undulating ridges. We have just had a pleasant shower which has left the air cool and refreshing and free from the sand which has been such an annoyance to us. Can see Wind river Mts.[53]

Sweet water

26th, Sabbath The morning was clear and pleasant. continued so until noon, wind raised, sand became very deep, and blew about so that it became nearly suffocating. One of the oxen gave out and fell down. We came near the rim this afternoon where it seemed entirely shut up by the high ridges of rock. We left it to the right. Came through a gap or gully in the hills, found some poor grass and camped. Sand.

Artemisia and mosquitos in plentiful abundance and the only characteristics of the camp ground.[54]

27th Wind high, and extremely cold, constantly blowing from the west. roads not quite so sandy. We seem to be gradually ascending toward the dividing ridge between the waters of the Pacific and the Atlantic.[55]

28th Morning cold and clear, wind still very high, coming directly from wind river mountains where snowy peaks glistened in the morning's sunbeams like huge drifts of snow. We have encamped on the banks of the Sweet water, and are again going to cross at noon. There is a pretty green bottom with sloping hills on either side. The stern black granite hills of rock have quite disappeared. Snowy peaks are still in full view, in the distance before us. if the weather was warm it would be very gratifying to look upon them, but as cold as it is, it seems as if we were about to enter the regions of perpetual cold where Old Father Winter himself forever sits upon his ice gemmed throne, commanding the snow and winds that fitfully chase each other through his hoary locks, or quietly nestle down in some icy crevice as smiles of sunshine light up each snow flake, that is mirrored like diamonds, in some mountain lake in its rock bound shore, so quietly resting in undisturbed tranquility in the mountain valley below.[56]

29th [Prospect Hill] Yesterday evening after coming over quite a long hill and rock ledge the face of the country became more rugged. To day we have come over a succession of seemingly inclined planes, sometimes over rocky ledges of granite, and sometimes trap rock. Crossed a small creek, along which was snow. also crossed one stream, one of the headwaters of the Sweet water coming down from the mountains, along which was a pretty green valley. Came over a long hill and camped in a large valley, seemingly almost at the foot of the snow capped mountains which lay in full view north west of us and Table Rock to the south west. On the hills several varieties of pretty mosses have appeared, and other flowers are scattered over hill and vale in gay profusion. Several ponds of milky colored water were passed by, of which they would not let the cattle drink, thinking they contained too much alkali. Some indians on pack horses passed us of the — [name of tribe not given]. The wind has moderated, leaving a cool, refreshing mountain breeze which is truly invigorating.

South Pass

1853 June 30th Thursday The air is still very cool, but weather clear and pleasant, the country beautiful undulating plains. We have crossed all three forks of the Sweet water which has its source north of us in Wind river mountains, whose tops we have seen for several days

Mort Sumberg

Two abandoned cabins and acres of rushes mark the still-flowing Pacific Spring, the first water west of the continental divide.

glittering like towering peaks of crystal, about six thousand feet above us. We have encamped immediately in the South pass, almost or quite on the dividing ridge between the waters of the Atlantic and Pacific, seven thousand, five hundred feet above the Gulf of Mexico. We have reached this mountain height by gradual ascent over good roads generally, and to day especially the most beautiful, hard, smooth and wide, resembling well graded roads in the states, and although now on the summit of the great range of Rocky mountains, have had to climb no rugged steeps or mountainous ascents, but have reached it by one long gradual ascent, almost imperceptibly coming into the region of perpetual snow. Grass is scarce and artemisia is still the prevailing plant. To the south of us is Table rock and mountain with green sloping sides — north is the range of Wind river mountains, the highest of the Rocky mountains in which the Colorado, Columbia, Missouri and Platte rivers have their source. We are in latitude 42 and nearly a half degree North, longitude 109 and about a half degree West Longitude. Three or four miles to the west are the Pacific Springs where we strike the head waters of Green river, and after which we no long see any waters flowing to the Atlantic — indeed we bid adieu to the last to day.[57]

Big Sandy

July 1 Morning cold and slightly rainy. A few miles after leaving the pass came to the Pacific Spring, head of one of the tributaries of the Green river. The road has been slightly descending, very smooth and hard. I never saw a more beautiful road. The plains are covered with low scrubby artemisia which always exclusively occupies a dry sandy soil. We have taken the rout to Salt lake, leaving another road to north of us.[58] We have encamped upon a large level plain, surrounded mostly by what appears to be elevated, detached table lands, which in the smoky distance toward the setting sun, give an air of obscure and romantic cast to the scenery. East of us rise in lofty grandeur, the snow peaks of the wind river chain of the Rocky mountains — a little south of them, the barren, rocky summits of Table mountain are a prominent object of interest. We met eight or ten mule and horse teams in full drive, from Salt lake, we supposed, which is a novel incident to us, almost.

July 5th

J 2nd Day pleasant — roads still excellent, and plains level and uninteresting, covered with nothing but artemisia, which has no resembalance to sage, save in color and form of the shrub. The forenoon in the dim, smoky distance we could see white and dark blue lines of mountains stretching far away in the distance, as far, almost, as the eye could reach. Crossed the little Sandy. Came to Big Sandy and encamped three oclock on its little green grassy bottom, the willow and a few other bushes giving quite a welcome and refreshing appearance to us after travelling so long in sand, and I experienced quite domestic and homelike feelings in picking gooseberries for supper. The mountains on the east have a more extended and lofty appearance to day than heretofore. Until yesterday morning passed over the same parched, sandy, grassless prairie, when we crossed Green river — it is pretty well timbered, but not much grass on its bottom. The ferry is owned by mormons, ferriage six dollars per wagon.[59] After crossing we came up the river about two miles, where we encamped upon a pretty, grassy bank near some trees, after which we prepared our *Fourth of July* dinner, all of the train joining and setting a long table on the green grass. We were quite delighted with our success in getting the dinner, having a much greater variety in the way of eatables than we could have anticipated, having quite a number of kinds of cake, preserves, pies, butter, cheese, sauce, rice, beans, susages, ham, biscuit, tea, coffee, &c Just at night they killed a veal, but not in time for our celebra-

The trail leading from present-day Farson, Wyoming, to the Green River.

tion which we should have liked. All seemed to be in good spirits, and I think enjoyed themselves quite as well as if at home, and indeed, perhaps, relished the dinner better, although the fare was more homely — I dread to leave the green spot we are on, in exchange for the barren, hot and dusty road we shall have to travel over for a few days again before coming to another verdant spot. We meet Californians, on their return to the states occasionally.[60]

Black's fork

6th Cacti has again made their appearance and their gay red and yellow flowers afford quite a relief, scattered here and there among the sage. We have just arrived at Black's fork where we stay a few hours to rest the cattle — it is a considerable stream, no timber save a few shrubs — mosquitos so bad I can hardly write at all. — Evening. Came up the stream. Crossed mountain fork and camped near Blacks fork, (I suppose) where we were met with myriads of mosquitoes. We had to fight constantly and then could not keep them off. After dark they became less annoying.[61]

7th To day crossed another stream called [blank] raining a little this evening. The weather has been hot and sultry for a few days.

National Park Service

William H. Jackson's painting of Fort Bridger, on the Black's Fork.

8th travelled all day without coming to water until this evening, where we encamped upon a swift running stream with banks fringed with several kinds of willow, currant bushes and some trees. I think it is called muddy fork of green river. We had a cool, pleasant breeze from Salt lake mountains which are immediately before us. The scenery is quite picturesque, and we might enjoy a cool retreat upon the green banks of the stream so wildly rushing by us, if it were not that we are annoyed by the mosquitoes. perhaps after dark they will cease their depredations as they do generally when the air becomes cooler. Some Utah indians, on their ponies, are in camp with whom our folks are amusing themselves, in trying to make trades with them. I have seen no indians yet that any advantage could be taken off in a trade. On the contrary, they generally want much more than the worth of any article, besides they think the whites duty bound to give them bread, sugar, &c.

10th Did not travel yesterday, but spent the day washing — in the morning we were awakened by the singing of birds, and the music of running water. The evening was pleasant and as I listened to the sub-duing tones of the violin, my heart stole from the quiet, green retreat, back to other days and scenes. Started pretty early this morning, left fort Bridger in a few miles, to the left, situated in a pretty green valley, through which the stream ran — our road became more hilly, and dwarf cedars grow plentifully on some of the hills. Mr. B. went to some

This is the view seen by Brigham Young and others of the Mormon pioneers in the summer of 1847, as they came down Emigration Canyon to behold the valley of the Great Salt Lake. The scene has been recreated by William H. Jackson.

snow, and brought us some, which we were very glad to have to put in some water as the day has been very warm. just after noon, passed over a high plateau covered with grass and surrounded by hills and snow covered mts., after which we descended a long hill into valley, crossed a pretty stream, camped in a pretty spot enclosed by hills.[62]

Salt lake mountains

11th Had a storm of wind and rain last evening, and slight rain this evening just before camping. A shower seems to be of daily occurence in these mountains, as in those east of the Rocky mountains. Our road has been highly picturesque to day. We are constantly descending or ascending hills, some of which are partly covered with cedars, service berry bushes and others with beautiful cotton wood groves. The day has been bright and pleasantly cool. We have passed beautiful springs of cool water — near one was another of Soda water. Crossed Bear river this evening. It is a swift cold stream here running to the north through a deep green valley. Along its banks are some pretty cotton wood trees, and its islands and banks fringed with willows.[63]

13th Yesterday traveled over hills, through deep valleys covered in many places with blue flax and good grass. Two of our men left us night before last, taking some bread and bacon — I suppose they were dissatisfied about something. To day our road has wound through a deep canon (kenyon).[64] A purling stream passes down the canon overhung with willow, currant and gooseberry bushes. Luxuriant grass lies at the foot of high, steep hills and rocky precipices that rise on either side of us to a great height. In some places the grass quite resembles a field of wheat, being higher than our heads, and of a kind that is called wild rye. The canon is twenty-two miles long, and every few rods a spring arises out of the ground by the road side, or gushes from the rocks. The great number of times that the creek has to be crossed, and the rivulets from the springs render the road a little bad and troublesome, but the weather is pleasant and the scenery wild and picturesque. It is said that we cross the creek nineteen times. We have crossed it a great many times today, and are not yet out of the canon, as we camped at three oclock, being now shut up mid high hills on every side of us. To the right up are high precipices of rock, composed of gravel and sand, or rather pebbles imbedded or mingled with sand, which have become hardened together, making a conglomerate rock.[65]

G.S.L. mountains[66]

14th Soon after starting this morning the Canon became narrower, the rocks bolder and overhanging. The stream found its way through over hanging willows, the whole bottom being occupied with them, through which G.S.L. mountains the road was cut. Roses & hops clambered up the tall willows, and some oak bushes grew at the foot of the rocks, the first I have seen. The high walls of the Canon are composed entirely of a red looking rock. on the left hand they are formed into high, bold hills, covered with grass and groves of small cotton wood which gives them a very green, fresh appearance. After a few miles we came to a large stream and a high wall running transversely, which proved to be another canon running a contrary course down which we came a short distance, crossed the river, called Weber river, and camped opposite the mouth of another canon which we enter in the morning. Saw a few poor looking habitations along the stream which is well timbered with cotton wood, willow, currant and rose bushes form a thick fringe along its banks.[67]

15th All day our road has lain through canons (kenyons), deep and narrow, so that the road has been very bad indeed — We have passed through some pretty groves of Quaking asp and others of cottonwood, one this afternoon was the thickest timber we have passed through since starting. The streams of water have had to be crossed many times, and are always shaded with a thick growth of willows, gooseberrys, roses &c. Beautiful springs have been innumerable, which with the rushing creeks and rivulets give a cool and inviting appearance to a traveller over these dusty roads. The nights are very cool and days warm. We have hardly room to camp to night, and the cattle have been driven up another hollow in order to get any feed.

16th Our road has been terrible to day. We ascended through a long Canon, with scarce room enough for the road to the summit of a hill, where we had a most splendid view of the mountains this side of Salt Lake valley, which we have yet to pass through, and a glimpse of the valley, and mountains beyond. In the (kenyon) we passed through groves of spruce pine, whose tall, regular spires, make it a beautiful tree. We also found some new flowers, a beautiful large white honeysuckle I thought very splendid. The hill was very long to descend, and we are encamped in a pretty open space, or valley in the Canon, surrounded by high peaks, which are covered with luxurient vegetation, as all the mountains we have passed to day have been. Gooseberry bushes almost entirely cover whole sides of peaks. In the valley, a family have a temporary residence, in order to sell vegetables out of a small garden they have penned in. There is also a small haystack close by, made from grass cut in the valley. The lady was at our camp a few minutes since, and told us she lived in Salt lake city which is only twelve miles distant, but bad roads yet to pass over. A very long hill is in sight.[68]

19th Yesterday morning left camp, ascended the hill, decended through a long canon, called Emigrant canon, and shortly after hove in sight of Salt lake city.[69] It is situated in a large valley surrounded by mountains. The valley looks tolerably green and luxuriant, but the hills or mountains have a dry, sterile appearance. The city is large, but no where closely crowded, and laid off very regularly. It is well watered by streams from the mountains which are turned so as to have a pretty little brook running each side of the street, and crossing each other as do the streets. The houses are generally small and built of sun burnt brick, looking like lead colored houses. There are a few trees along one of the mountain streams passing through the city. Save these and a few small ones planted along some of the squares, there are none in sight. The gardens are filled with vegetables, and have a luxuriant appearance, being watered by the streams, there being little rain ever. Wood is very scarce, fences being built of erth and poles which look very insufficient,

The Salt Lake Cutoff went north from the city, around the northeast shoulder of the lake, heading toward the California Trail out of old Fort Hall. This view is near the junction.

but seem to answer every purpose. The city has a neat, quiet appearance, and must be healthy. The river Jordan is in sight on the east side of the city.[70] After passing through the city we came to some warm springs. They were large, and beautifully clear, leaving a bright green deposit underneath, but they have a nauseating smell and taste. Near them and into which they empty, is a small lake called Hot Springs lake. From Utah lake, through this, or near, runs the river Jordan which empties into Salt lake, which is in sight to day. It is beautifully clear and calm. the silvery clouds are resting upon all the mountain tops that circle around us, and the sky above is of a beautiful deep blue, and the valley has a peaceful, tranquil secluded appearance and looks as if one might enjoy quiet rest away away from the busy world. There are large, golden fields of grain on the opposite side of the river.[71]

21st We have passed through a large thriving neighborhood. The farms are regularly laid off, lanes passing between each, and purling little brooks running along each fence and through the fields. Ditches are dug and the dirt thrown up, a few poles placed on top for fences. The houses look very neat and comfortable, gardens luxuriant, and indeed every thing bears an aspect of industry and propensity. People are just harvesting, and have promise of an abundant supply of the staff of life. Only a few years since this great and beautiful valley was a waste wilderness, over which roamed the indolent Savage. Its mysterious waters, so quietly resting in their mountain encircled home were visited

The "Twin Sisters" are the sentinels which stand at the junction of the Salt Lake and Fort Hall roads to California.

alone by him, and he ascended the arid mountain tops to view this broad expanse of of beautiful lake, and prairie. And now the busy hum of civilized life is every where heard, the reapers song, the cradler wheating his scythe, the ratling of wagons and the lowing of cattle. And instead of the narrow winding indian trails, innumberable broad, smooth roads checker the valley, and wind their way up the mountain sides and along lake shores.

G.S.L. valley July

23rd Crossed Weber river yesterday and passed Ogden City.[72] To day passed some large salt springs, so hot we could not hold our hands in more than a moment. There was a copperas colored desposit in the springs, and upon the ground. We will pass farms and houses. got some vegetables last evening, which were quite a treat. Had a wind storm last evening and are having one at present with a few drops of rain and thunder. I do not see much prospect of supper unless it ceases soon. Mother and sister unwell to day.

24th Sunday A very hard hail storm this afternoon. We have seen most beautiful grass most all day and are camped amid a large ocean of it, clear of woods and very fine and good.

[27th has been crossed out] Crossed Bear river 25th. It has deep banks, here, on timber, and runs slow, having quite lost it mountain character. Found a cold spring yesterday morning and last evening came to Blue Springs. The water is warm and does not taste very good. A few days since the other side of Blue Springs we came [upon] some springs, all within a few yards of each other, one being hot, another warm and another cold. They were all of different mineral quality, some very salt. The cold one nearly pure, and the hottest ones of a disagreeable taste and smell. We have left the beautiful valley of Salt Lake. The mountains have not yet assumed the ruggedness they had the other side of the valley, but are smoother, with large valleys between.[73]

29th Day before yesterday took dinner at Hensly's Springs — a pretty, cool and large spring — at night camped on Deep creek. Yesterday nooned and spent four or five hours at the sink, and at night after dark camped at Pilot Springs.[74] Water is quite scarce since leaving Bear river, it being generally between six and ten miles between watering places — the weather is very warm, and roads dusty, grass generally good. Sage plenty in places and some cedar, the trees hanging full of light green berrys, forming a pretty contrast to the dark green leaves.

31st Day pleasantly cool. Started from Decasure Creek this morning. nooned near City rocks where the F.H. and G.S.L. roads meet and camped tonight near Mountain Spring. Night before last we camped on Stamp Creek, a beautiful, swift, mountain stream, the water most excellent. This morning, several of us crossed over the creek from the camp to pick currants. before Sister returned back to camp the train had started, but as they had to cross the creek about a mile above, we concluded to keep on that side. While walking along the creek, and about a quarter of a mile from the train, we met an indian, armed with gun, and bow and arrows. We were some what frightened,

Thomas H. Hunt

Wagons proceeding down Goose Creek left a deep and lasting trail.

but found it of no use to avoid him. we walked boldly up, and shook hands "how-de-do". He asked quite readily for some clothing. I directed him to wagons, but he passed on not seeming inclined to go to them, or daring to harm us. We were quite relieved when he left us, as he did not appear any too respectful.[75]

Goose Creek

1st of August,   Came from Mountain Spring to Steep Hill creek, road over hilly, thence to Goose Creek on which we are encamped for the rest of the day. The country has a very rugged, mountaineous appearance.[76]

3rd Staid last night at the head of Goose Creek. The water was bad, so we started before breakfast, found some water off of the road and

Thomas H. Hunt

The ruts are still sharp and deep in Thousand Springs Valley.

stopped at ten oclock and got breakfast. Grass is becoming very scarce. Road very rough and hilly. Stopped to night at Rock spring.[77] Three strangers staying with us tonight.

5th   Camped last night on an Alkali creek, which we had to use. Passed some very warm springs to day and are now staying a few hours not far from them. Uncle has been back a few days hunting some cattle — we wonder why he does not overtake us and are afraid some accident has happened him. This valley (Thousand Spring valley) very much resembles G.S.L. Valley.[78] Uncle has just arrived.

August 7th   Encamped yesterday, a little after noon on the headwaters of Mary's river. Staid until to day noon, since which we have come through a narrow rock Kanyon. The road was very bad part of the way. Far, far away in civilized lands church bells have been sending forth their Sabbath peals, and sober, church going people have been wending their way peacefully, and quietly to the house of worship, and devout worshippers have held solemn and happy communion with their Maker. Blooming, and happy maidens, have beheld the glance of approbation cast upon them by manly and perchance ardent admirers. Sabbath-School children have joyously looked into the faces of their kind teachers for the ever ready look of approbation which accompanies good lessons, and appropriate conduct. Ministers have tried faithfully to discharge their high and solemn duties, and many can peacefully rest their heads upon a quiet pillow, feeling that a day has not been spent in vain, while the Emigrant has been slowly wending his way over dusty roads, or through winding, rock walled kenyons. A few, perchance, have thought it necessary to stop and try to hallow this day which God has commanded to be one of rest, but most are inclined to content themselves with the idea that it is quite *necessary* to travel all, or at least a part of the Sabbath. We are encamped upon a little creek coming through the kanyon, and leading to Mary's or Humbolt river. Grass is abundant here, and quite a plain stretches to our right mountains are on our left.[79]

Humbolt river

Aug 8th   Travelled over a beautiful, grass covered bottom through which ran a branch of the Humbolt river. Crossed over one branch coming from the right.[80]

10th   Crossed Humbolt yesterday, and after driving through a most luxuriant field of grass, camped on a pretty stream running into the Humbolt — tried to catch some fish, but there were only a few small ones caught. Started early this morning which was rather cool, and a little after noon camped on another beautiful mountain stream. One or two trout was seen, so we all got our lines and went to the creek, but caught but one or two little fish. We lay by quite often so that the cattle may recuit a little. The dust is still quite bad, with some salaratus on the ground in places, that, or that alkalie, makes our hands and faces chap some, otherwise we have a very pleasant, and easy time generally speaking.

11th   Started early this morning. Crossed five or six most beautiful, crystal clear streams just issuing from Canons and running very swiftly neath a beautiful shade of pretty trees and undergrowth. We have encamped neath the shade of some cottonwoods by a pretty little creek with a white pebbly bed. The road had been rather rough, being near the mountains, some very picturesque ones with snow on them, being just on our left.

16th   After crossing one large beautiful stream we struck off into mountains, travelling over barren sage valleys, over high mountains, and through deep, rough and rocky canons. We found a few springs of water, not much grass, and roads very dusty, and rough. The last weeks travel has been a tedious one. Night before last we struck the river where it passes through a deep Canon. Next morning we passed over some more hills, and came to it again. The valley is wide here, but grass poor. Greece-wood bushes plenty, the soil dry and barren & day very warm. It is now about noon, and we will lay by the rest of the day. Oh! how I wish there was a good spring of cool water, and some shade trees neath which we might rest us once more. The river water is warm and we do not find any more springs. We have most beautiful moonlight nights, also cool and pleasant.

17th Traveled along the river bottom, mostly, to day. The roads are very dusty. We are encamped on a pretty green, near willow bushes growing on a slough, and are having a shower of rain, which is quite a rare thing to us, and for what we have been wishing some time.[81]

Humbolt

18th Mr. Huntly has just met us from California. His wife is in the train. Uncle Henry received a letter from his wife. We also heard from Dr. Baker and Alkire's train. They were in Carson Valley. Smith, a man who left us, was in his train.

20th One of our men has been suddenly taken with reumatics so that he cannot walk scarcely. He came into the train this side of Bear river — seems to be a very good disposed person. The roads have not been so dusty for a day or two — the bottom has been broad and beautiful (within a day or) until this morning, the river passed through a short kenyon, and the road over a ridge. The weather is very pleasant, nights beautiful moonlight, but a little warm. This morning quite a number of cattle were missing, and some alarm was felt lest the indians had stolen them, but they were all found by hunting a few hours. We are encamped on the bank of the river to remain this afternoon, it being Sabbath, and the cattle needing rest and food.[82]

26th Laying by again this forenoon — the roads have been very dusty and sandy, and scarcely grass for the cattle. Some of them have given out, and one or two have died — the weather is very warm. Charlie gets no better of his reumatics which are very painful. I shall be very glad when we get off the Humbolt. We have met a good many men from California who have come to meet trains from the States which they were expecting. Many trains have got into California before this time.

Great Meadows[83]

29th Roads have been bad, dusty and sandy. No grass until last night when we arrived about nine oclock at the commencement of the meadows — little to be seen but a large field of Tules, or bull rushes, which grow very high and large, on the right of us where the river begins to spread over the ground. Otherwise there is nothing to be seen but dry, sandy desert, on which nothing grows but a little sage, or greece wood. Close along the river there is sometimes some bushes growing, which hang very full of a small, sour berry which make very good pies, resembling currant pies. They are called bear berries and are only eatable fruit, growing on the river that I have seen. We had a very pleasant shower, which has lain the dust, and made it cooler this morning.[84]

30th After cutting, and packing some grass in the wagons, to last over the desert, we again started this afternoon, came a few miles and

The brackish Humboldt flows into nothing but the ground. It was at the sink of the Humboldt that Lorena's train prepared for the arduous trek over the Forty-mile Desert.

camped on the only dry, grassy place in sight. there are many dead cattle in sight, and the water has a bad smell. The lake is in sight.[85]

Sept. 3rd After passing the lake which was quite a pretty sheet of water, with a pebbly edge, we followed down the slough, crossed it and then struck out onto the great desert. Traveled all night, nearly. In the morning the cattle were unyoked and drove onto a little dry bunch grass which was found off the road. About three oclock they were drove up and again we started our sandy pilgrimage. Stopped about two oclock on Carson river along which are some trees, I see — have not been down to it, no grass here for the cattle and we expect to go on before breakfast to grass as the cattle are very hungry and weak, quite a number having given out on the desert. There is quite a little village of tents &c here, called Ragtown of California. The weather is cool and windy this morning and last night.[86]

Carson river

4th, Sabbath Came about four miles yesterday, have been here ever since. It is quite a pretty spot — beautiful trees grow on the river, and there is pretty little grassy bottom with willow bushes scattered over it. On the desert about twelve miles the other side of Ragtown, night before last, a man was shot by another with whom he had a little difficulty about a steer. He had his trial last night, or was to have had it. It was supposed he would be hung in Ragtown, where the corpse was to be brought, and the trial to take place. It seems the father and son who shot the young man had but little provocation. The son made his escape.[87] Some of the lame and weak cattle in our train are to be left in the care of one or two hands this morning, while we proceed as usual. We hope to end our journey in two weeks or more.

Carson valley

7th Travelling sandy most of the way. Camped yesterday all day on the river banks Came over a desert of eight miles to day — again on the river — pretty shade trees along its banks.

10th We have at length arrived in Carson valley.[88] It is a pretty valley, though not so extensive as I had supposed, only thirty miles in length. The great Sierra Nevada towers up in front of us over which we shall soon have a toil, and from whose summit we shall take a view of the far-famed gold land, the land of our hopes. O! shall they be realized? Shall we be happier in our new home? It is not its mines of gold, its stores of treasured wealth that can give us happiness, unless we have the "Pearl of great price" in our hearts. If we have not found it, may we seek it earnestly, and Oh! may its sweet influence ever keep our hears pure and free from the numerous temptations that may surround us.

12th For several days we have travelled through the beautiful Carson valley and along the foot of the great Sierra Nevada. The valley is a peaceful, quiet looking place. There is a quite a number of ranches, and vegetables, fresh meat and groceries can be obtained. To night we have camped at or near the mouth of a large canon, near the river which comes foaming over large boulders from the canon.[89]

Sierra Nevada

13 This morning started in the Canon which is eight miles in length, the road filled with large rocks, and hilly. Walked all the way through the canon. We breathe the exhilarating mountain air, look at the towering pines and lofty mountain rocky peaks, and listen to the music of dashing waters, as they fitfully leap, and foam over their rocky beds, and hear the distant sighing and murmuring, and the now nearer loud roaring of the wind as it comes sweeping onward the pine trees, and we scramble over rocks and descend into quiet vales. In the afternoon we immerged from the canon into a pretty valley between two ranges of high mountains, pretty pine trees were scattered over a small, grassy lawn, and a beautiful mountain stream passed through it. The wind is high and cold coming off the snowy range just before us.[90]

14th A beautiful, calm sunny morn dawned on us. The winds seemed to have tired with their increasing play, and have quietly nestled away, to some more sequestered nook or dell, or have politely

California Historical Society, San Francisco

J. Wesley Jones painted this scene, showing one of the corduroy bridges over the Carson River in Carson Canyon.

taken themselves off to their more rightful home, up among the snowy, jagged, wintry peaks above us. After travelling a few miles we came to Red lake with its grassy border, lying just at the foot of the first summit. It was very steep and rocky to ascend, but not very long. In descending, one wagon was turned over — Aunt, and two children were in it, but did not get hurt. We came to a pretty lake, called Deer Lake, just at the foot of the next summit. Here we camped by moonlight, on a pretty green lawn mid the shadows of pinetrees, near the margin of the lake, encircled by snowy mountains — a truly romantic spot. Came 8 or 9 miles, walked it.[91]

15th Cloudy and misty in the morning. rained soon and before we were at the summit, it snowed, rained and blowed. We walked much faster than the teams could ascend. Got very wet and cold while waiting for them. Two wagons were broken, one left. The ascent was long, and difficult. Near the summit we were enveloped in a cloud, so that we could see neither above nor below us. A large snowbank lay

The high walls of the Sierra Nevada hem in the west branch of the Carson River in Carson Canyon.

along our road some distance. Just this side of the summit we became very much frightened, supposing that some of the females had taken a wrong course, and got lost among the rocks, But it was so foggy, they had got on ahead with out our notice, and were found after some little delay, by uncle who went on ahead. We had sent a man in the direction they were supposed to have went, but he soon returned and found us all together. The wind blew very hard, and was cold. We came about four miles, stopped all wet and cold, but got much colder before they got good fires built. The roads have been so bad that we walked all the way — nine or ten miles over mountains, through rain and snow. We have truly had a hard day of it.[92]

Sierra Nevada

16th Cleared off last night, was very cold, morning clear but some cold. The men have returned for the wagon — both will have to be repaired. We shall be detained to day.

18th Over hill and rough road as uual. Walked about twelve miles yesterday. We have left the Sacramento road to the right, and taken the Volcano road.[93] Got a slight view of Sacramento valley and the coast range.

Part 3—The California Years

The California Years 1853-59

T HE BEAUTIFUL IONE VALLEY, surrounded by low, rolling foothills, attracted farmers as well as miners during the early 1850s. Located between two gold-yielding rivers, the Consumnes to the north and the Mokelumne on the south, today it forms part of western Amador County on the edge of California's great Central Valley, close to both the state capital of Sacramento and the port city of Stockton. But when Lorena and her relatives arrived in late September 1853, Amador county did not yet exist. It was created the following May from sections of two adjacent counties, with part of another added three years later.[1]

Even then the Ione Valley portion of the new county remained in the 48,585-acre Arroyo Seco Rancho, a situation easily overlooked by settlers. Many assumed this Mexican land grant must have passed automatically into the public domain either in 1846, when California won independence from Mexico, or in 1850, when statehood was declared. With the "considerable village"of Ione as a focal point for the numerous mining camps nearby, this area of the central goldfields held out promises of a bright future for those who turned its soil, either to mine gold or to plant crops.[2]

According to one report written during the early summer of 1853 and reprinted by an eastern newspaper, the Ione Valley

> may well be called the Paradise of our country. The whole valley comprising several thousand acres is now laid out into farms and is under cultivation. The population is large and rapidly increasing and the Society is excellent. They have erected the finest church in the county, which is well attended, a large portion of the congregation being ladies. In the vicinity of the church there has sprung up a considerable village, with a new saw mill, hotel, stores etc. and village lots are in great demand.[3]

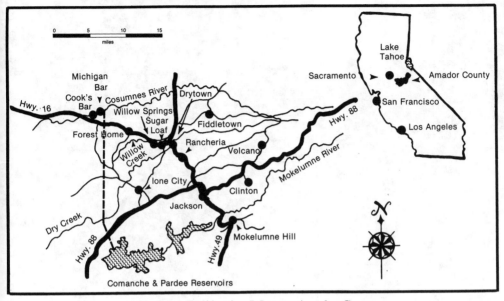

Lorena's California: Western Amador County

Several weeks later two additional reports also described the area where the Woodward, Hays, and Lithgow families decided to settle:

At Ione Valley, Dry Creek Valley and the neighboring ranches the sounds of busy labor are heard around and all is life, energy and exertion. Never before were such luxuriant crops presented to the eye of man. . . . The wheat crop is said to stand over seven feet high [and] the wheat head is six-and-a-half inches long.[4]

Although the Ione and Dry Creek valleys yielded such agricultural rewards to others, farming may have been considered impractical by the Hays women without the help of Lorena's only surviving brother, William Philander Hays, whose whereabouts remained unknown. Supposedly he was still hunting for gold somewhere in the northern mines, but nothing had been heard from him before his mother and sisters began their overland journey. So the six Hays women would have to rely upon their own resources to earn a living in new and different surroundings, although relatives established ranches nearby.

On September 23, as the Woodward-Hays-Lithgow wagon train rolled towards "Dry Town," the oldest mining camp in the hills northeast of the Ione Valley, they found Aunt Sarah Woodward waiting for them. She traveled a short distance up the road in anticipation of an early reunion, something frequently done by those awaiting the arrival of loved ones coming in off the overland trail. She joined the company for the last few miles, through Drytown and four miles farther to a place Lorena identified as "Sarrahsville."[5] The Hays women left the

The Cosumnes River at Michigan Bar, once a thriving gold rush community. This view was taken from the site of the Chinese miners' camp, looking west down the river toward Cooks Bar, where Lorena's mother ran a boarding house in 1854.

train here, "to look around before going elsewhere," while the rest of their party continued on towards Ione, which called itself a "city" in keeping with the booster spirit of the nineteenth century.

The Hays women settled near Dry Creek's north fork, not far from the Cosumnes River. This region had been extensively mined during the initial excitement of 1848 because of its proximity to Coloma, where gold was discovered at Sutter's Mill on January 24. In Lorena's time the Cosumnes River Valley, today considerably changed by subsequent hydraulic mining operations, was half-a-mile wide and sixty to seventy feet below the surrounding countryside. In spring, when the river overflowed, it became twenty to thirty yards wide and twenty feet deep, but during the rest of the year streams and creeks ran dry. So this part of Amador County turned into "dry diggings" without water readily available for washing gold from the soil. One description of the Cosumnes area reported:

> The bars are small & contain the fine gold — small scales, very pure. The hills are sparsely covered with oak & pine trees, the surface soil reddish from furrungenious clay & covered with loose broken pieces of

Streams in the Ione Valley often run dry in mid-summer. The area in the nearby foothills was known as "dry diggings" in the 1850s because water had to be brought in to work the mines.

quartz. The rock exposed here is a bluish slate, the strata standing on edge & showing occasional veins of quartz. No gold has been detected in the flint, though this is supposed to be the Matrix.[6]

Cosumnes gold, considered equal to that found along the Yuba and Feather rivers, was "so fine that we had to use a magnifying glass to see it." Although "small fortunes" of $200-300 a day could be made during the first summer, by the fall of 1849 miners began reporting "indifferent success" along this river, with the exception of Michigan Bar and three "rich placers" on the south fork. Miners believed "the richest diggins" had been "nearly cleaned out . . . although occassionally a man stumbles upon a pocket with thousands in it." But "unbounded richness" supposedly still existed in the "unaccessible deep holes with which the river abounds." In later years the Cosumnes was called, comparatively speaking, "probably the poorest in gold of all the rivers in the mines." Indeed, this part of California rated only a brief mention in accounts of the gold regions written by Hubert Howe Bancroft and Theodore H. Hittle, two of the state's most prominent nineteenth century historians.[7]

Soon after arriving in this gold region, Lorena's mother purchased a small house and prepared to take in boarders as she had done in Illinois. Lorena wished to teach but found no opportunity to resume this career because the nearest school, located in Ione City, employed only one instructor. So, as the eldest daughter, she stayed with the younger ones to help their mother while sisters Caroline and Sarepta found work in two of the many "public houses" which dotted the countryside. These "public houses" were situated at two-to-three-mile intervals along roads leading from Sacramento to the mines and on Sundays "were crowded with people from the City. . . ."[8]

Once Lorena had a roof over her head again she realized how much she missed the freedom of the overland trail. With little to do other than help at the boarding house, she might well have succumbed to ennui, as she had in Illinois, except life in the goldfields offered many more diversions. Lorena thoroughly enjoyed frequent "rambles" — sometimes on horseback — through the country and filled her diary with observations about new places and people, providing one of the few detailed records for the Cosumnes-Ione region during the 1850s. Apparently she soon became acquainted with the family of William Hicks, considered the first settler of the Ione area in 1848, because she wrote several times about visiting "Mr. and Mrs. H." on Dry Creek, where the Hicks' ranch was located. She also knew Capt. Charles Peters, who claimed to be "the oldest pioneer living in California who mined in the days of '49 . . ." when he wrote his autobiography in 1915.[9] Although at first Lorena limited her accounts to the local scene, during the next six years she also wrote about California politics and current events.

During her first weeks in California Lorena discovered that her earlier concerns about this "land of gold and wickedness" had not been unduly exaggerated and hoped the day of "sobriety, justice and truth" would soon arrive. But in writing about this aspect of life in the mines, she did not mention the most notorious robber-murderer of the year: Joaquin Murieta, whose career began in northern Amador County, according to local legend. In the spring of 1853 Murieta and his band terrorized the countryside between Jackson and Sutter's Creek. Pursued by a posse into the southern part of the Central Valley, Murieta and several of his followers were killed on July 26, two months before Lorena arrived in California. His head, preserved in alcohol, was widely exhibited that fall as proof of his death.[10]

Lorena did not have long to ponder similar incidents because almost immediately she was swept up in a social whirl such as she had never known in Illinois. Single young women were still a novelty in male-dominated mining communities in 1853, so their presence created quite a stir, as noted on September 4 by John Doble of Volcano:

"Several young ladies have stopped here to remain the winter and in consequence the young men are all on the *quivive* and looking for wifes."[11] And Abby Mansur, living in another mining camp, wrote earlier in the year to her sister:

> I tell you women are in great demand in this country no matter whether they are married or not . . . there is a first rate chance for a single woman . . . she can have her choice of thousands.[12]

Shortly after arriving at Sarrahsville in 1853, Lorena and at least one sister received invitations to a "social ball" at the nearby Willow Springs House, a "fine hotel" located on the road to Fiddletown. Printed on white paper with a border of embossed flowers, these invitations were issued by an all-male ball committee with the names of the "managers" listed by locale. Other invitations addressed to Sarepta and received by the Hays sisters still exist, helping to identify many of the people in Lorena's diary.[13] On the evening of November 9 a prim-and-proper Lorena declined to join in the dancing and later resolved not to attend other parties. But as the months passed, she overcame this reluctance and enjoyed an unexpected popularity.

An especially merry outing took place in mid-May 1854 when Lorena and some friends attempted to tease the three young men who played together as Walker's Cotillon Band, a group that "makes splendid music." The "Walker boys," with two violins and a clarinet, "have a call about every week to play," added Horace Seaver, then boarding at the Mountain House on the Drytown-Jackson Road. He identified them as Sole (Seaver), Frank, and Burt Walker from "Colwell's prairie," Wisconsin. When Lorena met them, the band was on the way to Fiddletown to play for a "cotillion party" at a place called the "Sign of the Star."[14]

In high spirits the young women promised to attend the party if they could have a ride but — "with great glee" — planned to revoke this decision upon reaching Lorena's house. When the carriage drove by without stopping, "we had no alternative but to go whether we would or not." Lorena's description of the day portrays the image of a happy, laughing group driving through a countryside just beginning to turn from green to gold with the approach of summer. The party that evening, she wrote, "was very pleasant & much enjoyed by most present."

By this time Lorena and her family had been living in Willow Flats, on the edge of Willow Springs Creek, for several months, having moved sometime in late January 1854. Their new home, again only a temporary one, was north of Dry Creek, somewhere between the road to Drytown and the community of Willow Springs. Located on a main road to Sacramento (today's Highway 16), Willow Springs prospered through copper mining as well as gold. Its fine hotel had developed

SOCIAL BALL.

Miss S. Hays

The Pleasure of your Company is respectfully solicited at a Social Ball, to be given at the

WILLOW SPRINGS HOUSE,

On Wednesday Evening, November 9th, 1853.

MANAGERS:

WM. GOODE,	J. R. MOHONE,
B. F. WAYNE,	A. M. PLUMMER,
Dry Town.	Cosumnes.
M. MILLER,	A. GILLMORE,
Amadore.	Forks Cosumnes.
Col. A. PLATT,	WM. Z. WALKER,
Sutter Creek.	O. PLUMMER,
A. A. HUMPHREYS,	Dry Creek.
Jackson.	CHAS. STONE,
J. P. DOUGLASS,	Buena Vista Ranch.
Mokelumne Hill.	J. H. ALVORD,
MR. HANFORD,	J. MOORE,
Volcano.	Ione Valley.
JAS. BURT,	WARNER,
Fiddle Town.	Mountain House.
T. D. HEISKILL,	S. LINDSEY,
Indian Diggings.	Somersett House.
DR. O. P. WHITE,	C. S. COOVER,
Cedarville.	H. A. CHASE,
N. MOWREY,	A. PERRY,
Michigan Bar.	R. MOREHOUSE,
JOHN KNIGHT,	Sac. City.
Big Bar.	

FLOOR MANAGERS:

DR. C. W. COX, | F. WALKER

COTILLON PARTY.

The pleasure of your Company is respectfully solicited at a Cotillon Party, to be given by

JOHN M. WARNOCK,

AT THE

SIGN OF THE STAR,

FIDDLETOWN,

ON FRIDAY EVENING, MAY 12, 1854.

COMMITTEE OF ARRANGEMENTS:

DR. J. H. PHELPS,	F. DELANEY,
CHARLES SLOAT,	Indian Creek,
J. KENDAL,	WM. JAMISON,
LAFAYETTE PHELPS,	Jamison's Ranch,
E. R. YATES,	W. GOODE,
Fiddletown.	Dry Town.
JOHN CABLE,	A. A. HUMPHREYS,
JOHN ELDRIDGE,	Jackson,
J. J. ARMSTRONG,	SAMUEL MANING,
JOHN McDONALD,	MR. ROSE,
Indian Diggins,	Amadore,
E. H. PERRY,	JOHN MYERS,
Perry's Ranch.	MR. HANDFORD,
WM. R. SMITH,	Volcano,
SAMUEL HAMET,	COL. A. PLATT,
Cedarville,	Ione Valley,
CHARLES STAPLES,	G. C. WILLIAMS,
Fair Play,	Willow Springs,
CAPT. BOGARAUS,	JOS. KING,
Cayoteville,	25 Mile House,
PAUL FERING,	MR. WARNER,
Fork Cosumnes,	Mountain House,
MR. WILCOX,	A. J. TREDWAY,
St. John,	Gold Spring Ranch
JAMES FOLDS,	S. RICE,
CHARLES DROWN,	Michigan Bar,
Pleasant Valley,	JOHN R. MAHONE,
MR. ARMSTED,	Slough House.

FLOOR MANAGERS:

LOYD SPAR, | PHIL RASPBERY, | W. H. DAIN.

Music, Walker's Cotillon Band.

California Historical Society

Lorena and her sisters were immediately invited to parties after arriving in Amador County. The 1853 invitation is addressed to her sister, Miss S[arepta] Hays. The invitations and the envelopes, both white and lavender, were embossed with flowers.

from nothing more than "a log hut on the edge of a swamp" in 1849, according to Bayard Taylor, a reporter for the *New York Tribune*.[15]

The Willow Springs House, which Lorena visited frequently, was considered "the best in the mines," wrote Rachel Frazier, who worked there in the mid-1850s as a chambermaid and then as housekeeper. She explained that the hotel, approximately twenty-five miles from Sacramento, employed a dining room attendant called "Irish Tom" and a cook. "Every luxury of the east was found at this hotel," noted Frazier, who made the trip from Philadelphia via Panama in 1855 and worked in the mining region "for her health." Upstairs the second floor was furnished with "iron bedsteads in the open with six blankets on each."[16]

As J. D. Borthwick, a Englishman who traveled through Amador County, observed,

The American system of using hotels as regular boarding-houses prevails also in California. The hotels in the mines are really boarding houses, for it is on the number of their boarders that they depend. The transient custom of travelers is merely incidental.[17]

Farther west along the Sacramento road flourished another similar community called Forest Home, which did a "thriving business in general commodities." Apparently one of Lorena's sisters worked there during the spring of 1854, and Lorena often stopped at Forest Home during her trips to the Ione Valley. Developed around a tavern of the same name, this settlement eight miles north of Ione had two stores, a billiard salon, a barber shop, and a second hotel by 1857.[18]

The country around Forest Home, Willow Springs, and Drytown was described as being an "Italian landscape and an Italian atmosphere" in September 1849 by William M'Collum during an expedition to the headwaters of the "Rio de Cosumnes." He also remarked upon the unusual appearance of many hills "in the form of sugar loafs, the ascent to their summits gradual and occassionally giving us extensive views over the surrounding country."[19]

Lorena and her family lived near one of these "sugar loaf" hills between Willow Flats and Drytown, perhaps the same one M'Collum climbed before his party "struck across the plains and camped on Dry Creek." M'Collum found "the view from it was like a scene of enchantment! Before us was an extended sweep of rolling prairies and a long narrow streak of timbered land skirting the banks of the Cosumnes."[20] On February 3, 1854, Lorena also admired the view from the top of Sugar Loaf, 1,106 feet above sea level, and then enjoyed "a fine race in coming down the mountain," wishing she could have more "such rambles."

In early May 1854 Lorena's mother decided to move again, this time to Cook's Bar, a mining camp established in 1849 by Dennis Cook on the south side of the Cosumnes River about two miles west of Michigan Bar. "What they call a Bar in California is the flat which is usually found on the convex side of a bend in the river," explained J. D. Borthwick. He added,

> Such places have nearly always proved very rich, that being the side on which any deposit carried down by the river will naturally lodge, while the opposite bank is generally steep and precipitous and contains little or no gold.[21]

At times the population of Cook's Bar, which had at least one hotel in 1854, reached 500 but this camp faded away in 1860 unlike Michigan Bar, "the most prominent of all the early gold camps on the Cosumnes river," as well as one of the richest.

Michigan Bar, whose 1,500 inhabitants in the early 1850s were once described as "remarkable for industry, sobriety and generous hospitality," was divided by the river with the Chinese miners' camp on the south side. Acclaimed as "one of the largest as it is now one of

Sugar Loaf looms above the plains of the California Central Valley between Sacramento and Dry Town, once another important mining region. Willow Flats, where Lorena lived for a few months, was located at its foot.

the prettiest and most orderly towns in California,'' the original town site has disappeared, washed away by hydraulic mining. When Lorena lived nearby, Michigan Bar had seven stores, five boarding houses, two blacksmiths, a wheelwright, a baker, and a butcher.[22]

Some idea of what life could be like for a woman in one of these mining communities along the Cosumnes River in 1854 can be ascertained from a letter written in May by Frances Castle of Forest Home. ''I feel a very contented disposition,'' she declared, but then admitted to ''an occasional regret that I cannot attend church, neither my boy school.'' And in a revealing statement Castle added, ''I like this country very well but see a great many discontented ladies. Ladies generally do not like this country, it is, pretty much, prety much the same story.''[23] While Lorena could not be called ''dissatisfied'' at this time, a certain degree of restlessness shows in her diary during 1854 as she tried to decide what to do with her life.

Lorena, like Castle, missed going to church regularly because none existed in the immediate area. That year mining camps along the Cosumnes River were served by itinerant ministers, who might ride a sixty-mile circuit each week to conduct services throughout the Cosumnes-Ione district. One of these was Rev. Peter Y. Cool, who came from New York in 1850 at the age of twenty-two planning to mine enough gold so he could finish his college education. As the first schoolteacher in Amador County, he helped raise funds to build a small church and school near Volcano. Cool, who received his license to preach in 1850 from Dr. Isaac Owen of the California Methodist Church, mined near Amador City with three other ministers at a site soon christened "Ministers' Gulch" in their honor.[24] When Lorena heard Cool preach on May 17, 1854, he was still an eligible bachelor, and she thought him a "young man of promising abilities."

To attend the nearest church, a Methodist one, required traveling ten to twelve miles in each direction. The frame building was constructed in Ione City during the spring of 1853 at a cost of $2,000. Lorena made this trip whenever possible. But during the summer of 1854, her mother — although a Baptist — opened their house at Cook's Bar for services conducted by Rev. Isaac B. Fish from the Ione Methodist-Episcopal Church. A native of Ohio, Fish entered the ministry in 1848 and three years later responded to a call for volunteers to do "pioneer work" in California. Before being assigned to the Ione church, the thirty-year-old preacher spent a year serving two other nearby congregations. Described as a "man of medium size," he had a "light complexion [and] a comely face though deeply marked by smallpox" contracted in Cincinnati after visiting a sick parishioner.[25]

Fish's "unexpected" assignment to the Ione post came at a time when he and his wife, Naomi, had been "home[les]s and itinarant" for quite a while. He had not anticipated anything until it was time for "an appointment for Eternity — which will be *home indeed!*" Fish succeeded his wife's brother-in-law, Rev. George B. Taylor, and received $1,200 a year from the California Methodist Conference. Due to the "press of labor" Fish did not keep up his diary during 1854 but wrote a summary of the year's activities on April 17, 1855.[26]

"At Ione City I found a good church and Parsonage," he wrote, "but had to ride 24-60 miles every week." Fish preached every Sabbath and forenoon, held Sabbath school at other locations every two weeks on alternate Sunday afternoons and nights during the summer and also took one or two other appointments. His comment that "the work was the hardest I had ever done" must have been somewhat of an understatement. What his wife, one of Lorena's friends, might have thought of his conscientious regimen is unknown, but it could not have been an easy year for her either, because their first child, a son, was born on September 30.[27]

A worker in the temperance cause, Fish served as master of the grand division of the California Sons of Temperance. In the fall of 1854 "gamblers etc. became very much enraged with me for my opposition from the pulpit" and withdrew from his Ione church. This so aroused the rest of the community that the "congregation became larger" and his support better than ever before, although "many would have done me bodily injury but the Lord restrained them." In later years Fish was remembered in Ione history as

> a fearless man, of good mind and great force of character who did not hesitate to denounce the popular vices of the age. At Ione, especially he won the enmity of saloon-keepers and gamblers.[28]

Because he did not keep his diary on a daily basis during 1854, Fish did not mention preaching at Lorena's home in Cook's Bar. Her diary augments his unpublished one in providing a more complete record of Methodist Church activities along the Cosumnes River and in the Ione Valley during the mid-1850s.

Lorena's diary also records information about the early Baptist Church of Amador County, since she attended the organizational meeting in Ione Valley on July 2, 1854, conducted by Rev. Myron Newell. Because the Baptists did not have a church building, "a large and attentive congregation" held services in the Union House.[29] At this July meeting Lorena and her family presented their "letters of dismission" from the Illinois Baptist Church in Barry, thus becoming charter members of the new congregation. Soon afterward Lorena attended a joint Sabbath school celebration on the Fourth of July with ministers from the Baptist and Methodist faiths participating.

This celebration provided Lorena with a topic for her first California newspaper article. Her account of the festivities appeared in the July 16 issue of *The Golden Era,* a weekly family paper printed in San Francisco "devoted to literature, agriculture, the mining interest, local and foreign news, commerce, education, morals and amusements." Printed in a column with the heading "Correspondence of the Golden Era," Lorena's letter was entitled "Notes from a Mountain Lassie" and signed with her initials "L.L.H."[30]

Lorena's brief but promising career as a newspaper writer began inadvertently. In mid-May while on a trip to visit a nearby ranch, she shared a stagecoach with an artist and an editor from *The Golden Era.* While the name of the artist remains unknown, the editor may well have been Rollin M. Daggett, noted for wearing a miner's red shirt and high-top boots while traveling through the gold country selling subscriptions and writing articles while his partner, J. Macdonough Foard, ran the paper in San Francisco. During this chance encounter, Lorena was asked to become a correspondent for *The Era.* Begun December 19, 1852, its circulation jumped to 2,000 after the first month of publication. *The Golden Era* has been called "the most important journal ever published on the Pacific Slope." It printed poetry and fiction as well as summaries of the news and "an occasional signed article" by a columnist, with about half the space in its four pages filled with advertisements. Contributors to this newspaper rarely received more than five dollars a column for prose and nothing for poetry.[31]

A favorable editorial comment appearing on page two of the July 16 issue greeted Lorena's first article, thus calling it to readers' attention as well. This "Correspondents' Column" appeared on the left side of the editorial page and included advice and comments upon stories and poems submitted for publication. Lorena must have been very pleased and encouraged to read: "Our fair correspondent at Ione City will find her spirited letter on the fourth page. Would be glad to receive a weekly correspondence from the same hand."

During the remainder of 1854 Lorena wrote three more articles for *The Era* and had the thrill of seeing two of these contributions printed on the front page. She wrote under the nom de plume of "Lenita," turning her middle name into a Spanish-sounding version, and also as "Our Mountain Lassie." To be known only by a pseudonym had been common practice in American and English literary circles for a long time, especially for women writers, many of whom have never been identified by their real names. Often beginning writers tried out a number of pen names before settling upon one they liked, thus adding to the confusion. Without Lorena's diary, the identity of "Lenita" would never be known, nor that of her sister Sarepta, whose poetry and articles were also printed by *The Golden Era* under the names of "Lida Woodvale," "Ethleberta," "Annie Lisle," and "Iona."

In her first article Lorena wrote about the Ione Valley as "a beautiful vale, quietly nestling 'neath the shadows of a wreath of encircling hills." Her description is one of the few written about this part of California in 1854. Readers were told,

. . .with its neat farm houses and fields of most luxuriant grain and vegetables, [it] presents a most welcome and refreshing sight to the eye of one approaching from the dry plains surrounding it. Beautiful trees with their inviting shade are scattered over the valley and the spirit of Peace and Love seems ever hovering over a scene of such beauty and promise.

Lorena also wrote about the Sunday school celebration with an account nearly identical to the entry in her diary and concluded by mentioning one of the "entertainments of the evening" had been "an exhibition of Harker's panoramic view of a Trip across the Plains."[32]

This "Grand Panorama" of the Overland Routes to California appeared in Sacramento on June 30 and July 1. Apparently it then moved to Ione for the July 4 showing. According to advertisements in the *Sacramento Pictorial Union,* this panorama was exhibited by J. W. Harker, "proprietor and manager," throughout California before he planned to take it to the Atlantic states.[33]

Lorena's second article arrived too late to be printed in the September 10 issue of *The Golden Era,* so the following notice appeared instead: "To our correspondent Lenita — Received your communication descriptive of matters and things in the dry diggings too late for insertion this week." Her letter appeared in the September 17 issue and reported, "Cook's Bar is beginning to assume quite a business air and contains a number of very good buildings." Lorena added, "Times are exceedingly dull owing to the scarcity of water." While many of the miners were leaving on "prospecting excursions", they would return "as soon as water will permit the washing of their claims here," she explained.

Lorena's use of the word "dull" in this context was the accepted California definition of the day to describe life in a mining community when there was little water available. She added, "We are promised lively times this coming winter, or as soon as water may be had in the ditch, which is now under repair." Here she referred to attempts, similar to one in 1851, to bring water into an area where camps and towns, "dependent upon the river beds," were abandoned during the dry season. One report of a similar endeavor in this area was recalled years later by a German visitor to the Sacramento Valley in 1849-50:

> From Coloma they are turning the South Fork [of the American River] into the Cosumnes so that the southern mines can then be expolited with water from the northern mines. Thus a mining region 15 miles wide which could not be worked because of insufficient water has been transformed into a new site of fortune for gold seekers.[34]

The last half of Lorena's second column concerned woman's role in reforming gold rush society, reflecting her continuing concern with the "wickedness" of California. Her views received an editor's comment commending this article to the "ladies of California" for "careful perusal" because of the "good suggestions" it contained. "Progress and reform are becoming the watchword of the times," Lorena wrote, but "where is the star that is to illumine our social horizon? WOMAN is beginning to awaken to her true position." Lorena added,

> It is her province and privilege to disseminate the blessings of purity and peace; and surely in California she can see there is work for her hands to do.

Lorena urged women readers "to engage in reformatory movements, and help to roll from our sunny land the dark waters of pollution which had so long hideously marked and sullied the brightness of our history."

She believed "Man, all-powerful as he is," could not do this alone and urged woman not to sit "supinely at her ease, her hands folded in luxury, thus tacitly giving consent to the vice and immorality that abounds.'' Woman's work, according to Lorena, "may be accomplished unostentatiously, for there is in the appropriate work an art of woman a wonderful influence for good.'' If the "secret power'' granted woman by God were used, wrote Lorena, "who can tell but that the gambler, duellist, sabbath-breaker and drunkard would soon cease to stalk in insolent dignity through the land." Lorena then suggested that women

> . . . should let the withering influence of her power and displeasure be felt and spur from her society, on all occasions, the contaminating presence of the willful desecrator of law and religion, and one who, perhaps, on the slightest occasion of offense, would not hesitate to imbuee his hands in the blood of her own husband, son or brother.

Lorena praised "those ladies who last winter petitioned the Legislature'' for a prohibition law but reminded readers "there remains much yet to be done, and some of the labor rests upon woman.'' Lorena raised the question, "Shall she plead inefficiency, or let ease and luxury long render her apathetic to her own best interests or her duty to others?'' She also stated that while woman "is indifferent, no reform will take place or the great work of the upheaving and overturning of long sanctioned customs and practices of a vitiated society be accomplished.'' In conclusion, Lorena wrote:

> Anxiously was woman looked for in California, as if when she came, her smile could chase away the darkness and gloom, that, despite its golden treasure, hang over the land and gladly was she welcomed to these desolate shores. The arm of welcome was everywhere extended to receive her and earnest and deep was the silent thanksgiving of every heart that went up to heaven, when she came to make this wilderness her home. Shall she, then, in any degree forget her mission or fail in her errand of mercy?

In this essay Lorena reflected the prevailing Victorian attitude towards "woman's mission'' as the primary "regenerator'' of society. As a "domestic angel'' woman had fewer worldly interests, so the "purity'' of her motives would be unquestioned as she extolled Christian virtues. At this time, women were supposed to have "great powers and widely-extended influence,'' which would be "most beneficial if allowed to flow in its natural channels, viz. domestic ones.'' However, these were to be exercised "with silent unostentatious vigilance.''[35]

Lorena's next contribution, dated October 20, was not published until nine days later because her "little budget'' arrived "too late for the present page'' of that issue. When it did appear in print, her article received space on the front page. Based upon her interest in education, Lorena wrote about the role played by newspapers, which she called "bright stars in our literary firmament," in bringing the world to her small mining community. Upon hearing the call "The Expressman has arrived," Lorena wrote, "now let ennui fly to the winds" because these "winged messengers" arrived "like gleams of sunshine through the clouds." She added,

> If you have the blues and find your spirits sunk below zero, let the last paper or magazine be brought and what a sudden glow of joy and satisfaction warms up your heart. You plunge into its contents and soon find yourself surrounded by an atmosphere that brings back elasticity of spirits and better feelings of your nature are again brought into active operation. It is mind holding sympathy with mind that brings happiness and in what better way do we find congenial spirits, sometimes, than through the press?

Lorena wondered what life would be like without newspapers to supply "sufficient mental food" and decided it "would cause a dreadful jog in this *fast* age." Her use of "fast" to describe the pace of life due to the mechanical inventions of the Industrial Revolution was also an appropriate Victorianism. In Lorena's opinion, without newspapers,

> Ignorance and superstition would again flap their dark wings around us . . . the Goddess of Wisdom would fold her shroud around her, and sit weeping o'er the grave of buried Hope — the downfall of learning and retrograde of man. I do not wonder that those were called the *dark* ages when no newspaper found its way to the family circle. What did they do all the long summer days, or how pass off the long winter evenings?

She asked what would happen without newspapers to "elaborate the qualities of books . . . or herald the discoveries of science . . . [because] the gospel is preached, education disseminated and science diffused through the newspaper press." And in this article Lorena made her first and only known comment acknowledging the existence of a "world of fashion" when she wrote, "How did the ladies used to get the fashions before 'Godey' or 'Graham' issued their magazines?"[36] Upon the arrival of the expressman, "A quiet reigns throughout the house," Lorena explained, adding,

> All, even the boarders, are quietly ensconced here and there with their papers spread out before them. No time now for the trifling jest in rational enjoyment. They are plucking sprays from the tree of knowledge — gathering pearls that have been washed up from the ocean of thought.

She recommended that in any "interval of spare time" it would be wise to "take up the neglected newspaper and carefully treasure the mental and moral lessons of its content." Upon ending this paean, Lorena wrote,

> Blessings rest upon the *Expressman:* May he be protected from danger

and ever find a glad welcome to our mountain home. And Heaven's choicest blessing also rest upon the Printer, whose assiduous labors are devoted to so worthy and noble a cause as that of diffusing happiness and intelligence over a field of such extent and beauty.

Lorena's last column for 1854, a rather melancholy but impressionistic "reverie" entitled "Autumn Harvests," was published on the front page of the November 12 issue "from our Mountain Lassie, Lenita." She wrote of "past joys and sunshine of childhood," telling for the only time about the setting of her family home in western Pennsylvania. She recalled an orchard behind the house, rose bushes and quince trees between the windows, and berry patches along the fence. Naming many varieties of trees, she wrote, "I knew them all and had my favorite" while the flowers in the garden "all are distinctly before my mind as if I had but today beheld them."[37]

In these reminiscences, Lorena also mentioned a "luxuriant" grapevine, supported by an apple tree along the walk, "whose purple clusters strongly tempted my little hands to break one of the commandments." She remembered gathering the "first blue violets" of spring from a grassy bank "by the little brook that pearled so joyously along its pebble bed" and from "the many beds that nestled so snugly amid the crooked roots of the great beech trees, underneath which we built our cosey play-house, and which we arranged with as much taste and pride as any bona-fide housekeeper." These memories were not recorded in Lorena's diary, although she often tried out ideas for her newspaper columns in it.

However, a draft similar to the rest of this column did appear in her diary. She then wrote of children, who "little think that clouds and shadows may fall on their future pathway. In the moaning winds of autumn and in the falling leaf, they read no lesson of the future." And, perhaps speaking for many far from home, she commented:

> The flower-clad prairies, artemisia plains and smiling vallies stretch
> far between Rocky's crystal peaks and Sierra's snow-clad heights loom
> up to the skies, yet do they not shut out bright reveries of the past, or
> erase the many pictures daguerrotyped upon the walls of memory.

Deciding not to "linger upon the past," Lorena declared, "the present also has its pleasures. Autumn has come again — autumn in this bright and sunny land! One might almost suppose we had no such season, they are so uniform here." She also noted a "preceptible change" as "Old Sol has moved from his vertical position and now throws his glances more obliquely upon us — we enjoy his smiles without fear of encountering the warmer rays of his displeasure." Lorena described her view as "the violet tint of the distant hills is deepening its shade and Sierra's snow-caps are enveloped in a mantle of etherial blue.'' She added,

> ...we know that all beauty must fade, all scenes of loveliness must
> pass away, yet we love them no less for their transientness...and we love
> the ''fall'' best of all the seasons for the life-lessons it conveys and be-
> cause it leads us from the fading beauty of earth to the contemplation
> of joys above, where no ''change'' or ''passing away'' is written on all
> we love.

Although Lorena's dream of a career as an ''authoress'' became a
reality in 1854, writing a few articles for *The Golden Era* did not take
too much time. So, at the request of Rev. Isaac Fish, she also submitted
at least one letter to the *California Christian Advocate,* published as the West
Coast edition of the Methodist Church newspaper.[38] No copies of issues
in which these letters might have been printed have been found in
Methodist archives, so what Lorena wrote for this publication remains
unknown.

Meanwhile, she also sought every opportunity to further her education by reading whatever books, magazines, and newspapers reached
Cook's Bar. She became interested in hydropathy, a popular health
reform of the Victorian era, after reading several copies of *The Water-
Cure Journal,* published in New York and distributed by a San Francisco
dealer. Hydropathy, also called the ''water cure,'' attempted to treat
diseases by the copious use of water, both internally and externally. It
focused upon helping to alleviate feminine health problems seldom
discussed publicly.[39] Water cure establishments, staffed by women, were
widely patronized and provided information in an open manner about
bodily functions and sexuality. In approving of the water cure, Lorena's
views coincided with those expressed by a number of prominent women
in the mid-1850s, including author-reformer Catherine Beecher.[40]

While helping with a boarding house did not provide exactly the kind
of educational opportunities Lorena desired, it enabled her to meet some
interesting people. In December 1854 a temperance speaker and a
theatrical troupe found accommodations at the Hays' boarding house.
Sarah Pellet, one of those ''strong-minded Females,'' lectured throughout
the Mother Lode region that year on political reform for women's rights
and against alcohol. Her crusade was noted by the *The Golden Era:*

> Within the last three months several ladies, remarkable for their
> masculine tendencies and for the total absence of those more refined at-
> tributes which lend to the female character its greatest charms, have come
> among us from the great hotbed of transcendentalism at the East — each
> bent on engrafting upon the tender stock of California her peculiar view
> of everything connected with our human economy.[41]

These women were characterized by the editor as having "a brazen look and unabashed carriage," but Miss Pellet, "who hails from Maine," was described by one listener as ". . . not bad looking, dressed in the Quaker style, has a fine voice and a great flow of language." He later decided Pellet talked "a perfect torrent" and "thanked our stars we were not tied to her for life."[42]

In spite of her views about woman's role in gold rush society, Lorena did not quite know what to make of Miss Pellet because of her independence in traveling alone and speaking out in public.

Lorena also was not sure what to expect from a theatrical family who became their next boarders. Although "The Robinson Family" had played in Pike County, Illinois, when she lived there, she had never attended their performances. Headed by Joseph R. Robinson, this family could be considered a troupe in itself, since everyone performed, including the Robinson children, Clara, "Miss Susan," and "Master William." The last two were billed as "the unequaled and celebrated Infant Prodigies." "Miss Susan," not yet ten years old in 1854, was also known as "The California Fairy Star" and "La Petite Susan." An actress, dancer, and singer, she was considered both a rival as well as an inspiration for Lotta Crabtree, another precocious child whose stage career began in the gold mining region during the mid-1850s.[43]

When not busy with boarders, Lorena's thoughts often turned to ways she might continue her formal education. At one time it seemed possible that she could attend the Sacramento Academy and Female Institute, taught by Miss M. S. Bennett, whom Lorena later met. In 1854 this institution advertised instruction in "English branches, miscellaneous exercises and penmanship" for ten dollars a month. A year later Bennett moved the school, renamed the Young Ladies Institute, a few blocks to L Street and offered, according to a newspaper advertisement, an enriched curriculum of English, liberal sciences, and vocal and instrumental music to day students, as well as to boarders, who paid thirty dollars a month. Without money of her own, Lorena could not attend and she declined an offer made by "a kind friend" to pay this tuition. Instead, as the year ended, she accepted a teaching position and prepared to leave home, venturing beyond the Ione Valley for the first time.[44]

Lorena's job required moving about twenty-five miles west of Cook's Bar to a place called Benson's Ferry, located on the Mokelumne River not far from where it is joined by the Cosumnes River and Dry Creek. This ferry, in operation since 1849, served travelers on a road between Sacramento and Stockton, a route also used by the California State Telegraph Company for its lines. It was purchased in 1850 by John Benson,[45] who employed Lorena in December 1854 to teach his children. At first she had three students but "a young Spaniard from Chile" joined the class, thus giving Lorena a chance to learn Spanish. During this time her sister Sarepta, working in Drytown, also studied Spanish, so she and Lorena exchanged at least one letter in this language. While the Hays sisters' interest in learning Spanish might be considered unusual, it reflects a continuing search for education and self-improvement. Three years later Elvira Bradway, whose husband made the overland trip in 1853, wrote from northern California that she also taught and studied Spanish.[46]

Because Lorena found it lonely to be so far from family and friends, her teaching career lasted only about six weeks. When an opportunity came to return to Cook's Bar, she accepted with mixed emotions, primarily because "a friend" came to escort her home. This "friend" is mentioned frequently in Lorena's diary during 1854, identified sometimes as "Mr. B.," and at others, as "Mr. Bomer." He was John Clement Bowmer, a six-foot-tall Kentuckian who claimed Lorena as his bride two weeks after her return from Benson's Ferry. They were married on February 25, 1855, by Rev. Isaac Fish in Cook's Bar.[47]

Clement, as Lorena called him, was described by a friend as "a gentleman of good disposition and tolerable high literary attainments . . . [he] is a man of good character and I would feel to trust him as a very confidential friend."[48] Clement must also have been a very patient man indeed because their courtship took more than a year. They met shortly after she arrived in California, but for months Lorena refused to acknowledge there could be anything more than friendship between them. When she received a diamond ring as a forfeit in an after-dinner game, Lorena would not even consider that it might possibly signify an engagement. Perhaps Lorena's hesitancy can be explained by the fact that John Clement Bowmer was ten years older than she and had been married before. His first wife died after he left for California in 1850 to mine gold in Eldorado County with his brother and their father. This left three children, a girl and two boys, back home in Grant County, Wisconsin.[49] When Lorena met her future husband, he was operating a general store in Ione City in partnership with Benjamin F. Wayne, also formerly from Wisconsin.

Lorena's diary tells how this friendship blossomed into love, but it does not explain why she spelled Clement's name without the "w" while he, and nearly everyone else, wrote it "Bowmer." Nor did Lorena give any reason why their marriage took place so suddenly and, to her, "unexpectedly." This occurred because Clement apparently wished to settle their relationship before he left for Wisconsin to visit his children. Nearly a year earlier, when he planned a similar trip, Lorena called him back only to keep him waiting while she tried to make up her mind about her feelings for him.

Although the newspaper announcement of their marriage reported that it took place in Cook's Bar, Lorena wrote only that the ceremony was performed "in church" and gave no other details about what should have been a festive occasion. Her brief honeymoon consisted of a quick trip to San Francisco to bid her husband farewell as he started the journey to his former home. Lorena did not record the name of the ship Clement sailed on, but the 3,000-ton *Golden Gate,* owned by the Pacific Mail Steamship Company and commanded by Allan McLane, was the only steamer to leave San Francisco Bay that week for Panama. It sailed from the Vallejo Street wharf "with mails, passengers and Treasure" on Thursday, March 1, at 9 A.M.[50]

It is difficult to imagine a more inauspicious way to begin married life, and Lorena may have felt this way, too, as she set about housekeeping in a single room. Without Clement to reassure her, Lorena worried and wondered what marriage might bring, hoping the "many little sacrifices" made in the name of love would be "sufficient recompense" for giving up her independence as a single woman. In her diary Lorena also confided her love and longing for her husband during his absence. Since these emotions were seldom recorded by women during the nineteenth century, according to one 1982 study about women's diaries of the overland journey, Lorena's account would be unusual in this respect.[51] And the use of her husband's middle name, rather than calling him "Mr. B.", is also worthy of note, although later, after the first glow of love faded, she did refer to him in this traditional Victorian manner.

During her husband's ten-week absence, Lorena filled the days as she had done before marriage by visiting friends, reading, and writing. She submitted another article to *The Golden Era* and it was printed in April. This received a special welcome from the editor, who had written on February 4 to remind "Lenita — We should be pleased to hear from the 'Mountain Lassie' again. Do not forget us." And in the April 1 edition, "Lenita" learned:

> We are most happy to hear from you. Your communication comes to us from who knows where — Heaven probably [or] from a sunny little valley near the "foot hills" where the soil yields harvests of virgin gold as well as turnips and where bright eyes write the name of "home" on every door and contentment on every bearded phiz.

In this letter Lorena fancifully portrayed the wind as "Old Boreas" and "The Storm King," a "stern, rough old fellow we think him." She told of his "mad frolic" in the mountains with "wild ravings and maniac shrikes" as spring storms swept the countryside. Lorena depicted this "wind God" as sending

> a few bright visitors down into the smiling valley to kiss the petals of some fairy flower, which in unconscious beauty nestles in its quiet

retreat, like domestic love, all heedless of the storms and commotions in the world abroad.

And, thinking of her husband, she wrote about the "homeward-bound one on the 'ocean wave' " during a storm at sea. But Lorena also noted how welcome were the spring "rain drops that follow dashing and splashing" after a storm to "bring gladness and hope to the heart of the miner." She added,

> Ditches and slucies are filled with water and he will go to work again with a light heart. The turbid rivers come rushing and roaring down from their homes in the mountains, bearing with them the golden sands that will help supply exhausted finances and give life and impulse to labor and business again. . . . [But] 'Tis startling to hear, as we have on two successive days, that the banks have fallen in and crushed the laborer at his work.

She again spoke of her continuing concern about the condition of local society, exclaiming that "the establishments here have sent forth a miasma that has polluted the moral atmosphere of all our towns." Then, realizing what a moral crusader she must sound like, even though this was an accepted role for a woman in the mid-nineteenth century, Lorena added:

> But I see, Messrs. Editors, I am forgetting that it is news you most desire in a letter and that you prefer the "sunny side" of a story to dull disertations on morality or other every-day-written upon subjects.

Nevertheless, the editors of *The Golden Era* printed her letter on page 1 of the April 8, 1855, issue.

While continuing to write for *The Era,* Lorena again received encouragement to resume her correspondence for *The Christian Advocate,* this time from Rev. H. H. Rheese, one of the editors who later served as superintendent of Amador County schools.[52] In addition she investigated the possibilities of submitting articles to *The Quincy Prospector,* but found it was "a very little bit of a sheet," with no room in its four pages for her letters. Published weekly between March 3 and November 17, 1855, *The Prospector* was one of the smallest newspapers ever printed in California. It measured five and three-fourths inches wide by six and three-fourths inches high. "Clark and Badlam, Editors and Proprietors," charged twenty-five cents a copy for this miniature.[53]

All this time, as she awaited her husband's return, Lorena lived in anticipation of "steamer day," when his ship would dock in San Francisco. Clement's round trip to Wisconsin, via Panama and New York City, took two and a half months, made easier and shorter by improvements in transportation, because in 1855 completion of the transisthmus railroad reduced the time required to cross Panama from

"Steamer day" was an occasion of great excitement in San Francisco during the 1850s. Lorena would have been in such a crowd when her husband returned in 1855.

several days to only hours. "Transit of the isthmus" was advertised in California newspapers "from ocean to ocean by railroad cars in six hours or less." In May 1855 this railroad was reported to be in "good order and the transit is made regularly in from three to four hours."[54]

Lorena, who had received several letters from Clement during his travels, reached San Francisco on May 14. She sailed from Sacramento on the small steamer *Hunt* with Samuel Seymour, who normally commanded another similar boat, serving as captain for this trip. Operated by the California Steam Navigation Company, these boats made three round-trips each week between San Francisco and Sacramento, with stops at the town of Benicia. In 1855 cabin passengers paid seven dollars for the trip while deck passage cost five dollars.[55]

Upon arriving in San Francisco, Lorena discovered the steamer *John L. Stevens,* owned by the Pacific Mail Steamship Company, had been delayed. The *Stevens,* under the command of R. H. Pearson, sailed from Panama on April 30 but stopped the following day to rescue passengers from the *Golden Age,* which had struck a reef. The *Stevens*

A view of Ione City by Mrs. E. W. Withington

Huntington Library

then returned to Panama to unload, sailing again for San Francisco at
5 A.M. on May 3. However, the steamer was again delayed, without
explanation, for thirteen hours at Acapulco and did not reach port until
noon May 16. Among the 801 passengers were 160 women and 151
children, including Mrs. Sarah J. Wayne, wife of Clement's partner,
and her two youngsters. According to the ship's passenger list,
Lorena's husband was identified as "J. C. Bowman."[56]

When the reunited Lorena and Clement returned to Ione City they
settled down to married life in a boarding house, which was not an
unusual thing for newlyweds to do in the 1850s, until they could afford
their own home. Less than a year later, in April 1856, they moved into
the house Clement purchased on "village lot no. 6 in block no. 1,"
valued at $600.[57] By this time Ione City had become "a very fine
place," according to miner Ben Bowen, who thought it "quite a pretty
little village, rather too flat but that is easily remedied." How, he did
not explain. Bowen, twenty-two, had been mining with "indifferent
success" in the wilds of Fort John, farther north on Dry Creek, so
when he arrived in Ione he discovered,

> things seem to be a little more settled than I am used to. There are quite
> a number of families in this place and I could scarcely look either way
> without seeing a pretty woman.[58]

Lorena's home was located in the same block as the "Bomer and
Wayne Store House." The store was built on the eastern part of lot

No. 1, which had been surveyed in 1854 as 100 feet deep with a twenty-five-foot frontage on Main Street. The partners paid $500 for the "fractional part" of this lot in early February 1854. Their store, which carried a wide variety of items according to one inventory, would have been built of wood, because in 1856 Daniel Stewart constructed the first brick store, which still stands on Ione's Main Street, although the facade has been changed over the years. By 1855 Ione City, never important insofar as its own mines were concerned, was fast becoming a major supply center for the southern gold region.[59]

Clement's return to storekeeping raised an immediate problem as he and his partner tried to settle the question of doing business on Sundays. Because Lorena had objected to traveling on the Sabbath during her 1853 overland trip, it is not surprising she also disapproved of this practice, which was widespread throughout the gold region. Spencer Richards, who ran one of seven stores in Fiddletown that summer, also wrote about the same situation:

> . . . the customers are different here . . . here we close from eleven to one o'clock and Sundays we dont get a chance to sit down all day. I wish it would get out of fashion to keep open on Sundays.[60]

Richards thought it would be years before Sunday would be "respected." At the Ione store the Bowmers' views seem to have prevailed because Lorena wrote that her husband settled this business "satisfactorily." This may have been the time that the Bowmer-Wayne partnership ended, with this issue perhaps a contributing factor.

Now Lorena began to write less frequently in her diary. In August she did record a long description of the "Rancheria Murders," later said to have occurred in retaliation for anti-Mexican activities in Amador County. These included blaming the Mexican population for the deaths of several travelers along the Drytown-Cosumnes Road earlier in the summer. When all Mexicans were ordered to leave the county they refused to do so. On August 6 a band of twelve men, described as predominately of "the Mexican type," robbed the Chinese camp near Drytown and headed for the community of Rancheria (which later disappeared from the Drytown-Jackson Road). At Rancheria the "banditos" killed six men, one woman, and an Indian, while wounding two others. They blew open the safe in the Francis store and escaped with $20,000.[61]

The next day "the atrocious character of the murders, the unprovoked and causeless attack, raised the anger of the mass of people almost beyond control." All Mexicans in the vicinity were rounded up and arrested, with thirty-five men to be tried and hanged. Only three were executed, according to vigilante justice, and the rest released if they promised to leave the area within four hours. Meanwhile, Sheriff W. A. Phoenix led a posse in pursuit. He finally caught up with the band on August 12, but "in the affray Phoenix was the first to fall," shot through the heart. Several days later forty Mexicans were arrested farther south, and one was identified as a member of the gang. Manuel Escobar became the "tenth and last" man to die on the famous hanging tree that stood in Jackson until 1862. Others of the Rancheria gang were cornered separately and killed.[62]

The Rancheria murders were reported by Ben Bowen from Fort John on August 7:

> There came past us to day 8 men who were after some greasers who in the most brutal and inhuman manner killed five men and one woman at Rancheria last night also broke open a safe and took out some 7 or 8,000 dollars. This makes the second tragedy within three weeks which has taken place in the neighborhood — three men, killed and robbed, one at Upper rancheria a short time ago and all made their escape.[63]

On August 11 Bowen added, ". . . the whole country is in a state of excitement yet and has been all week." Another view of the murders was later described by William Hubert Burgess, who wrote about "an awful tragedy enacted in the murdering line."[64]

As Lorena's diary and these accounts by Bowen and Burgess indicate, violence against the Mexican population did not subside quickly.[65] Lorena apparently never submitted her account of the Rancheria murders to a newspaper, nor the description she wrote about the 1855 state elections and subsequent inauguration ceremonies. However, later in September she again received encouragement to write for *The Golden Era* when the following message appeared in the correspondents' column: "Lenita — It would give us great pleasure to hear from you again. We have always a corner at your service."

In fulfilling this request Lorena wrote an essay entitled "A Chapter on Beards." It was certainly not what one would have expected after reading her diary for September 22. In it she gave vent to her feelings about women's rights when her husband, whom she nicknamed "Mr. Snooks" in this account, left her to attend a secret meeting. Perhaps this was a meeting of the Sons of Temperance, to which Clement belonged, or of the Settlers' League, which kept no minutes of discussions about the problems of land ownership in the Ione Valley. Lorena's uncles, Henry Woodward and Adam Lithgow, are known to have taken part in these discussions about the Arroyo Seco Grant.[66]

Although when single Lorena had been outspoken about women's role in reforming gold rush society, as a married woman she did not allow even a hint of her feelings on a similar topic to show in her article. But she was especially incensed when her husband "patted me on the head,"then told her to be a "good dear" and write her piece for *The Era*. Her "Chapter on Beards" was printed on page one of the October 7 issue. The editor was "pleased at hearing" from her again, despite the fact that "The subject is a funny one for Ladies but is pleasantly handled." Whether Lorena's husband had recently grown a beard or shaved one off cannot be discerned from this article.

Lorena's newspaper articles and diary entries provide many more details about impersonal events than about family matters. During the years, as three of her sisters, their mother, and a Lithgow cousin married, Lorena's diary tells when the ceremonies took place but not much else; she did not even record the names of the bridegrooms. Her reports about these events were nearly as brief as that of her own wedding. But when her youngest sister Sarah was married at the age of eighteen years, Lorena, who had been twenty-eight when she became a bride, felt this was too young to begin the responsibilities of married life. However, Lorena did recognize that her sister might not have had a very happy time with a new stepfather in the house. This sentiment also appears in a letter from their brother, William Philander Hays, who had joined the family in California as soon as possible after learning of their arrival.[67]

This same lack of detail in Lorena's diary is especially noticeable during the winter of 1855-56, when she wrote nothing about events leading up to a court case against her husband. At the same time, a similar case had been brought against his partner, Benjamin F. Wayne. These cases, listed as Nos. 79 and 80 in the Fifth Judicial District Court records of Amador County, included an inventory of goods carried in the Bowmer-Wayne store. These were attached on September 19, 1855, by Sheriff George Dunham. Wayne received a bill of $41.50 for his share of the costs involved in these attachment proceedings, while Bowmer's share came to only $14.50. Both cases involved repayment of a $1,000 debt incurred December 1, 1854, according to one statement. This might well have been just before or after the partnership was formed. Charles M. Fox, the lender, sued Wayne and won a judgment requiring repayment of the loan with interest of three percent a month from September 19, for a total of $1,350. But Fox was required to pay costs of the suit, which was settled November 12.[68]

In the second case, Wayne testified against Lorena's husband, since their partnership had been dissolved on July 21, 1855. It was heard by the Honorable Charles M. Creanor on February 27, 1856, when court sat in Jackson to hear sixty-three cases on the calendar. A trial by jury was waived on consent of all involved. Primary evidence took the form of a "certain written statement, herein filled," in the court records. It was signed "Bowmer & Wayne" on the first line. Written on blue paper in Drytown on February 3, 1855, this note still exists among court papers. It read:

> Two months from date for value rec'ed, We jointly and Severally Promise to pay Charles M. Fox 1,500 fifteen hundred dollars, together with three per cent per month until paid.

In an unknown hand on the back of this note were two notations: "Received on the written note 600 $ June 4, 1855" and "August 15th — $500 received on the written note."[69]

Part of the $1,500 borrowed was used to pay expenses incurred by Lorena's husband. His expense account for a round-trip via Panama, New Orleans, and New York City was also filed with the court. It showed he received $1,727.09 from Wayne, but his own expenses came to only $519.34; the rest covered transportation and accommodations for Wayne's family. When Wayne testified, Bowmer objected and his legal counsel, H. A. Carter of Ione City, moved for a new suit but lost.

The major defense witness, Josiah Heacock, testified that he worked as a clerk for Bowmer and Wayne at the time the note was signed. After dissolution of the partnership, Heacock bought out Wayne for $600 after being told it was needed so Wayne could "pay on the note."

During the trial Lorena's husband told the court, "I would rather pay the money if I had it than have a difficulty but I do not owe the money which Wayne had no authority to sign my name to the note." Bowmer added, "I never got a dollar of the money — I saw Wayne get the money." Although Bowmer did not win his case, Judge Creanor's verdict was that "Bowmer et al" had to repay only "the sum of six hundred and twenty nine 52/100 Dollars with Interest therein. . . ." Judge Creanor, whose district also included Calaveras, Tuolumne, Stanislaus, and San Joaquin counties, was noted for his efficiency, and it was later said, "no judge ever retired from the bench with a fairer record."[70]

Bowmer and his attorneys immediately appealed the case, but a notice that the case had been settled was issued on April 1, 1856. Shortly thereafter Bowmer sold his interest in the store and bought an Ione City house and nearby lot.[71]

Lorena's only comment upon the trial during this entire time was even briefer than usual, just two short sentences written on February 20. Perhaps she did not go into much detail because she had something more important on her mind — the birth of their first child, a girl, on April 23. In fact, Lorena's diary is more informative about her pregnancy than would be expected, either from her own reticence or that traditionally associated with the Victorian woman. Although she did not report frankly on her condition, anyone acquainted with code words used by Victorians to describe pregnancy can read between the lines, especially the entry for January 26, which Lorena called "Reflections." And, looking back through her diary for the preceding nine months, all the indications of pregnancy are there, hiding behind her frequent allusions to poor health.

Although the baby, whose name Lorena never entered in her diary, was born "well developed and healthy," she soon developed what may have been an abcess on the neck. All medical treatment failed and the baby died on June 26, leaving Lorena disconsolate. To give her a change of scene and something of interest to think about, Clement accepted an invitation from Lorena's sister, Amanda Malvina, and her husband, William Matthews, to visit them near Independence Flat in Calaveras County. Amanda, who wrote in late June to her mother, praised the beautiful country and wished "you were all up here. You have no idea how you would enjoy it." She added that she had made eighteen dollars recently "by washing," besides taking care of her baby and cooking.[72]

Lorena and Clement rented out their house in Ione and started for the mountains the last week of July, traveling through Jackson and Mokelumne Hill. The Bowmers decided to camp near the mining town of Jesus Maria, located about five miles southeast of the latter.[73]

The novelty of camping out while building their own cabin helped revive Lorena's spirits somewhat, and she enjoyed entertaining friends and relatives in this mountain retreat. She also visited the Calaveras Grove of Big Trees, seventeen miles away, and marvelled at the size of the giant sequoias, called "the mamoth trees of Calaveras." Discovered in 1852, it did not take long for this grove, which contains some spectacular specimens, to become a popular tourist attraction.[74]

Lorena's vacation lasted only about a month. Upon returning to the Ione Valley, she wrote infrequently in her diary, although she did note her support of "Fremont and Freedom," and would have voted that way if she could have.

By New Years Day 1857 the Bowmers were "situated" on a ranch, the location of which Lorena did not give, because their house in town was leased to a woman photographer. Mrs. E. W. Withington advertised her Ambrotype Gallery in the July 25, 1857, issue of the *Amador Ledger*. Withington's gallery, with "a large and well arranged skylight," was located on "Main street, first door west of the bridge." She hastened to "inform the citizens of Amador country and the public generally" that she did business on Tuesdays, Wednesdays, Thursdays, and Saturdays "at all hours suitable for operating, where all are invited to call and examine her specimens before getting pictures elsewhere.[75]

Withington announced that she had adopted "Excelsior" as her motto and was sure of providing "satisfaction to all who patronize her by giving them a *faithful likeness* as they can procure elsewhere." Her confidence was based upon having "recently visited not only Brady's celebrated Gallery in New York City but many of the most noted galleries in several of the Atlantic States." Amador County residents were invited to "Come and See, and if it pleases you, Secure the shadow ere the substance fade."

The Amador County newspaper greeted Withington's business venture by commenting:

> We are assured upon undoubted authority that she is an accomplished lady and most excellent artist. Just think of it — Your picture taken by a lady! We trust she may receive a liberal support.[76]

Withington also gave lessons in "Oriental Pearl Painting," one of many nineteenth century parlor art endeavors popular among women. Whether there was a great demand in Ione City for this type of instruction is unknown, but the fact that it was even offered would seem to indicate the community was quickly becoming civilized, according to Victorian views.

During 1857 Lorena's life centered upon housekeeping duties, visits to relatives, and church activities. Although she occasionally wrote a few sentences in her diary about current events, she could not find the energy or enthusiasm to resume her newspaper career, in spite of several such requests. However, in March she finally summoned up her courage and wrote what would be her final article for *The Golden Era*. This "Letter from Lenita," printed March 29 on page two, gave the editor "great pleasure to hear from you after a long silence." Apparently, Lorena cringed at such "public notice," fearing someday the correspondents' corner might include a statement that "So-and-so 'declined' or 'try again.'" If this occurred,

> Oh, I should never "try again" . . . as I have never been the recipient of such editorial condecension. I should shrink from it with considerable degree of timidity and would rather prefer "consignment to oblivion" to such a method of obtaining notoriety.

In repeating this "abhorence of such public attention," Lorena also told the editor he might use her letter "to light his cigar with" instead. And, in a statement providing another clue as to her personality, Lorena continued:

> . . . You must permit me to dash off in my own random style . . . I like freedom: freedom of the mind, heart, and hands; freedom from the conventionalities of society and fashion. One enjoys this feature of pioneer life.

Lorena then described the "beauty in Nature" of the Ione Valley, with "thriving farms occupy[ing] the whole of its rich bosom." Commenting upon "our little society," she wrote, "We have churches, schools and happy family circles, of course." The rest of her last letter told about recent social events:

> This winter the "dance" (the fashionable promiscuous balls) have been substituted by more substantial and innocent enjoyments. Whereas no indulgent papas and fast young men were compelled by "hard times" to curtail expenses and so exhilarated young ladies with dress decollete and bare arms, also compelled to forego the pleasures of polka and redowa, I know not but nevertheless our holidays were made merry and cheerful for the children, charitable calls have been answered and donation parties for our minister well attended by smiling faces and made pleasant and agreeable by well-loaded tables and a plentiful supply of the one thing needful, wherewith clerical wants, as well as others, must sometimes be purchased.

After this long sentence, one can only surmise the editor must have had a soft spot in his heart for Lorena to print her work unedited.

Her last article ended with the statement, "It is time to prepare dinner," almost an indication that in the future family responsibilities might occupy so much of her time she would not be able to continue her writing. On April 5 an unsigned poem about the death of a baby, "In Memory of Lily," appeared on page one of *The Era*. While authorship cannot be directly attributed to Lorena, who did write some poetry, these verses sound very much like the lamentations in her diary. And on April 10 she wrote that some of her poetry had been published in a newspaper.

About this time Lorena and her husband began to participate more actively in the Baptist Church of Ione Valley, with Clement serving alongside Uncle Adam Lithgow as a deacon. Rev. H. Holcomb Rheese, who had previously been a successful Stockton attorney, and his wife shared part of the Bowmers' home in 1857, after returning from a trip east. Rheese had "in every way labored arduously for the building up of the church and conversion of siners" by holding public service every Sabbath "or nearly so," according to minutes of the California Baptist Association. In 1857 it was reported by the Ione Valley church:

> Our congregations at public services have been more than usually large, always attentive and apparently exhibited a spirit of honest inquiry. The weekly prayer-meeting of late has been very well attended.[77]

At the May 1857 meeting of the Baptist Association in San Francisco, Rheese, chosen to serve as moderator pro tem as well as on committees for education and benevolent efforts, requested permission for the Ione Valley church to withdraw and help organize a new association for the Sacramento area. "Dismission for the purpose of effecting such organization" was granted, and the first meeting of the new Sacramento Valley Baptist Association was held September 12-14.[78]

Lorena's husband and uncle, along with three other deacons, represented the Ione Valley congregation at this session when "some 12 churches" met to form the new group. Rheese served as clerk of the association. Also present was Rev. Myron Newell, who helped organize the Ione church in 1854.[79]

Lorena, who had attended some previous church association meetings, stayed at home, and her diary made no mention of her husband's role in the Sacramento session. She was again bothered by poor health because she was three months pregnant. However, in October she did write about visiting the California State Fair, held in Stockton. This four-day event was the fourth such fair held in the state. New features included exhibits of manufactured goods and fine-blooded stock; for the first time discussion was underway about finding a permanent location for the state fair. Lorena, who had always enjoyed horseback riding, found the competition between the "lady equestrians" of special interest.[80] Later Lorena and her husband stopped at the gardens of Capt. Charles M. Weber, a German emigrant who came to California in the first overland company of 1841 and founded Stockton. The city was laid out according to Weber's plans, and he became a wealthy landowner and banker.[81]

Upon returning from Stockton, Lorena and Clement moved back to Ione City, where he apparently earned a living by working as a carpenter. One evening, while her husband was in Jackson, Lorena nearly burned down the house when a candle set laundry on fire, which also endangered the cloth ceiling. Such flimsy construction was common in California. One account of a public house on the Sacramento-Hangtown Road described it as "lined throught with Muslin, and would take but a few moments [for fire] to Spread through the whole House...."[82] A similar report of such buildings came from DeWitt Seaver, another 1853 emigrant, who wrote it was a "wonder" that

> more of the cities and villages do not burn up. They are built with the more inflammable materials composed of pitch pine and generally lined with cotton cloth as they get so dry in summer that it seems they would take fire from spontaneous combustion.[83]

While awaiting the birth of their second child on March 4, 1858, Lorena continued her reading program of self-improvement but did not write more than once a month in her diary. Again, her references to poor health and being an "invalid" can be translated as Victorianisms for pregnancy and childbirth. Lorena came through her second pregnancy with less "sickness," recovered her health quickly following delivery, and so was able to enjoy their son, Harry Livingston Bowmer. Lorena's joy shows clearly in the few diary entries she wrote during the remainder of that year.

Soon Lorena discovered what a difference a baby made in her life. She had little time to read or write. The nineteenth century "Cult of Domesticity" dominated her life (as it did that of most other Victorian women), and any thoughts of a career were clearly out of the question. Household duties filled her days.[84] Even trying to do the laundry became more difficult with a baby to watch or, later, a toddler to be kept away from the fire and tub of hot water. It was nearly impossible for her to write with young Harry, soon nicknamed "Bub" and "Livy" by his parents, pulling at her skirts, trying to climb into her lap and grabbing at the pen. Lorena despaired of ever finding time to do anything besides the required domestic duties. In January 1859 she hoped to take lessons at a new piano school but could not find the time, even though Harry was almost one year old. It is tempting to speculate whether Lorena could have successfully combined a career with marriage and motherhood had she lived 100 years later.

To give Lorena some relief, the Bowmers brought in a mother's helper, who turned out to generate more work than help. This young girl, called Sarah, was still of school age and did not often wish to mind the baby or help with many of the household chores. Since Sarah had to attend school, this made double work for Lorena, almost as if she had two children instead of one. However, in late February 1859 Lorena had a vacation of sorts when she took the baby for a visit to her mother in Volcano for two weeks. Lorena, whose thoughts had been filled with a premonition of death, returned home in better spirits after a change of scene, as well as her mother's companionship and help with Harry.

After writing about this visit in mid-March, Lorena did not turn to her diary again until four months later. On July 8, 1859, four short sentences filled all the available space left in the booklets she had begun eleven years earlier to record her innermost thoughts and hopes. If she started another diary, it has not survived. This final entry reveals that Lorena had come to terms with her ambition, accepting with some degree of resignation the course of her life.

"If Only I May Be Useful"

23RD ARRIVED IN DRY TOWN to day. It is a small place situated in the mines and has not a very pleasant appearance. Came on to Sarrahsville, four miles further — met Aunt Sarah before getting to Dry town as she came to meet us. Our journey is ended for a few days, as we will have to look around before going elsewhere.[1]

26th, Monday Went to church yesterday, about 10 or 12 miles down in Ione Valley.[2] It is a pretty valley and appears to be in flourishing condition, containing clusters of new buildings, and fine ranches. I enjoyed the preaching though there were few there, and the minister not the most intelligent, but a *good* man. We have met quite a number of old acquaintance and formed some new, which I hope may prove useful, interesting and agreeable. This is a wild, romantic and almost barbarous country. It seems as if all restraint were laid aside by every one when they arrive here. Kind admonitions, earnest prayers and good advice of pious, anxious parents at home are quite forgotten, and sober-minded young men of good habits become wild and reckless — husbands almost forget the anxieties of a confiding wife, and all go heedlessly rushing, hurrying on in wild strife for gold, yet few seem miserly. Money seems to be used prodigally and lavishly on all occasions, some in the promotion of Christianity, and morality. Yet females, who are to be a purifying influence upon society are cordially welcomed, and politely treated by all. In my ride yesterday I saw mistletoe growing upon some live oak trees. The scenery was quite pretty, the country being somewhat broken, the trees scattering and spreading, being mostly oak. The grass is all dry at present. weather dry and pleasant. We are not yet settled and do not know how we shall be situated, whether all together, or one in one place and another elsewhere. I hope though it may be in that way the we can be most useful to ourselves and others. May ever set a good example, and ever be ready to do any little kind act or speak a sympathizing word whenever an opportunity occurs.

Sarahs ville, Cal.

25th Attended preaching last evening at Mr. Tost's by Mr. Cleveland. He seems to be a sincere man. I hope he may do much good. The congregation was small but gave good attention. I believe that intelligent, earnest ministers could always gain large, and attentive audiences.[3]

Sister Sarepta has gone to Dry town to assist in a boarding house. She has fifty dollars per month.[4] We have been enquiring in reference to schools, but find them very scarce, and I fear shall have to engage in other business.

Sept. 29th Well, we are at last settled in a comfortable little home. Mother has purchased a small house, rough and homely, and now we are dependent upon our own exertions for a livelihood. We are left alone among strangers, our friends bade us adieu to day, having started for a more southern portion of the country where they can procure ranchos for their cattle. I felt lonely enough as I gave them the parting hand and now the wagons move slowly off. I could hardly realize that our train had gone and left *us*. It will hardly be the same train, so many of us are left behind. I am no longer to live a camp life, no longer to walk, ride and to be almost constantly in the fresh, free air of Heaven. A roof must now intervene between me and the blue dome above and the stars and bright moon that gem of the ether blue, can no longer look freely down upon us, but some stragling ray, or beam, must come slyly peeping through some loophole, or crevice. Oh! I shall be almost ''homesick'', I fear, to be travelling again. I can never feel so free, so independent any more. Truly we had a very easy and interesting journey across the plains. The last part of the journey was rough, and somewhat tedious, but I have no reason to regret it in the least — I feel that I have seen and learned enough to pay for all its troubles. Now I am situated in a strange land amid strangers. Society and its customs are very different. Many things are tolerated which I cannot like. Many people must be treated friendly whose habits we cannot approve off, yet I think I shall be quite happy, if I may only be useful, if I can ever set a good example, which may have an influence upon others, if I may grow wiser and better, surely I shall have no reason to complain. May Gods blessings rest upon us, and may *we ever* try to live to His honor and glory.

I had quite a pleasant little ramble yesterday with Aunt Sarah and a friend of hers along the diggings, but she is gone now, and there is not one left to guide and befriend me.

Sarah's ville

Oct 1st Two more days have passed off quite agreeably, though very warm. What few acquaintances we have formed are very kind and considerate. I think we shall like the place very well as soon as we shall get more acquainted.

Oct 2nd — Sabbath No church or Sabbath School to attend. I felt very low-spirited this morning though I hardly knew on what account. I think I do not have enough exercise since leaving off travelling. Mother talks some of opening a boarding house. I think I should like it on several accounts, especially as I could be more actively engaged, and should not be compelled to such sedentary habits.

I have been reading the Christian Advocate printed at San francisco[5] & found it interesting, especially facts relating to the moral habits of the country. Though people are every where reckless and wild, yet I never hear of any that are averse to hearing the gospel preached, but there is a general manifestation of interest and good attention every-where paid to preaching, so far as I have had opportunity of judging.

5th Yesterday rode to Dry town. Aunt Sarah came back to see us as they were camped only eight miles from us. She went with me to Dry town, we had a pleasant ride. Called on Sister and some of the ladies. Several old acquaintances have called on us this week and I enjoyed their company very much.

Sarahsville

8th Uncle Henry is up to see us to day. He expects to settle on a rancho near where he is camped — A friend just brought us in some nice bunches of most excellent grapes — they are brought from the vallies, and are surely very delicious. We eat flour, sugar and dried fruit brought from Chili[6] which seems very strange to a resident of the United States. The oranges we have are very large and nice. Afterall, in many respects, I can think this is a pleasant country — I should like the privilege of visiting the different parts of it, its sea coasts, cities and vallies.

Nov 4th It has been some time since I have written any, nothing out of the usual routine of every day life having occurred, save that we have been preparing and enlarging our house for boarders. We are nearly ready for opening it when, I suppose we shall have plenty to do. Mr. Israel called on us to night bringing some letters from the States, but they were written so long ago that they were not very interesting.

11th I have not been very well for several days. Wednesday evening I attended a ball at the Willow Springs. Did not participate in dancing, and do not intend making a practice of going to balls & parties. There were near three hundred persons present, quite a number from Sacramento were there. The music was excellent. Supper splendid, rooms very tastefully arranged, and the people polite and agreeable.[7]

17th We had some boarders the last two weeks, not enough yet to make very hard work. Most all are gone to night, and I feel a little lonely. I have some apprehensions lest not all will go well to night, as a new grocery & saloon is to be opened at Michigan Bar.[8] A ''spree'' most likely will be the consequence. Oh, what a foothold has intemperance gained in this land of golden hills & fruitful valleys. What a happy land it will be when sin no longer reigns so universally over its diversified surface. When the gambler, robber, murderer and drunkard shall hide their heads abashed from the presence of sobriety, justice and truth.

30th Nothing of very much interest has occurred since I last wrote. We have a few boarders, so our work is not hard, & we usually spend our time quite pleasantly during the leisure time of the day in reading good newspapers of which we ever have a plentiful supply ''just from the States''.[9] Our evenings are spent in writing and reading. Some of the boarders are taking lessons in penmanship, which they think a much more profitable way of spending time than in gambling & drinking saloons. I do not wonder at bad habits which young so soon form after arriving in this country, there being no profitable places of recreation and useful intellectual resorts for them to attend in their leisure hours. They have no female society with whom they might spend profitably & pleasurably their evening hours, which are usually spent in participating in or watching a game of cards. At first they are merely induced to enter the saloon in order to ''pass of time'' which, if there were other inducements, they would gladly spend otherwise. ''Lookers on'' soon get interested and then are not hard to be persuaded to participate in so fascinating an indulgence but which ends in such fatal & ruinous consequences to them. The society is truly deplorable here. There is no Sabbath, and all seem alike plunged in heathen darkness so far as religion is concerned. What a field for a missionary! What a field of usefulness for anyone who is desirous of benefitting his fellow man! Here is the degraded Digger, the Chilanean from South America, the Chinamen, Frenchmen & Spaniard, the escaped convict from Australia, and indeed there is no country without its representative here. Oh! what an example it is our privilege to set them that they may receive a favorable impression of the great blessings of a land of *liberty*. That their hearts may be impressed with a *due* respect and esteem for our holy religion. But, alas! most of us are selfish. We come for gold, and have no time for others. They come for it too, so all go hurrying on in the strife, gathering and spending it as they go.

12th Time passes off more & more pleasantly as new and kind friends gather around us. Sometimes incidents, unusual to us, occur, which for a little while cause unpleasant emotions, but they soon pass off and we are all happy again. I never at home have found friends who seemed more sincere and kind than most of our acquaintances do here.

Dec 13 I at least, never felt more confidence in them than in some I have found here who have manifested such tender and respectful interest for us, thereby showing that they are well aware of the influences by which we are surrounded in a country like this. I can never be too grateful for such kindness which far exceeds my greatest expectations. Sister S. and myself had, the other day, a pleasant horseback ride down to Ione Valley where our Uncles reside. They have a very pretty ranch, quite romantically situated. Our ride was quite a long one, but the day passed agreeably, and quickly away. Last evening heard the Rev. Baine preach.[10] It was the best sermon I have heard since leaving home. I wish I could hear such a sermon much oftener — We have had some little rain, but no cold weather, and the grass is every where springing up green and fresh as if it were spring. What an ever beautiful climate do we live in.

18th Sabbath This is a beautiful pleasant day. Uncle & Aunts were here last night. Had some letters from the States. It is pleasant to hear what is passing at home. Shall I ever visit it again? We have a happy home here, though, & I have no reason to complain. Friends are kind. Oh! may I ever act worthy of their friendship, may I ever be kind and affable to all, & be willing to make self sacrifices for others. I have plenty of books and papers to read and often get to much engaged in them, to pay as much attention to others as I ought to, sometimes, I fear.

Jan 11th, 1854 Christmas & New Years have passed with no stirring events to note. For four weeks an interesting young man lay sick in our house. He died on the morning before New Years. He became speechless three or four days before he died, or at least could not say many things which we could understand, although he tried very hard some times, which often brought tears to our eyes. I suppose he must have been conscious that he was going to die, although he could tell us nothing about it & he left no evidence that he had any hope in Christ. How hard it must be for one so young, and beautiful to die far away from home in this land of strangers. He has left a brother here, younger than himself. Oh! may he take warning in time & be ready when the messenger of Death shall come to summon him away. The weather is still mild and dry, no rain this winter, so far, which makes business very dull.[11]

Jan 22nd The weather has been exceedingly cold the last few days for California. The winter is said to be severer than has been known for years. Time passes of pleasantly, generally. I have been reading a number of the water-cure journals to day. It contained more valuable and interesting matter than usual. I do not think the system can be overated or too highly appreciated. I have read the Encyclopedia of Hydropathy,[12] and believe it worthy the study of every one. Oh! that I had the power and talents to aid in the great reforms these works advocate. Would that every one would interest themselves in these matters so immediately concerning themselves, yet upon which we too often maintain the most ignorance.

I have to read, and think by myself in these matters. There are none of my friends that I know of who would sympathize with me or enter into any views, and feelings in regard to the late reforms. If I try to argue the matter with them, I am only persecuted and laughed at, so I must submit in patience, and wait their slow, yet I think sure progress. I at least will have my own enjoyment in reading and thinking.

Feb 3rd Last Sabbath we took a stroll to the top of Sugar-loaf where we had a splendid view of the Sierra nevada covered with snow & also the far off Coast range just discernable in the dim, blue distance.[13] The air being smoky, our view was somewhat obscured, but it was a very pretty, romantic sight. From a steamer on the Sacramento river we saw the smoke curling proudly up. The valley looked peaceful & quiet. The broad expanse of country which we could behold had a truly romantic and picturesque appearance. I enjoyed our excursion very much — it was refreshing, and gave me quite an exuberance of spirits. I had a fine race in coming down the mountain. I wish I could have such a ramble every day.

Willow Flat[14]

Sunday, 5th "Charley" and "Jenny" have just come from the valley and I am going home with them. I anticipate a fine time rambling and rusticating for a few days.

15th Came home yesterday. enjoyed my visit very much, though it rained a good deal. On coming home, heard my friend, Mr. B. was going to the States.[15] I thought a good deal of it last night — I shall feel bad to bid him "good bye". He has been a *very kind* friend. I may never find another who will manifest so much interest and kindness for me, a poor orphan girl —

18th Made quite a pleasant call on the Willow Spring House to day. Weather is pleasant. Took a walk yesterday, after flowers, found but very few — has been to cold for them to grow.

21st Disappointed in a visit to the Willow Springs on account of the rain, although they sent for us.

22nd To night is the festival in the valley. It is so rainy I do not see how anyone can go. It will be a great disappointment to the fair ones who have taken so much pains to get it up, and then what a loss will be sustained as the proceeds were to be used for the finishing of their church. This has been very, very rainy day. I have been reading Graham's magazine and listening to the violin, and making some attempts to learn to play a tune, but what a dull musicioner! I don't think I need even entertain a hope that I can learn instrumental music, although I have always had a desire to learn, and always believed, too, that I could accomplish anything I really determined. All my time is running to waste, I fear, as I am neither acquiring or learning, save what I can glean from reading.[16]

March 3rd Have been talking with some young men in reference to Gambling. Do not know what effect it will have. I must always feel sorry after talking lest I do more harm than good.

Willow Flat

7th Took a walk after flowers, found but few, except a beautiful specimen of yellow violet which grow in great profusion, just as purple ones grow in the States. I found no purple ones here, though. I felt so sad and lonely to night, although we have not been alone — have had music and a little dancing, just for pastime. But I have felt as if I wanted some dear sympathizing friend with whom to hold sweet converse, one in to whose willing ear I might pour my deep soul thoughts, my hearts earnest emotions. 'Neath to night's pale, gentle moonbeams how I could have enjoyed the society of some gentle, loving heart — How eagerly liste'd to the soothing, gentle tones of a kind earnest friend. Yet, I must not complain. I have many kind friends, and there are those whose earnest heart-sympathies I might freely have, yet I do not earnestly & freely reciprocate. Do I do wrong? Is it not my duty to return a generous love that is lavishly bestowed upon me. I know not. Oh! Father in Heaven, guide me aright. I do thy will. Only show it me. A beautiful ring presented me for a Phillippine gift, I shall retain as a momento of the friendship and tender regard of one who has been most kind to me in a land of strangers. I have a Bible to present him as he won the last Phillippine off of me.[17]

9th To day is almost like summer, so calm & still, and such a beautiful, cloudless sky over head. What a beautiful climate we have.

20th Took a ride to the Forest Home[18] to see sister — met her coming home just as I got almost there. Did not enjoy my ride much, and have been sorry ever since that I went. Am almost getting tired of staying here, the society is distasteful, as there are but few of very refined habits. We have quite a number of boarders and cannot well change our situation at present, But I hope a better will soon offer itself, and I also hope that I may be able to live and act becomingly at all times here. I fear I often go astray.

22 Oh, dear. I have had a series of vexatious little troubles — I am all in a tremble. How little things affect us greatly sometimes. For dinner, quite a number of strangers came in, and it seemed as if our dinner was uncommonly poor. Nothing was right, and I was almost mortified to death about it. An old indian just now wanted some biscuit of sister. She said she would not give him any. He said ugh and seemed displeased. So I told him I would give him some, and flew off to get it he following me with delight, but upon his coming into the room where I was alone I got frightened, screamed and ran. The indian was very much amused at me and went off mimicking me to his comrad. He was a grotesque looking old man, had his bow and arrows. I do not know why I was so frightened, but I thought he was going to take hold of me, & I was siezed with a terrible panic. Just after he left an old drunk man came in a terrible, loathsome looking man he is. It is said he was once a very intelligent man.

Evening. Miss Orten visited us this afternoon. Mr. Waye and Bormer called. Mr. W. has consented for Mr. B. to go home. I feel sadly to have him go. He has been such a kind friend.[19]

23rd Have been almost sick from my excitement yesterday. Was so nervous I could not sleep well last night. Low spirited, and ate no supper last night or anything this morning.

26th Sarah & I went to see Mrs. H. on Dry-Creek, 2 miles from here —[20] found some new flowers & enjoyed the walk, though I was somewhat afraid of meeting Spaniards who, it is said, are not always respectful to females, and they often murder Americans for their money.

Willow Flat   Personal Journal

March 31st About sunrise this morning we heard the wailings of a camp of indians. I suppose some one of their number has dies, and if so, they will burn the corpse, and paint their faces black with the ashes or soot of the body. Yesterday a number of the captains met at Capt. Peters camp to partake of the feast & make arrangements for a fandango.[21] Some of them rode up here quite pompously, one had a bell on his horses neck.

I have felt too inactive to do anything for a day or so, except to read & loll about. Sometimes I feel lonely, and low-spirited and long for more congenial associates, or some amusement or exercise to pass time pleasantly. I believe I will go and hunt some flowers pretty soon, but feel too dull to enjoy them when I get them. I was last evening reading a few sketches from F. Bremer's Homes of America, which were very interesting. She writes with so much simplicity, ease and clearness. One would never weary of reading her pretty and vivid narratives.[22] O! I wish I could write like her. I'd be a dull, inactive, unknown, unthought off being no longer. I'd have a name, an influence, that should gather around me a cluster of loved & loving friends, beings of kindred spirits, only excelling in superiority of all that is good and intellectual that I might ever be drinking from the fountain of knowledge & love. But I'm an effeminate dreamer — too inactive, too inefficient for the world of stern necessity, and cold realities. There are only a few who can mount the pinnacle of human ambition, this desirderation of terrestrial happiness, and hold a happy sway over mind. I have not the genius, or talent even if I had the education.

April 4th O! what a lovely night. So mild — such soft moonlight — the air loaded with the perfume of flowers. It is so lovely it makes me almost sad. Indeed I've been but sad for several days. The only friend with whom I can hold sympathy and communion of heart is going to leave me, and alone in this sad world. I shall have no one to look to for love and sympathy, no one to guide. I must rely upon my own weakness & almost utter helplessness. I must try & be strong & brave though I feel so weak, and dependent. May my Heavenly Father support & guide me & give me wisdom how to act.

April 9th Aunt Sarah came up one day last week. Wanted me to go home with her. Got on to our horses to start. Mine commenced prancing so that became afraid to ride it. Mr. B. got a horse and went with us. We had a pleasant ride. I came home the next day with him. It was a beautiful day. An abundance of flowers are in bloom. I brought home some beautiful ones of a species I never saw before. Mr. and Mrs. H. came to our house next day. I went with them to Dry Creek. Have not enjoyed myself much for a week, but spent last evening *very* pleasantly.

10th Church last evening — did not go. Took a walk this afternoon in company with sisters and some gentlemen who travel with Mr. B., was my escort. I never had so tender & dear a friend, never was so *earnestly* and *devotedly* loved. I have always loved him as a dear friend & benefactor — he has been *so kind.* I never really admired him as a lover, but have learned to love him for his goodness of heart and purity of principle. O! that I may ever appreciate, and love him as tenderly as he does me. May I prove constant, and love him more, and more every day of his absence, & when he returns may I find him *everything* I could wish him to be, and may I be all to him I should be. How *much gratitude* I owe my heavenly Father for so many unexpected, undeserved blessings as are daily being showered upon me. I can never be sufficiently grateful that my most earnest desires are gradually being fulfilled.

If not disappointed by some unforeseen cause, I expect once more go to school that I may obtain some of those accomplishments I have always so earnestly desired that I may be fitted to move in a circle (society) I have ever wished to enjoy. I hope I may so improve as that my friends may be proud, and gratified with me, and make myself capable of exerting a useful influence in society. My *dear friend* brought me a pretty pair of California quail this morning.[23] I shall endeavor to take "good care of them" for his sake. He presented me with a beautiful natural specimen pin — two specimens connected by a little chain. I have never seen any prettier one. It is late. I go to bed hoping I shall find *much* happiness in the future. Oh! that my temperament were more sanguine. I am ever too fearful. God grant my cup of happiness may be full.

17th   What a world of wretchedness I have suffered since last writing. My *friend* started to the states expecting never to see me again. I gave up going to school, and expected to remain at home and spend a sad summer unless I got a chance to go to Sacramento or somewhere to earn a living. I felt sadly to bid *him* goodbye. Mother advised me to send him word to come back in the fall. I did so — but was fearful I did not yet love him as I ought to. Oh! how I suffered. He has came back *so happy,* having given up going entirely. I take a ride with him to day. Oh! that I felt such happiness as I want to. Is it my disponding temperament, or do I not *love* as I *ought* to? Oh! Father in Heaven, bless me and fill my heart with deep, earnest happiness such as I have hoped to feel on an occasion like this. Oh! I want to be *so proud, so happy* in him. — I close and go to the valley to see the store &c by his request.

23rd Sabbath Just returned from the valley. Oh! what a lovely place it is. So green and beautiful. So peaceful and quiet. I took some pleasant rambles. The scenery is varied and beautiful. There are sloping hills and nestling vallies dotted over with evergreen oaks, and flowers grow in profusion everywhere. In the far distance is the snow capped summits of the Sierra Nevada. Uncles and Aunts are busily engaged in making butter, & milking cows, & all sorts of domestic labor. In going down I went by Ione City, went in to the store. It is quite a pretty place. It is said to be one of the pleasantest in California. Mr. B. accompanied me home. We had a pleasant ride. The day is beautiful. My friend is so kind. I shall never be able to repay all of his goodness to me. Such deep and tender devotion, and yet how often I have wounded, and almost broken his heart of hearts. How could I bear to do so? Surely I do not appreciate him as I ought, or as I yet hope to. I must go to work tomorrow and get ready to go to Sacramento where I intend to spend a few weeks at least. Sister Sarepta is spending a few days at home. Sister Caroline is still at the Prairie House,[24] received a letter from her to day. She is not very well pleased with her situation. Mother does not know, hardly, what is best to do. There is no mining done here now, consequently we shall have no boarders, and cannot earn anything here.

28th My health is improving, but such an inexpressible sadness so irresistibly steals over me at times. Oh! what sufferings, what agony have I not endured within the last month? But it was my own fault, though I have not intentionally done wrong. O! no! I have wanted to do right. O! that I loved him as earnestly as I have believed *he* has loved me, or that I could at once tell him again that his deep devotion could not be reciprocated. But he has so often told me the consequences would be so sad and ruinous to him, and I cannot but believe at times that I shall yet learn to love him as he deserves, and as my own heart can love. It is through his kindness that I expect to go to the city. I almost feel that I am doing wrong to accept any more favors from him, but I know not what else to do. It would not be right to spend the summer in idleness. Yesterday afternoon and evening spent at the Willow-Springs House very agreeably. Met Mrs. Moore there. They called me Mrs. B. and wished me much joy having heard I was married — quite a mistake, though.

May 1st Mother & Malvina[25] gone to the valley. Sarah & I all alone. How very lonesome & sad I have felt to day. I *must* throw off these depressions if possible. I shall not be able to do anything if I continue to feel so. I do not think my health is fair, or I should not feel as I do. Heard a very intelligent gentleman preach last evening. He staid with us.

4th Mr. B. came to see mother while she was gone. I was agreeably surprized by his coming, and enjoyed his presence, as I was quite alone, and it was lonely. Mr. Jamisan, a stranger whom I had seen once before, called for dinner and to present a ball ticket for the 12th at Fiddletown. He was quite an agreeable gentleman. Mother has made up her mind to build a house at Cook's Bar — there seems to be a good opening for her to make money at that place. She can have a very pleasant situation in Ione Valley but prefers to go to Cook's Bar.[26] I hope she may do well. O! how I wish now I had a thousand dollars. I do so want to go to Sacramento, to school. I am not well & feel such mental depression at times. It seems impossible for me to throw it off, unless I could be employed in some congenial pursuit. I might go to school, if I would accept the generous offer of a kind friend. But I cannot do it conscientiously & so have got to wait until I earn some money, and that seems never to be my luck. Spent most of to day at Willow Springs. Am always treated very kindly there.

8th Yesterday received by mail a book entitled Hopes and Helps. I find it very interesting so far as I have read, & hope to profit by it. To day received a long, and kind letter from my *good* friend. We are preparing for a change in our residence. Shall leave this place, which is quite deserted — it is, however, a very pretty place. The scenery is pretty at this season of the year. The trees are scattered over the country here and there resembling an orchard. Flowers grow in great profusion almost entirely choking out the grass. Some are very pretty, and most are new to me. I am about to give up going to Sacramento again — I am sorry, but it is best most likely. I must work as hard as I can this summer so I can go next winter. "Hope on, hope ever" is my motto, though I often get quite discouraged. Surely I am not energetic or persevering enough.

17th Spent a part of the last week at the Forest Home — on Friday in company with sister & Mrs. Cook came up to the Willow Springs in tending to spend the afternoon with Miss Orton. Walker's Cotillion band on their way to the Fiddletown ball,[27] having called, Miss O. had fancied a desire for a ride, and requested that we all should favor the gentlemen with our company to the ball. None of us really intending to go except Miss O. when the announcement was made that the carriage was waiting. I jestingly said we were ready, got our bonnets, and went to the carriage with great glee, intending to stop at home & at least consult my mother, if not refuse to go at all. But when we came near our house, no entreaties, or threats could prevail on the gentlemen to let us stop, unless we would positively promise to go the rest of the way. This they would not do, so they refused to stop altogether, & we had no alternative but to go whether we would or not. The party was very pleasant & much enjoyed by most present. Fiddletown looks like a thriving and prosperous place, but is not a very pretty place or handsomely located, being situated in a narrow ravine with only room for one street and that is very narrow. Sabbath evening heard a good sermon from Mr. Coole. He is a young man of promising abillities.[28]

Yesterday went up to Brown's ranche on a visit. While in the stage, formed an acquaintance with two young men who were also on a visit to Mr. Smith at the ranche. One of them was an artist & had his sketch book along with him, the other one of the editors of the Golden Era. We spent the evening very pleasantly in interesting conversation. I had a very pressing invitation to become a correspondent with the Era. Desired to accept the invitation, but am fearful of my abillities as an editors correspondent.[29]

Cook's Bar

23 Have been ever since Thursday, at the Forest House. Miss Nanrankin was there. We had a very pleasant time. I do not know when I have romped so much. Mr. and Mrs. Cook are very lively. Last night they gave a social party. It was a very pleasant one indeed. I have found some interesting acquaintances. This morning came to Cook's Bar where we now live. The place is mostly composed of small canvas

houses, many of them placed in a grove of trees, which render them much more comfortable to live in then they would be if placed in the sun-shine. There is a ridge, or natural smooth embankment extending quite around the plat, or depression, in which the mines & habitations are situated, & which gives it the appearance of being shut away from other neighbourhoods, which are not far distant. The river is about a half a mile distant, but only a small portion of the bottom adjoining can be seen from our house.[30]

27th   Have been engaged in reading the Water-cure Journal of which I have just received several back numbers — it is an earnest advocate of all reform movements, especially the health reform. No one can read it without feeling benefitted and made wiser in reference to his own being and organization, or the laws of health and life. In "Hopes and Helps" I found most valuable lessons inculcated[31] Not a word or sentence but conveys a deep meaning. It contains no useless language, though its language is as beautiful as the lessons it conveys. As one has remarked of it, "it is a succession of gems and dew drops". With my reading I find, that every day, I become more, and more impressed, with a desire for different and more appropriate opportunities for mental culture. How I long for a situation, where everything would be favorable to progress, where there would be agreeable incentives, and stimulants to exertion, kind friends to teach and encourage, and *pecuniary wants* no drawback. It has scarcely ever been my lot to have many friends who cared to sympathize with or encourage me in mental acquirements. O! how I should prize nay *love* and *adore* one to whom I could look up for instructions, and guidance, coupled with affection, and love in return. I do not believe that any other can occupy a full place in my heart.

June 16th Sad and lonely has been my feelings for a few days. Went to Michign Bar last week. Was very sick part of the day. Monday went to Ione Valley with Mr. B. in a carriage. Came home Wednesday on horseback. Called on Mr. and Mrs. Fish in Ione City. They are pleasant & intelligent. He preaches at our house on monday evening.[32] We have a good many boarders, & of course a plenty of work to do. The house is nearly done & is quite pleasant & commodious. The weather is becoming very warm. We have poor water, but otherwise our situation is quite pleasant. There is a comfortable breeze most of the day, & the evenings are delightful. Have been trying to write an article for the Golden Era but can't get one written to suit me. O! dear: wish I could —

Sabbath Called at Mr. Newcomb's to see a sick man. He is quite low & may not get well, poor man, away from home, and most of his friends, he must feel lonely enough — Music is ever welcome to us after nightfall. It comes to me now in soft strains borne on the still air of evening. California is a land of music and seems adapted to the cultivation of all the fine arts. There is something in its very atmosphere that seems to call up the most passionate practicle feelings of our nature, something that makes more acute our sense of the beautiful & we unconsciously imbibe a love of grandeur & extravagance unknown to us before. California is a sunny, golden land, full of life and gaity & were it not that so many reckless and lawless characters have been lured by its golden treasure, it be the happiest and loveliest of lands. But sin & crime have darkened and cast a moral gloom over its hills and in its ravines and vallies, but we trust that the star of reform will ere long shine upon us, that the sun of righteousness will shed its bright rays upon us, & sweep immorality, & crime from our beautiful land.

Sad and pensive have been my thoughts & feelings. I can hardly throw off the depression which so weighs upon my spirits. There is *one* perhaps suffering even more than I do, suffering the pangs of unrequited love — no — not altogether unrequited. I love him very much for his goodness and kindness & feel the need of his love & sympathy quite as much as he desires my love. Oh! how often & deeply have I lacerated & torn afresh the wounds in his heart which have hardly been closed & which former afflictions had produced.

Rev. Fish preached at or house on monday evening. He is a good minister.[33]

Ione Valley

July 6th Came to Ione last Sabbath. Attended Church Organization by Mr. Newal. Handed in our letters.[34] On the fourth attended Sabbath School Celebration. Repaired to a grove a short distance south of Ione City where were assembled the scholars of the valley in waiting for the Jackson & Dry town Schools who were invited to participate in the celebrating of the fourth with them. After a few appropriate songs by the teachers and children the Jackson School arrived with their banner for the occasion. All were arranged in good order when another song was sung, then prayer by the Rev. — from Jackson, then singing again, then came the D.T. after which the Rev. Phillips was introduced by Rev. Fish (conductor of ceremonies) to the audience to deliver an address appropriate for the occasion, and a most appropriate and eloquent discourse it was. It was deep, profound & learned and eminently shaddowed forth the brilliant talents of the speaker. Interesting historical incidents were related, startling facts announced, and beautiful hearts lessons conveyed, and a closing appeal to the bachelors of California left the audience in a state of pleasant enthusiasm. After singing & prayer, the children were dismissed by

Mr. Fish to amuse themselves in swinging or rambling in the shade of the beautiful grove while the ladies arranged on the table the bountiful supply of refreshments which had been provided for the occasion. All prepared the bell was rung, when came the happy children in an orderly procession to partake of the festive cheer which they all seemed to enjoy and of which the was a bountiful sufficiency for all present. The repast over and order again restored, and some more beautiful Sabbath School songs by the teachers & children, the Rev. Reasoner was introduced. His remarks were witty, sparkling and vivacious and well adapted to the occasion. Being a bachelor he thought himself grievously dealt with by the speaker in the forenoon address, when Mr. Phillips remarked that his castigation was not intended for those who were not to blame for their situation, which produced general and reciprocal laughter. Rev. Newel was announced. The day being far spent he only made a few appropriate remarks, after which toasts were called for, and several quite witty and applicable ones given. The ceremonies of the day were closed by singing by teachers & children and benediction by Rev. Newel. Thanks tendered by Jackson and Dry town schools to Ione school for their hospitable invitations and entertainment. Ione school returned a note of thanks for their acceptance of the invitation, and attendance upon the occasion. When a procession was formed and headed by a band of music belonging to — ["Mr." crossed out] panorama, all proceeded in order and quiet to the village, where they dispersed to their homes, or to some of the several entertainments of the evening among which was an exhibition of — [left blank]'s celebrated panoramice view of a trip across the plains.[35]

18th Yesterday had the pleasure of reading one of my own letters in the "Golden Era" with the above description in it and a request from the editors for further correspondence. Also visited at the Rev. Mr. Fish's and the school taught by Mr. Peters. He is a very interesting young man.[36] I spent the day very pleasantly. Friends, though new, are kind and respectful. Mr. Fish requested me to write for the "Advocate." The weather is cool at present, though last week we had a few days of most exceedingly warm weather. The winds came over the plains like heated blasts from a furnace. I must try and write several letters this week.

Ione Valley

August The camp meeting commenced last Friday evening. I went Saturday evening & found it very interesting. It has continued to be so ever since and I think the meeting will continue through this week. I have formed many agreeable acquaintances, and generally enjoy myself in their society. Several of the ladies have called on me. I ride on horseback quite frequently. On two evenings six of us went to meeting on horseback. We ride at a tremendous rate sometimes. This is a *fast* country. Did not go meeting last night any of us, but Mr. Newell and myself both expressed it as our belief that they had a good meeting. I hope we shall all be benefitted.[37]

Wednesday 9th Visited Mr. Peter's school yesterday. Did not enjoy myself as well as I wished to for some reason — probably my own fault. Some little indiscretion of conduct or defect in manners will often occasion a whole days or weeks pain, and regret. Oh! that I could ever act in such a manner as that I might feel pleased altogether with myself. I am so often doing or saying something that gives me sorrow. When shall I become wiser? and do just right. Mr. B. has been sick the last week or over, So that I have not seen him, which I am anxious sometimes to do.

Aug 19 Weather very warm. I have been in the valley about six weeks. Have not seen Mr. B. for nearly three to speak to him. He has suffered very much with a severe felon[38] in his hand, and I have not had the privilege of bestowing even a sympathizing word. Mr. Peters spent one evening with us week. He is an intelligent young man. I called at Mr. Martins one day last week, otherwise time has passed off rather wearily. I do not feel as well as usual this week — perhaps have not had sufficient exercise. This morning took my book, and walked a short distance to some rocks to enjoy before breakfast the pleasant morning air. The gentle rustling of the wind through the yellow leaves of the buckeye trees that find a stinted and short existence among the rocks filled my heart with a pensive feeling and reminded that autumn was approaching. There is little difference between Summer and Autumn here save that the weather is not quite so warm. The foliage of most of the trees remains quite unchanged. The sky is clear, and beautiful, the air still and pure, and a serene stillness seems ever to reign in the valley and on the pinecovered mountain tops. It would seem that the spirit of peace and gentleness was ever hovering over our land, but alas, the deeds of man speak out his fallen nature here too, and the most beautiful portions of earth seem oftenest destined to wear the mark of the direct moral blight, and where the most bountiful blessings abound there is man, most ungrateful and disobedient.

20th Yesterday while with a book in my hand I lay carelessly reclining upon the floor, my little cousin announced that Mr. B. had come. I hastened up to meet him, which I did by a pressure of the hand, but in silence. He looked pale, but more spiritual for he has indeed had a time of suffering and pain. I had only seen him since sick at church one mourning, and then though I had looked and longed for his coming I scarcely returned the nod he gave me, but turned my head away as if I had met only the face of a stranger, so wayward are our hearts and so unaccountable are our actions sometimes to us. But I felt reproached afterwards, as he waited not as I had anticipated after services to speak to me, but hurried home, for so absorbed had he been in listening to the discourse that he became quite unconscious of his hand which had become much worse swollen, the swelling also having extended rapidly along his arm. He went home very sick and while walking the floor fell in a fainting fit and was quite delirious during the afternoon. I think he has born his affliction with much patience and fortitude, having had his hand lanced nine times.

He again pressed me to know if I returned his love. I ventured to give more encouragement than usual, though perhaps have done wrong. I love him dearly in once sense. I can feel such a trust in him. My weakness finds in him such a firm and strong protection, and his love for me is so pure and tender, that in contemplating the withdrawal of it, my heart can scarcely bear the desolation and loneliness that steals over it when he asks me, as he sometimes does, if I will not tell him that I do not love him, and thereby remove the suspense that he has had such struggles to bear up under.

25th   Came home day before yesterday. When arrived at the Buckeye Ranche,[39] were overtaken by Mr. Cook and Miss Reed who were on their way to our house. We got home before dinner. In the afternoon took a ride to Michigan Bar, after spending an hour or so in singing. We spent the day *very* pleasantly. Have been working to day some about the house which I think will do me good.

Ione Valley

Sept 1st Came to the valley last Sabbath. Am almost sick having had to hurry so much to prepare to attend a wedding party which took place last evening. It was a very pretty party. Every thing was arranged with good taste — the company was agreeable, and seemed to enjoy themselves very much.

Sabbath What a calm, and pleasant day. A peaceful quietness pervades over the scene of rural beauty, and domestic comfort. Quiet valley, surrounded by your barrier of golden hills, the snowy peaks of yon lofty mountains in the dim, blue distance, sentinel-like, ever guarding with ceaseless vigils your beauteous vales, rest on in your quiet, peaceful seclusion. The voice of man now gladdens your once still air, his hand has rendered still more beautiful and useful your once lonely, and valueless fields. Sabbath bells echo out on your once silent dales, but like the garden of Eden, thy beauty, and purity, too, must be darkened and shadowed with the sins and crimes of ever erring man. Perfect purity and goodness can nowhere be found in any of the beautiful vales of Earth.

Cook's Bar

8th Spent two days on a visit to the willow spring house, Forest Home & Mountain house.[40] While gone sent a letter to Mr. Daggett for publication in the Era if he should consider it worthy a place in the paper. I'm sure I had trouble enough in preparing it if that would add any to it's merits. Times are dull here now. Weather beautifully pleasant. Day before was election day, and of course, had it's usual accompaniments of noise, fights and &c.[41] Ive a large quantity of reading matter on hand, and am afraid I shall have to hurry over it too fast to have it do me that good I should desire it should. I wish I could remember all I want to.

16th Have been reading a good deal to day in different newspapers. I could spend all my time in reading them alone, and consequently have little time to devote to other studies which perhaps are more essential, though I seldom read any thing but such as I consider useful intelligence, general news, and &c. I have just read a description of the beauties of Hock Farm. It seems that Gen. Sutter is at present a poor man.[42]

26th Just one year since the 23 of this month we ended our long journey across the plains. There have been many changes since then. Time is ever leaving his impress upon all he touches as he hurries on in his swift career, and now I must ask myself the question, how have I improved time since my arrival in this golden land? Have I benefitted myself or anyone. Have I done all the *good* I might, and improved my own mind as I should have done. I fear I may not answer in the affirmative as heartily as I could wish. Yet I can say that I have truly tried to improve my advantages for learning. There may have opportunities where I might have done more for the benefit of others if I had had wisdom how to act as I should have done. It is possible I might have rendered less poignant the grief I have seen others suffer. But it is useless to indulge in regrets for the neglected duties of the past. I must gird on strength for the future, must make resolutions, not to be broken. There is little I can do here for others or myself. I must throw off the indecisions and inactivity that has so bound me down of late. I cannot be content to spend life so no longer. I *will do some thing* and trust to God for the consequences. I am only wasting life here, only throwing away my energies. I *must* do otherwise. Oh! that I may be guided in wisdom's ways, and in those paths that lead to *true* happiness.

Oct 21 Much has occurred since last I wrote that was of interest to me. First I was made glad by a visit from a *friend*. My *letter* to the *"Era"* was published and much eulogized by the editor in a letter to myself as well as recommended in the correspondents list in the *paper*.[43] Since then I have sent two other communications. Received Miss Bremer's

Homes.[44] About two weeks since we were joyfully surprised by receiving a letter from the states informing us where brother was in this state. He had written home, not knowing that we were in California. Since then he has paid us a visit, is with us at present — I feel very thankful that we have found him and in good health with his morals as *free* from *corruption* as could be expected in this land. I hope that he will *ever* conduct himself in a manner that will render his mother and sisters proud of him. There are many temptations for young men to resist in this country. We are expecting to have a singing school tonight here by Mr. Peters, an interesting young man, which will add much to the variety of our social amusements.

29 To days paper contained a letter from "our mountain Lassie."[45] The editor paid me a short visit last week. He is very fluent in conversation and seems to possess a considerable degree of knowledge. I was a little embarrassed and made one or two blunders which mortified me, besides I did not feel very well and so was not in the right mood to entertain any one with very good grace — I imagine he went away with the impression that I was a rather dull visitor, and that he will think my letters the same hereafter —

I am lonely and discouraged and know not what to do. I have made every effort to go to school that seems practible. My case seems hopeless — there's no use of my trying any further — I must give up to remain contented in the sphere I can and try to do what little good I may with my humble capactites. It is best, doubtless, and if I may only dwell in *content* and *love* I care not so much.

No 9th Attended a temperance lecture delivered by the Rev. Mr. Blain last evening.[46] It was interesting — I enjoyed it excessively. The Society is every day growing interesting here. But to day I have felt out of tune. Everything seems to strike a note of discord in my feelings, and nothing vibrates in unison with them. Every thing I have done, or said also, seems to create disunion and strife — where shall I go for sympathy and quiet? where find rest, & how learn to always act, and speak with propriety and exactness?

[N]o 19th Time passes all too swiftly; books are unread, letters unwritten, and studies unpursued. Oh! how shall I ever accomplish all that I wish to. Never, never will all be done that I wish to do. I progress too slowly. My time is all frittered away and nothing gained of great importance, yet I should not thus complain — I have many, so many advantages, and privileges which many have not & which I should sadly feel the need of if deprived of them. The weather is most delightful. The sky unclouded, air fine and mild as an Italian atmosphere.

Sabbath Mother gone to the valley. Expect to leave home soon to teach in a family nearly thirty miles from here — Am afraid I shall be homesick, but must do the best I can — feel very dull and stupid to day. Can't think of anything to write.

9th Heard Miss Pellet lecture on Temperance last Wednesday evening. She had a crowded house. Is an earnest-hearted, and intelligent woman. Speaks very well, possess a pleasant voice and graceful manners, and may do a great deal of good, though some think her out of her sphere in thus going about alone and speaking in public. Im sure I do not know just what to think upon this point.[47]

My last letter was published in the Advocate. Have not had time to write for two weeks as I have been making preparations to go from home. Shall probably go day after tomorrow. To day the ''Robinson'' family will be here. They play tonight. I have never attended a theater. They are popular — We shall be in a hustle — I hope they will stay but one night.[48] Miss P. was with us but one night, but she was quiet, interesting and easily satisfied. Her object seemed to be to do good. I doubt whether the ''theatricals'' have so laudable a purpose in view, and yet there are many of them supported in California —

Consumnes Valley 1855[49]

Jan 2nd Just three weeks I have been installed teacher in a family. Have three pupils. To day one was been added, a young Spaniard from Chile who now, with his mother, resides in Sac. I am teaching him English and he is teaching Mr. Benson and myself Spanish. This is a retired place, though on the telegraph road from Sac to Stockton, but not much traveled at present.[50] The plains are expansive but not interesting, too much sameness of scenery. The weather has been most delightful until within the last few days we have had a delightful rain, which has no doubt, rejoiced everybody, and will cause business and life to move on with more activity annimattion than it has hitherto throughout our beautiful land. Men will look up with hope again. The holy days are past but there has been nothing here to tell us they were different from others. I have been reading Fredrika Bremer's Homes, presented me by the Editor of the Golden Era Am delighted with it. She is constantly speaking of beautiful things, and saying pretty things too, and keeps her reader in contact with good, great & noble minds and people and institutions. It is as if one were associating with & listening to the conversation of the wisest & most intelligent people, with whom we may learn wisdom, as well as purity, and propriety of conduct. I have not heard from home since coming here. The Sunday before I came away Mr. Reese preached for us.[51] A good many of our friends from Ione Valley came with him. The Robinson family were there at the same time and staid three days. I did not attend their performances.

Jan 4th Last evening received a letter from Uncle Joseph, wants me to send him some gold for a ring. Sent a draft on Drexel & Co., of San Francisco. It is a small legacy from my grandfather's estate.[52] Also received a letter from Mr. B. of Ione Valley. Glad to get letters. Want to go home day after tomorrow if I can, on a visit.

7th It has become cloudy again to day after several days of beautiful sun-shine — Notwithstanding the sameness and monotony there is a sublimity and expansiveness in the scenery when one becomes accustomed to these plains, although upon first beholding them with thoughts of their being my home for a few months, a lonesome sickliness, a feeling of isolation crept over me, and I thought I should have to strive hard to enjoy myself, and so I have fought against the blues, but yet I am not so sad or lonely as I anticipated. Our thoughts will wander forth, and we soon find companions in the scense of nature, and objects become familiar and interesting, which at first seemed uncongenial and repulsive, or we dwell in fancy with those far away, or in hopes for the future. With the exception of a strip of timber along the Sacramento and Mokelumne rivers, the scenery is a perfectly level, dry plain, unless we look far away to the mountains, for Mount Diablo, the coast range are on one side of us and Sierra Nevada on the other. At this time the view of them is remarkably distinct and clear. They appear higher and nearer than usual, owing perhaps, to the great quantity of snow upon them which has fallen within a few days — Did not go home yesterday as I wished. I employ my spare time studying Spanish, have been trying to write some poetry, but have not succeeded to please myself, wanted to send a piece to the Era. How I long to be going to school, but when shall I get money enough to with? Why can I not come upon a fortune suddenly as others have done, and did not use it half so wisely as I *think I could?*

18th Was home on a visit last friday, staid until Sunday. Mr. Northop, a minister who had come to the Bar to preach very much desired me to go home with him and spend a week in the valley, as there was going to be a meeting there during the week —[53] wanted to go, but Mr. Benson did not think it would do to close school, on account of Juan, so I gave up and came back. Have just now received a letter from a friend, there, one from sister at Dry Town enclosing one from the states from My Dear friend, Annie —[54] Sister says she progresses in Spanish — does not know that I too am studying it. Have not been diligent this week. must study harder. Many expressions of kindness contained in the letters just received.

Sabbath Beautiful day, So still, and quiet, and warm. cannot go out to enjoy it, must read write and look at the glittering peaks of the Sierra Nevada.

Wednesday We are having such pleasant warm weather now, near the last of january. Beautiful, calm, tranquil moonlight nights. The sky

is deep blue, clear, and bright, night and day. What a beautiful country, and climate; its mountains and vallies. How much to the lover of
nature, the naturalist and philospher there must be in them, and yet it
needs the hand of cultivation and art to render it still more beautiful to
strip it of its barren and somewhat unclothed appearance, to give its
vallies and mountains a finishing stroke of beauty, a *homelike* charm and
attractiveness, and then what may not be the ideal for the future of
such a land with wise laws, and institutions.

Benson [crossed out]

25th Took a short walk this morning. A thin mist hung its draperies
upon the earth, through which struggled the dim rays of the rising sun,
and the dew-drops strung upon the tiny blades of grass, just peeping
up, glistened like thousands of infinitesimal diamonds. The mist is now
lifted up. The sun shines brightly from a deep blue, cloudless sky, and
we may see the line of trees in the distance and the dim outlines of the
mountains still farther distant.
 Sabbath Calm and beautiful as ever — I have yesterday and to day
looked for some of my friends. It is very lonesome here and I need the
companionship of more congenial friends sometimes. I sent last week a
letter to Sister S. written in Spanish which she is also studying. I have
been studying six weeks.[55]
 9th Yesterday it rained and to day nature is resplendent with beauty. The sun shines brightly and warm, the grass is more green, and the
birds sing sweetly. Have no letters yet, which I certainly expected this
week. I am often lonely in this great, silent valley, but nature ever
smiles serenely, no frown scarscely ever darkens her brow. She is never
angry or boistrous but reposes blissfully in the sunlight, with the
brightest and bluest of skies.

Cook's Bar

17th Last Saturday a friend came to bring me home — and what a
world of contending emotions have filled my heart since then —
sleepless nights and weary restless days have been passed. How much
to be preferred is physical pain, to mental anxiety and distress, and yet
my sickness is always of mental kind, yet partially proceeding, I doubt
not, from physical debility, which I should fail to notice, perhaps if not
for the effect upon my mind — and though I feel as though a little of the
burthen had fallen from my heart tonight, still I fear there are yet many
sad hours in store for me. Oh! how much of sorrow has it fallen to my
lot to share — And sometimes I can scarcely dare hope there is any
happiness in store for me in life — A request in the Golden Era to

"Lenita, not to forget them"—[56] How can I gather up effort enough to go to such a task again? But I must get up courage enough to do something. I must spend time in this useless manner no longer. What shall I do, what can I accomplish with so little energy? If it might be only something to do good.

March 3rd Now how shall I record the events of last week. I am no longer a girl, a free maiden to live, to act for self or at pleasure, or from freak or fancy. I can live no longer in anticipation of girlish joys, can no longer look forward with bright hopes to the time when I should be a *bride — that time is past.*

I am now one — am now a *wife*— what crowds of emotions fill my mind. Ah, shall I, shall I realize, shall experience the joy, the delicious, earnest, deep happiness, that I have hoped to do upon such a change? I know not what is in store for me — Friends, name, fame, all are given to husband — to one — and in that one shall I find an equivalent? Shall I find joy? Shall I find my souls deepest love longings realized, shall I find my souls treasure — will my heart find a sweet resting place — will it find an ocean of love in which to pour its troubled waters, will it find the deep, deep felicity it capable of realizing with one who can understand and read its hidden treasure of deep, earnest love. Oh! God, Oh! Merciful Father in Heaven, thou alone canst guide our destinies, Alone canst keep smoothly together two little streams that have been united. Oh! if those waters do not gently mingle together, if our hearts do not beat in unison, if there should come discord, and jars upon the harp string — then will these chords be snapt assunder, then will be a sacrifice, a sacrifice of life, for what is life where there is no love — it is a blank, a miserable, wretched blank. And may the clouds, which such contemplations shadow down, be lifted, be wafted away by rays of sweet love and trust.

Today is Saturday. last Sabbath was married,[57] rather unexpectedly, in church, owing to some misunderstanding taking place between self — and — *Husband.* Went to the Bay to see him start for the States. It was so stormy that our trip was not as pleasant as it might otherwise have been. I did not see a great deal of either city. Thursday the same carriage conveyed *Clement* myself to our respective boats which were expected to start the same hour, but ours pushed off first and we glided gracefully away over the smoothe waters of the bay leaving the great steamer still stationary.[58] The friends of each vessel saluted each other, by waving hats and pocket handkerchiefs. Several kind friends called on me, among which were judge Willis,[59] the Rev. Blain who ernestly solicited me to write for the Christian Advocate of which he is one of the editors. He wishes me to write at least as often as once in two weeks. When I write for the Era hereafter my pieces will not be headed "from our Mountain Lassie".[60] I am a lass no longer. My kind husband does not know how many hard struggles I have had to make for his sake, how *many* little sacrifices (and great ones they have sometimes appeared to me) — of ambition, and pride I have had to endure. Will *love* alone prove a sufficient recompense? Will domestic duties and joys supply the place of other pleasures I might have anticipated? Oh! if they should not! Then will my life be a miserable, crushed thing without beauty, or fragrance. But *he* is good, and kind, and devoted.

13th   Very stormy, windy and raining. Sister gone to a wedding. Went to Dry-town last week. formed an acquaintance with Mrs. Burt. She is agreeable and intelligent. At Michigan Bar on my return, became acquainted with Miss Bennet[61] — a school teacher. She also seems intelligent, and amiable. Clement is now experiencing a storm on the sea, though he must be nearing Panama. I think it must be sublime, and grand, to witness a storm on the Ocean, and no doubt it is terrific, quite too much so, perhaps to afford much pleasure to timid persons like myself, but for those who know nothing of fear, the dangers of the sea must afford a great deal of attraction. I must finish my letter to *him,* which should go into morrows mail, that he may get it while at home. I hope that he will have a good visit, and pleasant, and profitable journey. And Oh, may we have a joyful meeting when he returns. Old Boreas has once again ceased his wild frolics. His wild ravings have ceased to gentle, sighing murmurs —

20th   most beautiful is the weather yet. Took a long walk Sabbath, and twice since have walked a short distance. Do not feel very well for want of exercise, perhaps. Take lessons in Spanish, read, and write for the papers —

Ione City

23rd   Mr. Wayne here today — Says he thinks that Mr. Bomer has arrived home yesterday or to day. I hope that he is enjoying himself with his friends and dear children. To morrow I go to the Valley, and next day to the City, probably to help select furniture for my room.[62]

April 4th   Spent most of last week in the city. Went to the floral gardens whilst there. Mr. Wayne presented me with a beautiful boquet. Have now got located in my little room — found it too small for my furniture, but it is quite a pleasant room now. If *he* were only here to enjoy everything with me — but it will be six *long* weeks yet. Received a letter from Panama monday full of kind & tender sentiments, and telling how hard it is for him to bear this Separation. Though he has not murmured at it, I know he has suffered. Dearest, you will spend a few short weeks with your children, and then another painful, sad parting 'ere returning to your "Sweet wife" as you so kindly Style your unworthy one. But when we meet again may it be to enjoy each others society without alloy, and may we be blessings to each other, and those around us. Mrs. Reed and Carter called on myself and Mrs. Rees to day.[63] I am fortunate in getting among so pleasant people.

7th Heard the rev. Mr. Phillips preach the two past evenings. He is a fluent speaker and good man.[64] Did some washing yesterday for myself, felt quite tired after it — my room is too warm part of the day, on account of a stove pipe which passes through it. I have not yet my time so arranged as to have regular hours for study as I wish to, as I believe is essential in order to progress any in mental acquirements. I have many books to read, but whenever I attempt to commence one, I so wish to have my husband to read it with me that I am tempted to put it aside again until he returns.

15th The rain is pattering gently over my head, while I look from the window and see the turbid, swollen creek rushing by, its waters now spread out amid the green bushes along the banks, and the beautiful valley and green trees resting so quietly in the circlet of hills surrounding it. We have had considerable rain the past week which will prevent vegetation from dying so soon as is usual — There was a ministerial meeting held in the place last week, the exercises of which were very interesting, essays by the ministers being read and criticised. To day is the Sabbath — my *husband* is far away in Wisconsin. Is he sitting beside the fireside of some dear friend answering their many eager questions of California, while a dear child twines its arms caressingly about his neck, anxiously dreading the time when they shall have to be separated again — only a few days and he will have to tear himself away from them to start for California again — it is sad that parents and children must be so much separated.

Ione City

17th *Dearest* — your likeness is before me. How *often* and *long* have I pressed it to my lips to day and yesterday, trying to feel the warm pressure of yours in return, and sometimes I must imagine that smile of love most lights up its passive features, and that a blush of consciousness passes athwart the image of that dear face I so long once more to feel pressed against my own. How time wearies, love — the wide, wide ocean is yet between us — one long, lone month yet before I shall nestle in your bosom in sweet union and sympathy with yours. Oh! Shall we not be happy then, dear *husband!* Shall I not find that fulness of joy and sweet, blissful trust my heart has so longed for — Dearest will you not be all my pride, and love would have you — will you not seek to fill my heart with that deep, deep happiness it is capable of experiencing? Seek to infuse into it some of the deep, rich love that wells up from the fountains of your own? Oh! love — I have many, many thoughts, and dreams and ardent hopes for you. many desires have gone up to the Father of prayers that I have not told you of — Oh! that I had faith to remove mountains — but you *love me,* dearest, do you not? I do *not doubt it* — and you will for that *love's sake* do all that is right — but that will not be the only incentive to guide you. You are *noble,* and *good* yourself, and have desires that will lead you to love and cultivate all that is *beautiful* and great in your own nature. I kiss your picture again and try to be patient till you come and fold me in your warm and loving embrace again. I am shut up all most exclusively in my own little room — have been here two weeks, and begin to feel the need of more exercise — It has been raining so much that I could not ride out. The Rev. Mr. Phillips (editor) has repeatedly solicited me to write for the California Christian Advocate. my baptist friends think I ought to write for their paper — I scarcely feel that I have time, or inclination to write for either just now.

21st Yesterday and day before, attended examinations of Mr. Peter's school — It was interesting in some respects. To day, or yesterday, I think dear husband left New York on his return to California, and this beautiful night is he looking up at the bright moon that reflects her silver rays on the ocean's calm bosom, and as peaceful visions steal o'er him does he think of his loving one, to whom the days, and hours are growing weary in his long absence — to whom books and pleasures lose half their charms because he is not here to share them — Ah: yes He is thinking of his absent one and counting the moments as they fly all too slowly by, and impatiently measuring the long distance that holds him from her so unwillingly, yet in obedience to duty

Took a long ride yesterday and have felt some fatigue and lameness to day — hope to ride oftener, and not so far at a time — rode Mr. Bomers horse — he is gentle and easy in his gait.

23 Rode on horseback yesterday to the lower church — "Billy" was a little more playful, and consequently a little more tiresome to ride. I should not have disobeyed Mr. B's orders about rididing him, but I could seldom get another horse suitable to ride, and as other ladies had first rode him, I concluded that it would not be dangerous for me to ride him — Wonder if Clement received my letter while in Wisconsin. Will it not seem very strange to him, while perhaps in his *old home* where a few short years since he left a *loving wife* and children, now whilst there again, surrounded by associations that will recall former days of happiness spent with *her,* while the sad tale of her death in his absence is being told to him by those friends who witnessed it, while his heart is bleeding with anguish to think how she suffered, and *he* not there to soothe and support, whilst he is visiting those scenes, *her grave* for the first time since, that will bring fresh to his heart all those sad

memories, will it not seem very strange there to *receive* a letter telling him of the welfare, of the joys, and sorrows, of *inmost secret* heart — thoughts of *one* he has loved, and left in faroff California — will there not be a strange mingling of sorrow and joy. Will his heart not waver and almost hesitate whether to be true to the past, to the loved dead, or to seek solace in loving the living? Will he not almost be tempted to give up the "dear one" he has newly found, and remain with those scenes and friends that will cherish sweet memories of the past? Oh! dearest, I should not blame you if it were so — but love you all the better as I saw you faithful, and sorrowing for the past — love you all the better as I saw your heart agitated, and heaving with grief and sorrow caused by those sad memories — for it would only be another proof to me of how capable you are of loving — of how susceptible your heart is to the beautiful, true and good in life. Cherish all the sweet and *tender emotions* in your nature, dear — *cultivate diligently* your *mental endowments* and a love for all that is beautiful and true, and *thus* you will warm and bring into activity, the *deepest* and *best* emotions of my heart, thus you may make happy one who has linked her destiny with yours either for weal or woe, one that will *love you* in *proportion* as she discerns in you all *that is noble, intellectual and good,* who cannot *love truly* anyone who does not possess these attributes and yet one whose happiness *depends* upon loving *one* whose nature is so formed as to claim sympathy and superiority from him whom she would cherish as her hearts dearest earthly treasure, one who will never know true, earthly happiness, only as she finds that treasure worthy, and capable of receiving the deepest, and best affections of her own heart. Ah: what a world of inexpressible emotions, and reflections does not this theme bring up. May the time soon be when we may together talk and realize our hearts desire, when we may realize this bliss of loving, and being loved, and together live and act for each other so far as love and reason guides us truly.

2 of May Yesterday was May day — and the children had their festivities. The Rev. J. S. Diehl preached last Sabbath, spoke yesterday, and last evening on temperance. He is the G.W.P. of the Sons of temperance in California[65] — said he had read my newspaper productions and tried to form my acquaintance before, but had not succeeded in time as I was now married, &c. I am suffering with a cold and have felt sadly, and disheartened. Oh! why is it my lot even to have such, and so many sad moments, and so few real happy ones. I sometimes think that I never shall be truly happy, and yet I have friends, and those that truly love me — but I cannot be satisfied — my heart is not satisfied — There is something I have not yet found, that my being, my nature is constantly reaching out after, and I cannot quell these rising emotions, cannot keep down these unsatisfied longings, but it is *wrong* and 'tis the bitterest pang of all to feel that I err — I cannot dwell with

the reality, and be satisfied as I ought, but live to much in dreams, and thoughts that may not be realized.

4th Yesterday received a letter from Mr. Bomer — he had just arrived at N.Y. and had time but to write only a short letter — I look for him to return next Steamer, when I expect to meet him at San Francisco. Had a ride on horseback — went to Quincy. Saw the editor of the "prospector", A very little bit of a sheet, printed by a little press which was out of doors in a very little town[66] —

6th Sabbath just returned from the Union Church — had a good ride and heard a good sermon by Rev. Rheese.[67]

7th The time slowly draws near when I expect the return of *Clement*. Steamer Day! How many glad, or sad emotions does it bring to numbers in Cal. How many loved, and loving ones are united or disappointed in an expected meeting.

I am thinking of thee to day, love,
Am thinking oft of thee
And wonder if thou art thinking too, love,
Art thinking thus of me.

Art hurriedly treading the deck, love,
Counting the moments slow
That bear thee on to thy home, love
Where wearily they go?

Twill be a moment of bliss, love,
Will not forget again
When we meet with a warm sweet kiss, love,
And forget grief and pain.

14th San Francisco Arrived here last evening per Steamboat 'Hunt', Cap. Seymour[68] left Michigan Bar Saturday where I had staid a few days with Mr. Wayne — his health was better but he is not well enough to come to the Bay in order to meet his wife — I do not know how long I may remain here — I hope the Steamer will come to day, but it may not be for two or three days — if not I shall get very weary of waiting for my husband — It is raining and I have but a very poor way of passing off the time in this strange city.

Near five oclock, just through dinner. The Steamer has telegraphed and will be here in three hours — Shall I be disappointed? I hope not — are they on board, and anxiously expecting a happy meeting in a few hours? Mrs. Wayne will be disappointed in not meeting her husband here, but she will soon see him if she has come, and I trust she has. Today has been a dreary dull day to me, and if I have to spend any more such I dont know what I shall do.

15 It was a false report that the Steamer had telegraphed [69] — I was quite surprised this morning to see Mr. Wayne. I had left him sick in bed.

Ione Valley

Sabbath-20th On Wednesday the Steamer came in — it was a beautiful day — Our friends met us and I need not try to describe the meetings. Dr. Pardee[70] was married to a young lady of the same name who my Mr. Bomer brought out to him. Saw Lola Montez at the International. She is not handsome but rather ordinary in her looks — I have heard that she is fitting out a brig for Australia where she intends going.[71] Accidently formed an acquaintance with an old lady who very much interested me with her conversation. I should liked to have gone and seen her as she requested. Rec'd an invitation from the editor of the California Farmer to contribute to that paper.[72] Though I was gone a week I did not enjoy my excursion much. There are constant drawbacks upon my happiness — trifles affect me too easily perhaps and my health is not good.

14th Have been to a sister's wedding. Went to Sacramento. Attended association and dedication of Chinese Chapel by Elder Shuck.[73]

July 20 What a long time has elapsed since my pen has done any work! I am every day wishing that I could accomplish something, yet every day passes by leaving nothing done — I seem to have so little energy that I cannot come to the point of sitting down with the determination of accomplishing anything of a task. The weather has been very warm, and my health not good.[74] Last evening our boarding house narrowly escaped a conflagration — quite an excitement was created for a short time.

My husband has at last effected a settlement of his business quite satisfactorily to himself so that he need not do business in a manner contrary to his notions of propriety or else offend a partner. I[t] seems quite evident in most instances that those men who do business on strictly moral principles in California generally meet with the least success — there are always those in the community who will take advantage of his rectitude and sieze the custom that otherwise would have been his — for instance, if my husband will not trade on sunday he loses the custom of those who would prefer to trade with him, yet having no scruples, and it being more convenient they will go to other stores and trade on Sabbath what they would have done at his store, providing all stores were closed on Sabbath, yet he is determined not to violate his conscience, let the consequences be what they may, and it is my opinion that there is a class in community that will sustain him as there are many here who will not break the Sabbath and therefore will be more careful to give him all their trade rather than uphold those who have so little regard for the Sabbath.

Aug 13 We have had very exciting times this week — a band of mexicans entered the town of Rancharia and killed five men and one woman, ransacked & robbed the town and left several wounded — it was after reported that three hundred had conspired to kill all Americans that they could — many Mexicans have since been hung, and shot, and measures adopted to drive all out of the country — women and children have been greatly frightened by flying reports, and altogether it seemed as if we were going to realize some of the horrors of war, but the Mexicans are fast leaving as they are in much fear, and are all disarmed if found in possession of any weapons. I think the excitement will soon pass away.[75]

Aug 31 This last summer morning awakened to the sound of thunder and rain drops pattering against the window pane and upon the roof. ["It thundered two or three times also which is a rare phenomenon in some parts of California" crossed out] How refreshing and soothing is only a few drops of rain after such an excessively hot and dry period. Oh: how very warm the weather has been — enough almost to scorch and dry up the very life streams of one's system. How longingly I have looked toward the mountains or thought of the cool streams and recesses and wished for the snow from their glittering peak — Pacific breezes which play so wild and free near the rock bound coast. Within sight of us, all around us are situated most beautiful cool and delicious places (our country is well) where one might hie away from the bustle toil, heat and excitement of life — where one might sweetly rest neath delicious skies, quaff balmy breezes and drink in new life, and feel both body and soul refreshed and renewed. The blood would bound *healthfully* along it cause again and the exultant, hopeful joyous feelings of faculty come back again and with them happy remembrances of home and childhood, those remembrances as which keep the heart refreshed (and are as green spots in our life) but which the busy toilsome (life) California life too often obliterates — but alas the Californian has no time — He swelters, tugs and toils on in his struggle for gold until excitement disappointed hopes and unsatisfied ambition or a reckless life leads him to disapation, the insane asylum or a premature grave. Ah: how many high hopes have been wrecked, how many noble forms bowed, and found a resting place in the lonely grave amid the hill, ravines and vallies of California — They heeded not the green oasis, nor stopped at the watering places of life, so that they might have gained vigor and refreshment for their weary journey and lengthened out life to a time when they should see their pioneer efforts crowned with success, until they might have seen the land which afforded them so few comforts, affording happy homes, and birth places such as they left far away, to a time when (pratling) little children would hang about their knees, prattling their childish tales, or teasing for stories from the (gray headed) old man whose gray hairs and wrinkled brow they looked upon with awe and reverence, but such is life. We heed not its present comforts — we (can at) look back to those enjoyments we have missed, or forward to time when we thinke we shall have gathered happiness around us — this is partially right perhaps yet I do think we should not hurry through life so fast — as so heedless as to forget its duties, those duties we owe our hearts, bodies and minds — and I think often that the body is least cared for of all, or at least the abuse of our physical powers often in those (we think) the cause lays the foundation for the abuse and disease of other faculties, the mind and heart — I know not why men so neglect the study of their physical being, the laws of life and health and the affinity and influence they have to our higher faculties —

But I am forgetting my beautiful morning. this morning that seemed to whisper that the long heated dusty days of summer were about to leave us and (soon) that soon the dreamy delicious days of Autumn would come, when we shall forget the two or three hot months that have passed, and think again that we have the most beautiful climate in the world — and indeed we should never complain when we have only a few months that are uncomfortable while all the rest are so beautiful — The clouds of the morning have passed away, the rain-drops are glistening on the pines and trees the birds have been singing so charmingly — There seems a perfect "bridal of earth and sky" — and it would also seem that in this little hill wreathed valley (we were shut out) that no sin, and guilt might scarsely enter — but alas we and others of adjacent towns have lived through much excitement for the last few weeks. The fair smiling heaven has bent unmoved one dark and horrid scene — murders have taken place, roberies committed — in return men supposed to be the perpetuators have been hung without trial — peaceful inhabitants driven from their homes, their property destroyed houses and church burned — vigilance committees have been established companies sent-out and guard stationed in the towns.[76] one evening this week shortly (just) after the inhabitants had retired to rest for the night a perfect volley by deafening volley of yells, shouts and discharge of pistols hastened the inhabitants in consternation from their beds and houses. Women were panic struck — men hastened to sieze their arms — the prevalent thought was — the Mexicans are upon us, for false reports that had been circulated that they were preparing to burn our town and massacre the in habitants — when the men arrived in the street what should they discover but the effigy of a Mexican suspended to a tree. Some men had placed themselves at the upper end of town — one started in a run while the others commenced a chase after him shooting and filling the air with the most hideous yells and noises. This beautiful joke which would not have had its effect had it not been — was perpetrated by the town guard and a part of the vigilance committee instituted for the safety and peace of the inhabitants. Vigilance committees and not violence becoming detestation to the sober & reservable part of the community. We fear a great deal more disturbance from these committees and white greasers than from the Mexicans who have been driven from their homes. Due retribution has been visited upon those, who perhaps are not more culpable for the depredations committed by a lawless bandetti than are americans for acts committed by lawless characters — and if there is aught else to do why should not the law have its face? I am weary and heartsick of hearing of so many murders and crimes as are comitted daily in our land— but as if there were not enough we must be wearied and disgusted by the disgraceful conduct of men calling themselves law-abiding and civilized inhabitants.[76] These disgraceful outrages will reach the ears of my friends at home — for we would not deceive them — they are unpleasant to record — and the picture of California life would not be complete without the darker shades — There is a lacking in our society — where rests the responsibility — is it because of our peculair situation — the mixed and incongruous mass of our population or the vast predominance of the male element in society, or is the evil attributable to inefficient Legislation.

5 of September Election day — *The* day of all days for general excitement. What a jostling, hurrying and bustling. Democrats — Whigs — Know Nothings, Phalanxes, Temperance and whiskey parties (the latter, it is anticipated, will be victorious)[77] and I know not how many others whose deeds being evil will love the dark rather than light. How they swelter and tug and sweat.

Fanny Fern in speaking of hot weather (that she pitys)[78]— I pity omnibus horses and ministers, I pity the little victims of narrow benches and short recesses, I pity the Irish who huddle in a cellar and take boarders, I pity consumptive seamstresses who "sing the song of the shirt" for six cents per day, I pity cooks and blacksmiths and red-haired people, &c But I pity politicians who have to electioneer and make speeches, to ride in crowded stages in the hot sun and over dusty roads, drink toddies and talk blowing, who get weary and weary everybody, who talk and are talked against, who defame and get defamed, defeat and get defeated. But the contest is ended, the prizes are awarded, windy letters and labored speeches, and indescribable love for the "dear people" will alike come to an end. Men will have time to get off the sidewalk for persons or husbands to attend to the wants of their wives, and all mankind in general have a general respite — a time for reflection. Alas for disappointed ones who sigh over lost offices, lost bets, wasted speeches, wasted juleps, wasted time and strength.

22 Went this week to see a sick sister, found her a little better. Mother was quite unwell. I was quite well entertained by two other sisters who read me pieces of their compositions which were so good that they surprised me. I think they both may make writers some day. I have been very unwell for several days — to day a request in the Era to Lenita[79] alas my muse has been sadly neglected. Thank you kind Era for that corner you have reserved for me — I tell you it is a glorious thing to write for a paper — what should I busy myself about tonight if it wasn't for filling out that same little corner? while Mr. Snooks [her husband] is gone off to some secret redezvous — guess he didn't think when he patted me on the head and said, "there, that's a good dear, write your piece for the Era, I'll be back by ten", that I'd revenge myself for his staying out so late. I intend to say just what I please (in fun) and that isn't all, I'll set the foot stool in the door way, and blow out the light so he will hit his rheumatic limb against it when he comes home — Husbands can do just as they please, stay out six nights out of seven, attend secret organizations that their wives know nothing about, spend their money just how and when they wish, and nobody must say a word. Like to know what they'd say if we females were to have a dozen different secret societies to be attended every week. They'd think we were going to raise a rebellion right away, and I've no doubt but they would send a committee forthwith to examine in to our nightly proceedings, thinking we were concocting plans whereby to turn them all into cooks, nurses, or some household convenience. Why, we can't even have a women's rights convention in broad daylight but they make such a fuss about it that we are obliged to give up all hope of gaining our liberty, and have to promise that we will hereafter be dutiful wives and stay at home and take care of the babies.

20th of Dec

Ione City

Christmas night. At home all day. Nothing of interest took place here. Husband gone to Sacramento. Occupy much of my time in reading. Have not written much lately. Have been trying to write some poetry. Was composing much of the time in my sleep last night. My Newspaper laurels, I am affraid, will be stolen from me by my sister S. An acrostic to her last week in the "Era". "Lida Woodvale" is her signature.[80] Wish I could write something to benefit others. I do not think well to write merely for amusement.

27th A rainy and windy day. The trees by the roadsides which were covered with dust, are beginning to look washed and clean. The hills are looking more fresh and grass is beginning to show itself in the vallies. Very soon the dry, faded garb which the long, dry summer forced upon nature will be put aside for her resplendent robe of emerald profusely studded and decorated with flowers of every kind, either in size or color, from gorgeous golden coquettes down to those of the most tiny dimensions, delicate forms and modest colors. The rains will make times better, we hope. The mines will be worked and money become more plenty.[81] Soon our Legislature is to meet. We hope it will be a wise one. There is to be a grand Inauguration Ball. This is the commencement of the *necessary* expenditures with which the members are taxed. Poor fellows, how much champagne they will be obliged to force down their unwilling throats to toast the new governor. What fine clothes they will *have* to wear, and how much money they will be obliged to pay for the *necessary, small* quantity of moire antiques, brocades, jewelry, &c with which their wives must be decorated on the occasion. Wonder if the governor will think most highly of those dressed most extravagantly. Wonder if he appreciates fine clothes, graceful dancing, expensive parties, tempting viands, card tables, more than he does good Actions. It seems to me if *I* were governor or Legislator or any other great man placed authority in an exalted position I should try to have all my actions, ever public or private such as any man in the state might safely and proudly emulate. In return for the honor conferred upon me by the private and obscure yet discerning and virtuous, I would strive to set a worthy example to vicious and corrupt, yet often more popular and conspicuous men of the land. Then if I were traduced I should feel an inward consciousness of having done my duty.

Ione City

Jan sixth [1856] Weather uncommonly cold for the last few days, more mild to day. Last mail husband received letters from home. One contained a notice to heirs of John Bryan, deceased. Mr. Bomer is one of four heirs and anticipates coming into possession of property to some amount not yet estimated. If it should prove to be of some importance I trust we shall have wisdom to direct us in its disposal. May it prove a blessing to us.

Reflections

26th Oh! what weary and restless limbs. How like a caged bird with loosened pinions would I gladly fly away to the woods and fields to find freedom exercise and variety that bring vigor to my frame and hope and elasticity to my mind. Kindness will almost kill, sometimes. I am suffering daily and hourly for congenial employment and companion-ship. I have books & papers, and pen and paper, and these are indeed blessings beyond value, but lose half my *ardent* love and relish for them since I have no one, much of the time, to hold companionship with me in them. Why should I have ambition, or taste, or love for mental culture if *he* does not appreciate, or encourage it or has no time to devote to such things as will only satisfy my soul longings and desires. Ah, if he only knew the empty, aching void, the utter misery there is in the heart he loves so well — surely — but he does all he can, all that he has time to do and I should not complain. Ah, it is not physical wants that I do complain of, I could do without them. But I can only pray for strength to do *right,* and in the performance of *duty* there *may* be some comfort. I am in my little room alone, where much of my time is spent. In a few months my husband expects to go to the States again, and then will be many more restless, weary days and nights, dreary and com-panionless hours, no, perhaps not companionless this time. Maybe a tiny, helpless bird will then have nestled in my bosom. Perhaps its presence will give response to some of the voices of my heart which now cry "give, give". And perhaps 'ere then my own head may be pillowed on earth's cold bosom. Ah! I wake in the night-time, often in dread and fear of what a few months away may bring forth, but I must prepare for it with hopeful heart. I have much to do yet, will have much to learn — May God help me to realize and understand the duties before me, and may all of life's sad lessons teach me to be humble, obedient and acquiesent to His will. Then will I not have lived altogether in vain.

Feb 12th Last week visited Cook's Bar — went to the Social Tem-ple. Found it very pleasant. Also to the Lyceum in Katesville[82] which is very ably conducted. To day visited Uncle's. The weather is very beautiful at present. Dont feel like writing a bit, so will quit until I feel in a better mood.

20th Last friday a severe shock of Earthquake felt in San francisco[83] Court sits this week. Trial between husband and Mr. Wayne.[84]

Ione City

Feb 29th Last Monday was the anniversary of my wedding. Wonder if the average amount of *first years* of married life are enjoyed in dif-ferent degree than mine has been. There is much in one's disposition, no doubt, as well as health that causes happiness or unhappiness to flow into the heart. If there are no obstructions in the way numerous avenues are inviting its egress, but alas, into the hearts of many how streams of a different nature find access to embitter life and leave dark shadows on the memory. How many clouds are imaged where only sunlight it would seem should ever fall, and where we would have most beautiful impresses made, there will some viperous object be sure to throw its dark shade upon our hearts coveted treasure to obliterate its beauty and loveliness, and disappoint our soul-longings.

The weather is very beautiful. I wish I could be out to enjoy it more, but my husband is constantly employed in business so that he cannot devote much time to me. He has gone to the city to day and will be gone four days this time as he does not wish to come home on Sunday.

April 5th Since last writing my husband has sold his share in the store. Has purchased a house and lot which is quite pretty and very comfortable,[85] and for a week I have been experiencing the duties of a housekeeper. I have had but little opportunity of realizing the trials attended upon housekeeping yet presume I shall find them as all others do in course of time. I think the exercise will be beneficial to my health and hope it will increase my enjoyment also. I am alone this evening for the first time as husband has gone to the Division.[86] Am somewhat fatigued from the exercise of the day and consequently feel little in mood for writing. Tomorrow is Sabbath, a day of rest and improvement. I have been rather neglectful in mental pursuits for some time as I have had other duties to attend to, and *soon other* ones yet will require more of my time. May I be prepared to meet them and perform them *faithfully.*

14th Had fine rains this last week. Our yard and house is improving in appearance as Mr. Bomer takes much pains with it which is gratifying to me. His brother has been with us a few days.[87] Ione City is a still, quiet place as a general thing, and situated at the head of a beautiful little valley, is a healthful location, but in settling ourselves in a home I should have been glad to have found more variety and interest in the social and intellectual relations and pursuits of life. There seems to be too much sameness and apathy to keep one employed and awakened in mental and moral avocations necessary for selfculture and improvement. However, things may change very much in that respect as there are many permanent and worthy citizens in the valley and village. I often feel a want of a stimulus in these things which I could readily find in congenial and *superior* persons. The absence of this perfect culture and superior power in a *certain* one is the only drawback to my perfect *earthly happiness,* Yet I have no cause of complaint, and only that my nature seems so to crave *this one greatest* earthly blessing would I ever for a moment feel any thing but happy. It should be my greatest care now that I succeed in faithfully performing my various duties in life.

Ione City

May 7th My *babe* is just 2 weeks old to day. It was born the 23 of

April and is a well developed and healthy child, a pretty little girl. My own health is very good and I should have had a comfortable time since, if my breasts had not become so very sore. And now my great care must be to raise my child right. Shall I be able to do it? Not without wisdom from a higher source. May I have all that I need. Mother and sister M. were here whilst I was sick. Sister S. is staying with me and attending school.[88] Mr. B. is very proud of the babe — thinks it is a beautiful child as all new fathers and mothers do, of course.

June 1st With pain after so long time of suffering, I again resume my pen. My own health is little improved, and that of my babe has been very poor. It has been afflicted with a swelling on the side of the neck which has had to be lanced twice. It is not yet well, though I hope better. I am worn out with nursing, and feel that I have often been impatient and fretful, and fear that affliction does not make me better and more patient as it should. I have been out but once yet, though babe is almost six weeks old. Sometimes I am very much discouraged. I have not strength to write on the tragedies lately occurring at San Francisco[89] as I should like to do. Sister Carrie was married two weeks since, lives in the valley.[90]

27th My darling, sweet babe was too lovely for earth. It left us yesterday and to day lies in the cold ground. Never again will I feel its soft face nestle in my bosom, or will its tiny arm twine around my neck. Poor little sufferer. with what anguish did we watch it during its agonizing sickness, which lasted some one week. And now, and now, I have no innocent darling to love or to love me in return, no one on which to build up future hopes of comfort and happiness, but it has passed from a troublesome, sinful world. All its sufferings are ended and it is a bright little angel, now perhaps looking back upon us in our sorrow. If I could only realize these things as they are, only look hopefully to that time when I shall meet it in Heaven, if I am permitted to enjoy that place. As it is I mourn the absence of my precious one, an innocent angel which I thought to nourish as one to lead me upward and onward to greater perfection and usefulness.

10th To day my husband has gone away to remain a few days. I have longed for my dear babe. It is two weeks to day since it died — what a day of suffering and agony that — yet, I can see its patient, suffering little face, and hear its labored breathing. Beautiful angel, ye are free from Earth and its sorrows, and your mother would not bring you back although she so longs to fold your little form in her embrace again, so longs to see again those bright eyes and hear that baby voice. Oh; the joys of Earth: how transitory. Only a little over two months did my darling stay with me, and that time was on of much suffering and trouble to me. I was just recovering so that I thought I should enjoy its society and rejoice to see it soon well and robust. But alas! it was again taken sick after the swelling had healed, with the diarreah which ended in death, or rather its throat or lungs seemed affected two or three days before. It seemed to suffer a good deal, but I need not describe its sufferings or how faithfully we watched, and nursed it, especially its father who evinced a Mother's care and tenderness for it, and indeed in a great measure took my place as my health hardly permitted my nursing it much. He watched and held it night and day. The Dr. was also kind and attentive.

July 23 To day our dear babe would have been three months old. Tomorrow will be four weeks since it died. How our hearts yearn for it. I have been through a painful, yet pleasant dream. It has departed but left a precious image on my memory. My health is very good so that I visited my mother last week. Next week we go to the mountains. We leave a pleasant home not knowing when we shall return to it again. In looking from my window I see a large and happy group of school children partaking of a picnic prepared by their parents for them on the last day of school.

Monday prepared for starting to the mountains — in the afternoon made calls.[91] Yesterday went to church and in the evening visited the grave of my babe. How I wish to take it in my embrace once more. Tuesday — Started early. Saw Jackson and Mokelumne Hill for the first time. There are many good buildings in the latter place and many pretty cottages near both, some very diminutive ones. The road is very rough and in some places quite romantic. We came over some very high hills after leaving Independence Flat and are in a place surrounded by very high ones which separate us several miles from any habitation. It is a wild and romantic looking place, a narrow valley through which passes a pretty little stream.[92]

Sunday, Aug 3rd Majestic pines cover the hilltops which are in singular keeping with them. We have no house save a brush tent. and the first night I slept without any shelter except the tall trees above us, or rather, I did not sleep at all — there was something so wild and daring in the idea of so few risking themselves in the arms of sleep in so remote a place, but — since then I have slept soundly. Yesterday they hauled a part of the timber and laid the foundation for a log cabin.

Jesus Maria[93]

6th The doorway was sawed before breakfast, the ground leveled, and logs swept down. I helped gather fern for a floor, and oak bushes was spread for a roof, then we moved in. We have a cottage bedstead, a goods box for a table and cupboard, trunks for sofa, and chairs minus, for the mountains are so impassible that we made no attempt to bring our furniture. Most of the load we did bring had to be carried over the highest hills. "Will Wayward", alias Mr. Allen found his way to our mountain retreat yesterday. "Linda Woodvale" (Sister S.) is with us.[94] They have been fishing to day. I believe Will made a seine of willow bushes, waded the brook and dragged them out, anyway, they brought home a large mess of fine mountain trout which were much relished by all hands at supper. There are but three ladies and four men in our camp, and none other in many miles. For employment we cook, wash dishes, make butter and read or write. We sing, listen to music of the wind in the trees, the woodman's ax and the crash of the giant, prehistoric pine (monarchs of the mountains as they fall before the civilized hand) as it is felled to make boards for our cabin. At night we lie down looking up through the foliage above us at the blue sky and the stars ever shining so brightly above the tall pines.

12th I was out to day to see the men saw some boards cut from a tree which is as thick through as they are tall. It looks very large but it is on-ly one fifth as large as the famous "Big Tree".[95] What mamoth pro-ductions does not California display. (evening or two since I saw some snails which so astonished me that I was haunted in my dreams) There are momoth trees and vegetables, and momoth babies, we are mamoth people who have endured wrongs but who have (unfinished sentence), and an evening or two since I saw some momoth snails which so astonished me that all night my dreams were filled with horrible shapes of creeping reptiles. They are without shells,[96] and to me, have rather a repulsive appearance as an article of food for I am told many persons hold them a great delicacy.

20th Our house progresses slowly. The roof is now on, so we have a ceiling overhead of clean boards. The rafters are shaved so that no dirt or worm dust will be falling down, but the gable ends are not yet closed, nor the chinking in, and we are still minus a floor. My fine carpet became too good a harbor for worms and insects, so we gathered it up and put fire to it. The men are gone to cut down a redwood to make puncheons of. Well, I don't care much if the floor is rough so that it is a floor and free from dirt. Romance is not romance after all when one comes to the reality of it. "Distance lends enchantment to the view". "It would be so romantic to go to the mountains and camp out." There are shady woods and pleasant dells and purling brooks, and sublimity resting on the mountains, and every thing will be so quiet with nothing to trouble one, and then, too, one can have such fine horseback rides, but alas, we've no horses ladies can ride. But, dear me, who loves to live on a dirt floor or with no roof over them save such as would not prevent a California lion from pouncing upon you when

unconsciously locked in sleep. To be sure your sweet eyes is turned up
to the stars and the shadows of the leaves and moonlight are flitting
playfully in your face, and you might fancy such sweet things and importance to the moon, but you don't. Who can be poetic when half
trembling with fear? You wish again you were in your old home with
the surroundings of civilization to enclose you from wild beasts and
banditti. You'd rather have a roof over your head and hear the pattering of the rain, instead of the wind living in the tree tops, and a truce to
grassy carpets with wild flowers interspersed — you prefer brussels
with blue roses and red leaves.[97] Well, but the trees are grand and tall
there's music ever among them, and the mountains are rugged and
wild and the little vallies quiet and sunny. There's wild sublimity here,
and log houses look secure and comfortable, but papered walls are
somewhat cleaner.

24th It is Sabbath. No solemn bells call us to worship. In God's first
temples the heart here may hold its own silent, secret communings. No
worldly, splended trappings to distract the heart. No loud-toned music
to vibrate harsh discord along ones tortured nerves. No frescoed walls
or stained domes to shut out the free air and free light of heaven. No
satin lined, or velvet cushions to support drowsy frames, or fashionable
listeners to flowery sermons. There is music, heart unison music, in the
subdued, low murmuring voices of nature, in the rustle of the
refreshing breeze among the gently swaying branches, in the crystal rill
trickling along its pebbly bed. There is worship in the harmony and
Sabbath quiet that pervades. There is beauty all around, in the blue
dome above, majestic beauty in the tall swaying pines, in the tiny
blades of grass unbending their green fringe around the rocky brim of
some crystal lake, *mystic beauty* in the purple wreathed mountains, and
there are sermons eloquent in all, that not the drowsiest need ever tire
of sermons for the refined and the vulgar, sermons sublime and in-
tricate for the learned, and plain for the unlearned, the more learned,
the more fitting, for not the wisest will ever fully read the book of
nature. Here no wordliness, no blasphemy, no dissonance disturbs the
repose of the Sabbath, but for all this freedom from wordly turmoil one
may not always disregard his ties and obligations to humanity. The
heart cannot long rest in idleness, and though it come in contact with
repulsive vice it will seek again its abiding place within the poles of
civilization, will submit to the chains which society forces it to wear.

Sept 27th So, I have been down to the valley nearly a month. Oh!
that stage ride and that dark night, well, some appeared glad to see me.
Here watermelons, grapes, peaches and vegetables greeted me also,
but water is *so* scare and dust *so* plenty. There never was known so dry
a time.[98] The creek has not a drop of water in it, nor has it had for a
long time. Should there be no more rain the coming winter than has

been for several past, surely there will be a drought next summer. I have visited my mother and sisters, have made some preserves and done up sauce for the winter, and saved seeds for a garden next spring in the mountains. Mr. Bomer came down little more than a week since. He has finished the inside work of our cabin and made such necessary articles of furniture as we did not think expedient to haul over so bad a road. The walls are hewn, the boards shaved and nailed over the chinks. Won't we live cosily in our snug log cabin in the mountains. Great political agitation now. Fremont and the Dromedary line and Kanzas are the principal topics of conversation. I go in for Fremont and freedom. The Bucham & Fillmore men have had their conventions &c.[99]

O 8th   Night before last had a hard rain. The dust is laid, and though the weather is cold we look for pleasanter weather.

New Year's day, 1857   The prospects for our community for the coming year seem auspicious, most especially the religious prospects. There has not been a ball or any party of such character this winter, but on the opposite hand there has been two Donation parties given for the benefit of the two ministers residing in the valley, also an exhibition of the S.S. for the purpose of raising funds for the purchasing of books, all of which have been well attended and liberally contributed to. There have and will be soon several additions to the church by baptism. The rains have been abundant of late so that lively times are once more expected among the business portion of the community. The grass has started so that the hills already begin to look green and pleasant. We are now situated on a Ranche. Mr. B. is plowing, and as soon as spring opens I think it will be pleasant to raise chickens, make garden and watch the growth of plants vegetables &c &c.

Jan 29th   Whilst hanging out some clothes to day this morning I observed some very *tiny* white blossoms. The beautiful spring will soon be here, — indeed we have already been having some very fine weather. Last Sabbath Mrs. Hoyet was baptised and received into communion with the Baptist church. Our little church seems prospering in some degree. May I try and grow in grace that I may also be in some degree a more useful and worthy member — We are now about through the "Life of Judson"[100] what an example of holiness and persevereness was his whole life and how peculiar were its incident, both sorrows and blessings. Oh! that we would commit *our* ways unto the Lord and be more instant in serving Him, both in and out of season. Oh! for more *grace* and *faith*. Mr. and Mrs. Rhees (our minister who live in part of this house) are gone this week so that I am alone part of the time.

Was to visit my mother last week. She seems quite happy in her new husband. I trust he may prove a blessing to her, though he is much younger than she, and we felt to object somewhat to her marriage.[101] Sarah is teaching. We have been having rainy times. This is to be one of the wet winters. Much water is standing on the Ranch, but the plowing and geting in grain is about finished, so we can afford to let it rain until spring; as much rain is needed in California for all purposes, there having been so many dry seasons in succession. business had become dull and the interests of the country waning — Water, Water, is the great and constant cry of Californians.

Ione Valley

March I have been an invalid for a little over a week from over exertion, I suppose, as no other suitable reason can consistently be given for my sickness. I am very thankful that I suffered so little pain and am recovering rapidly. The weather is again pleasant but I often experience great sadness and depression of spirit.[102] I see but little company here and often find myself longing for a change. I wish for activity and variety. But there seems but little hope for change or congeniality here, but though I often feel these vague desires for something I have not, yet I also feel that I have little reason to complain. If I find not much to do, there is also less responsibility, and if I am not much in company I am less liable to wound or give offense and to suffer harassments.

21st Visited at Mrs. Carter's yesterday, it was my first trip from home since my sickness three weeks tomorrow — raining to day.

April 10th Sabbath. How unprofitable I have spent this day. My resolution to spend it well have nearly all been broken. I have read but little, meditated to no purpose. Company has partly prevented this, and I fear a walk in the morning had something to do with weakening my effort. Received some papers with some of my poetry in it, and further invitations to write hereafter.[103] Would that I could answer all these solicitations in such a manner as to do good to the readers. The face of the country is now most beautiful. The hills present a perfect garden of bloom of every variety of flower. All shapes, sizes and colors greet the eye.

May 3rd, Sunday Went this morning to two old people baptised, a man and his wife. It is pleasant to see people in their last days turning to God with subdued will in childlike simplicity obeying His commands. Would that I could realize that sweet faith, and humility that I observe in others. Oh! how much of the temptation I realize and how little true happiness — will the time ever come when we shall find true satisfaction? Sorrow upon sorrow overtakes us. Yet have we perhaps much to rejoice for — if we could look upon the sunny side more.

I have a niece nearly two weeks old. it was born just a year from the birthday of my own babe, the 23 of April. Mother is intend to move away this coming week. I do not expect to see her. Association is also this week, at San Francisco. We shall not be able to go.[104]

June 5th Another month has passed by and with it many and varied emotions and thoughts have passed also. Athwart life's horizon how many shadows like threatening clouds in a summer sky chase each other along, but the sky is again serene and calm if not *bright*. Last week we had a wedding, but not a joyful one to me. My youngest sister was married. I regretted it because she was too young I thought to assume the duties of married life under so unpromising circumstances.[105] But she knew what she was about, or thought she did, so I hope may find the happiness she anticipated. It is now nearly harvest time. Crops are promising and I hope will pay the labore for his work. My husband has been a hard laborer thus far having rented a farm this year. He failed in merchandising just managing to free himself from all liabilities and thought to try farming as promising the best facilities for making a raise at the present time — Yesterday I called on a lady who lives in our house in town. She has been home to the States on a visit, leaned the Ambrotype business and is going to establish herself at it soon. The thirteenth of this month the great comet appears, talked of so much as being in danger of striking the earth.[106]

Sabbath. Pleasant and beautiful it is to day. Indeed the weather has been comfortable so far. There is quarterly meeting at the village to day. I shall not go this forenoon preferring to remain quiet at home. Noise and confusion destroy the blessings of Sunday for me, and it has not been very quiet here for some days past owing to so many being about in harvest time. I have been reading the second volume of Miss Bremer's "Homes of the New World" which I find very interesting. Monday Went to Mr. Sesons to day. They have a very pretty place, good house, a large peach orchard, grapes, &c. Enjoyed it very well —

June 21st Sabbath. The comet did not appear. A part of the last week had been exceedingly warm. Yesterday was threshing day and we had all the threshers, horses and machines for company. What a saving of labor are machines. What would we do in this fast age without them? Two or three weeks' work can be done in one day, and thus one farmer may raise much larger crops and take care of them than as if he had to do it in the old fashioned slow way. The world literally goes by steam. What enormous strides we daily take in labor, in travelling, in communicating, in discovering, in educating, in investigating, &c &c. Are we not progressing to the end? Will not such rapid development soon bring about a new dispensation — will not the millenial day dawn with its Sabbath peace after this rushing turmoil and strife and active life?[107] How one should hasten to be prepared for the day of his change, for in a day when he thinketh not he may be summoned hence. How short is life. To live such we must live fast. Oh, that our meditation might be fastened upon the themes that delighted the midnight thoughts of the psalmist. How hard to fix the mind when the drama of life is so fast shifting it's various scenes. This rapid whirl that makes the brain grow dizzy, the eyes stare, and the mouth gape to catch the successive themes of interest that come rushing upon our wondering and awakened comprehensions.

Sabbath again. Another week of pleasantly beautiful weather has flown by upon the wings of time. I have little leisure for writing or reading — a household baby — what a pest and what a pleasure at the same time. We have had one here for several weeks, a nephew, a hearty, active, handsome child of fifteen months, busy and noisy as a chattering parrot for he is trying to say everything that he hears[108]— there, I've just had to stop and help his uncle have a spree with him — not many prettier things in life is there than a pretty baby. They are little stories in the history of life that fascinate us. Would my own little one, if it had lived, been this interesting? I know not, but to a mother it would, but it is in heaven out of the reach of Earths poluting breath. Oh! if they could only live and pass through manhood innocent and unstained into old age, how happy we should be to retain them, but they are bright sunbeams, and if they pass away the remembrance of them is beautiful — it is better than that the light should be turned into darkness.

The work of the farm progresses admirably under the vigorous efforts of an energetic man — I think my husband is a good farmer. The fences have not been built according to the rent agreement, which is somewhat annoying as there is danger of the beautiful crops being destroyed — What a country this is for vegetable growth, but the want of rain has caused a deficiency in the grain in some places, though there are beautiful fields in this valley, both of wheat, barley and hay.

Fourth of July

I have spent the forenoon day getting dinner as I usually do now-a-days. I cook, read and sew a little, which is about all I can do. I can get but little time to write. Reading is a great pleasure. I can live in a book or a newspaper. They may say what they please about newspaper reading and its bad tendency. It never been my misfortune to see one that I could not obtain much that was good and useful from. The bad I can let alone — it may not be so with others.

July 18 I have finished "Homes of the new World". Have lived and grown some, I hope, by their perusal. There is much in Miss Bremer's writing that is very beautiful because so natural. Very warm to day, but the sky is beautiful, a deep blue with white flakes of clouds scattered o'er it.

21st I do not know but that I am becoming morbidly sensitive or excessively irritable of late.[109] I have lived and boarded in families often and always got along with ladies in peace & harmony until living in this house a part of which is occupied by our minister and wife, and though she is an admirable lady yet have on several occasions felt myself agressed upon, and in return have treated her discourteously, although I think it was done half unwittingly, yet the temptation to resent it was so strong upon me that I have given away to my feelings very decidedly to my shame afterwards. Several circumstances, I think, have contributed toward rendering me so sensitive for I will not believe that she purposely intends to wound me. I should at least be too magnanimous to act discourteously in return, and this is the most mortifying point in the case to think I have shown such weakness. It is all for the want of grace and true Christian charity.

29th Day before yesterday Mrs. R. sent me a note wishing to know if she had offended me and how. I answered that I cherished no ill-will toward her, though I might have been momentarily wounded at some things she inadvertantly said, yet I blamed my own too sensitive nature — told her I had probably been too reserved and silent but it was natural for me to be so, &c. She answered me quite affectionately saying that she might have spoken too officiously but it was owing to her always having been with those who looked upon all her act — "love's parshal eye". She seemed to have been much affected at the coldness of my conduct, though I had not intended to wound her, and I hardly thought any one would care so much even if I had. As I seldom form warm attachments for others I expect others not to form any for me, but we cannot help being attracted or replused, as Mrs. R. said.

I have just finished the life of Horace Greeley.[110] There is much in his character that I like. He has a humanitary spirit and works diligently to effect good to his countrymen, yet there are some traits that we hardly would think proper to commend, especially his religious belief, yet that arises, no doubt, from his philanthropy —

Aug 12 O! the heated days of the past week — the heated air came across the plains like the hot breath from a furnace, and so prostrated did one become that to even read was an act into which one could infuse no spirit, not enough to be interested — to day is better last night and the forenoon were cloudy, and the air is somewhat cooled There are a few days of the California summer when the Atmosphere seems all aglow with heat, the air seems more dense and though the sunshine is intense the hot waves of air obscure the distant mountains. The hillsides and fields seem almost ready to ignite.

Oct Nearly the middle — nearly two months my pen has been perfectly still. Not a very industrious writer am I, and they would think so who say "write" if they knew this fact. The first of the month we were at Stockton to see my mother and to be present at the State fair.[111]

There was a goodly display of fruits for so young a state and also of many other things. The lady equestrians performed good feats of horsemanship. There were many people there. Stockton is not a very handsome city yet. We were at Mr. Webers gardens where were many grapes of which he gave to every one who wished to eat[112] About a week since we were blessed with a beautiful rain, so that we are no longer annoyed with dust — We are now living in town — to night I am entirely alone as Mr. B. has not returned from Jackson where he went to day. I came near meeting with a serious accident this evening. "How troublesome are these Aunts". They are in the habit of getting into my sugar bowl, and whilst getting tea I discovered some in the bowl on the table. I removed it to a chair and pretty soon took the candle to see if they had left it, and while engaged in removing them a light suddenly blazed around me. I immediately discovered that some clothes were on fire on a line over my head and they were about blazing up into the cloth ceiling above.[113] I had to do some lively snatching to get them down in time to prevent a general fire. There was no one in the house, and I had no time to call, so by my own efforts the fire was extinguished with the loss of two of Mr. B's. shirts which were on the line and caught by the candle in my hand, so intensely was I engaged with those little pests, the *Ants*. A new shirt that I had but a little while since made is every shred gone, and lies a blackened cinder in the yard where it finished its existence. So much for human toil.

Nov 23 We have had several fine rains. The hills are looking green. The atmosphere is soft and hazy. To day looks as if we should soon have more rain. I think this will be a wet winter. I have been washing and am too tired to write much although I must write sister who is keeping school in Stockton. I have much pleasant reading matter. I read with interest what others have achieved by industry and perseverence and am thus reminded of my own neglected efforts in literary matters. I have some straings of conscience, but my muse is lazy, or if the "spirit is willing, the flesh is weak", so a *long time* has gone by and nothing is done. It is my province? I begin to think not — I can hope to attain to no eminence and I am not wise enough to teach others. I would not like to wield a pen except to do some good, and so many write who are more capable. At present my duties lie in a humbler sphere — little honor is attached to it, but duty is duty, and when pleasanter ones call one it will be made known.

Ione City

Dec. 3rd Have finished "Dr. Kanes Artic Explorations." It is an interesting and exciting narrative. How much perserverence and energy he exhibited amid such varied distress and privation. How much sacrifices some men make and what is gained by it. Dr. Kane is now *dead,* and whatever were his motives throughout such arduous duties, it matters perhaps little to him now — we cannot tell. But the world is better off, perhaps, though it seems but little, too, for how can those regions be appropriated to good, and to what avail will be the scientific knowledge obtained, at least, to more than a few? But knowledge has been gained, and "knowledge is power". So, somehow in the course of human events *good* will come even from that barren land. As it is probably quite uninhabited we do not see how good can go to it, but that is not impossible, as Dr. K. was quite a good man and he made quite a little sojourn there.[114]

Dec. 27th Christmas is over, but it was not much of a holiday with us. We have a fire place just finished which sends out a cheerful firelight whether for Christmas or other days. Stoves are not cheerful nor so comfortable for sitting round. Have read "Dred" and "Hiawatha".[115] The former makes one indigent at slavery, besides gives fine portraitures of character. What a flitting beam of sunshine was Nina, so shortlived like all things beautiful and loved. Clayton proved how impractible seems any effort to ameliorate the condition of the slave. It is a black hanging cloud, and nothing but a mighty sweeping power seems capable of clearing it from our otherwise beautiful political horizon. "Hiawatha" is a sweet poem, and its greatest merit consists in its hormonizing a jingle of jawbreaking words, and perserving in story some interesting Indian legends which perhaps is as much as its author aimed at and it is as much as we could expect from a poetical history of a nation of no more cultivation than our North American Indians. Their manners and legends are simple and childish, therefore a truthful history must be somewhat of the same character. But there are many beautiful and prettily worded ideas in the book, though some might complain of repetition.

Jan 30th [1858] Have been an invalid a few days, am now convalescent, alone to day. How much I am alone & how blessed are others with congenial companionship, without such, one might as well be in solitude — and I can pass off the time in reading which everyone cannot do. Night before last our minister had a donation party. I could not go. Have been to no social party for a long time, one year, I think. I shall have to remain at home for some time to come. How I dread coming events. I sometimes think I cannot possibly pass through it all, but I must try.

Feb. 22nd Quite unwell to day. We have been favored with fine rains for a few days past. The weather is very warm and vegetation grows very fast. Peach trees are in bloom — we fear frost may come yet and destroy fruit. The hills are beautifully green and flowers are in bloom — How I long to be out to enjoy it all. I can hardly be still in the house all day, but may have to remain in *all spring.* I dread it and sometimes fear that I cannot endure all. People are improving their gardens, yards and houses and the town and country seems flourishing.

March 29th Baby almost four weeks old[116] he is healthy and active. I am well and have been very fortunate having no unusual sickness which is so much better than I anticipated that I am very thankful. We are having a fine rain after so continued a dry spell which rejoices the farmers very much. We have a woman hired to do the work which is a great relief to me. Mr. B. has had a new fence built around our yard. It is of lattice and when our shrubbery gets larger I think our place will be quite pretty.

May 29th — my birthday. I am thirty one years old; and how rapidly time seems moving along. How much I have thought of death lately, never have I thought of it as being so near and realized the shortness of life so much before — and what is death — how shall we be changed, or into what new scenes shall we be introduced? Are we prepared and shall we go cheerfully at the summons? Oh! that God will enlighten our mind and give us the true Christian's faith. How *few* feel their feet firm on the Rock of Ages.

Baby is almost three months old — he is improving and becoming interesting but when is not a babe interesting — to a mother's heart? Her eye catches every motion and watches every pain. Oh! that a time should ever come when she cannot protect, and soothe her darling, yet it assuredly must. And heartaches far worse than bodily sufferings must come — The little angel face must become worldworn and sin stained, the guileless trusting heart, so pure and tender will become distrustful and unloving. If a mothers love could shield her child from the evils to come, could keep him pure and undefiled until the day of his death; Alas, that sin should stain every heart that none can go through life without regrets and repentance.

18th June. We had a shower day before yesterday, or rather, the day was rainy. The weather is cool.

Aug first July has gone by — and little Hugh has two more cousins, one born the first, the other the fourth.[117] I was over to Cook's Bar last week. Saw two sisters and Mother. She is at Michigan Bar. Our hired woman has been away two days, again. She was at my sisters two weeks — It is quite warm to day — I have not much time to read and write, and have not been to church but a few times. I attended the funeral of Mrs. Lyons who, it is supposed, was murdered on the fourth of July by her husband. He was drinking and probably choked her to death, then, to hide it, hung her in the well saying she committed suicide. He is in jail awaiting his trial. Quite an excitement prevailed — how suddenly death comes somtimes.[118]

We weighted the baby today, he weighs 12 pounds and is five

months old in a few days, is rather delicate.

October 2 Two months have flown by, and in all that time I have
not found a spare moment to devote to writing. Reading I have also
had to lay by. I have had company (relatives) most of the time, and
almost all of my work to do and baby to take care of. I go scarce any
place yet do not get done half that I wish. I have had a wash woman to
day, and such a big ironing as I shall have to commence next week if
Livy is well enough. He had a very bad spell this afternoon — has a
severe cold — he is seven months old and weighs 16 pounds. He im-
proves very rapidly. I hope he will not get sick though I am a little
alarmed about him. I must go and see to him now — It is time I was in
bed with him as I did not sleep well last night. Sister S. left here yesterday with her babe which is very delicate and much trouble — she
herself was very unwell the week she was here. Camp meeting is over
— peaches and grapes plenty and almost gone. I have been to an orchard. Have been making some preserves. A large comet appears
nightly.[119]

January 16, 1859 It has been a long time since I have taken a pen to
write. I have read but little. My time is so occupied. Baby *must* be taken
care of and other domestic duties attended to. I can but just get a book
or pen in my hand before I am disturbed. Even now I am called. To
day I went to church for the first in a long time. Baby is a little one, ten
months old. He is trying to pull my book and pen away from me now.
A piano school has been commenced here — Mr. Goodrich, the
teacher, urges me to take lessons, but how shall I get time?

Monday Feb It is a bright and beautiful day. I thought to go to see
my mother tomorrow. It is so long since I have went any place except
the other day to see my sister — and I was wishing yesterday so much
that I *could go some where.* The air is so warm and pleasant and nature
looking so lovely after the rain — it seemed as if I could enjoy a little
jaunt so much. Mr. B. said he thought there would be a chance for us
to go to V.[120] we've been talking of it so long — well, this morning I
began to make arrangements about my work in order to be ready.
Sarah was to stay from school part of the day to do her own and help
me a little about washing. Mr. B. overheard and said Sarah should not
stay out of school. I said her clothes were dirty and she needed them
whilst I was gone and there would be no other chance to wash them.
"Well, she should not stay out of school — she might have washed
Saturday." It was in vain to tell him there were other things to do and
that washing around two days made more work than it saved — that I
took Sarah to help me take care of the baby and do chores — and
reserved the privilege of keeping home on necessary occasions, that I
had done so seldom, &c — men know but little about womens work. So
Sarah has gone to school — got on the last dress fit to wear — left me

three dresses to wash, two aprons and her underclothes. Baby must be left on the floor in another room, and every minute I must run to keep him out of the fire, or take him up to hold and warm him half an hour and get him in good humor again — poor little fellow, if he only knew what heart-aches there are in store for him — he would never want to leave his babyhood. But I know something about it — I never had a joy but was blighted right in the bud, never had a hope but was frustrated, never had a purpose but was met crosswise, never formed a Plan save to be disappointed — ah, inexpresible sadness rests down upon me sometimes. The gray dullness of hopelessness broods and settles heavily upon me, but my sorrows are those that may not be told — there is not *one* from whom I may draw sympathy. There is *no help*. I can only settle into stoical indifference until the cup overflows again. I could almost weep my life away sometimes, yet I never do weep at all. Oh! how many sad life mistakes there are. My child — if he could only escape them! He is asleep at last — I think sometimes I can see the germ of sad temperament in him — I hope he will avoid the shoals and thereby the anguish I have felt. But, to my washing. O dear — I have neither physical ability nor the mental organization for a drudge. I want to be busy, but to cook and wash dishes and sew all ones life is heart-sinking. Some can manage to get help from others, but I cant see how they do it. I took Sarah thinking to have some relief, but she can't tend 'buk when he is cross, or she don't feel like. She can't cook nor sweep clean nor wash. I have the making of her clothes to attend to, her washing and ironing, mending to see in order, and every thing she does to overlook — and she must never stay out of school lest someone will say she does not have justice done her.

March 13th Nearly three weeks since we started to Volcano to see Mother. It was a pleasant day but the next day after we got there it rained, and we had either rain or snow or wind most of the time we were there (two weeks). One Sunday we had a snow storm.[121] The flakes came down almost as large as little birds, and so softly and lightly as to cause one to feel as if silent pleasures were falling around him, as indeed they were for it is a pleasure to behold a snow storm when one is housed cosily in a warm room lazily looking out to see every thing gradually enwrapped in its beautiful covering of white, so cleanly and cheerful — quite different from a dreary, drizzling rain — The next Sabbath was pleasant and my husband came after me, but on Monday it rained steadily so that he was obliged to leave me to come in the stage the next day, a covered conveyance being preferred to an open one in a rain storm, so we had the expense of both all because I told my husband of his breaking the Sabbath. Tuesday was pleasant most of the day and after a ride of four hours we reached Jackson, stopped and had babies likeness taken.[122] He was tire, and fretful but we got a pretty good picture, next morning we started at four oclock in the dark and rain in a crowded stage and dreadful roads so that it would be no wonder if we had been turned over, but we have excellent drivers and a merry companion on this occasion so got home safe.

July 8th The Spring is past. Summer is here in its full heat. Harvest is over, and fruit will be ripe by and by. How swiftly passes the time.

Epilogue

LITTLE MORE IS KNOWN about Lorena's life after July 1859. According to the 1860 census the Bowmer family still lived in Ione City on June 9. Their assets were listed as $1,200 in real estate and personal property plus a milk cow valued at $30.[1] Thirteen days after this was recorded, Lorena and her husband sold their house and lot "together with all the singular hereditaments and improvements there unto belonging or in anywise appertaining" for $1,000 to Josiah Heacock, who had been one of Clement's business partners in the store. The agreement was signed on June 23 in the presence of J. Arnold Peters, justice of the peace, who certified Lorena was fully aware and understood the transaction. About this "conveyance" he wrote that Lorena

> acknowledged on examination apart from and without the hearing of her husband that she executed the same freely and voluntarily without fear or wish to retract the execution.[2]

Why Lorena and Clement sold the Ione property and moved away remains one of many unanswered questions.

Four months later, on October 30, 1860, Lorena died in San Francisco.[3] The cause of her death is unknown, but typhoid fever reached epidemic proportions in the city during the fall. No notice of her death has thus far been found in San Francisco newspapers and death records were destroyed in the 1906 earthquake and fire. Newspapers in the Sacramento-Stockton-Amador region that might be expected to carry such an announcement either no longer exist or did not report her death. The location of Lorena's grave is also unknown. If burial had been in San Francisco, the chances of finding the graveyard are not good because in the 1930s and 1940s many of these were reclaimed for

This reversible red, beige, and blue coverlet, dating between 1835 and 1850, has been handed down in Lorena's family. Made in two matching pieces, it could have been woven when the Hayses lived in Pennsylvania, or after they moved to Illinois in 1839.

Lorena's son, H. L. Bowmer, and his family, c. 1902

the land and the bodies reburied in mass graves on the San Francisco peninsula. Of course, it would seem more appropriate for Lorena to have been buried alongside her infant daughter perhaps in the Oak Knoll Protestant cemetery on a ridge above Ione City. However, a plat map of this cemetery has no names on it and many graves are now without markers because the original wooden ones have weathered and disintegrated.[4]

The only material evidence of Lorena's life and her contribution to the history of the westward movement rmains her diary, now at the Bancroft Library, and a summer-winter coverlet. Inherited by descendants of her youngest sister, this reversible red, blue, and beige overshot coverlet (c. 1835) crossed the continent with the Hays family from Pennsylvania to Illinois and then later to California, Lorena's "land of gold and wickedness."

The question of what happened to Lorena's husband and son is somewhat easier to answer. They moved to Reno, Nevada, sometime in the early 1860s, perhaps because Lorena's sister, Sarepta, taught school there before her marriage. Twenty years later Clement lived in Alturas, California, with his occupation given as "lawyer." According to one source, he had studied law and was admitted to the bar in Kentucky at the age of twenty-one years. Whether Clement became the "Judge Bowmer" of Deep Creek, who was described in one incident recorded by the historian H. H. Bancroft, is questionable. One of his great-grandsons did not believe that story although he reported Clement at one time served as constable in Weston, Oregon.[5]

Lorena's son began his successful newspaper career at the age of thirteen years by working as a "printer's devil" for the *Reno Crescent*. He also worked for the *Nevada State Journal* and the *Reno Gazette*. In 1881 H. L. (as he preferred to be called rather than Harry) moved to Washington state with his wife, Minnie M. Mann of Reno, and an infant son. The Bowmers also had two other sons and a daughter, named for her maternal grandmother.

In fulfilling Lorena's dreams of a newspaper career, Bowmer worked for twenty-two papers, fourteen of which he either founded, purchased or managed during a period of fifty-seven years. He also worked for the *Portland Morning Oregonian* under the editorship of Harvey W. Scott and in 1896 managed the Washington State Printing Office. When Bowmer retired from the newspaper world at the age of eighty-two in 1940, he was called the "dean of Washington journalism."[6]

One of Lorena's great-grandsons also helped carry out her dreams. Angus L. Bowmer, who grew up in Bellingham, Washington, founded the renowned Shakespearean Festival in Ashland, Oregon, in 1955. A former professor of English at Southern Oregon State College, he served as the producing director until 1971. Bowmer, who was appointed to the National Council on the Arts in 1974, continued as a consultant after retirement until his death in 1979. He acted in several Shakespearean roles in addition to directing the plays and "instilling his love of the theater" in students, some of whom went on to become well-known professional actors. Under Bowmer's leadership the Oregon Shakespearean Festival became America's third-oldest regional theater with the second-largest theatrical audience.[7] Throughout his life Bowmer treasured a special ring, inherited from his father. It contained two of the twelve tiny chip diamonds that once formed a cluster in Lorena's wedding ring.

Appendix

The Hays*

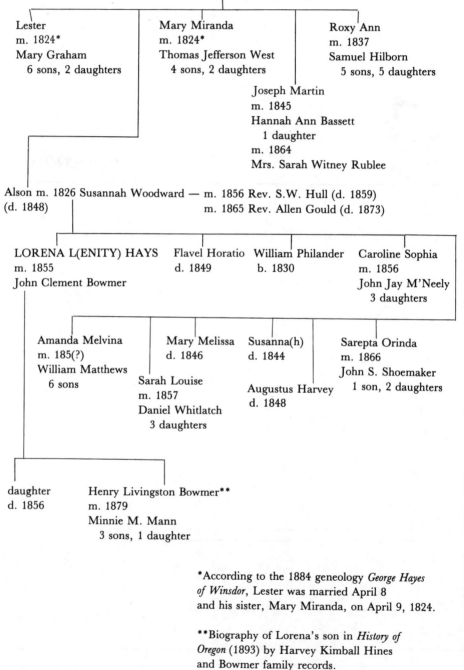

Martin Hays m. 1798 Mary Camp

Lester
m. 1824*
Mary Graham
6 sons, 2 daughters

Mary Miranda
m. 1824*
Thomas Jefferson West
4 sons, 2 daughters

Roxy Ann
m. 1837
Samuel Hilborn
5 sons, 5 daughters

Joseph Martin
m. 1845
Hannah Ann Bassett
1 daughter
m. 1864
Mrs. Sarah Witney Rublee

Alson m. 1826 Susannah Woodward — m. 1856 Rev. S.W. Hull (d. 1859)
(d. 1848)   m. 1865 Rev. Allen Gould (d. 1873)

LORENA L(ENITY) HAYS
m. 1855
John Clement Bowmer

Flavel Horatio
d. 1849

William Philander
b. 1830

Caroline Sophia
m. 1856
John Jay M'Neely
3 daughters

Amanda Melvina
m. 185(?)
William Matthews
6 sons

Mary Melissa
d. 1846

Sarah Louise
m. 1857
Daniel Whitlatch
3 daughters

Susanna(h)
d. 1844

Augustus Harvey
d. 1848

Sarepta Orinda
m. 1866
John S. Shoemaker
1 son, 2 daughters

daughter
d. 1856

Henry Livingston Bowmer**
m. 1879
Minnie M. Mann
3 sons, 1 daughter

*According to the 1884 geneology *George Hayes
of Winsdor*, Lester was married April 8
and his sister, Mary Miranda, on April 9, 1824.

**Biography of Lorena's son in *History of
Oregon* (1893) by Harvey Kimball Hines
and Bowmer family records.

The President and Lorena*

George Hayes m. (nd) Sarah (surname illegible)
m. 1683 Abigail Dibble of Winsdor, Conn.

6 daughters and 5 sons, including:

Daniel I (eldest son) m. 1716 Martha Holcombe** 1 son m. 1721 Sarah Lee 10 children	**II** (generation)	Samuel I (fourth son) m. 1719 Elizabeth Willcockson 9 children
Ezekiel (third son) m. 1749 Rebecca Russell m. 1774 Abigail Hitchcock Brown 10 children	**III**	Samuel II (eldest son) m. 1750 Rosanne Holcombe** 10 children
Rutherford (second son) m. 1779 Chloe Smith 9 children	**IV**	Martin (seventh son) m. 1798 Mary Camp 5 children
Rutherford II (second son) m. 1813 Sophia Birchard 5 children	**V**	Alson (second son) m. 1826 Susannah Woodward 10 children
RUTHERFORD B(IRCHARD) HAYES (third son) 19th President of the United States m. 1852 Lucy Ware Webb	**VI**	LORENA L(ENITY) HAYS (eldest) m. 1855 John Clement Bowmer

*According to the 1884 genealogy *George Hayes of Windsor*
**Martha Holcombe was an aunt of Rosanne Holcombe

The Woodward-Lithgow Families*

William(?) Oliver Woodward m. Lenity Segar   James (?) Lithgrow m. Elizabeth (?)

William
m.
?
1 daughter

Ebenezer
m.
Georgia (?)
3 daughters

Louise
m.
John Sweeney
1 son and (?)

Leah
m.
John Dehaven
1 son,
4 daughters

Arnold
m.
(?) Riggs
m.
Liza Riggs
1 son, 1 daughter

Henry
m.
Sarah (?)

Elizabeth
m. 1841 (?)
Lauristan Brown
3 sons, 2 daughters

Susannah
m. 1826
Alson Hays
10 children, including;

Caroline ———— m. 1833 ———— Adam C.

LORENA L(ENITY) HAYS

Louisa Elizabeth
d. 1853
(near North Platte
River bridge)

Mary Jane
m. 1857
Josephus Hoffman Rickey
3 sons, 4 daughters

Henry Martin
d. 1846

Caroline Victoria
m. 1873
Henry M. Bentzel
1 son
m. 1880
Samuel Warren Hackett
1 daughter

Helen Annette
d. 1863

James
d. 1840

*Information provided by Bernice Hoover,
a great-granddaughter of Adam and Caroline
Lithgow, and other members of her family.

ON THE WAY TO CALIFORNIA IN '53

By Sarah Louise Hays Whitlatch

Thirty years later, Lorena's youngest sister wrote this account. The folded, lined paper had previously been used for the beginnings of a letter, written in ink, addressed to "Dear Mary" and dated "Ione, Dec. 24th, 1883." Sarah, then forty-four years old, wrote in pencil over the inscription:

It was about eight o'clock on a bright summer morning — we had encamped over night in a pleasant spot in the valley of the "North Platte." The long train of ox wagons and the six hundred head of loose cattle had been set in motion on their Westward way. They had been traveling this same Westward way for months. California was the goal in view. The year was 1853 — Thers was a mixed company: a gentleman who had been in California & returned with plenty of gold to his family, who had found his eldest child, a daughter of seventeen, wasting with consumption and was returning to California now with the hope that the journey across the plains and the healthful climate of California would effect a cure. there was his wife and three daughters younger. another gentleman whose wife was in Cal and he had gone east & was bringing out stock on a speculation — a widowed sister of the same with 5 daughters, of whom I was the youngest, fourteen — a lady and daughter coming out to a husband and father who had made some money and sent for them, a widow with three sons, a Mosourian proprietor of an immense "prairie Schooner" and four hands and two hundred head of cattle, two Kentuckians, one Tennessean, a Missippian, a jolly irishman — a sedate dutchman and a dozen others, mostly young men & boys seeking their fortunes in the west.

The last to leave the camping ground was the "Carriage" fitted up for *our* invalid and occupied on this morning by the sick girl — her father and the driver. Wasted to a mere shadow of her once radiant self, the long-glossy waves of jet black hair thrown back from the smooth white brow, a hectic flush on the hollow cheeks — she lay back in the arms of her father her large appealing eyes looking in her fathers face with a last fond look, "O" papa how dark it is. Cannt see you. tell them good bye for me. Bury me where the wolves can not get me. The large eyes closed — the faint breath fluttered and was gone.

The order to *halt* was given by the driver of the carriage to the teamster of the wagon next him — and the word was passed on from wagon to wagon until the long train had come to a stand. [three words inserted here but illegible]. Soon all were informed of the cause and we turned out again only a short distance of our last resting place, after a

Sarah L. Whitlatch, Lorena's sister, around 1900.

few hours we moved on again for it had been decided to ley the dear
one to rest at the crossing of the North Platte where a new bridge had
just been completed and there were two men owners of the same living
— all was hushed — no noisy cracking of the long whips — no loud
talking or hallowing, even the cattle seemed to realize something
unusual had happened and were on their good behavior, just as evening fell was formed the circle with our wagons, pitched the tents in the
center and in one of them was placed the frail sweet form of our loved
one — the river rolled deep and somber close beside us. The willows
moved and whispered softly to each other along its banks. The high
[crossed out] mountains covered with a dense growth of evergreen pine
and cedar towered air giving [illegible word] the other side of us, the
bright stars came out and [two words illegible] the mystic milky way
spurred the cloudless sky large bands of cattle and horses [illegible
word] on the luxuriant grass in the plains around. Many camp fires

besides our own rose up ward casting an uncertain light on objects around. the sentinels paced to and fro near where to the stock was grazing — guns in their hand, pistols in readiness for use in case of attack from indians. four watchers sat throughout the lonely watchers of the night in the ten with the dead, while others slept calmly as usual in the tents with wagons around. While near and far on all sides it seemed yelped the demoniac cayote while a c cosinns a bank, slouchy grey wolf would come out [two words illegible] from the gray shadow nite — the flickering light of the fire and disappear again in the darkness.

cousin how our hearts longed to still carry you with us to our distant havin — but it could not be. the haven of rest for her had been reached — and tomorrow we would ley her away deep in the earth where the wolves could not get her — *robed in snowy white* the lovely wild flowers of the prairie *that* she loved so well nestling around her she indeed slept gently her last long sleep & as I tried in vain in my tumbled bed to fall asleep I wondered if her spirit still hovered near and see our grief and know of our loneliness.

A neat coffin had been prepared from material obtained from the bridgemen and at ten o'clock the following day a large company in attendance, services were held as ''at home'' — a long funeral procession filed across the long bridge & on a high mound on the opposite side, a prayer was offered — & that beautiful burial song was sung — ''sister thou wast mild & lovely'' — how appropriate it seemed tears fell fast and thick from the eyes of all present.

The deep grave was filled full and heaped up, willing hands gathered the large stone slabs so plentiful there and piled them high as they could reach over the still heart and her request to be buried where the wolves could not get her was complied with — a board with name and date was placed at the head of the grave and an evergreen from the mountain and sweet briar seed brought from her far away home were planted and all was done that kind hearts and willing hands could do. It is as fresh in my memory as if it had only happened yesterday, and although thirty years have passed and there were strangers present who did not even know her name no doubt many still remember the funeral of a young girl of eighteen they attended on the North Platte in '53 — while on their way to California.

At about the same time, Sarah also apparently wrote the following poem about the death and burial of their cousin, Louisa Lithgow:

In memory of L.E.L. who died of consumption on the ''plains'' in 1853 while journeying to California — and who was buried near North Platte river.

How fair was the morn that our darling lay sleeping
'Neath a white spreading tent — near a swift flowing stream.
How lone were our hearts and how sad was our weeping
As she in the white robes seemed sweetly to dream.

Far, far from her home and the scenes of her childhood;
We had journeyed for days o'er a flower-decked plain,
Had toiled up the Mountains and threaded the wildwood,
With many a pause (halt?) of our slow moving train.

We had hoped (that) kind nature would vowchsafe a healing,
That the bright glow of fever would leave that fair face —
Had prayed — Oh! so fondly! with hands clasped and kneeling
(That) Our dear one might linger lifes pathway to trace.

How often we gazed, as at nightfall we clustered
Reownd the light-covered wagon, on seat, tongue & wheel
At the (thin) face grown paler, the eyes brightly lustered
And feared that ere long we deep sorrow should feel.

Passed swiftly the hours with light song and with laughter —
Each told of the day — some bright coloring lent —
With hope and with gladness spoke of the "hereafter"
In the land we should dwell (when) our journeying spent.

Alas! all had changed! for Our dear one no longer
Could tarry with us — had preceded us home.
Though the eye had grown dim — the footsteps were stronger
She had "passed on before" and we were to come.

Far ahead stretched our train while the carriage lingered still
A few smoking faggots lay scattered around
Flowers trampled and dying — their fragrance had mingled
With the zephers that lulled to our rest profound.

"Dear Papa! Call Mama, how dark it is growing?
Hold me up in your arms, lay My head on your breast"
The eyes lost their brightness, the thin cheeks their glowing
"Where wolves cannot get me please lay-me-to-rest!"

From wagon to wagon — 'till at the one leading
Was heard the quick call —"Wait!, halt! stop the train!" —
Each ox at the wheel, all alert and quick herding
Sat firmly his feet with a sure, sturdy strain —

The strong arms, the true arms held closely their darling —
The quivering lips strove all vainly to cheer —
For dark as the night with no promise of dawning
Seemed this lovely morn with the sun shinning clear.

Faint and fainter the breath —sad eyes slowly closing —
While the fast paling lips spoke the last fond "Good bye" —
No word of regret for the life surely closing
But yealded it up with a tremulous sigh.

We strewed her white couch with flowers bright & glowing
They burdened the air with their odorous breath,
We kissed the pale lips, with eyes over flowing —
They wore a faint smile in the last sleep of death.

How simple the rites! few the words that were spoken
As we bore her across to the opposite shore
Then we sang a last song — our words sadly broken
And covered her up from our sight evermore.

Oh stranger! kind stranger, you helped us to gather
Slabs many and massive to place on her lone grave
Built higher and higher till strong arms no higher
Could build a high mound from the robber to save.

They bore from the mountain a sturdy young cedar
And planted it firmly near the low-lying head —
Dropped and watered with tears some seeds of sweetbriar
To arise and bloom on the grave of our dead.

Then left her to sleep near the swift flowing river
Where the lithe tassled willows droop lowly their heads,
Where gayly colored Lupines light tendrils quiver
And the fair valley lily sweet fragrance sheds.

Oh! Shades of yon mountain! watch over and guard her,
Oh! deep, sleepless river! still the waves on your breast.
Oh! wild winds that blow! cease your warring to hover
O'er our fair maid who here found haven of rest.

S.L.H.

LETTERS TO LOUISA

These two letters, dated March 12 and April 30, 1853, were written to Lorena's cousin, Louisa Lithgow. The first mentions both Lorena and her mother. It was written by a mutual friend, Ann Pressy, who had previously lived in Barry, Illinois. The second letter was received by Louisa when she reached Fort Laramie June 12-13. It came from twenty-year-old J. P. Grubb, whose family also lived in Barry. Both letters indicate what life was like for those left back home. They are among the Lithgow Family Papers belonging to Bernice Hoover of Ft. Collins, Colorado.

Pittsfield, March 12th, 1853

My Dear friend —

I hope you have not quite forgotten me. It is so long since I heard from you that I began to think that you were hardly in the lands of the living. Why have you not written and what are you doing? Come over and see us before you go to California and bring Lorena with you. Is your health any better? The last I heard you were quite unwell indeed. I heard I [illegible] sh was to be married soon in California is it so — [illegible] you can think and [illegible]. I have not been to school any this winter Just stayed at home at work. We have boarders a part of the time and have not had much leisure. *Come* up to the association won't you next month? We expect to have many pleasant meetings then — I suppose Mr. Kemmitt will be down as well as great many others — Mr Esty commenced a protracted meeting here last Tuesday not much interest, I think yet. The Baptist church is now quite small here but perhaps it will be revived. Mr. Esty had such a cold he could not preach every night last week but is now better he held conference meetings every other night. I have written this with a pencil because our ink is poor and it is sunday and I can't get any better. I am afraid it will pussle you to read it, read part and guess at the rest like a *zankie* would. Well then I am pusshed to find any more nonsense to write don't you think I might be. E. P. Barkers school will be out in about four weeks at Perry. cant you come and go to the examination. I will go with you if you will — We have had a great many weddings here this fall and winter one last week of Dr. Gorda (?) of Warsaw to Miss Emily Hodgen of this place were you acquainted with her? Matt Kook is tell them if you see him will you. There is not many young folks here now (I mean unmarried) not willing to be called old folks. I wish you would write to me and show me how to write a letter for if I ever did know how I have forgotten. Tell Lorena to write to me and give an account of herself. love to all whom it may concern — Goodbye Yours ever

L.A.H. Pressy

P.S. have you seen Aunt [illegible] and the baby She is now in Barry making a long visit. I look for her here soon. She thinks of calling it Alice. Isnt that a pretty name. Write soon and also after you get to California I should dread the journey very much don't you? There is Frank Sweet that was going to leave. Were you at the wedding & etc. A pretty long postscript this *I* think — Is all of Mrs. Hays family going to California? I have asked a great many questions and will stop. Ann — (Let no one see this poorly written letter but if you please burn it soon — When are you going to start I wish you would not go cant you stay *Do!*)

Weston Mo April 30th/53

Dear friend Louese

I have nothing of importance to write but I thot as I have an opportunity of sending you a line & to redeem a promise together with the anticipation of the pleasure it will give me to receive an answer, I thot I would write a few words any how. I wrote you a line to Kansas which I suppose you have rec' befor this time I suppose. I beat the letter to Kansas myself but as it was night when I passed there I did not have an opportunity of looking around to see if I could discover any familiar countinances. I am for the present stopping in the City of Weston and shall perhaps remain here during the summer. Nothing of interest transpired in Barry after you left up to the time of my leaving. The young Ladies & Gents anticipate rather a dull time there this summer owing to the decrease in their ranks caused by emigration of so many of their best associates. To me it began to look gloomy before I left partly in part to the cause already mentioned & in part to the discontinuance of the writing and day schools which necessarily deprived us some (at least one) of the "fairest flowers" which had for many months adorned our city. That "one" I have not seen since you left. She has commence teaching school on the Mississippi bottom when I left home. Her school house is in a few steps of the "Home of mi Childhood" Oh! that I could be there tomorrow to be fanned by the gentle breeze of a merry may while I listened to the soft accents of her voice rivaling in swetness that which the most extravigant imagination can conceive. But why indulge in thinking and writing of a thing so visionary, it reminds me of the old poem which says,

"How vain are all things here below

How false & yet how fair.''

Yes, fair indeed are the pictures of our imaginations but the realization is always far in the wake

I hope that ere you receive this you will have realized your fondest hopes in regard to the ''Brave'' Hope you will be true to your promise in sending on an invitation to attend the ''nuptials.'' For my part I shall certainly be true to mine but as I have told you before you hear will be ''blossoming for the grave'' before you receive the invitation. I must close as my time is limited, This will be left in the P.O. at Fort Laramie by a Mr. Addams, who is going to Salt Lake with a stock of goods from the house at which I am stopping He leaves this place in the morning. I hope I shall receive a long letter from you from the Fort direct to Weston, Mo.

My love to All
Truly your friend, J.P. Grubb

NEW CANTON STORE BILLS — 1848

Two stores in New Canton gave the Hays family credit in 1848. The following year the unpaid bills were charged against the estate of Lorena's father, who died Oct. 4, 1848.

A list of puchases for two months has been exerpted to show what one Illinois farm family bought at local stores in the late 1840s:

New Canton, Ill. — 1848
Alson Hays to James Shipman Dr.

Apr. 4 To 9 yds Calico @ 25 cents — 225 — 3 ½ yds @ 16	2 81
4 " 1 pr gaiter Boots	1 30
5 " ½ Bushell Dried Apples 63 Ballance on Tea 30	93
7 " 5 lbs Sugar @ 7	35
10 " 1 string Beads	10
11 " 1 pr Scissors	20
12 " 1 gl Molafses	45
14 " Ballance on Bbl Flour 25	25
14 " 2 Strings Beads 15 — 1 plug Tobacco 5	20
15 " ½ lb Tobacco 12 cents 1 paper pins 10	22
18 " 1 lb Saleratus	13
18 " 1 Bbl of Molafs more or lefs	3 00
18 " 10 lbs Coffee 100 & ½ lb Tea 50	1 50
Apr. 18 To 1 Jar	25
22 " 1 pr Shoes 100 — 3 plugs Tobacco 6	1 06
22 " 5 lbs Nails at 7 ½ cents — 1 Lawn Hdkf 38	75
25 " 25 lbs Nails 7 ½ — 187 — 2 crocks 25	2 12
25 " 2 tin pans @ 35 cents 70	70
25 " 6 lbs Nails — 7 ½	45
26 " ½ lbs Tobacco — 12	12

In May, 1848 the New Canton firm of H. Barker & Co. also extended credit to the Hays family:

Dr. to H. Barker & Co.   Estates of Alson Hays Deceased

May 3 ½ lb Tobacco 13 & 2 lbs Rice 20 ct	$ .33
8 Sundries Delivered wife	6.00
9 ½ lbs tobacco 13 & 1 P.L Hat self	.75
10 4 lbs Butter 40 (11) 1 lb Salaratus 13	.53
11 6 lights Glafs Del self	.30
12 4 lbs Butter Del daughter	.40

12	Paying Isa Howard for fish per your request	.25
13	135 lbs S fine flour 3.45 & Sack 40	3.85
13	½ lb Tobacco	.13
15	1 lbs 3 Nails son (16) Matches 6	.16
17	5 lbs Butter	.50
17	3 Combs for Caroline	.30
20	6½ lbs Butter	.65
22	3 yds Cottonade .75 3 yds Same of 30c 90	1.65
22	Thread &c	.10
23	10 Nails De per Self	.10
24	2 lbs Butter self	.20
25	Hooks & Eyes son	.10
27	Matches .6 son 5 lbs Butter	.56
30	1 paper beet seed	.10

1855 STORE INVENTORY

This inventory from the Bowmer-Wayne store in Ione City, California, provides information about the types of merchandise carried by general stores in Gold Rush communities of the 1850s. The list was made Sept. 20, 1855, by Sheriff W. Dunham of Amador County when the goods were attached for non-payment of a $1,500 debt.

1 Doz Axes
½ BBl Gin
½ BBl Whiskey
½ BBl Brandy
2 Cans Lard (20 lbs)
200 lbs Flour
4 Prs Blankets
7 Claw Hammers & 2 Augers
7 Pr Ladies Shoes
1 Doz Blanket Coats
9 Over alls
1½ Doz Woolen Drawers
½ Doz Cotton Drawers
½ Doz Calico Shirts
½ Doz Linen Pants
4 Silk Handkerchiefs
4 Remnants Gingham
1000 lbs Barly
32 Gal Vinegar

5 Gals Syrup
½ BBl Mifs Pork
5 Gal. Kegg of Pickles
15 Prs Boots
8 Prs Mens Shoes
60 Yds White Drilling
75 Yds Shirting
10 Pr Sat (?)tt Pants
1 Doz. Hickory Shirts
½ Doz Woolen Shirts
2 Pr Casmur Pants
4 Check Shirts
1 Remnant Blc Shirting
1 Remnant Blc Towling
1 Lincy Wolsey
13 White Shirts
1 Vest
4 Remnants Cotton Handkerchief
2½ Doz Mens Cotton Hoes

one Lot Ribbin

7 prs Mens Woolen Socks

2 Doz Table Spoons

4 Bottles Pain Killer

½ Doz Leather Belts

25 lbs Olive Soap

2 Boxes Cigare

1 Pr Gold Scales

1 Doz Coffee Potts

9 Ten Pails

1 Doz Pick Handles

½ BBl Orleans Sugar

17 long handled Shovels

11 Broomes

½ Doz prospects Pans

30 lbs Table Salt

8 Bottles of Peppermint

10 lbs Smoking Tobaco

3 hams Meat

2 Doz Ink

4 Neck Ties

8 Linen Coats

1 Reem letter Paper

Bunch Thread

1½ Doz Ladies hoes

2 Doz Tea Spoons

8 Boxes Pills

½ Doz Paper Taxs

20 lbs Tea

30 lbs. Candles

1 Doz Pepper Sauce

4 Small Tubs

1 Coffee Boiler

1 Doz Tin Pans

10 Picks

5 Wooden Pails

½ Doz Sluice Forks
(long handles)

7 Camp Kettles

4 Bake Ovens

2 Hoes & 1 Friing Pan

50 lbs Corn Meal

One Iron Safe & 2 Atc Books

1 Box Starch

3 Doz Knives & Forks

1 Lot of Screwe & Buts

2 Doz Yeast Powders

½ BBl Butter

25 lbs Crushed Sugar

50 lbs Grun Coffee

1½ Doz Cans of Hunney

1 Dox Cans Ground Coffee

1½ Doz Cans Roast Chicken

1½ Doz Cans Roast Tukey

1 Doz Black Pepper

1 Doz Cans (?) pour Powder

20 lbs Tobaco

6 lbs Cream Tartar

75 lbs Rice

1 BBl Crackers

25 lbs Chillie Peaches*

7 Cans Peaches

12 lbs Saleratus

1 Doz Cans Ground Mustard

1 Doz Cans Allspice

½ Doz Caster Oil

15 Cans Lobsters

*During the Gold Rush dried fruit was imported from Chili, so perhaps this is what was meant by "Chillie Peaches." In 1849, Mrs. James Caples recalled, "there were plenty of dried apples and dried pealed peaches from chili, pressed in the shape of cheese, to be had." She made fruit pies, rendering salt pork into the lard for crusts, and sold them to Placerville miners for one dollar and a quarter each. (Caples, 1911 typescript, California State Library, Sacramento)

The 1855 promissory note resulted in a court case one year later. John Clement Bowmer testified that he was not aware that it had been signed by his partner, B. F. Wayne, and was not responsible for it.

Also attached were:

"One Ranch known as the Map (?) Ranch containing about 320 Acres more or lefs Situated & being in Buck Eye Valley joins Store on the north and Kay on the west side:

133 sheep
3 American Mars
25 Tons of Hay
1 Waggon
1 Coat & Harnefs
2 one 80th in Macosumnes Ditch"

A CHAPTER ON BEARDS

By Lenita

One of the rare instances when Lorena let her sense of humor surface occurred in 1855. This essay was written under a nom de plume, the journalistic custom of the day. It appeared on the front page of the Oct. 7 issue of *The Golden Era* printed on Sundays in San Francisco as "A California Family Newspaper — Devoted to Literature, Agriculture, the Mining Interest, Local and Foreign Intelligence, Commerce, Education, Science and the Fine Arts."

Great events sometimes come from little causes.

"When Louis VII, to obey the injunctions of his bishops, cropped his head and shaved his beard, Eleanor, his consort, found him looking very rediculous. She revenged herself as she thought proper, and the poor shaved king obtained a divorce. She then married Count of Anjou, afterwards Henry II, of England. She had for her dowry the rich provinces of Poiton and Cuienne*, and this was the origin of those wars which for three hundred years ravaged France, and cost the French three millions of men. All this had probably never occurred had Louis not been so rash as to crop his beard, by which he became so disgusting in the eyes of Eleanor."

There! You see a forcible illustration of a woman's opinion on the beard question, and the dreadful consequences resulting from this toilet neglect in one instance alone; this non-compliance to a *wife's wishes* in reference to wearing of this gracful appendage; and who knows how many family jars, discords and estrangements may have had their origins in a like cause? I shouldn't like to say it was sufficient reason, providing all other differences were properly adjusted; but 'tis strange — passing strange — this fancy women have, and ever have had, for bearded faces, even back to the days of Abraham, Isaac and Jacob, for it is said they wore long flowing beards, and wer'n't Sarah, Rebekah and Rachel model wives? And, then, when "the question was popped" it didn't take the fair patriarch*esses* always to say *yes*. This *might* have been owing to an "exquisite pair of whiskers", just as is often the case now-a-days; but I wouldn't be *positive* that Providence and parents didn't make "special interpositions" in those days in affairs of this kind. However, this is all the *Scripture proof* I shall attempt to aduce in favor of my position.

But seriously, women are admirers of beards, and are they not allowed to possess good taste, and the finer discriminating powers? Speaking of fireside quarrels — "There, didn't you promise not to shave them off?" and the little beauty pouts and cries, and keeps her husband at a "respectful" distance until he promises to let them grow out again, better and *bigger* than ever. He came home looking as sheep-faced as though he were really guilty of theft, as indeed he had been robbing nature of a gift bestowed upon him as a distinguishing badge of his superiority over the rest of God's cratures. 'Tis well if this first experience learns him a lesson, and he faithfully promises never to perform a like mutilation again.

How many a maiden has proved faithless to her first vows of love and constancy, all because a fine pair of whiskers has stepped in and stolen first her admiration, then her affections from her beardless lover! No matter if he had the best hart and head, too; there is a nameless charm in these appendages that causes them to outweigh heart and brains both, sometimes, in a lady's estimation. Perhaps "she don't show her good sense" — and I admit she does not on all occasions; but you should show yours by cultivating your beard, and thus outweighing those brainless fops, for if such ornaments add charms to one who is deficient, how much more will they enhance the beauty and manliness of one who possesses real worth of heart and mind! Though *some* women are dazzled with appearances, yet few are wholly blind to true worth and integrity of character, either with or without fine looks, and we consider it no disparagement to a good man to be a fine looking man. Then, if good men were to pay more attention to their personal appearance, we think the chances would be more than double in their favor, and many women might be prevented from being "taken in by false appearances." They would thus make it necessary for worthless characters to reform, or keep their proper places, as they would be convinced that appearances only wouldn't always "weigh."

As I said before — although I cannot tell exactly why — there is something in a finely adjusted head of hair and properly cultivated beard, that most women cannot help but admire. Perhaps it imparts nobleness and dignity, and a look of strength, which we do not see in effeminate and beardless faces always. Women love to see in men in-tellectual beauty and physical strength blended, and man loves woman for her beauty and helplessness, which, perhaps, gives him a sense of his superiority. Then let him wear the emblem of his strength. But let him select a becoming style, for one sees such outlandish faces now-a-days to disgust him with all bearddom. Some faces resemble ferocious tigers, others silly goats or senseless buffoons. We think a beard-less phiz. preferable to these burlesques upon mankind. The hair may be arranged a little loosely upon the forehead, thus slightly shading the face, and giving to the countenance an expression of softness and refinement. Every man's beard may be arranged tastefully, and as best suits the contour of the features. But my advice to all husbands is, to cultivate their beards as tastefully and handsomely as they may. And wouldn't it be an item worthy of the consideration in the next Know Nothing Convetion, viz.: — *Resolved,* That we, as true Americans, do solemnly pledge ourselves, that henceforth we will maintain and practice the custom of wearing beards, lest American ladies, not finding suitable husbands at home, be induced to seek *foreign commodities.* '' Yes, Americans, add this new *platform* to your *plank,* and you will no doubt find a ready *home consumption* for all your marketable wares — viz: old bachelors with hearts to let, or those in search of their *other halves.*

*These were probably printers' errors made while hand-setting the small type used by *The Golden Era.* Lorena meant ''Poitou'' and ''Guienne'' in southern France.

J.C. BROWMER'S EXPENSE ACCOUNT

Written on a torn sheet of blue ledger paper, this list shows the expenses Lorena's husband incurred on his 1855 trip to Wisconsin to visit the children of his first marriage. On the return trip he was accompanied by his partner's wife, Mrs. Sarah J. Wayne, and her two children. The original bill was filed as evidence in Case No. 80, California Fifth Judicial District Court, Jackson (Amador County), California, February Session, 1856, Judge Charles M. Creanor presiding.

"General Expense from Sanfrancisco to Wisconsin

J. C. Bowmer

Fare to N Y.	300.00	
Bill at Hotel in N Y	17.50	
Omnibus fare Do	5.00	
Sundries *(Medicens)* Do	11.50	
Expenses to L N.Y.	27.75	
" Galena[1]	38.25	
	$400.00	
		$200.00

General Expense from Wisconsin to Sanfrancisco	
Expenses to DuBuque[2]	9.50
" " on wagon	5.75
Paid for expenses in Galena	13.00
Fare to Chicago	15.00
Bill at Hotel at Chicago	6.00
Fare from Chicago to NY	55.00
Bill at Cleaveland[3]	7.50
" Dunkirk[4]	4.50
" Hotel	5.00
2 Umbrellas	2.50
Dinners	1.50
Paid Porter & Omnibus N.Y.	2.50
" Bill at Hotel "	17.50
" Freight on trunks	5.57
" Steamer fare to S.F.	720.00
Omnibus & Porter N.Y.	2.00
" S.F	2.50
Sundry Expenses from N.Y. to S.F.	126.50
	1002.00

Amount of JCB. Expenses	334.00	167.00
JC Bowmer's proportion of Expenses		$367.00

1855 Statement of Cash Recd by J.C. Bowmer
March 1 From B. F. Wayne

Coin	550.00	
Dust	860.09	
April 11 Cash from John Wayne	300.00	
" 13 " " Mrs. Wayne	17.00	
Whole amt Recd	$1727.09	

J C Bowmer   Dr

To Expenses appr Statement	367.00
Cash used	152.34
	$519.34

1. Galena, Illinois, in the north-west corner of the state.
2. Dubuque, Iowa, across the Mississippi River and to the north of Galena, at the Wisconsin border.
3. Cleveland, Ohio.
4. Dunkirk, New York on the shores of Lake Erie between Erie, Pennsylvania, and Buffalo, New York.

THE CALIFORNIA BELLE

The ordeal of a six-month trip west exacted a toll upon emigrants, whose appearance upon arrival in California combined exhaustion with dirt and tattered garments. Many left extra clothing along the trail when superfulous items had to be abandoned. Luzena Stanley Wilson commented in 1849 upon the condition of her dress when she met miners near the end of the Carson Emigrant Road. Lamenting her ragtag appearance, Luzena commented upon the torn skirt that revealed her ankles and her lack of gloves, both important concerns for a properly dressed Victorian lady.

In 1853, while traveling along the Humboldt River, Harriet Ward mentioned the effects of dust and alkali, both hard on hair and skin. A year earlier John Doble, mining in the community of Volcano, observed that "sun burn dust etc. in crossing the plains makes [the emigrants] all look verry black & dirty about like a person would look after working charcoal all day in June or July."

Another view of how the trip effected women appeared in the Sacramento *Pictorial Union* of January 1, 1853, in "An Ode to the 'California Belle'," illustrated with drawings showing her crossing the plains and in town. The deep-brimmed sunbonnet worn during the overland trip featured a long "curtain" that protected the neck from sunburn. According to this article:

> Very many of the ladies who now grace the first circle of California society have endured the privitations and hardships of a journey across the Plains. In almost every instance, however, they have not only born fatigue without a murmur but have suffered less than their male companions. The novelty of the trip, and the natural curiosity peculiar to their sex, have furnished them with constant subjects of interest. They have been trained in a thorough school too and no women in our land are so well adapted for a California mode of life as those females who have made the overland tour.
>
> A large proportion of them although accustomed to every luxury at home and moving in the most refined circle have here cheerfully performed those household duties which usually devolve upon servants. They have invariably made excellent wives and contributed greatly toward establishing society upon a permanent bases. Such women are invaluable in our youthful commonwealth and we heartily give them our hearts and our hands.
>
> One of the portraits that embellish the present number of our pictorial represents a female of one of the trains pleasantly trudging along with her box of clothing and provisions and clad in apparel designed more for comfort than ornament. The other presents her completely metamorphased, and in the "entirely new dress." She has doffed her homespun frock and sun bonnet, thrown away her staff and plain shawl and now

Illustrations of the California belle in town and crossing the plains.

appears in the latest fashion. The mantua maker, milliner, dry goods merchant, shoe dealer and hair dresser have all drawn upon the "pile" of her California lover and she is now on the eve of exchanging her career of single blessedness — in other words, she "is in town." The great curiosity in California is "caught" so suddenly that the report has never had time to circulate.

Notes

INTRODUCTION

1. Gas lights first flickered and flared along St. Louis streets on November 4, 1847. Two months later, when Lorena was in the city, the *Daily Union* boasted "not more than one half of the retorts for the manufacture of gas are, at present, required to light this city. The gas district will, however, doubtless be extended this spring." J. H. Sloss, *St. Louis Directory for 1848* (St. Louis: Charles and Hammond, 1848), xi; *History of St. Louis, Annual Review and Improvements for the Year 1853* (St. Louis: Republican Steam Press, 1854), 10; *St. Louis Daily Union,* Jan. 10, 1848.

Weather reports were not a daily feature of newspapers in the 1840s and 1850s but the winter of January 1848 was so "mild and pleasant" that the St. Louis, Missouri, *Daily Republican* commented upon it Jan. 1 and Jan. 15. The St. Louis newspapers that month also carried notices in their "Amusements" columns for daily performances of circus acts at the amphitheater of E. Rockwell & Co. for 25 cents a seat. Meanwhile, at the Odd Fellows Hall every Tuesday and Thursday evenings a large audience enjoyed a "rare intellectual feast" in the form of historical lectures by Rev. F. Post, formerly professor of languages at Middlebury College, Vermont, who had moved to St. Louis the fall of 1847 to become minister of the Third Presbyterian Church. Lecture topics of "the highest order" included "The Nature and Aims of History, Principles, Methods and Objects of Historic Study and Criticism" and "The Philosophy of the Progress of Civilization and the Historic Relation of the Different Ages and Nations to It." *Daily Union,* Nov. 3, 1847; Jan. 1, 3, 10, 12, 1848.

A picture of the Second Presbyterian Church as it looked in 1848 appears in its 70th anniversary pamphlet. The church was built at the cost of $55,000 in 1839 on land given by Pierre Chouteau, Esq. and dedicated October 11, 1840. *Church Manual (1857) for the Communicants of the Second Presbyterian Church of St. Louis,* No. IV (St. Louis: S. Spencer, 1858); *Daily Republican,* Oct. 12, 1840, reprinted in the 70th Anniversary pamphlet.

2. This revival was announced in the *Daily Union,* Jan. 10 and the *Daily Republican,* Jan. 8, 1848. The later newspaper reported: "We learn that Dr. Hall will continue to preach in the Second Presbyterian Church this night and every night next week. Exercises to commence at 7 o'clock. Pews free." Apparently overwhelmed by the revival meeting, Lorena neglected to describe the circumstances surrounding her visit to St. Louis, a busy port city considered the "Gateway to the West." The trip, although in January, must have been relatively easy because the weather "had every appearance of spring." The first hard snow occurred January 8, but three days later it was again "pleasantly warm," so the river remained open for ships. The unusual weather continued well into February, when Lorena returned to her family in Pleasant Vale Township. The expense of this trip might be why her parents sold approximately twenty-six acres for $150 on February 5. Aside from one other brief 1848 entry, Lorena did not write again until December 2 the following year. Then, emotionally numb with shock and grief because of seven deaths within the family circle, she again sought consolation in her diary.

3. Harvey Newcomb in *The Young Lady's Guide to the Harmonious Development of Christian Character* (4th ed., Boston: James B. Dow, 1842) devoted fifteen pages to the topic of "self-examination," plus another nine pages in the appendix with questions to ask oneself: "How was my heart improved by last Sabbath? How have I since improved the impressions I then received? . . . What temptations have I encountered? What victories have I gained? . . . Did I yesterday make all needful preparations for the holy Sabbath? What was my frame of mind on retiring to rest at the close of the week? . . . How were my thoughts employed during the wakeful hours of the night? . . . Have I manifested a morose, sour, and jealous disposition towards others? Have I been easily provoked? . . . Do I harbor ill-will towards any being on earth? . . . In all my intercourse with others, have I manifested a softness and mildness of manner, and a kind and tender tone of feeling?" The list of such questions to be answered by someone as conscientious as Lorena was endless.

4. Lorena's religious intensity matches that of many other nineteenth century diarists, including Elizabeth Duncan of Jacksonville, Ill. See Elizabeth Caldwell Smith Duncan "Diary," 1824-48 [fragmentary] ed. by Elizabeth Duncan Putnam, *Illinois State Historical Society Journal,* 21 (1928): 1-84; Don Harrison Doyle, *The Social Order of a Frontier Community, Jacksonville, Illinois, 1825-70* (Urbana, Ill.: University of Illinois Press, 1978), 160-61.

5. A group of Jacksonville, Ill., women organized the "Ladies Association for Educating Females" in 1833 to raise funds to help girls attend the Jacksonville Female Academy, which in 1846 became MacMurray College for Women, now a coeducational four-year institution, ibid., 160-61. Advertisements for female seminaries in Pike County, Illinois, appeared in *The Union* and *The Free Press* during the 1840s and 1850s, listing courses of study and tuition per quarter.

6. The 1853 manuscript letters of Dr. J. R. Bradway are part of the Rollins Collection at the Princeton University Library.

7. *Pike County Free Press,* July 24, 1851.

8. These issues are missing from the newspaper files at the Library of Congress and at the Illinois State Historical Library.

9. Franklin Walker, *San Francisco's Literary Frontier* (New York: Alfred Knopf, 1939), 116-43.

10. Women in bloomers were an evocative sight, even on the trip west when such a travel costume might seem practical. Such overland travelers in 1853 caught the attention of Dr. J. R. Bradway, John Haas, and Harriet Sherrill Ward. See Bradway Letters, Princeton University Library; John B. Haas, "Autobiography," *The Pony Express Courier,* June-October 1938; Harriet Sherrill Ward, *Prairie Schooner Lady* (Los Angeles: Westernlore Press, 1941).

11. For information about the origins and impact of "the cult of domesticity," see Barbara Berg, *The Remembered Gate* (New York: Oxford University Press, 1978).

12. Ruth E. Finely, *The Lady of Godey's — Sarah Josepha Hale* (Philadelphia and London: J. B. Lippincott Co., 1931); estate papers of Alson Hays, Pike County Courthouse, Pittsfield, Ill.

13. The ratio of white women to men between the ages of fifteen and twenty years was 97.4 per 100 in the United States, according to the 1850 census. In the twenty-to-thirty age group there were 100 men for every 94 women. The population of Pike County, Ill., that year was given as 9,670 men and 9,106 women. In Illinois the ratio of marriages that year was "very nearly one person married to every 200 persons [listed in the census]." J. D. B. Debrow, *Statistical View of the United States* (Washington, D.C.: Beverly Tucker, 1854), 56, 57, 104, 218-29, 696, 714; *Bi-Centennial Historical Statistics of the United States* (93rd Congress, First Session, House Document No. 93-78, 1975), 19.

14. *Pike County Union,* July 28, 1852.

15. Charles Wells Hayes, *George Hayes of Windsor and His Descendants* (Buffalo, N.Y.: Baker, Jones & Co., 1884).

16. Ibid.

17. Ibid., 72, 228.

18. Ibid.

19. Ibid., 72, 228. According to one account, the Lake Pleasant Road was opened from Erie, some twenty-six miles away, to the Martin Hayes place in the winter of 1821-23 and did not extend further until four years later. *Nelson's Biographical Dictionary and Historical Refernce Book of Erie County, Pennsylvania* (Erie, Pa: S.B. Nelson, 1896), 650.

20. Ray Allen Billington, *Westward Expansion* (New York: Macmillan, 1950), 259.

21. Ibid.; *Nelson's Dictionary* 650; Estate papers and will of Martin Hays, County Courthouse, Erie, Pa.

22. Hayes, *Hayes,* 149-50.

23. Considering the Hays family background, it would be expected that Alson Hays, Lorena's father, had an education. He signed fourteen promisory notes between 1845 and 1848, which are still among his estate papers. In the early nineteenth century, a woman was considered educated if she could read but not necessarily write. See Nancy F. Cott, *The Bonds of Womanhood, "Women's Sphere" in New England, 1780-1835* (New Haven and London: Yale University Press, 1977).

24. Bernice Hoover, Lithgow Family Genealogy; Census, 1830, Erie County, Pa., Vol. 5, 280.

25. Hayes, *Hayes,* 149-50.

26. Ibid.; U.S. Census, 1830, Vol. 5, 249, 254, 261, 267.

27. Billington, *Westward Expansion,* 290.

28. Adam Lithgow was born in Lancaster, Pennsylvania, in 1808. A James Lithgow family is noted in the 1810 Pennsylvania Census for Leacock Township and appears in the 1830 Census for Erie, as James "Lithgo." Hoover, Lithgow-Woodward Family Papers; Index to the 1810 Census (Cleveland: Ohio Family Historians, 1966 microfilm), 161.

Lauristan Brown was nine years older than his wife, the former Elizabeth Lithgow. Whether they were married in Pennsylvania or in Illinois is unknown. The 1840 Census for Pike County lists their son, John H., as three years old. Hoover, Lithgow-Woodward Family Papers; 1840 Illinois Census, 183A, 1.35; 1872 *Pike County Atlas* (Davenport, Iowa: Andreas, Lyter & Co., 1975), 14.

29. Adam Lithgow is listed as the sixth person baptized by the Baptist church in Barry, Ill., in August 1838; another member of the Lithgow family (first name not given) was the twenty-first person baptized in 1837. The Lithgows' second son was born in 1841 and died five years later. Hoover, Lithgow-Woodward papers; "Organization, 1829-60," (Barry Baptist Church), 25, 34.

30. 1872 *Pike County Atlas,* 14; U.S. Census Records for Erie County, 1830; Pike County, 1840 and 1850.

31. Billington, *Westward Expansion,* 372-75; "United States Economy, 1837-1860," *Business Annals, 1926* (National Bureau of Economic Research) reprinted in *The Oregon Trail* (Federal Writers' Project, New York: Hastings House, 1939), 224-27.

32. U.S. Census Records, 1840: 115, 150.

33. J. M. Peck, *A Gazetteer of Illinois in Three Parts* 2nd ed., (Philadelphia: Gregg & Elliot, 1837), vi., 321, 323, 326; William Oliver, *Eight Months in Illinois with Information for the Emigrant, 1848* (Ann Arbor, Mich.: University Microfilms, 1966), 123.

34. Oliver, *Eight Months,* 99; Peck, *Gazetteer,* 1st ed., (Jacksonville, Ill.: R. Goudy, 1834), 77; Billington, *Westward Expansion,* 295-96; J. M. Peck, *A New Guide for the Emigrants to the West,* 2nd ed. (Boston: Gould, Kendall and Lincoln, 1837); Peck, *Gazetteer,* 2nd ed., 328.

35. Although West was only four years old at the time, he later wrote they did not travel at night but tied up to trees along the river banks. The steering was done with a helm on the back of the raft. West gave his father's name as "Josiah" and identified him as a carpenter by trade. However, the 1884 genealogy of the Hayes family lists West's father as Thomas Jefferson West "of New Hampshire parentage." West added that his father made the trip to California in 1852 "by water" and settled in Amador County, Calif., where he died in 1854. (According to the Hays genealogy, he died in Drytown on December 23, 1853). West's mother, Mary Marinda Hays West, died August 3, 1846 in Barry, Ill. After her death West lived with "different families, getting my board and clothing and some schooling." Later he worked "by the month" until he was sixteen years old "when I crossed the plains" with the Adam Lithgow family. Wells Wallis West, "Autobiography," Bancroft

Library, University of California-Berkeley; Hayes, *Hayes,* 72-73.

36. *Pike County Atlas,* 14.

37. Peck, *Gazetteer* (1834), 151; *New Guide,* 303.

38. Ibid.

THE ILLINOIS YEARS/INTRODUCTION

1. Deed Book 29, Pike Co., Ill., 34, Courthouse, Pittsfield, Ill.; Federal Tract Book S-701 (Quincy, Ill.); personal correspondence from Wayne Temple, 1977; Illinois State Archives, Springfield (hereafter called ISA).

2. Federal Tract Book S-701.

3. Nicholas Biddle Van Zandt, *A Full Description of the Soil, Water, Timber and Prairies of Each Lot or Quarter Section of the Military Lands Between the Mississippi and the Illinois Rivers* (Washington City: P. Force, 1818), 77; Temple letter, 1977.

4. New Canton was located in Pleasant Vale Township, one of the earliest settled areas in western Pike County. It consisted primarily of Mississippi River bottomland, but the timbered areas were supposed to be as fertile as the prairies. However, the uplands were "very rough and broken," better for grain and fruit trees than for large-scale farming. A major attraction for early settlers was Keyes Creek with its salt spring twenty feet in diameter which "boils from the earth and throws off a stream of some size, forming a salt pond in its vicinity." Willard Keyes, for whom the creek was named, and John Wood, who later became governor, arrived in this area about 1820, two years after Illinois was admitted to the Union. M. D. Massie, *Past and Present in Pike County* (Chicago: S. J. Clarke, 1906), 86-87; Peck, *Gazetteer* (1837), 274; Jess M. Thompson, *The Jess M. Thompson Pike County History, 1935-1939* (Pittsfield, Illinois: Pike County Historical Society, 1968), 206-07; Thomas Ford, *A History of Illinois from its Commencement as a State in 1818 to 1847* (Chicago: The Lakeside Press, 1945); Pike County Records and Deeds, Deed 8, mf roll 7, ISA; Record Book 30, 16205; Alson Hays estate papers, Pike County Courthouse, Pittsfield, Ill.

5. Rev. Jesse Elledge, a pioneer preacher in Pike County, was known as a "hardshell" Baptist who preached "hellfire." He came to Illinois in the mid-1820s, conducting camp and protracted meetings and serving as first clerk of the Sandy Creek (Winchester) church of Scott County, considered the forerunner of Baptist churches on both sides of the Illinois River. His grandfather, Edward Boone, was a brother of Daniel Boone and also a Baptist preacher in North Carolina. Elledge served the Barry Baptist Church (a United Baptist Church of Christ) for nearly twenty years, until replaced by Rev. S. F. Holt in June 1853. Thompson, *History of Pike County,* 299-325; Billington, *Westward Expansion,* 306-08; for information about the English settlement in eastern Pike County, see Rebecca Burlend, Milo M. Quaife, ed., *A True Picture of Emigration* (1831) (Chicago: The Lakeside Press, 1936); Barry Baptist Church Records; Thompson, *Pike County History,* 12, 14; Peck, *Gazetteer* (1834), 152; *History of Pike County, Illinois* (Chicago: Chas. C. Chapman & Co., 1880), 838.

6. Barry Baptist Church Records, 1840; Hayes, *Hayes,* 72-73, 228.

7. Oliver, *Eight Months,* 30; Doyle, *Frontier Community,* 157.

8. Hoover, Lithgow family papers.

9. Barry Baptist Church Records, 1850.

10. Ibid., 1848; The widely-held nineteenth century belief that women should not speak in public was based upon a Biblical injunction and this was used by opponents of higher education for women. Women were told they should be "modest in all things including intellectual attainments." Joan N. Burstyn, *Victorian Education and the Ideal of Womanhood* (New Brunswick, N. J.: Rutgers University Press, 1984), 146.

11. Barry Baptist Church Records, 1848, 1853.

12. Federal Writers Project. *Erie, a Guide to the City and County,* American Guide Series (Philadelphia: The William Penn Assoc., 1938), 57; *Nelson's Dictionary,* 312; *History of Pike County* (1880), 838; Thompson, *Pike County History,* 472.

13. In 1836 enrollment in the Chicago Female Seminary, directed by Frances Willard, jumped from seventeen to thirty-eight women students within three months. See Katherine Clinton, "Pioneer Women in Chicago," *Journal of the West* (April 1973): 317-24; Josephine L. McLaughlin, *Through These Hallowed Halls, A Trip Down Memory Lane and A Brief Glimpse of Life through the Past 100 Years of the Griggsville Schools* (Bluff, Ill.: Jones, 1976), 19, 95, 121.

14. *Pike County Union,* Sept. 1, 1852; Illinois Methodist Episcopal Church, *Minutes of the Illinois Annual Conference, 1852* (St. Louis: Intelligencer, 1852). The fourth annual catalogue of the Female College at Jacksonville is included in these records.

15. *Pike County Atlas* (1872), 115; Hays estate records.

16. Ibid.

17. Ibid.

18. Ibid.

19. Ibid.

20. *Business Annals* (1926), 224-27; Hays estate records.

21. William A. Grimshaw, "History of Pike County — A Centennial Address," delivered at Pittsfield, July 4, 1876, Illinois State Historical Society Library, Springfield (hereafter called ISHL); Oliver, *Eight Months,* 65; *History of Pike County* (1880), 348; Hayes, *Hayes,* 72-73, 150.

22. Hays estate records. Dr. A. C. Baker, born in 1813 in London, emigrated to the U.S. in 1815 and ten years later moved with his parents first to White County and later to Greene County, Ill. He studied medicine with Dr. Worthington of Pittsfield and after graduating from Ohio Medical College in Cincinnati in 1837, returned to Pike County to begin practice. During the winter of 1850-51 Dr. Baker accompanied laborers to Panama where they cut and graded for the Panama Canal. In 1853 he "crossed the plains to California with a herd of cattle from Berry and returned without accident the following year." His only recorded comment about this trip noted that while hunting along the Humboldt River he found himself in the "midst of Indians and was always well treated." Thompson, *Pike County History,* 805. Dr. P. M. Parker, a native of New York, studied under Dr. Higgins of Griggsville and was graduated from the State University of Missouri at St. Louis. He came to New Canton in 1846 and practiced in Barry 1853-64. *Pike County History*

(1880), 805, 828.

23. Hays estate records.

24. For a discussion of dower rights, see Joan Hoff Wilson, "Hidden Riches: Legal Records and Women, 1750-1825" in Mary Kelley, ed., *Woman's Being, Woman's Place* (Boston: G. K. Hall, 1979), 7-25. This "widow's exclusion property" consisted of:

4 Beds and Numerous Bedding
3 Common Bedstead & 1 Trundle Bedstead
1 Common Table
1 Spinning Wheel
1 Rocking Chair
2 Cows & calves
2 Shoats
1 cooking stove & furniture
2 small pigs
1 Candle Stand
1 Reel
4 Kitchen Do.
1 Pitchfork
2 Hens
A small lot of kitchen utensils
2 cows
2 calves

The one "reel" in this inventory may have been a "clock reel," used to wind and count yards of thread or yarn. Another fourteen items were listed in the "schedule marked A," which Lorena's mother wished to keep. These included "1 Gray Mare," purchased for $31.99 in February 1847, but now valued at $12, plus carpenter-cooper's tools such as an adze, axe, knives, jointers, a bucksaw and a handsaw, grindstone, hatchet, and 2,000 staves. The total lot was valued at $70.97, but Lorena's mother agreed to accept $10 less. Administrator Barker requested the probate judge to let him know "at as early a time as convenient if she [Susannah Hays] will be entitled to all in the schedule if she is and you set it apart to her I will fully agree to it." He added that he had advertised the raminder of Alson Hays' personal property for sale. An announcement of a public auction of the Hays land in Pleasant Vale Township and New Canton appeared in the county newspapers. It was held at 10 A.M. and 5 P.M. at the courthouse in Pittsfield. *Pike County Free Press,* Jan. 3, 1850; Hays estate records.

25. Alson Hays' silver watch, valued at $2.50, was bought back by his wife for 87.5 cents. Philander Hays bought his father's "long Jointer" for 30 cents, 75 cents less than the appraisal. Two Hays' brothers-in-law also attended the sale: Adam Lithgow purchased "1 old Plough" for $1 and Thomas Jefferson West acquired a workbench for 50 cents. The light one-horse wagon, valued at $10.50, sold for $16.10, but the "Ten Plate Stove & Pipe" valued at $3 was considered merely an "old stove" and sold for $1.70. It included an oven and was constructed from ten pieces of iron, hence its name. A forerunner of the free-standing kitchen range, the ten-plate stove was found in many American homes before 1850, according to William Seale, *Recreating the Historic House In-*

terior (Nashville, Tenn.: American Association for State and Local History, 1979), 59.

Even the auctioneer could not resist a bargain and purchased a bushel of rock for ten cents. Also sold was a note payable to Lorena's father for $20 worth of lumber at the mill of L. R. Marshall. Valued at only $10, it sold for $15.25. In an undated staement, the administrator declared the amount of the sale $68.743/4, or almost $5 more than the total shown on the sales sheet of the auctioneer. Hays estate records.

26. *Pike County Free Press,* Mar. 1, 1848.

27. Hays estate records.

28. Ibid.

29. Amador County, California, Deeds Book D, 475, 583-84, Amador County Courthouse, Jackson, Calif.

30. William Grimshaw was adjutant general of the Seventeenth Illinois Milita in 1833. As a Whig and a Republican, he authored the provision in the 1847 state constitution to prevent dueling and was a delegate to the convention that nominated Abraham Lincoln for the presidency. Grimshaw was in partnership with his brother until 1857. *History of Pike County* (1880), 682-83; Hays estate records.

31. Ibid.

32. *Business Annals* (1926), 224-27; Special Illinois Census, 1850, mf roll 31-97, 797, ISA.

33. *Weekly North-Western Gazette and Advertizer,* Galena, Ill., 1849; Patrick E. McLear, "The St. Louis Cholera Epidemic of 1849," *Missouri Historical Review* 63 (1969): 173, 179.

In May 1849 the *Pike County Union* carried a warning about cholera: "We have heard of but an isolated case of this disease in our county . . . be watchful of the first approach of any of its syptoms. It is on the increase not only in St. Louis but on almost every boat passing up our rivers and it will be fortunate, indeed, if our country should escape from this scourge." Three months later, cholera extended into the interior, "severly visiting" Pike County and "many valuable citizens have been carried off." May 16; Aug. 1.

34. Debrow, *Statistical View,* 340; *Pike County Union,* July 4, 1849. First known as Worchester, Barry was rechristened when it was learned that another Illinois town had the same name. The name Barry was selected by B. D. Brown, Lorena's distant relative by marriage. It is thought that he intended the name to be "Barre" for the town in Vermont where he once lived. Local legend claims that when Dr. A. C. Baker (the Hays family doctor) drew up the petition for the change, the clerk spelled it with a "y." Since this was the name of President Andrew Jackson's postmaster, the altered spelling was accepted.

The village of Barry was laid out by agents for Calvin R. Stone, who then owned the land in the northern half of Section 25 of Barry Township. He was also a partner in the St. Louis firm of Stone, Field, and Marks, which erected the first grain mill, sold in 1836 to B. D. Brown and his partner McTucker. Two years later they acquired a sawmill northeast of the public square and in the mid-1840s Brown and McTucker owned another sawmill. It was surrounded by eighteen dwellings, a meat packing house, and three large stores.

This comprised the community of Barry before 1850. *History of Pike County* (1880), 798.

35. Ibid.; *Pike County Union,* July 4, 1849; Debrow, *Statistical View,* 730; 1850 Census: township 4, section 6 West, Barry, Illinois The steam flour mill was established by William Wike, who also built a woolen factory that handled part of the 38,450 pounds of wool clipped from Pike County sheep and valued at $16,516 in 1850. The factory was located two miles west of Barry in an area known as "Snake Holler" due to the onetime presence of a rattlesnake on the site. With the aid of steam, this factory, whose buildings were still standing in 1978, undertook "carding, spinning, weaving, fulling and dressing of various woolen fabrics."

36. Census, 1850, Barry, Ill.

37. *Pike County Union,* July 4, 1849; Special 1850 Census for Pike County, mf roll 39-97, 797, ISA; *History of Pike County* (1880), 799. A Methodist deacon taught the first school classes, which were held in a small frame building. It moved so often that in later years no one could agree upon its original location.

38. Pike County land records and deeds: 8, 38, and 40 (1836-1853); *Pike County Atlas* (1872), 108.

39. Doyle, *Frontier Community,* 113-15; Census, 1850, Pike County, Ill. A carpenter was paid $1.75 a day without board in the 1850s in the western division of Pike County while a farm hand made $12 a month with board. The average daily wage for a laboring man was sixty-two cents with board and eighty-seven cents a week without. A female domestic servant received seventy-five cents a week plus board. Special Industrial Census for Pike County, 1850.

40. Finely, *The Lady of Godey's,* 234-35.

41. Doyle, *Frontier Community,* 204; Women teachers in Indiana in 1850 were paid $6.00, half the monthly salary for male teachers in that state. Kathryn Kish Sklar, *Catharine Beecher, A Study in American Domesticity* (New York: W.W. Norton, 1973) 312, fn. 34.

42. *Pike County Free Press,* 1848, June 1, June 22, July 6. In 1850 the western section of Pike County had fifty-five common schools with the same number of teachers for 1,642 pupils. Special Census, 1850, Roll 31-97, ISA.

43. Ibid.; *The Eclectic Fourth Reader,* published by the American Book Company, was part of the popular series of McGuffey readers, which were widely used by teachers for elocutionary drills. The six McGuffey readers, which dominated the textbook market and introduced students to the world of literature, contained selections now considered to be classics. The fourth reader, suitable for students in the fourth through sixth grades, included a fable by Nathaniel Hawthorne as well as selections from *Little Men* by Louisa May Alcott and Daniel Defoe's *Robinson Crusoe.* Diane Ravitch, "Where Have All the Classics Gone?", Book Section, *New York Times,* May 17, 1987, 46.

44. *Pike County Free Press,* May 30, 1850.

45. Ibid, September 1850.

46. Professor Turner's vision became reality in the 1860s with the establishment of the land grant colleges. A biographical sketch of Turner states he began his campaign when he first spoke at the 1850 Pike County Teacher's In-

stitute held in Griggsville. However, he did not speak at that meeting, according to Pike County newspapers, although he did speak in Barry three months later. Turner served on the Illinois College faculty from 1833 until he resigned in 1847. Dumas Malone, ed. *Dictionary of American Biography* (New York: Charles Scribner, vol. 19, 1933) 68.

47. Massie, *Past and Present; History of Pike County,* 597; *Pike County Free Press,* April 22, 1853.

48. *Pike County Free Press,* April 24, 1853.

49. Ibid.

50. McLaughlin, 3, 24.

51. Letter to Louisa E. Lithgow (last page with signature missing), Feb. 7, 1853, Hoover, Lithgow family papers.

52. Jeanne H. Watson, "The Cult of Domesticity," *Nineteenth Century* 7 (1982), 37-39.

53. Charles B. Johnson, *Illinois in the Fifties or a Decade of Development* (Champaign: Flanagan-Pearson Co., 1918), 70-72; According to a letter received by Lorena's cousin, one community in Pike County spent the winter of 1852-53 caught up in a round of religious activities. The first "protracted meeting" of three to four weeks was held by the Presbyterians, followed by five weeks at the Baptist Church and then it was the turn of the Methodists and Campbellites (the Disciples of Christ). These protracted meetings were immediately followed by the quarterly meetings of each faith.

54. Joseph R. Gusfield, *Symbolic Crusade, Status, Politics and the American Temperance Movement* (Urbana: University of Illinois Press, 1972), 44-49; *The Cyclopaedia of Temperance and Prohibition, a Reference Book . . .* (London and New York: Funk and Wagalls, 1891), 611-12; *Pike County Free Press,* May 18, 1848, printed the constitution and bylaws of the Pittsfield Division, Sons of Temperance.

55. Watson, "Cult," 38; *Uncle Tom's Cabin* by Harriet Beecher Stowe was first printed in the *National Era,* an anti-slavery newspaper in Washington D.C. as a serial between June 5, 1851, and April 1, 1852. Immensely popular, it was published in March 1852 by John P. Jewett as a two-volume work. It sold 10,000 copies in less than a week. *Dictionary of American Biography,* vol. 18, 117.

56. Doyle, *Frontier Community,* 52; Debrow, *Statistical View,* 218-29; Thompson, *Pike County History,* 152.

57. *Dictionary of American Biography,* Vol. 3, 175-76; Orville Hickman Browning, *Diary,* Vol. 1 1850-64, ed. Theodore C. Pease and James G. Randall (Springfield: ISHL, 1925), 67.

58. Known as the "pioneer shakes," malaria was prevalent in the Mississippi River valley and considered part of the initiation into fronteir life for newcomers. *History of Pike County,* 348; John Mack Faragher, *Sugar Creek, Life on the Illinois Prairie* (New Haven: Yale University Press, 1986), 89-90.

59. Faragher, *Sugar Creek,* 59, 125-26; George R. Stewart, *Ordeal by Hunger: The Story of the Donner Party* (Boston, 1960).

60. William T. Stackpole, Diary (ms), Beinecke Library, Yale University. Earlier in 1849 Charles Gilman of Pike County reported the "California train left yesterday morning (February 1) . . . about twenty in all. Another train leaves about the first of April, comprising about thirty more." Charles

Gilman to Horace S. Cooley, Feb. 2, 1849 (ISHL). Another eight wagons left from Perry on April 10 and joined with other adventurers in St. Joseph to form a train of fifty-six wagons, soon reduced to fifty-one when five withdrew because this company was considered too large, according to James Daigh. Pike County gold rush pioneers arrived in California in mid-September and J. J. Mudd wrote his brother, "We led most of the emigrants from Pike, a very short distance, however, as most of them came in within three days." James M. Daigh, *Nuggets from '49, an Account of Pike County Men in the Gold Rush,* condensed from his diary by Owen Hannat (Chambersburg, Ill., privately printed, 1949). *Pike County Union,* January 2, 1850.

61. Hoover, Lithgow family papers.

62. Ibid.

63. Census for Pike County, 1840, 25, 1-17; Census, 1850, 372, 1-29.

64. *Pike County Free Press,* June 12, 1851; John Regan, *The Emigrant's Guide to the Western States of America or Backwoods and Prairies,* 2nd ed. (Edinburgh: Oliver and Boyd, n.d. [1852?]), 350; Special Industrial Census, 1850, for Pike County.

65. Hinton Rowan Helper, "On the Land of Gold," ed. B. F. Gilbert, *Journal of the West,* (1973), 530.

66. *Christian Advocate,* Aug. 25, 1853, reprint of "16th instant" from the *Chicago Journal.*

67. *Pike County Free Press,* Dec. 23, 1852.

68. The Lithgow land, purchased with gold brought back by Adam Lithgow, consisted of nearly 102 acres divided between Section 3, just west of Barry, and Section 27, to the south in Pleasant Vale Township. He sold the land to David J. Wicke. Pike County Deed Book 38, 488.

69. At one time this shortage of women in California resulted in attempts to bring a company of women west, lured by promises that a laundress in San Francisco could make $1,200 a year while wages for clerks, bookkeepers and nurses were "proportional." *New York Times,* Feb. 22, 1853; Octavius T. Howe, *Argonauts of '49* (Cambridge, Mass., and London: Harvard University Press, 1970), 10.

70. Christiane Fischer, *Let Them Speak for Themselves, Women in the American West, 1849-1900* (Connecticut: Archon Books, 1977), 12.

71. *Frankie's Journal* by Frances Elizabeth Ward Gates, ed. Florence Stark DeWitt (Los Angeles: Western-Lore Press, 1960), 267.

72. Mary Fetter Hite Sanford, "A Trip Across the Plains and Biographical Sketch of Abraham Hite and Family," typescript, California State Library, Sacramento. (Hereafter referred to as CSL.)

73. Henrietta Reynolds, *The Reynolds-Salmon Train: Pioneers of the Sand Plains in San Joaquin County, California* (Angles Camp, Calif., privately printed), 14; Virginia Wilcox Ivins, *Pen Pictures of Early Western Days* (n. p., 1905), 55.

74. Henria Packer Compton, *Mary Ellen Murdock Compton* (privately printed, 1953), 10; Walter R. McIntosh, *An Overland Honeymoon in 1853* (Caldwell, Ida.: The Caxton Printers, 1938), 22, 33, 47.

75. The letter was signed "your sincere friend, E. A. Thaite" (or perhaps "Waite"). An advertisement for "Messrs. Clark & Son" appeared in the March 2, 1853, edition of the *Pike County Union,* announcing their daguer-

rotype studio was now located in "rooms over Hicks & Smiths store" in Pittsfield. The Clarks claimed they had "eight years of constant practice." The
Pike County Union of March 9 carried a similar ad. Hoover, Lithgow family
papers.

76. Adam Lithgow, who served as clerk for two years, wrote his last minutes
in the church records for the meeting of January 1853 and led his last prayer
at the meeting held the end of March. A deacon of the Baptist Church, he
was also a member of the building committee (at the February meeting the
congregation agreed "to sell the meeting house property to help defray expenses
of building a new House of Worship"). He left Barry before the new church,
which still stands, was built on the corner of Main and Rodgers streets. Hoover,
Lithgow family papers. Baptist Church records, 1853, 125.

77. Doyle, *Frontier Community,* 167.

78. Hoover, Lithgow family papers.

79. Pike County Deeds (microfilm): Roll 13, deed 40, March 10, 1853, ISA.
Brown, an unsuccessful candidate for sheriff in 1844, was an ardent booster of
the area. When Pike County was threatened with division in the mid-1840s,
he came to the defense because he could not "bear the idea of clipping her
wings . . . I do firmly believe that it would be much to our interest to inlarge
our Territory rather than diminish noble Old Pike." The intended division
never materialized and Brown, who later played an important role in the
development of Barry, acquired real estate valued at $4,000 by 1850. Brown
to William Blair, January 17, 1845, Blair Corresponence, ISHL; Pike County
Census Records, 1850, 146, 7-17.

THE ILLINOIS YEARS/DIARY

1. Lorena's agonies over publicly confessing her faith may seen extreme in
the 1980s, but in the nineteenth century religion played a dominant role in
everyday life. Because her frequent lamentations and indecision can detract
from her story, this first section of the diary has been edited to decrease the
repetition. The content has not been altered. The intense religious tone of the
diary reflects the spirit of a time when listening to a sermon provided genuine
intellectual and emotional pleasure for women such as Elizabeth Caldwell
Smith (Mrs. Joseph) Duncan, who moved from New Jersey to Jacksonville,
Ill., in 1830. She regretted that there was only one session of Sunday school to
attend on the Sabbath. At that time, anyone wishing to "get religion" was expected to "seek, implore and agonize 'till sins were forgiven." Duncan
"Diary," 2-4; Johnson, *Illinois in the Fifties,* 72.

2. According to the January 10, 1848, edition of the *St. Louis Daily Union,*
"The Rev. Mr. Hall will continue to preach at the Second Presbyterian
church for several evenings. Quite a revival is going forward under his
ministration." Although Lorena noted at least one session was held in a tent,
newspaper accounts do not include this information. The use of the terms
"mourners" and "enquirers" to describe those seeking to join a church was
typical of the 1840s and 1850s. They were expected to kneel at the "mourners"
or "anxious bench," a long seat without a back, placed in front of the pulpit.
Johnson, *Illinois in the Fifties,* 72.

3. Lorena did not record either the title or the topic of this sermon.

4. Lorena's father, Alson Hays, died October 4, 1848, in Barry, Ill., while the death of her grandfather, Martin Hays, occurred April 19, 1847, in Greene, Erie County, Pa. Her youngest brother, Augustus Harvey Hays (seven-and-a-half months old), also died in Barry, August 14, 1848, and Flavel Horatio Hays, twenty-one years old, died November 6, 1849, in Galena, Ill. Only one of the three cousins whose deaths Lorena mentions can be identified: Mrs. Mary Janet West Hart (daughter of Lorena's paternal aunt) died October 27, 1849, in Barry, leaving a son Alvin; she was the first wife of Orlando Hart. Hayes, *Hayes,* 72, 148-150; *Pike County History,* (1880) 819.

5. Designed as the Methodists' answer to *Godey's Lady's Book* and first published in 1841, the *Ladies Repository* featured sentimental fiction and French fashions. For thirty-five years it offered serious essays, poetry and literary chitchat with an "undisguised moral purpose." This was a "venture into the field of more worldly magazines but without the worldliness to which the Methodists strenuously objected." The monthly periodical was edited by Rev. B. F. Tefft and printed in both Cincinnati and New York City. *Christian Advocate,* September 27, 1956.

The books of Washington Irving (1783-1859) were immensely popular in his own day and he was known for his wit and humor as well as for his travel accounts. Although remembered for such works as *The Sketch Book, Bracebridge Hall, A History of New York* and *The Alhambra,* Irving also wrote about the American West. These books included *A Tour of the Prairies,* which described an 1832 expedition to the land of the Osages and the Pawnee. He also wrote a book called *Astoria* (1836) and *The Adventures of Captain Bonneville, U.S.A.* (1837). Lorena's description of her reading does not provide enough clues to identify which of Irving's books she enjoyed in February 1850. *Dictionary of American Biography,* vol. 9, 505-11.

6. The joke was really upon Lorena's brother because ipecac, a creeping plant found in South America, causes vomiting. Its root, as a medicinal extract, was used as an emetic as well as a purgative. The March 23 issue of the *Pittsfield and Griggsville Free Press* noted the marriage of Dr. P. Parker to Celia Dunham. Since the ceremony was conducted by Hugh Barker, Esq., a friend of the Hays family, this may be the wedding Lorena wrote about.

7. "Sister C." was Caroline Sophia Hays, born September 13, 1832. In California she married John Jay M'Neely, a mining engineer, who had served in the Mexican War. A native of Pennsylvania, he emigrated to California in 1849. "Cousin M." would have been Myron Augustus Hays (b. 1827), the son of Lorena's paternal uncle, Lester. This branch of the Hays family remained in Pennsylvania. Hayes, *Hayes,* 8-49. Lorena's use of initials when referring to someone is a typical Victorianism.

8. May Day parties, including a May queen and her attendants, played an important role in Pike County schools in the early 1850s. On this occasion mothers brought frosted cakes to school and these were a "luxury no one had more than two or three times a year." McLaughlin, *Through These Hallowed Halls,* 22.

9. Although a Teachers Association met in July 1849 in Pittsfield, the Normal School of May 1850 is considered the first Teachers' Institute to be held in Pike County. Professor S. R. Sweet from New York was in charge, providing

"instruction during the day in the common and higher branches, introducing the modern improvements." Considered "capable of importing scientific instruction," in 1837 he had "instituted such meetings in eastern states." He was considered "a warm and efficient advocate of the cause of popular education." "Lectures and discussions in which all are invited to participate" took place in the evenings and the Institute was open to "all persons now teaching or intending to teach." The local newspapers "earnestly recommend to our teachers in Pike the propriety of dismissing their schools for two weeks to attend." At a citizens meeting May 9, the decision to establish a Teachers' Institute for "the public welfare" received a unanimous vote. However, a July letter signed "Theta" questioned the value of such an Institute because "it is a temporary affair . . . and will not do all that an establishment of more pretensions or a college could do . . . " but concluded "still it will be of much benefit." *Pike County Free Press,* May 2 and 9; July 26.

10. It is interesting to note that early childhood education caused as much concern in the mid-nineteenth century as it does today.

11. Teachers attending the institute also agreed the school day should be no longer than six hours. The use of fourteen and fifteen-year-olds to serve as teachers for five and six-year-old students was also defended because this "monitorial system" would create teachers within the school itself. Lorena neglected to mention that teachers were advised never to "indulge," especially before pupils, in "chewing, smoking and snuffling practices" because "personal habits" should be "worthy of the imitation of his scholars and whereas the use of tobacco in all its forms should be discouraged among children as detrimental to health and personal cleanliness." *Pike County Free Press,* July 26. Lorena's nineteen-year-old cousin, Milo Milton Hays, died April 13, 1850, in Erie County, Pa. Hayes, *Hayes,* 148.

12. "Aunt C." was Caroline Woodward (Mrs. Adam) Lithgow, a sister of Lorena's mother.

13. According to the July 4 *Pike County Free Press,* "This anniversary, which will be remembered while the Republic exists, will be celebrated by the people of our county in a proper manner — We hear of various arrangements made for its commemoration and hope all may have 'a good time.' "

14. In the nineteenth century, a colporteur was a hawker or, more specifically, someone who distributed or sold religious tracts and books door-to-door.

15. Lorena apparently managed to overcome her aversion to immersion, which most Baptist churches accepted as the only scriptural form of baptism. The records of the First Baptist Church of Barry state, "Since August the Church meetings kept up regularly at one of which Sister Lorena Hays was received by experience and Baptism." Book One: Organization, 1829-1860, 106; Mary Ellen Finfrock Morris, "Religion on the American Frontier — Baptists and Methodists," typescript, The Huntington Library, San Marino, California.

16. The second Teachers' Institute convened in Barry September 23-October 5, 1850, with Professor Jonathan Baldwin Turner (1805- 1897) in charge. The local press hailed this meeting with "Success, say we, to all endeavors to raise the standard of education in the west." Fifty-five teachers

attended, with thirty-three from Barry, and two "honorary members." (There were twenty-one men and thirty-four women.) The major topic of discussion concerned the "best modes of teaching and governing schools." Teachers also discussed establishing a special library for their own use through "subscriptions and books," as well as which books to use for classroom instruction. In 1834 Turner was named professor of rhetoric and belles-lettres. A leader in the public school movement, he helped organize the Illinois State Teachers Association in 1836. In January 1853 he petitioned the Illinois State legislature to ask Congress to appropriate land for a state university "for the industrial classes" and this led to the founding of the University of Illinois at Urbana in 1867. Turner also supported the "free school law" of 1855 and helped establish the first Normal School in 1857. He was elected president of the Illinois State National Historical Society in 1858. *Dictionary of American Biography,* vol. 19, 68; *Proceedings of the Second Session of the Pike County Teachers' Institute* (Pittsfield, Ill.: Free Press Print, 1850).

17. Six years later in California these sentiments would be repeated by Lorena in an article published by *The Golden Era.*

18. The Sons of Temperance, organized in 1842 in New York City, served as a fraternal and benevolent organization as well as advocating the cause of abstinence. Its goals were to "reclaim the inebriated, rescue the moderate drinker and save the youth from the power of the drink habit." Membership was open to everyone, regardless of "sex, color, wealth or former condition." Only men could belong prior to 1866, but later women had "every right and privilege accorded to any member and are eligible to every office in the gift of the Order." A voluntary association with no power to enforce its point of view, the Sons of Temperance held impressive ceremonies promoting the principles of "Love, Purity and Fidelity" as well as revival style meetings to eradicate "Demon Rum." Parades, complete with banners and flags, became the standard form of persuasion. In addition, this organization provided financial assistance to its members and their families in times of sickness and death. Gusfield, *Symbolic Crusade,* 44-47; *The Cyclopaedia of Temperance,* 611-12; *Cyclopedia of Temperance, Prohibition and Public Morals* (New York and Cincinnati: Methodist Book Concern, 1917), 351.

19. According to Lithgow family records, Uncle Adam made his first overland trip to California sometime in 1849, but his name was not included in local newspaper accounts of Pike County residents who formed or joined wagon trains. These articles seldom listed the members of such companies, however, so it is impossible to document this story. The name of his nephew is also unknown.

20. Lorena's handwriting in this instance leaves something to be desired because it is difficult to decipher the name: it could have been either Ihm (or Wm.) Dunham or Jhn DeHaven. A family named Dunham lived in Pike County and a William Dunham went to California in 1850. John DeHaven, who is listed in the Pike County census for 1840, died October 11, 1849. He was the husband of Leah Lithgow DeHaven, a sister of Adam Lithgow (Lorena's uncle). An announcement that his estate would be settled appeared in the April 17, 1850, issue of *The Union* with his wife named the "Administrix." Michael Shunk, who lived in Fulton County in 1850, represented

the Perry Methodist Episcopal Church (part of the Griggsville district) at the Illinois Conference meeting in November 1852. Thompson, *History of Pike County*, 159; *Pike County Union*, Nov. 3; Records of Pine Lawn Cemetery, Old Section, Barry, Ill., 1961-62 (courtesy of Norton Walther, Barry General Store).

21. Nathaniel P. Hart, 24, and Louisa A. Blair were married November 21, 1850, with Rev. Jesse Elledge officiating. The ceremony was held in the home of the bridegroom's father, Nathaniel Hart, near Barry. The Nov. 28 *Pike County Free Press* announcement included the follow verse:

"May Hymen's siren dove descend
with love's enchanting power
and all its richest pleasures lend
To cheer their nuptial bower."

22. An advertisement in the *Pike County Union* of June 6, 1850, announced that William McCormick of Perry would "manufacture California gold into jewelry." All orders were to be placed through P(eter) V. Shankland of Pittsfield.

23. Articles about Jenny Lind, "the Swedish Nightingale," and her successful tour of America appeared in the September 26, 1850, issue of the *Pittsfield and Griggsville Free Press* and the September 11 edition of the *Pike County Free Press*.

24. Rev. C. S. Cady served as minister of the Congregational Church in Summer Hill, Pike County, 1853-55. The Illinois special census of 1855 lists a C. S. Cody as a resident of Hanover Township, Cook County. Lorena spelled his name with both the "o" and the "a."

25. Pittsfield, fifteen miles east of Barry, is the county seat for Pike County.

26. Two years later when Mrs. Barker taught school in the community of Perry her class was visited by Jon Shastid, a teacher in Barry who played an important role in the Pike County public school movement of the 1850s and 1860s. He reviewed her school in a newspaper article entitled "A Jaunt of a Pedagogue," giving her "credit for her energy." Shastid found the examinations to be "highly creditable to both scholars and teacher." Barker's curriculum included "dialogues, reading, composition and singing." Shastid added, "The little girls and most of the young ladies knew how to hold their tongues and enunciated clearly." *Pittsfield Free Press*, April 21, 1853.

27. "Uncle Henry" (Lorena's maternal uncle Henry Woodward) had been in California but returned to Pike County; his wife, Sarah, remained in California. William Philander Hays, Lorena's twenty-one-year-old brother, apparently decided to try his luck in Oregon because newspapers that summer printed stories that "gold has been discovered in abundance in the valley of the Klamath. Lumps valued at from $450-500 have been taken out and exhibited." *Pittsfield and Griggsville Free Press*, June 12, 1851.

28. The *Pike County Free Press* of March 20, 1851, announced that "W. M. Brown" would preach at the Christian Church in Pittsfield the following evening "at early candlelight." However, the pastor at the Perry Christian Church that year was Alpheus Brown, who also worked as a carpenter; in 1849 he was listed as a justice of the peace in Brown County. *Pike County History*, (1880) 479; Illinois Census, 1850, 187.

29. Hazen Pressy, 41, and his wife, Susan, 47, who lived in the community of Derry, were natives of New Hampshire, according to the 1850 Illinois census (170B-11 and 12). In 1846 he had been a candidate for coroner and four years later was elected to the county's first board of supervisors. Although Lorena does not mention it, another Teachers' Institute was held May 19, 1851, in Pittsfield, which she did not attend. Her cousin Louisa E. Lithgow and twelve others from Barry were present but the Institute "adjourned at the end of one week instead of the scheduled two for various reasons none of them being sufficient to warrant an adjournment," according to the March 20 and May 29 issues of the *Pittsfield and Griggsville Free Press.*

30. Laura Ann Wike, the wife of George Wike, died June 14, 1851, and was buried in the Park Lawn Cemetery. Consistency in the spelling of certain names and words was not one of Lorena's strong points. Cemetery records; to Jeanne Watson, Oct. 4, 1978 letter from Norton Walther.

31. Although 1851 was not considered to be a "cholera year," as compared with 1849, 1850 and 1852, any illness sweeping through a community caused great concern. The "flux" was a form of dysentery. The June 12, 1851, issue of the *Pittsfield and Griggsville Free Press* reported: "We regret to learn that the cholera is again scourging many towns in the west [in this context "west" refers to the western part of Pike County]. We have some doubt as to its being the cholera, but the Faculty so call it and of course they know best." On July 3 the *Pike County Free Press* announced: "It cannot be denied that the cholera to a limited extent is prevailing in our towns and the surrounding country. . . . We can only recommend vigilant caution. Almost all of our citizens feel more or less symptoms of cholera and they cannot too soon use preventatives . . . but if they allow themselves to become alarmed, the case becomes hopeless. Be cleanly, temperate and keep cool, and there is no danger." Only four fatal cases were subsequently reported in Pike County.

32. William Montgomery Blair, at one time a "New-Light minister,"came to Pike County in 1828 and built the first log cabin in Kinderhook as well as the first mill and first distillery in the area. It was said he made two-thirds of a barrel of whiskey per day by "steam distilling." M. Blair was listed as a dry goods merchant in the 1860 *Pike County Atlas.* There were also two other Blair families in Pike County at this time but little is known about them. The Universalist Church of Barry shared a minister with the one at New Salem, Ill. The congregation was "not numerous or wealthy," but the Barry church building was dedicated in 1854. *Pike County History* (1880),213, 629, 807; Illinois Census, 1850, roll 124, no. 675.

33. The Triplet(t) family belonged to the Barry Baptist Church. Miss Mary Ann Triplet, 22, died September 27, 1851. Park Lawn Cemetery Records, Old Section. According to Thompson's *History of Pike County,* no birth or death records were kept for Illinois until 1870 and none in Pike County until seven years later.

34. Lorena's sister Sarepta suffered from the contagious disease also known as "St. Anthony's fire," which could become epidemic. Symptoms included inflammation of the skin and mucous membranes.

35. Perry and Atlas are both small communities in Pike County.

36. Although novel reading was not approved in the Victoria Era because

such books presented a false view of life and duty, many young ladies ignored this warning and enjoyed them anyway. Watson, "Cult," 38.

37. The other two Hays sisters, Malvina and Sarah, had joined the Baptist Church in April, 1851, "upon a relation of their Christian experience before Baptism, all of which was Baptized the next day," Baptist Church Records, April 10. In February 1852 the Baptist congregation began a six-week meeting with "Brother Estee from Belvidere." It included the regular covenant meeting. "During which time the Lord poured out his spirit upon us in the revival of his work to the edification of the church and accession to the church of the following named Brethern," who included Caroline Hays "by experience and Baptism." A total of forty-eight new members joined. Rev. Stephen A. Estee, 44, lived in Boone County, Ill., in 1850. Barry Baptist Church Records; Census, 1850, for Boone County, Ill. 9B.

38. Lorena and Jon (also spelled John) Shastid, both twenty-five years old, taught in adjoining rooms at the Barry school. Shastid, who came to Pike County in 1836, graduated from Illinois College in Jacksonville. His teaching career spanned twenty-four years at schools in Pittsfield, Griggsville, Perry, Barry, Mt. Sterling and Lewiston. In later years a nephew recalled that at a time when corporal punishment was regarded as "more necessary to schooling than was reading, writing and arithmetic," Shastid "never could administer [it] to a student." In later life called "Professor John," Shastid in 1854 held a contract for tri-weekly mail delivery between Winchester, Beardstown and Quincy; in 1856 when Barry was incorporated he became the city clerk. This "school teacher of remarkable ability" left the profession in 1869 to join his father-in-law as wholesale and retail dry goods merchants and later owned a hotel in Perry. *Pike County History,* (1880) 597; *Pike County Atlas,* (1872) 16, 34; Thomas Hall Shastid, *My Second Life* (Ann Arbor, Mich.: University of Michigan, 1944), 642.

39. Rev. William Carter served as the first minister of the Pittsfield Congregational Church. An 1828 graduate of Yale College and Theological Seminary, as it was then known, he helped fellow students found Illinois College at Jacksonville. He also served congregations at Summer Hill and Rockport, both in Pike County, and served on the board of directors for the Chicago Theological Seminary. Carter died in 1871 at Pittsfield. Rev. A. H. Fletcher was also a Congregational minister at the Summer Hill church 1850-53. *Pike County History,* (1880), 668, 673, 783. Four Methodist ministers named Rutledge served in western Illinois during the 1840s and 50s, according to church records. Lorena probably heard Rev. George Rutledge, the eldest of three brothers (the other two were Edward and William J.). Born in Virginia, he was transferred from Baltimore to the Sagamon, Ill., circuit in 1835. Rev. George Rutledge moved to the Griggsville district in 1852 and then served in Jacksonville between 1853 and 1856. A special friend and advocate of the Illinois Female College in that community, he died in 1871 and was buried in Jacksonville. Rev. Edward Rutledge came to Fulton County in 1834, receiving his license to preach in 1850 and ordained a deacon in 1852 and as elder two years later. He served in the Civil War as did the youngest brother (William J.). Rev. James Rutledge, apparently not related to the others, served in Peoria in 1858. Methodist Records, Drew University; 1871

Annual Meeting Minutes, Methodist Conference, Illinois (Carrollton, Ill.: Carrollton Gazette, 1871), 47; *Journal and Records of Sixty-second Session, Illinois Annual Conference* (Jacksonville, Ill.: Illinois Courier, 1885), 107, 110; 1850 Pike County Census.

40. Harriet Bulkley, a native of New York, died April 17, 1852, at the age of twenty-nine. Park Lawn Cemetery Records.

41. By 1852 enthusiasm for the Teachers' Institutes had begun to wane and no report was printed in the county newspapers about the session that opened April 26 in Perry. Tuition cost "not more than 50 cents — perhaps nothing" while expenses of boarding would be $1.50 a week for gentlemen but for "ladies it would be without charge." Lorena did not attend this institute. A month later the Barry schools were described as "in a very flourishing condition," by "A Traveller" in a letter to the *Pike County Free Press.* "Both teachers and scholars seem to take a great interest in the advancement of the schools," this letter concluded. June 2, 1852.

42. Mary Camp Hays died March 17, 1852. Born in 1773 to Rev. Samuel and Hannah Guernsey Camp of Ridgebury, Conn., she was seventy-nine years old. Hayes, *Hayes,* 70.

43. The author was Rev. Charles Augustus Goodrich, (1790-1862) a Congregational clergyman from Hartford, Conn. His 414-page book told the history of the United States from the "first discovery" until March 4, 1825. It was printed that year by Russell Robbins of New York, and continually updated for a total of 150 editions. A Yale graduate of 1812, Goodrich served as state senator in 1838. His chief occupation was writing children's books and informational works. *Dictionary of American Biography,* vol. 7, 397.

44. "Mr. S." would probably be fellow teacher John Shastid while "Mr. B." might well have been E. P. Bunce, a thirty-seven-year-old school teacher who boarded at Mrs. DeHaven's house. He served as both singing master and deputy sheriff at the September 1850 Teachers' Institute held in Barry. J. Ballard served as minister of the Congregational Church of Griggsville. *Pike County History* (1880), 521.

45. Lorena was reading *Lectures on the Scientific Evidences of Natural and Revealed Religion,* published in 1850 by William Clark Larrabee (1802-1859). A Methodist Episcopal clergyman, he was licensed to preach in 1821 and seven years later was graduated from Bowdoin College. Larrabee taught school at the institution which later became Wesleyan University in Connecticut and also at the forerunner of DePauw University in Indiana. In 1852 he became the editor of the *Ladies Repository.* Larrabee, twice elected superintendent of the Indiana public schools, has been credited with founding the public school system in that state. *Dictionary of American Biography,* vol. 11, 7.

46. Slavery was a hotly debated issue in Pike County during the 1820s. The anti-slavery party won in the 1824 election, 261 votes to 23. Thompson, *Pike County History,* 10, 11, 20, 27. A notice appeared in the December 1, 1852, edition of the *Pike County Union* announcing that the publication of *Uncle's Tom's Cabin* "has an unprecedented run. Some 200,000 copies have been published in the country while the number issued in England is over 400,000." The editor added that it had already been translated and published in German.

47. Orville Hickman Browning, a Whig candidate for the United States

Senate, spent the week of September 6, 1852, campaigning in Pike County and spoke at meetings in seven communities. Browning supported the candidacy of Gen. Winfield Scott for the presidency during his two-and-a-half hour speech in Barry. Browning's interest in Pike County dated to 1837 when he bought half interest in the Philips Ferry and 200 adjacent acres of land. He laid out a town called Velasco with 200 lots on the Pike County side of the Illinois River and served as its proprietor. Thompson, *Pike County History,* 347.

48. This magazine was published for "Universalist Sunday schools and families" in New York between 1851 and 1854.

49. Leah Lithgow (Mrs. John) DeHaven, a widow in 1852, had been visiting in Erie, Pa. The DeHaven family apparently emigrated to Illinois about the same time as their neighbors and relatives, the Hays and Lithgow families.

50. A seventeenth century Protestant theologian, August Hermann Francke taught at the University of Halle for thirty-six years.

"Grace Greenwood" was the pen named used by Sarah Jane Clarke Lippincott (1823-1904). The youngest daughter of a "physician of some prominence," she grew up near Rochester, N. Y. Her family moved to the Pittsburgh area in 1842. She wrote both prose and poetry and in 1850 published *Greenwood Leaves: A Collection of Sketches and Letters,* the first of six books. In 1853 she married Leander K. Lippincott of Philadelphia. Over the next several years she helped edit the *Young Pilgrim,* a juvenile monthly, and contributed to *Health and Home, Atlantic Monthly, Harper's New Monthly Magazine* and both the *New York Times* and the *Tribune,* becoming one of the first American women to be a regular newspaper correspondent. During the Civil War, she visited army camps to talk and read to the soldiers. President Abraham Lincoln called Greenwood the "patriot propagandist for the advancement of women." *Greenwood Leaves* was the most popular of her books; in 1849 several of her letters were printed as "A Sketch from Life" in the *Pike County Union. Dictionary of American Biography,* vol. 11, 288-89.

51. The *Pike County Union* was originally called *The Union.* Printed in Pittsfield by M. H. Abbott, it was "devoted to politics, literature and general intelligence." Unfortunately, the files of this newspaper at both the Library of Congress and the Illinois State Historical Library, Springfield, do not include the issues that contained Lorena's first articles and no other record of them seems to exist.

52. Pike County newspapers devoted considerable space to events of national importance in the 1850s. For example, the death of Daniel Webster on October 24, 1852, was reported under the headline "National Calamity" in black-bordered columns. When Henry Clay died in June 1852 black borders were used throughout the paper, even for the advertisements.

53. Almost all the books Lorena read can be identified, including the popular novel *The Sunny Side, or The Country Minister's Wife.* Published anonymously in 1851, the author was Elizabeth Stuart Phelps (1815-52). It had an estimated readership of nearly 500,000 and received international recognition. Detailing the domestic trials and triumphs of a married woman, this book provided what was then considered a realistic and sympathetic view of daily life. In addition, this author wrote children's books as well as

newspaper and magazine articles. (Her daughter, who also became a popular author, wrote first under her mother's name and then as Elizabeth Stuart Phelps Ward.) On March 2, 1853, the *Pike County Union* printed "Why One Husband Went to California by the author of *Sunnyside*" on page 1. *Dictionary of American Biography*, vol. 19, 417-19; Langdon Lynne Faust, *American Women Writers* (New York: Frederick Unger Co., 1977, Vol. 2) 146-47.

54. Cousin Orlando Hart married Lorena's cousin, Mary Janet West, who died in 1849. Born in 1829 in Massachusetts to Nathaniel and Clarissa Hill Hart, he was one of eight children; the family came to Barry in 1838. A member of the Independent Order of Odd Fellows, Orlando died in 1879. Information about him in various histories of Pike County does not mention that he had been to California in the early 1850s. *Pike County History* (1880), 815, 819.

55. Clara, a sister of Orlando Hart, married Samuel Davis, a local merchant, October 14, 1851.

56. A "donation party" provided supplementary supplies and funds for ministers to augment their low salaries. The congregation contributed food stuffs and sometimes money. These social occasions often included a potluck supper. Seldom a surprise party, these events were frequently publicized in advance by the press. Contributions brought to a donation party could last a minister and his family many months. James Woods, *Recollections of Pioneer Work in California* (San Francisco: Joseph Winterburn & Co., 1848), 46-48; *Amador* [Calif.] *County Ledger*, 1858. Elder Wallace was probably Hardin Wallace, a member of the Illinois Conference of the Methodist Episcopal Church for the Griggsville District. *Pike County Union*, Nov. 3, 1852.

57. Among those bidding Lorena farewell was twenty-two-year-old Catherine Foot, who lived in the Barry household of the B. D. Brown family. Mary Shields' husband, David, was a Barry merchant as was the husband of Harriet Crandall Angle, Lewis C. Angle. In 1849 Shields and Angle were partners "at the sign of the Red Flag." (Later, Angle was in partnership with B. D. Brown). He stayed in Barry and by the 1870s had become a prosperous partner in the woolen mills. Described as a prominent and energetic businessman, Angle also had interests in dry goods, groceries, pork packing and the lumber trade as well as the Barry Exchange Bank. Both couples were in their twenties in 1853. A schoolteacher friend, Mary Hull, had attended the 1850 Teachers' Institute with Lorena; her parents were Daniel D. and Lydia Hull.

Mrs. Leah DeHaven opened her new Barry Hotel in partnership with D. D. Gray in January 1853. "The proprietors flatter themselves that by strict attention to business and by constant effort to render their guests comfortable and by moderate bills they may receive a liberal share of the public patronage."

Lewis Harvey ran the rival Buckeye Hotel and announced in the *Pittsfield Free Press* that he would "strive to render his house a home" to all visitors. Both hotels provided accommodations for horses; the proprietors of the Barry Hotel also offered to convey passengers to "different points with speed and reasonable rates." Pike County, Ill. Census, 1840, 1850; *History of Pike County* (1880), 802; *Pike County Free Press*, May 30, 1850; *Pittsfield Free Press*, Feb. 3, l0, 1853.

An announcement that the estate of a Robert W. Liles would be settled appeared in the March 2 *Pike County Union* but nothing was mentioned about the fact that he might have been a California emigrant. Lorena's concerns about death on the California Trail were not without reason. In 1850 and 1852 cholera claimed the lives of many overland emigrants. As many as forty percent of those on the trail in 1852 died of the dread disease. Lorena might also have been remembering the fate of former Illinois residents: in 1846 members of the Donner-Reed Party, which left from Springfield, Ill., were trapped by winter snows in the Sierra Nevada mountains. Of the eighty-seven pioneers in this company only forty survived. George Stewart, *The California Trail* (New York: McGraw Hill, l962), 182.

THE TRIP TO CALIFORNIA/INTRODUCTION

1. Harriet Sherrill Ward, *Prairie Schooner Lady, A Journal . . . of 1853,* ed. Ward G. and Florence Stark DeWitt (Los Angeles: Westernlore Press, 1959), 76.

2. William Taylor, "Reminiscences," microfilm, 281. For a detailed account of hardships encountered on the overland trail in 1852 see Herbert Eaton, *The Overland Trail* (New York: G.P. Putnam's Sons, 1974).

3. Browning, *Diary,* 95-96.

4. The records of boiler inspections for ships included the names of crew members. Records of the Bureau of Marine Inspection and Navigation, St. Louis, Missouri, July 29, 1850, National Archives, Record Group 41, BMIN, enrollment No. 93. Thomas Flint, "Diary," Historical Society of Southern California *Annual Publications* 12, 1923: 72-74; St. Louis *Daily Morning Herald,* April 7, 1853.

5. St. Louis *Missouri Daily Republican,* March 12 and 14. Unless otherwise indicated, all newspapers cited were published in 1853.

6. "A Citizen," *A Brief Sketch of St. Louis* (St. Louis: Ustick, Studley & Co., 1853), 4, 11; Calvin Graham, "Journal: Pennsylvania to California," typescript, 2.

7. Celinda Hines, Diary, Oregon Pioneers Association *Transactions* 46 (June 1918): 73; Basil Longworth, Diary, typescript, 5, 6.

8. James B. Cooper, Bird Notes and Diary, manuscript, 197.

9. Longworth, Diary, 5, 6.

10. Louise Barry, *The Beginning of the West, Annals of Kansas, Gateway to the American West, 1840-1854* (Topeka: Kansas State Historical Society, 1972): 1102, 1109, 1110, 1116, 1125, 1127, 1128, 1133, 1148.

11. Ibid.; *Republican,* March 12, 14.

12. Ibid.

13. Graham, Journal, 3; Longworth, Diary, 5.

14. Barry, *Beginning of the West,* 143; Hines, Diary, 82.

15. Hines, Diary, 78-82; Pheobe Judson, *A Pioneer's Search for an Ideal Home* (Bellingham, Wash.: 1925), 14.

16. William Keuenhof, *History of Kansas City Diocese in Historic Missouri* (Kansas City: American Federation of Catholic Societies, 1917), 8; Barry, *Beginning of the West,* 1180.

17. Hines, Diary, 82; Barry, *Beginning of the West,* 566-67.

18. Thompson, *Pike County History,* 805.

19. Lorena referred to John Charles Fremont's *Report of the Exploring Expedition to the Rocky Mountains in 1842 and to Oregon and Northern California in the Years 1843-44* (Washington D. C.: Gales and Seaton, 1845). However, she might also have been reading the popular, shorter version of the *Fremont Report,* printed the following year by D. Appleton & Co. of New York. Without the maps and scientific tables, this edition contained only 186 pages as compared with 693 in the "official copy." See "Books that Won the West, Guidebooks of the Forty-Niners and Fifty-Niners" by Ray Allen Billington, *American West* 4 (August, 1967): 25-32.

20. Eckland Family Papers.

21. Wells Wallis West, "Autobiography," photocopy of manuscript.

22. Ibid. and Hayes, *Hayes,* 72-73.

23. Elizabeth Goltra, Journal, typescript, 3.

24. Ibid.

25. Cornelia Ferris, *The Mormons at Home with Some Incidents of Travel from Missouri to California* (New York: Dix and Edwards, 1856).

26. See Lucy Cook's letters for March-June, 1853 in *Covered Wagon Women: Diaries and Letters from the Western Trails,* Vol. 4 (Glendale, Calif.: Arthur H. Clark Co., 1985): 282-95.

27. Copies of the typescript of Dr. Joseph R. Bradway's diary can be found at both the Wisconsin State Historical Society and the California State Library, but his manuscript letters are part of the Rollins Collection at Princeton University. Bradway's letters were intended for publication by the Delavan, Wisconsin, newspaper and so provide more details than do the entries in his diary.

28. With James Linforth, Frederick H. Piercy compiled *The Route from Liverpool to the Great Salt Lake Valley* (reprint, Cambridge, Mass.: Harvard University-Belknap Press, 1962).

29. Restricted use of the Hall pencil sketches stated in March 27, 1979, letter from the Wyoming State Archives and Historical Department to Jeanne H. Watson (a 1985 request for clarification remains unanswered). However, these sketches have been printed in 1968 and 1970 issues of the *Annals of Wyoming* as well as in Robert L. Munkres, *Saleratus and Sagebrush, The Oregon Trail Through Wyoming* (Cheyenne: Wyoming State Archives, 1974).

30. *New York Times,* November 4, reprint from the *Missouri Daily Republican.*

31. Maria Parsons Belshaw, Diary, Part I, in George P. Hammond, *New Spain and the Anglo-American West,* Vol. 2 (privately printed, 1932): 220; William Gilbert, Diary, typescript: See "Notes taken in 1919 from author by Ethel B. Virtue" at beginning.

32. Henry Allyn, "Journal of 1853," Oregon Pioneer Association *Transactions,* 49th Annual Reunion (1924): 389-90; Hannah Cornaby, *Autobiography and Poems* (Salt Lake City: J. C. Graham & Co., 1881), 34.

33. *New York Times,* May 11, reprint of story from the *Alton* [Ill.] *Telegraph.*

34. John D. Unruh, Jr., *The Plains Across — The Overland Emigrants and the Trans-Mississippi West, 1840-60* (Urbana: University of Illinois Press, 1979), 119-20; *New York Times,* July 28, August 1.

35. *New York Times,* July 9, reprint dated May 31 from St. Louis. Both the Ward and Williams parties began their overland trips from Arkansas. Ward, who left Arkansas the end of March, traveled with four wagons and provisions that included "one three gallon cask of best proof brandy for medicinal purposes." Joining a train of eighteen wagons, Ward followed the old Santa Fe Trail along the Arkansas River to Bent's Fort and continued northwest to Denver before crossing the Rocky Mountains. Upon reaching the Green River, the Ward company "struck the main traveled road — and what a change! We now found ourselvs on a broad highway from twenty to 500 feet in width — a main thoroughfare." Ward added that only four additional parties planned to attempt this route in 1853. Joseph Williams with his wife and their five children would have been in one of these companies because they

followed almost the same route from Batesville, Ark. After joining a larger wagon train, they traveled with twelve prairie schooners as well as freight wagons and drove both sheep and cattle. This group joined the Overland Trail eighty-five miles west of "old Fort Laramie." D. S. Stanley, with the US Second Company of Dragoons, left Fort Smith, Ark., on July 24 to join the railroad survey team of Lt. A. W. Whipple for the trip to San Diego, arriving in March 1854. Dillis B. Ward, *Across the Plains in 1853* (reprint, Seattle: The Shorey Book Store, 1965), 1-30; Joseph Williams, Diary, and "Reminiscences of a Covered Wagon" by Sarah Williams Spooner, typescript, 1-11; D. S. Stanely, Diary, typescript.

36. Unruh, *The Plains Across,* 119-20.

37. The anonymous writer never recorded the total number in the Forsgren Company but did note eighteen deaths and six births between the time they left Denmark and April 21 when the first group of 135 emigrants made the trip from St. Louis to Iowa (three members left the company before it reached Keokuk). This company arrived at St. Louis in late March "to go into the town to a place which has been prepared for us." Perhaps William Gibson, president of the St. Louis Conference of the Church of Jesus Christ of Latter-Day Saints, took in some of them. His diary, dated "Winter, 1852" followed by the date of April 29, 1853, records, "The first company of Saints from Denmark stopped at my house and in an adjoining empty room while they staid in St. Louis & I went with them & helped them to make their purchases as one or two of them could speak in broken English so that I could understand them." Forsgren Company, Diary, photocopy of manuscript, 17, 25.

Gibson also traveled to Salt Lake City in 1853, leaving Keokuk shortly ahead of the Forsgren Company, which joined with a party of English Mormons for the journey. The size of this joint company can be determined from the July 10 entry when it was reorganized: "In as much as there was nearly 100 men, he [Forsgren] had decided to have 1 captain over 100, 2 captain over 10 each in 3 wagons — in the first company of 50. And in the second company of 50 — 3 captains over each in 4 wagons, and 1 captain over 10 each in 3 wagons." William Gibson, Journal, photocopy of manuscript, 110.

38. To help in determining how many emigrants followed the overland trails in 1853 see stories from the following newspapers: *Missouri Daily Republican,* May 20, 31; June 6, 28; July 4; August 1, 15; *Weekly Missouri Statesman* (Columbia, Mo.) June 4; *St. Joseph Gazette,* July 5. These stories were reprinted by the *New York Times* on June 9, 21, 22, 23 and 24; July 27; Aug. 3, 23; Nov. 4. Several were also reprinted in the *New York Tribune* on June 3 and 17 as well as in August. The figures for Oregon appeared in the *New York Tribune* of Dec. 13. Among the 1853 emigrants who copied records available at Forts Kearny and Laramie were J. Soule Bowman, Celinda Hines, Michael Luark and Agnes Stewart.

However, records of the westward emigration, kept at Fort Kearny and at Fort Laramie by the military had disappeared by 1853, leaving only figures reported in newspaper stories and copied into emigrant diaries. Such statistics had been available for 1852 but on June 14, 1853, at Fort Laramie Andrew McClure reported, "We found the register destroyed and all commenced on a new scale." No estimates of the 1853 emigration were included in the official reports from Fort Kearny and Fort Laramie that year. Few attempts were ever made to record the number of emigrants who traveled along the north bank of the Platte River. Returns from U.S. Military Posts, 1800-1916, National Archives Microfilm Publication, copy 617, roll 595. Barry, *Beginning of the West,* 1158-59. Andrew McClure, Diary, typescript, 25.

A letter from a "friend at Fort Kearney" in the June 30 edition of the *New York Times* reported that, according to "Capt. Wharton," the emigration as of May 31 totaled: 4,937 men; 1,900 women; 2,630 children; 4,360 horses; 1,637 mules; 81,660 cattle; 2,984 wagons, and 11,000 sheep.

39. *New York Times,* August 23, Letter from "The Plains." The *New York Times* of July 1, reported the escape of a black from the Pawnees. Harriet Gill, *Diary,* ed. Eva Turner Clark (New York: Downs Printing Co., 1922), 34. The names of three other black emigrants of 1853 were also recorded later. Mrs. Susan Wilson made the trip with five children from Wayne County, Mo., to Texas and then to Mariposa, Calif., in a train of a hundred wagons. Traveling to Oregon as a child "with some white people," Mrs. Cloye Burnett Logan-Flood ran away at the age of eleven to California. Henry Mills came from Baltimore to Calaveras County, Calif., where he owned several mines. At one time he also owned 500 acres about fourteen miles from Stockton before moving to San Francisco, where "he contracted to do the grading of the city, employing a great number of teams." Delilah L. Beasley, *The Negro Trail Blazers of California* (reprint, New York: Negro Universities Press, 1969), 122-24.

40. The letter from Kit Carson was reprinted by the *Missouri Daily Republican;* Barry, *Beginning of the West,* 1150.

41. On June 8 the Stevens party left St. Paul, Minn., to explore a northern route along the forty-seventh parallel to the Washington Territory. Twelve days later Capt. John W. Gunnison's company departed from Camp Shawnee Reservation, about five miles west of the Missouri border, without any intuition that death awaited them. Gunnison and his companions, instructed to explore between the thirty-eighth and the thirty-ninth parallels, were surprised by the "Pah Utah" Indians at Sevier Lake. The Indians also captured most of the expedition's papers and intruments. The rest of the Gunnison party, under the leadership of Lt. Edward G. Beckwith (who had been assigned the territory between Salt Lake City and the Humboldt Valley), returned to Salt Lake City for the winter. Nearly as well known was the expedition conducted by Lt. A. W. Whipple to explore a southern route along the thirty-fifth parallel via Fort Smith, Ark., to San Diego, Calif. The other three 1853 government-sponsored railroad surveys have been almost forgotten but all concerned a southern route with Lt. R. S. Williamson leading one company from Santa Fe, N. Mex., to California's San Joaquin Valley (which included exploring Walker's Pass). The Williamson party was later taken over by Lt. J. G. Parke, who continued to explore along the thirty-second parallel as did the expedition led by Captain John W. Pope. The best remembered artists with these exploring expeditions were John M. Stanley of the Stevens party; Heinrich Balduin Mollhausen, "topographer and draughtsman" for the Whipple survey, and Richard H. Kern, one of the Gunnison company killed by Indians. Barry, *Beginning of the West,* 1155, 1161, 1167-69, 1172, 1176,

1188; Allen Nevins, *Fremont, The West's Greatest Adventurer,* Vol. 1, 2 (New York and London: Harper & Brothers, 1928), 461; Robert Taft, *Artists and Illustrators of the Old West, 1850-1900* (New York: Bonanza Books, 1953), 1-35; 254-63.

42. Spencer F. Baird, *Appendix of Journal of Proceedings of the Board of Regents* (ninth annual report), House Misc. Documents No. 37, series 807, 33rd Congress, Second Session, 85-86. A journal about Edward F. Beale's 1853 trip was written by his cousin Gwinn Harris Heap as the *Central Route to the Pacific from the Valley of the Mississippi to California* (Philadelphia: Lippincott, Grambo & Co., London: Truker & Co., 1854). Beale had been appointed to his new post by President Millard Fillmore in November 1852; on March 3, 1853, Congress voted him an appropriation of $250,000. The 1853 expedition, which ended disastrously, was Fremont's fifth and final one. The story of this attempt to find an all-weather pass for the trans-continental railroad was told by S. N. Carvalho, who served as the expedition's "artist and daguerreotypist": *Incidents of Travel and Adventure in the Far West with Col. Fremont's Last Expedition* (New York: Derby and Jackson, 1857); Nevins, *Fremont,* 463-72.

43. This identification was provided by an October 16 letter printed in the November 7 issue of the *Missouri Daily Republican;* the writer signed it "Snooks." The title "Prince of Nassau" does not mean this individual was related to the House of Orange-Nassau (the Dutch royal family) but refers instead to Wiesbaden, Germany, which in 1744 became the seat of government for the principality of Nassau-Usingen, annexed by Prussia in 1866. However, the Dutch royal House of Orange descended from this principality. An intriguing possibility is that an offspring of this "Prince of Nassau" might still live in the Midwest. Prince Paul of Wuerttemberg, a naturalist and traveler, visited the Missouri River country in 1823 and 1830. In 1851 he undertook a scientific expedition as far as Fort Laramie. According to this letter, "Snooks" thought the prince died in 1852 in Paris at his hotel near the Place Vendome. *Missouri Daily Republican,* Nov. 7; Barry, *Beginning of the West,* 95, 99, 101-03, 110-13, 129, 154, 167-68, 199, 1034, 1036-37, 1049-50; March 4, 1980, letter from Th. J. M. van den Muysenberg, Consul for Press and Cultural Affairs, Consulate General of the Netherlands, New York City, to Jeanne H. Watson; Lillian Langseth-Christensen, "Wiesbaden's Nassauer Hoff," *Gourmet* (November 1983): 24-25; *Harper's Book of Facts* ed. Charlton T. Lewis (New York and London: Harpers & Brothers, 1905).

Count Cipriani, who served as Sardenia's consul for California in 1852, left Wesport on June 3 with twenty-four men, eleven covered wagons and an "all-purpose ominibus" along with 500 head of cattle, 600 oxen, 6 horses, 40 mules and 20,000 pounds of cargo. Leonetto Cipriani, *California and Overland Diaries . . . ,* trans. and ed. Ernest Falbo (Portland: The Champoeg Press, 1962), 72.

44. Joseph B. Chiles has been remembered as a "trail-blazing pioneer." Chiles & Co. consisted of twenty members with Joel Franklin Chiles in charge and included five wagons and twenty animals [horses and mules]. Whether the two Chiles brothers met on the overland trail is unknown as is the date of Joel's return to Missouri, although Joseph married his second wife at Joel's home on Christmas day, 1853. It is known that Joel, who died three years

later, acted as his brother's livestock commission merchant in 1852. Joseph Ballinger Chiles, *Trail-Blazing Pioneer,* ed. Helen Griffen (San Francisco: John Howell Books, 1969), 83-87; Unruh, *The Plains Across,* 351-53; Barry, *Beginnings of the West,* 299, 429, 458, 484, 722, 747, 1147, 1151-52, 1210.

45. Hudspeth's company of thirty men with eight wagons, thirty animals and 700 head of cattle also left from Independence, Mo. Hudspeth's Cutoff in southern Idaho started six miles west of Soda Springs and ended due west at the Raft River. It was also known as Myers Cutoff because J. J. Myers accompanied Benoni Hudspeth of Jackson County, Mo., in trail breaking this shortcut by driving wagons through uncharted territory in 1849. The Hudspeth's or Myers' Cutoff diverted California bound traffic from Fort Hall. Barry, *Beginning of the West,* 1147, 1151-52; Irene Paden, *The Wake of the Prairie Schooner* (New York: Macmillan Co., 1943), 277, 307-10.

46. Barry, *Beginning of the West,* 1112-14, 1135, 1166-70, 1174-75, 1182, 1186; Kit Carson, *Autobiography,* ed. Milo Milton Quaife (Chicago: R. R. Donnelley & Sons Co., 1935), 147; William Rowe, "Ho for California, Personal Reminiscences," *Waterford* [Wisc.] *Post,* part 3. "Major Fitzpatrick, agent for the Sioux," according to a letter in the *Missouri Daily Republican* (October 7), "deserves much credit for the able manner in which he conducted the last and we hope final step with this discontented tribe" when the treaty was finally signed in the fall and the Indians "received their presents."

47. D. A. Shaw, *El Dorado or California as Seen by a Pioneer* (Los Angeles: R. R. Baumgardt and Co., 1900), 75-76. If accurate, the reminiscences of Shaw and Rowe are unusual because no one else seems to have noted the "fancy looking covered carriage" or the lady-in-question: Josefa Jaramillo Carson, daughter of one of the most prominent Spanish-Catholic families in the southwest and Carson's wife of ten years. Even her husband overlooked her possible presence, although he named three other 1853 traveling companions when he prepared his autobiography three years later with the help of a collaborator. Apparently a man of few words, Carson condensed months of activity into brief paragraphs, omitting information about his private life because the book was designed to capitalize upon his career as a western hero. So it is most intriguing to speculate upon Josefa's whereabouts during the spring, summer and fall of 1853, since her first child was born October 1 the preceeding year. Carson, *Autobiography,* introduction by Milo Milton Quaife, xxii-iii; M. Morgan Estergreen, *Kit Carson, A Portrait in Courage* (Norman: University of Oklahoma Press, 1962), 207-09.

Did Josefa, who was then twenty-five years old, tire of being left behind by her husband during his many exploring expeditions and so decide to join him in 1853? And did they leave six-month old William (the first of seven children) with relatives in Taos or take him to show off to Carson relatives in California? It seems unlikely that Shaw would not have remembered the presence of a baby in the mountain camp, but Josefa's invisibility might be more explainable. Since Carson was driving sheep, other wagons may not have traveled with his party so Josefa could stay out-of-sight in the covered carriage and not be noticed by someone like Rowe who only wanted to shake hands with a hero.

It is known that when Carson reached California he visited at least two brothers, possibly a third, as well as a nephew, and also his daughter by his first marriage, Adaline (Mrs. Louey) Simmonds or Simmons, who was born in 1837. A year before Carson married Josefa, he took this five-year-old daughter to relatives in Missouri. She attended the Howard-Payne Female Seminary until 1851 when Carson brought her back to live in New Mexico. At fourteen, Adaline was the same age Josefa had been when she and Carson first met. Sometime in 1852 Adaline married and moved to California but during the months in New Mexico a close friendship could easily have developed between the teenager and Josefa, who was still childless at that time. While such suppositions cannot be documented, those two 1853 reminiscences of Rowe and Shaw are suggestive, especially if consideration is given to the combination of a strict Spanish-Catholic upbringing with the Victorian view of retiring womanhood. Estergreen, *Kit Carson,* 76, 79, 86, 90, 100, 104, 124, 179, 181, 205-09, 273.

48. See Cornelia Woodcock Ferris, *Life Among the Mormons* and her husband, Benjamin G. Ferris, *Utah and the Mormons* [1856] (reprint, New York: Ams Press, 1971), 338-39.

49. Almost no information is available about Studebaker's overland trip in 1853. Brief accounts presented by various books about the family and their automobile company differ considerably and are not considered to be particularly accurate by the staff of the Discovery Hall Museum in South Bend, Ind., where the Studebaker Archives are now located. For example, both August 13 and August 31 have been given as the date for his arrival in California. The route he took across the Sierra Nevada is also subject to debate, depending upon which source is consulted but supposedly he followed the Carson Route. When Studebaker returned to Placerville in 1912, the celebration at the Ohio House focused upon his life there, rather than his trip fifty-nine years earlier. Studebaker built a wagon, with "extra-large wheels" in ten days for an emigrant train that originated in South Bend with the understanding he would drive it in return for three meals a day. On March 23 sixteen wagons left South Bend and joined twenty-two others from Chicago for a company of 210 men, women, and children. One story claims Studebaker became involved in gambling when he reached Council Bluffs and lost everything except fifty cents at three-card monte. *Who Was Who in America* (1942), 1202; "Reunion of J. M. Studebaker and A. T. Gage of Oakland," *San Jose Pioneer* (May 1898): 65; Edwin Corle, *John Studebaker, An American Dream* (New York: E. P. Dutton and Co., 1948); Stephen Longstreet, *A Century of Wheels, the Story of Studebaker* (New York: Henry Holt & Co., 1952); The Centennial Book Committee, *Alpine Heritage* (South Lake Tahoe: Anchor Printing, n.d.), 46; Wells Drury, *To Old Hangtown or Bust* (Placerville: privately printed, 1912); Diane Davis, "Portrait for a Western Album," *American West* 14 (July/August 1979): 33; letter of October 17, 1979, from Richard Welch, then director of Discovery Hall Museum, South Bend, Ind., to Jeanne Watson.

50. Unruh, *The Plains Across,* 185; *New York Times,* June 30.

51. Esther B. Lymon, Journal, typescript, 2. Every emigrant who kept a diary or later wrote about the overland trip in 1853 described these storms. On May 31 Bradway reported at sundown there were showers and a "perfect gale" of hail, thunder and lightning that "annihilated all our fire." Dr. J. R.

Bradway, Letter, manuscript, dated May 24 but mailed later at Fort Laramie.

52. John Smith, Journal, manuscript, April 23 and 24.

53. Horace Seaver, "Gold Rush Letters," manuscript: August 12 letter from Sacramento City to his father in Darien, Wisc. Seaver was one of three brothers and two brothers-in-law who made the 1853 overland trip together to California.

54. *New York Times,* May 24, June 9, (reprint of May 31 story from St. Louis).

55. H. Gill, Diary, 34; *New York Times,* June 30, July 1.

56. *New York Times,* ibid., and reprint from *Alton* [Illinois] *Telegraph,* May 11.

57. Unruh, *The Plains Across,* 394; Amelia Stewart Knight, "Diary," Oregon Pioneer Association *Transactions,* 56th Annual Reunion (1933), May 31.

58. *New York Times,* Aug. 23.

59. *New York Times,* Aug. 23, and Nov. 4 reprint of Aug. 15 story from St. Louis. Although driving a large herd of sheep in 1853, Dr. Thomas Flint and his cousin Llewellyn Bixby (of Flint, Bixby and Co.) later made a practice of purchasing stock along the Carson Emigrant Road in California to become extensive stock raisers. Once, when miners near Volcano claimed escaped livestock were "strays" Flint was advised by his laywer to avoid the costs of a suit by taking them by force. J. D. Mason, *History of Amador County* (Oakland: Thompson and West, 1881), 206; Sarah Bixby-Smith, *Adobe Days* (Cedar Rapids, Iowa; The Torch Press, 1925).

60. *New York Times,* Feb. 11; Cipriani, *California and Overland Diaries,* 71-72.

61. Flint, "Diary," 72; Robert Eccleston, Diaries, Vol. 7, 8 and 9, manuscripts, Vol. 7, May 17, 25; Col. William W. Hollister, 1878 Statement, manuscript, 3; Estergreen, *Kit Carson,* 209; Carson, *Autobiography,* 147.

62. *New York Times,* Jan. 29.

63. George Himes, "An Account of Crossing the Plains," *The Morning Oregonian,* June 23, 1907; also quoted by Harvey W. Scott, *History of the Oregon Country,* Vol. 3 (Cambridge, Mass.: The Riverside Press, 1924), 257-58; Mrs. M. A. Looney, *A Trip Across the Plains in 1853* (Albany, Oregon: privately printed), 2. The Himes and Looney families were among the first emigrants to cross the Cascade mountains of Oregon via the Natches Pass in 1853; also in the same large company was Van Ogle, who wrote his reminiscences as well.

64. The cause of "Asiatic cholera" was considered "absoltuely inscrutable" in the 1850s although some hint that contaminated water supplies could be at fault had begun to be discussed. Recommendations that using cistern and rain water exclusively would keep people free of cholera appeared in the newspapers. Cholera usually spread through polluted drinking water and burning, cleansing, praying, and quarantining had no apparent effect. According to one story, symptoms included a thickening of the blood which impaired circulation to the lungs, thus resulting in death due to a "want of oxygen." Doses of calomel (mercurous chloride) with castor oil might help overcome cholera if taken immediately upon the onset of the symptoms, according to some 1850s medical opinions. *Christian Advocate and Journal,* July 6, July 20, 1854; Hollister, Statement, 6; Patrick E. McLear, "The St. Louis Cholera

Epidemic of 1849," *Missouri Historical Review,* 63 (January 1969): 171-79.

65. Very few emigrants wrote about the problems of personal hygiene. Either everyone knew how to take care of these matters or else did not consider it appropriate to record this kind of information for posterity. Charlotte Pengra's comments concerned setting up tents in an area that resembled a "barnyard at home." She added, ". . . I should as soon think of setting a table there as in such a place. The stench is sometimes almost unendurable, it arises from a ravine that is resorted to for special purposes by all the Emigration, but such things we must put up with." Harriet Ward might have been thinking of just such a place when she noted, "Our camping ground nice and clean compared with those of the few previous nights." While men often bathed in the rivers and streams, women seldom recorded what they did in this respect. But in early June, Rebecca Ketcham wrote, "I was undressed in the tent washing myself and cleaning up." Mrs. Ward also recorded at least one instance when her daughter and another woman in their wagon train "took a pleasant bath in the creek," while traveling along the north side of the Platte River. And with a sense of humor, she described a storm near Fort Bridger, "a little like our old Platte river storms" when the "young ladies took a bath and were caught in the shower." In Salt Lake City, Harriet indulged herself in a "warm sulphur bath just before leaving" on August 1 but "had a sick night in consequence . . . ." While some nineteenth-century women might enter a code of special markings in their diaries to indicate menstrual periods, this was something Lorena did not do. Charlotte Pengra, Diary, typescript, 52; Rebecca Ketcham, "From Ithaca to Clatsop Plains," *Oregon Historical Society Quarterly* 52 (1961): 268, 270, 276, 280; John Mack Faragher, *Women and Men on the Overland Trail* (New Haven and London: Yale University Press, 1979), 169-70; H. Ward, *Prairie Schooner Lady,* 58, 105, 107, 121.

66. May 31 letter reprinted June 21 by St. Louis newspapers and in *New York Times,* July 1.

67. Bradway, Letter, manuscript, May 24; Diary, typescript, May 15 and 31.

68. Michael Luark, Diary, manuscript, 47. Keeping a record of the number of graves along the overland trail was not unusual or considered morbid in the mid-nineteenth century when death was a frequent visitor to every home. Lorena's diary for 1848-52 reveals that death was a major concern and topic of conversation in settled communities as well as along the overland trail.

69. John B. Haas, "Autobiography," *The Pony Express Courier* 1 (September 1938), 9; Frederica B. Coons, *The Trail to Oregon* (Portland: Binford & Mort, 1954), 64.

70. Henry J. Hazard, Dictation for H. H. Bancroft, manuscript, 8. James Cowden noted the same type of reticence and commented, "Some of the women don't take kindly to buffalo chips for fuel but it is all there is to be had." Some men did not mention using buffalo chip fires, either. James Farmer, a Mormon from England, was one of these but he had nothing to do with food preparation. Hired as a teamster, his concerns centered upon herding livestock and standing watch. James Cowden, Diary, manuscript, June 11; James Farmer, Journal, Parts 1 and 2, typescript.

71. Haas, "Autobiography," (September 1938): 7.

72. Ketcham, "From Ithaca to Clatsop Plains," 255.

73. Only Charlotte Pengra lamented in writing her belated discovery that "those who come this journey should have their pillows covered with dark calicao and sheets colored, white is not suitable." She partially remedied this on May 18 by making a pair of calico cases for pillows. Needlework filled long hours of travel for Maggie Hall's mother, whose "hands were never idle" because she "knit all the way across . . . to keep us all in stockings." Pengra, Diary, 20; Maggie Hall, Journal, microfilm.

74. Esther B. Lymon, Journal, 1 and 2.

75. Ibid.

76. Anyone who has ever made cutout cookies on a hot and humid day can only admire the skill and fortitude of Kate's mother. She probably outlined the animal figures with a knife and then removed the excess dough from the cookie sheet rather than using cookie cutters. Henrietta Catherine McDaniel Furniss, "From Prairie to Pacific," typescript, July 4.

77. Ibid.

78. For comments about women's responsibilities based upon their marital status see Lillian Schlissel, *Women's Diaries of the Westward Journey* (New York: Schocken Books, 1982); Bradway, Letter, May 24.

79. "The Mansions of Happiness," considered one of the earliest American board games, originated in Salem, Mass., supposedly designed by a minister's daughter. It was published by S. B. Ives in 1843 and provided an "instructive moral and entertaining amusement" while focusing upon virtuous and evil traits. The goal was to reach the mansion in the center by moving chips along a path of colored squares, each representing a different trait. According to the rules, "Whoever possesses PIETY, HONESTY, TEMPERANCE, GRATITUDE, PRUDENCE, TRUTH, CHASTITY, SINCERITY, HUMILITY, INDUSTRY, CHARITY, HUMANITY or GENEROSITY, is entitled to advance six numbers" while "whoever possesses AUDACITY, CRUELTY, IMMODESTY, or INGRATITUDE, must return to his former situation till his turn comes to spin again, and not even think of Happiness, much less partake of it." Players were expected to take to heart these sentiments advocating Christian goodness and apply such lessons to everyday life. Ward, *Prairie Schooner Lady*, 70, 80, 93, 97, 115; *A Century of Childhood, 1820-1920,* (Rochester: The Margaret Woodbury Strong Museum, 1984), 8, 9.

80. Ward, *Prairie Schooner Lady*, 68.

81. Bradway, Letters, May 24, June 9.

82. Haas, "Autobiography," 9.

83. According to Rebecca Ketcham, a traveling companion dressed for Sunday wore a "light gingham dress, white stockings and low shoes." Ketcham, "From Ithaca to Clatsop Plains," 263, 268. "De-laine," a form of "mousseline", was a thin textured muslin made with wool and could be either printed or plain. *The Ladies Treasury* of 1894, quoted in Anne M. Buck, *Victorian Costumes and Costume Accessories* (New York: Universe Books, 1970), 83-84.

84. Ketcham, "From Ithaca," 260.

85. Clarissa was the wife of S. H. Taylor. Her one surviving letter can be found among his correspondence to the Watertown, Wisc., newspaper. S. H. Taylor, "Oregon Bound," *Oregon Historical Society Quarterly* (March-December 1921): 137-38. Also traveling with Clarissa and S. H. Taylor were his brother, the Rev. Sylvester P. Taylor, and family, which included his wife, a son and two daughters, one of whom (Rachel Taylor) also kept a diary of the trip to Oregon.

86. Within sight of Chimney Rock on June 6, the Dinwiddie brothers passed by "a dog city, dogs and owls inhabit together. The dogs are a yellow color and the owl is a small bird [that] keeps near the hole." The brother who kept this diary did not mention the frequency of rattlesnakes on the prairies and neither did Lorena, although Harriet Ward recorded such information several times. However, Velina Williams calmly wrote of one such encounter when she "found myself standing on a copperhead snake coiled . . . my foot was across the coil so that the head was fortunately too nearly under my foot to injure me." John or David Dinwiddie, "Journal Overland," ed. Margaret Booth, *The Frontier* 7 (March 1928): 6; Velina Williams, "Diary of a Trip," *Oregon Pioneer Association Transactions,* 47th annual reunion (1922): 197.

Bowman's letters from the overland trail were published in the *Missouri Daily Republican;* copies of letters written to him by Spencer F. Baird, assistant secretary of the Smithsonian Institution, are in the Smithsonian's archives. Intensely determined to make a career for himself in the field of natural sciences, Bowman talked his former university professor into sponsoring his second consecutive trip west. Secretary Baird tried to explain to Bowman, a graduate of Dickinson University who also studied at Harvard, that Smithsonian funds had already been committted to other explorations. Finally, he gave in to this persuasive former student, who in 1852 once sent, via express mail, "two horned frogs & the lizard, all alive and apparently well" along with "alcoholic specimens" for the "rather high charge of $10.75." Letterpress copies in the Smithsonian archives show that in March Baird advised Bowman to buy a barrel of alcohol in St. Louis for preserving specimens but "by all means put in some tartar emetic to keep the men from drinking it."

His mentor assured Bowman, "whatever you send in will be described as having been presented by you and you can then go down in posterity on the back of a turtle or some other powerful beast." Fate was not that kind. Bowman died of typhoid fever November 24 in San Francisco at the age of twenty-five. This left his brother with the problem of what to do with the un-catalogued collection, much to Secretary Baird's distress. In the end Bowman never achieved the recognition he sought, even on the back of the promised turtle. It was far easier for his brother to add the specimens to those collected by Lt. A. W. Whipple during his 1853 exploration of a southwestern route for the transcontinental railroad. The two collections, bundled up as one and sent east, remain together today with Bowman's specimens never separated or identified. *Missouri Daily Republican,* June 23; Nov. 1; Dec. 21; Spencer F. Baird, "Report of American Exploration, 1853-54" in *Appendix of Journal of Proceedings of the Board of Regents of the Smithsonian Institution,* Ninth Annual Report, House Miscellaneous Documents No. 36, series 807, 33rd Congress,

Second Session, 86.

87. Cowden, Diary, May 22; John A. MacMurphy, "Thirty-Three Years Ago," *Transactions and Reports of the Nebraska State Historical Society* 3 (1982): 276. The anonymous author of the MacMurphy diary added their company had lost 148 head of cattle in a storm but "have recovered most of them." Only the section about crossing Nebraska has been printed; whereabouts of the rest of this diary is unknown.

88. The combined Royal-Taylor wagon train was a large one: 190 wagons, 468 men, 183 women, 407 children, 1,500 cattle, 173 horses, 53 mules and 500 head of sheep. It divided into two companies late in the trip, arriving in Jacksonville, Oreg., in October. Rachel Taylor, "Overland Trip . . . ," typescript, June 4; Taylor, "Oregon Bound," 127-28; James H. B. Royal, "Journal While Crossing the Plains," typescript, Forward.

89. Dinwiddie, "Journal Overland," 5; Benjamin Franklin Owen, Diary, typescript, May 26.

90. N. C. Fanaker, "Early Day Reminiscences," *Pioneer History of Kansas* (Kansas: Adolph Roenigk, 1933), 15.

91. Beeson also recorded another story about Indians taking a sick cow, which resulted in the murder of the Indian chief. Twenty-eight of the thirty soldiers sent out from Fort Laramie to investigate this incident also died, according to Beeson. Neither story can be documented and no mention of these events appears in the diary of Beeson's son, Welborn, who accompanied him to Oregon. It sounds as if Beeson were referring to the Grattan Massacre of 1854 rather than to any specific problems with the Indians in 1853. John Beeson, *A Plea for the Indians* (New York: John Beeson, 1858), 20; Welborn Beeson, *On the Oregon Trail,* ed. Bert Webber (Lake Oswego, Oregon: Smith, Smith & Smith, 1986).

92. Unruh, *The Plains Across,* 380.

93. Henry Allyn, "Journal," 400. By the time Dr. Smith made this purchase, he had already spent $608.57 since leaving his Indiana home. These costs included the expenses of outfitting at Council Bluffs, where he also purchased such medical supplies as "operim," "apafacitida," "sal amonia" and "Tincture Spanish flu." John Smith, Journal, manuscript, Huntington Library, June 18, "Account Book Supplement," 86-87.

94. Owen, Diary, June 14; J. Beeson, *A Plea for the Indians,* 11.

95. Owen, Diary, June 14.

96. Cornaby, *Autobiography,* 35.

97. Barclay's career also included serving as the superintendent of Bent's Fort; in addition, he built Barclay's Fort on the Santa Fe Trail in 1848. George P. Hammond, *Alexander Barclay, Mountain Man* (Denver: Old West Publishing Co., 1976), 101 (n. 44), 105, 106; Eccleston, Diaries, Vol. 7, 12; Bowman, June 23 letter from Fort Laramie, *Missouri Daily Republican,* Aug. 1.

98. Goltra, Journal, June 14, 15.

99. Wlliam Zilhart, "Missouri to Calfornia," manuscript, June 11; Jotham Newton, Diary, manuscript, June 13; Bradway, Letter, June 9.

100. Bradway, Ibid.; W. Taylor, Reminiscences, 287; Taylor, "Oregon Bound," 137; Piercy, *The Route to . . . ,* 252.

101. McClure, Diary, 27; Hines, "Diary," 98; Cipriani, *California and Overland Diaries,* 86; Farmer, Diary, Part 2, 28; Flint, "Diary," 85; Helen Stewart, Diary, typescript, 16. Helen was one of four sisters making the overland trip in 1853. The others were Agnes and Annie Stewart and Mrs. Elizabeth Stewart Warner.

102. Merrill J. Mattes, *The Great Platte River Road* (Lincoln: Nebraska State Historical Society, 1969), 513-14; *Missouri Daily Republican,* July 26.

103. In the October 7 issue of the *Missouri Daily Republican* "Yankton" repeated a story told him by an emigrant about another party of sixteen men, one woman and a boy returning from California who were "attacked at Fallon's Bluff at dark by some 50 Indians, who drove off mules and horses."

104. Mattes, *Platte River Road,* 513-14.

105. Andrew McClure, also at Fort Laramie on June 14, did not report the "incident" either, probably because he was too busy crossing the Laramie River. Although he noted problems with ferry boats on both the Laramie and North Platte Rivers on June 14 and 15, none of these matches the description given in "Yankton's" letter. McClure, Diary, 25-26; Samuel Handsacker, Letters, typescript, June 14; Bradway, Letter, June 21.

106. Allyn, "Journal," 401-02; Owen, Diary, 12; James Woodworth, "Across the Plains," typescript, 19; Smith, Journal, June 21.

107. M. Belshaw, "Diary," 225, 227.

108. Longworth, Diary, 23-24; Pengra, Diary, 28; H. Stewart, Diary, 14.

109. George Belshaw, Journal, typescript, 228.

110. Longworth, Diary, 23-24.

111. Flint, "Diary," 23; Pengra, Diary, 28.

112. Eckland Family Papers.

113. W. Taylor, Reminiscences, 285; William Hoffman, "Overland Diary," manuscript, July 20; M. Belshaw, "Diary," 228.

114. Cipriani, *California and Overland Diaries,* 89; Barry, *Beginning of the West,* 415, 486, 539, 686, 987, 988; Unruh, *The Plains Across,* 250, 270, 285, 278-79, 290-91, 297, 300, 489 (footnote 76), 490 (footnote 98); William K. Sloan, "Autobiography of . . . A Western Pioneer," *Annals of Wyoming,* 4 (July 1926): 245-46.

115. Bradway, Letter, June 24; Graham, Journal, 10; Luark, Diary, 49; Flint, "Diary," 90; Michael Luark also reported that 905 wagons had already crossed this bridge as of June 13. The Richard-Reshaw bridge, used until 1867, was augmented in 1858-59 by another built at Old Fort Caspar by Louis Guinard. Within six miles of the other, the new Guinard bridge was ready for use in the 1860 season. It was 1,000 feet long, 13 feet wide and supported by 28 log cribs filled with stones; this was the North Platte River bridge depicted several years later in a painting by William Henry Jackson. Unruh, *The Plains Across,* 250, 270, 278-79, 285, 290, 297-300, 489 (footnote 76); Gregory M. Franzwa, *The Oregon Trail Revisited* (St. Louis: Patrice Press, 1972), 250-55.

The site of the Richard-Reshaw bridge was identified in 1918 by Richard's daughter, Josephine (Mrs. Pat) Pourrier, wife of a military scout, according to newspaper stories. The south abutments were uncovered in 1963 while four-teen and fifteen-foot timbers, found on the north side of the river in 1966, measured 6' x 11" and 6' x 10", respectively. At the same time a few hundred feet below the bridge site, stone steps six inches thick (measuring 3' x 5" on the surface) were also found. In the late 1970s part of the bridge was reconstructed by the city of Evansville, Wyo., with cooperation from the state. Tom Nicholas, "Timbers from Old Reshaw Bridge Found," *Casper Star-Tribune*, Oct. 9, 1966; undated, unidentified newspaper page in Lithgow Family Papers and "History of Adam Lithgow" by Bernice Hoover; Nov. 19, 1986, letter from Dennis Chapman, curator, Fort Caspar Museum, to Jeanne Watson. According to a footnote in an 1852 travel guide, "It is understood that the United States government have erected a bridge across the north fork of the Platt at this point [the Upper Mormon Ferry]." P. L. Platt and N. Slater, *Traveler's Guide Across the Plains upon the Overland Route to California* (San Francisco: John Howell Books, 1963), 11.

Between 1855 and 1859, military camps were located on the south side of the Richard Bridge and in this area the skeletons of six white persons (later reburied in a mass grave in the nearby school yard) were discovered during construction of a new subdivision in 1962-63. Two were identified by a physician as being those of females, one a woman in her mid-forties. Military clothing found in this casket indicates she might have had some connection with troops stationed at Fort Payne, where archeaological studies have been conducted in recent years. The other female skeleton was described as that of a woman about five feet, six to seven inches tall and between sixteen and nineteen years old. Known as "Burial No. 5," the coffin was some distance from the others and closer to the south end of the bridge but apparently no other information was recorded. Could it be that at some time Louisa Lithgow's body was moved from the north to the south side of the river? Equally intriguing is a 1981 report of the possible existence of rock cairns, indicating burials, on the north side of the bridge. No clues as to their whereabouts could be found in 1987, while exploring the area around the north end of the Richard Bridge with Art Randall of the Natrona County Historical Society. Interview with Art Randall in August 1987 by Jeanne Watson; David Reiss, "A Cultural Resource Inventory of a Proposed Cemetery Site in Natrona County, Wyoming," typescript.

116. Robert Eccleston reported the charge for loose cattle was eight cents per head but Newton's company paid twelve-and-a-half cents. It cost three cents for each sheep, according to Eccleston, but horses and men were free of charge in mid-July. William Sloan reported that here cattle dealers took lame stock off emigrants' hands for $2.50 a head, while charging $100 for each fresh animal. Sloan, "Autobiography," 245-46; Newton, Diary, June 23; Eccleston, Diaries, Vol. 8, July 22.

117. Agnes Stewart, "The Journey to Oregon," *Oregon Historical Society Quarterly* 29 (March-December 1938): 90.

118. Richard's partners in the 1853 bridge were the firms of Bissonnete, Kenceleur & Co. and Ward & Gurrier. Barry, *Beginning of the West*, 1140, 1148.

119. Cowden, Diary, July 11; Eccleston, Diaries, Vol. 8, July 22; Unruh, *The Plains Across*, 267-301.

120. Rachel Taylor, "Overland Trip Across the Plains," typescript, July

16; Woodworth, "Across the Plains," 24, 25; Flint, "Diary," 93.

121. R. Taylor, "Overland Trip," July 21; H. Ward, *Prairie Schooner Lady,* 90.

122. Henry Allyn noted on June 29 it was "as cold as January." H. Ward, *Prairie Schooner Lady,* 97; James Compton, "Illinois to California," typescript, July 7; Pengra, Diary, 30; Allyn, "Journal," 406; Catherine Washburn, Journal, typescript, June 27; Zilhart, Journal, June 27.

123. Enos Ellmaker, Diary, typescript, 12.

124. George B. Currey, "The Occassional Address," Oregon Pioneer Association *Transactions,* 15th annual reunion (1887): 38. Earlier in the trip Rebecca Ketcham commented upon wearing goggles when "the sand blew in perfect clouds" and observed "no one should start without these. If I had known they were no more expensive than they are I should have had some. I can see through them perfectly well, and they are but twenty-five cents. The rest had on veils but they are not much protection from the sand." Ketcham, "From Ithaca," 338.

125. Ketcham, "From Ithaca," 354; Handsacker, Letters, July 1; McClure, Diary, 46.

126. Owen, Diary, 19.

127. Isaiah W. Bryant, Diary, typescript, July 27.

128. The number of women who were pregnant during the trip west can not be estimated because no hint of this condition appears in their diaries. Births were recorded by both men and women but these announcements provide almost no additional information aside from noting if the wagon train halted for a few hours or a day to allow the mother to recover. So Esther Lymon's heart-breaking account of the birth and death of a daughter Aug. 21 is atypical. Ill with fever and diarrhea six weeks before the birth, Lymon later reported "the Dr. said there was no use to give me any more medicine as I could not live longer than twenty four hours at the most, as at that time I could not speak above a whisper or raise my hand to my head, of course they had to stop awhile, and thanks to a kind providence in the course of a week I began slowly to recover." Lymon, Journal, 3; Longworth, Diary, 28; Haas, "Autobiography," July 4; Knight, "Diary," 45; Dillis Ward, *Across the Plains in 1853* (Seattle: Shorey Book Store, 1911), 40; Pengra, Diary 35.

129. Haas, "Autobiography," July 4; Knight, "Diary," 45; Allyn, "Journal," 409; Hoffman, "Overland Diary," July 31; Royal, Journal, 11; R. Taylor, "Overland Trip," July 31. The father of James Royal "administered the sacrament to five ministers and fifteen or twenty members." Both James Royal and William Hoffman noted that a Rev. Gray preached. He was identified as a Methodist preacher from the Missouri Conference, who wanted to join the Royal-Taylor company on July 29.

130. Newton, Diary, July 1; Eccelston, Diaries, Vol. 8, July 31.

131. Newton, Diary, July 5.

132. Handsacker wrote for the *Alton*[Illinois] *Telegraph.* Elizabeth Goltra's company decided to take the Kinney cutoff, which she described as the "left hand road after crossing the little Sandy, thence across to Big Sandy, then leave Big Sandy for 17 miles and strike it again for last time. Fill kegs and start for Green River 15 miles ahead." It took two days for the Goltras to reach the

Green River. Handsacker, Letters, August 5; Goltra, Journal, July 12. L. Humphreys' "Overland Guide from Kanesville to Oregon City" (undated except for a May 2, 1853, testimonial) explained the junction of the Great Salt Lake and California and Oregon roads would be found beyond the Dry Sandy. The right-hand one was "the old California and Oregon road and leads over the great Desert of 49 1/2 miles." Upon reaching the Big Sandy, pioneers found the left-hand road led to the "City of the Great Salt Lake and is also part of the Kinney cut-off to California and Oregon." The guidebook continued: "this cut-off avoids the Great Desert and many bad Hills and is about 15 miles the nearest. . . ." Humphreys, "Overland Guide," manuscript No. 266, Coe Collection.

133. *Missouri Daily Republican,* May 22, reprinted in May 31 issue of the *New York Times;* Elias Baldwin, *Lucky Baldwin* by C. B. Glasscock (Indianapolis: Bobbs-Merrill Co., 1933), 67.

134. H. Ward, *Prairie Schooner Lady,* 101; Gilbert, Diary, 37.

135. George West reported three ferry boats "controlled by the public [were] run on long rawhide ropes." "G. M. West, A Portion of His Memories" by Ira F.M. Butler, manuscript. Celinda's father drowned Aug. 26 while crossing the Boise River in western Oregon. He had been helping swim cattle across when his horse reared and threw him into the swift current. Celinda wrote that "most of the men were near, but none dared to go in, the danger was too great." Indians with a canoe "made every exertion to get the body, but were unsuccessful." She added, "It seems Pa had a presentiment that something was to happen as he had often spoken of his dread of crossing at this crossing." James H. Compton, "Illinois to California," July 12; Hines, "Diary," 115, 133; Phoebe Judson, *A Search for an Ideal Home,* 47.

136. Phoebe Judson recalled that their Fourth of July dinner, enjoyed while camping near Independence Rock, featured a "savory pie of sage hen and rabbit with a crust of raised yeast dough and rich gravy." This elaborate menu included three kinds of cake (fruit, pound, and sponge) as well as pickles, dried beef, preserves, rice pudding, beans, dried fruit, tea, coffee and "pure cold water." Judson, *A Search,* 42; Elias Draper, *Autobiography of a Pioneer of California* (Fresno: Evening Democrat, 1904), 25.

137. Eccleston, Diaries, Vol. 9, August 10; Piercy, *Route to Salt Lake City,* 124; Hass, "Autobiography," (September), 9.

138. Gilbert, Diary, 38; Handsacker, Letters, July 14; Flint, "Diary," 97; Unruh, *The Plains Across,* 294.

139. Frederick Piercy added, "The old [road] in Clayton's Guide led to the left of the bluff west of the fort." Piercy, *Route to Salt Lake City,* 124; Platt and Slatter, *Guide,* 42; Bradway, Diary, 53; Ivins, *Pen Pictures,* 87; Haas, "Autobiography," (September), 9.

140. Haas and Bradway, ibid.

141. J. Compton, "Illinois to California," July 31; Eccleston, Diaries, Vol. 9, August 14; Cipriani, *California and Overland Diaries,* 104. Upon reaching the Weber River on July 16, Samuel Handsacker observed "here for the first time saw a house and garden with vegetables growing. They looked well in such a country and made us feel almost like we were at home farming again." Handsacker, Letters, July 16.

142. Platt and Slater, *Guide,* 49; Hass, "Autobiography," (September), 9

143. Newton, Diary, July 13; Woodworth, "Across the Plains, "; Gilbert, Diary, 42. Harriet Ward also mentioned this Mormon quarantine, "where we were requested to report of the health of our company." Ward, *Prairie Schooner Lady,* 119.

144. Gilbert, Diary, 43; Piercy, "The Route to . . . ." 287-88; Handsacker, Letters, July 19.

145. Gilbert, Diary, 42.

146. Jacob H. Schiel, *Journey Through the Rocky Mountains and the Humboldt Mountains to the Pacific,* ed. Thomas N. Bonner (Norman: University of Oklahoma Press, 1957), 77.

147. William Carter wrote that the Mormons calculate the Temple "will cost two millions to build it and to finish it . . . the people give one-tenth." The United States Hotel was run by a Mr. Little, according to Irvin Ayres. James Woodworth identified him as a relative of Brigham Young as well as a former merchant in St. Louis, who went to Salt Lake City in 1849. William Carter, manuscript, Letter to his wife, Seaver Gold Rush Letters; Eccelston, Diaries, Vol. 9, Aug. 19; Rowe, "Ho for California," part 3; H. Ward, *Prairie Schooner Lady,* 120; Irvin Ayres, "Notes to H. H. Bancroft," manuscript, 3; Woodworth, "Across the Plains," 30-31; Bradway, Diary, July 20.

148. Stephen Forsdick, *On the Oregon Trail to Zion in 1853,* ed. Fletcher W. Birney Jr. (Denver: The Denver Westerner Brand Book, 1953), 47.

149. Eccleston, Diaries, Vol. 9, Aug. 19; H. Ward, *Prairie Schooner Lady,* 120; Woodworth, "Across the Plains," 30.

150. William Browder, Diary, microfilm, July 19; Baldwin, *Lucky Baldwin,* 67-70.

151. Baldwin, ibid.; Shaw, *El Dorado,* 74.

152. Eccleston, Diaries, Vol. 9, Aug. 18; H. Ward, *Prairie Schooner Lady,* 115.

153. Seaver, Letters, Aug. 12, to father; Haas, "Autobiography," (September), 10; Arthur Pendry Welchman, Journal, photocopy of manuscript, 78.

154. The next day William Gilbert reported that Brigham Young's sermon focused "principally on the Indian affairs." Gilbert, Diary, 42-44.

155. Harriet Ward reported meeting "a big half naked Indian with his axe, bow and arrow at his back" on Aug. 5 about a mile from the nearest camp. He told Harriet he was "a Utah Mormon." Ward, *Prairie Schooner Lady,* 122.

156. Ibid., 123, 126.

157. *New York Times,* Sept. 5.

158. Gwinn Harris Heap, *Central Route to the Pacific,* ed. Leroy R. and Anne W. Hafen (Glendale, Calif.: Arthur H. Clark Co., 1951): 226.

159. Heap, ibid., 211-30; Schiel, *Journey Through the Rocky Mountains,* 47-71. Heap also reported "Walker had made war and killed several men and drive off upward to 300 head of cattle." According to a September 5 article in the *New York Times,* which had been reprinted from a San Francisco newspaper, Walker "had sent word the war was to continue four years and he was determined to capture all the horses and cattle." Schiel reported the "most impor-

tant topographical notes [representing six months of work] and some expensive instruments fell into the hands of the Indians." Through "intercession of the Mormons, who had only a short time before, concluded a treaty of perpetual peace with the tribe," the papers were returned. On July 26 Heap noted the "Utahs, who the night before, were apparently so friendly, showed a disposition to be insolent." Six days later he explained that "shortly before our arrival in the Territory, hostilities had broken out between Walkah and the Mormons. . . ." Heap described Walker as "a man of great subtlety and indomitable energy . . . his movements are so rapid and his plans to skillfully and so secretly laid that he has never once failed in any enterprise . . . [his] principal object is to drive off horses and cattle." The extent of the damage caused by this war can be judged by a petition, signed by seventy-three Mormons in July, 1855, asking $18,538.70 as reimbursement for "moving houses, stables, barnyards, stock yards, standing guard at night, loss of houses and cattle, building fort wall &c." Samuel Stephen White, July 24, 1855, letter to Col. Peter W. Conover, from Pleasant Grove City, Utah, manuscript No. 521, Coe collection.

160. C. Ferris, *The Mormons at Home, Life Among the Mormons,* 221; Handsacker, Letters, July 26.

161. Draper, *Autobiography,* 28; C. Ferris, *The Mormons at Home,* 23; Ivins, *Pen Pictures,* 93. Mrs. Ferris described the ferry at the Bear River to be "a rough, crazy-looking craft."

162. Nathaniel Myer, Diary, typescript, July 14; Bradway, Letters, Aug. 5, and Diary, Aug. 2.

163. J. Compton, "Illinois to California," Aug. 15; R. Taylor, "Overland Trip," Aug. 26; Joseph Williams, "Reminiscences of a Covered Wagon," typescript, Aug. 16.

164. Woodworth, "Across the Plains," 36; J. Williams, Aug. 16.

165. Hoffman, "Overland Diary," Aug. 26.

166. R. Taylor, "Overland Trip," Aug. 27.

167. C. Ferris, *The Mormons at Home,* 241.

168. Newton, Diary, July 30, Aug. 2; Royal, Journal, Aug. 30.

169. Bradway, Diary, 61; Cowden, Diary, Aug. 25; John Pratt Welsh, Diaries, Vol. 3, manuscript, July 13; Hoffman, "Overland Diary," Sept. 12; Bryant, Diary, Aug. 25.

170. Near the end of Thousand Springs Valley the trail divided. Joel Miller "took the new road, the one leading to the right" while Isaiah Bryant followed the left fork which was "seven miles the nearest and best road but not so near the water." James Woodworth also took the left fork when he walked ahead of his company, which followed the right-hand road instead. When he "concluded to *turn in,*" Woodworth built "a bed of sage brush . . . [and] went to bed without coat arms or supper." The next morning Woodworth "passed the place where the two roads come together," approximately 30 miles beyond Thousand Springs Valley. (In pioneer days the name of this valley was also written as Thousand Spring Valley — without the "s.") Joel Miller, Journal, manuscript, July 25; Newton, Diary, Aug. 3; Bryant, Diary, Aug. 26; Woodworth, "Across the Plains," Aug. 16.

171. Platt and Slater, *Guide,* 23. For detailed information about the Hum-

boldt River see Dale Morgan, *The Humboldt, Highroad of the West* (New York: Rinehart & Co., 1943).

172. H. Ward, *Prairie Schooner Lady,* 145-46; Graham, Journal, 16.

173. Cowden, Diary, Sept. 5, 7; Velina Williams, "Diary of a Trip," Oregon Pioneer Association *Transactions,* 47th annual reunion (1919): Sept. 5; R. Taylor, "Overland Trip," Sept. 15; Rowe, "Ho for California," part 3; Welsh, Diaries, Vol. 3, July 17; C. Ferris, *The Mormons at Home,* 257; Newton, Diary, Aug. 16.

174. Welsh, Diaries, Vol. 3, July 17; Bradway, Diary and Letters, Aug. 7-12; Woodworth, "Across the Plains," 44.

175. Ward, *Prairie Schooner Lady,* 145; Zilhart, "Missouri to California," July 28.

176. Woodworth, "Across the Plains," 44.

177. H. Ward, *Prairie Schooner Lady,* 145.

178. Eccleston, Diaries, Vol. 9, Sept. 30.

179. B. Ferris, *Utah and the Mormons,* 338; C. Ferris, *The Mormons at Home,* 275; Miller, Journal, Aug. 2, 3; Eccleston, Diaries, Vol. 9, Sept. 30. In a letter of Aug. 29, Hugh Dixson of Chilicothe, Ohio, reported, "The Humboldt is very high and emigrants are compelled to keep on the ridge road on the north side all the way down." A second report [dated June 25] in the same issue of the *Missouri Daily Republican* had noted the Humboldt "rising rapidly." This same article "From the Plains and Salt Lake" reported that B. G. Ferris was a member of the second group described in the newspaper. Hugh Dixson, Letter, *Republican,* Aug. 29.

180. Royal, Journal, Sept. 11, 19.

181. Gilbert, Diary, 54.

182. R. Taylor, "Overland Trip," Sept. 7; Hoffman, "Overland Diary," Sept. 16; S. H. Taylor, *Oregon Bound,* 155.

183. Cook, Letters, 293.

184. James Woodworth passed "Hoopers trading post, which consisted of 12 or 15 large wagons" on Aug. 17 after crossing the west branch of the Humboldt River. Woodworth, "Across the Plains," 40; Bradway, Diary, 67.

185. Royal [Journal, Sept. 25, 26] reported the "Rev. Gray and company left, too," as did the family of the Rev. Sylvester P. Taylor, father of diary writer Rachel Taylor.

186. Rich diggings had been discovered at "Shasta City" [in Shasta County] by 1851 and this community, once known as Reading Springs, became the "metropolis of the nothern mines." Located at a cross roads leading to the Trinity River and to Oregon, it became the trading center for the placer mines along tributaries to the Sacramento River. Although in 1851 Lorena's brother left Illinois for Oregon, he eventually ended up mining in the Shasta area before rejoining the Hays family in the Ione Valley of California. Bryant, Diary, Sept. 12; Ward, *Prairie Schooner Lady,* 152; Eccleston, Diaries, Vol. 9, Sept. 24; Erwin G. Gudde, *California Gold Camps* (Berkeley: University of California Press, 1975), 315.

187. Cowden, Diary, Sept. 12; Hoffman, "Overland Diary," Sept. 22; William Carey Bailey, Diary, typescript, 4.

188. Newton, Diary, Aug. 16; C. Ferris, *The Mormons at Home,* 276-77.

189. Eccleston, Diaries, Vol. 9, Sept. 30.

190. Cook, Letters, 294.

191. Miller, Journal, Aug. 8; Bryant, Diary, Sept. 15; Zilhart, Journal, Aug. 15; Seaver, Letters, Aug. 12.

192. Zilhart, Journal, Aug. 18; Woodworth, "Across the Plains," 48. Hugh Dixson estimated he passed fifty wagons per day from the time he left Lassen's Meadow to the sink of the Humboldt. He also reported "a great many families on the road and a goodly number of young ladies." Dixson, Letter, *Republican,* Aug. 29.

193. Ward, *Prairie Schooner Lady,* 154; Eccleston, Diaries, Vol. 9, Sept. 30; C. Ferris, *The Mormons at Home,* 281.

194. Ferris, ibid.; Ivins, *Pen Pictures,* 100; Newton, Diary, Aug. 23; Browder, Diary, Aug. 29; Eccleston, Diaries, Vol. 9, Sept. 30.

195. Zilhart, "Missouri to California," Aug. 20; Graham, Journal, Aug. 24.

196. J. Compton, "Illinois to California," Sept. 9.

197. Bryant, Diary, Sept. 18.

198. Newton, Diary, Aug. 27, 28.

199. Remembrance Hughes Campbell, *A Brief History of Our Trip* (privately printed, 1905), 22; Gilbert, Diary, 61.

200. Feb. 15 letter from W. Wadsworth. *Missouri Daily Republican,* Apr. 13.

201. Washington Bailey, *A Trip to California in 1853* (LeRoy, Ill: LeRoy Journal, 1915), 21.

202. Count Leonetto Cipriani could afford to be humorous since he had shed all responsibility for the livestock at South Pass and spent a number of days in Salt Lake City before rejoining his company. Cipriani, *California and Overland Diaries,* 126.

203. Gilbert, Diary, 62; C. Ferris, *The Mormons at Home,* 284; *Missouri Daily Republican,* Sept. 14 reprint from the *Placer* [Calif.] *Times.*

204. Mary Hite Sanford, "A Trip Across the Plains," typescript, 10.

205. *New York Times,* Dec. 26, Nov. 14 letter from Portland, Oreg.

206. Draper, *Autobiography,* 28-29.

207. Irene Paden, *Wake of the Prairie Schooner,* 435; Unruh, *The Plains Across,* 374; Nevada Emigrant Trail Marking Committee, Inc., *The Overland Emigrant Trail to California, A Guide to Trail Markers Placed in Western Nevada and the Sierra Nevada Mountains in California* (Reno: Nevada Historical Society, 1980), 32; Gilbert, Diary, 62; Newton, Diary, Aug. 28; Baldwin, *Lucky Baldwin,* 72. According to Shaw, "Ragtown" received its name from a party of Californians "who came over the mountains with a pack train of provisions to supply 'hard-up' emigrants, as a money-making scheme." Shaw "squandered four bits for thin soup, served in a tin cup and $1 each for two biscuits. (It was the best place for catching suckers that I have ever seen.)" D. A. Shaw, *El Dorado,* 117-18.

208. Baldwin, *Lucky Baldwin,* 72; Campbell, *A Brief History,* 22; W. Bailey, *A Trip to California,* 21.

209. Zilhart, "Missouri to California," Aug. 25.

210. C. Ferris, *The Mormons at Home,* 290; Newton, Diary, Sept. 5.

211. Bryant, Diary, Sept. 28; C. Ferris, *The Mormons at Home,* 292; B. Fer-

ris, *Utah and the Mormons,* 339.

212. Newton, Diary, Sept. 1, 7.

213. For the story of opening the Carson Emigrant Road in 1848 by members of the Mormon Battalion see William Henry Bigler, *Bigler's Chronicle of the West,* ed. Erwin Gudde (Berkeley: University of California Press, 1962); Gilbert, Diary, 63; *New York Times,* July 26.

214. Thomas Hunt, *Ghost Trails to California* (Palo Alto, Calif.: American West Publishing Co., 1974), 156; Gilbert, Diary, 64; Graham, Journal, 21; Unruh, *The Plains Across,* 355. Although a few emigrants followed the Johnson Cutoff in 1853, the "main route [the Carson] is considered preferable by our informant. . . , "according to the *Missouri Daily Republican* of Sept. 14, "News from California."

215. Both Gilbert and Graham, who took the Johnson Cutoff, saw Lake Tahoe, which they called "Lake Truckee." Gilbert described it as a "very beautiful Sheet of water." Discovered in 1844 by John C. Fremont, who saw it from the top of a mountain peak south of the lake, it was described in 1846 as "a magnificent Laguna, 50-60 miles in length, containing several inhabitable islands," by Lt. Joseph Warren Revere of the U.S. Navy. Lt. Revere made a trip into the Sierra with Joseph Chiles and saw Lake Tahoe from a closer mountain peak to the north of the lake. He predicted: "In the course of time, it will become famous and perhaps the 'tired denizens' of the Atlantic cities may yet make summer excursions to its glorious shores." *A Tour of Duty in California, including a Description of the Gold Region* (New York: C. S. Francis & Co., 1849), 139; Gilbert, Diary, 65; Graham, Journal, 21.

216. Mrs. Ferris' account of crossing the Sierra has, in the past, been attributed to describing the Lassen cutoff because she mentions reaching a trading station run by a "Mr. Lason." However, having stopped at Mormon Station, it would be unlikely that her party backtracked so far. While she omitted names of locations along the Carson Emigrant Road across the Sierra summit, some of her descriptions more closely match those given by other emigrants for this trail than for the Lassen route. According to a map of the Carson-Mormon route, emigrants who took the Johnson Cutoff might not have visited Mormon Station. While William Gilbert and Calvin Graham, who took this cutoff, did not mention Mormon Station, Mrs. Ferris did not write about seeing Lake Tahoe. It would be difficult to overlook this large body of water but she could have forgotten to note it in her July 26 letter, written after she reached San Francisco. Place names included in her diary for this section of the California Trail included the Carson River, Eagle Ranch, "Wassau" Valley and Carson Valley; she concluded the overland trip at Diamond Springs, in Eldorado County. Bryant, Diary, Oct. 1; C. Ferris, *The Mormons at Home,* 288-99.

217. Wooden corduroy bridges built across the west fork of the Carson River in the Carson Canyon were reported in 1849 and 1850 with three bridges existing in 1852, according to one guidebook. Jasper Morris Hixson, "Diary" in *The Great Trek* by Owen C. Coy (Los Angeles: Powell Publishing Co., 1931), July 29; Newton, Diary, Sept. 6; Bryant, Diary, Oct. 2; Bernard J. Reid, *Overland to California with the Pioneer Line,* ed. Mary McDougall Gordon (Stanford: Stanford University Press, 1983), 140; Thomas J. Orr, *Life*

History, ed. Lillie Jane Orr Taylor (privately printed, 1930); Platt and Slater, *Guide,* 29.

218. Platt and Slater, ibid.; Newton, Diary, Sept. 9.

219. Bryant reported that at the top of this steep ascent a trader awaited weary emigrants. Bryant, Diary, Oct. 3; Newton, Diary, Sept. 10; C. Ferris, *The Mormons at Home,* 295. Nevada Emigrant Trail Marking Committee: *The Overland Emigrant Trail to California,* 42-46.

220. Newton, Diary, Sept. 10; Charles True, *Covered Wagon Pioneers* (Madison: College Printing Co., 1966).

221. The second dividing ridge of the Sierra Nevada had several different names during pioneer days. It could be referred to as the "Snowy Mountain" or "The Snow-Topped Mountain" while the large snowbank across its face was known as the "eternal snowbank," often ten to twenty feet deep in August and September during the 1850s when ice could also be found on the water buckets at Red Lake. Watson, Hiking Notes, 1968-87, typescript; Bryant, Diary, October 4; Platt and Slater, Guide, 30.

222. Newton, Diary, Sept. 11; Watson, Hiking Notes; Platt and Slater, *Guide,* 30.

223. Upon reaching the summit of the Carson Trail, D. A. Shaw recalled: "We found the main traveled road turned to the left along the ridge and a plain pack trail leading directly down the slope which we felt would interesect the principal thouroughfare at no great distance and accordingly we decided to save time by taking what proved to be another 'fool's cut-off'." C. Ferris, *The Mormons at Home,* 296; Seaver, Gold Rush Letters, August 12; Shaw, *El Dorado,* 127; Platt and Slater, *Guide,* 30.

224. John Doble, *Journal and Letters from the Mines* (Denver, Old West Publishing Co., 1962), 165, 182.

225. *New York Times,* Aug. 10, reprint from the *Sacramento* [Calif.] *Union.*

226. Cowden, Diary, Jan. 1, 1854.

THE TRIP TO CALIFORNIA/DIARY

1. Lorena meant the *Die Vernon,* one of three steamboats with this name on the Mississippi River in the 1850s. By 1853 one had become a tugboat and so could hardly be her "very pleasant boat"; another was not built until 1859. Lorena's *Die Vernon* was built in 1850 in St. Louis without a mast and with a cabin above the single deck. She was 250 feet long with a 31 foot beam and displaced 445 74/95 tons. Rufus Ford served as the master of the *Die Vernon* in March 1853. Among the businessmen listed as owners was Lyman Scott, an 1830s settler of Pike County and a former Hays' neighbor during the 1840s. The Hays family caught the *Die Vernon* at Hannibal, Mo., after crossing the Mississippi River on the ferry. The existence of this ferry is documented by a notice in the Jan. 27, 1853, issue of the *Pike County Free Press.*

Lorena's "Capul Gray" was the Cap au Gris, known in frontier days as the "Grindstone." A limestone bluff or headlands, it is located to the west of the junction of the Illinois and the Mississippi rivers above St. Louis. The site of a 1680 massacre of the Illinois Indians by the Iroquois, it had become a French settlement by 1700 with some twenty families cultivating a common field of 500 acres. A fort was established on the Missouri side to protect settlers from

Indian attacks during the War of 1812. John Ward and Willard Keyes met at Cap au Gris in the winter of 1819-20 to explore north into Pike County, establishing the first settlement in the new Illinois Military Tract. Until 1848 this area was known as the Cap au Gris election precinct of Pike County. National Archives Record Group 40. Records of the Bureau of Marine Inspection and Navigation: enrollment 93, St. Louis, July 20, 1850; 30, 1852; 13, 1853; Thompson, *Pike County History,* 24, 25, 50, 72, 73; J. H. Colton & Co.: 1855 Map of Missouri.

2. The *Clara,* a "new and splendid" steamer in 1851, was built in Pittsburgh with a deck of 183 feet. She made her first voyage up the Missouri River in mid-summer with Joshua Cheever as captain. The *Clara* and the *Isabel* were designated as the regular St. Joseph-St. Louis packets that year. In 1853 she carried gold from the eastbound trade of the Santa Fe Trail. This was the same steamboat John C. Fremont took in September 1853, when he returned to St. Louis for medical care before setting out on his fifth expedition to demonstrate that a central railroad route to the Pacific would be practical during winter. The *Clara,* a side-wheeler, met her end when she encountered ice at St. Louis in 1856. Barry, *Beginning of the West,* 1034-35, 1093, 1180.

3. Conditions of steamboat travel on American inland waterways apparently had changed very little since 1828 when Frances Trollope described her trip up the Mississippi River. While she thought steamboats might be "delightful" if the "social arrangements" were improved, she was not impressed with the passengers, infinitely preferring to share the space "with a party of well conditioned pigs." Celinda Hines was a bit more restrained in her comments about passengers on the steamboat *Robert Campbell* when she sailed March 16, 1853, from St. Louis to Kansas City. She did find there were "very few with whom I would care to cultivate an acquaintance with" and added, "I think no more motley throng can surely be seen than one can see on board a steamboat on the Ohio or Mississippi Rivers." Mrs. Frances Trollope, *Domestic Manners of the Americans* [1839]. Reprint. (New York: Dodd, Mead & Co., 1927), 11, 13, 22; Hines, "Diary," 73.

4. Surveyed in 1838 and "situated on a fine, rocky bluff" with an elevation of 100 feet above the river, Kansas City, Mo., first served the Santa Fe traders. In the late 1840s wagon trains began to leave from the area of Kansas City, then known as Westport Landing, rather than Independence, because they could avoid eighteen miles of bad roads and several "inconvenient" creek crossings. Kansas (not referred to as a "city" until 1854) was located between the Missouri and Kansas rivers about a mile from the boundary line between the state of Missouri and the Indian Territory. The "spacious landing" with its one wide street provided space for "blocks of store-houses and other buildings. Here many thousands congregate in the spring season to make preparations for their long line of march. . . . Artisans supply them with wagons and gearing, stores furnish groceries and provisions, and farmers throughout the western part of Missouri are here with mules, horses, oxen and cows for their teams. Here, too, are found 'black legs' and other sharpers with spotted bits of pasteboard and other contrivances to filch the money and outfit from the wild and thoughtless. . . ." From the lower end of the town site a "wide ravine furnishes a pathway to the back country with a convenient grade

to the top of the bluffs, where a beautiful plateau extends to some distance.''
An engraving of Kansas City, c. 1853, drawn from ''Nature for the Proprietor
Herrmann J. Meyer, 164 William Street, New York,'' shows a steamboat ap-
proaching the landing. Henry Howe, *The Great West* (New York: George F.
Tuttle, 1851), 515; A. Theodore Brown, *Frontier Community, Kansas City to
1870,* Vol 1. (Columbia, Mo.: University of Missouri Press, 1963), 31-45, 55;
Charles Dana, *The U.S. Illustrated, The West or the States of the Mississippi Valley
and The Pacific* (New York: Herrimann J. Meyer, c. 1853-4), 133-34; J. M.
Peck quotation in I. N. Phelps Stokes and Daniel C. Haskell, *American
Historical Prints, Early Views of American Cities, 1497-1891* (New York: New
York Public Library, 1933), 116.

5. The Gilliss House, also known as the Union Hotel, provided accommodations for many emigrants during the 1850s. William G. Barclay served
as the proprietor in 1851 but in August 1852 William Gilliss, a native of
Maryland and formerly a trader with the Delaware Indians, advertised it for
rent, identifying it as the Union Hotel. It was described as a large hotel or
tavern and as ''a commodious and roomy house,'' located on the Missouri
River, just above the steamboat landing. An 1852 report claimed it was ''new,
built of brick, and contains forty-six rooms, with a pump in the kitchen and
every room furnished.'' In addition, the facilities included a large brick stable,
100 feet long, with an adjacent cattle yard. The first hotel in Kansas City was
built in 1846 at Wyandotte and Delaware streets by Dr. Benoist Troost. [Ap-
parently this had been known as the Troost House, a ''magnificient and commodious hotel containing over 100 apartments.''] The principal hotel until
about 1856, the Gilliss House at times was also referred to as both the Western
and the American Hotel. Celinda Hines, called it the Union House; she found
it ''very comfortable and nice'' on March 24. A hotel register for the Gilliss
House for 1869-70 is in the collection of the Kansas City Museum of History
and Science but the whereabouts of others is unknown. Barry, The *Beginning of
the West,* 575, 1105, 1120-21; Theodore S. Case, *History of Kansas City, Missouri*
(Syracuse: Mason & Co., 1888); Brown, *Frontier Community,* 36, 62; Hines,
''Diary,'' 78.

6. Since the Baptist Church of Kansas City was not organized until April
1855, Lorena could have attended the Methodist Episocpal Church, built
three years earlier on Walnut Street, if services were not held at the home of a
member of the Baptist congregation. Case, *History of Kansas City,* 300.
However, by 1851 Kansas City had attracted congregations of these two
faiths as well as the Presbyterians and also had a large Catholic community.
''A large number of stores'' along the main street, which was thirty feet above
the level of the river, served a population of approximately 800. According to
an 1860 real estate map, Water Street, a short road, ran parallel to the river
landing on the eastern part of the community. The houses in this ''lively little
place'' were constructed of both baked brick and board. Kansas City supplied
emigrants as well as the ''semi-civilized'' Indian tribes nearby. Barry, *Beginning of the West,* 1054; 1978 Letter from William Crowley, former curator of
history at the Kansas City Museum of History and Science, to Jeanne Watson.

The Kansa (Caw) Indians, once described as ''unquestionably the best hunters on the Missouri," had acquired a long-standing reputation for begging and stealing. In 1831 neighboring Indians reported the Kansa "infest us constantly: they beg everything from us and what we do not give them, they steal from us." The Kansa were said to have resisted repeated attempts to turn them into an agricultural people because they preferred to hunt. Twice [1825 and 1846] they ceeded land to the United States to make room for Indian nations immigrating across the Mississippi River. In the 1830s, the government began to hire farmers to grow crops for the Kansa until they started to cultivate small fields and build houses themselves. However, a successfull battle with the Pawnee in 1840 discouraged further efforts and a missionary wrote "the prospect of reforming these people is truly gloomy at present." By 1843 the Kansa were "in a state of starvation" and cholera two years later left them in a "deplorable condition." A "destitute and starving nation" was removed in 1847 to a new reserve near Council Grove in upper Neosho County. In 1854 there were an estimated 1,375 Kansa Indians living eighty miles above the mouth of the Kansas River. One report noted "they are making little or no exertion to better their conditions." Because there were no towns or villages, "each person or head of a family selects or makes his location where he chooses . . . [they] follow the chase and subsist upon buffalo, deer and turkeys." Barry, *Beginning of the West,* 33, 119, 169, 174, 183, 203, 250, 322, 366-67, 423, 470, 485, 564, 569-70, 649, 689; Henry Rowe Schoolcraft *History of the Indian Tribes of the United States, Their Present Condition and Prospects and a Sketch of Their Ancient Status* (Philadelphia: J. B. Lippincott & Co., 1857); Reprint by order of Congress, under direction of the Department of the Interior-Indian Bureau, Historical American Indian Press, n.d., 705, 543-44.

The Wyandot [also spelled Wyandotte] Indians belonged to the Woodland culture and came from a confederacy of four tribes of the Huron nation that joined together for protection from the Iroquois League. In 1815 they signed a peace treaty with the United States and eighteen years later began to move west from Ohio, where they had been given a large tract of land although they had supported the British in the War of 1812. The Wyandot were noted for adopting captives into the tribe. When 600 Wyandots arrived at Westport Landing the end of July 1843, they brought with them a code of laws, the Methodist Church, and a Free Mason's Lodge. [Membership in the Methodist Church totaled 240 in 1847.] The Wyandots purchased land at the forks of the Kansas and Missouri rivers from the Delawares and had their own school and trading store. According to the Office of Indian Affairs, there were 553 Wyandots in the Kansas City region in 1854. The following year they dissolved as a tribe to became citizens of the United States despite the objections of some who later resumed tribal relations. At that time they gave up their rights to their land as a tribe so it could be subdivided and assigned in fee-simple to individuals. Barry, *Beginning of the West,* 74, 209, 377, 493, 729, 864, 1196; William E. Connelly, *History of Kansas,* Vol. 1 (Chicago: The American Historical Society Inc. 1928), 232-37; Connelly, *The Provisional Government of the Nebraska Territory and the Journals of William Walker. Proceedings and Collections of the Nebraska State Historical Society* (1897): 1, 4, 16; *Encylopedia Britanica,* (1973), 615; Charles J. Koppler, *Indian Treaties, 1778-1893* (New York: Inteland Publishing, 1972), 534-35, 587, 678.

7. The Rev. Benedict Roux, a native of France and a Jesuit missionary from the St. Louis diocese, came into the region in 1833 to establish the first Catholic congregation. He acquired land at the mouth of the Kansas River where a log structure, 20 ' x 30 ', plus a matching parsonage were built after he left. [Father Roux was transferred to Kaskaskia, Ill., thirteen months after he arrived in Kansas.] Funds came from the prominent Chouteau family of St. Louis: probably from Francois Chouteau of the American Fur Company, which was staffed by a number of French employees. Originally known as "Chouteau's Church," it was used for nearly twenty-five years, replaced in 1857 by a brick structure. Father Roux's church was located at present-day Eleventh Street and Pennsylvania Avenue, with the Catholic cemetery, on land he also obtained as part of a ten-acre tract, extending west to Jefferson Street. However, another, earlier Catholic cemetery apparently existed on Grand Avenue. The Very Rev. William Keuenhof, *A History of the Kansas City Diocese* (Kansas City: American Federation of Catholic Societies, 1917), 5; Barry, *Beginning of the West,* 253, 257, 292; Brown, *Frontier Community,* 14; Kansas City Chapter, Daughters of the American Revolution, *Vital Historical Records of Jackson County, Missouri 1826-76* (Kansas City: Lowell Press, 1933-34), 264; Crowley letter. Lorena's description of the altar decorations is an interesting reference to the use and availability of artificial flowers (probably made from either wax, paper, or fabric, including silk) in frontier communities.

8. Now part of Kansas City, Wyandott(e) City was established on the Wyandot Indian reservation at the mouth of the Kansas River in 1843. Two years later it included a school for both Indian and white children, a Methodist Episcopal church, store, and council house. In describing Jefferson City, the capital of Missouri since 1821, and Booneville, both steamboat stops on the Missouri River, Lorena recalled her recent trip to Kansas City. On March 27 Basil Longworth visited Jefferson City and found the state capitol to be "a fine building on the outside but is not well finished on the inside." Built of polished limestone, this 200 ' x 120 ' building had a circular portico with columns nearly "four feet in diameter and nearly 45 feet high." Jefferson City itself did not impress Longworth, who added it "has a very poor and uneven location, and is tied to the earth by extreme poverty. The city being unsurpassed in native ugliness." The following day Longworth visited Bonneville, "a business-like place with perhaps two thousand inhabitants, its situation rather rough." Barry, *Beginning of the West,* 567, 790-91, 1053; *Kansas, A Guide to the Sunflower State* (New York: Viking Press, 1939), 207; Charles R. Tuttle, *A New Centennial History of the State of Kansas* (Madison: Inter-State Book Co., 1876), 209-10; Longworth, Diary, 7, 8.

9. Mrs. Margaret Clark Northrup, wife of a prominent Kansas merchant and Indian trader, lived in a log house near the corner of Main and Fourth Streets. Her husband, Hiram N. Northrup, who had been adopted by the Wyandot tribe, settled in the Westport area in 1844. They were married the following year on Nov. 27 in the parsonage of the Wyandot Methodist Church. A year younger than Lorena, Mrs. Northrup [1828-1887] was born in Ohio, the daughter of Thomas Clark, a Wyandot Indian. Mrs. Northrup's husband, who was born in 1818 in New York, had been licensed to trade with

the Sac, Fox, and Pottawatomie tribes and in 1853 was a partner in the firm of Walker, Northrup, and Chicks, described as a "large and profitable" merchandising business which later became a private bank. The Northrups were the parents of five sons. Barry, *Beginning of the West,* 526, 566-67, 1016, 1171; Case, *History of Kansas City,* 686, 689; Patrick McLear, "Economic Growth and the Panic of 1857 in Kansas City," *Missouri Historical Review* (January 1970): 151.

10. Peace medals of copper, silver, and pewter had been given to prominent Indians by the French, Spanish, British, and American governments for nearly 300 years to promote peace and friendship with the whites. They were also issued between 1789 and 1889 by fur trading companies and individuals supposedly authorized by the Secretary of War to make such presentations. No accurate records exist because Indian agents handed out many medals. Possession supposedly indicated allegiance to the United States and Indians considered them to be charms with supernatural powers; these medals were often handed down in families. Presidential medals were also distributed with no two alike because they were hand-engraved. From Lorena's comment it is impossible to determine what kind of a medal she referred to or how she knew it had been given by a "gentleman of Hartford, Conn." Bauman L. Belden, *Indian Peace Medals Issued in the United States* (New York: The American Numanistic Society, 1927), 2-11, 14-16, 39-44; 1978 Letter from Henry Riely, Wadsworth Antheneum, Hartford, Conn., to Jeanne Watson.

11. The need for a transcontinental railroad to the Pacific became an important public concern in the early 1850s. In December 1852, citizens of Kansas City met to discuss the possibilities and endorse the "great work" of the Pacific Railroad Company. On Oct. 27 that same year a convention had been held in Platte City by "friends" interested in promoting construction of a railroad between Kansas City and St. Joseph; they pledged to "aide by every means" its "speedy completion." The 1853-54 Army Appropriations Act authorized the Secretary of War to employ the corps of topographical engineers and "such other persons as he may deem necessary" to survey the "most practicable and economical route" from the Mississippi River to the Pacific ocean with $150,000 to pay expenses. Barry, *Beginning of the West,* 1136, 1141.

12. The Lithgow family left Barry, Ill., on April 5, nearly three weeks behind Lorena's company. Wells West, her cousin, recalled "many neighbors and friends came to bid us goodbye. Some of them went with us the first days journey." The Lithgow party crossed the Mississippi River on a steam ferry to Hannibal and then made their way across Iowa to Parkville. At the Missouri River they found a "6 oared row boat with 6 row men." He remembered that two wagons made up "a load." According to this account, the ferryboat would drift downstream to a sandbar, about 100 yards below on the west bank, so "the men would have to tow the boat up stream until opposite the landing on the east side." The company "layed by until the first day of May" in Kansas, starting on the overland trip with only grass for the stock. Eighty miles from the Missouri River they "met by appointment Henry Woodward and his train. He had outfitted at Independence." W. W. West, Autobiography, typescript.

13. According to the 1850 census, three families named Israel lived in Pike County, Ill. It seems most likely that Lorena referred to Isaac G. Israel of Barry rather than to the two families in the Griggsville area. A native of Louisiana, Isaac operated the second mill to be built in Barry in 1845 and also packed pork. With him would have been his wife, Elizabeth, and two children, ages ten (daughter Mary) and seven (son David). No one named Alkire appeared in the 1850 census but in later years a biography of Barton W. Alkire appeared in the *History of Pike County*. This noted that Alkire, a bachelor, had been in California in 1849-50 "gold-mining, in which he was quite successful." 1850 Census: Township 4 South, Range 6 West, 183B; 1880 *History of Pike County*, 741, 799.

14. In 1833 John Calvin McCoy, son of Baptist preacher Isaac McCoy, laid out Westport about four miles south of present day Kansas City and offered lots to newcomers if they would "build and conduct a business." This community had been a trading post, established in 1821 by either Francois or Pierre Chouteau, Jr. (both names are given in sources) of the American Fur Company; the post was swept away by floods the following year. William Chick, a prosperous farmer who also took over the general store, purchased McCoy's interests in 1836. Ten years later disagreement among investors resulted in reorganization and the sale of additional lots. The site offered a "good steamboat landing and suitable starting point" for caravans to New Mexico. Westport, which had a "narrow rock landing," soon rivaled Independence as the eastern end of the Santa Fe Trail, but became part of Kansas City after it was incorporated in 1853. Brown, *Frontier Community*, 27-61; Kent Ruth, *Great Day in the West — Forts, Posts and Rendezvous Beyond the Mississippi* (Norman: University of Oklahoma Press, 1963), 102-03; Federal Writers Project, WPA, *Missouri* (New York: Duell, Sloan and Pearce, 1941), 244-46.

15. Once emigrants left the Westport-Kansas City area, they were in what was then called "Indian Territory," so Lorena used this as a descriptive heading for these pages in her diary.

16. Very few pioneers correctly spelled the name of the Wakarusa River, located approximately sixty miles beyond Westport-Kansas City. Variations included "Wahkaloosa," "Wakorusah," "Wappaloosa," "Wak-ka-russi" and even "Waggerousse." The name supposedly came from a root found in abundance on the river banks and used as a food source by the Indians. Another possibility is that the name came from a Kaw (Caw) word meaning "hip deep" or "River of Big Weeds." According to an 1856 map of eastern Kansas, branches of the California Trail crossed this river at two points, converging near Lawrence. Several alternative routes then lead along the south side of the Kansas River towards present-day Topeka. Barry, *Beginning of the West*, 346, 482, 541, 982; Mattes, *The Great Platte River Road*, 138-39; E. B. Whitman and A. D. Searl, *Map of Eastern Kansas* (Boston: J. J. Jewett & Co., 1856); George A. Root, "Ferries in Kansas," *Kansas Historical Quarterly* 6 (February 1937): 18.

17. Missionaries of many faiths began to arrive in Kansas in the early 1830s. The Baptist Mission, which served the Pottawatamie Indians, was established in 1837 by Rev. Isaac McCoy [1784-1846], who had built Indian

missions in Indiana and Michigan. The site of this mission changed twice and by Mar. 20, 1848, it was located in temporary quarters a half mile south of the Kansas River and nine miles below Uniontown. It was also one-and-a-half miles west of the "great California road." That October a contract signed with the government called for establishing a manual labor school for ninety students with $5,000 given for the building and $4,500 annually for operations. By September 1849 a stone building, 85' x 35' with two cross walls of stone, was nearing completion. The three-story structure had twelve rooms with sixty doors and windows; it was finished in 1850 at a cost of $4,800. Barry, *Beginning of the West,* 252, 336, 531, 741, 800, 889, 930, 1061-62.

18. Along this section of the trail emigrants found a number of ferries across the Kansas River. The Lower Ferry at Topeka was run by Joseph and Louis Papin; next came Smith's Ferry, operated by Sydney Smith for eight years, located six miles below Uniontown. A rope ferry at Uniontown, built by Kennedy and Freeman, was called the Upper Crossing. The road ran west from the old Baptist Mission through the river bottom, where the mission farm served as a favorite emigrant camping place. In addition, another known as the Pottawatomie "National Ferry" had been established about two miles west of Uniontown in 1850; Louis R. Darling, "ferryman for the Pottawatomie nation," ran this one until January 1854. Barry, *Beginning of the West,* 795, 952, 1088, 1137, 1177; Mattes, *The Great Platte River Road,* 139; Root, "Ferries in Kansas," *Kansas Historical Quarterly* 3 (February 1934): 15.

19. Lorena's diary indicates at least one additional ferry across the Kansas River existed in May 1853. However, the Uniontown ferry, nine miles above the Baptist Mission, was considered the "main emigrant route" across the river. Two other ferries started in 1853 in the same vicinity, all located within a quarter of a mile of each other, but it is not known if these were above or below Smith's Ferry. Hiriam Wells and John Ogee operated the only deck ferry boat on the Kaw River that year while Joseph and Louis Ogee started another ferry in the immediate area. Root, ibid., 16-17; Barry, *Beginning of the West,* 931, 952, 1177.

20. Once the Woodward and Lithgow companies met they traveled together, making between fifteen and twenty miles a day, according to Wells West, Lorena's cousin. They started about 8 A. M., "taking a rest at noon and going into camp early enough for the stock to feed before dark. . . . We usually layed by one day a week." Almost every emigrant diary mentioned accidents caused by careless handling of firearms, which resulted in a number of serious accidents and deaths. W. W. West, "Autobiography."

21. St. Mary's Catholic Mission on the north side of the Kansas River also served the Pottawatomies. Originally on the south side of the river, it had been moved to its present site 120 miles "from the settlements," today the location of St. Mary's College. The church had been designated a cathedral in 1851 while the mission boarding school, established by Sisters of the Sacred Heart. provided care for Indian children as well as religious and secular instruction. In 1852 some 3,500 Indians lived in small villages on thirty square miles of land; St. Mary's was the first and largest with a population of 1,500 converted Indians. The mission farm consisted of 170 acres with 95 under cultivation: 60 in corn, 25 in oats and six in potatoes with the rest used for turnips, hemp,

buckwheat and cattle. Count Leonetto Cipriani arrived at St. Mary's June 17 and declared it was one of the few missions that had "succeeded in civilizing an Indian tribe." He attended Mass, requesting a prayer for an "auspicious journey." Fremont, who stopped at St. Mary's in late October, described "well-built, whitewashed houses" and noted a cross on the spire of the church. Barry, *Beginning of the West*, 773-74, 1007, 1036, 1060; Cipriani, *California and Overland Diaries*, 77; Nevins, *Fremont*, 408-20.

22. Both Celinda Hines and Rebecca Ketcham noted a bridge existed across the Vermillion River in 1853, thus making it unnecessary to contend with the steep banks as in other years. While Lorena does not specifically describe the location of the grave she saw by the roadside, it could have been that of T. S. Prather, who died of cholera on May 27, 1849, or one of the other forty-nine emigrants buried near the Vieux crossing of the Big Vermillion River. Celinda Hines described another nearby grave, that of H. L. Blinns of Michigan who died in 1852. A third alternative might have been the grave of Sarah Keyes, a member of the 1846 Donner Party buried near Alcove Springs. However, Lorena did not write about seeing these springs, a notable spot on the Overland Trail. The graves of Indians always attracted the attention of emigrants. Hines, "Diary," 91; Ketcham, "From Ithaca," 259; Franzwa, *The Oregon Trail Revisited*, 151, 159.

23. From St. Mary's Mission, this branch of the Overland Trail led to the Big Blue River and the Independence or Lower Crossing, below present-day Marysville, Kans. Although Lorena and Elizabeth Goltra reported little problem in fording this stream on May 13, six days later Celinda Hines' company could not cross because of high water; instead they went seven miles farther north to a ferry, established in 1849 by Francis J. Marshall, who founded the community of Marysville. A number of 1853 emigrants reported crossing the Big Blue by using the Marshall ferry. The roads from St. Joseph and Independence joined after crossing the Big Blue River. Hines, "Diary," 90-91; Cipriani, *California and Overland Diaries*, 89; Haas, "Autobiography," (August 1938), 9; Barry, *Beginning of the West*, 1149, 1067-69.

24. After crossing the Big Blue River, emigrants found themselves following the Little Blue River through southeast Nebraska towards the Platte River. They traveled along the north side of the Little Blue, crossing a number of small streams, two with names similar to those in Wyoming: the Big and the Little Sandy. According to Dr. J. R. Bradway, Turkey Creek took its name from the "fact that wild turkey are said to have been quite numerous along its banks." Dr. Bradway crossed the Big Sandy on May 18, a day after Lorena's company, and reported it "tolerably high and very turbid," following a "perfect gale" the night before. Bradway, Letters, May 17, 18.

25. A wind storm one night "blew down our tents and nearly upset some of our wagons," according to Wells West. He also recalled another evening near Fort Kearny "all but 2 of our horses (which were staked out) took a stamped and ran back on the road about twenty miles. when found the next day one was dead and the others pretty badly used up, which caused us to do much walking during the rest of the trip." W. W. West, "Autobiography."

Helen Stewart's account of the May 21 storm reported "it is lightening round and round . . . the thunder begins to role the lightning flash and the

[t]erefick black clouds moves in all there terifying grand. . . . I think evry minit the covers will be torn of or the wagons upset I sit in the wagon in despair and hold the door shut which was no easy job and indeed it was laughable to look out and see the fellows that was sleeping in the tent for it blew over and they crawled out under it they stood and tried to hold it but they could not" H. Stewart, Diary, typescript, 5.

Another record of this same storm was written by Mrs. Goltra on May 22: "The heavy wind last night might be called a hurricane . . . the Heavens were a perfect blaze and thunder rolled from one side to the other." The Goltras had to turn their "wagons back to the wind and lock both wheels and run tung in the ground to keep the wagon still. . . . next morning found some kettles and pans that was not lost and some clothing was blown about quarter of mile from camp." Goltra, Journal, May 22.

26. On May 23 Dr. Bradway described an experience similar to Lorena's on the same day: "Mirage very abundant, producing in every direction at a few miles distant the appearance of beautiful lakes. The deception is at times perfectly astounding." Both were traveling along the same section of trail between the Little Blue and the Platte rivers. Upon reaching Fort Kearny on June 3, Celinda Hines discovered, "People are forbidden to camp within three miles of the Fort." Bradway and Hines visited the fort and described it as "a sort of relief and trading post . . . for the accommodation of emigrants" rather than "a regularly and liberally endowed military establishment." Bradway, Letters, May 23, 24; Hines, "Diary," 93.

27. Esther Lymon, who began her journal at Fort Kearny, promised relatives in Michigan "a description of the Platte River . . . a large stream, being three quarters of a mile wide on an average . . . it has numerous islands, something like an Archepelago, which are more or less covered with small timbers, while the shores of the stream are almost entirely destitute of it. The Platte is a shallow stream, but very swift." She added, " . . . had no wood but Willows and they were afforded only by wading across a part of the river to an Island." Lymon, Journal, 1. On June 1 Elizabeth Goltra summarized her ten-day trip "up Platte Bottom," which covered an estimated 125 miles, with these words: "Grass quite good most of the way . . . had considerable rain . . . see plenty of wolves, antelope, buffalo, prairie dogs and dog towns etc." Goltra, Journal, June 1.

Almost every emigrant of 1853 wrote about seeing graves from other years as well as "new" ones, but Michael Luark and Dr. John Smith also mentioned burials along the trail. On June 2, after passing Chimney Rock, Luark "stopped a spell" with an Indiana family preparing to bury a young woman. Dr. Smith passed a "company [from Arkansas] digging a grave for a woman who died yesterday evening [June 27] leaving a Babe four days old." Years later John Haas recalled the funeral of a five-year-old girl from Missouri who had fallen out of a wagon, which ran over and killed her. Luark, Diary, 47; Smith, Journal, June 28; Haas, "Autobiography," (August 1938), 10.

28. Dr. Bradway on June 1 reported a story similar to Lorena's about lost hunters who "found shelter night before in another camp." Overland trail diaries of men and women differ significantly when reporting a first encounter with the huge herds of buffalo that roamed the Valley of the Platte. Little of

the excitement connected with hunting and killing of the first buffalo is reflected in women's accounts, as compared to the details given by men. Since women were passive spectators of these events, this reaction would hardly be surprising and Lorena's brief report can be considered typical. Bradway, Letters, June 1.

Although the following day, May 29, was Lorena's birthday she did not mention this fact in 1853; perhaps she was too busy with the details and problems of overland travel. In other years she noted the occasion but without recording any type of celebration. During the trip west, her cousin Wells West observed his seventeenth birthday but did not mention it either. Several other 1853 overland trail diaries note birthdays but do not provide enough information to determine if these were considered festive occassions in the mid-nineteenth century.

29. Upon reaching the south fork of the Platte River, some emigrants admired its "green livery of cottonwood," according to Henry Allyn. On May 28 he reported the river "high and full to two feet of the top of the bank . . . runs like a mill race."

Emigrants did not suffer too greatly from the almost constant rains of 1853 but Dr. Bradway discovered one distinct disadvantage: "The frequent rain renders buffalo chips, which are abundant, entirely useless." He gave the following weather report on June 6: "The last two weeks drenched with rain, pelted with hail and chilled with the cold." Allyn, "Journal," May 28; Bradway, Letters, June 6.

30. Whether on the north or south side of the Platte River, emigrants commented upon the exotic flowers of the prickly pear cactus. "Its blossom would do honor to any flower garden," wrote Henry Allyn. Allyn, "Journal," June 13.

31. Emigrants of 1853 described three crossings of the South Platte River: a lower, a middle, and an upper ford, all leading to the south side of the North Platte River and on to Ash Hollow. (The lower ford, according to Merrill Mattes, would be slightly west of North Platte City with the middle one located just east of Ogallala while the upper crossing was west of Brule, Nebr.) Jotham Newton, who mentioned both the lower and the upper fords, made two trips cross the South Platte River with double teams. He found the bottom to be quicksand, "the current swift, the depth of water varying about three-quarter of a mile wide and one to three feet deep, the water muddy but wholesome." Mattes, *The Great Platte River Road*, 265; Newton, Diary, June 3.

According to Wells West, Lorena's company crossed the South fork of the Platte River "a short distance above the junction of the two rivers." He described the South Platte as about half a mile wide but "shallow for so large a river." It took a day to cross, "having to Block up the wagon beds." Another day's travel brought the Lithgow-Hays-Woodward company to Ash Hallow where they "layed by one day." West recalled they "layed in enough wood to last us to Scotts Bluff." W. W. West, "Autobiography."

32. In his professional opinion, Dr. Bradway decided "without the rain and cold the emigration would have been much less healthy and more annoyed by dust gnts and mosketoes &c." Bradway, Letters, June 6.

33. Most emigrants who crossed the South Platte River above the forks cut

across to the south side of the North Platte River, a route that brought them to Ash Hollow, "fifteen miles from the upper ford of the river," according to Dr. Bradway. He described a 200 to 300 foot descent along a "steep and very winding road" and found Ash Hollow to be a very "rough and picturesque place." Lorena's description is similar to those of everyone else who came this way in 1853.

Rebecca Ketcham considered Ash Hollow to be a "wild, desolate looking place," one which she could compare to nothing else: "When we first entered it we were in doubt whether it took its name from the ashy appearance of the earth or from there being ash trees in it. As we saw nothing but a few cedars we thought it must be the former, but as we came on we saw the ash trees." Ketcham decided she could "not ride down in the carraige because of the holes and ravines, precipes and gorges," She added, ". . . we came along of the top of a ridge with a deep gorge on each side. The soil is sandy and the water has washed out these gorges and ravines. We came down two very steep long hills . . . [and] ran on ahead to look for anything we could find that was curious." Ketcham also discovered a "new flower," which she described in detail, comparing the straw-colored, wax-like blossoms that clustered around the stem as hanging down "like the flox crown imperial." Dr Bradway commented upon seeing a "low species of pholox" at Ash Hollow but this might have been different from the flower Rebecca described. Bradway, Diary, 33, Letters, June 5; Ketcham, "From Ithaca," 286-87.

Pioneers now traveled over "small ridges of deep sand (the deepest found on the road from the States to Fort Laramie), which makes heavy wheeling." Platt and Slater, *Guide,* 7.

34. Regardless of the route followed, 1853 overland trail diaries contain many references to seeing other wagon trains across both the Platte and North Platte rivers. Also noted were times when companies camped within sight and sound of each other, when visits could be made and information exchanged. The traditional stereotype of the solitary wagon alone on the vast plains is not an 1853 view. Jotham Newton observed, "The emigration on the road is very thick since leaving Ash Hollow. The emigration on the other side of the river seems to be very large. We have seen waggons on the other side of the river most of the way since leaving Fort Kearny." Newton, Diary, June 8.

35. Lorena's brief descriptions of two of the most famous landmarks along the Overland Trail is puzzling, considering how much was written by other emigrants in every year of the westward emigration. Almost no one wrote so short an account about these spectacular monuments of the North Platte River valley. Her "singular rock" near Courthouse Rock had its own name: other emigrants called it "Jail" or "Jailhouse" Rock.

However, Lorena's comment about the resemblance of Chimney Rock to "Pompey's Pillar" is most unusual, especially since it refers to Egyptian and Roman history. Standing on an "eminence about 1,800 feet" south of the walls of Alexandria, Pompey's Pillar "consists of a capital, shaft, base and pedestal, which last rests on a substructure of smaller blocks once belonging to older monuments." The total height of the column was ninety-eight feet, nine inches while the shaft, "a monolith of red granite," measured seventy-three feet long with a circumference of twenty-nine feet, eight inches. The name cannot be explained. According to one source, it was given "by an ancient traveler for no assignable reason," but the inscription on the base showed Pompey's Pillar erected by "Publius, the prefect of Egypt in honor of Diocletian," Roman emperor, 284-305 A.D., probably to commemorate the capture of Alexandria. The summit "contains a circular depression of considerable size, intended to admit the base of a statue." How Lorena knew about Pompey's Pillar can not be determined, but the comparison would be very apt. Whether it still stands is unknown. *Encyclopedia Americana,* Vol. 22, 345.

36. Also called the "Solitary Tower" by other emigrants, Chimney Rock, three and a half miles southwest of Bayard, Nebr., received more space in Lorena's diary than did Courthouse Rock. Every emigrant had a different estimate of its height. Today the column, composed of Brule clay with layers of volcanic ash and sandstone, stands 500 feet above the North Platte River. It could be seen from thirty to forty miles away by pioneers, whose numerous reports about this curiosity would fill volumes. First described in 1813 by Robert Stuart and his band of traders en route back from Astoria, Chimney Rock probably received its name fourteen years later when Joshua Pilcher reported on his journey to a fur trappers rendezvous. An 1852 guidebook remarked upon its resemblance to the "long chimneys of some factories" but James Farmer, a Mormon emigrant from England, thought it "has the appearance of an old church." Chimney Rock, designated a National Historic Site in 1956, retains no evidence of the many names known to have been inscribed here during the years of the westward movement. Over the years erosion, which originally caused its detachment from the main ridge of the bluffs edging the valley along the North Platte River, has altered its appearance somewhat from pioneer days of the mid-nineteenth century. National Park Service, *Chimney Rock—National Historic Site* (U. S. Department of the Interior, 1978); Mattes, *The Great Platte River Road,* 378-420; Farmer, Diary, 23; Platt and Slater, *Guide,* 7.

While most emigrants enthused about Chimney Rock, William Hoffman only grumbled: he found it to be "greatly exaggerated both as to its appearance and deminisions; it is an uncouth mass of sand Rock with a peak (which is split) and altogether at a distance it presents a rather interesting appearance, yet when approached, it is altogether unsightly. 'Distance lends en-enchantment to the scene'." Hoffman, Overland Diary, June 29.

37. Long descriptions of the Sioux Indians appear in many emigrant diaries and in 1853 a number of accounts mirror those written by Lorena. Unlike other tribes, the Sioux elicited respect and even praise from a number of travelers that year, although the possibility of hostilities could never be discounted or taken lightly. According to a July 24 report from Fort Kearny, some of the Sioux participated in a battle with other tribes against the Pawnee and their allies, who were victorious although outnumbered. Later that summer, the Sioux would gather at Fort Laramie, awaiting the arrival of Indian agent Thomas Fitzpatrick, who did not set out for that fort until August 2, after negotiating another treaty first at Fort Atkinson. Fitzpatrick, named Indian agent for the Upper Platte in 1846, had been commissioned to negotiate treaties with Plains tribes and left Kansas City on June 20 with a large wagon

train of treaty goods. In 1853 the Sioux were described as being "in a starving state" due to the rapid decrease of the buffalo. In June a large encampment with as many as 400 lodges existed on the north bank of the North Platte River near Fort Laramie, and reports began to come in about the Sioux harassing emigrants and demanding presents.

These two incidents might well explain the large number of Sioux along both sides of the North Platte River in June and July of 1853. In the fall when Fitzpatrick arrived the Sioux had become resentful and demanded satisfaction for their wrongs, including the immediate removal of Fort Laramie, but were mollified by Fitzpatrick, who died the following year. Barry, *Beginning of the West,* 1166-67, 1172, 1175, 1193. See also Remi Nadeau, *Fort Laramie and the Sioux Indians* (Englewood Cliffs, N. J.: Prentice-Hall Inc., 1967), 83-90.

38. In 1853 emigrants faced a decision upon reaching Scotts Bluffs, another landmark of the Overland Trail, because two routes existed past these towering bluffs. The "old" road led through Robidoux Pass while the "new" road went through Mitchell Pass, which was closer to the North Platte River; both were used that year. Robidoux Pass took its name from that of Antoine Robidoux, a trader who established a post and blacksmith shop not far from two springs near Scotts Bluffs in 1849. Mitchell's Pass, today the route of Nebraska State Highway 92, was widely used after 1850; it was named for Brig. Gen. Roger B. Mitchell, a commander of volunteers recruited to fight Indians, according to Merrill Mattes, who tells the detailed story of these two routes in *The Great Platte River Road,* 421-79.

Many emigrants compared Scotts Bluffs to the fanciful ruins and fortifications of medieval cities. They also found distances along the North Platte River valley deceiving. According to an 1852 guidebook, "It is here more than anywhere else previously, that inexperienced travelers on this route begin to be deceived in relation to distances and the size of objects." Platt and Slater, *Guide,* 7.

Of Scotts Bluff, Dr. Bradway wrote: "The great gate constitutes the main entrance to the city on either side are fortifications which guard the approach to that entrance and throu it is plainly visible the castle or tower that guards the entrance." He found the new road "very rough and winding for about 1½ miles when came on the bottom where it was very beautiful." Bradway explained this road led directly through "what appears to be the gateway of the fortified city." Although the Mitchell Pass trail supposedly saved about eight miles, Bradway noted it was traveled by "but very few emigrants the present season." Both Bradway and Robert Eccelston mentioned a bridge crossing a "dangerous dry Ravine near the Bluffs" (which many emigrants apparently refused to use) as well as trading posts and a Sioux Indian village in this area. Bradway, Letters, June 9, 10, Diary, 35; Eccleston, Diaries, July 9.

Rebecca Ketcham found this route to be "several rods wide, and such a screwing and twisting as there is to get through, it is not often seen. There are small rocks of every size and shape all over the bed of the opening, and on each side the bluffs assume every imaginable form." Ketcham, "From Ithaca." 340.

On June 19 James Woodworth's company passed "a trading lodge kept by Robidoux" before arriving at Scotts Bluffs at noon to stop near the "top of a

spring which ran down a shady ravine about 300 yards, to get wood & water.''
After climbing one of the bluffs and admiring the view, Woodworth continued
"over the bluffs and encamped to the right about a mile from the road . . .
near a ravine which was full of little springs. The grass here was the finest we
have had yet.'' After following up a ravine looking for a spring, Celinda Hines
passed a trading post of "several log buildings connected together'' as well as
a blacksmith shop but wrote "the whole was deserted.'' She added, "Near by
was one of the most beautiful springs I have ever seen.'' Because Lorena
describes the springs and valleys but not the rough and twisting road, her company appears to have followed the road through Robidoux Pass. Woodworth,
"Across the Plains,'' 16; Hines, "Diary,'' 97.

39. Lorena's description of how wagons were parked while waiting to cross
the Laramie Fork to reach Fort Laramie provides an unusual dimension to life
on the Overland Trail and indicates the lack of privacy that resulted. By ignor-
ing and not writing about what took place in nearby wagons, emigrants could
manage some measure of privacy for themselves and others.

40. The name given to a river, the fort and a 10,247-foot mountain peak,
came from that of a French fur trapper and trader, according to one tradition.
Supposedly, Jacques La Ramie, was killed in the early 1820s by Indians near
the stream known as the Laramie Fork of the North Platte River. Robert
Stuart passed the site of the future fort in 1812-13. Fort Laramie's history included replacing two previous forts nearby: Fort William (1834) and Fort
John (1841). The names of almost every person important in the history of the
west can be associated with Fort Laramie, which in 1849 became a military
post. Ruth, *Great Day in the West*, 280; Mattes, *The Great Platte River Road*,
480-520. Arriving at Fort Laramie, nearly 650 miles from the Missouri River,
emigrants felt they had accomplished a major part of their journey. Although
great numbers of emigrants visited the fort, many traveling along the north
side of the North Platte River did not make this effort. Lorena's comment
about the location of Fort Laramie is augmented by James Farmer, who
wrote, "it lies in the hollow high Bluffs all round.'' Her reference to the officers' quarters might have been to the building known as "Old Bedlam,''
built in 1851 by the government for $70,000 with lumber hauled by ox team
from Fort Leavenworth. Farmer, Diary, 17; Federal Writers Project, *The
Oregon Trail* (New York: Hastings House, 1939), 172.

In 1853 John S. Tutt and Lewis B. Dougherty ran the store at Fort
Laramie. "Prices range tolerably high here just now,'' wrote J. Soule
Bowman in a June 23 letter to the *Missouri Daily Republican.* "The traders and
speculators in this county are all bound to be rich,'' he added, noting that
bacon sold for twenty cents a pound with a pound of either sugar or coffee
priced at forty cents. When George Belshaw visited the fort on June 17, he
found dried apples priced at twelve dollars a bushel with vinegar at two dollars
a gallon. Samuel Handsacker thought it an "excellent store — get nearly
everything you wish.'' James Woodworth purchased "a common pencil such
as in the states would have cost about 2 cts for which I paid 20 cts.'' He also
recorded prices charged by the blacksmith: "shoeing a horse 4 a mule 5 and an
ox 6 Dollars for setting a shoe 75 cts.'' Rather than buying dried buffalo meat
and horseshoes, Elias "Lucky'' Baldwin worked out a trade for some of the

brandy, tobacco and tea he had brought from Wisconsin. Barry, *Beginning of the West,* 1141; Bowman, Letter, *Republican,* Aug. 1; G. Belshaw, Journal, June 17; Handsacker, Letters, June 14; Woodworth, "Across the Plaines," 17-18; Baldwin, *Lucky Baldwin,* 50.

41. Although Lorena did not receive any mail at Fort Laramie, her cousin Lousia Lithgow did. A letter from a young man she had known in Barry is among the family papers treasured by Lithgow descendants; it has been printed in full in the Appendix to Lorena's diary. In May and June, 1853, it took William Allison approximately twenty-five days round trip to deliver mail between Fort Laramie and Independence, Mo. While most emigrants used the fort's post office, Henry Allyn found he could "deposit letters without crossing to Fort Laramie for 10 cents" on the north side of the river. Hoover collection; Barry, *Beginning of the West,* 1160, 1169; Allyn, "Journal," 401.

42. These warm springs, about twelve miles from Fort Laramie, would be the ones near Guernsey, Wyo., at the foot of a hillside which retains a set of some of the most spectacular of all wagon ruts on the overland trail. The temperature of the water was sixty-eight degrees, according to Dr. Bradway, who wrote "After leaving the spring passed a hard hill." James Woodworth described the road at this point as winding "round among the rocks & cliffs and after crossing the rim of the spring we passed up a kanyon about a mile & encamped. . . ." No one in 1853 seems to have mentioned Register Cliff, located between the fort and Warm Springs, where many emigrants carved their names in the soft stone. A 1933-41 survey on file at the Bancroft Library of the then still-legible names and initals at nearly a dozen places along the overland trails lists those of at least thirteen 1853 pioneers at Register Rock. Of the approximately eighty names included in this survey for 1853 only two were those of women, both of whom were unmarried. Bradway, Diary, 38; Woodworth, "Across the Plains," 19; Charles Kelly, typescript, research notes and photographs.

43. Lorena's assumption about the origin of the name of the Black Hills was correct; according to an 1852 guidebook, "The Black Hills are so called on account of the dark colored pines which grow upon them." They were located about fifteen miles beyond Fort Laramie. In 1853 Dr. Bradway described three routes from the fort: 1) the "river route" which followed the banks of the Platte; 2) the "middle" road that led "over the points of the hills, only a part of the time in sight of the river and is less sandy," and 3) a route passing directly over the hills, "which is some eight miles the shorter but is reported to be very high and very hard on cattles feet." Platt and Slater, *Guide,* 9; Bradway, Letters, June 15.

44. Many emigrants noted the red soil along this section of the trail but this was not the Red Buttes, which are located beyond Fort Casper, Wyo. Instead, Lorena's company had reached a small stream called Red Bank Creek. Platt and Slater, *Guide,* 10.

45. This bridge, a new one across the North Platte River, had been built in the spring of 1853 not far from the site of present-day Evansville, Wyo. Here emigrants who had been traveling up the south side of the river crossed to join with those coming along the other bank as the two trails converged to form

essentially one route leading to the Sweetwater River and on to South Pass.

46. When Jotham Newton reached Deer Creek he found the grass "eat off" and so turned down the creek to camp in a spot "overlooked by earlier emigrants." He spent the afternoon fishing and caught enough for "one good meal although we were poorly supplied with hooks." Across the creek he saw a blacksmith and wrote "we occasionally meet with these mechanics — they charge very high, sometimes a dollar for setting a shoe." Newton, Diary, June 21.

It was a "common sight to see dead Indians buried up in trees on platforms with perhaps two or three buffalo robes over them," according to the reminiscences of an unidentified member of the Reynolds-Salmon wagon train from Wisconsin. On July 14 Rachel Taylor "passed a place where a dead Indian warrior was placed on a scaffold, their way of burying. A band of feathers [had] fallen down and we took each of us one, in memory of the departed brave." James Royal, traveling with the Taylor company, added, "saw dedded Indian on the ground who had been buried in a tree." Since these descriptions were written after the Royal-Taylor company had passed Deer Creek, it seems likely this was the same Indian burial described by Lorena. Reynolds-Salmon Company, *Pioneers of the Sand Plains in San Joaquin County, California,* 15; Royal, Journal; R. Taylor, "Overland Trip," both July 14.

In recounting his experiences along the overland trail in 1849, William L. Manly explained such burials were customary among the Sioux. He saw a number of such platform graves in the cottonwood trees not far from Scotts Bluff and decided while this "seemed a strange sort of cemetery" it was preferable to the "desecrated earth-made graves." William L. Manly, *Death Valley in '49* (New York: Wallace Hebberd, 1929) 62.

47. Louisa Lithgow had been "an invalid all the way from Illinois," according to her distant cousin Wells West. In his memoirs, West added, "She was buried in a rough board Coffin on the north side of the Platte River near the Bridge. It was a very sad funeral." W. W. West, "Autobiography."

48. Lithgow Family records contain no information about whether this promise was ever fulfilled during the lifetime of Louisa's parents. Attempts to locate her grave have failed and as of 1987 no mention of it has been found in the 1853 overland trail diaries consulted. Five days after Louisa was buried, Maria Belshaw passed the bridge in "the forenoon" but did not add this grave to her trail statistics nor was it mentioned by her brother-in-law, George Belshaw. In the 1960s six bodies were discovered on the south side of the Reshaw Bridge but these appear to be associated with two army camps located at this site during the late 1850s. Hoover collection; M. Belshaw, "Diary," June 27; G. Belshaw, Journal, June 27; Art Randall, "Geology of Camp Payne-Richards Trading Post Site;" David Eckles, "The Archaeology of Camp Payne," and Skylar Scott, "Military Camps at Camp Payne," *The Wyoming Archaeologist* (Fall 1985): 9-107.

49. Lorena referred, of course, to the famous *Report* written by "the pathfinder," John Charles Fremont, about his first expedition in 1842 to the Rocky Mountains. The report had been printed separately but the U. S. government reprinted it in 1845 along with Fremont's report of his second

(1843-44) expedition to Oregon and Northern California. The Senate and House each ordered 10,000 copies of the 1845 edition while the secretary of state (Asbury Dickins) requested an additional 10,000 in March of that year. The Fremont *Report* became immensely popular and was reprinted in various forms for a number of years. Many emigrants of the 1840s and 1850s consulted the Fremont *Report,* as William L. Manly pointed out. In 1849 he believed "most of them going to California had fortified themselves before starting by reading Fremont." Lorena's interest in this book would not be unusual for a nineteenth-century woman with an inquiring mind. In 1849 Maria Wade of Buffalo, N. Y., received a copy of Fremont's 1848 *Geographical Memoir upon Upper California in Illustration of his Map of Oregon and California* "with the respects of Dr. Everett." The wide variety of books Lorena read documents her continuing search for a better education, despite the fact that it includes several romantic novels. "Notice to Readers," 1845 edition of the Fremont *Report;* Manly, *Death Valley in '49,* 118; inscribed copy of Fremont's *Geographical Memoir* in editor's collection.

50. For information about women's reactions to meeting Indians along the overland trails, see Glenda Riley's *Women and Indians on the Frontier, 1825-1915* (Albuquerque: University of New Mexico Press, 1984). Mrs. Kate McDaniel Furniss remembered meeting the fifteen-year-old daughter of a Sioux chief named "Lola," clad in a "loose white buckskin gown, soft as silk . . . similar to our slip-on dresses with no sleeves and cut low in the neck." The edge of the skirt, which came to the knees, was deeply fringed above "long leggings." Lola's bridle and saddle of white leather were "decorated as beautifully as her clothing." Kate added that Lola had been killed "by a careless white" two weeks after the McDaniel family left the Sioux country. Furniss, "From Prairie to Pacific," typescript.

51. Jotham Newton described the Sweetwater River as "20 yards wide and commonly fordable." In 1853 emigrants reported a bridge about a mile below the "old fording place" with a charge of $2 per wagon but Newton added that it "suffered some injury by high water" so he had to ford the river anyway. Maria Belshaw decided despite its reputation for good water, the Sweetwater while "clear" did not have a "pleasant taste" but Charlotte Pengra's view was the reverse: she called the Sweetwater "a swift but not very clear stream of good water." Newton, Diary, June 25; M. Belshaw, Diary, June 30; Pengra, Diary, 32.

For some unexplained reason Lorena neglected to mention several sites along this part of the overland trail usually noted by other diary writers. Those she omitted include: Willow Springs, the Red Buttes, large alkali lakes where a "good many cattle dead by the way side, caused no doubt, by drinking the waters," according to Samuel Handsacker, and Prospect Hill. Although she did not identify it by name, Lorena did describe the trail at this location. Handsacker, Letters, June 25; Goltra, Journal, June 24-30.

Known as the "Great Record of the Desert" because of the thousands of names once clearly visible on its surface, Independence Rock was a trail landmark almost no one missed describing. However, James Royal gave Independence Rock "only a passing notice." Between 167 and 193 feet high, depending upon which end was measured, its circumference came to 1,552 yards. Independence Rock, fifty-five miles southwest of Casper, Wyo., supposedly received its name in 1832 when members of the Ashley-Henry expedition camped there on July 4; another account credits the name to a July 4, 1847, celebration by some 1,000 Oregon and California emigrants encamped on the banks of the Sweetwater. Ruth, *Great Day in the West,* 286; Robert Spurrier Ellison, *Independence Rock, The Great Record of the Desert* (Casper: Natrona County Historical Society, 1930); Royal, Journal, July 21.

Maria Belshaw climbed Independence Rock on June 30 and "felt very dizzy when I reached the top." But Agnes Stewart, who enjoyed the climb, wrote on July 7, "on top of Independence Rock: How often I have read and thought about it, and now I am on top of it. The wind blows very hard. That is the reason it is so unpleasant for those wearing skirts. It is quite easy to ascend, but I think it will be much more difficult to descend." M. Belshaw, Diary, June 30; A. Stewart, "The Journey to Oregon," 91.

52. A "prairie schooner," smaller than the Conestoga wagon from which it developed, had a bed fourteen feet long and four-and-a-half feet wide; its wooden sides measured five-and-a-half feet high. With a raked white canvas top, blue body, and red wheels, when new it must have attracted considerable attention, but even after weeks of travel its shape would have made it stand out. In the 1840s the prairie schooner began to be seen on the Oregon Trail. It was designed and made in the east and transported by steamboats to Independence, Westport, Fort Leavenworth, and St. Joseph. The prairie schooner, with iron tires two-to-three inches wide, carried a maximum load of 2,500 pounds, as compared to the larger Conestogas that hauled freight first to Santa Fe and then across the continent. Lorena's comment, as well as that of her youngest sister, indicates that in 1853, at least, the prairie schooner had become an unusual wagon on the overland trail. The Lithgow-Hays-Woodward company apparently used primarily "ox wagons," according to Lorena. These might have been similar to the wagons used by Velina Williams' family that had a wagon box with "an extension top that was a foot or more wider than the lower part of the box, with sides about 8 inches high. The lower box was divided into compartments for food and clothing with tight canvas so the upper part could be used for sleeping purposes." The Williams' wagon, made by her father, had a "hinged endgate and step for easy access," while the covers were made from oiled canvas. This family also took along extra running gear for the wagons as well as a supply of homemade ox yokes and wagon bows. Foster-Harris, *The Look of the Old West* (New York: Bonanza Books, 1960), 159, 160; Nick Eggenhofer, *Wagons, Mules and Men, How the Frontier Moved West* (New York: Hastings House, 1961), 101-02.

Devil's Gate, which Velina Williams called "Hell's Gate," also rated considerable space in many emigrant diaries, although some pioneers did manage to remain rather noncommittal about this 350 foot granite-walled gorge, six miles beyond Independence Rock. William Taylor would later remember that at both Independence Rock and Devil's Gate "we painted our names high up under shelving rock where they are to this day if not obliterated from someone else." Jotham Newton called it an "awful chasm," estimating the average width "must be about 70 feet and the distance about 500 feet with perpendicular walls of rugged granite rock. . . . One at the top can scarcely hear the

roar of the water — he looks down the fearful abyss with awe and wonder.''
To Basil Longworth, Devil's Gate "truly looks like an eternal map of masonry
built by the Great Architect of Heaven and Earth, and is the most imposing
and grand natural scenery I ever saw," while Dr. Bradway called it "an awful
place in a mountain of granite." Ruth, *Great Day in the West,* 288; V. Williams,
"Diary," July 15; W. R. Taylor, "Reminiscences," 288; Newton, Diary,
June 26; Longworth, Diary, 27; Bradway, Diary, 44.

53. In his entry for Aug. 2, 1842, Fremont wrote: "The country here is exceedingly picturesque. On either side of the valley, which is four to five hundred miles broad, the mountains rise to the height of twelve and fifteen hundred or two thousand feet." In exploring the Wind River chain of mountains,
the highest in Wyoming, Fremont climbed the peak, afterwards named in his
honor, which rises to 13,730 feet. Here he planted a special American flag,
made by his wife, with an eagle in place of the stars. Fremont, *Report,* 57;
Nevins, *Fremont,* 112-14.

54. This was Lorena's first mention of mosquitoes, which had plagued a
number of emigrants earlier in the journey. John Haas called them "the Platte
monsters" and compared them to the notorious New Jersey mosquitos, which
"could sting through a copper kettle." When Haas was stung through woolen
pants, he decided "even a copper kettle could not be immune" to these
overland trail pests. Haas, "Autobiography," August, 10.

55. The Lithgow-Hays-Woodward company had begun the gradual approach to South Pass in the Rocky Mountains, across a flat, gravelly stretch
sloping gently east and west. Henry Allyn found the trail here to be over "very
high ground, rocky enough to shake a rickety wagon to pieces." Lorena did
not describe either Ice Slough or Strawberry Creek, which other emigrants included in their travel accounts. Paul C. Henderson, *Landmarks on the Oregon
Trail* (New York: Peter Decker, 1953), 46-59; Allyn, "Journal," 408.

56. The writing style of the mid-nineteenth century could be very romantic
as well as sentimental but this was not a characteristic only of women. Henry
Allyn earlier in his trip wrote, "Old Boreas breaths upon us in great fury all
day." Allyn, "Journal," 388.

57. Table Rock and Mountain were not well-known landmarks along the
Oregon-California Trail, as a spot check of fifty-six diaries written between
1846 and 1859 reveals. However, Byron N. McKinstry in 1850 specifically
mentioned "a singular kind of table hill to the south, leaving a pass 18-20
miles wide." His grandson (Bruce L. McKinstry of Illinois) in retracing the
trail between 1948 and 1973 identified this "table hill" as Oregon Butte,
about six miles from the summit of South Pass and 8,612 feet high. Several
other diaries mention two and three mounds in this region but do not describe
any with a table-like appearance.

Lorena would have been on the look-out for Table Rock because she was
reading the 1842 Fremont *Report:* "From the broken ground where it commences at the foot of the Wind river chain, the view to the south-east is over a
champaign country, broken, at the distance of 19 miles, by the Table rock,
which, with the other isolated hills in its vicinity, seems to stand on a com-
parative plain. This I judged to be its termination, the ridge recovering its
rugged character with the Table rock." Bruce L. McKinstry, *The California*

Gold Rush Diary of Byron N. McKinstry (Glendale, Calif.: Arthur H. Clark Co., 1975), 171; Fremont, *Report,* Aug. 7, 59-60.

Alkali lakes, often the only water along some sections of the Overland Trail, concerned emigrants because cattle died from drinking it. Velina Williams wrote the water, "when disturbed, is black and smells bad where it has evaporated there is a white crust of Saleratus in some places quite pure and others it is mixed with sand." The water in these alkali ponds looked like lye to James Cowden. V. Williams, "Diary," 207; Cowden, Diary, July 16.

In 1842 Fremont estimated the altitude of South Pass at "about seven thousand feet above the sea" and compared this with "the ascent of the Capitol hill from the avenue in Washington." The following year, using a "good barometer," he was more precise and reported a 7,490 elevation above the Gulf of Mexico. Lorena's longitude and latitude figures appear to be rounded off from those given by Fremont in both his 1842 and 1843-44 *Reports.* At his Aug. 7, 1842, encampment, six miles from the summit of South Pass, he reported: longitude 109° 21′ 32″ and latitude 42° 27′ 15″. The next year he noted the South Pass longitude as 109° 26′ 00″ with a latitude of 42° 24′ 32″. Fremont, *Report,* 59-60, 128-29.

Credit for discovering South Pass goes to Robert Stuart and his "returning Astorians," who came from the Columbia, across the Rocky Mountains to the Sweetwater and then the North Platte rivers in 1812-13. The South Pass route was "rediscovered" in 1823 by Jedediah S. Smith but the first wagons did not cross here until nine years later with Captain Benjamin L. E. Bonneville's expedition. Barry, *Beginning of the West,* 70, 115, 213.

Pioneers were amazed at the "long, gradual ascent" and often would not have known they had reached South Pass unless this was called to their attention by others or by guidebooks. Here Isaiah Bryant "bid farewell to the Atlantic waters and likewise the great Mississippi valley, the valley of the wide world and the home of peace and plenty." Hannah Cornaby remembered "the pleasurable part of our journey came to an end" as they approached Pacific Springs. She added, ". . . provisions became scarce, the grass failed, and many of our oxen died; some wagons were abandoned, and the contents cached, or buried; we also encountered some heavy snow storms at the springs, when our buffalo robes came in requisition." At Pacific Springs, Wells West and some other men in the Lithgow-Hays-Woodward company "took a hunt that day saw a grizzly Bear but got no meat." Bryant, Diary, July 26; Cornaby, *Autobiography,* 35; W. W. West, "Autobiography."

58. William Zilhart thought the road between Pacific Springs and the Little Sandy the "finest and prettiest" he had ever seen but Lorena's description of crossing this area to the Green River is more complete than most in 1853. Her company kept on the main road to Salt Lake City and did not venture upon either the Sublette or the Kinney cutoffs; these also led to the Green River, where there was more than one crossing place and more than one Mormon-owned ferry doing business, each charging a different price. In 1853 ferry rights across the Green River on the Salt Lake City route had been granted to Daniel H. Wells, who also ran another at the crossing on the Sublette Cutoff; he was to pay ten percent of all proceeds to the Mormon's Perpetual Emigrating Fund to help others of the faith reach their destination. Zilhart,

"Missouri to California," June 30; Fred R. Gowans and Eugene E. Campbell, *Fort Bridger, Island in the Wilderness* (Provo, Utah: Brigham Young University Press, 1975), 64-66.

59. Even with two cutoffs in use in 1853, some emigrants, including Calvin Graham, still followed the Oregon Trail towards Fort Hall and then took the Hudspeth Cutoff to reach one branch of the California Trail. Elizabeth Goltra described the Kinney Cutoff as a two day drive after crossing the Little Sandy. Emigrants taking this route crossed the Big Sandy twice, according to Goltra, with a seventeen-mile stretch in between. For the last fifteen miles to the Green River she advised "fill kegs." Dr. John Smith chose the Sublette Cutoff, forty-five miles without water. According to John Welsh, the Salt Lake road and the Sublette Cutoff both crossed the Little Sandy about five miles apart with "willow all the way between." Goltra, Journal, July 12; Smith, Journal, June 16; Welsh, Diaries, Vol. 3, June 17.

60. Many 1853 diaries do not report any special attention being given to July 4, although a number of companies did celebrate the holiday to the best of their abilities. Samuel Handsacker stayed up until "a late hour" because the "boys were quite merry [with] Fourth of July speeches, singing etc." Harriet Ward and her daughter, Frankie, took a "pleasant walk" on July 4 to "gather an Independence Bouquet for our dear ones at home." Andrew McClure awakened that morning to the sounds of the "men discharging their revolvers and striving in a feeble manner to commemorate the birthday of our National Independence." For Lorena's cousin, a highlight of his Fourth of July feast was a fruit cake baked in Barry and saved for just such an occasion. Handsacker, Letters, July 5; H. Ward, *Prairie Schooner Lady,* 87; McClure, Diary, 42; W. W. West, "Autobiography."

61. Black's Fork of the Green River ran "very high" on July 7 according to Jotham Newton, who "suffered intensely" from the mosquitoes. Dr. Bradway wrote that Black's Fork, between perpendicular banks about three feet high, was six rods wide and two-and-a-half feet deep with a rapid current but the bottom was "rather soft." James Woodworth took time out to fish with a seine, catching "a wetting and one fish." Before reaching this stream, emigrants also had to cross Ham's Fork, another tributary of the Green River. Some 1853 emigrants, including William Zilhart and the Royal-Taylor company, detoured here, crossing to the Bear River to come into the Sublette Cutoff and rejoin the California Trail along the Raft River. In this area also, the "road from Arkansas joins the California Trail," according to Isaiah Bryant. He found "a great many horses, cattle, sheep and long trains of immigrant wagons from Arkansas are now in the valley." Bradway, Letters, July 9; Woodworth, "Across the Plains," 26; Bryant, Diary, Aug. 7.

62. Fort Bridger, located on 3,898 acres and described by emigrants in 1853, was not the first trading establishment in this region nor was it the first with that name. The third one had been burned by the Mormons in 1843. Its location on Black's Fork, at 6,665 feet above sea level, meant the area was well watered from snows in the Unitah Mountains, so the valley could support large herds of horses for trade with the emigrants and Indians. In 1853 Fort Bridger, as described by Frederick H. Piercy, could be considered "unusual" because it was built in the "form of pickets with lodging apartments opening

into a hollow square . . . a high picket fence encloses the yard.'' Piercy explained the unwelcoming sign reported by several travelers had been put up so the pasture would not be overgrazed by emigrants' stock. The use and sale of liquor at Fort Bridger had been legal until the beginning of the ''Walker War'' during the late summer of 1853 when Gov. Brigham Young revoked all trading licenses. Young apparently believed Jim Bridger and his partner Louis Vasquez lied about the Mormons and the Indians to each other, stirring up trouble. In August 1853 a warrant was issued for Bridger's arrest and a posse of 150 men sent out to bring him to Salt Lake City. Bridger escaped to Fort Laramie and later claimed he lost $100,000 worth of property. Piercy, *The Route . . . to Salt Lake Valley,* 124; Gowans and Campbell, *Fort Bridger,* 1-63.

There were three men, all identified as ''Mr. B.,'' in Lorena's life. The first, perhaps E. P. Bunce, a school teacher in Barry who conducted the local singing school as well, might be the second ''Mr. B.'' mentioned in this entry. However, he was not the third ''Mr. B.,'' whom Lorena met and married in California.

63. Fed by melting snow, the Bear River could be sixty yards wide. According to *Dr. J. Tarbell's California Guide,* which sold for thirty-five cents, the Bear River ''melts while the sun shines and [is] freezing at night, which causes the river to ebb and flow daily.'' It was said to be ''too deep to ford'' in the morning ''but it will fall.'' This guidebook outlined the route from Council Bluffs, by way of South Pass, to Sacramento City and also pointed out ''the mineral water is much to be dreaded by the Emigrant.'' J. Tarbell, *The Emigrants Guide to California* (Keokuk, Iowa: Whig Book and Job Office, 1853), 16.

64. ''A 'canon' (pronounced kanyon) is a Spanish word signifying a piece of artillery, the barrel of a gun, or any kind of tube,'' according to Fremont. He then explained ''in this country [it] has been adopted to describe the passage of a river between perpendicular rocks of great height, which frequently approach each other so closely overhead as to form a kind of tunnel over the stream, which foams along below, half chocked up by fallen fragments.'' Emigrants used both spellings as well as a number of variations. Fremont, *Report,* 73.

65. Frederick Piercy, busily compiling his own guidebook for use by future Mormon emigrants, noted a ''new road, now altogether traveled'' in 1853 that led to the right of Fort Bridger while the ''old one'' went to the left of the bluff. The road east of Muddy Fork, Piercy claimed to be the ''steepest and roughest hill on the road.'' Then came Echo Creek with between fifteen and twenty ''difficult'' crossings within twenty-five miles. James Woodworth thought the ascent and decent here came to ''perhaps 1000 feet.'' Piercy, *The Route to. . . ,* 125; Woodworth, ''Across the Plains,'' 27.

66. Lorena's abbreviation stands for the ''Great Salt Lake mountains.''

67. Along the east bank of the Weber River, Piercy described ''Witches Bluff,'' a rock outcropping that resembled ''gigantic and rude pieces of statuary in the form of women.'' No one else seems to have mentioned this feature, especially using such a picturesque description, perhaps because they were too busy coping with the problems of getting wagons over this route, which ran up hill and down, through ''canons'' and over streams requiring

multiple crossings. Piercy, *The Route to. . .* , 125 ; Woodworth, "Across the Plains," 27-30.

68. Lorena's "long, high hill" was probably the one James Woodworth called the "Summit" at an altitude of 7,400 feet. On July 18 he wrote, "The last half mile is very steep and it was as much as the teams could do to hold the wagons with two wheels dragging." Woodworth, "Across the Plains," 28; W. Clayton, *The Latter-Day Saints' Emigrants' Guide,* ed. Stanley B. Kimball (St. Louis, Mo.: Patrice Press, 1983), 79-82.

69. The next day Woodworth again described problems encountered at another long steep hill nearly as bad as the summit before descending into another "kanyon," which would be Lorena's "Emigrant canon." Both crossed this section of the trail on July 19, arriving at the mouth of the canyon with its view of the Valley of the Great Salt Lake only after a harrowing day. Woodworth wrote, "The road here is in some places dug round the side of a steep mountain with barely room for a wagon to pass and here a false drive of a feu inches would precipitate the whole team and wagon into the boiling stream which runs at the bottom of the Canon below." Woodworth, "Across the Plains," 29.

70. The view of Salt Lake City that greeted emigrants brought tears of joy to Hannah Cornaby: "When at length, from the top of the Little Mountain, we caught a first glimpse of the 'Valley,' our delight and gratitude found vent in tears of unfeigned joy." When her company of Mormons from England emerged from the mouth of "Emigration Canyon" on Oct. 12 and "beheld the City of the Saints," she recalled, "we felt more than repaid for the nine months of travel and all the hardships we had endured. We seemed to inhale the restful spirit of the beautiful city, spread out in peaceful loveliness before us." Cornaby was also thankful her journey had ended because she walked "more than one thousand miles" from Council Bluffs. What James Farmer's reaction was upon seeing Salt Lake for the first time will never be known because twenty-one pages are missing from his diary; the unidentified recorder for the Forsgren Company merely noted the Sept. 30 arrival of the Danish Saints in the "Valley of the *Great Salt Lake,* the land of Zion." The emotions of Hannah Tapfield King, a Mormon from England, were revealed upon reaching "the goal for which we had so long panted" by the punctuation she used when her company reached the "Valley of the Great Salt Lake!!!" on Sept. 15. Cornaby, *Autobiography,* 36; Farmer, Diary [pages 377-398 missing]; Forsgren Company, Diary, 35. Hannah Tapfield King, "My Journal" in *Covered Wagon Women, Diaries and Letters from the Western Trails, 1840-1890,* Vol. 6, ed. K.L. Holmes (Glendale, Calif.: Arthur H. Clark Co., 1986), 222.

According to the reminiscences of Wells West, the Lithgow-Hays-Woodward company arrived in Salt Lake City on July 24, the day the "Mormons celebrate, it was the seventh anniversary of their arrival in the Salt Lake Valley." Because the Lithgow-Hays-Woodward company did not spend any time in Salt Lake City this would explain Lorena's brief account of what it looked like in 1853, as compared with the diaries and letters of other emigrants that year. W. W. West, "Autobiography."

71. The trail from Salt Lake City crossed a number of springs as it swung

around the north side of the Great Salt Lake, where Jotham Newton took time out and "bathed in its waters," finding it "very salty and consequently very buoyant. It is almost impossible to sink in it." Newton, whose company spent only one day in Salt Lake City, also wrote about passing "another large settlement" where wheat was being harvested on July 17. Newton, Diary, July 16, 17.

72. This was the second time emigrants had to cross the Weber River: the first took place several weeks earlier on the eastern side of the Salt Lake Valley. James Woodworth recorded this fact in his journal while camped under the shade of some cedars and also reported catching "several fine strings of trout" with hooks rather than the seine. Dr. Bradway reported Ogden City to be "a small collection of houses situated on a small but fine stream of the same name." Ogden, the 1845-46 site of Fort Buenaventura, had been built by Miles Goodyear to supply emigrants with vegetables and also to provide corn and wheat to the Indians. Goodyear, who had been at Fort Bridger in 1846, according to James Frazier Reed of the Donner Party, sold his log buildings and stockade to the Mormons for $1,950 in 1847. Woodworth, "Across the Plains," 33; Bradway, Letters, July 25; Dale Morgan, *The Great Salt Lake* (Indianapolis and New York: The Bobbs-Merrill Co., 1947), 148, 174, 204, 208.

Woodworth did not mention Ogden City by name but reported, "The settlers are collecting here with their property in consequence of the alarm about the indian troubles and an order from the Governor to collect and build forts through the settlements. They are preparing to build a fort here." The so-called "Walker War" did not reach Mormon settlements north of Salt Lake but fears of Indian attacks led many to move "houses, stables, barn yards and stock yards" while building fortifications. As an example, expenses incurred plus the losses of houses and cattle sustained in the community of Pleasant Grove City "growing out of and consequent upon the Indian difficulties in the years AD 1853 and 1854" came to a total $18,538.70 for seventy-three residents. Woodworth, "Across the Plains," 33; July 24, 1855, letter from Maj. Samuel Stephen White to Col. Peter W. Conover, manuscript, Coe Collection.

73. Prior to crossing the Bear River, emigrants passed a "collection of mineral springs, twenty in number," according to Dr. Bradway, which came from a small basin to the left of the road and formed a "fine stream." He ferried the Bear River because it was too deep to ford with a "tolerably swift current and water quite turbid." According to James Woodworth the Bear River ferry consisted of "two old skiffs fastened within a foot of each other and covered with puncheons being pulled over by a rope. . . . " for $3 a wagon. Dr. Bradway thought the water of Blue Springs (with a temperature of 80 degrees) "answered very well for stock" and William Browder reported the water to be "salty and brakish" as well. According to an 1852 guidebook the water "is somewhat blue." Bradway, Letters, July 28, 29; Woodworth, "Across the Plains," 34; Browder, Diary, July 27; Platt and Slater, *Guide,* 53.

74. Hensell's Spring, located about thirteen miles from Blue Springs, was "quite cold and very palatable." Jotham Newton observed, "Never was pure

water more welcome to man and beast'' and Harriet Ward agreed, especially "after our long toilsome ascent up a circuitous path.'' According to one account, the name of this spring is attributable to Samuel Hensley, returning to California in 1848 after testifying at the Fremont court-martial. When he gave up on taking the Hastings' Cutoff, Hensley went north of Salt Lake City and around the lake, finding this a much "nearer" route. Originally the Hensely Cutoff, it soon became known as the Salt Lake Road or Cutoff; while actually longer, it was less hazardous because grass and good water could be found throughout the year. Several other streams, including Deep Creek, had to be crossed before reaching Pilot Springs where Newton dug a foot and a half to find good water. Bradway, Letters, July 29; Newton, Diary, July 25, 26; H. Ward, *Prairie Schooner Lady*, 128; Morgan, *The Great Salt Lake*, 217.

75. Although few emigrants besides Jotham Newton mentioned it in 1853, this route crossed Stoney or Oregon Creek, the "first waters flowing into the Columbia.'' Then came De Casure Creek, eight miles further, with "precipitous banks'' which the Ward company overcame with "shovels, axes, willows, etc.'' Newton, Diary, July 27; Platt and Slater, *Guide*, 53; H. Ward, *Prairie Schooner Lady*, 128.

Pyramid Circle, also known by various other names including "City of Rocks,'' is located in southeast Idaho. Nathaniel Myer found it "really delightful to see the many Pyramids of rock standing in a plain as they are.'' William Zilhart camped here on July 21 and admired the "magnificent scenes of rocks'' too. Pyramid Circle was five miles long and three miles broad according to William Hoffman, with "many isolated masses of rocks of a great variety of shapes and forms — some like a dome, others pyramidal and some over-hanging.'' Two miles further Isaiah Bryant described Steeple Rocks as similar to those of Pyramid Circle only higher. Zilhart, "Missouri to California,'' July 21; Hoffman, "Overland Diary,'' Aug. 26; Bryant, Diary, Aug. 20.

With many routes now converging to form the "main California road'' a number of emigrants reported seeing wagon trains that had taken different trails to reach this point. William Hoffman also reported, "The grass near the road has been grazed off'' and so took his stock about two miles from the road to find feed. Hoffman, "Overland Diary,'' Aug. 27; Dr. Howard Ross Cramer, *The Emigrant Trails of South-East Idaho* (U.S. Department of the Interior, Bureau of Land Management, 1976).

76. The Goose Creek valley, a half a mile wide and twenty-two miles long (in present-day Nevada) was described by Dr. Bradway as a "carpet of beautiful green.'' " It contains several table bluffs, mountain-high with their smooth, level tops, breaking off square at their edges, then gradually and smoothly sloping down to the level of the valley,'' according to Platt and Slater's 1852 guidebook. The crossings of Goose Creek were "somewhat miry.'' Bradway, Letters, Aug. 5; Platt and Slater, *Guide*, 20, 21.

77. Rock Spring, near the beginning of Thousand Springs Valley in Nevada, took its name from a stream coming from under a ledge of rocks. Platt and Slater, *Guide*, 27.

78. A "great variety of springs — exceedingly cold and hot, and some very

strongly impregnated with alkali," according to Jotham Newton, gave Thousand Springs Valley its name. Approximately thirty-five miles wide, the ground was "marshy" while "springs rose to the surface and stand in sort of clear pools," Isaiah Bryant reported. William Gilbert thought Thousand Springs Valley "very beautiful" while Newton reported "grass may be found in this valley by the early but those that come late cannot find much." A stream "of tolerable good water, though somewhat tinctured with alkali" which ran northeast, was known as both Alkali Creek and Cold Water Creek. Many emigrants provided more detailed descriptions than did Lorena and Harriet Ward along this part of the California Trail. However, after leaving Thousand Springs Valley, the Lithgow-Hays-Woodward company encountered a steep hill where "we took all but one yoke of oxen from the front of the wagons and hiched them to the hind axle with chains so that all could hold back the wagons," according to Lorena's cousin. Newton, Diary, Aug. 25; Bryant, Diary, Aug. 25; Gilbert, Diary, 52; Platt and Slater, *Guide,* 22; W. W. West, "Autobiography."

79. The Humboldt River through Nevada has had several different names, some of them not terribly complimentary. Once called "Ogden's River," for its 1829 discoverer Peter Skene Ogden, a fur trapper and leader of the Hudson's Bay Company, it was also known as Mary's River, supposedly for his wife. While following it for more than 300 miles, many emigrants decided it deserved to be called "Humbug" or even "Hellboldt" River. The name Mary's River should have referred to only one fork of the Humboldt but was often used to identify the whole river. The Humboldt received its name in honor of Baron Alexander von Humboldt, a German natural scientist, from John Charles Fremont during his 1843-44 expedition. A guidebook warned emigrants about the Humboldt route: "Fordings difficult owing to the banks being steep and muddy with many pools of standing water . . . also Indians are thieveish along this river . . . the grass is good for the first 100 miles. . . ." Harold Curran, *Fearful Crossing, The Central Overland Trail Through Nevada* (Reno: Great Basin Press, 1982), 48-49; Dale L. Morgan, *The Humboldt, Highroad of the West* (New York: Rinehart & Co., 1945), 5-6, 108; Tarbell, *Guide,* 13.

The headwaters of Mary's River led through a "most beautiful valley," thus deceiving emigrants about what lay ahead despite a warning that the Humboldt mountains would be covered with "everlasting snows, while you are in the valley below, melting under the scorching rays of the sun, during the longest days of the summer." Platt and Slater, *Guide,* 23.

Lorena's memories of a Sunday back home in this entry of her diary would later serve as the basis for one of her newspaper articles in *The Golden Era.*

80. Emigrants crossed back and forth, traveling on both sides of the Humboldt River depending upon how full the river was and where grass could be found most easily. They could expect to cross as many as four times in ten miles and were told "The crossings are not bad in low water, but difficult in high water." To Jotham Newton the Humboldt seemed "very crooked — the most irregular stream I ever saw" as it serpentined back and forth while the "crooked, winding road can be seen for many miles." These trails also led

through sloughs as well as over dry, barren ridges and through valleys and deep ravines, often leaving the river for miles before returning to it. On Aug. 6 Newton observed that at least they were now "a little nearer California than when we started this morning." He found some consolation in that thought, feeling "quite encourag[ed]," adding, "This is certainly a long and tedious journey." Platt and Slater, *Guide,* 23; Newton, Diary, Aug. 6, 8, 17.

81. Soon, however, emigrants found the country becoming "very barren, the roads heavy and sandy . . . the water begins to taste of alkali." Grass could be found "only in patches" and the "sun pours down its intense heat [while] dust forms a heavy cloud." and "jaded" cattle now required "constant urging to keep moving." William Hoffman found this part of the journey "very trying to our cattle and more especially to our horses, which have failed very much in the last two weeks." He also noted "a large number of dead cattle are met with daily," but reported an "abundance of excellent grass" along much of the river. Tarbell, *Guide,* 13; Hoffman, "Overland Diary," Sept. 5.

82. Along the Humboldt River, when livestock strayed or disappeared, emigrants automatically assumed the Digger Indians had driven them off. According to James Woodworth on Aug. 22, "We here some report of the indians causing some trouble in this neighborhood and stealing some of the emigrants stock." Three days later, Isaiah Bryant reported Indians had driven off a number of horses and cattle; the cattle were found but there was "no news of the stolen horses." On Sept. 18 James Royal recorded a visit from a number of Indians who brought "large strings of fish to swap for almost anything. Poor degraded human beings. How I feel for them." The fish must have been especially welcome because the Royal-Taylor company was "short of provisions." Woodworth, "Across the Plains," Aug. 22; Bryant, Diary, Aug. 25; Royal, Journal, Sept. 18.

83. Because Lorena did not keep her diary on a daily basis while on the Humboldt River, many details and landmarks mentioned by other emigrants are missing from her account. By "Great Meadows," she meant the one at the end of the river, not Lassen's Meadow where the trail divided with one road leading across the Black Rock desert to the northern gold mines as well as to the Rogue River in southern Oregon. In 1853 a number of wagon trains followed this route.

84. Rain along the Humboldt in August would be unusual for any year but in 1853 several emigrants wrote about this kind of weather. On Aug. 17 Jotham Newton encountered "a slight mist of rain and this evening a little shower — just enough to lay the dust," which must have been a welcome relief. Newton, diary, Aug. 17.

85. At the end of the Humboldt River a lake and large meadows greeted emigrants, who were advised "If you should happen here in a dry time, take in a supply of water, for the water at the Sink becomes brackish when the river gets low." Emigrants also cut grass to feed livestock while crossing the dread Forty-mile Desert to the Carson River. The trail led across a small ridge to a valley, "where a part of the Mary's river, having escaped from the lake, sinks." Therefore, the number of miles across the desert became less and the trip somewhat easier in 1853 than in previous years because "the waters of the

Humboldt were never higher." That year a number of emigrants also followed another, older trail across the desert to pick up the Truckee or Donner Route near Reno, Nev., and cross the Sierra Nevada north of Lake Tahoe. Tarbell, *Guide,* 14; Platt and Slater, *Guide,* 27; Letter from "Mr. Bernard to the *Dessert News,*" reprinted in *New York Times,* July 13.

86. Sixty-eight years later in his autobiography Wells West described crossing the desert from the Humboldt Sink to the Carson River with Lorena's company. After traveling all night, they were still fourteen miles from the Carson River at sunrise. Because the cattle were tired, "we lay by all day and gave them a rest. We started again in the evening. Some of the men and cattle reached the River by two oclock. A. Lithgow and I stayed back with the cattle that gave out and did not reach the River until ten oclock the next day. the cattle that gave out would lie down and rest awhile. they could smell the water and get up and start on again." W. W. West, "Autobiography."

After reaching the Carson River, Jotham Newton reconsidered his company's strategy and decided "we should have started on the desert in the morning instead of the evening, by that means [we] could have passed the last twelve miles in the cool of the morning." Like so many emigrants before him, Newton commented upon the number of dead animals and remanents of broken wagons along this desert route. Newton, Diary, Aug. 28.

87. Lorena's description of this incident sounds remarkably like one witnessed by Elias Draper and recounted in his memoirs. Ragtown, at the end of the desert road and on the Carson River, "is quite a little town built here by the Californians," according to Newton. John Haas found Ragtown consisted of "tattered canvas tents, close to a corral, the like of which I do not believe could be found on either side of the Rockies. There was no timber close by and the practical owner of the town had gone out on the desert and gathered a lot of riffle barrels and log chains . . . for posts and rails." He said the resulting corral would hold "any horse or cow left behind or traded for." William Gilbert was glad to reach the Carson River because it was a "great rarity to get good water again." Newton, Diary, Aug. 29; Haas, "Autobiography," (Jan. 1939), 11; Gilbert, Diary, 62.

88. From Ragtown, the route Lorena followed led over dry, sandy bluffs, returning every few miles to the Carson River until it reached the Carson Valley, about twenty miles south of Reno, Nev. Considered the "largest fertile spot found on the route since leaving the head-waters of Mary's river," the Carson Valley by 1853 had already been developed into a number of ranches where emigrants could purchase supplies to last them until they crossed the Sierra Nevada. On Sept. 1 Jotham Newton described this "pleasant valley" as a "strange contrast to the dry sage plains and sear, brown and gloomy mountains" that bordered it. By 1851 a number of Mormons had already settled in the Carson Valley with Mormon Station (present-day Genoa) described as "a considerable trading establishment" by Isaiah Bryant. Another division of the California Trail occurred in the Carson Valley: the Johnson Cutoff over the mountains to Lake Tahoe lured a number of 1853 emigrants while the route across Walker River, further to the south, brought others to the Sonora Pass. In 1853 an estimated thirty-four wagon

trains crossed the Sonora Pass. Platt and Slater, *Guide*, 28; Newton, Diary, Sept. 1, 5; Bryant, Diary, Sept. 28; George Stewart, *The California Trail* (New York: McGraw-Hill, 1962), 310.

89. A number of small streams had to be crossed in the Carson Valley, about forty miles in length. The road ran along the low foothills on the west side of the valley at the foot of the mountains to avoid the sloughs of the river itself. Emigrants were advised to "stop in this [Carson] valley and recruit their teams before crossing the Nevada mountains." Platt and Slater, *Guide*, 28.

90. Entering the Carson Canyon, pioneers discovered the "worst road on the journey" crisscrossed the west branch of the Carson River several times and led "through the most difficult passes, over rocks and quagmires." The river was "enclosed on both sides by high rocky cliffs, the stream comes rushing down from the mountains roaring like a cataract. The road is so very rocky that it is difficult in many places to get along with a wagon." At the mouth of the canyon, both Isaiah Bryant and William Zilhart reported the existence of a saw mill, "built this spring and the only one in the valley." Zilhart added that a tavern and blacksmith shop were also located here in 1853. He reported rocks in the roadbed, which in places was the stream itself, ranged from six inches to four feet, presenting problems for wagons. Platt and Slater, *Guide*, 29; Tarbell, *Guide*, 16; Bryant, Diary, Oct. 1; Zilhart, "Missouri to California," Sept. 6.

Although Lorena did not mention it, three bridges across the Carson River helped make it easier to follow the steep, winding trail through the canyon. Hope Valley, at the head of the Carson Canyon and today a forty-minute drive from the south end of Lake Tahoe, served as a welcome camping spot along this part of the California Trail since it provided "some good grass and water." Platt and Slater, *Guide*, 29.

91. Above Red Lake the trail twisted and climbed with numerous short turns. Wells West provided additional details about this section of the road: "in climing the Mountain [above Red Lake] we crossed Slippery Rock where we had to unhich the oxen from the wagons and drive them up over the Rock and then hich them to the end of the tongue with long chains and pull them up. near the top one of the wagons upset." Red Lake Hill was considered "the terror for everyone who made the trip," according to the reminiscences of Annie [Mrs. William] Hagerman Vela in recounting the story of her parents' 1853 trip. According to this account, oxen were taken off and led around the rocks in "corkscrew fashion" to the top where "huge chains were wrapped about a tree and dropped to those below." Then the wagons were "attached and oxen driven forward, the wagon making slow progress." These recollections are of special interest because they supply otherwise unknown details about how wagons were taken up this mountainside. Before undertaking the next summit of the Sierra, many emigrants camped overnight by a small lake in a valley, today covered with the waters of Caples Lake [named for Mr. and Mrs. James Caples, who made the overland journey twice, in 1849 and 1850]. Watson, Hiking Notes; W. W. West, "Autobiography"; Elizabeth Ann Sargent, *Amador County History* (Jackson, Calif.: The Amador Ledger, 1927) 56-57.

92. Again, Lorena's diary and her cousin's account provide detailed information about crossing the second summit of the Sierra as compared to the very brief descriptions given by both Bryant and Zilhart. Such omissions might well reveal the difficulty presented by this ascent; it might also be an indication of how tired emigrants had become as they neared the end of their journey and had also used up nearly all writing supplies. Whatever the reason, many did not write more in detail about this section of the trail. Today seventeen miles of the Carson Emigrant Road, beginning on the west side of Caples Lake, is included in the Mokelumne Wilderness and designated a National Recreation Trail. It has also been renamed the Emigrant Summit Trail by the U. S. Forest Service.

According to Wells West, the Lithgow-Hays-Woodward company began the ascent of the "Main Summit" in the rain. "Before we reached the top it was Snowing, on the Summit the Snow was about six inches deep with a strong wind and very cold. Were right in the clouds. We came down two miles from the Summit to the timber line and had rousing big camp fires that night." West was one of the men returning for the wagon that broke down near the summit. Watson, Hiking Notes; W. W. West, "Autobiography."

93. Upon leaving the summit, emigrants considered themselves to be in California, at long last. "We crossed the line into California about two oclock," wrote William Zilhart on Sept. 9. From here the rough, rocky descent led through five miles of desert along the top of the mountain ridge with meadows and water located off the trail on both sides. Few emigrants in any year wrote detailed reports about this part of the route but after swinging around the Silver Lake basin, both Zilhart and Jotham Newton mentioned passing Tragedy Springs. However, neither explained the name given to this location where three Mormons were buried in 1848. Former members of the Mormon Battalion, they had been working at Sutter's Mill when gold was discovered in 1848. Ordered by Brigham Young to report to Salt Lake City, these men had been scouting a new route over the Sierra when attacked by either Indians or whites masquerading as Indians. Tragedy Springs and grave site, located just off State Highway 88, today are maintained by the Daughters of Utah. Zilhart, "Missouri to California," Sept. 9; William Henry Bigler, *Chronicle of the West,* ed. Erwin G. Gudde (Berkeley: University of California Press, 1962).

Eight miles beyond Tragedy Springs emigrants came to "the junction of the road," as Bryant explained: "The left leading to Volcano [then a prosperous gold rush community in Amador County] and the right to Placerville." Lorena's company took the left fork, as did Bryant, Zilhart and Newton, to reach "Volcano City and the Golden Land." And William Warner concluded, "Of all the animals that cross the plains, man is the toughest and can endure the most." Sept. 23 letter from Nevada City, Calif., to "Dear Mother" in Huntington, Ind., *California Historical Quarterly* (1926) 289-92; Bryant, Diary, Oct. 9.

THE CALIFORNIA YEARS/INTRODUCTION

1. *New York Times,* June 10. Amador County was formed from sections of adjoining Sacramento and Calaveras counties. Running west to east between the Cosumnes and the Mokelumne rivers, it marked the southern-most boundary of the central gold region. The new county's major trading center remained the state capital rather than nearby Stockton, which served instead as the trade area for the southern mines. In 1856-57 a section of Eldorado County was added to form the present-day county boundaries. J. D. Mason, *History of Amador County, California* (Oakland: Thompson & West, 1881), 7, 226; E. G. Gudde, *California Gold Camps* (Berkeley: University of California Press, 1975), 414.

2. Settlers first came into the Ione Valley in the late 1840s to ranch, but the name of Ione City did not appear in print until about 1852. The first frame building in Ione was brought around the Horn in 1850 for Judge H. A. Carter. The area was named after the heroine in the popular romantic novel *Last Days of Pompeii* by Edward Bulwer-Lytton, having previously been called an assortment of names including "Bedbug," "Freezeout," "Rickeyville," "Hardscrabble," and "Woosterville." The Arroyo Seco (Spanish for "dry creek") consisted of a tract of land equal to eleven leagues in 1840, when it was granted to Teodocio Yuba (or Yorba) by the Mexican government, a fact unknown to settlers until about 1853. It included Sacramento, Amador, and San Joaquin counties, with Ione in the center. Mason, *History,* 48-49; Gudde, *California Gold Camps,* 169; Robert G. Cowan, *Ranchos of California* (Fresno: Academy Library Guild, 1956), 17, 242-43.

3. *New York Times,* June 10. In 1853 the Methodists built "a neat church and parsonage" at Ione and, according to church records, "All paid for, thank God." Built on Church Street between Main and Jackson, it opened for worship on March 6 of that year. C. V. Anthony, *Fifty Years of Methodism* (San Francisco: Methodist Book Concern, 1901), 124; *Centennial of Methodism in Ione City* (n.d.), pamphlet collection, Bancroft Library.

4. *New York Times,* July 13.

5. The location of Lorena's "Sarrahsville" (which she also spelled with only one "r") is unknown; maps of Amador County in the early 1850s do not show a place of that name in the vicinity of Drytown. Since "many little settlements started near a spring where water could be obtained," perhaps Sarrahsville was one of the many ephemeral gold rush camps that flourished briefly before disappearing forever. No mention of it seems to exist outside Lorena's diary and after the fall of 1853 she never referred to it again. From her accounts of frequent trips between Sarrahsville, Drytown, Fiddletown (the location for one of Bret Harte's stories), Ione and the Cosumnes River mining camps of Cook's Bar and Michigan Bar, it must have been somewhere in this area because of the short distances she traveled. In the 1850s two other gold rush communities were also called Sarrahsville, but it seems unlikely that either could be the one Lorena wrote about. One was located in Placer County to the north while the other, later renamed Clinton, was situated in southeastern Amador County. Called Sarahsville in the U. S. Post Office records of

1856-59, this camp, which once had a population of 2,000, flourished in hydraulic mining days on the south fork of Jackson Creek, eight and one-half miles east of the community of Jackson. During trips to Ione City and Valley, Lorena never mentioned Jackson, although the road from Sarahsville/Clinton led directly through the county seat. Lorena did not travel through this part of Amador County until 1856, when she visited Jackson for the first time. Gudde, *California Gold Camps,* 309; Walter N. Frikstad, *A Century of California Post Offices, 1848-1954* (Oakland: Pacific Rotoprinting Co., 1955), 6; *Early Day History of Drytown, Plymouth, Fiddletown and Vicinity,* monograph, Amador County Chamber of Commerce, vertical file, University of the Pacific.

6. In May 1850 Franklin Starr reported making $4-6 a day mining on the "Macosma River" but "calculate on an ounce or more when the river goes down." He added, "We made one day not long ago in a ravine $122.20 of very coarse gold." William Rich Hutton, *Glances at California, 1847-53* (San Marino: Huntington Library, 1942), 12; Franklin Starr, May 16, 1850, Letter, ISHL.

7. Letters to the *Marietta* [Ohio] *Intellegencer,* Mar. 21, 28, May 30, 1850, in Elisha Douglass Perkins, *Gold Rush Diary,* ed. Thomas D. Clark (Lexington: University of Kentucky Press, 1967), 169-74, 192-93; Mason, *History,* 226; Hubert Howe Bancroft, *History of California,* Vol. 6 and 23 (San Francisco: History Co., 1888), 353; Theodore H. Hittel, *History of California,* Vol. 3, (San Francisco, N. J. Stone and Co., 1897), 109-10; Jacques A. Moerenhout, *The Inside Story of the Gold Rush* (San Francisco: California Historical Society, 1936), 13-16, 26.

8. Franklin A. Buck, *A Yankee Trader in the Gold Rush* (New York: Houghton Mifflin Co., 1930), 66.

9. William Hicks' "rawhide house," constructed of hide-covered poles, was the "only improvement" reported in the Ione Valley during the summer of 1848. A farmer from Missouri, Hicks came to California in 1843 and had been at Mormon Island; he turned the Ione house into the first store with Moses Childers as his manager. Hicks, who mined in the Ione area in 1846, later declared that these mines "were not within the richest gold belt and so this settlement did not enjoy the prosperity of neighboring places." Later engaged in stock raising, Hicks brought cattle from southern California to the Ione Valley to fatten for market. 1852 Special California Census, 215 in original; 103 in DAR typed copy; Mason, *History,* 182-83; Owen C. Coy, *In the Diggings in '49* (Los Angeles: California State Historical Association, 1948), 46; Charles Peters, *The Autobiography of . . . .* (Sacramento: The LaGrave Co., 1915). A colorful character, Peters, born on an island off the coast of Portugal, participated in the whaling trade before coming to California in 1848. He mined in Amador County until the late 1850s when he took up ranching.

10. Joaquin Murieta's name has been spelled various ways, including with two "r"'s. A "chronicle of a series of atrocities unexampled for villainy and cruelty" between Jackson and Sutter's Creek appeared in the March 29 issue of the *New York Times,* with additional reports throughout the spring and summer of 1853. *New York Times,* Mar. 29, Apr. 8; Richard Rodriguez, "The Head of Joaquin Murrieta," *California* (July 1985): 55-62, 89.

11. This French word used by John Doble has several meanings. *Quivive*

translates as either "long live who?" or "whom do you favor?" It has also been defined as the "challenge of a French sentinel or patrol" equivalent to "who goes there?" Doble, *Journal and Letters,* 177. The arrival of women in the mining areas was considered a force for improvement and John P. Clough, Jr., wrote from nearby Stockton on July 28, 1853: "The Society is becoming much better but nothing compared with that at home." John P. Clough, Letter, manuscript.

12. Abby Mansur, "Letters," reprinted in Fischer, *Let Them Speak for Themselves,* 48-58.

13. Gudde, *California Gold Camps,* 372. These invitations were given in the 1940s to the California Historical Society Library, San Francisco, apparently by a descendant of one of Lorena's sisters. No further information about the donor is available.

14. The Mountain House was located about thirteen miles from the Ione Valley, according to Horace Seaver, an 1853 emigrant who had turned to threshing rather than mining in the summer of 1854 due to a lack of water. Seaver, who stayed at the Mountain House during the spring and summer, identified the Walker brothers (Frank and Burt who came from near Racine, Wisconsin) in a June 12, 1854, letter; however, "Sole" was his brother Solon Seaver, "one of the best violin players there is in this part of the country." Solon, who also came to California in 1853, and his wife, Amanda, became proprietors of the Mountain House in 1855. Seaver, "Letters," manuscript, June 12, 1854; Oct. 21, 1855. Dance invitations, California Historical Society Library.

In 1854 en route to Drytown, Maj. Edwin A. Sherman met "an old lady in a stage coach who claimed to be the first female to settle in Fiddletown." She had "a large house and kept a tavern and people came there to dance," he added. According to Sherman, this lady claimed "my husband and my two sons and a daughter all play the violin and two of them could play the flute and one the flageolet," thus explaining why Fiddletown could be considered "Violin City." Edwin A. Sherman, "Reminiscences: Sherman Was There," Vol. 24, California Historical *Quarterly* (1945); 167.

15. Bayard Taylor, *Eldorado* (New York: Alfred A. Knopf, 1949), 197.

16. The Willow Springs House began as a cottage run by "John Craig, county clerk, and Berry." Rachel Frazier, *Reminiscences of Travel* (San Francisco: Francis and Valentine, 1871), 11-14.

17. Borthwick's "first hand picture of life in California mining camps in the early fifties" appeared in print in 1857 as *The Gold Hunters.* He reported the average rate of board per week was $12-15 while the charge for a single meal came to $1-1.50. Borthwick, *The Gold Hunters.* Reprint. (New York: MacMillan Co., 1917), 168.

18. At one time there were also a winery and a stage stop, as well as the dance halls and saloons of a typical mining community at this location. Although the Forest Home Inn, a two-story stone building with walls two feet thick, was reportedly built in 1856 by the Castle family from Lansing, Mich., some sort of accommodations run by them also existed earlier. In May 1854 Mrs. Frances A. Ferry Castle wrote, "We rented our house on the first of the year. It is kept in the best of style [and] rents for $100 per month." Although

"transient," the "custom is very good yet," she added and one day served dinner "at the price of $1 per meal" to forty-one persons but the average number was "more often 17." Nine months later there could be no question about the Castle family running such a business at Forest Home because she wrote, "We has somewhere between 16 to 18 for dinner, I can't tell which, and 13 tonight." Joseph Henry Jackson, *Anybody's Gold* (New York: Appleton-Century Co., 1941), 376; Mrs. J. L. Sargent, *Amador County History* (Jackson, Calif.: Amador Ledger, 1927), 47; Otheto Weston, *Mother Lode Album* (Stanford: Stanford University Press, 1948), 124-25; Castle Family papers, manuscript, May 27, 1854, Feb. 24, 1855; Gudde, *California Gold Camps,* 119; *Amador Ledger, May 9, 1857.*

19. William M'Collum, *California As I Saw It* (Los Gatos: Talisman Press, 1960), 167; Gudde, *California Gold Camps,* 338-40; *Register of Mines and Minerals, Amador County* (San Francisco: State Mining Bureau, 1903), map.

20. Ibid.

21. Borthwick, *The Gold Hunters,* 167.

22. Both Adams Express Company and the Michigan Bar Canal Company also had offices in Michigan Bar, alongside two saloons, a drug store, a tenpin alley and a livery stable. Although the Sons of Temperance Hall, used as a church, was built later, at one time a "flourishing school" existed as well as the private residences of twenty-one families. All this information appears on an undated California pictorial letter sheet designed for miners to use when writing the folks back home. Visible in the cover illustration of Michigan Bar are signs for "Drugs, Hawley & Co., the Canal Company, the Valentine Company and the Cosumnes House." Mildred B. Hoover and H. E. Rensch, *Historic Spots in California* (Stanford: Stanford University Press, 1966), 301; Joseph A. Baird, Jr., *Bibliography of Pictorial Letter Sheets, 1849-69* (San Francisco: David Magee, 1967).

23. Castle Family papers.

24. Mason, *Amador County History,* 39. In 1855 Rev. Peter Y. Cool, a Methodist minister, married Sarah Mahala Aram, daughter of Col. Joseph Aram, an 1846 pioneer. He kept a small pocket daybook of his mining and church activities in Amador County in 1851 and his wife wrote a biographical sketch of him in 1883. Peter Y. Cool, Pocket Day-Book and Letters, manuscript, The Aram Papers 27; Sarah Mahala Aram Cool, "Biographical Sketch and Frontier Life, Incidents and Work," manuscript; Richard Coke Wood, *Calaveras* (Sonora: Mother Lode Press, 1955), 96; for information about the Aram family's overland trip see also Margaret Hecox, *California Caravan* (San Jose: Harlan-Young Press, 1966).

25. Gudde, *California Gold Camps,* 398; Records of nineteenth-century Methodist ministers, Methodist Archives, Drew University; Methodist records, Pacific School of Religion, Berkeley, Calif.; Anthony, *Fifty Years of Methodism,* 93.

26. Apparently the two brothers-in-law exchanged pulpits frequently during their first year in California. Rev. George B. Taylor, who came to California via Panama with the Fish family, began his ministry at Drytown. He served as minister for Ione in 1853. According to Fish, in Jan. 1854, "last week the trustee purchased a building for the church instead of the canvas house [used]

for two years." Isaac Fish, Journal, Vol. 2, 1852-54, manuscript, (Feb. 10, 1853) 51, 52; Anthony, *Fifty Years of Methodism,* 93-94; Ione Methodist Church, *Celebration of the 93rd Year* (Ione: the Community Methodist Church, 1945), 7-8.

27. Naomi Fish, Journal, manuscript.

28. I. Fish, Journal, 55; Ione Methodist Church, *Celebration of the 93rd Year,* 7-8.

29. Sandford Fleming, *God's Church* (Philadelphia: The Judson Press, 1949), 133.

30. *The Golden Era,* a literary weekly published in San Francisco, prided itself on providing "something worthwhile to read." A chatty and informal journal, *The Era's* eight narrow columns of small type served as a forum for many writers, including a number who became prominent, such as Ambrose Bierce, Ina D. Coolbirth, and Joaquin Miller. However, the majority of the routine writing was done by women, who did not use their real names. Aside from teaching, a literary career was the only respectable profession open to women before the Civil War. It could provide an independent, albeit small, source of income as well as friendships outside the family while being a self-sufficient and creative activity. It was the one place where feminine ambition could be allowed public exposure, but only with the use of a pen name. Franklin Walker, *San Francisco's Literary Frontier* (New York: Alfred Knopf, 1939), 20, 24, 29, 130, 135, 180, 187; Ann Douglas, *The Feminization of American Culture* (New York: Alfred Knopf Inc., 1977), 113.

31. Encouraging aspiring writers from Arizona to Oregon, *The Era* has been credited with doing more to develope writers on the Pacific coast than any of its rivals and almost everyone served an apprenticeship with this journal. It was considered "indispensible to miners and farmers in the hinterland." In 1860 Daggett and Foard sold *The Era,* which was resold six years later; it was published until 1893. Walker, *San Francisco's Literary Frontier,* 117, 119, 145.

32. According to Rev. Isaac B. Fish in 1854, "Our sabbath school and society here have been as interesting as any I ever had charge of in my life." Fish, Journal, 55.

33. Sacramento audiences "appeared to be well pleased with the various views presented . . . the unbounded success which the Panorama has met with is a guarantee of its intrinsic merit," wrote on reviewer. This panorama was painted in "transparent oil colors at enormous expense" by George M. Weaver and featured forty scenes, running a total length of half a mile. In Sacramento it was shown first at McNulty's Music Hall and then in a "Pavilion on the Alley between I and J [streets]." The "Grand Panorama" was first shown in San Francisco in January 1854. After the Sacramento and Ione showings, the panorama would be shown in the southern mining region. "As there is now an unusual dearth of amusements among us, the Panorama will doubtless attract crowds," according to the newspaper story. John Doble paid $1 when he attended a show in Volcano Oct. 5, 1853, which he called "a panoramic view of crossing the plains." These gigantic panoramas were apparently highly popular amusements because in 1852 another, "The Great National Revolving Mirror" of 2,000 scenes in California and the "Routes to and from by land and sea," toured the Midwest. Advertised as the "only

reliable and correct series of Panoramic views ever painted of the Land of Gold," it covered 190,000 feet of canvas and cost $11,000. *Pike County Union,* Nov. 3, 1852; *Sacramento Pictorial Union,* June 27, July 1, July 3, 1854; George R. MacMinn, *The Theater of the Golden Era in California* (Caldwell, Ida.: The Caxton Press, 1941), 226.

34. Carl Meyer, *Bound for Sacramento* (Claremont, Calif.: Saunders Studio Press, 1938), 220. Five months later, William Lobenstein, who sold "groceries and implements" to miners for three years, wrote from a camp near Dry Creek: "As miners mainly depend upon the rain to wash their dirt, have up throughout a period of nine months, a failure of it in Winter when it is anxiously looked for is a great disappointment to the miners all over the county. When mining is stopped, everything else is dull and depressed." As a result of dry weather during the fall and winter of 1854, Lobenstein added, "There appears to be at present a general depression in business all over the county, money tight and provisions dear and labor scarce." William Lobenstein, *Extracts from the Diary of. . . .* (privately printed, 1920), 67.

35. Daughters from nineteenth-century evangelical families often felt they led useless and meaningless lives while their brothers were encouraged to be dedicated to service in the name of God. Yet charitable work required a woman to be "too worldly to be considered moral" while politics was not considered women's sphere. This left few alternatives aside from attempting to reform society by both word and deed as evidenced through a "missionary spirit." Exactly what "woman's mission" encompassed resulted in much debate both in England and America during the nineteenth century by men as well as women. These views were widely promoted by Sarah Lewis, whose *Woman's Mission* had been reprinted in thirteen editions by 1849. For additional information about women's role, see Sarah Lewis, "Woman's Mission," in *Strong Minded Women & Other Lost Voices,* ed. Janet Murray (New York: Pantheon Books, 1982), 23-28; Harvey Green, *The Light of the Home* (New York: Pantheon Books, 1983); Burstyn, *Victorian Education and the Ideal of Womanhood,* 138.

36. *Godey's Lady's Book,* edited by Sarah Josepha Hale, was one of the most popular and long-lasting of the nineteenth century magazines for women. It included fiction, poetry, commentary, book reviews and advice on social etiquette as well as needlework patterns and hand-tinted fashion plates. Hale, who assumed the editorship in 1836 (a position she held for forty years), advocated women as public school teachers, fought for married women to retain property rights, started the first day nursery and, among numerous other causes, helped with the establishment of Vassar College. *Graham's Magazine* was published by George Rex Graham (who invented the graham cracker) beginning in 1841; both Edgar Allen Poe and Bayard Taylor served on its staff at times. This magazine also offered light essays and fiction, travel articles, verse, biography, art criticism, and editorial commentary as well as colored fashion plates. Originally a men's magazine, it appealed more to women. Finley, *The Lady of Godey's,* 17, 63; *Dictionary of American Biography,* Vol. 7, 473-74; Taylor, *El Dorado,* ix.

37. This was the only time Lorena mentioned her childhood in Pennsylvania during the 1830s. Her use of the word "daguerrotyped" near the end

of this column refers to both an early form of photography as well as the resulting image, produced by exposing a silver or copper-covered plate, made sensitive with iodine and bromine and developed with the vapor of mercury.

38. *The Christian Advocate and Journal* served as the official voice of the Methodist Church. Although 1853 editions carried news about "California Affairs," the Methodists also published regional newspapers.

39. These establishments were more sympathetic in treatment than many in the male-dominated medical profession of the nineteenth century. The water cure also allowed for the termination of unwanted pregnancies while seeking to aide the wide variety of ailments and diseases of the reproductive system. Participating with others in the water cure, which treated the whole person rather than just the symptoms, also helped alleviate the isolation of American domestic life for women while providing mutual support. The *Water-Cure Journal,* later called *The Herald of Health,* was published intermittently between 1845 and 1910. In 1854 the subscription price was $1.00 a year. Kathryn Kish Sklar, *Catherine Beecher—A Study in American Domesticity.* (New York: W. W. Norton & Co., 1973), 206-07; Joseph S. Van Why, "Introduction" in Catherine and Harriet Beecher Stowe, *The American Woman's Home.* Reprint. (Hartford, Conn.: Stowe-Day Foundation, 1975); *The Pacific,* July 28, 1854.

40. Ibid.

41. This editorial entitled "Strong-Minded Females" appeared in *The Golden Era* during the fall of 1854 and is quoted in MacMinn, *The Theater of the Golden Era in California,* 285.

42. On another occasion, after speaking twice, Pellet took up a collection to "defray her expenses" and received $71, which Franklin A. Buck considered "a pretty good day's work." When this "Yankee trader" heard Pellet speak another time, he added: "Women's rights appear to be a hard ticket but I think they will vote *in mass* in a few years . . . as the women here are in the minority they have the right to do just as they please. So Miss Pellet has dropped that subject and lectures on temperance. She is so pleased at the perfect state of freedom in which women live here that she is getting up a scheme to liberate 5,000 New England girls from the slavery in which they live and bring them out here. Glorious idea!" Buck added, "When she took her stand on a dry goods box and commenced talking everyone ran. The saloons and stores were deserted. No dog fight ever drew together such a crowd. . . . Great country for women, isn't it? What an opportunity this state presents for a woman of genius . . . while we poor men have to work at least three days in the week to get a living." Buck, *A Yankee Trader in the Gold Rush,* 135, 149.

Major Edwin A. Sherman provided a post-script when he wrote, "Miss Pellet lectured on temperance for a short time and then went to Nicaragua as aid or something to the filibuster William Walker, who was captured and forfeited his life, being shot. What her career was after that I am not informed." Sherman, "Reminiscences," 165. "Strong-minded" was the adjective applied to any woman who spoke her mind openly and publicly during the 1850s and was used both in America and in England. See Muray, *Strong Minded Women and Other Lost Voices.*

43. When the Robinson Family, identified as F. L. Robinson & Co., played in Pike County, Ill., in June 1851 a featured performer was "La Petite Em-

ma, a beautiful and accomplished Danseuse.'' The two entertainments at Pittsfield were given by thirty-six persons and horses in an ''immense waterproof pavilion capable of accommodating 11000 persons.'' The fifty cents admission included a ''moral domestic Temperance Drama'' entitled *The Fallen Saved.* MacMinn, *The Theater of the Golden Era,* 452; *Pike County Union,* June 11, 1851.

44. Mary S. Bennett's seminary for fifty boarding students opened in March 1854 and was originalliy located on N Street. *Sacramento Illustrated,* reprint ed. Caroline Wenzel (Sacramento: Sacramento Book Collectors Club, 1950, 97; *Sacramento Daily Union,* Feb. 21, 1854; *Quincy Prospector,* June 2, 1855.

45. Benson's Ferry, one of several across the Mokelumne River, was started in 1849 by Edward Stokes and A. M. Wood. They sold it the following year to John A. Benson, murdered in 1859 by an employee. Hoover and Rensch, *Historic Spots in California,* 374. A magnetic telegraph line, one of two in northern California during the 1850s, connected San Francisco and Sacramento via San Jose and Stockton. Built in 1852-53 by the California State Telegraph Company, it crossed approximately 210 miles and began operation in October 1853. Joseph A. McGowan, *History of the Sacramento Valley,* Vol. 1 (New York: Lewis Publishing Co., 1961), 167.

46. When Elvira Bradway joined her husband, Dr. Joseph R. Bradway, an 1853 emigrant, in California is unknown but only a handful of her letters survive in a collection of his correspondence. E. and J. R. Bradway, Letters, manuscript, May 23, 1857.

47. *Sacramento Daily Union,* Feb. 28, 1855.

48. Feb. 8 and 14, 1855, letters from Dr. Enoch H. Pardee to his fiance and distant cousin Mary Pardee of Cuyahoga Falls, Ohio. Dr. Pardee, a San Francisco oculist whose office was located at 202 Pacific Street, treated Lorena's husband for an eye problem in January-February, 1855. Three letters in the archives of the Pardee Home Museum in Oakland, Calif., provide information about the doctor's arrangements for John Clement Bowmer of ''Iohone'' to escort Mary Pardee and her brother to California that spring.

49. According to Dr. Pardee, his patient, whose ''eyes will be well in about 2 or 3 weeks,'' was ''going to return after his family about the middle of March — he says it will afford him the greatest pleasure of awaiting on my most esteem friend, *Mary.''* Dr. Pardee explained a week later that he meant Bowmer's ''previous family — his children . . . he is a widower.'' The 1850 California census shows John C. Bowmer with his younger brother, William J., and their father, William, in Eldorado County. According to the 1850 census for Grant County, Wisc., John C. Bomer, a native of Kentucky, owned property valued at $600. He and wife Betsey were the parents of Martha 11; Thaddeus S., 9, and John Bomer, 7. The firm of Bowmer and Wayne had been in business before 1854 and the Store House stood on Lot No. 1 in Block No. 1 of Ione. In 1855 the firm's property was assessed at $1,300 and the lot valued at $600; they paid a total tax of $19.90. Benjamin F. Wayne, Bowmer's partner, was a native of Indiana. In the 1850 California census he was listed as being in Placerville and vicinity while the 1854 Sacramento County assessment rolls show him as living in Cosumnes with personal property totaling $1,500. Pardee Letter, Feb. 14, 1855; *Index to the California Census*

of 1850 (Baltimore: Genealogical Publishing Co., 1972), 149; 1850 Wisconsin Census, roll 998, line 291; l850 California Census, 256; Hayes, *Hayes,* 149; 1855 Amador County Assessment Rolls, 82; 1854 Sacramento County Assessment Rolls, 99.

50. The *Golden Gate,* with C. P. Pattison as commander, was a new addition to the Pacific Mail Steamship Company fleet in 1851 and made her first trip December 1. Built in New York by William H. Webb, this vessel was 270 feet long with a beam breadth of forty feet. She could accommodation 300 passengers with cabin space and carry a total of 800 should "sofas and steerage" be pressed into service. *San Francisco Daily Herald,* Feb. 26, 1855; Ernest A. Wiltsee, *Gold Rush Steamers of the Pacific* (Lawrence, Mass.: Quarterman Publications Inc., 1938), 61-62.

51. For comments about what nineteenth century women did and did not include in their diaries, see Lillian Schlissel, "Diaries of Frontier Women" in *Woman's Being, Woman's Place,* ed. Mary Kelley (Boston: G. K. Hull & Co., 1979), 53-66.

52. Rev. H. Holcombe Rhees[e], formerly a successful Stockton attorney, joined the Baptist Church in 1853, submitting his letter from the Mt. Holly, N. J., church. He served as Sunday school clerk, superintendent and trustee of the Stockton Church before being ordained to the "work of the gospel ministry" Nov. 4, 1854. He went to the Ione Valley congregation that December and received his official appointment from the Baptist Home Mission Society March 1 the following year. Sandford Fleming, *God's Gold, The Story of Baptist Beginnings in California* (Philadelphia: The Judson Press, 1949), 123-24; Mason, *History of Amador County,* 269.

53. Lorena found the community of Quincy to be small, also, although it boasted about the houses being numbered. At one time Quincy consisted of ten to twelve dwellings. The remains of thirty fireplaces supposedly have been found along the wide main thoroughfare, appropriately called Broadway. A stage stop on the road north out of Ione, it had a population of about twenty-five when Lorena visited there. According to other reports, this settlement also included saloons, stores, several real estate agencies, offices for doctors and lawyers, a hotel and a lyceum. Quincy disappeared from Amador County assessment records in 1856, a casualty, along with nearby Muletown, of "Ione's Bloody Squatters War" over ownership of lands in the Arroyo Seco Grant. When given a choice, residents of the valley agreed that Ione should survive so the "twin towns" were vacated, all brick buildings and structures destroyed and the land completely cleared, leaving little evidence that Quincy and Muletown ever existed. The most complete file of the *Quincy Prospector* is located at the Huntington Library. Mason, *History of Amador County,* 192; "Ione's Bloody Squatters War," *Focus Magazine, Stockton Sunday Record,* May 18, 1969.

54. Plans for a railroad across Panama were first discussed in 1849 with work beginning in 1850, financed by a group of New York businessmen. During the first year more than 600 workmen were employed on this project and William Swain, returning East late in 1850 reported construction underway for a number of railroad depots. Although the 1855 advertisement quoted a six-hour trip, eventually this was reduced to three hours when the railroad was

completed that year. During its ten years of operation, an estimated 400,000 travelers enjoyed an easier trip, avoiding the necessity to walk or ride mules along jungle trails before transferring to boats to reach the coast. In 1855 Rodney Glisan, an Army assistant surgeon, found it took six hours "in tranistu" to cover forty-nine miles due to "difficult of passing over steep grades . . . at these places engines are reversed and the train runs back some distance when the effort was renewed with increased force." When Glisan made this trip the railroad was "in good order," according to a May 16 report. J. S. Holiday, *The World Rushed In* (New York: Simon and Shuster, 1981), 418, 435n, 437; *San Francisco Daily Herald*, Feb. 26, 1855; Rodney Glisan, *Journal of Army Life* (San Francisco: A. L. Bancroft & Co., 1874), 180; *Sacramento Daily Union*, May 16, 1855.

55. This steamer would have been the *Wilson G. Hunt* rather than the *Thomas Hunt*, although both were owned by the California Steam Navigation Company (the later was disposed of in 1855). Built in New York as a Coney Island excursion steamer in 1849, the 450-ton *Wilson G. Hunt* had a white enamel and gold leaf cabin interior with stained glass windows. In 1858 she went to British Columbia, returning to San Francisco nearly twenty years later but burned in 1890. *San Francisco Daily Herald*, Feb. 26, 1855; Jerry Mac-Mullen, *Paddle-Wheel Days in California* (Stanford: Stanford University Press, 1944), 50, 53; *Sacramento Daily Union*, June 7.

56. The *John L. Stevens* (the name was also spelled Stephens) was a "new and splendid first-class" steamship in January 1853, "intended to shortly sail for the Pacific." Owned by the Pacific Mail Steamship Company, she registered at 2,500 tons with a "great breadth" that "produces a wonderful improvement in the deck accommodations . . . [it is] vastly more agreeable and spacious than . . . any modern vessel." There were 350 "commodious" berths but a most unusual and luxurious feature was the "extensive suite of baths . . . which can be supplied with hot or cold water in a moment." The *Stevens* could also supply fresh water for passengers, crew, and machinery. Designed to meet the competition of the Vanderbilt Line on the Panama run, the *Stevens* finally arrived in San Francisco April 4, 1854. Although fares had decreased due to competition, in February 1855, the cost, including transportation across Panama, on similar ships came to $300 for first cabin and $250 for second cabin accommodations with a $150 fee for steerage. Rodney Glisan, an army assistant surgeon, thought the *Stevens,* commanded by Capt. R. H. Pearson, "a magnificent vessel — very large and kept in perfect order with fine airy staterooms and a promenade on the hurricane deck." He reported the food was good but he paid twenty-five cents a pound for ice. *The Illustrated News,* Jan. 8, 1853; Wiltsee, *Gold Rush Steamers,* 103, 130, 160; Glisan, *Journal of Army Life,* 190.

The *Golden Age* ran aground on Apr. 28, 1855, near Jicaron Island, 216 miles north of Panama, staving in her bottom. Glisan, a passenger on the *Stevens,* reported she was found "securely on a sand beach with her bow almost out of the water." The *Stevens* was initially delayed because "we are now reshipping her passengers and freight" and Glisan estimated returning to Panama would detain them three days. This meant nearly 1,900 passenger on board when the *Stevens* turned around, not to leave for San Francisco again until May 3, with a stop at Tobago to take on more coal. Glisan, *Journal of Army Life,* 190-94; Marine Intelligence, *San Francisco Daily Herald,* May 17, 1855; *Sacramento Daily Union,* May 16, 1.

Lorena's husband also escorted Mary Elizabeth Pardee and her brother, Horace, who met him at Dunkirk, N. Y. In a letter of introduction to Miss Pardee, her future husband, Dr. Enoch H. Pardee, wrote: "Mary you can place implicit confidence in what Mr. B. tells you as he is a man of honor and integrity he brings with him his partners family & a young lady who is a relation — I think you will find them to be the best of company and will feel much pleased in their society . . . Mr. Browmer has been lately married so he will have a load-stone to call him back as soon as possible." E. H. Pardee, Letter, Feb. 29, 1855. Lorena did not mention any female relative coming west with John Clement Bowmer so this plan may have fallen through. *San Francisco Weekly Bullentin,* May 17.

57. The Amador County Assessment Roll for 1856 shows J. C. Bowmer owned personal property valued at $300. He paid a poll tax of twenty-five cents but no military tax. Assessment Roll, 13.

58. Ben Bowen, "A Record of Life Commenced at Fort John," manuscript, 41.

59. Daniel Stewart and Company began business in Ione in April 1852. The Stewart store of 1856 had iron shutters and was built of brick made in nearby Muletown. Mason, *Amador County History,* 49.

60. Spencer Richards, June 26, 1855, letter to "Friend Warren," manuscript.

61. Mason, *Amador County History,* 36, 83-88; Gudde, *California Gold Camps,* 282-83.

62. Ibid.

63. According to Bowen: "There came past us to day 8 men who were after some greasers who in the most brutal and inhuman manner killed five men and one woman at Rancheria last night also broke open a safe and took out from 7 or 8,000 dollars. This makes the second tragedy within three weeks which has taken place in the neighborhood — three men, killed and robbed, one at Upper rancheria a short time ago and all made their escape." Bowen, "A Record of Life," manuscript, 81.

64. Burgess' version tells of "A party of several Mexicans having two Americans for leaders entered a small camp called Rancheria, broke into a house and killed all of its men and one woman. The next day they pursued them. The whole counties of Calaveras and Amador were in arms and awful were their doings. Alike, innocent and guilty, were shot or hung wherever they could be found." William Hubert Burgess, Letters and Note Book, manuscript.

65. Chile Flat, part of Drytown, inhabited by Chilenos who had nothing in common with the Mexicans, was set afire, including the Catholic Church, while all houses belonging to the Mexicans in Rancheria were destroyed. Mexicans were escorted across the Mokelumne River as well as into Eldorado County to the north. As a result of the Rancheria murders, according to a local history: "The community became terribly excited and moved to deeds which were afterwards looked upon with regret. . . . Most of this wanton kill-

ing, arson and driving people from their homes was to allow the attackers to seize control of the property, basically the rich gold claims of those they so ran off. Mason, *Amador County History,* 83-88.

66. The Settlers' League was formed in Amador County to protest the existence of the Arroyo Seco land grant, which had been purchased from the original owner in 1843 by Andres Pico (brother of the last Mexican governor of California) for "500 heard of long horn cattle." Although Pico sold off some of the land, he fought to keep the rest. The court case reached the U. S. Supreme Court in October 1856 but was dismissed two years later, apparently without ever being considered. The Arroyo Seco, one of many Mexican land grants in California before 1846, was called "a floating grant" because the lines shifted each time an improvement was made. The problems over ownership of the land within this grant continued well into the 1860s, when many settlers gave up their claims and left Amador County. In 1856 Henry S. Woodward, Lorena's uncle, served on a committee to "prevent Don Andres Pico from locating a pretended Spanish land grant upon the lands we have chosen for our homes." A mass meeting was held in Ione on June 17. *Focus Magazine;* Cowan, *Ranchos of California,* 242-48; *Amador Ledger,* June 21, 1856.

67. All of the women in Lorena's family married in California. In 1856 her sister, Caroline, became the wife of John J. M'Neely, a veteran of the Mexican War who came to California in 1849, while sister Amanda, married William Matthews (date uncertain). Their mother, Susannah, married her second husband, Rev. S. W. Hull, a Baptist minister, in 1856. The cousin referred to was Mary Jane Lithgow, married in 1857 to Josephus Hoffman Rickey, whose family were early settlers of the Ione area. Lorena's youngest sister Sarah Louise became the bride of Daniel Whitlatch May 28, 1857. Hayes, *Hayes,* 149-50; Hoover, Lithgow Genealogy and papers; Eckland Family papers.

68. Court Records, Amador County Courthouse, Jackson, Calif.

69. According to the court records, Lorena's husband claimed the note had not been signed with his "permission or consent and said he did not owe" Fox, who believed the money had been used by the partners (Wayne and Bowmer) to pay Bowmer's expenses "home & back again & of Wayne's family coming to this country." The plaintiff added he had "no knowledge or suspicion that Wayne had no right to use the name of the firm in signing the note." He claimed Lorena's husband had not "denied his liability and promised to pay it soon." C. H. Misner, who signed the promissory note, testified that Wayne had "no authority to sign his [Bowmer's] name to the note. He understood from Wayne that the money . . . was for partnership purposes of the firm." Court Records.

70. The Fifth Judicial District was divided in 1859 although three years earlier the State Legislature considered a proposal to limit it to only Amador and Calaveras counties. Mason, *Amador County History,* 284; *Amador Ledger,* Feb. 23, Mar. 2, 1855.

71. No legal notice about the dissolution of the Bowmer-Wayne partnership appeared in the local newspaper.

72. Independence Flat, adjacent to Railroad Flat, in Calaveras County was located on a tributary to the south fork of the Mokelumne River. Prospecting

began here in 1852 but without much success. Gudde, *California Gold Camps,* 166; Eckland Family papers.

73. Reputed to be one of the wildest places in Calaveras County, Jesus Maria, settled in the early 1850s by Mexicans, was part of a large placer mining region. The one long street with business houses on either side included several stores, a blacksmith shop, hotel, dance halls, and fandango houses. Jesus Maria once served as a trading center for other mining areas and had its own Chinese miners' colony. William H. Burgess, who visited this settlement while on a hunting trip four years earlier, reported it "a lively mining camp." He provided the following colorful description of Jesus Maria: "The place can be summed up in the following words: tents, gambling, whiskey, cigarritos, guitars and spanish speaking people of both sexes, in and around the place Fandangos [dance houses] red sashes round men's waists, knives, pistols, drunken men with mexican spurs on; horses tied to tent poles here and there, loafers everywhere. All mexican or chilian mining camps are about the same character. . . ." Burgess, Letters and Note Book, 117; Emmett P. Joy, "Echoes from Calaveras Ghost Towns," typescript, 1966.

74. The "Big Tree Grove" is located beyond Murphy's in Calaveras County, along a road described in 1857 as "mountainous yet in fine condition for a horseback or buggy ride." In addition to the giant sequoias, another tourist attraction was the hotel at the base of "the Big Tree." There "a fine spring floor had been laid to dance upon, which with the stump was covered with a large arbor of evergreens, beautifully illuminated with many candles among the boughs." Thirty-two people could dance on top the stump, which measured seventy-six feet in circumference, according to a San Francisco newspaper story. It took five men twenty-five days to cut down this tree and a fifty-foot section was taken to New York and Paris for exhibition but the entrepenuer, a Captain Handford, "has met a just reward for his vandalism by losing a fortune in the enterprise. . . . Upon the trunk, about one hundred feet from the base is situated a bar-room and ten pin alley." *San Francisco Weekly Bulletin,* June 20, 1857; "The Mammoth Trees of Calaveras" in J. M. Hutchings, *Scenes of Wonder and Curiosity in California* (San Francisco: Hutchings & Rosenfield, 1860) 1-55.

75. Seven of Mrs. Withington's "views of Ione City and Valley," perhaps taken later than when this photo artist rented Lorena's house, survive as steroptican cards in the photo collection of the Huntington Library. *Amador County Ledger,* July 25, 1857.

76. Ibid.

77. The Baptist congregation still needed "a house of worship of our own in the village — we cannot sustain a Sabbath School." This annual report concluded "the most complete harmony and unanimity in our relations as a church" prevailed as well as "some prosperity" while the outlook for the future was considered more encouraging "than ever before since our organization." *Minutes* of the 1857 annual meeting, San Francisco Baptist Association, May 7-10 in San Francisco, Appendix — Digest of Letters, 9, 10.

78. Ibid., 16, 17; *Minutes,* Sacramento Valley Baptist Association, Sept. 12-14, 1857, typescript among research notes of Sandford Fleming (location of original unknown).

79. These churches had "long felt that we ought to have more association so as more conveniently to accommodate our churches in their widely separated localities and the more efficiently to promote the interests of the Redeemer's Kingdom." Ibid.

80. This state fair offered premiums amounting to $7,981 as compared with $4,660 paid during the first fair of 1854 at the San Francisco Music Hall with a cattle show at the Mission Dolores. These fairs were organized by the State Agricultural Society, which had 866 members by 1857. The 1857 fair was well attended with accommodations even provided by Stockton churches as well as by the fair managers, with mattresses on the floors. In addition to specimens of sugar from the San Francisco Refinery, the exhibits included "some ears of corn from Ione Valley [that] would tickle the fancy of a man from the region of 'hog and hominy' . . . one hundred and nine bushels of such corn was gathered from one acre." The fair ended with a ball, attended by 400 couples and "the sight was magnificent — seldom in California has there been an assemblage of ladies as were there present." Rudy Miskulin, "History of the California State Fair," typescript; *San Francisco Weekly Bulletin,* Oct. 3, 10.

81. Captain Charles M. Weber (1814-1881) developed the city of Stockton on land purchased from his partner, who had obtained the French Camp grant in 1843. The subject of many biographies and historical works, Captain Weber's career has been extensively researched. His home still stands in Stockton but the majority of the furnishings have been given by descendants to the San Joaquin County Historical Society and are currently exhibited in the new Weber Rooms, opened in 1986 at the Museum in Lodi, Calif. See George P. Hammond, *The Weber Era in Stockton History* (Berkeley: Friends of Bancroft Library, 1982).

82. Cloth ceilings and walls were not uncommon for houses built during the 1850s in California both in the mining regions as well as in the cities. In describing an 1854 fire at the Western House, located on the Sacramento-Placerville Road, Morris Sleight wrote, ". . . the House was on Fire, it is lined throught (like all California Houses) with Muslin, and would take but a few moments to Spread through the whole House. . . ." Mar. 11, 1854, letter from Morris Sleight to his wife, Hannah, of Naperville, Ill., manuscript.

83. Sept. 14, 1856, letter from Dewitt Seaver to his father in Darien, Wisc., Seaver Gold Rush Letters, manuscript.

84. Lorena now faced a problem encountered by nearly every woman during the Victorian Era because the widely-held ideal of womanhood meant that "once married [she] received little respect for her accomplishments." She also had little or no role in helping her husband with his business, according to the dictates of the prevailing "Cult of Domesticity," which relegated her back into the home as her primary place of duty and influence. Burstyn, *Victorian Education and the Ideal the Ideal of Womanhood,* 138.

THE CALIFORNIA YEARS/DIARY

1. The road Lorena's company followed after leaving the Carson Emigrant Trail across the Sierra took them through Volcano, a prosperous mining community of 300 houses and businesses "situated in a very pretty Valley surrounded by high pine capped hills." In 1852 a "new emigrant road" joined the old one at Leek Springs; this route led along the dividing ridges between Sutter and Dry Creeks. Doble, *Journal and Letters,* 76.

Wells West, Lorena's cousin, recalled, "Our road was mostly down hill to the mining country. We arrived at Willow Spring flat, Amador County, California, September 23, ending a 2,200 mile journey of five months and nineteen days." West, who spent the first winter with a brother in a mining camp near Ione, later mined at Michigan Bar. He spent two years "riding after cattle" in the San Joaquin Valley near Firebaugh but enlisted in 1862 in the "California 100," a company recruited to fight on the Union side in the Civil War; West was one of only twenty-three men in the original company to survive. After working as a carpenter in Chilicothe, Mo., he returned to California, settling in the Lakeport area. West, "Autobiography"; A. O. Carpenter and Percy H. Milberry, *History of Mendocino and Lake Counties* (Los Angeles: History Research Co., 1914), 860.

Located on California State Highway 16, Drytown took its name from nearby Dry Creek, so-called because in summer water disappeared, making this a gold mining region of dry diggings. The first site in Amador County where gold was discovered, Drytown's mines could yield as much as $100 of gold in a single pan and "an average good return" ranged from nothing to $114 in two days. This area, "just on the skirts of the rough mountain region and the country of canons, gulches, canadas and divides" was mined so extensively that by 1857 its prosperity came to an end. In 1849 Bayard Taylor found 200-300 miners at Drytown during the winter season and the village "laid out with some regularity with taverns, stores, butchers' shops and monte tables." John Doble reported Drytown in 1852 had 200 houses as well as the first stamp mill and post office. Gudde, *California Gold Camps,* 101, 102; Taylor, *Eldorado,* Vol. 2, 16-17; Doble, *Journal and Letters,* 108; Hoover and Rensch, *Historic Spots in California,* 30.

Drytown, twelve miles from Jackson on the road to Sacramento, was the oldest town of any size in Amador County. Because of its proximity to Sutter's Mill, where gold was discovered, mining began in the Drytown area in 1848. Its ravines and gulches yielded rich gold deposits near the surface. Drytown consisted of a motley collection of log cabins and shake shanties. Rev. Peter Y. Cool in November 1851 wrote about the dance halls and noted, "We saw the degradation of females as we passed up the sidewalk." By 1854 several brick buildings had been constructed, along with a Catholic church and a general meeting hall, also used as a school. However, Drytown was considered "a worked-out place" by 1856 and never recovered following a fire the next year. Mason, *Amador County History,* 229; Gudde, *California Gold Camps,* 102; Cool, Journal, Nov. 4, 1851.

2. The Methodist Church in Ione Valley was built in 1853 on land pur-

chased for $1,000 from Thomas Rickey. Rev. William Hurlburt had been sent from Sacramento to organize a congregation the preceding year. When church services were held in March 1853 the initial membership totaled seventeen. Although a Baptist, Lorena may well have held the same views as Charles Peters, a miner in Jackson who helped organize the Methodist Church there. Although baptized a Baptist, Peters announced, "All religious creeds look alike to me . . . there may be some differences in the route taken but all the paths lead to the same destination." Apparently many former residents of Pike County, Ill., settled in Amador County, because graveyards contain names of families known by the Hays, including Uriah Francis Elledge, a member of the extensive Elledge clan of Barry, Ill. California Census records for the Ione area in 1860 also contain names similar to those of 1850s residents of Pike county. *Celebration of the 93rd Year,* Ione Methodist Church 1,6; Charles Peters, *Autobiography,* 16, 17.

3. In 1855 a Rev. J. J. Cleveland was listed as the Methodist Episcopal minister for Mariposa. 1855 *Minutes* of the California Annual Conference (San Francisco; Alta California Pioneer Press, 1855), 2.

4. Working as a domestic servant was one of the few ways a woman could earn money in the nineteenth century but was not considered suitable employment for a "lady." Sarepta's wages of a $50 a month would have been considered good because six years later a servant girl in Weaverville was being paid $40, while in San Francisco one could be hired for $25-30 a month. Buck, *A Yankee Trader,* 179. Schools were not established at Ione, Volcano, and Sutter Creek until 1853. According to a local history of Amador County, "School teaching, though holding so important a position in social economy, is a profession that is little honored." Mason, *History of Amador County,* 17.

5. This was a regional publication of the Methodist Church, edited by M. C. Briggs and S. P. Simonds of San Francisco. Peter Y. Cool, Journal.

6. Because gold attracted so many miners from all walks of life, California farms were neglected and could not provide enough food for the growing numbers of emigrants. Imported food stuffs carried by stores in the mines included "dried apples and dried pealed peaches from Chili, pressed in the shape of cheese," according to Mrs. James Caples, an 1849 pioneer. In 1853 almost everything "consumed in California" came from the eastern states or from foreign countries, according to a newspaper clipping in the scrapbook compiled by J. Winfield Davis. Fresh fruit was imported from Manila and Tahiti with dried fruit, beans, and flour from Chile and tea and rice from China. Caples, Reminiscences, typescript; *San Francisco Chronicle,* Sept. 11, 1881, in second volume of Davis scrapbook.

7. Willow Springs was the name given to a community, a creek and a "flat" in Amador County about five miles northeast of Amador City on the road to Fiddletown. While gold and copper were both mined here, it was better known for its fine hotel, the Willow Springs House, built by William Jennings and a partner remembered in history only by the last name of Richardson. On the main road from Drytown and Fiddletown to Sacramento, it changed hands frequently. The printed invitation to the "Social Ball" of Nov. 9, 1853, listed the names of twenty-eight managers form nineteen communities with Dr. C. M. Fox and F(rank) Walker serving as "floor managers." It was addressed

to "Miss S. Hays," who had also received an earlier invitation to an Oct. 21 ball at the United State Hotel, located in Fiddletown. The handwritten invitation arrived in a lavender envelope embossed with roses and was addressed to Sarepta Hayes at Cooks Bar. Apparently neither of the sisters attended the October party. In the 1850s tickets for these events usually cost $5 and $6, including supper. (Sister Sarepta also received invitations to a Dec. 1, 1854, ball at the "Kremlin Hall" in Cook's Bar and a Jan. 8, 1855, party held at 5 P.M. in Nebraska Hall, Michigan Bar. This last was to benefit the Michigan Bar and Cook's Bar Division of the Sons of Temperance.) Sarepta was the last of the Hays sisters to marry when she became the wife of John Scudder Shoemaker, a Reno, Nev., druggist, in November 1866. Gudde, *California Gold Camps,* 372; Mason, *History of Amador County,* 232; Ball invitations, California Miscellaneous file, California Historical Society Library; Peters, *Autobiography,* 23; Doble, *Journal,* 179; Hayes, *Hayes,* 149.

8. Located twenty-six miles east of Sacramento, Michigan Bar, in Sacramento County, was the most prominent and largest of all the early gold camps along the Cosumnes River, where a toll bridge operated. It began with the arrival of two miners from Michigan in 1849 and had a population of close to 1,500 in the early 1850s. The first claims were small, only about sixteen feet, in this placer area but the first ditches to bring water into dry diggings were built here and the total gold production eventually totaled at least 1,700,000 ounces. The original townsite, located a mile north of the historic marker on Highway 16, was washed out by hydraulic mining which changed the countryside drastically. Hoover and Rensch, *Historic Spots,* 301; Gudde, *California Gold Camps,* 214; Wright, *History of Sacramento County,* 214; D. W. Carlson, "Sacramento County Gold Dredging," *California Journal of Mines and Geology* Vol. 51 (Sacramento: State Department of Mines), 90, 135-142.

9. Although weeks late, newspapers from the East and Midwest were sent to California by ship, to be picked up at post offices or delivered by mail carriers to mining communities. Many who received newspapers from home commented in diaries and letters about how welcome these were, even when weeks out of date. In 1855 J. Heacock, agent for the Pacific Express Co., advertised "The latest Eastern papers always on hand" at his Ione City office. *The Quincy Prospector,* May 1, 1855.

10. Henry Woodward and Adam Lithgow owned land adjacent to each other along the south side of Sutter Creek not far from Ione City, where "first class bottom land" sold for $10 per acre. The Lithgow holdings, purchased from Woodward for $1,300, came to eighty acres but no record exists of how many acres the Woodwards had in 1855. In 1860 the Woodward land holdings of 320 acres were valued at $15,000 with an additional $7,125 in personal property, according to the 1860 California special census. The Lithgow family property, with fifty-three acres improved and forty unimproved, totaled $6,000. Lorena's uncles took an active role in the 300-member Settlers' League, which fought to save their lands located in the Arroyo Seco grant, but the confusion surrounding the court cases could not be settled satisfactorily. As a last resort settlers, who had "honestly believed" the land had been owned by the "general government," appealed to President Abraham Lincoln, stating that if this failed "we will endeavor to reconcile ourselves to our hard

fate and at once quit our humble homes.'' When all efforts to obtain clear title
to the land failed, the Lithgow and Woodward families left Amador County
in the mid-1860s to relocate in the San Diego area. An ''Elder Blain'' of the
Methodist Episcopal Church held services in Fiddletown, where the church
was built during the winter of 1852-53. In 1853 Rev. J. D. Blain[e] served as
the presiding elder for the Sacramento District. 1860 Census, Township No.
2, (''Production of Agriculture'', Reel II); Cowan, *Ranchos,* 248-49; Amador
County Deeds 583 and 584, recorded Nov. 13, 1860; Lithgow Family papers;
Mason, *Amador County History,* 225.

11. John Doble in nearby Volcano also commented about the January 1854
weather and its effects upon business: ''. . . the times are more dull now than
they have ever been in California nearly all are waiting for water and in consequence money is scarce . . . most of the retail trade is now done on time here
and from what I can hear it is generally so throughout California, such
however is the effect of a dry winter like the present.'' Several days later rain
started, followed by snow so that on Jan. 20, Doble described the morning as
''the coldest within the memory of the oldest inhabitant with the thermometer
down to one degree above zero.'' Doble, *Journal,* 199-202.

12. The 1853 *Hydropathic Encyclopedia* by Dr. R. T. Trall was designed as a
''guide for families and students and a tez [sic] book for physicians'' which included 300 engravings and colored plates. ''Substantially bound,'' it could be
ordered pre-paid by mail for $3.00. A review in the *New York Tribune* called it
the ''most comprehensive and popular work'' published on the subject as well
as ''well-arranged'' and of ''general utility.'' It contained information on
hygiene, anatomy, and physiology of the human body, dietetic and
hydropathic cookery, the treatment of ''all known diseases'' and application of
its system to ''midwifery and the nursery.'' A popular and widespread
medical reform movement, the water-cure treated the whole person, internally
as well as externally, rather than just symptoms. It also advised women about
contraceptive methods at a time when almost every newspaper carried thinly
disguised advertisements for abortion pills. The *Water-Cure Journal,* founded
1845 with the motto ''Wash and Be Healed,'' also supported women's rights
and temperance. Hydropathy began to decline in the 1890s as the medical
profession instituted reforms to meet state licensing requirements. Advertisement, *Pike County Union,* Mar. 7, 1855; Sklar, *Catherine Beecher,* 206-08,
318-20.

13. To find Lorena's ''Sugar-loaf,'' follow California State Highway 16
east from Sacramento past the intersection at Waits Station. Before reaching
the junctions of Highways 104 and 49, this formation, called Sugarloaf Peak
on modern maps, will be seen ahead and to the right. Several other smaller
''sugarloafs'' exist in this area, too, while a much more prominent one is
located to the north in Eldorado County.

14. Like Sarahsville, Willow Flat must have had an extremely short existence because no other reference to it can be found, aside from the comment
made by Wells West, Lorena's cousin (see note 1). Lorena's family lived there
a little less than four months before moving to a nearby mining camp on the
Cosumnes River.

15. ''Mr. B.'' was John Clement Bowmer, Lorena's future husband. He

was considering returning to his former home in Wisconsin to visit his children since his first wife died while he was in California.

16. Lorena's desire to play a musical instrument met approved Victorian dictates concerning suitable activities for young women, who were expected to perform at a moment's notice regardless of time, inclination, or talent. Music provided solace and consolation as well as pleasure and entertainment, thus becoming an attractive showcase for the performer. Watson, "Cult of Domesticity," 37.

17. Here Lorena describes a "custom in the northern states at dinner or evening parties" when almonds or other nuts were served, a game reputedly of German origin. Those nuts that were double or contained two kernels were called "Fillipeens" or "Phillipina." The name apparently had a biblical reference to conciliation between different religious faiths. However, in the 1850s if a lady found an almond with two kernels she gave one to the man to eat. Then, when the two met again each tried to be the first to exclaim "Fillipeen" for "by doing so, he or she is entitled to a present from the other." A Bible was considered a suitable present according to this custom. *A New* [Oxford] *English Dictionary,* Vol. 7 (1909), 775.

18. Forest Home, about six miles from the junction of Highways 16 and 49, was the center of a mining district in the northwest part of Amador County. It has been described as "perhaps the poorest in gold of any portion that was extensively worked" since the paying claims on the Cosumnes River were farther down at Michigan Bar. However, a small settlement there did a thriving business with the old stone inn built about 1856 by the Castle family from Michigan, at one time also listed as operating the Willow Springs House. That year a new ditch brought water from the Cosumnes River and Michigan Bar ditch to the mines, which were worked for more than ten years. An undated picture at the Bancroft Library shows a two-story stone building with a balcony and central chimney and two windows on either side of a middle doorway. Gudde, *California Gold Camps,* 119; Mason, *Amador County History,* 47, 213; also see Castle Family papers.

19. Although called "Diggers" by the pioneers, these Indians of Amador County were probably from either the Northern Miwok or the Hill Nisenan cultures since both could be found between the American and Cosumnes rivers due to demands for their labor at Sutter's Fort beginning in 1847. However, members of the Washo tribes also crossed the mountains from Nevada; all three groups hunted in summer along the Sierra summits. According to one report, a large Indian village once existed near Buena Vista and there were 5,000 Indians in the Ione area. Attempts to ranch or raise cattle on the east side of the San Joaquin River supposedly failed because Indians would appropriate the livestock and destroy the rest. Little trouble with these Indians could be expected because when their lands were appropriated by the whites, they retired higher up in the mountains. However, John Doble reported the Indians along Dry, Sutter, Amador and "Rancherie" creeks and the "Lower settlements," a district of "some eight miles square in which there are no mines and consequently no whites settled in, are said to be getting verry troublesome to travelers," supposedly incited to rob and steal by bands of outlaws, including that of Joaquin Murieta. Mason, *Amador County History,* 26;

Doble, *Journal,* 148.

Benjamin F. Wayne and John Clement Bowmer were partners in a store located on the south side of Ione's Main Street, about forty feet from the corner of Buena Vista Street, when Lorena met them in 1854. They paid $500 for the lot "on which the store house now stands" in October that year. Apparently Wayne, whose middle initial was sometimes written as a "T," had been in business previously in Drytown. Amador County Deed Book A, 225; Delinquent Tax List, *Amador Sentinel,* Dec. 20, 1854.

20. According to the 1852 special California census, William Hicks and his wife had both lived in Missouri before coming to California. A post office was added to the Hicks ranch in 1857. Special California Census (1852), 103; Thompson and West, *History of Sacramento County.* Reprint (Sacramento: Howell-North, 1960), 217.

21. Charles Peters might well have been called captain because he had been on whaling expeditions in the Atlantic and Pacific before sailing for California in 1848 from New London, Connecticut. In his autobiography, written in 1915 as the "oldest pioneer living in California who mined in the Days of '49," Peters recorded major gold discoveries throughout the state but only one for the Cosumnes River: a boat-shaped nugget four inches long and weighing over a pound (valued at $240) found in 1855. The name "fandango" and the dance came from the West Indies to Spain and back again to Central and South America. As a lively dance, it was done in 5/8 or 6/8 time. In Mexico the word also meant a ball or general dance. A not-too exaggerated description of such an event was written by "Henry Vizatelly," a pen name for a doctor (J. Tyrwhitt Brooks) who supposedly had never been to California. See *Four Months Among the Gold-Finders* (London: David Bogue, 1849), 81-82; Peters, *Autobiography,* 3, 4, 93.

22. Frederika Bremer (born 1802), the well-educated daughter of a wealthy Swedish merchant, had already achieved recognition in both the United States and Europe as a novelist when she came to American in 1849. More than nine books as well as stories, tracts, and articles depicted both village and fashionable life in Sweden. In 1853 a review of her two volume work *Homes of the New World, Impressions of America* appeared in the *Christian Advocate and Journal,* translated by Mary Howitt. Reprinted from *Harper's,* this book "contains many just views of society, manners, custom, laws and politics as found in many states of the Union with some light gossip. Upon the whole, Miss Bremer is a pleasing writer. Her reflections are often very sensible and always forcibly expressed." The author was described in 1850 by another periodical as "decidedly plain . . . her spare, sallow features lighted up by a look full of intelligence and sweetness and her meager form is set off by the neat simplicity of her attire." Apparently well aware of her appearance, she "always positively refused to have her likeness taken" so the only picture was an imaginary one by a German painter. *Christian Advocate and Journal,* Nov. 3, 1853; *The Ladies Repository,* January 1850, 270-72.

23. Pet quail could be found in many California households, apparently, because in July 1857 Mrs. Elvira Bradway had a pair of them at her Red Bluff home. Mrs. Bradway explained: "The quail is a California bird and many keep them as pets." She and her husband, Dr. Joseph R. Bradway, planned

to take some quail home with them should they return to Delavan, Wisc. Mrs. Bradway thought the mountain quail "more beautiful than the valley ones." July 10, 1857, Bradway Letters.

24. The Prairie House was located on Alder Creek, two miles south of Folsom in the community known as Prairie City. While Prairie Diggings were just north of this "city," the Prairie House was about two miles south on the Placerville Road. This mining camp began in 1853 and within a year its population had grown to 1,000 as compared to an estimated 140 inhabitants in the spring of 1854 with 400 others buying supplies there. However a "Prairie Cottage" existed between 1852 and 1864 on the Ione Road; which one sister Caroline worked at can not be determined. Gudde, *California Gold Camps,* 276; G. Walter Reed, *History of Sacramento County* (Los Angeles: Historic Record Co., 1923), 115.

25. Malvina was Lorena's third sister, whose full name was Amanda Malvina Hays.

26. John M. Jamison came to California in 1850 from St. Louis and settled in the area of Amador County known as the Shenandoah Valley near Plymouth on Big Indian Creek. He operated a horse-powered sawmill in 1851 but the following year moved to Pigeon Creek where he had a steam-powered mill instead. When his family joined him, Jamison built a house nearby. In 1852 Jamison was accused of trying to drive away Mexican miners at gun point but denied involvement in what later became known as "the Jamison affair." Jamison apparently took the law into his own hands because Mexicans accused of cattle stealing were whipped and then brought to trial at his ranch; when the sheriff attempted to free them, he was ordered to leave. Jamison and his son William were subsequently arrested and taken to Coloma, where they pleaded guilty, paid a small fine and were dismissed but others involved in this example of vigilante justice were never apprehended. Sargent, *Amador County History,* 71-72; Mason, *Amador County History,* 227.

The mining camp of Cook's Bar was located on the north side of the Cosumnes River, about two miles west of Michigan Bar. Named for miner Dennis Cook, who ran a trading post there between 1849 and 1859, it once had a population of 500 in the early 1850s but had disappeared by 1860. In 1854 a hotel, the Cook's Bar House, had been built there by Chenault and Hall. Although gold was discovered almost simultaneously at Cook's and Michigan Bars, the richest locations were the bars at the main forks of the Cosumnes River. Gudde, *California Gold Camps,* 81; Hoover and Rensch, *Historic Spot,* 32; George Wright, *History of Sacramento County* (Sacramento: Thompson and West, 1880), 214, 216; *An Improved Topographical Map of the Northern and Middle Mines* [1854] in Carl I. Wheat, *The Maps of the California Gold Region* (San Francisco: The Grabhorn Press, 1942) No. 265, 120.

27. The invitation to this cotillion party listed thirty-four men from twenty-two mining communities in Sacramento and Amador counties as members of the committee of arrangements with John M. Warnock as the host. Floor managers were Loyd Spar, Phil Raspberry, and W. H. Dain. Members of Walker's Cotillion Band were identified as Solon Seaver and Frank and Burt Walker by Solon's brother, Horace Seaver, in a June 12, 1854, letter. Horace and Solon Seaver had made the trip from Darien, Wisc., to California in 1853

along with their brother, DeWitt, and two brothers-in-laws: David L. Hastings and William Carter. Miscellaneous File, California Historical Society; Seaver, Letters.

28. Forty-niners from Missouri settled Fiddletown, also called Oleta, but the early records no longer exist, leaving only rumors about the origins of its name. The wide streets of this community, a trading center for a number of rich mining camps, were once lined with 100 houses of brick, wood and stone, as well as several stores and saloons. According to one record, before 1852 a drug store was also located in Fiddletown, perhaps the 136-year-old Chinese herb shop undergoing restoration in 1987. The Chinese population of Fiddletown in the 1850s ranged from 5,000 to 10,000 making it second only to the San Francisco community. The first hotel in Fiddletown, kept by a "Capt. Stowers with Carter and Curtis," boasted of having "real glass windows"; the United States Hotel, operated by McDevitt & Cope, opened in 1852. The community received widespread fame when the author Bret Harte wrote a short story entitled "An Episode at Fiddletown." Gudde, *California Gold Camps*, 70; Mason, *Amador County History*, 221-22; "Nuggets of History in Chinese Herb Shop," *Newark Star-Ledger*, Apr. 26, 1987; Henry L. Walsh, *Hallowed Were the Gold Dust Trails* (Santa Clara: University of Santa Clara Press, 1946), 106.

Rev. Peter Y. Cool of the Methodist Episcopal Church along with four other ministers mined near Amador City, where gold mixed with quartz was discovered in 1851 along a creek. The claim, known as "Ministers' Gulch," was the site of a stamp mill built in September 1851, which made "dividends as well as wages for the ministers who were all workers." Organized as the South Spring Hill Company, they took out seventy-five ounces of gold a week, thus becoming the first successful quartz mining operation in the county. Cool with Thomas Rickey and his son, James, were among the first to find gold at Fort John near Volcano, where they built a small church and also the first school in Amador County. Mason, *Amador County History*, 39, 47.

29. John A. Brown, a native of Missouri, came to California in 1848, settling first on Bear River near Marysville. In 1849 he moved to Amador City with his family to farm near the community of Sutter Creek for fourteen years. His ranch was located on the road east of Sutter Creek, according to an 1866 map. Mason, *Amador County History*, 300; *Official Map of Amador County, California*. J. M. Griffith, County Surveyor, 1866.

In 1853 the first stage line in Amador County was operated by John Vogan and Charles Green, who later moved to the Q Ranch. The trip from Jackson to Sacramento, via Drytown, was made in one day and later extended through Mokelumne Hill to Sonora with the trip taking the same time. Because expenses were high — horses cost at least $300 each while coaches came to $3,000 and drivers were paid $150 a month — these stages were usually filled to capacity. The route followed the trails, zigzaging around dust holes in summer and mud holes in winter. In January 1854 the line was taken over by the California Stage Company with coaches traveling the 120 miles between Sacramento and Mokelumne Hill. The fare from Jackson to Sacramento was $10. Mason, *Amador County History*, 69, 183, 322, 327.

Rollin M. Daggett, co-editor of *The Golden Era*, made a practice of tramping through the mines, selling subscriptions and writing articles about the areas visited under such pen names as "Blunderbuss," "Korn Kob" and "Old Zeke." Born in St. Lawrence County, N. Y., in 1831, he came to California in 1849 at the age of eighteen years. Daggett, who learned the printing trade in Ohio, worked as a compositor for the *Sacramento Times* before going to the mines, supposedly making enough to found *The Era* with F. Macdonough Foard in 1852. Daggett also published the short-lived *San Francisco Mirror* and in 1864 worked for the Virginia City, Nev., *Territorial Enterprise.* He also served in Congress and later as U. S. minister to Hawaii. Daggett died in 1901. Lawrence E. Mobley, "The Golden Era," microfilm, 182; Walker, *San Francisco's Literary Frontier,* 380.

30. Houses constructed of canvas or cloth could be found throughout California mining communities as well as in cities such as San Francisco.

31. The full title of this book was *Hopes and Helps for the Young of Both Sexes.* Written by Rev. George Sumner Weaver (1818-1908), it "related to the formation of character" and included information on the choice of advocation, health, amusement, music, conversation, cultivation of the intellect, moral sentiment, and social affection as well as hints about courtship and marriage. The first edition was printed in 1852 with another edition three years later by Fowlers and Wells of New York and Boston.

32. Rev. Isaac B. Fish was born in 1824 near Cincinnati, Ohio, and joined the Methodist church in 1839. Eleven years later, after attending Augusta College in Kentucky for three years, he received his license to preach from the Ohio Conference; he was ordained a Deacon in 1850 and as Elder the following year. Fish and his wife, Naomi, were married in 1850 and came to California the following year when he answered a "call made for volunteers to [undertake] pioneer work" in the far west. Assigned to the Mokelumne Hill circuit, he organized and built the Methodist Church in Jackson, where his wife taught at the free school, sustained by voluntary contributions. Fish and Rev. George B. Taylor of the Ione Church were brothers-in-law and often exchanged pulpits. In April 1854, Fish was assigned to the Ione Church while Taylor moved to the Placerville-Diamond Hill area. The Fish and Taylor families purchased side-by-side three acre lots in Ione from Thomas Rickey. It cost $500 for the lot plus $600 to construct board fences around both homesteads. Fish, allowed $1,200 a year by the Conference, remained in Ione until mid-May 1855, when he was transferred to Sonora. Before his retirement in 1880, he had served a number of churches including Marysville and again at Ione in 1863-64. Fish, who had also been active in the temperance cause, died Dec. 24, 1884, in Watsonville, Calif., where he was buried. Methodist Church Records; *California Christian Advocate,* Apr.6, 1854; Rev. Isaac Owen, "Account of Individual Preachers," manuscript pocket notebook; Methodist Episcopal Church, *California Conference Minutes,* September 1885, 39; Richard Coke Wood, *Calaveras, the Land of Skulls* (Sonora: Mother Lode Press, 1955), 98; *Watsonville Register-Pajaronian,* Dec. 25, 1884.

33. The Cosumnes Circuit of the Methodist Episcopal Church included Ione, Drytown, Sutter Creek, Muletown, Michigan Bar, and Cook's Bar. Because this required traveling twenty-four to sixty miles a week, Fish did not

write in his journal during the year 1854 "through press of labor." To judge from Lorena's diary, he visited Cook's Bar on Mondays.

34. Until 1853 no Baptist church had been established in any mining region although a number of Baptist ministers preached throughout the area. The Ione Valley Baptist Church was constituted July 2, 1854, with eight members, under the leadership of Rev. S. Myron Newell, who remained there until December when he was assigned to the Nevada Church. Because they had no building, the "large and attentive" Baptist congregation met at the Union House. Newell participated in the September 1854 Baptist State Convention in Santa Rosa, serving on several committees including one for resolutions. Fleming, *God's Gold*, 133; California Baptist State Convention, *Minutes*, 1854, 5-6.

Although Lorena and her mother became members of the Ione Baptist congregation at the July 2 meeting, her uncle Henry Woodward joined the Methodists, serving as a trustee and steward of the Ione Church in the early 1860s. He was also a member of the 1861 building committee and a "neat and beautiful church" was constructed near his home "two miles west of Ione." *Celebration of the 93rd Year*, 11, 15, 16.

35. Both George S. Phillips and Nelson Reasoner were ministers of the Methodist Episcopal Church. Reasoner, who came to California in 1853 from New York, later served the Mokelumne Hill Church and then the Stockton District. A native of Pennsylvania, Phillips transferred to California in 1852 and served as editor of the *California Christian Advocate* and later as president of the female department at the University of the Pacific. Phillips also served churches in North Carolina and Colorado. During the Civil War he was a chaplin with an Ohio regiment under Gen. William T. Sherman. Phillips died in 1865 in Ohio at the age of forty-six years. Methodist Church Records.

This entry in Lorena's diary served as the basis for her first California newspaper article, printed in *The Golden Era*.

36. The first public school in Ione, held in a private home by a man named Meade, was established in 1853 along with the ones at Volcano, Jackson, and Sutter Creek, making a total of five schools in Amador County that year. In 1854 enrollment totaled 208 students, slightly less than half the children between the ages of four and eighteen years in the county; the following year there were four teachers for 865 students. Lorena's diary indicates that J. A. Peters (twenty-seven years old in 1854) taught in Ione at least four years earlier than the date given in a county history. A native of New York, he was listed in the California Special Census of 1852 as having been a farmer before he arrived in the gold fields. In 1859 he was elected justice of the peace for Township No. 2. Mason, *Amador County History*, 92, 185, 268; *The State Register and Year Book* (San Francisco: Henry G. Langley and Samuel A. Mathews, 1857), 123.

Here Lorena referred to the *Christian Advocate and Journal*, the official newspaper of the Methodist Church published in New York with regional editions. Her report of the summer weather contradicts a booster-inspired description that "when the plains are sweltering in heat, when the scanty herbage is withering under a scorching sun, Ione is green and delightful." Mason, *Amador County History*, 182.

37. According to Fish: "We have had a glorious Camp Meeting in Ione where sixteen souls were converted." Considered social events and held several times a year, these camp meetings provided families with a place and time for vacations. Board was usually provided for the men and feed for their horses. *Celebration of the 93rd Year,* 29.

38. John C. Bowmer suffered a painful inflammation of the last joint of one finger, the medical definition for a "felon." Mr. Martin might well have been J. P. Martin, an early settler of the Ione Valley, who crossed the plains in 1843 and also engaged in stock raising along with William Hicks and Moses Childers. A native of Virginia, this prosperous rancher owned property valued at $75,000 in 1860. Mason, *Amador County History,* 183; 1860 Census for Jackson, California.

39. The Buckeye Valley was considered inferior to Ione Valley for "cultivation of crops but furnished an abundance of the finest quality of hay." Although a number of places called Buckeye existed in California at this time, the one Lorena visited must have been located between Drytown and Fiddletown, probably on Laguna Creek near the present community of Carbondale on the Ione Valley road. A Buck's Ranch was located on the south side of the Cosumnes River in an area divided by the Sacramento-Eldorado county line not far from Michigan Bar. Mason, *Amador County History,* 192; Gudde, *California Gold Camps,* 49; George H. Baker, *Map of the Mining Region of California* (Sacramento, Barber and Baker, 1855); 1854 Map of El Dorado County in Carl I. Wheat collection, Bancroft Library.

40. The Mountain House, built in 1850 by James Gordon, was located on the Drytown Road about twenty-five miles from Sacramento and thirteen miles from the Ione Valley. In 1852 this was a temporary trading station where hay and other articles could be obtained by recently arrived emigrants. Horace Seaver in an Aug. 20, 1854, letter written from the Mountain House commented that mining had stopped "at present" because "the water has given out." He noted considerable excitement existed about the potential of hill diggings with the range of hills along the Cosumnes River "staked off for over two miles in length." His brother, Solon Seaver, planned to "run a tunnel into the hill about one mile from this place they think they will find something that will pay but it is uncertain they commence operations tomorrow." He added philosophically, "It will be with that as it is with other mining — some will pay and some will loose." Reed, *History of Sacramento County,* 115; *The California Pictorial Almanac* (San Francisco: Hutchings & Rosenfield, 1857) 47; Platt and Slater, *Guide,* 32; Seaver Letters.

41. In the election of 1854 Amador County was expected to vote a Democratic ticket but the Know-Nothings, a Native American party of nationwide influence, had been well organized and so played an important role. This group, which excluded anyone born outside the United States as well as Catholics and Jews, was a secret organization and the name supposedly originated from claims that people knew nothing about it. The Know-Nothing vote for J. Neely Johnson for governor of California totaled 2,035 in Amador County with the Democratic candidate, John Bigler, receiving 1,719 votes. However, Amador County elected a Democratic state senator and two Whig assemblymen that year. Mason, *Amador County History,* 82, 88; Alice Felt

Tyler, *Freedom's Ferment* (New York: Harper & Brothers, 1962), 385-93.

42. John A. Sutter (1803-1880), host to hundreds of emigrants who found his fort in the Sacramento Valley a refuge at the end of their long overland journeys during the 1840s, lived in poverty as a result of the gold rush. A prosperous landowner, the former Swiss citizen extended help to many but in return had lost nearly everything he once owned by the early 1850s. Sutter, who came to the United States at the age of thirty-one in 1834, reached California by way of Missouri, Fort Vancouver, the Sandwich Islands, and Sitka, Alaska. Arriving in 1837, he received permission from the Mexican government to settle in upper California in return for becoming a citizen. His 50,000 acre land grant, known as New Helvetia, included Sutter's Fort (the site of the city of Sacramento, which became the state capitol in 1854) with many acres in wheat and extensive livestock herds. At the site of his sawmill in Coloma James Marshall discovered gold on Jan. 24, 1848. The gold rush destroyed Sutter's possessions and dreams as workmen deserted him to mine for themselves and emigrants took over his lands as their own. Sutter left his former empire to live quietly with his family at the Hock Farm, located on the west bank of the Feather River near Marysville in the upper Sacramento Valley. In the fall of 1853 Ida Pfeiffer, one of the intrepid women travelers of the Victorian era, visited Sutter's farm during her "second journey round the world." She reported "quantities of abundant and fine corn and vegetables" being raised there.

According to an article printed by the San Francisco *Argonaut,* Sutter wrote: ". . . thousands upon thousands made their fortunes from this Gold Discovery — for me it turned out a folly . . . without having discovered gold, I would have become the richest and wealthiest man on the Pacific shore." For years Sutter petitioned Congress for restitution; in 1880 the claim was presented for the sixteenth time, but Congress adjourned without taking action two days before Sutter's death in Washington D. C. Gudde, *Sutter's Own Story* (New York: G. P. Putnman's Sons); Julian Dana, *Sutter of California* (New York: Halcyon House, 1934); Mason, *Amador County History,* 39-45; Ida Laura Reyer Pfeiffer, *A Lady's Visit to California in 1853* (New York: Harper Bro., 1856), 25.

43. *The Golden Era,* Sept. 17, 1854.

44. This would be *Homes of the New World, Impressions of America* (by Fredericka Bremer, a renowned Swedish author), which Lorena had been reading earlier.

45. *The Golden Era,* Oct. 29, 1854.

46. In 1854 "nearly all social intercourse was based upon 'drinks all around' - and drinks were always in order," especially in the mining camps. Blaine and Fish were not the only Methodist preachers to denounce from the pulpit the use of alcohol. Rev. Peter Y. Cool, whom Lorena also knew, once preached at an 1851 temperance meeting on the effects of liquor as "being a national evil" and proved "so conclusively that I took my seat amid great applause." In Volcano in December, 1853, John Doble witnessed a torchlight procession held by forty members of the recently organized Sons of Temperance "wearing Regalias and they looked verry well. Their appearance so unexpected in the street created some astonishment which soon however

subsided.'' He also took part in several temperance meetings that year, including ones held in the Methodist church and reported that they were well attended and that the "Temperance order is increasing rapidly." The Ione division of the Sons of Temperance was organized in April 1854 with forty-four members. Rev. H. H. Rheese, a Baptist minister, also took part in these activities. Mason, *Amador County History,* 76; Cool, Journal, Oct. 22, 1851; Doble, *Journal,* 163, 165, 182, 190, 192; Sons of Temperance, *Proceedings of the Grand Division* (San Francisco: Whitton, Towne & Co., 1855), 28, 44.

47. Sarah Pellet, a lecturer for women's rights and political reforms, apparently created quite a sensation wherever she spoke. She was described as "quite prepossessing in her appearance, mild and graceful in her manner . . . an amiable and talented person. Young, intelligent, good-looking and pure," Miss Pellet, who also spoke out against alcohol, combined eloquence and "earnestness" with "true feminine delicacy and most becoming demeanor.'' Shortly after Lorena heard her speak, the following report appeared in *The Owl,* one sheet allocated by the editor of the *Amador Sentinel* in the Dec. 30, 1854, issue: "The State Superintendent (of Education) has just made arrangements with Miss Pellet for the importation of 5,000 Yankee girls to be consigned to the different E Clampus Vitus Lodges throughout the State. The Independent Order of Owls of Snougerville have ordered 100 from the first ship load that arrives and the next census report from Amador County will be looked for with great interest as the crop of tow-heads and damp noses is expected to be enormous the coming season. Every well-disposed citizen will be glad to aid in a cause of so much importance to unborn generations." Apparently *The Owl* was published sporadically at Jackson but only one copy, edited by William Logan and incorporated into the *Amador Sentinel,* is known to exist. *Amador Sentinel,* Dec. 30, 1854; MacMinn, *The Theater of the Golden Era in California,* 285.

48. For information about this theatrical troupe see note 38 in introduction to the California years of Lorena's diary.

49. The Cosumnes Valley, although not widely known by that name today, consists of the land between the Cosumnes and the Mokelumne rivers, which, along with Dry Creek, form the major channel of the Mokelumne River, emptying ultimately into the San Joaquin River. The Cosumnes Valley, west of Amador County, today is divided by the Sacramento-San Joaquin County line.

50. Among the first to reach the goldfields were miners from Chile, since they received the news earlier than did many from other countries; their transportation was also somewhat easier to arrange.

The location of Benson's is shown at the junction of Dry Creek and the Cosumnes River on an 1852 map of the Southern Mines. This same map shows a road between Sacramento and Stockton crossing the Mokelumne to the west of Benson's.

The California State Telegraph Company, with offices in San Francisco, charged $2 for the first ten words and seventy-five cents for each additional five for messages sent between Stockton, Sacramento, and Marysville. It began operation Oct. 24, 1853. Abraham P. Nasatir, "Chileans in California . . . " *California Historical Quarterly* (Spring 1974): 52-70; C. D. Gibbes' map in

Jane Bissell Grabhorn, *A California Gold Rush Miscellany* (San Francisco: The Grabhorn Press, 1934); *San Francisco Directory,* 1854, 261; *The State Register and Year Book of Facts,* 154.

51. Rev. H. Holcomb Rhees(e), who had been a Stockton attorney before becoming a Baptist minister, was invited to assume the pastorate in the Ione Valley in December, 1854, and was appointed the following March by the Home Mission Society. Between 1854 and 1856 a number of church revivals, including ones at Ione City, were considered as "preludes to the Great Revival of 1857-58," with numerous conversions reported. Fleming, *God's Gold,* 123, 124, 125.

52. Lorena's grandfather, Martin Hays of Greene, Erie County, Pennsylvania, died Apr. 19, 1847. Her Uncle Joseph, born in 1812, was his third and youngest son and had been a Presbyterian minister. In later years he moved from Pennsylvania to La Crosse County, Wisconsin, where he was living in 1884 with his second wife. Hayes, *Hayes,* 72, 149-50.

One of several prominent California financial firms, Drexel & Co. (the full name was [F. M.] Drexel, [Pader] Sather and [E. W.] Church) made a specialty of shipping specie, according to a listing in the *New York Times* for 1853. Located on Montgomery Street at the corner of Long Wharf in San Francisco, it could "draw bills of exchange at sight or on time, in sums to suit on fifteen banks," including Drexel & Co. in Philadelphia, as well as upon banks in Stuttgart and "Frankfurt-on-the-Maine" in Germany. *New York Times,* Aug. 10, 1853; *San Francisco Directory,* 1854, 29; *Alta California,* Feb. 27, 1855.

53. Rev. Charles H. Northup of the Methodist church traveled throughout California for fourteen years before retiring in 1866. His "high moral integrity, clear intellect and persistent and unwavering fidelity" were praised following his death in 1870 in Healdsburg. *Minutes of the California Conference* (San Francisco: Cubery & Co., 1870), 33.

54. No other reference was made by Lorena to this friend, so the identity of Annie remains unknown. Perhaps she was Ann Pressy of Pike County, Ill., who would have been about Lorena's age.

55. Unfortunately, Lorena left no evidence of her lessons in Spanish aside from four references in her diary. Nor did she use a single Spanish phrase in anything she wrote, aside from signing "Lenita" as her middle name.

56. *The Golden Era,* Feb. 4, 1855.

57. Although no official marriage record can be found, the following announcement appeared in the Feb. 28, 1855, issue of the *Sacramento Daily Union:* "Married at Cook's Bar, Sacramento County, February 25 by the Rev. Isaac B. Fish, Mr. J. Clement Bowmer of Ione City to Miss Lorina L. Hays of Cooks' Bar." Because Fish did not keep a daily journal in 1854-55, he did not report this wedding, but two years earlier he wrote about receiving $20 for conducting a marriage ceremony. *Daily Union,* Feb. 28, 1855; Fish, Journal, Sept. 20, 1853.

58. Steamers operated by the Pacific Mail Company left San Francisco from the Broadway Wharf the first and sixteenth of each month for Panama, while the smaller Sacramento steamers left from Pacific Wharf at 4 P.M. daily. This schedule meant that Lorena's husband would have sailed on March 1;

the only ship to sail that week for Panama was the *Golden Gate,* scheduled to leave at 9 A.M., but apparently delayed by several hours that day. *San Francisco Directory,* 1854, 178, 202, 231; *Alta California,* March 2.

59. Judge Edward Jefferson Willis served in Sacramento County from 1851-53 and presided at the hearings involving disputes between "Squatters" and John Sutter over land claims. Willis came to California in 1849 from Virginia. A graduate of the University of Virginia, he studied law in Charlottesville. Judge Willis started practice in Sacramento and began his judicial career in 1850, serving until he retired four years later to help organize the First Baptist Church of Sacramento. In association with others Willis began publication of a weekly Baptist paper, which survived only a year, losing $3,000. In 1854 Willis was elected vice-president of the state Baptist convention in Santa Rosa. Later he returned East to raise funds for the church. Due to illness he never returned to California. He served as a Civil War chaplain with a Virginia infantry regiment in the Confederate Army. William J. Davis, *An Illustrated History of Sacramento County* (Chicago: Lewis Publishing Co., 1890), 54, 182; *Baptist Conference Minutes* (San Francisco: Whitton, Towne & Co., 1854) 2; Fleming, *God's Gold,* 123.

60. Lorena used this pen name as well as "Lenita" for her articles in *The Golden Era,* which sometimes combined both in the same byline. This resulted in the comment that appeared in the Apr. 1, 1855, issue of *The Era:* "By the way the little place (Cook's Bar) is becoming celebrated for its large number of lady correspondents. The similarity of diction observable among the different signatures is quite remarkable." Whether she used these same pen names for articles printed in other newspapers remains unknown because issues containing her articles have not been found.

61. Mrs. Burt would be the wife of James Burt, who came from Vermont to California in 1849. He arrived in Amador County in 1851 and built the first brick store in Fiddletown. Burt was listed as one of the managers for the November 9, 1853, social ball at the Willow Springs House which Lorena attended. His ranch was located on Rancheria Creek, below Dry Creek and above Plymouth. Miscellaneous Files, California Society of Pioneers and California Historical Society; Mason, *Amador County History,* 343; 1866 Map of Amador County. For information about Miss Bennett and her school in Sacramento see introduction to the California years and note 39.

62. During the 1840s and 1850s it was not unusual for newlyweds to begin housekeeping in rented quarters, usually a room in a boarding house. This meant a new bride did not have to immediately display her knowledge and skill (or lack of both) in cooking. Where in Ione Lorena boarded while her husband made his trip to Wisconsin is unknown. Nor is it known if her reference to "the City" refers to Sacramento or to San Francisco. However, she mentions visiting the floral gardens, which might indicate that it was indeed Sacramento, since Smith's Pomological and Floral Gardens were located on the American River east of the community. This was a public resort with a great variety of plants, including 3,000 peach trees. Russell Lynes, *The Domesticated Americans* (New York: Harper & Row, 1963) 39-50; *Sacramento Directory and Gazetter, 1857-58* (San Francisco: S.D. Valentine & Son, 1857), xiii.

63. The letters Lorena received from her husband apparently no longer exist, since they were not handed down in her sister's family along with her diary.

Mrs. Rees would be the wife of the Baptist minister, but Mrs. Reed cannot be easily identified.

Mrs. Eliza Carter was the wife of H. A. Carter, a native of New York who studied and practiced law there before coming to California in 1849. The Carters lived in the first frame house in the area, brought by ship from the East Coast. Carter, who later served as the first district attorney for Calaveras County and in 1875 was elected to the State Assembly, was remembered in Amador County for "always giving advice to avoid a lawsuit." He represented Lorena's husband in 1856 in a partnership dispute. Mason, *Amador County History,* 286; 1860 Census for Ione, 2.

64. In her first article for *The Golden Era,* Lorena described Rev. George S. Phillips of the Methodist Church as presenting a "deep, profound and learned" address for the 1854 Fourth of July picnic. She added that this "eminently shadowed forth the brilliant talents of the speaker." *The Golden Era,* July 16.

65. Fish described this May day celebration in more detail: "We had a Sabbath school festival here. It was indeed a pleasant time . . . sixty children with parents and teachers spent the day in the woods, singing, swinging, playing, eating and hearing addresses from the Reverend N. Reasoner and J. S. Diehl. I am greatly attached to the Sabbath school here. At night we had a very interesting Temperance meeting here. Addresses were delivered by the above named brethren." A week later Fish "closed up my labor for this conference at Cook's and Michigan Bar." Although the society voted unanimously for his return, he had completed his year's work and at the May conference meeting was assigned to Sonora. With a heavy heart he wrote, "It was a trial to part with friends whom we had at Ione." When Fish left Ione, the Methodist congregation numbered sixty-five members and the church owned property valued at $4,000.

At that time Reasoner was identified as being from the Mokelumne Hill Methodist Church. Lorena heard him speak at the 1854 Fourth of July celebration in Ione and thought his remarks "witty, sparkling and vivacious, and well adapted to the occasion."

Diehl, Grand Worthy Patron of the Sons of Temperance, served the Placerville church and a year later was assigned to the Cosumnes congregation. Fish, Journal, 58; *Minutes of the California Annual Conference, Methodist Episcopal Church* (San Francisco: Alta California Power Press, 1855), 6.

66. Today the exact location of the former community of Quincy in Amador County might be difficult to find but it served as a stage stop about two miles north of Ione between the site of Muletown and the Boston Store. A "dry diggins," the Quincy mines relied upon rain and runoff from Mule Creek, a tributary of Dry Creek. Fifteen issues of the *Quincy Prospector,* issued weekly for twenty-five cents, were published between Mar. 3 and Nov. 17, 1855, by Alexander Bedlam, who became the 1881 city assessor for San Francisco, with Clark as his partner and W. I. Wallace as the printer. In December this miniature newspaper was moved to Sacramento, where it was printed in a slightly larger format as *The Times* until Feb. 5, 1856, when it apparently

ceased publication. Mason, *Amador County History,* 192; files of the *Prospector* are located at the Huntington Library.

67. Between 1854 and 1856 a number of Baptist Church revival meetings were reported throughout California, including several at Ione City. Fleming, *God's Gold,* 125.

68. In 1854 a steamship usually made the trip between Acapulco and San Francisco in seven days as compared to forty-seven days required for a sailing vessel two years earlier. Mildred Throne, ed., "The California Journey of George D. Magoon" *Iowa Journal of History* (April 1956): 165 fn. For information about the boat Lorena took to San Francisco and the reason for the delayed arrival of the *John L. Stevens* see notes number 49 and 50 to background information about Lorena's California years.

69. The arrivals and departures of steamboats to Panama were widely reported in California newspapers. Many of these steamers were owned by the Pacific Mail Steamship Company, organized in 1848 by the New York firm of Howland and Aspinwell to take gold seekers by sea to California. A steamer carrying mail received an especially enthusiastic reception twice a month with a signal from Telegraph Hill announcing the ship's approach to the entrance of San Francisco Bay. On "Steamer Day" the ordinary routine of business would be suspended as the whole population headed for the wharf. B. E. Lloyd, *Lights and Shades in San Francisco* (San Francisco: A. L. Bancroft & Co., 1876), 423-24, 519, 521-22.

Lorena's husband brought with him the wife of his partner, Sarah J. Wayne, and their seven-year-old son and six-year-old daughter. Three years later, Mrs. Wayne, a native of Illinois, took an unusual step when she filed a statement declaring her intent to carry on "in my own name and on my own account" the business of "raising and dealing in stock together with that of ranching stock." She stated the amount invested in her business "does not exceed five thousand dollars." 1860 Census; *Sacramento Daily Union,* May 17; Separate Property of Wives, Mar. 29, 1858, 44, Amador County Recorders Office, Jackson, Calif.

70. Dr. Enoch Pardee and his distant cousin Mary Elizabeth Pardee were married when she reached California, accompanied by her brother Horace. Their first son, George Cooper Pardee (1857-1941) became governor of California. Portraits of Dr. and Mrs. Pardee hang in the parlor of the family home, in 1987 undergoing restoration, in Oakland, Calif. In making arrangements for Lorena's husband to escort Miss Pardee to California, Pardee provided a letter of introduction to this "good company and responsible parties." They were supposed to meet in Cleveland and travel together to New York. February 1855, letters from Enoch Pardee to his fiance.

71. The celebrated actress Lola Montez came out of retirement in Grass Valley that spring to prepare for an "artistic tour of Australia, the Philippine Islands, Manila, Calcutta, Etc." The "divine Lola," also known as the Countess of Landsfeldt, was staying at the International House while preparing to sail in early July. Lorena was not impressed by this famous European entertainer, noted for her spider dance, although she never attended one of Lola's performances. According to the California press, "Mme. Lola's day has gone by. Her name is no longer sufficient to attract a crowded house; and

as to her dramatic talent — it is not equal to her skill as a *danseuse.* '' For the story of Lola Montez see Doris Foley, *Lola Montez, the Divine Eccentric* (New York: Ballantine Books, 1969); MacMinn, *The Theater of the Golden Era,* 355, 376.

72. A weekly, *The California Farmer and Journal of Useful Science* was originally printed in San Francisco in 1854 but moved to Sacramento a year later. Warren & Son with J. K. Phillips & Co. served as publishers; in July 1856, the paper returned to San Francisco. Whether Lorena ever submitted anything for its columns is unknown. Davis, *History of Sacramento County,* 85.

73. Although the Hayes Family genealogy gives June 9, 1853, as the wedding date for Amanda Melvina Hays and William Matthews, a farmer from Kentucky, Lorena's diary indicates the ceremony took place in June 1855. Hayes, *Hayes,* 149.

The Chinese Baptist Chapel in Sacramento was established as a mission in 1853 with $15,000 subscribed for building a school and church. Devoted to moral and religious instruction, it was under the direction of the See Yup Company; at that time the Chinese population in the Sacramento area numbered between 10-15,000, primarily from Canton. Also known as the Chinese Bethel Chapel, it was located on the northwest corner of Sixth and H Streets. The three-story building in the Gothic style was dedicated June 10, 1855, at a meeting held in Sacramento by the San Francisco Baptist Association with Rev. J. Lewis Shuck, a Southern Baptist, officiating. Shuck served in China in 1835 as a missionary in Macao and Hong Kong; after his wife's death in 1844 he returned to the United States but was assigned again to China. In 1853 he was appointed to work with Chinese on the Pacific Coast and become pastor at the First Baptist Church of Sacramento until 1860. During his time in Sacramento, Shuck baptized fifteen Chinese and served as managing editor of *The Baptist Circular. New York Times,* Aug.10, 24, 1853; Fleming, *God's Gold,* 121; Edgar A. Stickney, *1850-1950 Centennial History of the First Baptist Church of Sacramento* (privately printed); *Sacramento Illustrated,* 102.

74. Lorena's comment about her poor health provides the only indication that she was pregnant with their first child. Few Victorian women openly disclosed their pregnancies, only hinting at their conditions through the use of certain words and phrases. In later months of pregnancy, women were advised to retire from society to the seclusion of their own homes, reappearing only with the new offspring in tow, supposedly to the great surprise of male acquaintances. Lynes, *The Domesticated Americans,* 69.

75. Lorena referred here to the excitement surrounding the ''Rancheria murders,'' which did not easily or soon subside. Reaction to this incident resulted in forcing nearly all Spanish residents out of Amador County, whether they were originally from Mexico, Chile, or other Latin countries. The community of Rancheria, which no longer exists, was located southwest of Drytown on a creek with the same name. ''Rancheria'' meant ''Indian village'' in Spanish and was spelled a number of ways in the 1850s. In 1853 a water driven quartz mill was built in Rancheria, then called Lower or Old Rancheria (with a population of about 600) to distinguish it from Upper Rancheria, five miles northwest of Volcano. Relationships with the Spanish com-

munities of Amador County in the 1850s had never been very good because whenever gold was discovered, Mexican miners were run off their claims; later these lands were converted into farms with Mexican-owned herds no longer allowed to graze at will. Roads known to be frequented by Mexicans were considered dangerous to travel, especially between Drytown and Cosumnes. Previous attempts to banish the Spanish-speaking residents from the county had failed because they moved from camp to camp and then returned. So the Rancheria murders served to force them to resettle in the Jenny Lind area of Calaveras County next door. Mason, *Amador County History,* 83-88; Gudde, *California Gold Camps,* 282-83.

76. When Rafael Escobar was captured and accused of participating in the Rancheria murders, Charles Peters witnessed what happened next. Escobar was taken to Jackson for trial on August 22, when vigilante justice took over and he was "met by a reception committee and less than thirty minutes afterwards" hanged from the live oak tree that shaded Main Street until 1862 when it was destroyed by fire. Peters, *The Good Luck Era,* 21.

77. Major Edwin A. Sherman described a mass meeting held at Michigan Bar during the 1855 election campaign and attended by several thousand people. For this evening meeting a large platform to accommodate a hundred was erected. "Double chairmen were chosen to preside alternately, presenting their speakers likewise alternately," Sherman wrote, adding the "arguments and oratory were splendid excepting on the part of [David] Higgins . . . it reached the highest degree in the political thermometer without coming to blows." Candidates included Vincent Geiger, editor of the *Democratic State Journal;* William S. Long, an attorney, and Higgins "who was trying to be one," according to Sherman. The "American state and county ticket was elected," wrote Sherman, who won as Sacramento County surveyor, a position he held for two years. Sherman, *Recollections,* 170-71, 177.

78. Sara Payson Willis wrote under the pen name of "Fanny Fern" and had an article a week published in the *New York Ledger* for eighteen years. Born in 1811 in Portland, Maine, she received her education at the young ladies seminary run by Catherine Beecher in Hartford, Conn. Willis married three times, having been widowed in 1847 and divorced in 1853; in 1856 she married her third husband, James Parton, a noted historian and writer. Fanny Fern's first literary effort appeared in 1851 and led to a series of brief one- or two-page essays published in book form as *Fern Leaves from Fanny's Portfolio* in 1853. More than 130,000 copies sold in the United States and another 48,000 in Great Britain. In 1854 Mrs. Parton's first novel, *Ruth Hall,* received praise in the *New York Protestant Episcopal Quarterly Review* and 50,000 copies were sold within eight months; her second book, *Rose Clark,* the following year was also successful. Mrs. Parton, who died in 1872, wrote *Fresh Leaves,* a sequel to her first book in 1857. *The National Cyclopedia of American Biographical History of the United States,* Vol. I (1898), 392.

79. *The Golden Era,* Sept. 23, 1855. Although outspoken in her newspaper articles about women's role in reforming corrupt and dissolute gold rush society, Lorena did not champion the cause of women's rights in print so this Sept. 22 entry in her diary is especially significant. What prompted her to write "A Chapter on Beards" is unknown but her partisanship as an admirer of a

"properly cultivated beard" was in direct contrast to opinions expressed in *Godey's Lady's Book*. According to this publication, an unshaven man was a "Whiskerando" and might well have caught "the mustache rabies," while trying to conceal something. Lorena did not write again until more than a year had passed, a delay that caused the editor of *The Era* to write: "We occasionally hear from Lenita but not as often as we would desire. The last from our contributor was an article on beards, in which she took occasion to give the wiskerless a few very disagreeable facts to ponder over." Finely, *The Lady of Godey's*, 147-48; *The Golden Era*, Oct. 28, 1855.

80. Lorena's sister, Sarepta, also wrote for *The Golden Era* and in the Dec. 9, 1855, issue the following message appeared in the Correspondent's Column: "Lida Woodvale—looking for something from you for some time. If the weather is unfavorable to poetic inspiration, try prose." Her poem entitled "Musings" appeared on the first page of the Oct. 28, 1855, issue and was called "musical and pretty." Sarepta also learned "we will make room for others as we find proper space for them . . . we have placed them in a drawer marked 'accepted'." *The Era* published her second poem, "A Lesson," in the Feb. 10, 1856, edition and the following week Lida Woodvale's sentimental memorial "Chimney Rock — A Reminiscence" also appeared on page 1. *The Golden Era*, dates and pages as indicated above.

81. The fall of 1855 in Amador County had been exceptionally dry with no rainfall in October and with only sprinkles reported for September and November. So the December rains of two inches were especially welcome since without water mining became almost impossible. Earlier in the year when the same situation occurred, "houses which enjoyed the greatest public confidence and patronage" suspended payment, according to William Lobenstein, a merchant at French Hill located on Dry Creek half a mile from "Camp Secco." He ascertained that "gold diggins are getting scarcer all the time and as living is almost as dear as in forty-nine and fifty, when it was easier to make an ounce than it is at the present day to make a dollar — it is easy to imagine how oppressive the hard times must be." Mason, *Amador County History*, 242; Lobenstein, *Extracts from the Diary*, 65, 69.

82. Katesville, located near the Cosumnes River twenty-three and a half miles from Sacramento, was established as a community in 1854, although mining there began two years earlier. Never incorporated, it was three miles south of Arkansas Creek in Sacramento County. Katesville, not far from Cook's Bar, had a hotel, at least one boarding house, stores, a blacksmith shop, several saloons and dwelling houses. However, Katesville was deserted by 1862. Lorena's is the only mention of the existence there of a Lyceum, considered an essential indication of education in nineteenth-century America. An association for debate and literary improvement, a lyceum program also included lectures by prominent men. During the early 1850s appropriate topics discussed at Amador County lyceums included "Which Gives the Most Happiness — Pursuit or Possession?" and "Which Has the Greatest Right to Complain of the Whites — the Indians or the Negroes?" Davis, *History of Sacramento County*, 216; Hoover and Rensch, *Historic Spots*, 301; Cool, *Journal*, Oct. 25, Nov. 8, 1851.

83. The weather during the year 1856 in California exhibited all extremes: a

severe drought, intense summer heat, earthquake shocks and thunderstorms, as well as severe sandstorms. However, Ione farmers did not suffer from the "drouth, unlike the vallies below," so crops of grain and hay were abundant. The "beautiful valley is the garden spot of the world," according to the *Amador Ledger* in May and June. In August a visit to this "thriving village" revealed "vegetation is suffering severely for want of water, still business appeared to be lively — the crops have been abundant." *Amador Ledger,* May 24, June 28, Aug. 9; "Water and Weather in California," *California Historical Courier,* Vol. 29 (March 1977): 5.

The earthquake of Feb. 15, 1856, occurred "at 24 past five o'clock" [apparently 5 A.M.] and "every building shook to its foundations. Houses were swayed and rolled as vessels in a heavy sea." The shock was so violent that "some were thrown from their beds, furniture was thrown through windows . . . vessels containing liquid were turned over and horses tied in stalls fairly shrieked with terror." The first shock lasted fifteen seconds, according to the papers, and hundreds of San Francisco residents rushed to the public squares. The quake, which apparently did not equal the 1857 one of an estimated 8.0 on the Richter scale or the 8.3 of the 1906 earthquake, still did considerable damage with major cracks reported in walls of the San Francisco City Hall, the Mission Dolores and several business firms, while plaster was stripped from buildings near South Park. Reports of severe damage also came in from Oakland and Contra Costa County. In Stockton the shock had "sufficient force to produce nausea of the stomach in some and awake others who experienced it. The vibration was horizontal and from east to west." *San Francisco Weekly Bulletin,* Feb. 16; *San Francisco Herald,* Feb. 18; *New York Times,* July 20, 1986.

84. This trial concerned repayment of money borrowed in the name of the Bowmer-Wayne firm to help defray expenses of bringing Wayne's wife and two children to California in 1855. The plaintiff testified he had "no knowledge or suspicion that Wayne had no right to use the name of the firm in signing the note." One witness stated he believed the money had been borrowed for "partnership purposes" but later "saw that Wayne had no authority to sign his name to the note." Testifying for the defense, Josiah Heacock stated "the note was never charged to the firm and never was used in the firm . . . . During the partnership between Wayne and Bowmer the outdoor business of the concern was generally done by Wayne." When Lorena's husband learned about this note, "He seemed surprised and said he never gave or authorized any such note and would not pay it." Later, Heacock bought Wayne's share for $600 so the debt could be settled. Bowmer appealed the case, being willing to abide by the judgment of the California Supreme Court to pay in full or in part, as well as the costs. The attorney's fee would have been an additional $300 but H. A. Carter, the lawyer who represented Bowmer, apparently convinced him to settle out of court. Cases No. 79 and 80, Fifth Judicial District Court records.

85. When Lorena commented that her husband had purchased a house and lot she meant her name did not appear on the deed or on the county assessment rolls, which showed that J. C. Bowmer paid $600 for the town lot three doors from the Methodist Church. In April 1856 his personal property

amounted to $300. 1856 Amador County Assessment Roll, 13; 1860 California Census for Amador County.

86. By "Division," Lorena meant the local branch of the Sons of Temperance. This was perhaps the "secret" group to which her husband belonged, since records of the Amador County Masonic Lodge and the Independent Order of Odd Fellows do not list him as a member. She might also have been referring to the Settlers' League, which kept no records of its members or its meetings.

87. Lorena's brother-in-law was William Bowmer, Jr., born in 1825 in Missouri. *Index to the California Census of 1850* (Baltimore: Genealogical Publications Co. Inc., 1972) 149.

88. No records of the birth, death or burial of Lorena's baby can be found. In America during the 1850s and 1860s births were not routinely announced by the newspapers as they are today. This was according to the dictates of Victorian etiquette, which varied from decade to decade but it is unusual to find such printed announcements because they were not considered in good taste. The death of an infant apparently was not reported in the newspapers either, unless a member of a prominent family. Lorena's expressions of grief were typical of the sentimental Victorian era, which considered deceased children to be innocent angels. Lynes, *The Domesticated Americans,* 96.

89. Here Lorena referred to the May 14 shooting of James King of William, editor of the San Francisco *Evening Bulletin,* and its aftermath. His assailant James P. Casey edited the rival *Sunday Times* and was a member of the San Francisco board of supervisors. Casey had also spent eighteen months in Sing Sing Prison for larceny and had been accused of ballot-box fraud. He became enraged when King planned to publish this information. After King's death, the newly organized second vigilante committee seized control, sentencing Casey to be hanged immediately. The same sentence was also given gambler Charles Cora, awaiting a retrial for murder of a U. S. marshall. On June 3 Gov. J. Neely Johnson declared San Francisco in a state of insurrection and all attempts to disband the vigilantes failed. Within three months, the vigilante committee hanged four men and banished at least twenty-six others, while frightening away additional criminals. Not until August 12 did some 8,000 vigilantes give up their arms, according to L. H. Woolley, a member of this 1856 vigilante committee. Woolley, *California, 1849-1913* (Oakland: DeWitt & Snelling, 1913), 11-23; Herbert Asbury, *The Barbery Coast* (New York: Capricorn Books, 1968), 79-94; John Bruce, *Gaudy Century, 1848-1948* (New York: Random House, 1948), 35-37, 44-47.

90. Caroline Sophia Hays became the bride of John Jay M'Neely, a native of Pennsylvania, on May 17, 1856. The ceremony was held at Cook's Bar, as was the 1855 wedding of her sister, Amanda. Hayes, *Hayes,* 149.

91. Nineteenth-century women devoted considerable time and attention to the etiquette of "calling," which was surrounded by rigid and elaborate rules. Calling took place not only in socially prominent circles of eastern cities but also, as Lorena's diary indicates, within small western communities as well. Pages in Victorian etiquette books were devoted to the many fine points, including an edict that calls must always be paid upon friends by one planning to leave the community. Watson, "Life in a Doll's House — The Victorian

Lady.''

92. One of the most important centers of the Mother Lode during the early years of the gold rush, Jackson has been the Amador County seat since 1854. In 1848 it was called Bottilleos because many visitors to its springs left behind empty bottles. Located on State Highway 49 between Sutter Creek and the Mokelumne River, the community began in 1849 with sixty people and the following year had 100 tents and houses. The name came from Col. Aldan Apallo Jackson, who mined there briefly in early 1849 at a time when the average amount of gold per day came to a half ounce for every miner. Although the population was predominately French in the spring of 1853, two years later ''the principal street is literally covered with Chinese stores.'' A number of large and profitable mines existed in the Jackson area: the Argonaut (1850-1943) yielded more than twenty-five millon dollars while the Kennedy, located at ''The Gate'' northeast of town and in operation between 1856 and 1875 and again from 1885 to 1942, has been credited with 34.2 million. This was the deepest gold mine in the United States with a 5,912 foot shaft. Gudde, *California Gold Camps,* 172-73.

Mokelumne Hill, the Calaveras County seat from 1852-66, was also a leading gold rush community. On the south side of the Mokelumne River, it can be reached by following Highway 49 beyond Jackson. A toll bridge across the Mokelumne River existed in the mid-1850s but was destroyed by the 1862 flood. Six miles east of Mokelumne Hill Lorena and her husband would have passed Rich Gulch with another six miles bringing them to Railroad Flat and then to neighboring Independence Flat. A placer and quartz-mining center, prospecting began in this region in 1852 with a number of small but rich ledges worked by Mexican miners. Gudde, *California Gold Camps,* 166; Hoover and Rensch, *Historic Spots,* 45.

Lorena's sister, Amanda Hays Matthews, described Independence Flat that summer as being ''fresh and green . . . with excellent water'' while ''I suppose everything is dried up below.'' Her husband, Will, was going to help ''bring in a ditch about six miles from here into some new diggings lately discovered.'' Amanda added that times ''are pretty dull now but I think we can make our board until water comes in.'' Apparently Will and his brother-in-law ''Phlan'' (William Philander Hays) considered going into ranching together because they had been looking at property, according to Amanda. June 19, 1856, letter from A. M. Matthews to ''Dear Mother and Sister.''

93. Jesus Maria, by 1852 a sizeable placer mining camp, is located on Calaveras Creek, a tributary to the north fork of the Calaveras River. It was named for a Mexican who raised melons and vegetables for the early miners. About five miles southeast of Mokelumne Hill, Jesus Maria once served as a trading center for other mines and included a justice court, livery stable, dairy, and sawmill, with a school established in 1858. Fire destroyed most of the community sometime after that. Gudde, *California Gold Camps,* 177; Joy, ''Echoes from Calaveras Ghost Towns,'' typescript.

94. Here Lorena identified another contributor to *The Golden Era.* S. B. Allen, Amador County pioneer newspaperman, used ''Will Wayward'' as his pen name. 1n 1857 Allen was at Jackson, ''editing the *Ledger,* which has removed from Volcano to that place,'' according to Lorena's brother. A year

later, "heartily tired of the newspaper business," Allen bargained to take charge of a sawmill three miles from Jackson, leaving the newspaper field "although I have accomplished all that I expected to do when I went into it yet I feel unsatisfied — feel as though I had wasted a year of valuable time. . . ." Letter from William P. Hays to Sarah L. Hays, Apr. 29, 1857; Letter from S. B. Allen to Friend [Daniel] Whitlatch of Michigan Bar, Mar. 22, 1858. At the time the second letter was written Daniel Whitlatch and Sarah Hays had been married almost a year. Eckland Family papers.

95. The Calaveras Grove of Big Trees [*Sequoia gigantea*] is located twenty miles northeast of Murphy's, where mining began in 1848. Also called "The Mammoth Trees of California," this is the largest of the two California groves of sequoias. Credit for its discovery has been given to A. T. Dowd, a hunter employed by the Union Water Company, who came across the immense trees in 1852, although many others insisted they saw them at least two years earlier. (John Bidwell stated he had seen the grove during his overland trip of 1841 but that has always been debatable.) In 1853 the *New York Times* reported "the mammoth tree of Calaveras county, the greatest and most wonderful production the vegetable kingdom has ever known, has been sacrilegiously cut down for speculative purposes." The "Father of the Forest, although long since bowed his head to dust," measured approximately thirty-two feet in diameter and 300 feet in length. The Big Tree Cottage Hotel, built in 1852 by James L. Sperry, was destroyed by fire in 1943. The fifty-acre grove contained 103 trees "of goodly size, twenty of which exceed twenty-five feet in diameter at the base, and, consequently, are about seventy-five feet in circumference!" *New York Times,* Aug. 10, 1853; Hoover and Rensch, *Historic Spots,* 45, 46; *San Francisco Weekly Bulletin,* June 20, 1857; Hutchings, *Scenes of Wonder and Curiosity,* 10, 40-41, 43.

96. Lorena's comments about "mammoth vegetables" probably referred to those exhibited at the 1855 state fair in Sacramento. These included ten-pound carrots, a seventy-eight pound beet, tomatoes seventeen inches in circumference and a three-pound onion. *California Almanac* (San Francisco: Carrie & Damon, 1856), 22. Her reference to the large snails without shells might be to the so-called "banana slugs" that can be found at this altitude throughout the California foothills.

97. This comment provides the only clue about Lorena's taste in interior decoration. A Brussels carpet, made in twenty-seven to thirty-six-inch strips, had a pile of uncut loops. First manufactured in Wilton, England, in the mid-eighteenth century, the weaving process resulted in elaborate patterns with curving floral designs. In America Brussels carpets, produced as early as 1807, became the type of fine carpeting most frequently used in homes during the 1850s when the new aniline dyes produced vivid colors. Seale, *Recreating the Historic House Interior,* 79-81.

98. Ione obtained early fame for its watermelons and by 1854 its economy began to flourish, based upon the sale of melons, vegetables, hay, and barley to the miners. Years later Charles Peters remembered in 1851 he paid $2 for an Ione watermelon and saved the seeds, which he called a high priced commodity, to sell at twenty for $1.00. Mason, *Amador County History,* 76; Peters, *The Good Luck Era,* 19.

Even less rain fell in Amador County in 1856 than in the previous year, which had also been very dry. The official record, corrected for Sutter Creek, showed 23.684 inches of rain that year as compared with 32.026 in 1855. Mason, *Amador County History*, 242.

99. The election of 1856 was the first nationwide trial for the new Republican Party, which replaced the Whigs, with John C. Fremont, the famed western explorer, as its first presidential candidate. Fremont, who lost, challenged Millard Fillmore and James Buchanan. Fillmore, a former Whig who stepped up to the presidency following the death of Gen. Zachery Taylor in 1850, ran in 1856 on a combined Whig and Know-Nothing ticket while the Democratic Party selected as its nominee Buchanan, the election winner. In Amador County the Republican Party nominated a full slate at an October 4 meeting in Drytown with seventy-five in attendance; later, mobs threatened Republican supporters at Volcano. Amador County voted for Buchanan with Fremont coming in third since Republicans cast only one-sixth of the ballots. Issues in the 1856 election focused predominately upon slavery with emphasis upon the Kansas-Nebraska Act of 1854 which repealed the 1850 Missouri Compromise. This created the territories of Kansas and Nebraska and opened the Northern territories to slavery. The result was "Bleeding Kansas," with battles over land and slavery becoming a national issue as the Republicans endorsed admitting this territory as a free state. Lorena's "Dromedary line" is an obscure term which can not be easily identified but might well be a satirical reference to the Mason-Dixon Line that defined the boundaries of slavery under the Missouri Compromise. Nevins, *Fremont*, 473-518; Mason, *Amador County History*, 89.

100. An 1857 "tabular view" of the Ione Baptist congregation reported in May "baptized four, received two letters, received one by experience, one dismissed" for a total of twenty-one members, an increase of seven from the preceding year. A family named Hoyt lived northwest of Ione City. In 1856 the Baptist congregation had "lamented that so little fruit has been produced by their labors" because they were "few in number and limited in means," although services were held nearly every Sabbath. Their pastor, Rheese, who was from New Jersey, apparently took a leave of absence to return to "the States" and Lorena's diary documents his return to the Ione area by January 1857 but it would still be three years more before the Baptist had their own building.

Her latest reading material described the career of Baptist missionary Adoniram Judson, Brown University graduate who was one of the first four American missionaries to Burma in 1811. Although ordained a Congregational minister, he and his wife, Ann, joined the Baptist faith the following year. Judson developed an 1849 English-Burmese dictionary and translated the Bible. After a trip back to the United States, he returned to Burma in 1846 but died en route and was buried at sea. By 1857 at least four books had been written about him; which one Lorena was reading can not be identified, although the title that most closely matches is *A Memoir of the Life and Labors of the Reverend Adoniram Judson* written by Francis Wayland and published in 1853 by the Boston firm of Phillips, Sampson & Co. Lorena's interest in books meant that she was also interested in those available through the local Sunday

School libraries and at this time there were 250 volumes at the Methodist Church, although there were no public libraries in Amador County in 1860. *Minutes of the San Francisco Baptist Association,* 1857, 9; 1856, 14; 1866 Map of Amador County; *Dictionary of American Biography,* Vol. 5, 234-35; *Celebration of the 93rd Year,* 28; Social Statistics, 1860 California Census, Film 67/20c, Reel 1, 11.

101. Susannah Woodward Hays married her second husband, Rev. S. W. Hull on May 26, 1856. A Baptist minister, Hull, a native of Texas, had been licensed to preach at Cook's Bar in 1851. Where his career took him during the next five years is unknown but in 1856 he served the Judson Baptist Church (no location given) and two years later was listed as pastor of the Union Baptist Church in Sacramento. He was recognized as one "whose faithful admonition and pious zeal for the Lord of Hosts, won for him a large place in our hearts." In 1859 Hull wrote from Volcano, "We learn that the prospects of the Volcano Baptist church are brightening. Four new members received and the house of worship is undergoing extensive repairs." In February 1860 it was reported that the Olive Branch Church of Volcano with eighteen members had lost their pastor, who "left them in prostrated health and some two months ago he went to his rest." Hull was "highly esteemed and deeply lamented." Six years later Lorena's mother married her third husband, Rev. Allen Gould (d. 1873), also a Baptist minister. Hayes, *Hayes,* 148; Minutes of the Baptist Church: San Francisco and Sacramento Conferences, 1851-60.

102. Lorena might well have had a miscarriage, to judge from the words she used to describe her health the end of February and the first part of March 1857.

103. *The Golden Era* of Mar. 22, 1857, noted the editor's pleasure at again hearing from Lorena and her "Letter from Lenita" appeared in the March 27 edition. She had "thought once more to write you a letter . . . not that I can write anything very interesting, useful or beautiful, but that my 'unoccupied energies' are wishing for something to do." The April 5 issue contained an unsigned poem on the first page about the death of a baby. This, of course, would not be an unusual topic for Victorian sentimental poetry and a similar poem "The Baby (ANN)" appeared in August that year, written by Lorena's friend S. B. Allen under the alias Will Wayward. *The Golden Era,* Mar. 22, 1857; Mar. 27; Apr. 5; Aug. 3.

104. This niece was Ella Caroline M'Neely, first daughter of her sister Caroline. Hayes, *Hayes,* 149. The San Francisco Baptist Association held its 1857 meeting May 7-10 at the First Baptist Church with Lorena's minister, Rheese, as the moderator pro tem and the Reverend Mr. Shuck as moderator. *Minutes,* (San Francisco: B.F. Sterett, 1857), 7.

105. The marriage of Sarah Louise Hays and Daniel Harvey Whitlatch on May 28, 1857, was among the first fifty to be recorded at the Amador County Courthouse in Jackson. The ceremony took place "at the home of John C. Bowmer in the presence of Mr. and Mrs. Bowmer, Mr. and Mrs. Matthews, Mr. and Mrs. Lithgow and others in accordance with the laws of the state of California." Rheese officiated. The bride was eighteen years old; her husband, a native of Indiana and later a mining overseer at Ione, was eight years

older. Perhaps they had met at an anniversary ball held Sept. 14, 1855, at Nebraska Hall in Michigan Bar when Whitlatch served as one of two managers from Willow Springs. An April 29 letter from brother William P. Hays, then at Railroad Flat in Calaveras County, indicated that Sarah did not have an easy time with their new stepfather nor had any of the other sisters. William consoled Sarah about the situation, commenting, "You alone have faced the storm boldly and stood with true courage what we shrank from encountering." He suggested Sarah live with one of her sisters instead, adding he had also written to her fiance suggesting that Whitlatch should join him because "I believe he can do better here than at the [Michigan] Bar." Amador County Marriage Records, No. 32; Hayes, *Hayes,* 150; Miscellaneous File, California Historical Society; Eckland Family papers.

106. Seven stereoviews of Ione City and Valley by Mrs. E. W. Withington, "Photo Artist," depict ranches and houses, identified in pencil on the back. Three photographs, dated 1874, show threshing activities by W. L. Bailey & Co. while two others depict the T. M. Stephens dairy and the lower dairy of J. B. Scott with 84 and 134 milk cows respectively. In one view the Grant House is shown in the distance and in another the Grant home in Ione City is featured with children and women playing croquet while others watch from the balcony. The seventh photo shows a live oak tree and the resident of J. (or I.) B. Gregory and an unpaved street. The style of the dresses worn by the women tends to agree with the early 1870s dates written on the back of two cards since they appear to be those of the late 1860s and early 1870s before the bustle became fashionable.

It was predicted that a great comet would arrive on Saturday, June 20, but there was "no scientific evidence that it would collide with the earth," according to Professor Benjamin Pierce of Harvard University. He took to task the French astronomer Mons. Babinet [or Rabinet] who had made errors in his calculations so "people may safely wager that the world and mankind will survive June next." Thomas S. King, editor of the *San Francisco Weekly Bulletin,* added on May 9 "it is a pitiful case that mankind should be frightened into fits because doctors or astronomers differ." This comet supposedly returned every 300 years, with the last appearance in 1556; it had been predicted for 1848 and also for August 1852 but had an "uncertainty of two or more years." *San Francisco Weekly Bulletin,* May 9, 1857; *Pike County Free Press,* May 26, 1857.

107. The idea of a forthcoming "millennial day" of judgment when the dead would rise from the grave became widespread in the 1830s and early 1840s. This belief in the second coming of Christ influenced a large number of people and the Second Advent was predicted for 1843. The major advocate was the revivalist William Miller, who became a Baptist minister in 1833 and converted crowds throughout New England and the Middle West. When the Second Advent failed to materialize in 1843, Millerite leaders selected Oct. 22, 1844, as the Day of Judgment. In anticipation of "immediate translation to a blissful heaven," chores were left undone and crops unharvested. Hundreds of people camped on hilltops the night of October 21 eagerly awaiting this event. When nothing occurred, the disillusioned rejected the millennial doctrine and the movement faded. Lorena's use of this term indicates a linger-

ing belief had survived. Tyler, *Freedom's Ferment*, 70-77.

108. Apparently Lorena had just finished reading the May 10, 1857, issue of *The Golden Era* which featured a poem "The Household Baby" on page 6. The author was Grace Greenwood, the pen name used by Sarah Jane Lippincott. Lorena's description of "what a pest and what a pleasure" coincides with those in the poem. This nephew was probably her sister Amanda's oldest son, Charles Herbert Matthews, born in 1856. (The birth date in the Hayes family genealogy does not agree with the information in a letter written by Amanda in that year.) *The Golden Era*, May 10, 1857; Hayes, *Hayes*, 149; Eckland Family papers.

109. Lorena's "morbidly sensitive or excessively irritable" conduct may well be attributable to the fact that she was pregnant with her second child. The "Mrs. R." mentioned in these entries was Mrs. Rheese, wife of the minister; the two families shared the house.

110. Published in 1856, *The Life of Horace Greeley* has been called a "landmark in the history of American biography." It established the reputation of the author James Parton (1827- 1891), the third husband of Fanny Fern. This was the first biography written about Greeley, then forty-four years old, and contained "an abundance of amusing and interesting details" about the career of this illustrious newspaperman who became editor of the *New York Tribune* in 1831 at the age of twenty. More than 7,000 copies sold before publication with an additional 23,000 within a few months thereafter. At least one other contemporary, who had also made the overland trip in 1853, found this book of interest. DeWitt Seaver, who had left the Cosumnes area to mine in Nevada City, wished "every young man in the land would read it." *Dictionary of American Biography*, Vol. 7, 528, 534; Vol. 14, 279-80; Seaver, *Letters*, Nov. 16, 1856.

111. In 1852 the *Alta California*, the first daily newspaper in California, supported organization of a state Agricultural Society and an exposition to show off the variety and quality of California produce. A year later the first state fair was held at the Music Hall in San Francisco with the cattle show at the Mission Dolores, while the second in Sacramento in 1856 included industrial exhibits at the county courthouse, a stock show and races at the Louisiana race track. A four-day fair was held in San Jose in 1856 with prizes for best orchards, farms, and nurseries; a jury traveled on horseback in order to select winners. By 1857 some 850 members belonged to the Agricultural Society and the fair opened with an address by Judge Henry Eno of Calaveras County. A pavilion 200 feet by 75 feet was constructed on the courthouse square in Stockton. The equestrian events at the race track included "twenty reckless horsemen upon unbroken animals including (on a wild prancing colt) little Miss [Lucy] Phelps, a child of eight years who showed skill and courage." In another trial of skill and horsemanship, five women competed but the "crowd upon the track was so dense [they] had but poor change to exhibit their skills." However, "after they had started they delighted everybody by the perfect ease with which they controlled their animals and the grace of their movements. Miss Phelps [of San Jose] sat her horse like a veteran trooper both sideways and astride." Miskulin, "History of the State Fair"; *San Francisco Weekly Bulletin*, Oct. 6, 1857.

112. At first known as Tuleberg, Stockton was renamed in 1848 for Commodore Robert Stockton of the U. S. Navy who had played an important role, in the Bear Flag Revolt two years earlier when California won its freedom from Mexico. This San Joaquin County community was founded by Capt. Charles Maria Weber, an 1841 California emigrant from Germany, who became a prominent figure in the state's history. In 1845 Weber, then living in San Jose, purchased 48,000 acres in the French Camp grant and moved there two years later with a large livestock herd. The city of Stockton was laid out according to his plans. In 1850 Weber married Helen Murphy, daughter of 1844 pioneer Martin Murphy of San Jose. In the mid-1850s Weber's interests turned to horticulture with his garden becoming a major hobby. Often he brought back plants from his excursions to grow experimentally in his own yard, which featured flowers and trees from many different places. *National Cyclopedia,* Vol. 7, 455; Hammond, *The Weber Era in Stockton History,* 156.

113. Fires destroyed many early California communities and cities, including San Francisco, primarily because houses as well as hotels were constructed with canvas and cloth walls and ceilings.

114. Published as two volumes in 1856, Elisha Kent Kane's *Arctic Exploration: The Second Grinnell Expedition in Search of Sir John Franklin in the Years, 1853, '54, '55* joined the Bible as a favorite book on almost every American parlor table for a decade. Kane, an assistant surgeon in the navy, served as medical officer with the 1853 government expedition to search the Arctic for Sir Franklin, missing for eight years. This was the second search party by Kane, who had previously served in China as well as in Africa and Europe. The expedition reached Cape Constitution, its farthest point north in the western hemisphere, and charted Kane Basin and Kennedy Channel, used fifty-four years later by Robert E. Perry. Trapped by the weather, the Kane expedition, which failed to find Franklin, was rescued off southern Greenland in the fall of 1855. Kane died two years later in Havana at the age of thirty-seven. *Dictionary of American Biography,* Vol. 10, 256-57.

115. Here Lorena provided brief reviews of two new popular books. Harriet Beecher Stowe published *Dred, A Tale of the Great Dismal Swamp* in 1856 (Boston; Phillips, Sampson) while *The Song of Hiawatha,* based upon Indian legends, by Henry Wadsworth Longfellow was printed the preceding year.

116. Lorena's son, Harry Livingston Bowmer, was born in Ione on Mar. 4, 1858. Lorena referred to him by such different nicknames as "Hugh," "Livy" and "buk."

117. One cousin would have been Susan Elizabeth Whitlatch, born July 4, but the other cannot be identified in the Hayes family genealogy unless the year given there is wrong for Effie Elizabeth M'Neely, whose birth date was reported as Oct. 5, 1856. The care of her son took so much time and attention that Lorena neglected to write about the outside world, but that year Ione was considered as a place "doubtless improving to a greater extent than any other village in Amador County." It was surrounded by a "permanent farming community" and its "advantages for schools, churches, society, cheapness of articles and nearness to market, render it one of the most desirable places for a family resident in the State." That summer crops in the Ione Valley looked "very well," including the farms of Lorena's uncles, where "there is a promising good yield" with the season's premium corn coming from this region. In

answer to the perennial problem of water, plans were being made to dig wells near the creek and raise it by pumps worked by wheels set in the stream. Hayes, *Hayes,* 149-50; *Amador Ledger,* Jan. 23, July 5, 1858.

118. Dr. L. G. Lyon, Ione farmer and physician, was reported to have drowned his wife in a well in their yard. "The case has occasioned much feeling among the people of the locality." The circumstances were considered "peculiar," especially since the doctor was "found in the well with the deceased and refused to come out. When he did he appeared to be intoxicated." Lyon claimed he had been out hunting when his wife killed herself but a witness testified the doctor had accused her of "the habit of getting drunk" with a boarder. Following this most sensational crime, he was placed under a $2,000 bond but left town for parts unknown. His bondsmen had secured a mortgage on his farm, according to the *Amador Ledger,* but the intentions of the doctor and actions of the grand jury remained "a mystery." After a three-day inquest, the coroner's jury was prepared to render a verdict but "were awaiting further testimony when the accused ran away." Lyon was subsequently acquitted and left Amador County. *Sacramento Daily Union,* July 9, 1858; *Amador Ledger,* Nov. 8, 1855; Mason, *Amador County History,* 80.

119. Lorena refers to the comet expected to appear earlier. See note 106.

120. Volcano, fifteen miles north of Jackson on a fork of Sutter Creek, was so named because early miners believed, correctly, that there had been a volcano in the area. Once a prosperous mining camp, in 1852 its 300 buildings of clapboards and pine poles, "make very comfortable houses in this country," according to John Doble. He described Volcano as "situated in a very pretty Valley surrounded by high pine capped hills those on the north presenting to the view from the Valley a rugged, rocky appearance as the sides are of a whitish kind of rock thrown up in rough piles and high cliffs — both piles and cliffs reach nearly to the top of the Hills." The town extended from a bridge across the main stream, up the valley in a single row of houses for about 200 yards, an area called "shirt tail bend," Doble reported. By 1853 Volcano had eleven stores, three hotels and three private boarding houses, three bars and gambling houses — one of the bars was actually an apothecary shop — three bakeries, and one restaurant. Volcano had its own social set composed predominately of well-educated midwesterners who enjoyed cultural improvement and included a library association, a thespian group, and debating societies. Hydraulic mining began in the Volcano region two years later and by 1858 eight stamp mills and six Mexican-style "arrastres" took up two miles of land along the stream. Doble, *Journal,* 76, 101, 102, 156; Gudde, *California Gold Camps,* 360-61; Walsh, *Hallowed Were the Gold Dust Trails,* 108, 116.

121. March 14-17, 1859, was the "coldest spell ever experienced" in Amador County. The ground in shady places "remained frozen all day," as much as two inches thick while a dry north wind helped reduce the temperature. This unexpected cold spell nipped an early spring season because it destroyed the fruit trees that were in full bloom and also killed grass and grain. Mason, *Amador County History,* 241.

122. Wallace Kay, pioneer photographer-daguerreotyper, and his brother William had been in Jackson since 1855. However, this photograph of Lorena's son, who would have been a year old, apparently has not survived,

although her diary has been handed down in the family of her youngest sister. Perhaps one of the photographs of unidentified infants in long white dresses that fill two family photo albums may be of Harry Livingston Bowmer. Information from the Bowmer family indicates some mementos and photographs might have survived but Lorena's Bible cannot be found. As so often happens in many families, when Lorena's namesake granddaughter died in the 1950s these may have been discarded because their whereabouts remains unknown. Mason, *Amador County History*, 105; July 1979 letter from Mrs. Angus L. Bowmer to Jeanne Watson.

EPILOGUE

1. 1860 Census, Vol. 1-152, Amador County, 276. According to this record Lorena's husband had been working as a carpenter, because that was the occupation recorded by the census taker, who misspelled her name as "Lavina."

2. The Bowmers owned the house on Village Lot No. 6 in block No. 1 of Ione City, one of 468 structures in the community. The justice of the peace who questioned Lorena on June 22 was the same J. A. Peters, whose school she had visited in 1854. Amador County Deeds, No. 475, filed June 23, 1860; 1860 Census.

3. To date, the only record known to exist about Lorena's death appears in the Hayes family genealogy. She was thirty-three years old at a time when the average life expectancy for the late 1850s was about forty years: 38.7 years for men and 40.9 for women. Hayes, *Hayes*, 149; *Dictionary of American History*, Vol. 4, 149-50.

4. This map is in the collection of the Haggin Museum and Art Gallery in Stockton, Calif.

5. One story claims that when vigilante justice in Modoc County threatened to take over in an 1856 murder case, Judge Bowmer "felt himself called upon to lay down his life for the constitution of his country," stating he would rather let the mob "make him into a piece of honeycomb before he would yield to their unhallowed demands." However, in June of that year Lorena and John Clement Bowmer were in Ione City, grieving over the death of their first child. Bancroft, *California Inter-Pocula — The Works of Popular Tribunals* Vol. 37 (San Francisco: The History Co., 1888), 554; for another version see the autobiography of Lorena's great-grandson, Angus L. Bowmer, *As I remember, Adam* (Ashland, Oregon: The Oregon Shakespearean Festival Association, 1975), 15-17.

6. Hayes, *Hayes*, 149; Harvey Kimball Hines, *An Illustrated History . . . of Oregon* (Chicago: The Lewis Publishing Co., 1893), 451. Undated newspaper clippings, including interview with H. L. Bowmer, from Mrs. Angus L. Bowmer of Ashland, Oregon.

7. In 1970 an indoor theater was built for the Oregon Shakespearean Festival and named for Lorena's great-grandson, Angus L. Bowmer. "Western theater . . . bravo!" *Sunset* (March 1985): 264; "Shakespeare at its Best," *Travel & Leisure* (January 1986) E12-14; "Angus L. Bowmer, 74, Founder of Oregon Shakespeare Festival," *New York Times*, May 29, 1979; Bowmer, *As I remember*, 15-17.

Bibliography

Key to location of primary sources:

BL   Bancroft Library, University of California, Berkeley
BY   Bienecke Library, Yale University, New Haven
CaHS California Historical Society, San Francisco
ChHS Chicago Historical Society, Chicago
CSL   California State Library, Sacramento
HL   Huntington Library, San Marino, California
ISHL Illinois State Historical Library, Springfield
ISHS Iowa State Historical Society, Iowa City
KSHS Kansas State Historical Society, Topeka
LC   Library of Congress, Washington D.C.
LCHS Lane County Historical Society, Oregon
LDS   Historical Department, Church of Jesus Christ of
      Latter-Day Saints, Salt Lake City
MoHS Missouri Historical Society, St. Louis
NatA National Archives, Washington D.C.
NL   Newberry Library, Chicago
NSHS Nebraska State Historical Society, Lincoln
OHS   Oregon Historical Society, Portland
RCP   Rollins Collection, Princeton University, New Jersey
USHS Utah State Historical Society, Salt Lake City
UW   University of Washington, Seattle
WHS   Wisconsin State Historical Society, Madison

SOME ADDITIONAL
1853 OVERLAND TRAVEL ACCOUNTS

NOTE: Travel accounts written on a day-to-day basis while following emigrant trails west are indicated with (T), while all reminiscences are marked with (R) and letters by (L).

(T) Allyn, Henry. "Journal of 1853, Fulton County, Illinois, to Willamette Valley, Oregon Territory." Oregon Pioneer Association *Transactions,* 49th Annual Reunion (1924): 372-435.

(R) Ayres, Irvin. Notes to H. H. Bancroft, 1886 interview by James Morrison. Typescript, BL.

(R) Bailey, Washington. *A Trip to California in 1853, Recollections of a Gold Seeking Trip by Ox Train Across the Plains and Mountains by an Old Illinois Pioneer.* LeRoy, Ill.: LeRoy Journal, 1915.

(R) Bailey, William Carey. Diary. Typescript, CaHS. William Carey Bailey and Washington Bailey were not related.

(R) Baldwin, Elias Jackson. *Lucky Baldwin, The Story of an Unconventional Success* by C. B. Glasscock. Indianapolis: Bobbs-Merrill Co., 1933. Baldwin traveled at times in the overland company of D. A. Shaw.

(R) Beeson, John. *A Plea for the Indians.* New York: John Beeson, 1858.

(T) Beeson, Welborn. *On the Oregon Trail in 1853.* Ed. Bert Webber. Lake Oswego, Oreg.: Smith, Smith & Smith, 1986. Welborn was the son of John Beeson.

(T) Belshaw, George. Journal from Indiana to Oregon. Typescript, BY.

(L) _____. May 10, 1853, letter from Council Bluffs, Iowa, to Henry Belshaw. Typescript, HL.

(T) Belshaw, Maria Parsons (Mrs. Thomas). "Diary: Part I - Council Bluffs to Soda Springs" in *New Spain and the Anglo-American West,* Vol. 2. George P. Hammond. Privately printed, 1932. "Diary." Ed. Joseph W. Ellison. *Oregon Historical Quarterly,* (1932): 318-33. Maria was the wife of one of George Belshaw's three brothers.

(R) Bixby, Llewellyn. *Adobe Days* by Sarah Bixby-Smith. Cedar Rapids, Iowa: The Torch Press, 1925. Bixby made overland trips in 1851 and 1853 with his cousin and partner Dr. Thomas Flint. The Flint-Bixby train joined that of Col. William W. Hollister for part of the journey between Salt Lake City and San Bernadino.

(R) Bond, Allen and Rachel. *An Overland Honeymoon in 1853* by Walter H. McIntosh. Caldwell, Ida.: The Caxton Press, 1938. The Bonds, married the evening before their trip west, traveled in the McClure train to Oregon.

(R) Boren, Lucine Mecham. "Journal" in *Treasures of Pioneer History.* Salt Lake City: LDS, 306-09.

(L) Bowman, J. Soule. Letters to the the *Missouri Daily Republican:* "June 6, Ft. Kearny from the Plains," June 23; "June 23, Ft. Laramie, Trail of the Emigrant,"'Nov. 1; "Death Notice," Dec. 21; "Report of American

Exploration, 1853-54" by Spencer F. Baird, *Appendix of Journal of Proceedings of the Board of Regents of the Smithsonian Institution,* 9th Annual Report, House Misc. Documents No. 37, series 807, 33rd Congress, Second Session, 86.

(L) Bradway, Joseph R. and Elvira. Letters, 1853-57. Manuscript, RCP.

(T) Bradway, Joseph R. Journal from Delvan, Wisconsin, to California. Typescript, WHS and CSL.

(T) Browder, William. Diary (incomplete) from Warsaw, Missouri, to Sonora, California. Microfilm, BL.

(T) Brown, William R. *An Authentic Wagon Train Journal of 1853 from Indiana to California.* Ed. Barbara Willis. Mokelumne Hill, Calif.: Privately printed, 1985.

(T) Bryant, Isaiah W. Diary, Muscatine, Iowa, to California. Typescript, Merrill J. Mattes papers, NSHS.

(R) Bushell, Joseph Corydon. The Narrative of. . . . Typescript, LCHS.

(T) Butler, Mrs. Ashmun J. (America E. Rollins). "Diary." Ed. Oscar O. Winther and Rose D. Galey. *Oregon Historical Quarterly* (December 1940). Butler's trip in 1853 took her from Yreka, California, to Medford, Oregon. She and her husband made the overland journey the previous year.

(R) Butterfield, Thomas. "An Interesting Account of a Trip Across the Plains in 1853." *The Grizzly Bear,* January 1908.

(R) Campbell, Remembrance Hughes. *A Brief History of Our Trip Across the Plains with Ox Team in 1853.* Privately printed, 1905.

(R) Carson, Kit. *Autobiography.* Ed. Milo Milton Quaife. Chicago: The Lakeside Press, 1935. M. Morgan Estergreen. *Kit Carson, A Portrait in Courage.* Norman: University of Oklahoma Press, 1962. Harvey Lewis Carter. *Dear Old Kit, The Historical Christopher Carson with a New Edition of the Carson Memoirs.* Norman: University of Okalahoma Press, 1968. Charles Burdett. *Life of Kit Carson, The Great Western Hunter and Guide.* Philadelphia: John E. Potter and Co., 1865. Dewitt Peters. *The Life of Kit Carson, Nestor of the Rocky Mountains.* New York: W. R. C. Clark & Co., 1860. Mar. 27, 1853, letter from C. Carson to William S. Allen, *Missouri Daily Republican,* Apr. 28. For contemporary reports on Carson's trip see reprints from various California newspapers in *New York Times,* Aug. 2, Aug. 24, Sept. 10, Oct. 10.

(T) Carvalho, S. N. *Incidents of Travel and Adventure in the Far West with Col. Fremont's Last Expedition.* New York: Derby and Jackson, 1857.

(T) Cipriani, Leonetto. *California and Overland Diaries of. . . , 1853-71.* Ed. Ernest Falbo. Portland, Oreg.: The Champoeg Press, 1962.

(T) Compton, James H. "Illinois to California in 1853." Typescript, BL.

(R) Compton, Mary Ellen Murdock (no relation to James Compton). *Mary Ellen Murdock Compton* by Henria Parker Compton. Privately printed, 1953.

(T) Comstock, Noah D. Diary (undated but thought to be written in 1853) from Ash Hollow to California. Manuscript, Coe colletion, BY.

(L) Cook, Lucy Rutledge. "Letters, March-June, 1853," in *Covered Wagon*

Women: Diaries and Letters from Western Trails, 1840-1890. Vol. 4. Ed. Kenneth L. Holmes. Glendale, Calif.: The Arthur H. Clark Co., 1985. The Cook family made the overland journey as far as Salt Lake City in 1852 and spent the winter there, completing the trip in the spring and early summer the following year.

(T) Cooper, James G. Bird Notes and Diary. Manuscript, BL.

(R) Cornaby, Hannah. *Autobiography and Poems.* Salt Lake City: J. C. Graham & Co., 1881.

(T) Cowden, James S. Diary. Manuscript, CaHS.

(R) Currey, George B. "The Occassional Address." Oregon Pioneers Association *Transactions,* 15th Annual Reunion, 1887; excerpts in *The Oregon Trail* by Ingvard H. Eide. Chicago: Rand McNally & Co., 1973.

(T) Dinwiddie, John (or David). "Journal Overland from Indiana to Oregon." Ed. Margaret Booth. *The Frontier,* Vol. 7, No. 2. Missoula: State University of Montana, 1928. The name of which brother wrote this diary has never been determined.

(L) Dixson, Hugh. "From California" in *Missouri Daily Republican,* Aug. 29, 1853.

(R) Draper, Elias J. *Autobiography of a Pioneer of California.* Fresno, Calif.: Evening Democrat, 1904.

(T) Eccleston, Robert. Diaries, Vol. 7, 8, 9. Manuscripts, BL.

(R) Ellmaker, Enos. Diary, Biographical Sketch and Letters. Typescript, LCHS.

(R) Fanaker, N. C. "Early Day Reminiscences," *Pioneer History of Kansas.* Kansas: Adolph Roenigk, 1933.

(T) Farmer, James. Journal, Parts 1 and 2. Typescript, USHS. Twenty-one pages in Part 2 are missing, so this account of the trip west ends September 10 on the Sweetwater River, resuming nearly a year later. Farmer, a Mormon emigrant from England, reported progress of the Forsgren company of Danish Saints because the two emigrant groups traveled close together. Other pages in Part 1 were either missing or so damaged they could not be transcribed in 1936 for the Utah Historical Records Survey, Federal Writers' Project-WPA.

(L) Ferris, Cornelia Woodcock (Mrs. B. G.). *The Mormons at Home with Some Incidents of Travel from Missouri to California.* New York: Dix and Edwards; London: Sampson Low, Son & Co., 1856. Mrs. Ferris and her husband spent the winter of 1852 in Salt Lake City and continued the journey to California during the early summer of 1853.

(R) Ferris, Benjamin G. (husband of Cornelia). *Utah and the Mormons.* 1856 reprint. New York: Ams Press, 1971.

(L) Fish, Charles. Letters. Manuscript, New-York Historical Society Library. Fish, whose family lived in Batavia, New York, made the 1853 trip via Nicaragua.

(T) Flint, Thomas. "Diary: California to Maine and Return, 1851-1855." Historical Society of Southern California *Annual Publications* (1923): 53-127.

(R) Forsdick, Stephen. "On the Oregon Trail to Zion in 1853." Ed. Fletcher W. Birney Jr. Denver: *The Denver Westerner Brand Book* (1953): 33-55.

(T) Forsgren Company. Diary, translated from the Danish. Typescript, LDS. This journal was kept by an unknown emigrant in John Erich Forsgren's company.

(R) Furniss, Henrietta Catherine (Kate) McDaniel. From Prairie to Pacific, A Narrative by Aunt Kate. Ed. Mai Luman Hill. Typescript, CSL.

(T) Galloway, James Hezlep. Diary, Iowa to the Humboldt, March 31-August 17. Microfilm, BL.

(T) Gaylord, Orange. Diary. Oregon Pioneer Association *Transactions,* 45th Annual Reunion, 1917.

(T) Gibson, William. Journal from 1851-54. Manuscript, LDS.

(T) Gilbert, William W. Diary, Milwaukee to California. Typescript, NL.

(T) Gill, Harriet Tarleton (Mrs. William). Diary, (incomplete) in *California Letters of William Gill.* Ed. Eva Turner Clark. New York: Downs Co., 1922.

(T) Gill, William. *California Letters of . . . .* Ed. Eva Turner Clark. New York: Downs Co., 1922.

(R) Gill, Thomas A. (no relation to Harriet or William Gill). "Across the Plains in the Early Days." *Stanislaus Weekly News,* Aug. 14, 1903, from earlier account in *California Elk,* photocopy, CSL.

(T) Goltra, Mrs. Elizabeth Julia Ellison. Journal of Her Travel Across the Plains. Typescript, LCHS.

(T) Graham, Calvin. Journal: Pennsylvania to California. Typescript, KSHS.

(T) Gunnison, John W. and E. G. Beckwith. *Reports of Exploration and Surveys to Ascertain the Most Practicable and Economical Route for a Railroad from the Mississippi River to the Pacific Ocean.* Vol. 2. Washington D. C.: A. O. P. Nicholson, 1855. 33rd Congress, Second Session, House Ex. Doc. 91, Serial No. 792. Gunnison kept his diary between June 4 and July 12 while traveling along a short section of the Overland Trail through Kansas. It. was included in the report written after his death by Beckwith. Nolie Mumey. *John William Gunnison, 1812-53, the Last of the Western Explorers.* Denver: Artcraft Press, 1955.

(T) Haas, John B. "Autobiography" from notes taken by Charles E. Hass. *The Pony Express Courier,* June 1937-October 1938.

(T) Hall, Cyrenius. "Pencil Sketches of Scenes Along the Overland Route to California: Chimney Rock, Court House Rock, Scotts Bluff, Storm in Rocky Mountains, Crossing the Barrier." *Annals of Wyoming* (October 1968): 252; (April 1970): 56; (October 1970): l92. These sketches also appear in Robert Munkres' *Saleratus and Sagebrush, The Oregon Trail Through Wyoming,* 1974, but further publication has been restricted, according to Mar. 27, 1979, letter from Katherine A. Halverson of the Wyoming State Archives to Jeanne Watson (1986 letter of request for permission to use the Hall sketches remains unanswered).

(R) Hall, Maggie. Journal: Texas to California — Crossing the Plains. Microfilm, BL.

(R) Hamilton, Mrs. Sarah Jane Watson. *A Pioneer of Fifty-Three* (poem). Albany, Oreg.: The Herald, 1905.

(L) Handsaker, Samuel. Letters to the *Alton* [Ill.] *Telegraph.* Typescript journal and reminiscences, LCHS.

(R) Hazard, Henry J. Dictation for H. H. Bancroft and biographical sketch. Typescript, BL.

(T) Heap, Gwinn Harris. *Central Route to the Pacific from the Valley of the Mississippi to California, Journal of the Expedition of E.F. Beale, Superintendent of Indian Affairs in California.* Philadelphia: Lippincott, Grambo & Co, 1854. *Central Route to the Pacific with Related Materials on Railroad Exploration and Indian Affairs* by Edward F. Beale, Thomas H. Benton, Kit Carson, and Col. E. A. Hitchcock, 1853-54. Ed. Leroy and Anne Hafen. Glendale, Calif.: Arthur H. Clark Co., 1951.

(R) Himes, George. "An Account of Crossing the Plains in 1853 and the First Trip via Natchess Pass." *The Morning Oregonian,* June 23, 1907, magazine section. Himes, secretary of the Oregon Pioneer Society in 1907, gave this address for the 35th reunion. His family traveled with that of Mrs. M. A. Looney, who identified him as George Hines of the Oregon Historical Society in her 1907 recollections of their trip west. Van Ogle was also a member of this company of 155 emigrants.

(T) Hines, Celinda (Mrs. H. R. Shipley). "Diary." Oregon Pioneers Association *Transactions,* 46th Annual Reunion (1918): 69-125.

(T) Hite, Abraham. "Diary of a Trip Across the Plains." Typescript, CSL. He was the grandfather of Mary Fetter Hite Sanford, who also made the trip in 1853.

(T) Hoffman, William. "Overland Diary — Across the Plains and Rocky Mountains in 1853." Manuscript 537 (microfilm), OHS. Hoffman traveled with the Royal company and so his diary also augments those kept by S. H. Taylor and his niece, Rachel Taylor, providing four accounts for this one wagon train.

(R) Hollister, William W. 1878 Statement of a Few Facts on California, 1852-60. Manuscript, BL. The town of Hollister, California, is named for him.

(T-R) Ivins, Virginia Wilcox. *Pen Pictures of Early Western Days.* Privately printed, 1905.

(R) Judson, Phoebe Godell. *A Pioneer's Search for an Ideal Home.* Bellingham, Wash.: 1925. The Judsons traveled with the Hines company.

(R) Kent, Deborah (Mrs. Horace A.). Her Story, as remembered by granddaughter Eva Holden. Manuscript, OHS.

(R) Kennedy, George W. *The Pioneer Campfire: Anecdotes, Adventures and Reminiscences.* Portland, Oreg.: Privately printed, 1914.

(T) Ketcham, Rebecca. "From Ithaca to Clatsop Plaines, Miss Ketcham's Journal of Travel." Ed. Leo M. Kaiser and Pricilla Knuth. *Oregon Historical Quarterly* (1961): 237-87, 337-402.

(T) King, Hannah Tapfield. "My Journal" in *Covered Wagon Women, Diaries & Letters from the Western Trails, 1840-1860.* Vol. 6. Ed. Kenneth L. Holmes. Glendale, Calif.: The Arthur H. Clark Co., 1986. Mrs. King and her family were Mormons who made the trip from England to Salt Lake City.

(R) Kleiser, James Abram. Autobiography. Manuscript, BL.

(T) Knight, Mrs. Amelia Stewart. "Diary." Orgeon Pioneer Association *Transactions,* 56th Annual Reunion (1928): 38-53.

(R) Larson, Thomas. 1887 Statement for H. H. Bancroft. Manuscript, BL.

(R) Lewis, John I. *My Garden of Roses or Footnotes on Life.* Berkeley: Privately printed, 1913.

(R) Longmire, James. "Narrative." *Tacoma* [Washington] *Ledger,* Aug. 21, 1892; *Washington Historical Quarterly* (1932): 47-60, 138-50. Interview, "1853 to Washington" by Mrs. Lou Palmer in *The First Three Wagon Trains.* Portland, Oreg.: Binford and Mort, 1961. Robert A. Bennett. "James Longmire" in *A Small World of Our Own.* Walla Walla: Pioneer Press Books, 1985. Longmire was also in the first wagon train to cross the Cascade mountains at Naches Pass in 1853, as were George Himes, Mrs. Looney and Van Ogle.

(T) Longworth, Basil. "Diary of . . . an Oregon Pioneer." Typescript. Historical Research Survey, Works Project Administration, 1938, NatA. His name has also been spelled "Longsworth."

(R) Looney, Mrs. M. A. *A Trip Across the Plains in 1853.* Portland, Oreg.: Privately printed, 1912. Looney traveled in the same company as George Himes, Van Ogle and James Longmire.

(T) Luark, Michael Fleenen. Diary — Overland Trip to Washington. Manuscript, UW.

(T) Lymon, Esther Brakeman. Journal (begins at Ft. Kearny). Typescript, LCHS.

(T) MacMurphy, (first name unknown). "Thirty-Three Years Ago, Through Nebraska Before Any Settlements," in *Transactions and Reports* (1892): 270-77. In 1886 John A. MacMurphy read this paper, based upon his family's diary, "Journal of a Journey to California in 1853," for a meeting of the Nebraska State Historical Society. Nothing else is known about this diary. July 11, 1978, letter from David Hoober, then NSHS manuscripts curator, to Jeanne Watson.

(T) McClure, Andrew S. Diary. Typescript, LCHS and OHS.

(T) McIntyre, Peter. Autobiography. Typescript, LDS.

(T) Miller, Joel. Journal to Santa Rosa (partially destroyed by flood). Typescript, BL.

(T) Mollhausen, H. Baldwin. *Diary of a Journey From the Mississippi to the Coasts of the Pacific* [1858]. Reprint. New York: Johnson, 1969.

(T) Myer, Nathaniel. "Diary, with Account of Experiences while Crossing the Plains in 1853." Typescript. Southern Oregon Historical Society.

(T) Newton, Jotham. Diary of a Trip to California Overland in 1853. Manuscript, BL.

(R) Ogle, Van. "Memory of Pioneer Days." *Washington Historical Quarterly* (1922): 269-81. Ogle and George Himes were members of the first company of Oregon emigrants to cross the Cascade mountains at Natches Pass, as were Mrs. M.A. Looney and James Longmire.

(T) Owen, Benjamin Franklin. Diary. Typescript, Lane County [Oregon] Museum. Owen joined the McClure train for the last part of the trip.

(R) Parker, Basil G. *The Life and Adventure of. . . An Autobiography.* Plano, Calif.: Fred W. Reed, 1902.

(T) Pengra, Charlotte Stearns. Diary. Typescript, Lane County Museum. Traveling part of the way in the same company were relatives D. A. Stearns and Velina Williams.

(T) Perkins, Sarah (Sally). "The Jottings of . . . ." in *Covered Wagon Women, Diaries & Letters from the Western Trails, 1840-1860.* Vol. 6. Ed. Kenneth L. Holmes. Glendale, Calif: The Arthur H. Clark Co., 1986.

(R) Peter, Ann E. "A True History of My Life, including a Brief Account of 1853 Journey to California." Microfilm, BL.

(T) Piercy, Frederick Hawkins and Linforth, James. *Route from Liverpool to the Great Salt Lake Valley.* 1855. Reprint. Cambridge: Harvard University Belknap Press, 1962.

(R) Rea, Thomas. "Biographical Information." *The Pioneer and Historical Review* (1897-1901): 96, 103, 282.

(L) Read, L.H. "Letter from Great Salt Lake City," June 23, 1853. *Missouri Daily Republican,* Sept. 1.

(R) Reeves, Elijah and Martha Caroline Lamphier. "Memories of Pioneer Life in Lake County" by William and Mary Ellen Reeves Nobles. Typescript, BL.

(R) Reynolds-Salmon Train. *Pioneers of the Sand Plains in San Joaquin County, California by Henrietta Reynolds.* Angels Camp, Calif: Privately printed, 1953.

(R) Rowe, William, Sr. "Ho for California, Personal Reminiscences." *Waterford* [Wisconsin] *Post,* May — June, 1905. RCP.

(T) Royal, James Henry Bascomb. "Journal While Crossing the Plains in 1853." Typescript, Southern Oregon Historical Society. This diary augments those kept by William Hoffman, S. H. Taylor, and Rachel Taylor.

(T-R) Sanford, Mary Fetter Hite. "A Trip Across the Plains and Biographical Sketch of Abraham Hite and Family." Typescripts, CSL. Mary's grandfather, Abraham Hite, also kept a record of this trip.

(T) Schiel, Jacob H. *Journey Through the Rocky Mountains and the Humboldt Mountains to the Pacific.* Ed. Thomas N. Bonner. Norman: University of Oklahoma Press, 1957.

(L) Seaver Brothers. Gold Rush Letters of three brothers: Dewitt C., Horace Everitt, and Solon L. Seaver; and their two brothers-in-law: David Hastings and William Carter. Manuscript, RCP.

(S) Shaw, D. A. *El Dorado or California as Seen by a Pioneer, 1805-1901.* Los Angeles: R. R. Baumgardt & Co., 1900.

(R) Sloan, William K. "Autobiography of . . . Western Pioneer." *Annals of Wyoming* (1926): 235-64.

(T) Smith, John. Journal, Pittsburg, Indiana, to Oregon. Manuscript, HL.

(T) Sparks, J. H. "A Manuscript Map for the Overland Journey from Salt Lake City to Sacramento City" (undated but assigned to either 1852 or

1853). Ed. John R. Purdy, Jr. *Western Historical Quarterly* (January 1975): 47-62.

(T) Stanley, D. S. "The March of the United States Second Dragoons from Ft. Smith, Arkansas, to San Diego, California." Typescript, MoHS. Stanley (along with Mollhausen) was a member of the Whipple company exploring a southern route for the transcontinental railroad.

(R) Stearns, Orson A. "Annotation and Appendix for the Diary of His Aunt, Velina Williams." Oregon Pioneer Association *Transactions,* 47th Annual Reunion (1922): 227-28. Stearns and Mrs. Williams were in the same company as Charlotte Pengra, Mrs. Williams' sister.

(T) Stewart, Agnes. "The Journey to Oregon, A Pioneer Girl's Diary." Ed. Claire Warner Churchill. *Oregon Historical Quarterley* (1938): 77-98.

(R) Stewart, Annie. Her Story as told by Lillian Schlissel in *Women's Diaries of the Westward Journey.* New York: Schocken Books, 1982. Annie was one of three sisters who kept records of their 1853 overland adventures, while a fourth wrote about her experiences in a letter several years later. This account by Annie also provides information about their mother. Indications are that Annie may have kept a diary, but no information is provided about its location.

(T) Stewart, Helen. Diary (incomplete). Typescript, Lane County Museum. Helen, Annie, and Agnes Sewart were sisters of Elizabeth Stewart Warner.

(R) Studebaker, John M. *Who Was Who in America.* Chicago: A. N. Marques Co., 1942; "Reunion of J. M. Studebaker and S. T. Gage of Oakland." *Pioneer,* May 1898; Edwin Corle. *John Studebaker, An American Dream.* New York: E. P. Dutton and Co., 1948; Stephen Longstreet. *A Century of Wheels, the Story of Studebaker, 1852-1952.* New York: Henry Holt & Co., 1952; The Centennial Book Committee. *Alpine Heritage, One Hundred Years of History, Recreation and Lore in Alpine County, California.* South Lake Tahoe, n.d.; Wells Drury. *To Old Hangtown or Bust.* Placerville: Privately printed, 1912; Diane Davis. "Portrait for a Western Album." *The American West* (1979): 33; Oct. 17, 1979, letter from Richard Welch, then director of Discovery Hall Museum, South Bend, Indiana, to Jeanne Watson.

(L) Taylor, Clarissa E. July 6, 1853, letter from Fort Laramie in "Oregon Bound." *Oregon Historical Quarterly* (1922): 136-38. Clarissa was the wife of S. H. Taylor and the aunt of Rachel Taylor.

(T) Taylor, Rachel. "Overland Trip Across the Plains from Rockford, Illinois, to Rogue River Valley, Oregon." Typescript, Southern Oregon Historical Society. The Royal and Taylor families traveled together.

(L) Taylor, S. H. "Oregon Bound." *Oregon Historical Quarterly* (1921): 117-60.

(R) Taylor, William. Reminiscences, 1884. Microfilm, BL. William was not related to the S. H. Taylor family.

(R) Teal, Mary Elizabeth Coleman. "Crossing the Plains in '53, The Story of the Nathan Coleman Party as Told to Her Son, Joseph Nathan Teal." Typescript, N. J. Teal papers, University of Oregon Library.

(R)   Ward, Dillis B. *Across the Plains in 1853*. Seattle: The Shorey Book Co., 1911.

(T)   Ward, Harriet Sherrill. *Prairie Schooner Lady, A Journal . . . of 1853*. Ed. Ward G. and Florence Stark DeWitt. Los Angeles: Westernlore Press, Great West and Indian Series, 1959.

(L)   Warner, Elizabeth Stewart. Unfinished letter describing trip to Oregon in Lillian Schlissel, *Women's Diaries of the Westward Journey*. New York: Schocken Books, 1982. Elizabeth, who wrote this letter sometime in 1856-7, was the sister of Agnes, Helen, and Annie Stewart.

(L)   Warner, William. "Overland in 1853." *California Historical Quarterly* (1926): 289-292.

(T)   Washburn, Catherine Amanda Stansbury. Journal of 1853. Typescript, NL.

(R)   Welchman, Arthur Pendry. Journal. Typescript, LDS.

(T)   Welsh, John Pratt. Diaries, Vol. 3. Manuscript, HL.

(L-T)   West, Calvin B. *Calvin B. West of the Umpqua*. Ed. Reginald R. and Grace D. Stuart. *Pacific Historian* (1960): 48-57.

(L-R)   West, George Miller. "Memoirs of the Butler Wagon Train to Oregon," including letters of Isaac and Margaret Smith, Isaac M. Butler, and Peter Butler. Microfilm, BL. Letters from Eliza A. Ground and Elizabeth M. B. Hutchinson, also members of the Butler company, are included in *Covered Wagon Women, Dairies & Letters from the Western Trails, 1840-1860*. Vol. 6. Ed. Kenneth L. Holmes. Glendale, Calif: The Arthur H. Clark. Co., 1986.

(R)   West, Wells Wallis. Autobiography. Manuscript (photocopy), BL. West, one of Lorena's cousins, accompanied the Adam Lithgow family to California. He observed his seventeenth birthday on the overland trail but did not write his reminiscences until 1921, three years before his death.

(T)   Whipple, A. W. *Pathfinder in the Southwest, The Itinerary of Lt. A. W. Whipple during His Explorations for a Railroad Route from Fort Smith to Los Angeles*. Ed. Grant Foreman. Norman: University of Oklahoma Press, 1941.

(T-R)   Williams, Joseph T. Reminiscences of a Covered Wagon, including his diary, by Sarah Williams Spooner. Typescript, BL.

(T)   Williams, Velina. "Diary of a Trip." Oregon Pioneer Association *Transactions*, 47th Annual Reunion (1922): 178-226. The Williams and Pengra families were related through the marriages of the Stearns sisters, Velina and Charlotte, but not to Joseph T. Williams (listed above).

(T)   Woodworth, James. Across the Plains to California in 1853, Typescript, LCHS.

(L)   "Yankton." Letter from the Plains, Fort Laramie, Sept. 15, 1853. *Missouri Daily Republican,* Oct. 7.

(T)   Zilhart, William. "Missouri to California (Journal)." Manuscript, BL.

Note: Brief accounts about four other families who made the overland trip to California in 1853 are included in Elizabeth Ann Sargent's *Amador County History*. Jackson, Calif.: The Amador Ledger, 1927. These were the Henry Barton family; the family of Annie Hagerman (Mrs. William Vela); the Franklin Herman family; and the family of Carrie Sanborn (Mrs. Fayette Mace). Three other overland diaries have been misdated for 1853: John Joseph Callison went to Oregon in 1852, while Rev. Isaac Foster of Plainfield, Ill., made his third trip to California in 1854, after spending the winter of 1853-54 in Council Bluffs, Iowa. Solomon Zumwalt's account was written about his family's 1850 trip west, which included spending the winter in Salt Lake City, reaching Oregon June 1, 1851, and includes only a brief mention about the 1853 emigration.

PRIMARY SOURCES

Abbey, James. *A Trip Across the Plains in the Spring of 1850.* New Albany, Ind.: Jno. R. Nunmacher; Louisville, Ky.: C. Hagan & Co.; Cincinnati, Ohio: Wm. H. Moore and Co.; and Philadelphia, Pa.: Lippincott, Grumbo and Co., 1850.

Abbott, Carlisle E. *Recollections of a California Pioneer* [1850]. New York: Neale Co., 1917.

Alden, Bradford Ripley. "The Oregon and Calfornia Letters of. . . ." *California Historical Quarterly* (1949): 199-232.

Alspaugh, Hannah Ditzler. *Reflections on a Bygone Era, 1848-1875.* Naperville, Ill.: Bank of Naperville, n.d. Includes letter from sister Libbie Ditzler Cable, who went to California in 1854 as an eighteen-year-old bride.

Amador County, California: Cemetery Records, CETA project, Jackson Public Library. Card file and 1936 plat map for Ione cemetery (without names) at Haggin Art Museum, Stockton.

American Bible Society. *The New Testament.* New York: National War Work Council of the Young Men's Christian Association, 1918.

Armstrong, J. Elza and Banks, John Edwin. *The Buckeye Rovers in the Gold Rush* [1849]. Ed. Howard L. Scamehorn. Athens, Ohio: Ohio University, 1965.

Bacon, Henry, ed. *The Ladies' Respository.* Vols. 17 and 18, June 1848-50.

Baird, Spencer F. Copies of correspondence, 1851-54. Letters from Lt. A. W. Whipple, J. Soule Bowman and S. M. Bowman. Smithsonian Institution Archives, Washington, D. C.

Bailey, Mary Stuart. "A Journal. . . ." [1852] in *Ho for California!* by Sandra L. Myres. San Marino, Calif: Huntington Library, 1980.

Baker, Hozial H. *Overland Journey to Carson Valley & California* [1859] San Francisco: The Book Club of California, 1973.

Ballou, Sylvester A. "Explorer Returns to Live in Naperville," *A View of Historic Naperville from the Sky-Lines of Genevieve Towsley.* Naperville, Ill.: Naperville Sun, 1975. Biographical file, CaHS.

Barber & Baker. *Sacramento Illustrated.* San Francisco: Monson and Valentine, 1855.

Barry [Illinois] Baptist Church Records — Organization and Minutes, Book I, 1829-60. Manuscript.

————. Park Lawn Cemetery Records, Old Section. Typescript.

————. Community School Unit District No. 1: Feb. 4, 1977, letter to Jeanne Watson.

Barry, C. (Mrs. John Van Antwerp). "1851 Letter to Sister." *California Historical Quarterly* (1926): 203-05.

Bennett, James. *Overland to California* [1850]. Indiana: New Harmony, 1906.

Bidwell, John. *Journal of . . . A Journey to California* [1841]. Berkeley: The Friends of the Bancroft Library, 1964.

Bigler, William Henry. *Bigler's Chronicle of the West — Conquest of California, Discovery of Gold and Mormon Settlement.* Ed. Erwin G. Gudde. Berkeley: University of California Press, 1962.

Bloom, Henry S. "Tales of the Pioneers of the Kankakee" [1850]. Typescript, BL.

Blue River [Illinois] Association of United Baptists. *Minutes* 1833-42.

Booth, Edmund. *Forty-Niner, The Life Story of a Deaf Pioneer.* Stockton, Calif.: San Joaquin Pioneer and Historical Society, 1953.

Borthwick, J. D. *The Gold Hunters — A First Hand Picture of Life in California Mining Camps in the Early Fifties.* New York and Cleveland: Macmillan, 1917.

Bowen, Ben. "A Record of Life Commenced at Fort John, California September, 1854." Manuscript, BL.

Bowmer, Angus L. *As I remember, Adam, an Autobiography of a Festival.* Ashland, Oreg.: The Oregon Shakespearean Festival Association, 1975.

Bowmer, Mrs. Angus L. Family photographs and newspaper clippings; Sept. 11, 1979, and Feb. 13, 1980, letters to Jeanne Watson.

Breyfogle, Joshua D. Diary [1849]. Typescript, BL.

Brewer, William H. *Up and Down California, 1860-4.* Ed. Francis P. Farquhar. Berkeley: University of California Press, 1966.

Brooks, J. Tyrwhitt. *Four Months Among the Gold Fields in Alta, California.* London: David Bogue, 1849. Supposedly written by Henry Vizatelly and David Bogue, neither of whom had ever seen the California mines.

Brooks, Elisha. *A Pioneer Mother of California* [1850]. San Francisco: H. Wagner, 1922.

Brooks, Noah. "The Plains Across," *The Century Magazine* (1902): 803-20. Brooks gives no dates for his overland trip, but, from his description of Fort Bridger it must have been after 1853.

———. *The Boy Emigrants.* New York: Charles Scribner's Sons, 1900. Fiction.

Brown, B. D. Jan. 17, 1845, letter from Barry, Ill., to William Blair concerning the division of Pike County. William Blair correspondence. Manuscript, ISHL.

Brown, John Evans. "Memoirs of an American Gold Seeker," [1849] *Journal of American History* (1908): 129-54.

Browning, Orville Hickman. *Diary 1850-64.* Ed. Theodore C. Pease and James G. Randall. Springfield, Ill.: ISHL, 1925.

Bruff, J. Goldsborough. *Gold Rush — Journals and Drawings.* Ed. Georgia Willis Read and Ruth Gaines. New York: Columbia University Press, 1949.

Buck, Franklin A. *A Yankee Trader in the Gold Rush — The Letters of. . . ,* compiled by Katharine A. White. Boston and New York: Houghton Mifflin; Cambridge: The Riverside Press, 1930.

Burgess, William Hubert. Letters and Note Book. Manuscript, CaHS.

———"California Is Quite a Different Place Now, The Gold Rush Letters and Sketches of. . . ." by Gary Kurutz. *California Historical Quarterly* (1977): 250-69.

Burlend, Rebecca. *A True Picture of the Emigration* [1831]. Ed. Milo Milton Quaife. Chicago: The Lakeside Press, 1936.

Burrows, Thomas. "Letters from California, 1853-58." Typescripts, Vera Conover collection, Monmouth County Historical Association, N. J.

Burton, Richard F. *The City of the Saints and Across the Rocky Mountains to California* [1860]. New York: Alfred A. Knopf, 1963.

Cain, Joseph and Brower, Ariah C. *The Famous Mormon Way-Bill to the Gold*

Fields of California from Pacific Springs. Great Salt Lake City and Desert: W. Richards, 1851.

California Baptist Church — San Francisco Association:

Minutes, First Annual Meeting: June 13-16, 1851, Sacramento City. New York: Holman and Gray, 1851.

Minutes, June 11-14, 1852, San Jose. New York: Holman and Gray, 1852.

Minutes, June 9-11, 1855, First Baptist Church, Sacramento. San Francisco: Whitton, Towne & Co., 1855.

Minutes, June 7-9, 1856, Baptist Church, Oakland. San Francisco: Sterett & Co. 1856.

Minutes, May 7-10, 1857, First Baptist Church, San Francisco. San Francisco: B. F. Sterett, 1857.

Minutes, May 8-10, 1858, First Baptist Church, Stockton. San Francisco: G. W. Stevens, 1858.

_____State Convention:

Minutes, Sept. 28, 1854, Santa Rosa. San Francisco: Whitton, Towne and Co., 1854.

Minutes, Feb. 2-4, 1860, First Baptist Church, San Francisco. San Francisco: Towne & Bacon, 1860.

Minutes, May 11-13, 1867, Marysville. San Francisco: Towne & Bacon, 1867.

_____Sacramento Valley Association:

Minutes, Sept. 12-14, 1857, First Baptist Church, Sacramento. Typscript, in research notes of Sandford Fleming, American Baptist Seminary of the West Library, Berkeley, Calif.

Minutes, Sept. 8-10, 1860, Sacramento Baptist Church. San Francisco: Towne & Bacon, 1860.

California Methodist Episcopal Church:

Minutes of the California Annual Conference, third session, March 16-22, 1855. San Francisco: Alta California Pioneer Press, 1855.

Minutes, fourth session, Aug. 27-Sept. 3, 1856, San Jose. San Francisco: Sterett & Co., 1856.

Conference Minutes, 33rd session, Central Methodist Episcopal Church, Stockton, 1885. San Francisco: Methodist Book Depository, 1885.

California Pictorial Almanac, 1858. San Francisco: Hutchings and Rosenfield, 1858.

California Pictorial Letter Sheets, 1849-67, introduction and bibliography by Joseph A. Baird. San Francisco: David Magee, 1967.

California State Almanac and Annual Register for 1856. Sacramento: Democratic State Journal, 1856.

California State Register and Year Book of Facts for the Year 1857. San Francisco: Henry C. Langley and Samuel A. Mathews, 1857.

Canfield, Chauncey L. *The Diary of a Forty-Niner* [1849-50]. Stanford: James Ladd Delkin, 1947.

Caples, Mary Jane (Mrs. James). "Overland Journey to California" [1849]. Typescript, CSL.

Carpenter, Helen. "A Trip Across the Plains in an Ox Cart" [1857] in *Ho for*

California! by Sandra L. Myres. San Marino, Calif.: Huntington Library, 1980.

Carr, John. *Pioneer Days in California* [1850]. Eureka, Calif.: Times Publishing Co., 1891.

Carrie & Damon's California Almanac, 1856. San Francisco: Carrie & Damon, 1856.

Carstarphen, James E. *My Trip to California* [1849]. Fairfield, Wash.: Ye Galleon Press, 1971.

Carter, William. March 8, 1847, letter from Pittsfield, Ill., Congregational Church to James R. Wick. Manuscript, ISHL.

Casler, Mel. *A Journal Giving the Incidents of a Journey to California in the Summer of 1859.* Fairfield, Wash.: Ye Galleon Press, 1969.

Castle Family Papers, including 1854-60 letters of Frances A. (Ferry) Castle. Manuscript, BL.

Chandless, William. *A Visit to Salt Lake, Being a Journey Across the Plains and a Residence in the Mormon Settlement of Utah.* Reprint. New York: Ams Press, 1971.

Charleville, F. A. 1857 Letter to "Dear Dan" from Fiddletown, Calif., Gold Rush Letters, No. 106. Manuscript, BL.

Cheney, J. "The Story of an Emigrant Train" [1858], *Annals of Iowa* (1915): 80-97.

Child, Andrew. *Overland Route to California* [1850]. Reprint. Los Angeles: N. A. Kovach, 1946.

Chiles, Joseph Ballinger. *Trail-Blazing Pioneer.* Ed. Helen Griffen. San Francisco: John Howell Books, 1969.

Christy, Thomas. *Road Across the Plains* [1850]. Ed. Robert Becker. Denver: Fred A. Rosenstock, 1969.

Clapp, John T. *A Journal of Travels to and from California with Full Details of the Hardships and Privations; also a Description of the Country, Mines, Cities, Towns, &* [1850]. Kalamazoo: Kalamazoo Public Museum, 1977.

Clappe, Louise Amelia Smith. *The Shirley Letters from the California Mines, 1852.* New York: Alfred A. Knopf, 1965.

Clark, John Hawkins. "Overland to the Gold Fields of California in 1852." Ed. Louise Barry. *Kansas Historical Quarterly,* (1942): 227-96.

Clark, Sterling B. F. *How Many Miles from St. Jo?* [1849] with commentary by Ella Sterling Mighels. San Francisco: privately printed, 1929.

Clayton, William. *The Latter-Day Saints' Emigrants' Guide . . . from Council Bluffs to the Valley of the Great Salt Lake.* St. Louis: Missouri Republican, 1848. Reprinted in Leander V. Loomis *A Journal of the Birmingham Emigrating Company* [1850]. Salt Lake City: Legal Printing Co., 1928.

Clough, John P., Jr. July 28, 1853, letter to "Friend Vira" from Stockton, Calif. Manuscript, BY.

Cole, Gilbert. *The Overland Trail in Nebraskas Territory in 1852.* Kansas City: Franklin Hudson Co., 1905.

Comstock, Loring Samuel. *A Journal of Travels Across the Plains in the Year 1855.* Ed. Mrs. Stillman T. Clark. Oskaloosa, Iowa: Mahaska County Historical Society, n.d.

Conyers, E. W. "Diary of A Pioneer of 1852," Oregon Pioneer Association

Transactions, 33rd Annual Reunion, 1905.

Cool, Peter Y. Pocket Day-Book and Letters. Manuscript and typescript, Aram Papers 27, HL. Copies at Methodist Library, Drew University, N. J.

Cool, Sarah Mahala Aram. "Biographical Sketch of Her Husband, the Rev. Peter Cool, and Frontier Life, Incidents and Work in California, 1883." Manuscript, HL.

Crawford, J. G. Ledger Book — Accounts, 1837-1850s, Griggsville, Ill. Private collection.

Cresswell, John M. "Getting off from Iowa to California in the Spring of 1850," *Annals of Iowa* (1935): 71-73. This letter to his brother mentions the name of Tom Christy, whose diary is listed above.

Cross, Samuel E. Unfinished letter with additions by Dwight Hollister, printed Mar. 21, 1850, in the Marietta, Ohio, *Intellegencer;* reprinted in *The Gold Rush Diary* of Elisha D. Perkins. Ed. Thomas D. Clark. Lexington: University of Kentucky Press, 1967. Cross, who died Jan. 8, 1850, had begun the letter earlier and Hollister finished up the sheet.

Daigh, James M. *Nuggets from '49, An Account of Pike County Men in the Gold Rush,* condensed from diary by Owen Hannat. Chambersburg, Ill.: Privately printed, 1949.

Daughters of the American Revolution. Amador County Cemetery Records, Vols. 16, 17, 18.

_____. Vital Statistics compiled from the San Francisco *Daily Evening Bulletin,* 1860-61.

Decker, Peter. *Diaries, Overland to California and Life in the Mines* [1849]. Ed. Helen S. Griffen. Georgetown, Calif.: Talisman Press, 1966.

DeWolf, David. Diary and Letters [1849]. Manuscript, ISHL.

Doble, John. *Journal and Letters from the Mines: Mokelumne Hill, Jackson, Volcano and San Francisco.* Ed. Charles L. Camp. Denver: Fred A. Rosenstock, 1962.

Doyle, Simon. April 22, 1853, letter to his father from Union Bar, on the Feather River, Calif. Manuscript, BY.

Duncan, Elizabeth Caldwell Smith. Diary, 1841-48. Illinois State Historical Society *Transactions* (1928): 1-84.

Early California — Northern Edition. Portland, Oreg.: Binford & Mort, 1974. Compilation of old photographs and maps, 1830-1920.

Eckland Family Papers, including letters and records.

Eno, Henry. *Twenty Years on the Pacific Slope, Letters from California and Nevada, 1848-71.* Ed. W. Turrentine Jackson. New Haven: Yale University Press, 1965.

Evans, Burrell Whalen. Diary [1849]. Microfilm, BL.

Ewer, Ferdinand Cartwright. Diary [1826-60]. Manuscript, CaHS.

Fairchild, Lucius. *California Letters* [1849-50]. Ed. Joseph Schafer. Madison: Wisconsin State Historical Society, 1931.

Fern, Fanny (Mrs. James Parton). *Fern Leaves from Fanny's Port-folio.* Auburn, New York: Derby and Miller; Buffalo: Derby, Orton and Mulligan; Cincinnati: Henry W. Derby, 1853.

_____*Twelfth Thousand Fern Leaves from Fanny's Port-folio.* Auburn and Buffalo, New York: Miller, Orton & Mulligan; London: Sampson Low, Son & Co., 1854.

Fish, Issac B. Journal, Vol. 2 [1852-55]. Manuscript, Pacific School of Religion, Berkeley, Calif.

Fish, Naomi (Mrs. Issac). Journal, c. 1850 (incomplete). Manuscript, Pacific School of Religion, Berkeley, Calif.

Foster, William C. "Gold Rush Journey: A Letter" [1850]. Ed. Dwayne Bolling. *Nebraska History* (Fall 1981): 400-10.

Frazier, Mrs. Rachel. *Reminiscences of Travel from 1855-57.* San Francisco: Francis and Valentine, 1871.

Fremont, John Charles. *Report of the Exploring Expedition to the Rocky Mountains in 1842 and to Oregon and Northern California in the Years 1843-44.* Washington D.C.: Gales and Seaton, 1845.

_____*Narrative of the Exploring Expedition to the Rocky Mountains (1842) and to Oregon and Northern California (1843-44),* "reprinted from the official copy." New York: D. Appleton & Co; Philadelphia: Geo. S. Appleton; Cincinnati: Derby, Bradley & Co., 1846. This edition, without the maps and scientific tables, contains only 186 pages as compared to 693 pages in the "official copy," printed in 1845.

_____*Geographical Memoir upon Upper California, in Illustration of His Map of Oregon and California, Address to the United States Senate.* Washington, D.C.: Wendell and Van Benthuysen, 1848.

Frink, Margaret. *Journal of the Adventures of a Party of California Gold-Seekers, Overland to California in 1850, under the Guidance of Ledyard Frink.* Oakland, Calif., 1897.

Frizzell, Mrs. Lodisa. *Across the Plains to California in 1852* (incomplete). Ed. Victor Hugo Paltsits. New York: The New York Public Library, 1915.

Gates, Frances Elizabeth Ward. *Frankie's Journal.* Ed. by Florence Stark DeWitt. Los Angeles: Western-lore Press, 1960.

Geiger, Vincent and Bryarly, Wakeman. *Trail to California* [1849]. New Haven: Yale University Press, 1962.

Geological Reconnaissance in California. Report of the Secretary of War, 1850, 31st Congress, first session, Senate Executive Document No. 47, 1850.

Gillette, Martha Hill. *Overland to Oregon [1852] and in the Indian Wars of 1853.* Ashland, Oreg.: Lewis Osborne, 1971.

Gilman, Charles. Feb. 2, 1849, letter from Quincy, Ill., to Horace S. Cooley. Manuscript, ISHL.

Glisan, Rodney. *Journal of Army Life.* San Francisco: A. L. Bancroft & Co., 1847.

Gould, Charles and Staples, David Jackson. *The Boston-Newton Party, From Massachusetts to California in 1849.* Ed. Jessie Gould Hannon. Lincoln: University of Nebraska, 1969.

Gray, Charles Glass. *Off at Sunrise* [1849]. Ed. Thomas D. Clark. San Marino, Calif: Huntington Library, 1976.

Green, Jay. *Diary of. . .* [1852]. Ed. Merrell Kitchen. Stockton, Calif.: San Joaquin Pioneer and Historical Society, 1955.

Grindell, John. "The Overland Narrative of . . . from Platteville, Wisconsin, to California in 1850." Typescript 233, Coe Collection, BY.

Hartronft, Abraham. "A Professional Man's Diary" [1854]. *Naperville* [Ill.] *Sun*, Feb. 19, 1970.

Harthshorne Letters. Correspondence from California, 1849-55, of Charles Minturn, Robert Hartshorne and Benjamin Minturn Hartshorne. Manuscripts, Hartshorne Family papers, Monmouth County Historical Association, N.J.

Hastings, Lansford W. *The Emigrant's Guide to Oregon and California.* Reprint. New York: Da Capo Press, 1969.

Hatch, Lewis. "Journal from Home to California [1850]." Manuscript, Lake County Museum, Ill.

Haun, Catherine. "A Woman's Trip Across the Plains in 1849" in *Women's Diaries of the Westward Journey* by Lillian Schlissel. New York: Schocken Books, 1982.

Hayes, Charles Wells. *George Hayes of Windsor and His Descendants.* Buffalo, New York: Baker, Jones & Co., 1884.

Hays, Alson. Estate Papers and Records, Pike County Circuit Court, Pittsfield, Ill.

Hays, Martin. Will, Sept. 2, 1846. Will Book C, 187, Erie County Court House, Erie, Pa.

Hecox, Margaret M. *California Caravan* [1846]. San Jose: Harlan-Young Press, 1966.

Helper, Hinton Rowan. "On the Land of Gold" [1851]. Ed. Benjamin Franklin Gilbert. *Journal of the West* (1973): 521-62.

Henderson, Lucy Ann. "Young Adventurer," *Nevada Historical Society Quarterly* (Summer 1973).

Hildreth, George D. Dec. 24, 1849, letter in the Marietta, Ohio, *Intellegencer*, Mar. 28, 1850, reprinted in Elisha Perkins. *Gold Rush Diary.* Lexington: University of Kentucky Press, 1967.

Hine, Robert V. and Lottinville, Savoie. *Soldiers in the West, The Letters, 1845-53, of Theodore Talbot during His Service in California, Mexico and Oregon.* Norman: University of Oklahoma Press, 1972.

History of Saint Louis City. Vol. 1. Philadelphia: Louis H. Everts & Co., 1883.

History of St. Louis and Improvements of the Year [1853] and Annual Review. St. Louis: Republican Steam Press, 1854.

Hittel, Theodore H. *History of California.* Vol. 3. San Francisco: Stone & Co., 1897.

Hixson, Adrietta Applegate. *On to Oregon— A True Story of a Young Girl's Journey into the West* [1852]. Fairfield, Wash.: Ye Galleon Press, 1971. The reminiscences of her mother, Mary Ellen Todd, written after her death by her daughter.

Hixson, Jasper Morris. "Diary" [1849] in *The Great Trek* by Owen C. Coy. Los Angeles: Powell Co., 1931.

Hixon and Co. *Plat Book of Pike County, Illinois.* Rockford, Ill.: ca. 1907.

Holley, C. A. Letter from Frenchtown, Calif., 1853, to his parents. Manuscript 82, Gold Rush Letters, BL.

Horn, Hosea J. *Overland Guide from Council Bluffs to Sacramento, California.* New York: J. H. Colton, 1852.

Howe, Henry. *The Great West*. New York: George F. Tuttle; Cincinnati: Henry Howe, 1857.

Howe, Octavius T. *Argonauts of '49*. Cambridge, Mass., and London: Harvard University Press, 1970.

Humphreys, L. Overland Guide from Kanesville to Oregon City (undated except for May 2, 1853, testimonial as to its usefulness). Photocopy of manuscript map and mileage, 266, Coe collection, BY.

Hunt, Nancy. "By Ox-Train to California, A Personal Narrative" [1854]. Ed. Rockwell D. Hunt, *Overland Monthly* (April 1916): 317-26.

Hutchings, James Mason. *Seeking the Elephant, 1849, Journal of His Overland Trek to California including His Voyage to America, 1848, and Letters from the Mother Lode*. Ed. Shirley Sargent. Glendale, Calif.: The Arthur H. Clark Co., 1980.

———. *Scenes of Wonder and Curiosity in California*. San Francisco: Hutchings & Rosenfield, 1860.

Hutton, William Rich. *Glances at California, 1847-53, Diaries and Letters*. San Marino, Calif.: Huntington Library, 1942.

Illinois Manuscript Land Book, [1850]. Maps, descriptions, and valuations, ISHL.

Illinois Methodist Episcopal Church. *Minutes of the Illinois Annual Conference*, 1852, 29th session, Winchester, Ill. St. Louis: The Intelligencer, 1852. Includes fourth *Annual Catalog* of the Illinois Conference's Female College at Jacksonville, Ill.

———. *Journal and Records*, 1885, 62nd session of the Illinois Annual Conference, Rushville, Ill. Methodist Serials, 1885-95. Jacksonville, Ill.: Illinois Courier, 1885.

Ingalls, Eleazar S. *Journal of a Trip to California by the Overland Route across the Plains in 1850-51*. Waukegan, Ill.: Tobey & Co., 1852.

Ingersoll, Charles. *Overland to California in 1847*. Fairfield, Wash.: Ye Galleon Press, 1970.

Irwin, I. N. *Sacramento Directory and Gazetter-Years 1857-58*. San Francisco: S. P. Valentine & Sons, 1857.

Isham, Giles S. *Guide to California and the Mines* [1849]. Fairfield, Wash.: Ye Galleon Press, 1972.

Jefferson, T. H. *Accompaniment to the Map of the Emigrant Road from Independence, Mo., to St. Francisco, California (1849) — Brief Practical Advice to the Emigrant or Traveler*. Reprint. Photocopy of the 1849 eleven-page original published by the author in New York with *Introduction to the Map of T. H. Jefferson* by George R. Stewart. San Francisco: California Historical Society, 1945.

Johnston, William G. *Overland to California, First Wagon Train to California in 1849*. Oakland: Biobooks, 1948.

Jones, J. Wesley. "Pantoscope of California," *California Historical Quarterly* (1927). Includes three views of the Emigrant Trail across the Carson Pass.

Josselyn, Amos Piatt. *The Overland Journal of . . .* [1849]. Ed. William Barrett II. Baltimore: Gateway Press Inc., 1978.

Kappler, Charles J., ed. *Indian Treaties, 1778-1883*. New York: Interland Publishing Inc., 1972.

Keller, Agnes DuVal and Shafter, Roberta Liles Zachary. Pike County, Illinois, Marriages, Vol. 2, 1846-53. Typescript, ISHL.

Kelly, Charles. "Emigrant Register — Names and Dates Found Along the Old Emigrant Trails." A listing of approximately 3,000 names recorded between 1933 and 1941. Typescript plus research notes and photographs, BL.

Kelly, William. *Across the Rocky Mountains from New York to California* [1849]. London: Simmons and M'Intrye, 1852.

Kilgore, William H. *Journal of an Overland Journey to California* [1850]. Ed. Joyce R. Muench. New York: Hastings House, 1949.

Knox, Reuben. *A Medic Fortyniner, Life and Letters of* . . . [1849-51]. Ed. Charles W. Turner. McClure Press, 1974.

Langworthy, Franklin. *Scenery of the Plains, Mountains and Mines.* Ed. Paul C. Phillips from 1855 edition. Princeton: Princeton University Press, 1932.

Lithgow-Woodward Family Genealogy, records and letters. Collection of Bernice Hoover.

Leeper, D. R. *The Argonauts of Forty-Nine.* South Bend, Ind.: J. B. Stoll & Co., 1894.

Lobenstein, William C. *Extracts from the Diary of* . . . [December 31, 1851-58] , with biographical sketch by Belle W. Lobenstine. Privately printed, 1920.

Loomis, Leander V. *A Journal of the Birmingham Emigrating Company* [1850]. Ed. Edgar M. Ledyard. Salt Lake City: Legal Printing Co., 1928.

Loveland, Cyrus Clark. *California Trail Herd* [1850]. Ed. Richard H. Dillon. Los Gatos, Calif.: Talisman Press, 1961.

McAuley, Eliza Ann. Diary [1852]. Typescript, ISHS.

M'Collum, William. *California as I Saw It* [1849-50]. Ed. Dale Morgan. Los Gatos, Calif.: Talisman Press, 1960.

McDarmid, Finley. Letters [1850]. Manuscript, BL.

McGuffey, Wm. H. *McGuffey's New Fourth Eclectic Reader — Instructive Lessons for the Young.* Cincinnati: Sargent, Wilson & Hinkle; New York: Clark and Maynard, 1857.

McKeeby, Lemuel Clark. *The Memoirs of* . . . [1850]. San Francisco: California Historical Society, 1924.

McKinstry, Byron N. *The California Gold Rush Diary of.* . . [1850-52]. Ed. Bruce L. McKinstry. Glendale, Calif.: The Arthur H. Clark Co. American Trail Series, 1975.

Madarasz, Martha A. Cemetery Inscriptions, Pike County, Ill. Typescript, ISHL.

Magoon, George D. "The California Journey of. . . ." [1852- 54]. Ed. Mildred Throne. *The Iowa Journal of History* (April 1956).

Manly, William Lewis. *Death Valley in '49.* New York and Santa Barbara: Wallace Hebberd, 1929.

Marcy, Randolph B. *The Prairie Traveler — A Handbook for Overland Expeditions* [1859]. Williamstown, Mass.: Corner House Publishers, 1968.

Marietta Company. Letter of Apr. 9, 1850, from "some of the young men" in Longtown, El Dorado County, Calif. Reprinted in Elisha Perkins' *Gold Rush Diary* [1849]. Ed. Thomas D. Clark. Lexington: University of Kentucky Press, 1967.

Marryat, Frank. *Mountains and Molehills* [1855]. Reprint. Philadelphia and

New York: J. B. Lippincott Co., Keystone Western Americana Series, 1962.

Maxwell, William Audley. *Crossing the Plains* [1857]. San Francisco: Sunset Publishing House, 1915.

Meeker, Ezra. *The Ox Team or The Old Oregon Trail, 1852-1906.* Indianapolis: 1906.

_____. *Kate Mulhall — A Romance of the Oregon Trail* [1852?]. New York: Ezra Meeker, 1926.

Megquier, Mary Jane. *Apron Full of Gold, Letters from San Francisco, 1849-50.* Ed. Robert Glass Cleland. Los Angeles: Ward Richie Press, 1949.

Methodist Church. Ministers File (names and information about nineteenth century ministers). Methodist Library, Drew University, N. J.

Meyer, Carl. *Bound for Sacramento,* translated from the German by Ruth Frey Axes. Claremont, Calif.: Saunders Studio Press, 1938.

Mitchells, Lyman. Journal [1849]. Microfilm, BL.

Moerenhout, Jacques Antoine. *Inside Story of the Gold Rush.* Ed. Abraham P. Nasatir. San Francisco: Special Publication No. 8, California Historical Society, 1935.

Moorman, Madison Berryman. *The Journal of . . . 1850-51.* Ed. Irene D. Paden. San Francisco: California Historical Society, 1948.

Morgan, Martha M. *A Trip Across the Plains in the Year 1849.* Reprint. Fairfield, Wash: Ye Galleon Press, 1983. The author was actually her husband, Jesse Morgan, killed August 14, 1850, in Sacramento, according to Dale Morgan. (See *The Overland Diary of James A. Pritchard, 1849.* Denver: Fred A. Rosenstock, 1959.)

Murray, Janet, ed. *Strong-Minded Women and Other Lost Voices from 19th Century England.* New York: Pantheon Books, 1982.

Naper, Robert. Letters [1850]. *Naperville* [Ill.] *Recorder,* 1850. Typescript of DuPage County [Ill.] history compiled by the Daughters of the American Revolution. Caroline Martin-Mitchell Museum — Naper Settlement. Al Frink. *Aurora* [Ill.] *Beacon News,* Apr. 20, 1971. Naper, who ran a hotel in Placerville in July 1850, was a friend of Morris Sleight [also from Naperville] whose letters are at the Chicago Historical Society. The DAR typescript also contains brief information about other men from Naperville who participated in the California gold rush, as do the files at the Martin-Mitchell Museum.

Nevada Emigrant Trail Marking Committee Inc. *The Overland Emigrant Trail to California, a Guide to Trail Markers Placed in Western Nevada and the Sierra Nevada Mountains in California.* Reno: Nevada Historical Society, 1975.

Newcomb, Harvey. *The Young Lady's Guide to the Harmonious Development of Christian Character.* Boston: James B. Dow, Fourth Edition Revised and Enlarged, 1842.

Nobles, William H. *Speech of . . . Together with Other Documents Relative to an Emigrant Route to California and Oregon through the Minnesota Territory.* St. Paul: Omstead & Brown, 1854.

Oliver, William. *Eight Months in Illinois, with Information for the Emigrant.* Newcastle upon Tyne: William Andrew Mitchell, 1843. Reprint. Ann Arbor: University Microfilm Inc., 1966.

Orr, Thomas, Jr. *Life History.* Ed. Lillie Jane Orr Taylor. Privately printed, 1930.

Owen, Isaac. "Account of Individual Preachers [Methodist] and Biographical Sketches," Pocket Note Book. Manuscript, Pacific School of Religion, Berkeley, Calif.

Packard, Major Wellman. *Early Emigration to California* [1849]. Fairfield, Wash.: Ye Galleon Press, 1971.

Page, Elizabeth. *Wagons West — A Story of the Oregon Trail* [1849]. New York: Farrar & Rinehart Inc. 1930.

Palmer, Joel. *Journal of Travels over the Rocky Mountains in 1845-46 to Oregon.* Reprint. Ann Arbor: University Microfilm Inc. facsimile edition.

Panabaker, W. R. "Tells of Trek to California during '49 Gold Rush,"in *A History of Lawrence County, Illinois, Physicians and A Review of Medicine as Practiced 100 Years Ago* by Dr. Tom Kirkwood. Lawrence County, Ill.: Lawrence County Historical Society, 1975.

Pardee, Enoch H. February 8, 14, and 27, 1855, letters. Pardee Home Foundation, Oakland, Calif. The "Mr. Bowmer" mentioned in these letters was Lorena's husband, a patient of Dr. Pardee.

Parkman, Francis. *The Oregon Trail* [1846]. Reprint. Chicago: Longman's Green and Co., 1914.

Peacock, William. *The Peacock Letters, 1850-52.* Stockton, Calif.: San Joaquin Pioneer and Historical Society, 1950.

Peck, James Mason. *A Gazetteer of Illinois in Three Parts.* Second edition. Jacksonville, Ill.: R. Goudy, 1834; Philadelphia: Grigg and Elliot, 1837.

———. *A New Guide for the Emigrants to the West.* Second edition. Boston: Gould, Kendall & Lincoln, 1837.

Perkins, Elisha Douglas. *Gold Rush Diary, Being a Journal of . . . on the Overland Trail in the Spring and Summer of 1849.* Ed. Thomas D, Clark. Lexington: University of Kentucky Press, 1967.

Peters, Charles. *The Autobiography of . . ., the Good Luck Era — Placer Mining Days of the '50s (in 1915 the oldest pioneer living in California who mined in the days of '49 also historical happenings, interesting incidents and illustrations of the old mining towns).* Sacramento: The LaGrave Co., 1915.

Peters, Henry H. January 21, 1853, letter written from Sacramento. Manuscript, New York Public Library.

Pfeiffer, Ida Laura Reyer. *A Lady's Visit to California, 1853, from her Second Journey Round the World.* New York: Harper Brothers, 1856, and Oakland: Biobooks, 1950. She arrived in San Francisco from southeast Asia en route to New Orleans.

Pike County, Ill., Superintendent of Schools. *Proceedings of the Second Session of the Pike County Teachers' Institute, held at Barry, commencing Sept. 23, and closing Oct. 5, 1850.* Pittsfield, Ill.: Free Press, 1850.

———. *Programme of Teachers Institute in Eldara,* January 24 (no year). Private collection.

Platt, P. L. and Slater, N. *Travelers' Guide to California* [1852]. San Francisco: John Howell Books, 1963.

Pritchard, James A. *Overland Diary of . . . from Kentucky to California* [1849]. Ed. Dale L. Morgan. Denver: Fred A. Rosenstock, 1959.

Prouty, William H. "Reminiscences of a Trip West, circa 1852," talk given to Native Sons and Daughters of the Golden West "around the turn of the century." *Amador* (Calif.) *Ledger, Dispatch and Progress News,* Jan. 6, 1982, and *Progress News,* Jan. 13, 1982.

Pruess, Charles. *Exploring with Fremont* [1843-44]. Trans. and ed. Erwin C. and Elisabeth K. Gudde. Norman: University of Oklahoma Press, 1958.

Reed, George Willis. *A Pioneer of 1850.* Ed. Georgia Reed. Boston: Little, Brown and Company, 1927.

Register of Mines and Minerals, Amador County. San Francisco: State Mining Bureau, August 1903.

Ressler, Theo. C. "Across Iowa in 'Forty-Nine." *The Palimpsest* (January-February 1974): 2-17.

Richard, Spencer. 1855 Letter to "Friend Warren," Fiddletown, Calif. Manuscript No. 26, Gold Rush Letters, BL.

Richardson, Alpheus. Diary [1852]. Microfilm, BL.

Richardson, Caroline [not related to the above]. Day Book and Journal [1852], Poems and Receipes. Manuscript, BL.

Robinson, Fayette and Street, Franklin. *The Gold Mines of California — Two Guide Books* [1849 and 1850]. New York: Promontory Press, 1974.

Robinson, Harriet H. *Looms & Spindles or Life Among the Early Mill Girls.* Reprint. Kailua, Hawaii: Press Pacific, 1976.

Robinson, Zirkle D. *Journey to the Gold Fields of California* [1849]. Ed. Francis C. Rosenberger. Iowa City: The Prairie Press, 1966.

Royce, Sarah. *A Frontier Lady.* New Haven: Yale University Press, 1932.

Rudd, Lydia Allen. "Notes by the Wayside En Route to Oregon, 1852" in *Women's Diaries of the Westward Journey* by Lillian Schlissel. New York: Schocken Books, 1982.

San Joaquin Genealogical Society. "Gold Rush Days — Vital Statistics from early newspapers of Stockton, Calif., 1850-55." Introduction by Mildred Fitts Pyle. Typescript.

San Francisco Directory, 1854.

Sawyer, Mrs. Frances H. Overland to California [1852]. Typescript, BL.

Sawyer, Lorenzo (no relation to the above.) *Way Sketches, Containing Incidents of Travel Across the Plains from St. Joseph to California in 1850.* New York: Edward Eberstadt, 1926.

Schoolcraft, Henry Rowe. *History of the Indian Tribes of the United States, Their Present Condition and Prospects and a Sketch of Their Ancient Status.* Reprint. Published by order of Congress, under the direction of the Department of the Interior, Indian Bureau. Philadelphia: J. B. Lippincott & Co., 1857. Historical American Indian Press, n.d.

Schwartz, Alois and Ferdinand. Letter of June 20, 1895, in *The Pioneer,* Aug. 15, 1895. Interview by Jeanne Watson, Oct. 5, 1974, with Naperville, Ill., descendants.

Searls, Niles. Diary of a Pioneer and Other Papers [1849]. San Francisco: n.p., n.d.

Shastid, Thomas Hall. *My Second Life.* Ann Arbor: George Wahr, 1944.

Shaw, Pringle. *Ramblings in California: Containing a Description of the Country, Life at the Mines, State of Society &c. Interspersed with Characteristic Anedotes and*

Sketches from Life, Being the Five Year's Experience of a Gold Digger. Toronto: James Bain, n.d., Reel No. 192, American Culture II, University Microfilm, Ann Arbor, Mich.

Shaw, Ruben Cole. *Across the Plains in Forty-nine.* Ed. Milo Milton Quaife. Chicago: The Lakeside Press, 1948.

Shepherd, J. S. *Journal of Travel Across the Plains to California and Guide to the Future Emigrant.* Racine, Wisc.: Mrs. Rebecca Shepherd, 1851.

Sherman, Edwin A. "Sherman Was There — Recollections of. . . ." *California Historical Quarterly* (September 1944): 259; (January 1945): 67-69; (February 1945): 165-80.

Sleight, Morris. 1853-54 letters from Aurum City, Sacramento, the Western House, and San Francisco to his wife and family in Naperville, Ill. Manuscript, ChHS.

Sloss, J. H. *The St. Louis Directory for 1848.* St. Louis: Charles & Hammond, 1848.

Smith, C. W. *Journal of a Trip to California* [1850]. Ed. R. W. G. Vail. Manchester, N. H.: Standard Book Co., 1920.

Spalding, C. C. *Annals of the City of Kansas and the Great Western Plains.* Kansas City: Van Horn & Abeel, 1858.

Spooner, E. A. Diary [1849]. Microfilm, BL.

Sprague, Paul E. "Inventory of Architecture before World War II in Pike County, Ill." Illinois Historic Structure Survey, October 1974, Illinois Department of Conservation. Typescript, ChHS.

Stackpole, William T. Diary [1849]. Manuscript, BY.

Stansbury, Howard. *An Expedition to the Valley of the Great Salt Lake.* London: Sampson Low, Son & Co., 1852. Reprint. Ann Arbor: University Microfilm Inc., facsimile copy, 1966.

Starr, Franklin. Letter of May 16, 1850. Manuscript, ISHL; Diary [1850]. Microfilm, BL.

Swain, William. *The World Rushed In, The California Gold Rush Experience, An Eyewitness Account of a Nation Heading West* [1849]. Ed. J. S. Holliday. New York: Simon and Schuster, 1981.

Tarbell, J. *Dr. Tarbell's California Guide.* Keokuk, Iowa: Whig Book, 1853.

Taylor, Bayard. *Eldorado or Adventures in the Path of Empire.* New York: George P. Putnam & Co., 1854.

Thornton, J. Quinn. "Five Months and 2,000 Miles to Oregon," in *Western Wagon Wheels* by Lambert Florin. Seattle: Superior Publishing Co., 1970.

Tourtillott, Jane Augusta Holbrook Gould. Diary [1862]. Microfilm, BL.

Trollope, Frances. *Domestic Manners of the Americans.* New York: Dodd, Mead & Co., 1927.

True, Charles F. *Covered Wagon Pioneers* [1858]. Ed. Sally R. True. Madison: College Printing Co., 1966.

Turnbull, Thomas. *Travels from the United States across the Plains to California* [1852]. Ed. Frederic L. Paxson. Madison: Wisconsin Historical Society, 1913.

Udell, John. *Incidents of Travel to California* [1850-52-54]. Jefferson, Ohio: 1856.

van den Muysenberg, Th. J. M. Mar. 4, 1980, letter and enclosures concerning "William Nicholas, Prince of Nassau," from the Consul for Press and Cultural Affairs, Consulate General of the Netherlands, New York City, to Jeanne Watson.

Van Zandt, Nicholas Biddle. *A Full Description of the Soil, Water, Timber and Prairies of Each Lot or Quarter Section of the Military Lands between the Mississippi and the Illinois Rivers.* Washington City: P. Force, 1818.

Verdenal, John M. and Dom[ini]que (Dominick). "Journal [1852] from St. Louis, Mo., to Placerville, Calif., by Land." Photocopy of manuscript. Mrs. Verdenal Johnson, Madison, N. J.

Walker, William. "Journals" in *The Provisional Government of the Nebraska Territory.* Vol. 3. William E. Connelly. Lincoln: Nebraska State Historical Society Proceedings and Collections, 1899.

Walker, Zachariah. Diary [1850-51]. Photocopy of manuscript, ISHS.

Ware, Joseph E. *The Emigrants' Guide to California* [1849]. Reprint. Princeton: Princeton University Press, 1932.

Watson, William C. and Jeanne H. Observations, notes and photographs taken while hiking and marking forty miles of the California Trail across the Carson Pass, 1968-87.

Wayman, John Hudson. *A Doctor on the California Trail* [1852]. Ed. Edgeley W. Todd. Denver: Old West Publishing Co., 1971.

Welch, Adonijah Strong. "Three Gold Rush Letters of. . . ." [1849-50]. Ed. William H. Hermann. *Iowa Journal of History* (January 1959): 61-73.

White, Samuel Stephen. July 24, 1855, letter to Col. Peter W. Conover, from Pleasant Grove City, Utah. Manuscript, No. 521, Coe Collection, BY.

Willis, Ira. "Best Guide to the Gold Mines, copied by E. A. Spooner in his Journal." Manuscript, microflim, BL.

Wilson, Luzena Stanley. *Luzena Stanley Wilson, '49er.* Mills College, Calif.: Eucalpytus Press, 1937.

Wilkins, James F. *An Artist on the Overland Trail, Diary and Sketches* [1849]. Ed. John Francis McDermott. San Marino, Calif.: Huntington Library, 1968.

Wintermute, Hampton. "Diary of a Trip to California during the Gold Rush" [1850], a supplement to the Wintermute family history. Typescript, ISHS.

Wood, John. "Along the Emigrant Trail" [1850]. *Motor Land,* December 1928 — April 1929.

Woods, James. *Recollections of Pioneer Work in California.* San Francisco: Joseph Winterburn & Co., 1878.

Woodman, David. Letters and Papers [1852]. Manuscript, Michigan State University.

Woolley, L. H. *California, 1849-1913, or Rambling Sketches and Experiences of Sixty-four Years Residence in the State.* Oakland, Calif.: DeWitt and Snelling, 1913.

Wooster, David. *The Gold Rush Letters from California to the Adrian, Michigan, Expositor, 1850-55.* Mt. Pleasant, Mich.: The Cumming Press, 1972.

Wyman, Walker D. *California Emigrant Letters, The Forty-Niners Write Home.* New York: Bookman Association, 1952.

Yager, James Pressley. "Diary of a Journey Across the Plains" [1863]. *Nevada Historical Society Quarterly,* (Spring 1970-Summer 1971).

Young, Brigham. Letter [from] Salt Lake City, *New York Times,* May 31, 1853.

MAPS

California

Amador County. Survey of J. M. Griffith, 1866, BL.

Army Map Service (SX), Corp of Engineers, Washington D. C. Three dimensional maps of the western United States, 1963, 1:250,000 Series V502: Sacramento, California-Nevada, edition 3-AMS, sheet NJ 10-6, 1961; Walker Lake, Nevada-California. Ed. 2-AMS, sheet NJ 11-4, 195.9

Calaveras, Amador and Tuolumne counties. Map (n.d.) showing the settlement of these counties, compiled from records in the Tuolumne County Courthouse, BL

Baker, George H. Map of the Mining Region of California, 1855. Sacramento: Barber & Baker, BL.

Buell, P. A. Map of part of California showing the Mother Lode mineral belt with railroad and stage line connections to the city of Stockton. Stockton, Calif.: P. A. Buell, 1898, BL.

Colton, Walter. Colton's Map of California (1849), with "particulars of routes, distances, fares, etc. to accompany map of California and the Gold Region," and Aug. 29, 1848, letter to the *Philadelphia American.* Private collection.

Camp, Charles. Map of Central Mines, in the diary of John Doble. Denver: Fred A. Rosenstock, 1962.

Gibbs, C. D. Map of the Southern Mines, 1852, in *A California Gold Rush Miscellany* Jane Bissell Grabhorn. San Francisco: The Grabhorn Press, 1934.

Jackson, W. A. Map of the Gold Regions, 1849, with appendix, in *Inside Story of the Gold Rush* by Jacques Antoine Moerenhout. San Francisco: California Historical Society, 1935. Reprint. San Francicos: John Howell, 1936.

Milleson, M. Improved Topographical Map of the Northern and Middle Mines, 1854. San Francisco: Alex Zakreski, 1854, reprinted in Carl I. Wheat. *Mapping the Transmississippi West.* San Francisco: Institute of Historical Cartography, 1959.

Pierce, Parker H. Official Map of the Washoe Mining Region, with tentative distances from the principal places of California, 1860, BL.

Wheat, Carl I. *Mapping the Transmississippi West, from the Mexican War to the Boundary Survey, 1846-54.* Vol. 3. San Francisco: Institute of Historical Cartography, 1959.

————. *The Maps of the California Gold Region, 1848-57, A Biblio-cartography of an Important Decade.* San Francisco: The Grabhorn Press, 1942.

Illinois

Pike County. 1860 Map. Buffalo, N.Y.: Holmes and Arnold, 1860. (Includes business directory and pictures.) ISHL.

Andreas, Lyter, & Co. Atlas Map of Pike County, Compiled, Drawn and Published from Personal Examinations and Surveys. Davenport, Iowa: Andreas, Lyter & Co., 1872.

Atlas of the State of Illinois, 1876, tracing of Pike County, plus 1907 letter from A. C. Matthews of Pittsfield to Mrs. Jessie Palmer Weber, ISHL.

Cowperthwait, Thomas and Co. Map of the State of Illinois, c. 1850. Philadelphia: Thomas Cowperthwait & Co.

Van Sandt, Nicholas Biddle, Map of Military Lands between the Mississippi and Illinois Rivers. Washington City: P. Force, 1818, BY.

Kansas

Whitman, E. B. and Searl, A. D. Map of Eastern Kansas. Boston: J. J. Jewett & Co., 1856.

Missouri

Colton, J. H. and Co. Map of Missouri. New York: Colton & Co., 1855.

Overland Trail

Harris, Everett W. Overland Emigrant Trails to California, Oregon, and Salt Lake City. Reno: Nevada Historical Society, 1970.

Hulbert, A. B. Map in *Forty-Niners, The Chronicle of the California Trail.* New York: Blue Ribbon Books, Inc., 1931.

Nevada Emigrant Trail Marking Committee Inc. Maps in *The Overland Emigrant Trail to California, A Guide to Trail Markers.* Reno: Nevada Historical Society, 1975.

Paden, Irene. Maps in *The Wake of the Prairie Schooner.* New York: Macmillan Co., 1943.

NEWSPAPERS

California

Jackson: *Amador Ledger,* Oct. 27, 1855, to July 17, 1858 (formerly the *Volcano Weekly Ledger,* 1855). Microfilm, BL.

Amador Sentinel, Vol. 2, No. 1, Dec. 30, 1854.(This is the only known copy; it includes one page entitled "The Owl.") HL.

Quincy (This Amador County gold rush community disappeared in the early 1860s and is not to be confused with present-day Quincy in Plumas County.): *The Prospector,* Vol. I, No. 1-15, Mar. 3-Nov. 17, 1855.

HL. The newspaper then moved to Sacramento and ceased publishing in February 1856. The complete file of this miniature newspaper, which measured 5 3/4 " x 6 3/4 ", is at Huntington Library. June 2 and Sept. 22, 1855, CSL.

Sacramento: *The Baptist Circular,* January 1859, American Baptist Seminary of the West, Berkeley, Calif.

The Pictorial Union, Jan. 1, April-July 4, 1853; April-July 4, 1854, CSL.

The Union, 1854-60. Microfilm, BL.

San Jose: *The Pioneer and Historical Review,* 1897-1901. California Society of Pioneers.

San Francisco: *Alta California,* January-June, 1855, and July-December, 1860. Microfilm, LC.

Daily Herald, 1855-56. Microfilm, LC.

The Golden Era, A California Family Newspaper, 1853-59. Microfilm, BL.

The Pacific, 1853-54 and 1860 (Congregational Church). Pacific School of Religion, Berkeley, Calif.

The Young America, "A Messenger from Home," June 20, 1857. Published semimonthly by D. F. Verdenal, this miniature newspaper measured 5¼ " x 3¾ ". Verdenal Johnson, Madison, N. J.

Weekly Bulletin, 1857-58.

Stockton: *Daily San Joaquin Republican,* January-June 1856, 1860. Microfilm, BL.

Watsonville: *Register-Pajaronian,* Dec. 25, 1884.

Illinois

Galena: *Weekly North-Western Gazette and Advertizer,* 1849. Microfilm, BL.

Ottawa: *Illinois Free Trader,* July 30, 1841. LC.

Pike County: *Free Press* (printed in both Pittsfield and Griggsville) 1846-53, incomplete file. LC.

The Journal, Pittsfield, January 1860-February 1862. Microfilm, ISHL.

Republican, Pittsfield, June 10, 1842. HL.

Sucker and Farmer's Record, June 1, 1842. LC.

The Union, 1849-53. Incomplete file, LC. Microfilm, ISHL. (Ten issues missing for the fall of 1852.)

Missouri

St Louis: *Daily Republican,* January-February 1848, and 1853. Microfilm, BL and MoHS.

The Daily Union, Sept. 22, 1847-Mar. 25, 1848. Microfilm, MoHS.

Independent Apr. 28-Aug. 12, 1853. Microfilm, MoHS.

Daily Morning Herald, 1853. Microfilm, MoHS.

St. Joseph: Gazette, Jan. 7, 1852-Oct. 4, 1854. Microfilm, MoHS.

New York

The Christian Advocate and Journal, 1853-54, and Sept. 27, 1956 (last issue).

Methodist Library, Drew University, N. J.

New York Times, 1852-54. The California news appeared every ten to fifteen days depending upon the arrival of steamships from the West Coast. It also reprinted articles from the Midwestern and Western newspapers. Microfilm, Summit Public Library, Summit, N.J.

Recorder and Register, Mar. 15, 1854, and Jan. 3, 1855. American Baptist Seminary of the West, Berkeley, Calif.

Undated Newspaper Clippings

"Heart of the Mother Lode — Amador County," History Room, Wells Fargo Bank, San Francisco.

"Pico Grant Lands of Ione," August 18, 1960, *Oakland Tribune.* Miscellaneous file, Society of California Pioneers, San Francisco.

"Forest Home," 1948 photograph and 1920s (?) newspaper clipping. Picture file, BL.

"History of Sutter Creek" and "History of Ione," Haggin Art Museum, Stockton, Calif.

"Ione's Bloody Squatters War - The Fall of Quincy and Muletown," *Stockton Sunday Record,* Haggin Art Museum, Stockton, Calif.

"History of Quincy" by Larry Cenotto, *Sacramento Bee.* Amador County miscellaneous file, CaHS.

CENSUS RECORDS

Bi-Centennial Historical Statistics of the United States, Colonial Times to 1970, Part I, U.S. Department of Commerce, Bureau of the Census, 93rd Congress, first session, 1975, House Doc. No. 93-78.

DeBrow, J. D. B. *Statistical View of the United States* ("embracing its territory, population — white, free, colored and slave — moral and social condition, industry, property and revenue, the detailed statistics of cities, towns and counties, being a compendium of the 7th census to which are added the results of every previous census, beginning with 1790"). Washington D.C.: Beverly Tucker, 1854.

California

Bowman, Alan P. *Index to the California Census of 1850.* Baltimore: Genealogical Publishing Inc., 1972.

Journal of the Fourth Session of the Legislature of California, Doc. 14, Appendix, the 1852 special state census. Manuscript on microfilm, CSL and BL.

Daughters of the American Revolution. Typed copy of the 1852 special California census. Microfilm, CSL and BL. This copy does not match, page-by-page, the manuscript copy, so it is difficult to check against the microfilm copy of the faded and torn original listed above.

1860 — 8th annual census for Amador County. Microfilm. Vol. 1- 153, Roll 55, National Archives depository, Bayonne, N. J.

1860 — Special census: Products of Industry, Amador County, during the year ending June 1, 1860; Social Statistics, and Production of Agriculture, Township No. 2, Ione City, June 3-5, 1860. Microfilm, BL.

Illinois

Illinois State Archives. Census Index [card file] for 1850 and 1860 federal census records, plus 1855 special state census. A card has been made up for each name in these census records, with reference by county to the page upon which it appears.

1840-1850-1860 — Annual census records for Pike County, Illinois. Microfilm, National Archives depository, Bayonne, N. J.

1850 — Special census, Pike County: Industry and Social Statistics, Roll no. 31-97, and Agricultural Census, Roll no. 31-33, by township. Microfilm, Illinois State Archives.

Pennsylvania

Index to the 1810 Census, compiled by Ohio Family Historians. Cleveland: Bell & Howell Co., 1966. Microphoto, LC.

1830 — 5th annual census for Erie County. Microfilm no. 19, Roll 147, National Archives depository, Bayonne, N.J.

Wisconsin

1850 — 7th annual census for Grant County. Microfilm no. 432, Roll 998, National Archives depository, Bayonne, N. J.

OTHER RECORDS

Federal

Records of the Bureau of Marine Inspection and Navigation, St. Louis, July 29, 1850. Record Group 41, BMIN, enrollment No. 93, NatA.

Returns from U.S. Military Posts, 1800-1916, Fort Laramie, June 1849-December 1860. Microfilm, copy 617, roll 595, NatA.

California

Amador County Court House, Jackson:

County Deeds (August 1854 to October 1872) Book A, 174, 225; Book D, 475, 583-84.

Marriage Records, Book A, 1856-57, 32.

Court Records Docket for 1854-60.

County Court Register of Actions [undated, but lists cases for 1855-56].

Fifth Judicial District Court Records, Feb. 19, 1856.

Court of Sessions Records, April term, 1856.

Assessment Rolls. 1855, 82, 88; 1856, 13, 115, 263.
Separate Property of Wives, 1858, 44.
California State Archives, Sacramento:
Sixth District Court Records, 1852-53.
Assessment Rolls, 1855, 82, 88; 1856, 13, 115, 263.

Illinois

Federal Tract Book S-701 (Quincy), 1830s and early 1840s, Illinois State Archives.
Delinquent Tax List for 1849, Pike County. Manuscript, ISHL. Index for southwest quarter of Section 3, Township 5, Range 6, and Books No. 29, 30, and 38. Clerk's Office, Pike County Court House, Pittsfield.
Records and Deeds, 8, 38, and 40, 1836-1853; also on microfilm (rolls 7, 13, and 19), Pike County Court House and Illinois State Archives.

PHOTOGRAPHS AND ILLUSTRATIONS

California Society of Pioneers. Jackson, 1857, No. 7, *California Mining Town Series*. California Book Club, 1934.
California State Library. Photographs of Adam Lithgow taken from a portrait. Picture file. Information (erroneous) supplied by descendant J. Q. Rickey.
Bowmer, Mrs. Angus L. Lorena's son and family.
Eckland, Ellis E. Hays-Whitlatch family photo albums.
Hoover, Bernice. Lithgow family mementos.
Wells Fargo Bank, History Room, San Francisco. Drytown in 1854, from the July 4, 1854, *Sacramento Pictorial Union;* Michigan Bar, by Anthony and Baker, negative 12; and Volcano, two 1850s tintypes made into a postcard.
Withington, Mrs. E.W. Views of Ione City and vicinity (seven stereoptican views, 21498-41504), undated but probably early 1870s. Photo file, HL.

SECONDARY SOURCES

Abernethy, Thomas Perkins. *From Frontier to Plantation in Tennessee, a Study in Frontier Democracy*. Chapel Hill: University of North Carolina Press, 1932.
Allen, W. W. and Avery, R. B. *California Gold Book — Its Discovery and Discoverers and Some of the Results Proceeding Therefrom*. San Francisco and Chicago: Donohue & Henneberry, 1893.
Altman, Lawrence K. "Gulf Coast Monitored for Cholera," *New York Times*, Mar. 20, 1979.
Amador County, California, chamber of commerence. Early Day History of Drytown, Plymouth, and Fiddletown, mimeographed pamphlets, undated, vertical file, Holt-Atherton Center, University of the Pacific, Stockton, Calif.
Andrews, John R. *The Ghost Towns of Amador*. New York: Carlton Press Inc., 1967.
Anthony, C. V. *Fifty Years of Methodism: History of the Methodist Episcopal*

Church. San Francisco: Methodist Book Concern, 1901.

Arlington, Leonard J. *Great Basin Kingdom.* Lincoln: University of Nebraska Press, 1966.

Asbury, Edith Evans. "Angus L. Bowmer, 74, Founder of Oregon Shakespeare Festival." *New York Times,* May 28, 1979. The obituary of Lorena's great-grandson.

Asbury, Herbert. *The Barbary Coast.* New York: Capricorn Books 1968.

Barry [Illinois] First Baptist Church. *Centennial Book.* Barry, Ill.: 1954.

Barry, Louise. *The Beginning of the West, Annals of Kansas, Gateway to the American West, 1840-1854.* Topeka: Kansas State Historical Society, 1972.

Bancroft, Hubert Howe. *The Works of . . . History of California.* Vol. 24. San Francisco: The History Co., 1890.

———. *The Works of . . . Popular Tribunals.* Vol. 17. San Francisco: The History Co., 1890.

Beasley, Delilah L. *The Negro Trail Blazers of California.* Reprint. New York: Negro Universities Press, 1969.

Belden, Bauman L. *Indian Peace Medals Issued in the United States.* New York: The American Numismatic Society, 1927.

Berg, Barbara. *The Remembered Gate: Origins of American Feminism: the Woman and the City, 1840-1860.* New York: Oxford University Press, 1978.

Berry, Joy and Cowan, Natalie. "Weather and Water in California An Historical Perspective," *California Historical Courier* (March 1977).

Berry, Thomas, Sr. "Gold! But How Much?!," *California Historical Quarterly* (Fall 1976): 246-55.

Billington, Ray Allen. "Books that Won the West, Guidebooks of the Forty-Niners and Fifty-Niners," *American West,* (August 1967): 25-32.

———.*Westward Expansion, A History of the American Frontier.* New York: Macmillan Co., 1950.

Bitton, Davis. *Guide to Mormon Diaries and Autobiographies.* Provo: Brigham Young University Press, 1977.

Bradley, Lenore and Crowley, William: *Trekkin' West: An Emigrants Guide to Oregon.* Kansas City: Kansas City Museum, n.d.

Brown, A. Theodore. *Frontier Community, Kansas City to 1870.* Vol. 1. Columbia, Mo.: University of Missouri Press, 1963.

Brown, Terry. "An Emigrant's Guide for Women, 1850 Edition: Making the Necessary Preparations for the Arduous Five-Month Journey Along the Oregon Trail," *American West* (September, 1970): 12-17. This is a fictional composite from many original sources; such a book for women never actually existed.

Bruce, John. *Gaudy Century, San Francisco Journalism, 1848-1948.* New York: Random House, 1948.

Burstyn, Joan N. *Victorian Education and the Ideal of Womanhood.* New Brunswick, N. J.: Rutgers University Press, 1984.

California Historical Society. *California Pictorial Lettersheets, 1849-59, Museum Reproductions of Unique Writing Paper used in Gold Rush California, selected from Rare Originals in the CHS Archives.* San Francisco: Reynard Press Inc., 1961.

———. Scrapbook — Description, Biography (a collection of newspaper clippings) and Obituaries, Vol. 13. This includes an *Oakland Tribune* story of

July 25, 1940, concerning the Ione Methodist Church and its dedication.

Carlson, D. W. "Sacramento County Gold Dredging," *California Journal of Mines and Geology,* Vol. 51. (Sacramento; 1955): 135-42.

Carson Valley Historical Society. *Along the Carson River Route, A Segment of the Emigrant Trail.* Ed. Grace Dangberg. Carson City, Nev.: 1973.

Case, Theodore S. *A History of Kansas City, Missouri.* Syracuse, N. Y.: Mason and Co., 1888.

Cathcart, William D. *The Baptist Encyclopedia, A Dictionary.* Philadelphia: Louis H. Everts, 1883.

Centennial Book Committee: *Alpine Heritage, 100 Years of History, Recreation and Lore in Alpine County, California.* South Lake Tahoe: Anchor Printing, n.d.

Chicago Historical Society. "The United States of 1856," *Chicago History* (Spring 1956). "Illinois in 1856," *Chicago History* (Summer 1956).

Clark, William B. *Gold Districts of California,* Bulletin 193. San Francisco: California Division of Mines and Geology, 1970.

Clinton, Katherine. "Pioneer Women in Chicago, 1833-37," *Journal of the West* (April 1972): 317-24.

Connelly, William E. *History of Kansas.* Vol. 1. Chicago and New York: The American Historical Society Inc., 1928.

Coons, Frederica B. *The Trail to Oregon.* Portland, Oreg.: Binford & Mort, 1954.

Cott, Nancy F. *The Bonds of Womanhood, "Women's Sphere" in New England, 1780-1835.* New Haven and London: Yale University Press, 1977.

Cowan, Robert G.. *Ranchos of California, A List of Spanish Concessions, 1775-1822, and Mexican Grants, 1822-1846.* Fresno: Academy Library Guild, 1956.

Coy, Owen D. *Guide to the Archives of California.* Sacramento: California Historical Survey Commission, 1919.

———. *In the Diggings in '49.* Los Angeles: California State Historical Association, 1948.

Cramer, Howard Ross. *Emigrant Trails of Southeast Idaho.* U.S. Department of the Interior, Bureau of Land Management, 1976.

Curran, Harold. *Fearful Crossing, The Central Overland Trail through Nevada.* Reno: Great Basin Press, 1982.

Dana, Charles A. *The United States Illustrated — The West, or the States of the Mississippi Valley and the Pacific.* New York: Herrmann J. Meyer, ca. 1853-4.

Davis, J. Winfield. Scrapbooks, No. 1-4 (of 18), newspaper clippings and articles from various papers, starting in 1882, HL.

———. *An Illustrated History of Sacramento County, California.* Chicago: Lewis Publishing Co., 1890.

Davis, W. N. "Research Uses of County Court Records, 1850-79, and Incidental Intimate Glimpses of California Life and Society," *California Historical Quarterly* (Fall-Winter 1973).

Devoy, John. *A History of the City of St. Louis and Vicinity.* St. Louis: John Devoy, 1898.

Dictionary of American Biography. Ed. Dumas Malone. New York: Charles Scribners Sons, 1933.

Dobson, R. Calvin. *The Romance of the Pioneer Church: The First Presbyterian*

Church of St. Louis, Missouri, 1817-1960. Privately printed, 1960.

Douglas, Ann. *The Feminization of American Culture.* New York: Avon Books, 1977.

Doyle, Don Harrison. *The Social Order of a Frontier Community — Jacksonville, Illinois, 1835-70.* Urbana, Chicago, and London: University of Illinois Press, 1978.

Eaton, Herbert. *The Overland Trail* [1852]. New York: G. P. Putnam's Sons, Capricorn Books, 1974.

Eckles, David. "Introduction to Camp Payne, Wyoming" and "The Archaeology of Camp Payne, Wyoming." *The Wyoming Archaeologist* (Fall 1985) 5-7, 20-96.

Edwards, Malcolm. "The War of Complexional Distinction: Blacks in Gold Rush California and British Columbia." *California Historical Quarterly* (Spring 1977): 34-45.

Egan, Ferol. "Incident at Tragedy Springs," *American West,* (January 1971).

_____. *Fremont, Explorer for a Restless Nation.* Garden City, N. Y.: Doubleday & Company, Inc., 1977.

Egenhoff, Elizabeth L. *The Elephant as They Saw It, A Collection of Contemporary Pictures and Statements on Gold Mining in California.* Sacramento: Centential supplement, California Journal of Mines and Geology. California Division of Mines, State Department of Natural Resources, 1953.

Eggenhofer, Nick. *Wagons, Mules, and Men, How the Frontier Moved West.* New York: Hastings House, 1961.

Eide, Ingvard Henry. *The Oregon Trail.* Chicago, New York, and San Francisco: Rand McNally and Co., 1973.

Eklund, Richard A. Reshaw Burial Site. Typescript. Private collection.

Ellison, Robert Spurrier. *Independence Rock.* Casper, Wyo.: Natrona County Historical Society, 1930.

Engle, I. A. *Men Who Dug for Gold and Men Who Preached for God — There's Gold Ahead!* Commission on Archives and History, California-Nevada Conference, United Methodist Church, 1973.

Faragher, John Mack. *Women and Men on the Overland Trail.* New Haven and London: Yale University Press, 1979. Faragher's percentages for the 1853 emigration (Table A 1.11) do not agree with the numbers given in his source materials: *Publication No. 20.* Ed. Albert Watkins. Lincoln, Neb.: Nebraska State Historical Society, 1922.

_____. *Sugar Grove, Life on an Illinois Prairie.* New Haven: Yale University Press, 1986.

Farquhar, Francis P. *Notes on Joaquin Murrieta* in *The Brigard Chief of California, A Complete History of His Life from the Age of 16 to the Time of his Death in 1853.* San Francisco: The Grabhorn Press, 1932. This is a copy of a serial from the *California Police Gazette,* Sept. 3 to Nov. 5, 1859, with reproduction of poster announcing exhibition of "The Head of the Renowned Bandit Joaquin! and the Hand of Three-fingered Jack!"

Federal Writers Project, Works Progress Administration. Amador County. Typescript, Haggin Art Museum, Stockton, Calif.

_____. *California, A Guide to the State.* New York: Hastings House, American Guide Series, 1939.

_____. *Erie, a Guide to the City and County.* Philadelphia: The William Penn Association, 1938.

_____. *Kansas, A Guide to the Sunflower State.* New York: Viking Press, American Guide Series, 1939.

_____. *Missouri, A Guide to the "Show Me" State.* New York: Duell, Sloan and Pearce, 1941.

_____. *The Oregon Trail, the Missouri River to the Pacific Ocean.* New York: Hastings House, 1939.

Finley, Ruth E. *The Lady of Godey's: Sarah Josepha Hale.* Philadelphia and London: J. B. Lippincott and Co., 1931.

Fischer, Christiane. *Let Them Speak for Themselves — Women in the American West, 1849-1900.* Connecticut: Archon Books, 1977.

Fleming, Sandford. *God's Gold, The Story of Baptist Beginnings in California, 1847-60.* Philadelphia, Chicago, and Los Angeles: The Judson Press, 1949.

_____. Ninety-five Years Beside the Gold Gate. Typescript and research notes. American Baptist Seminary of the West, Berkeley, Calif.

Ford, Thomas. *A History of Illinois, from Its Commencement as State in 1818 to 1847.* Ed. Milo Milton Quaife. Chicago: The Lakeside Press, 1945.

Franzwa, Gregory M. *The Oregon Trail Revisited.* St. Louis, Mo.: Patrice Press, 1972.

Frickstad, Walter N. *A Century of California Post Offices, 1848-1954.* Oakland: Pacific Rotoprinting Co., 1955.

Foley, Doris. *Lola Montez, the Divine Eccentric.* New York: Ballantine Books, Comstock Edition, 1969.

Funk and Wagnalls. *The Encyclopedia of Social Reforms.* Ed. William D. Bliss. New York and London: Funk and Wagnalls, 1898.

_____. *The Cyclopaedia of Temperance and Prohibition, a Reference Book of Facts, Statistics and General Information on All Phases of the Drink Question, the Temperance Movement and the Prohibition Agitation.* London, New York, and Toronto: Funk and Wagnalls, 1891.

"Games and Toys," Madison, N.J.: Museum of Early Trades and Crafts, 1984.

Ghent, Jocelyn Maynard. "The Golden Dream and the Press: Illinois and the California Gold Rush of '49," *Journal of the West* (April 1978): 16-27.

Glass, Mary Ellen and Al. *Western Nevada.* Reno: Nevada Historical Society Guide Book Series, 1975.

Gowans, Fred R. and Campbell, Eugene E. *Fort Bridger, Island in the Wilderness.* Provo: Brigham Young University Press, 1975.

Gregory, Winifred. *American Newspapers, 1821-1936, a Union List of Files Available in the United States and Canada.* New York: The H.W. Wilson Co., 1937.

Greuner, Lorene. *Lake Valley's Past.* South Lake Tahoe: Lake Tahoe Historical Society, 1971.

Grimshaw, William A. "History of Pike County, A Centenial Address Delivered at Pittsfield, Illinois, July 4, 1876," ISHL.

Grodin, Joseph R. *Silver Lake, High Sierra Hiking Guide No. 17, Between Carson Pass and Ebbetts Pass.* Berkeley: Wilderness Press, 1976.

Gudde, Erwin G. *Sutter's Own Story.* New York: G. P. Putnam and Son, 1936.

————. *California Gold Camps, A Geographical and Historical Dictionary of Camps, Towns and Localities Where Gold Was Found and Mined; Wayside Stations and Trading Centers.* Ed. Elisabeth K. Gudde. Berkeley: University of California Press, 1975.

Gusfield, Joseph R. *Symbolic Crusade, Status, Politics and the American Temperance Movement.* Urbana, Chigaco, and London: University of Illinois Press, 1972.

Hafen, Leroy R. and Young, Francis Marion. *Fort Laramie and the Pagent of the West, 1834-1890.* Glendale, Calif.: The Arthur H. Clark Co., 1938.

Hammond, George P. *Alexander Barclay, Mountain Man, from London Corsetier to Pioneer in Canada, Bookkeeper in St. Louis, Superintendent of Bent's Fort, Fur Trader and Mountain Man in Colorado, New Mexico, Builder of Barclay's Fort on the Santa Fe Trail, N.M., 1848 — A Narrative of His Career, 1810-50, and His Memorandum Diary, 1845-50.* Denver: Fred A. Rosenstock, 1976.

Harper's Book of Facts. Ed. Charlton T. Lewis. New York and London: Harper and Brothers, 1905.

Hartman, Mary S. *Victorian Murderesses.* New York: Simon and Schuster Pocket Books, 1977. Includes information upon the popularity of hydropathy in England and America.

Haucke, Frank. *The Kaw or Kansa Indians.* Topeka: Kansas State Historical Society, 1952.

Henderson, Paul C. *Landmarks on the Oregon Trail, from Court House Rock to Pacific Springs.* New York: Peter Decker, 1953.

Heininger, Mary Lynn Stevens. ''Children, Childhood, and Change in America, 1820-1920'' in *A Century of Childhood, 1820-1920.* Rochester: Margaret Woodbury Strong Museum (1984): 1-32.

Hines, Harvey Kimball. *An Illustrated History of the State of Oregon.* Chicago: The Lewis Publishing Company, 1893.

Hinkle, George and Bliss. *Sierra Nevada Lakes.* Indianapolis: Bobbs-Merrill Co., 1949.

History of Erie County, Pennsylvania. Chicago: Warner, Beers & Co., 1884.

History of Pike County, Illinois, Together with Sketches of Its Cities, Villages, and Townships, Educational, Religious, Civil, Military and Political History; Portraits of Prominent Persons and Biographies of Representative Citizens. Chicago: Chas. C. Chapman & Co., 1880.

Hodge, F. W. *Handbook of the American Indian.* New York: Pagent Books Inc., 1960.

Hoover, Catherine and Sawchuck, Robert. ''from the place we hear about . . . : a descriptive checklist of pictorial lithographs and letter sheets in the CHS collection,'' *California Historical Quarterly* (1977-78): 346-67.

Hoover, Mildred Brooks; Rensch, Hero Eugene; and Ethel Grace. *Historic Spots in California,* third edition revised by William N. Abeloe. Stanford: Stanford University Press, 1966.

Horridge, Patricia E.; Smathers, Diane G.; and Vachon, Diane L. *Dating Costumes: A Check List Method.* Technical leaflet No. 102. Nashville: American Association for State and Local History, 1977.

Horan, James D. *The Great American West — A Pictorial History.* New York: Bonanza Books, 1949.

Hunt, Thomas H. *Ghost Trails to California, a Pictorial Journey from the Rockies to the Gold Country.* Palo Alto: American West Co., 1974.

Hulbert, A. B. *Forty-Niners, the Chronicle of the California Trail.* New York: Blue Ribbon Books, Inc., 1931. A fictional composite from original sources.

Ione [California] Methodist Church. *Celebration of the 93rd Year: A History of the Church, 1852-1945.* Ione: The Community Methodist Church, 1945.

Ione, Our Home Town. Ione Public Library.

Ione Annual Homecoming Picnic, Souvenir of Amador's 100th Birthday, 1854-1954. Ione Public Library.

Jackson, Donald Dale. *Gold Dust, the Saga of the Forty-Niners.* New York: Alfred A. Knopf, 1980.

Jackson, Joseph Henry, ed. *The Western Gate — A San Francisco Reader.* New York: Farrar, Straus and Young, 1952. Includes essays on "Lola Montez, Mid-Victorian Bad Girl" by Oscar Lewis and "San Francisco in the '50s" by H. H. Bancroft.

_____. *Anybody's Gold, the Story of California's Mining Towns.* New York and London: D. Appleton-Century Co. Inc., 1941.

Jackson, W. Turrentine. *Wagon Roads West, 1846-69, Study of Federal Road Surveys and Construction in the Trans-Mississippi West.* New Haven: Yale University Press, 1965.

Jacobson, Ronald V. and Teeples, Gary R. *Pennsylvania 1820 Census Index.* Bountiful, Utah: Accelerated Indexing System Inc., 1977.

Jeffery, Julie Roy. *Frontier Women, The Trans-Mississippi West, 1840-1880.* New York: Hill and Wang, 1979.

_____. "Frontier Letters: A Perspective on Women's World," paper presented at 1980 meeting, Western History Association.

Jensen, Andrew. *Encyclopedic History of the Church of Jesus Christ of Latter-Day Saints.* Salt Lake City: Deseret News, 1941.

Johnson, Charles B. *Illinois in the Fifties, or a Decade of Development.* Champaign: Flanagan-Pearson Co., 1918.

Joy, Emmett P. "Echoes from Calaveras Ghost Towns." Typescript, BL.

_____. "Drytown," *Grizzly Bear,* n.d. History Room, Wells Fargo Bank, San Francisco.

Kammen, Michael. "A Question of Values," *New York Times,* Jan. 9, 1980.

Kaufman, Martin. *Homeopathy in America, the Rise and Fall of a Medical Heresy.* Baltimore and London: The Johns Hopkins Press, 1971.

Kaufman, Polly Welts. *Women Teachers on the Frontier.* New Haven and London: Yale University Press, 1984.

Kelley, Mary. *Women's Being, Women's Place, Female Identification and Vocation in American History.* Boston: G. K. Hall, 1979.

Kemble, Edward C. *A History of California Newspapers, 1846-58.* Reprint. Los Gatos, Calif.: Talisman Press, 1962.

Keuenhof, William. *History of the Kansas City Diocese in Historic Missouri.* Kansas City: American Federation of Catholic Societies, 1917.

Langseth-Christensen, Lillian. "Wiesbaden's Nassauer Hoff," *Gourmet* (November 1983): 24-25.

Laut, Agnes. *The Overland Trail, the Epic Path of the Pioneers to Oregon.* New York: Frederick A. Stokes Co., 1929.

Lorch, Fred W. "Iowa and the California Gold Rush of 1849," *Iowa Journal of*

History and Politics (July 1932): 307-76.

Lottinville, Savoie. *The Rhetoric of History.* Norman: University of Oklahoma Press, 1976.

Lynes, Russell. *The Domesticated Americans.* New York: Harper & Row, 1963.

MacMullen, Jerry. *Paddle-Wheel Days in California.* Stanford: Stanford University Press, 1944.

MacMinn, George R. *The Theater of the Golden Era in California.* Caldwell, Ida.: The Caxton Press, 1941.

McGlashan, C. F. *History of the Donner Party.* Sacramento: H. S. Crocker Co., 1902.

McLaughlin, Josephine Laird. *Through These Hallowed Halls, A Trip Down Memory Lane and a Brief Glimpse of Life through the Past 100 Years of the Griggsville* [Illinois] *Schools.* Bluff, Ill.: Jones Publishing Company, 1976.

McLear, Patrick E. "Economic Growth and the Panic of 1857 in Kansas City," *Missouri Historical Review* (January 1970): 151-52.

_____. "The St. Louis Cholera Epidemic of 1849," *Missouri Historical Review* (January 1969): 171-79.

McGowan, Joseph A. *History of the Sacramento Valley.* Vol. 1. New York and West Palm Beach: Lewis Publishing Co., 1961.

Maino, Jeannette Gould. *Left Hand Turn, A Story of the Donner Party Women.* Privately printed, 1987.

Marzolf, Marion. "The History of Women Journalists," *Matrix,* (Winter 1977-78): 22-30.

Mason, J. D. *History of Amador County, California, with Illustrations and Biographical Sketches of its Prominent Men and Pioneers.* Oakland: Thompson & West, 1881.

Massie, M. D. *Past and Present in Pike County.* Chicago: S. J. Clarke, 1906.

Mattes, Merrill J. *The Great Platte River Road.* Lincoln: Nebraska State Historical Society, 1969.

_____. *Fort Laramie and the Forty-Niners.* Estes Park, Colorado: Rocky Mountain Nature Association, 1949.

_____. *Scotts Bluff National Monument.* Washington D. C.: National Park Service Historical Handbook, 1958.

Miskulin, Rudy. "A History of the State Fair." Typescript, California State Fair, Sacramento.

Mobley, Lawrence E. *The Golden Era, Its Contents and Significance plus Representative Selections and Index of Contributors.* Microfilm, BL.

Morgan, Dale L. *The Great Salt Lake.* Indianapolis and New York: The Bobbs-Merrill Co., 1947.

_____. *The Humboldt, Highroad of the West.* New York and Toronto: Rinehart & Co., Inc., The Rivers of America Series, 1943.

Morris, Mary Ellen Finforck. "Religion on the American Frontier: Baptists and Methodists." Typescript, HL.

Morton, Stratford Lee. *In the Days of the Covered Wagon in St. Louis.* St. Louis: Connecticut Mutual Life Insurance Co., 1923.

Moynihan, Ruth Barnes. "Children and Young People on the Overland Trail," *Western Historical Quarterly* (July 1975): 279-94.

Murray, James A. H., ed. *Oxford English Dictionary,* Vol. 7. Oxford: Clarendon Press, 1909.

Murray, Robert A. "Trading Posts, Forts and Bridges of the Casper Area — Unraveling the Tangle on the Upper Platte." *Annals of Wyoming* (1972): 6-30.

Myres, Sandra L. *Ho for California! Women's Overland Diaries from the Huntington Library.* San Marino, Calif.: Huntington Library, 1980.

_____. Comments on papers presented at session on Frontier Reminiscences at 1980 meeting, Western History Association.

Nadeau, Remi. *Fort Laramie and the Sioux Indians.* Englewood Cliffs, N. J.: Prentice-Hall Inc., 1967.

Nasatir, Abraham P. "Chileans in California During the Gold Rush Period and the Establishment of the Chilean Consulate." *California Historical Quarterly* (Spring 1974): 52-70.

National Bureau of Economic Research. "The United States 1837-1860," from *Business Annals* [1926]. Reprinted in *The Oregon Trail,* Federal Writers Project-WPA. New York: Hastings House, 1939.

National Cyclopedia of American Biography, History of the United States. New York: James T. White and Co., 1898.

Nelson's Biographical Dictionary and Historical Reference Book for Erie County, Pennsylvania. Erie: S. B. Nelson, 1896.

Nevins, Allan. *Fremont, The West's Greatest Adventurer.* New York and London: Harper & Brothers Publishers, 1928.

"New Look at Richard's Upper Platte Bridge and Trading Post at Evansville, Wyoming, 1852-1867." Typescript, private collection.

Norton, Wesley. "Like a Thousand Preachers Flying: Religious Newspapers on the Pacific Coast to 1865." *California Historical Quarterly* (Fall 1977): 194-209.

Notable Names in the American Theater. Clifton, N. J.: James T. White and Co., 1976.

Olmsted, Roger and Nancy. "Letters of Gold — California Letter Sheets." *American West* (May-June 1976): 13-19.

Paden, Irene. *The Wake of the Prairie Schooner.* New York: Macmillan Co., 1943.

_____. *Prairie Schooner Detours.* New York: Macmillan Co., 1949.

Perry, John. *American Ferryboats.* New York: Wilfred Funk Inc., 1957.

Pickett, Deets. *Cyclopedia of Temperance, Prohibition and Public Morals.* New York and Cincinnati: Methodist Book Concern, 1917.

Pooley, William V. *Settlement of Illinois from 1830-50.* Madison: University of Wisconsin Bulletin No. 220.

Quaife, Milo Milton, ed. *Pictures of Gold Rush California.* Chicago: The Lakeside Press, 1949.

Randall, Art. "Geology of Camp Payne-Richards Trading Post Site, Natrona County, Wyoming." *The Wyoming Archaeologist* (Fall 1985): 97-106.

Rawls, James J. "Gold Diggers: Indian Miners in the California Gold Rush." *California Historical Quarterly* (Spring 1976): 28-45.

Reed, G. Walter, ed. *History of Sacramento County.* Los Angeles: Historic Record Co., 1923.

Regan, John. *The Emigrant's Guide to the Western States of America, or Backwoods and Prairies.* Edinburgh, Scotland: Oliver and Boyd, n.d. (attributed to 1852).

Reid, John Phillip. *Law for the Elephant, Property and Social Behavior on the Overland Trail.* San Marino, Calif.: Huntington Library, 1980.

Reiss, David. "A Cultural Resource Inventory of a Proposed Cemetery Site in Natrona County, Wyoming." Typescript, Office of the Wyoming State Archeologist.

Reiter, Joan Swallow. *The Women.* Alexandria, Va.: Time-Life Books, The Old West series, 1978.

Report of Explorations and Surveys to Ascertain the Most Practicable and Economical Route for a Railroad from the Mississippi River to the Pacific Ocean. Executive Document No. 78, Senate, 33rd Congress, 2nd session, Vol. 5. Washington D.C.: Beverly Tucker, 1856.

Richmond, Robert W. "Development along the Overland Trail from the Missouri River to Fort Laramie, before 1854," Part 1. *Nebraska History* (September 1952): 54-79; "The Mormon Trail," Part 2, (December 1952): 237-47.

Ricketts, Norma B. *Tragedy Spring and the Pouch of Gold.* Sacramento: privately printed, 1983.

_____. *Mormons and the Discovery of Gold.* Sacramento: Primm Printing, 1982.

Riley, Glenda. "Through Women's Eyes: Indians in the Trans-Mississippi West," paper presented at 1980 meeting, Western History Association.

_____. *Women and Indians on the Frontier, 1825-1915.* Albuquerque: University of New Mexico Press, 1984.

_____. *Inventing the American Woman, A Perspective on Women's History, 1607-1877.* Arlington Heights, Ill.: Harland Davidson, Inc., 1986.

Rodriguez, Richard. "The Head of Joaquin Murrieta," *California* (July 1985): 5-62, 89.

Root, George A. "Ferries in Kansas," Part 2: Kansas River. *Kansas Historical Society Quarterly* (August 1933): 251-93; Part 2 Continued: Kansas River (February 1934): 15-42; Part 3: Blue River (May 1934): 115-44; Part 13: Wakarusa Creek (February 1937): 16; and Turkey Creek (February 1937): 19-20.

Rosales, Vincente Perez. "We Were Forty-Niners! The Gold Rush Though Chilean Eyes," *American West* (May-June 1976): 46-51.

Ross, Nancy Wilson. *Westward the Women.* San Francisco: North Point Press, 1985.

Ruth, Kent. *Great Day in the West — Forts, Posts and Rendezvous Beyond the Mississippi.* Norman: University of Oklahoma Press, 1963.

Sargent, Mrs. J. L. *Amador County History.* Jackson, Calif.: Amador Ledger, April 1927.

Schlissel, Lillian. *Women's Diaries of the Westward Journey.* New York: Schocken Books, 1982.

_____. "Diaries of Frontier Women: On Learning to Read the Obscured Patterns" in *Woman's Being, Woman's Place.* Ed. Mary Kelley, Boston: G. K. Hall & Co. 1979.

_____. "Women's Diaries on the Western Frontier" in *American Studies*

(Spring 1977): 7-100.

Second Presbyterian Church of St. Louis, Missouri. Miscellanneous materials, including 70th anniversary pamphlets, October 11-12, 1908, MoHS.

———. *Church Manual for the Communicants,* No. 4. St. Louis: S. Spencer, 1857.

Scott, Harvey W. *History of the Oregon Country.* Vol. 3. Cambridge, Mass.: The Riverside Press, 1924.

Tyler, Alice Felt. *Freedom's Ferment, Phases of American Social History from the Colonial Period to the Outbreak of the Civil War.* New York: Harper & Brothers Torchbooks, 1944.

Unruh, John D. Jr. *The Plains Across — The Overland Emigrants and the Trans-Mississippi West, 1840-60.* Urbana, Chicago and London: University of Illinois Press, 1979.

Van Why, Joseph S. Introduction to *The American Woman's Home* by Catherine Beecher and Harriet Beecher Stowe. Reprint. Hartford: Stowe-Day Foundation, 1975.

Volcano Stands . . ., Souvenier from Volcano, Calif.

Wagner, Henry F., *The Plains and the Rockies, A Bibliography of Original Narratives of Travel and Adventure, 1800-65,* third edition revised by Charles L. Camp. Columbia, Ohio: Long's College Book Co., 1953.

Walker, Franklin. *San Francisco's Literary Frontier.* New York: Alfred A. Knopf, 1939.

Walsh, Henry. *Hallowed Were the Gold Dust Trails, A Story of Pioneer Priests of Northern California.* Santa Clara, Calif.: University of Santa Clara Press, 1946.

Watson, Douglas S. *California in the Fifties, 50 Views of Cities and Mining Towns in California and the West, Originally Drawn on Stone by Kuchel and Dresel and Other Early San Francisco Lithographers.* San Francisco: John Howell, 1936.

Watson, Jeanne H. "The Cult of Domesticity," *Nineteenth Century* (Winter/Spring 1982): 37-39.

———. "Life in a Doll's House — The Victorian Lady," paper presented at 1977 Annual Meeting, American Association for State and Local History; 1979 Victorian Album Seminar, National Archives — Victorian Society in America; 1984 lecture series on "Nineteenth Century Women," co-sponsored by the Iowa Chapter, VSA; Iowa Committee for the Humanities, and the Des Moines Women's Club; and 1985, Museum of American Folk Art, New York City.

———. "The Carson Emigrant Road," *Overland Journal* (Summer 1986): 4-12.

Webb, Todd. *The Gold Rush Trail and the Road to Oregon.* New York: Doubleday & Co., 1963.

Weston, Otheto. *Mother Lode Album.* Stanford: Stanford University Press, 1948.

Whettemore, Margaret. *Sketchbook of Kansas Landmarks.* Topeka: The College Press, 1936.

White, Stewart Edward. *Old California, in Picture & Story.* Garden City, New York: Doubleday, Doran & Company, Inc., 1937.

Wilson, Joan Hoff. "Hidden Riches: Legal Records and Women, 1750-1825" in *Woman's Being, Woman's Place.* Ed. Mary Kelley. Boston: G. K. Hall & Co., 1979.

Wiltsee, Ernest A. *Gold Rush Steamers of the Pacific.* Lawrence, Mass.: Quarterman Publications Inc., 1938.

Wood, R. Coke. *Big Tree-Carson Valley Turnpike, Ebbetts Pass and Highway 4.* Murphys, Calif.: Old Timers Museum, 1968.

———. *Calaveras, the Land of Skulls.* Sonora, Calif.: Mother Lode Press, 1955.

Index

Jeanne Hamilton Watson

Hiking and marking the Carson Emigrant Road across the Sierra Nevada has been a family enterprise for Bill and Jeanne Hamilton Watson for more than two decades. They have "adopted" the top two miles over West Pass and work as summer volunteers with the U.S. Forest Service. Both are Charter Life Members of the Oregon-California Trails Association. Since 1979 Jeanne has been executive director of the Morris County Historical Society in New Jersey. In 1983 she received the Award of Recognition from the New Jersey Historical Commission for "outstanding contributions to public knowledge and the preservation of New Jersey's history." A graduate of the University of California-Berkeley, she served on the national governing council of the American Association for State and Local History (1986-1990).